The Latin American Studies Book Series

Series Editors

Eustógio W. Correia Dantas, Departamento de Geografia, Centro de Ciências, Universidade Federal do Ceará, Fortaleza, Ceará, Brazil

Jorge Rabassa, Laboratorio de Geomorfología y Cuaternario, CADIC-CONICET, Ushuaia, Tierra del Fuego, Argentina

Andrew Sluyter, Louisiana State University, Baton Rouge, LA, USA

The Latin American Studies Book Series promotes quality scientific research focusing on Latin American countries. The series accepts disciplinary and interdisciplinary titles related to geographical, environmental, cultural, economic, political and urban research dedicated to Latin America. The series publishes comprehensive monographs, edited volumes and textbooks refereed by a region or country expert specialized in Latin American studies.

The series aims to raise the profile of Latin American studies, showcasing important works developed focusing on the region. It is aimed at researchers, students, and everyone interested in Latin American topics.

Submit a proposal: Proposals for the series will be considered by the Series Advisory Board. A book proposal form can be obtained from the Publisher, Juliana Pitanguy (juliana.pitanguy@springer.com).

More information about this series at http://www.springer.com/series/15104

Juan Bautista Belardi · Damián Leandro Bozzuto ·
Pablo Marcelo Fernández ·
Enrique Alejandro Moreno · Gustavo Adolfo Neme
Editors

Ancient Hunting Strategies in Southern South America

Editors
Juan Bautista Belardi
CIT Santa Cruz
Consejo Nacional de Investigaciones
Científicas y Técnicas (CONICET)
Universidad Nacional de la Patagonia
Austral, Unidad Académica Río Gallegos
(UNPA-UARG)
Rio Gallegos, Santa Cruz, Argentina

Pablo Marcelo Fernández
Instituto Nacional de Antropología y
Pensamiento Latinoamericano (INAPL)
Consejo Nacional de Investigaciones
Científicas y Técnicas (CONICET)
Universidad de Buenos Aires (UBA)
Buenos Aires, Argentina

Gustavo Adolfo Neme
Departamento de Antropología
Museo de Historia Natural de San Rafael
Instituto de Evolución
Ecología Histórica y Ambiente (CONICET
- Universidad Tecnológica Nacional-UTN)
San Rafael, Mendoza, Argentina

Damián Leandro Bozzuto
Instituto Nacional de Antropologia y
Pensamiento Latinoamericano (INAPL)
CONICET
Universidad de Buenos Aires (UBA)
Buenos Aires, Argentina

Enrique Alejandro Moreno
Centro de Investigaciones y Transferencia
Catamarca (CITCA—CONICET/UNCA)
Escuela de Arqueología
Universidad Nacional de Catamarca
(UNCA)
San Fernando del Valle de Catamarca
Catamarca, Argentina

ISSN 2366-3421   ISSN 2366-343X   (electronic)
The Latin American Studies Book Series
ISBN 978-3-030-61186-6   ISBN 978-3-030-61187-3   (eBook)
https://doi.org/10.1007/978-3-030-61187-3

© Springer Nature Switzerland AG 2021
This work is subject to copyright. All rights are reserved by the Publisher, whether the whole or part of
the material is concerned, specifically the rights of translation, reprinting, reuse of illustrations, recitation,
broadcasting, reproduction on microfilms or in any other physical way, and transmission or information
storage and retrieval, electronic adaptation, computer software, or by similar or dissimilar methodology
now known or hereafter developed.
The use of general descriptive names, registered names, trademarks, service marks, etc. in this publication
does not imply, even in the absence of a specific statement, that such names are exempt from the relevant
protective laws and regulations and therefore free for general use.
The publisher, the authors and the editors are safe to assume that the advice and information in this book
are believed to be true and accurate at the date of publication. Neither the publisher nor the authors or
the editors give a warranty, expressed or implied, with respect to the material contained herein or for any
errors or omissions that may have been made. The publisher remains neutral with regard to jurisdictional
claims in published maps and institutional affiliations.

This Springer imprint is published by the registered company Springer Nature Switzerland AG
The registered company address is: Gewerbestrasse 11, 6330 Cham, Switzerland

Ancient Hunting Strategies in Southern South America: An Introduction

Food obtaining strategies and tactics have always played a central role in archaeological investigations. Among them, knowledge about hunting and fishing activity has attracted particular interest. As Lee and Devore (1968) early pointed out, 90% of the time involved in human evolution was characterized as hunter-gatherer societies. This implies a vast number of human groups throughout time and space focused their economies on hunting and fishing practices along with food gathering. The socioeconomic hunting-fishing-gathering systems persist, and this has to do both with their higher benefits compared to other economic alternatives, and with the social cost of ceasing hunting (Kramer and Codding 2016). Beyond the historical depth and persistence of this way of acquiring resources, research interest was placed on understanding activities and social relations developed in hunting practice. Among them, one can find planning and knowledge on prey's behavior and environment particularities, socioeconomic motivations that involve food procurement, obtaining raw materials such as leather and bones and the search for prestige by hunters (Binford 1978–2012–, 1991; Borrero 2013; Churchill 1993; Foley 1983; Frison 2004; Laughlin 1968; Mithen 1990; Speth 2010). Besides, the particular roles of the people involved should be considered, whether as hunters/fishermen, beaters, carriers, and/or apprentices. Technology involved carrying out hunting, such as weapons systems, which may require components of different designs, raw materials, and geographical origin (Fenenga 1953; Ratto 1994, 2003; Shott 1997; Thomas 1978) and the construction of structures is also taken into account. Once the hunt has taken place, decisions about prey's butchering and transport are relevant. Combination of prey, landscapes and distances, number of hunters, tactics employed and technology available translates into hunting structures and the formation of different archaeological contexts, which are an excellent example of the spatial continuity of human behavior. Hunting/fishing activities influences and nourishes all the members and components of the social system, being crossed by multiple symbolic aspects like songs, rituals, dreams, that supplement and outline its realization. Last aspect of this practice and archaeological research, highlights the relevance of regional contexts. In this volume, we ask about the archaeological record of hunting, fishing, and gathering small animals in southern South America—taking into account the heterogeneity of this space—and on the strategies and tactics which were implemented by human populations.

A few years ago, we thought of convening a meeting to bring together the Argentinean research groups that were studying hunting/gathering/fishing practices combining multiple lines of evidence. Starting with conversations held in the framework of the IV Congress of Argentine Zooarchaeology at Ushuaia, Tierra del Fuego in 2016, the proposal was materialized in August 2018. The 1st Workshop "*Estrategias y tácticas de procuramiento de presas en el pasado: su discusión a partir de la integración de distintas líneas de evidencia*" (Strategies and tactics of prey procurement in the past: its discussion based on the integration of different lines of evidence) was held at Los Reyunos, Universidad Tecnológica Nacional (San Rafael, Mendoza, Argentina) and the meeting gathered 17 papers, which are the source of this book.

Workshop participants at Los Reyunos, San Rafael, Mendoza, August 2018

During Workshop, research carried out in very diverse sectors of the landscape of southern South America were presented, from the high deserts, such as the Puna to the steppes of northern Tierra del Fuego, and from Pampa plains to the central mountains and the forests of the Patagonian Andes. There were also multiple temporalities crossed, since the initial peopling of these landscapes to the current forms of hunting. Also, they integrate different archaeological lines of evidence from an interdisciplinary perspective. Ethnographic, anthropological, and historical data are pieced together with information brought by geneticists, biologists, zoologists, chemists and physicists, among others.

Ancient Hunting Strategies in Southern South America: An Introduction

Volume Chapters

The first chapter (Chap. 1) focuses on the northwest of Argentina, and more precisely at Puna of Catamarca province. Enrique Moreno, Jorge Martínez, and Carlos Aschero propose a compendium of information on hunting strategies through the Holocene, center on data obtained from zooarchaeological sites, weapons systems and landscape characteristics and their transformations in two different regions of Antofagasta de la Sierra department. In this case, the main prey would have been the vicuña (*Vicugna vicugna*). The authors develop a theoretical and methodological proposal to study hunting strategies, focusing on the relevance of collective hunting and the construction of hunting blinds on a regional scale. Also, the information obtained of projectile points design allows them to discuss those models along the Holocene.

In the second chapter (Chap. 2), Matías Medina and Imanol Balena advance on a technological and functional study of projectile points recovered from different sites in the Córdoba province corresponding to the late pre-Hispanic period (1500–360 years BP). The authors evaluate the importance of hunting in contexts where agriculture introduction would have diminished the importance of this activity. This implies populations with flexible economies throughout the annual circle, prioritizing in some moments cultivation and others hunting and gathering activities. Economic intensification would have been accompanied by multiple sociocultural changes, including the adoption of bow and arrow as a weapon for camelid hunting and the performing of individual hunts, as a clear reference to the emergence of centrality on family groups.

Chapter 3 takes place at Pampa area, more precisely, in zones related to the Samborombón and Salado rivers, María Isabel González, Paula D. Escosteguy, Mónica C. Salemme, Magdalena Frère, Celeste Weitzel and Rodrigo Vecchi focus on the study of coypu obtaining (*Myocastor coypus*), a large rodent that has been repeatedly used by human populations for at least the last 2500 years. Currently, it is required mainly for its skin, but also for its caloric contribution. The authors, based on experimental and ethnoarchaeological studies, focus on the stages of obtaining, consuming, and discarding these animals today. These data are compared with archaeological evidence, especially with lithic technology and zooarchaeological assemblages. It is argued that, while it is still possible to hunt coypu with a stick, in the past "*bolas*" and other weapons like projectile points were frequently used. All this suggests the incidence of changes in the different strategies for obtaining this resource over time.

In Chap. 4, Cristian Kaufmann, María Clara Álvarez, Pablo Messineo, María Barros, Mariano Bonomo and Guillermo Heider, study hunting strategies for obtaining guanacos (*Lama guanicoe*) during the late Holocene in the south-east pampas. They compare data from two periods, the early stages of Late Holocene (3400–1700 years BP) and it's the final stage (1300–800 years BP). They established the great importance of guanaco for the populations that lived there, and the changes in the technology of obtaining them. Thus, while in the earliest archaeological sites, weapons would have been "*bolas*" and atlatl darts, for the final period bows and arrows would have been used, evidenced by the presence of small triangular projectile points. Despite the technological change, continuity of the spaces used to hunt, such as river junctions and dunes as hunting traps, is observed.

Regarding other activities and prey, in Chap. 5 Romina Frontini, Cristina Bayón, and Rodrigo Vecchi ask about strategies to catch marine fish during the Middle Holocene in the area of Monte Hermoso, Buenos Aires province, corresponding to the Pampa area. Through the study of archaeofaunal fish remains, lithic technology, paleoenvironmental reconstructions and ethological characteristics of fish, the authors propose that weights for nets and lines were used in the sites. Fishing worked as alternative to obtain marine resources, at a time when environmental conditions were favorable to this.

Chapter 6, by Silvina Castro, Lucía Yebra, Valeria Cortegoso, Erik Marsh, Agustín Castillo, Agustina Rughini, María Victoria Fernández, and Raven Garvey, proposes an analysis located at central west Andes of Argentina, but which has a potential discussion on a wider scale, such as the adoption of bow and arrow and the replacement of weapons system previously used. Despite focusing on projectile points, the authors also use environmental, chronological, and paleoenvironmental data to frame the discussion. Through projectile point analysis from six archaeological sites, they pose the presence of bow and arrow from 3080 years BP in the sites located North of the study area, while just about 1000 years BP makes its appearance at sites located to the South. This technological change would respond to population growth, reduced mobility, low-scale food production, and the implementation of pastoral economies.

Miguel Giardina, Clara Otaola, and Fernando Franchetti develop in Chap. 7 their study about hunting, processing, and consumption of Rheidae. This proposal is based on ethnographic and ethnohistorical data that allow them to know the traditional strategies of obtaining this bird and its implications for archaeological investigations. From interviews with local people "*puesteros*" and the participation in a traditional hunting event, the authors emphasize the economic importance of this bird for the *puestero* populations, especially the fat, but feathers, skin, and bones too. This chapter shows the importance of the use of boleadoras together with horses and dogs for hunting execution. That is why they pose the possibility that this practice is relevant for the local economy after the Spanish conquest, while for the pre-Hispanic period it would have focused on eggs obtaining.

In Chap. 8, Diego Rindel, Florencia Gordón, Bruno Moscardi, and Iván Pérez deal with on the importance of small prey (armadillos, fish, mollusks, birds, small carnivores, and rodents) for human population diets at northwestern Patagonia. The authors seek to understand and evaluate the role of these animals in the food choices of these populations. They used stable isotope values and zooarchaeological data, which are discussed with ethnohistorical evidence on the nutritional supply of these animals. The results suggest that the importance of small prey in human population diets during the Holocene had been much greater than originally thought. In this way, it is proposed that hunters would have supplemented guanaco with small prey, according to availability and nutritional benefits of these small animals, and despite its processing and capture costs.

Mariana Carballido Calatayud and Pablo M. Fernández established, in Chap. 9, the differences in hunting strategies developed in the forest and the steppe of North-Central Patagonian for the last 3500 years. Based on environmental, ethological, ethnographic, and historical information, they propose three models of hunting strategies, one linked to the forest, another to the steppe, and a transitional one. The models contemplate the hunting of guanaco, huemul (*Hippocamelus bisulcus*), and lesser rhea (*Rhea pennata*), and are tested by the analysis of lithic materials and faunal remains from archaeological sites located along the rain shadow gradient of Patagonia. The authors propose some differences in the strategies employed, as the prevalence of huemul hunting in the forest, while the guanaco would have been the main prey in the steppe. Also, they state the use of bow and arrow as a useful weapon to gain an advantage in the forest, but not in the steppe.

In Chap. 10, the archaeological landscape of the Patagonian plateaus of Santa Cruz and Río Negro provinces are the focus of the study. Laura Miotti, Laura Marchionni, Darío Hermo, Enrique Terranova, Lucía Magnin, Virginia Lynch, Bruno Mosquera, Jorgelina Vargas Gariglio and Natalia Carden propose to study on changes in hunting strategies through time and space. They focus on information on lithic technology, archaeofaunal remains, rock art, and hunting structures (hunting blinds). Once again, the main prey would have been guanacos and propose the articulation of four factors to be taken into account for the interpretation of hunt: the participation of hunting groups, the ethological characteristics of prey, the diversity of weapons employed, and topography, a category that includes landforms, objects, and beings. Based on this proposal, they observe changes in hunting strategies through the Holocene, as well as in the different plateaus on which the research focuses. The authors' highlights the importance that hunting blinds would have had over time as hunting-related constructions, while the main difference would have been in the use of different weapons systems, with the appearance of "*bolas*" during the middle Holocene and the bow and arrow during the late Holocene.

In Chap. 11, Josefina Flores Coni, Juan Dellepiane, Gisela Cassiodoro, Rafael Goñi, and Agustín Agnolin centralize their study on guanacos hunting strategies in the Patagonian plateaus of Santa Cruz and give account on the changes these strategies experienced along the last 2500 years. Changes are related to demographic growth, the use of more effective technologies, and changes in the mobility patterns of hunters. The differences were mainly materialized in the construction of hunting blinds on these plateaus configuring inherited archaeological landscapes. Hunting grounds are established in open and closed areas, but spaces for social interaction between hunter populations are also configured. Thus, by opposing paleoenvironmental, spatial, lithic technology, and archaeofaunal information, it is proposed that these plateaus were spaces used by guanacos in times of greater aridity and that hunters modified their hunting strategies and technologies by delineating hunting grounds through the construction of blinds.

Also, with an important focus on the articulation of hunting strategies with hunting blind construction, Nora Franco, Lucas Vetrisano, Brenda L. Gilio, Natalia A. Cirigliano, and Pablo Bianchi, in Chap. 12 discusses the characteristics of human occupation of the southern end of Deseado Massif, located in the center of Santa Cruz province, and the realization of communal guanaco hunting. Intensive surveys show the presence of hunting blinds in a limited sector of the landscape, while they would be absent in the rest of the study area; they are registered more than 100 km away. This information, added to the data obtained from lithic technology analysis, leads the authors to propose that these places would have been used during the late Holocene mainly as hunting grounds.

Finally, in Chap. 13, Juan Bautista Belardi, Flavia Carballo Marina, and Gustavo Barrientos describe and discuss the hunting strategies and tactics implemented during the late Holocene to obtain guanaco and Rheidae as a complementary prey. To achieve this goal, the authors use archaeological evidence at different altitudinal levels on the northern margin of Lake Viedma basin, Santa Cruz province. These altitudinal and environmental variations—ranging from the shore of the lake to the basaltic plateau—seem to have generated different hunting strategies. The distribution, density, and variability of artefacts related to hunting—projectile points and "*bolas*"—the differential presence of hunting blinds and the environmental characteristics of different altitudinal levels allows the authors to propose a seasonal and complementary model of landscape use, which allowed the occupation of the basin throughout the year.

Ancient Hunting Strategies in Southern South America: An Introduction

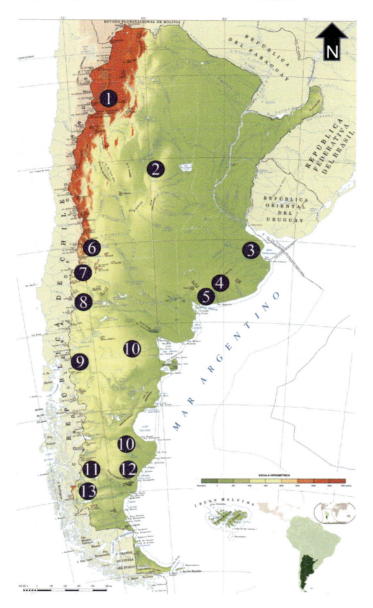

General reference map with the location of research areas reflected in each chapter (Map modified from Instituto Geográfico Nacional Argentino)

Cross-Interests and Study Trends

First of all, we would like to highlight the geographic variability covered by the different chapters and the way multiple lines of evidence have been articulated to try to understand the strategies for obtaining resources and the contribution that this configures to understand the human societies. We would like to highlight some other aspects in which the different chapters intersect and we believe that they summarize the interests in the study of the acquisition of resources through hunting, fishing, and gathering of small animals in Argentina. The first of these is the importance of camelids—guanacos and/or vicuñas—as the main prey in most of the landscapes investigated. This highlights the outstanding role played by these animals throughout history for the human populations at different latitudes of South America. Nevertheless, strategies for the production and processing, consumption, and disposal of huemul, rheids and smaller species such as fish, rodents, small birds, and carnivores have also been discussed. The great diversity of prey on which the chapters concentrate shows the importance of the obtaining of different species for both diet and the establishment of strategies for obtaining them.

The treatment of changes and continuities in hunting strategies through time and space is another aspect treated along the volume, either covering the entire Holocene or on shorter time scales. Different strategies, changes in weapon system or in social organization, and even the impact of the Spanish conquest are some of the themes that intersect the chapters. Also, geography and landscapes play a preponderant role in several chapters, analyzing how hunting strategies impact environmental diversity within study regions. This shows the importance of assessing local contexts and their relevance to regional archaeological interpretations.

Also, it is noteworthy the integration of ethnographic, ethnohistorical, and experimental data. The articulation of these sources allows the building of frames of reference to discuss the archaeological information and also to expand the chronological and interpretative backgrounds. Finally, we would like to stress the role played by the construction of hunting blinds and its imprint on the landscape, and the reason for weapon systems change, specifically the adoption of bow and arrow.

This volume provides a broad compilation of articles that brings together the effort of many years of fieldwork and laboratory analyses done by different research groups; thinking, discussing, and generating multiple lines of evidence to interpret how hunting and fishing strategies were organized and developed by human populations in southern South America. In this way, this volume can be grouped with other compilations dealing with hunting strategies at a global level (Bar-Oz and Nadel 2013) and at a regional scale (Martínez and Bozzuto 2011; Martínez and Rivero 2013).

Finally, we would like to thank the many actors who were of central importance, both in the realization of the workshop and in the development of this volume. In the first place, to all the research groups that accepted the proposal and the challenge of bringing together different lines of evidence to deal with a special topic such as hunting, fishing, and collecting different faunal resources. To the reviewers, for their readings and suggestions that have enriched chapters, helping with their knowledge and playing an important role in this book. To Springer/Nature editors, for allowing us to publish the volume, and particularly to Jorge Rabassa, editor of the Latin American Studies series of Springer/Nature. To the Consejo Nacional de Investigaciones Científicas y Tecnológicas (CONICET), Universidad de Buenos Aires, Universidad Nacional de Catamarca and Universidad Nacional de la Patagonia Austral, for all the support offered for the organization of the workshop and the edition of the abstract's volume. To the Dirección de Turismo of the Municipalidad of San Rafael and to the team of the Executive Unit IDEVEA that offered itself totally to the organization of the event. In particular, we would like to thank the Universidad Tecnológica Nacional of San Rafael for providing its facilities to carry out the workshop where we were able to develop such enriching discussion moments around animal hunting and fishing strategies in the past.

Juan Bautista Belardi
Damián Leandro Bozzuto
Pablo Marcelo Fernández
Enrique Alejandro Moreno
Gustavo Adolfo Neme

References

Bar-Oz G, Nadel D (2013) (Guest editors) Worldwide large-scale trapping and hunting of ungulates in past societies. Special volume of *Quaternary International* (Vol 297)
Binford LR (1978–2012–) Nunamiut ethnoarchaeology. Foundations of archaeology. Percheron Press, New York
Binford LR (1991) When the going gets tough, the tough get going: Nunamiut local groups, camping patterns and economic organization. In: Gamble CS, Boismier WA (eds) Ethnoarchaeological approaches to mobile campsites. Hunter-Gatherer and pastoralist case studies. International Monographs in Prehistory. Ethnoarchaeological Series 1, Ann Arbor, pp 25–137
Borrero LA (2013) Estrategias de caza en Fuego-Patagonia. *Comechingonia* 17(1):11–26
Churchill S (1993) Weapon technology, prey size selection, and hunting methods in modern hunters-gatherers: Implications for hunting in the palaeolithic and mesolithic. *Archaeological Papers of the American Anthropological Association* 4:11–24
Fenenga F (1953) The weights of chipped stone points: A clue to their functions. Southwestern. *J. Anthropol.* 9:309–323
Foley R (1983) Modelling hunting strategies and inferring predator behavior for prey attributes. In: Clutton-Bock J, Grigson C (eds) Animals and archaeology 1 Hunters and their prey. Bar International Series 163, Oxford, pp 63–76
Frison GC (2004) Survival by hunting. prehistoric human predators and animal prey. University of California Press, Berkeley
Kramer KL, Codding BF (2016) Hunters and gatherers in the twenty-first century. In: Codding BF, Kramer KL (eds) Why forage? Hunters and gatherers in the twenty-first century. School for Advanced Research. Advenced Seminar Series. University of New Mexico Press, Albuquerque, pp 1–14
Laughlin WS (1968) An integrating biobehavior system and its evolutionary importance. In: Lee RB, De Vore I (eds) Man the hunter. Aldine Publishing Company, Chicago
Lee RB, DeVore I (1968) Man the hunter. Aldine Publishing Company, Chicago
Martínez J, Bozzuto D (comp) (2011) Armas prehispánicas: Múltiples enfoques para su estudio en Sudamérica. Fundación de Historia Natural, Félix de Azara, Buenos Aires
Martínez J, Rivero D (eds) (2013) Estrategias y técnicas de caza prehispánicas. Dossier. *Revista Comechingonia* 17(1)
Mithen SJ (1990) Thoughtful foragers. A study of prehistoric decisión making. Cambridge UniversityPress, Cambridge

Ratto N (1994) Funcionalidad versus adscripción cultural: Cabezales líticos de la margen norte del estrecho de Magallanes. In: Lanata J, Borrero L (eds) Arqueología de Cazadores-recolectores. Límites, casos y aperturas. Arqueología Contemporánea, Buenos Aires 5:105–120

Ratto N (2003) Estrategias de caza y propiedades del registro arqueológico en la Puna de Chaschuil (Departamento de Tinogasta, Catamarca, Argentina). Unpublished doctoral thesis. Facultad de Filosofía y Letras, Universidad de Buenos Aires, Argentina

Shott M (1997) Stone and shafts redux: The metric discrimination of chipped-stone dart and arrow points. *American Antiquity* 62(1):86–101

Speth JD (2010) The paleoanthropology and archaeology of big-game hunting. Protein, fat, or politics? Interdisciplinary contributions to archaeology. Springer

Thomas D (1978) Arrowheads and atlatl darts: How the stones got the shaft. *American Antiquity* 43:461–472

List of Reviewers

Pablo Ambrústolo, Consejo Nacional de Investigaciones Científicas y Tecnológicas (CONICET)—División Arqueología, Facultad de Ciencias Naturales y Museo, Universidad Nacional de La Plata. Museo de La Plata.

Ramiro Barberena, Instituto Interdisciplinario de Ciencias Básicas (ICB) CONICET—Universidad Nacional de Cuyo Laboratorio de Paleoecología Humana.

Federico Bobillo, Instituto Superior de Estudios Sociales (ISES-CONICET/Universidad Nacional de Tucumán (UNT)).

Natacha Buc, Instituto Nacional de Antropología y Pensamiento Latinoamericano (INAPL), Consejo Nacional de Investigaciones Científicas y Técnicas (CONICET).

Marcelo Cardillo, IMHICIHU-CONICET-Universidad de Buenos Aires (UBA).

Mercedes Corbat, Universidad Nacional de la Patagonia "San Juan Bosco".

Isabel Cruz, Instituto de Ciencias del Ambiente, Sustentabilidad y Recursos Naturales (ICASUR-UARG-UNPA).

Luis del Papa, CONICET, Facultad de Ciencias Naturales y Museo, UNLP.

Alejandra Elías, CONICET-INAPL.

Alejandra Gasco, ICB-CONICET/UNCuyo, Laboratorio de Paleoecología Humana—LPEH.

Adolfo Gil, Instituto de Evolución, Ecología Histórica y Ambiente (IDEVEA—CONICET UTN).

María Gutiérrez, Instituto de Investigaciones Arqueológicas y Paleontológicas del Cuaternario Pampeano (INCUAPA-CONICET), Facultad de Ciencias Sociales, UNICEN.

Heidi Hammond, División Arqueología, Facultad de Ciencias Naturales y Museo, UNLP.

Lucía Magnin, CONICET—División Arqueología, Facultad de Ciencias Naturales y Museo UNLP.

Gustavo Martínez, INCUAPA-CONICET. FACSO-UNICEN.

Diana Mazzanti, Laboratorio de Arqueología (Universidad Nacional de Mar del Plata (UNMDP)).

Sebastián Muñoz, Instituto de Antropología de Córdoba-CONICET/Universidad Nacional de Córdoba (UNC).

Javier Musali, Ministerio de Transporte de la Nación.

Clara Otaola, Instituto de Evolución, Ecología Histórica y Ambiente (CONICET-Universidad Tecnológica Nacional-UTN).

Gisela Sario, IDACOR-CONICET y Museo de Antropología, FFyH, UNC.

Luciana Stoessel, INCUAPA-CONICET (Facultad de Ciencias Sociales, UNICEN).

Martín Vázquez, Centro Austral de Investigcaciones Científicas (CADIC-CONICET).

Atilio F. Zangrando, CADIC-CONICET.

Leandro Zilio, División Arqueología, Facultad de Ciencias Naturales y Museo, UNLP.

Contents

1 Ancient Hunting Strategies of Wild Camelids Through the Study of Multiple Lines of Archaeological Evidences at Southern Argentine Puna 1
Enrique Moreno, Jorge G. Martínez, and Carlos A. Aschero

2 Tiny Arrow Points, Bone-Tipped Projectiles, and Foraging During the Late Prehispanic Period (Sierras of Córdoba, Argentina) 33
Matías E. Medina and Imanol Balena

3 Assessing Strategies for Coypu Hunting and Use in the Salado River Depression (Buenos Aires Province, Argentina) 59
María Isabel González, Paula D. Escosteguy, Mónica C. Salemme, M. Magdalena Frère, Celeste Weitzel, and Rodrigo Vecchi

4 Guanaco Hunting Strategies in the Southeastern Pampas During the Late Holocene 83
Cristian A. Kaufmann, María C. Álvarez, Pablo G. Messineo, María P. Barros, Mariano Bonomo, and Guillermo Heider

5 Fish Capture Strategies in Atlantic Littoral of Monte Hermoso District (Pampean Region Argentina) During Middle Holocene 113
Romina Frontini, Cristina Bayón, and Rodrigo Vecchi

6 The Introduction of the Bow and Arrow Across South America's Southern Threshold Between Food-Producing Societies and Hunter-Gatherers 137
Silvina Castro, Lucía Yebra, Valeria Cortegoso, Erik Marsh, Agustín Castillo, Agustina Rughini, María Victoria Fernández, and Raven Garvey

7 Hunting, Butchering and Consumption of Rheidae in the South of South America: An Actualistic Study 159
Miguel Giardina, Clara Otaola, and Fernando Franchetti

xix

Contents

8   The Role of Small Prey in Human Populations of Northwest Patagonia and Its Implications 175
Diego D. Rindel, Florencia Gordón, Bruno Moscardi, and S. Ivan Perez

9   Hunting Techniques Along the Rain Shadow Gradient in North-Central Patagonia, Argentina 209
Mariana Carballido Calatayud and Pablo Marcelo Fernández

10 Changes and Continuities of Hunting Practices from the Late Pleistocene to the Late Holocene Among Nomadic Societies of the Patagonian Plateaus 259
Laura Miotti, Laura Marchionni, Darío Hermo,
Enrique Terranova, Lucía Magnin, Virginia Lynch,
Bruno Mosquera, Jorgelina Vargas Gariglio, and Natalia Carden

11 Technological Strategies and Guaranteed Return: Hunting Blinds and Patagonian Plateaus 293
Josefina Flores Coni, Juan Dellepiane, Gisela Cassiodoro,
Rafael Goñi, and Agustín Agnolin

12 Hunting Blinds in the Southern End of the Deseado Massif: Collective Hunting Strategies During the Late Holocene 313
Nora V. Franco, Lucas Vetrisano, Brenda L. Gilio,
Natalia A. Cirigliano, and Pablo E. Bianchi

13 Hunting Landscapes in the North Margin of Lake Viedma (Southern Patagonia, Argentina): Preys, Strategies and Technology 343
Juan Bautista Belardi, Flavia Carballo Marina, and Gustavo Barrientos

Index 361

Contributors

Agustín Agnolin Instituto Nacional de Antropología y Pensamiento Latinoamericano (INAPL), Consejo Nacional de Investigaciones Científicas y Técnicas (CONICET), Buenos Aires, Argentina

María C. Álvarez Instituto de Investigaciones Arqueológicas y Paleontológicas del Cuaternario Pampeano (INCUAPA-CONICET), Facultad de Ciencias Sociales, Universidad Nacional del Centro de la Provincia de Buenos Aires, Olavarría, Argentina

Carlos A. Aschero Instituto Superior de Estudios Sociales (ISES) CONICET, Instituto de Arqueología y Museo, Universidad Nacional de Tucumán, San Miguel de Tucumán, Argentina

Imanol Balena Consejo Nacional de Investigaciones Científicas y Técnicas (CONICET), División Arqueología, Facultad de Ciencias Naturales y Museo, Universidad Nacional de La Plata, La Plata, Argentina

Gustavo Barrientos CONICET, UNLP-FCNyM, La Plata, Argentina

María P. Barros Instituto de Investigaciones Arqueológicas y Paleontológicas del Cuaternario Pampeano (INCUAPA-CONICET), Facultad de Ciencias Sociales, Universidad Nacional del Centro de la Provincia de Buenos Aires, Olavarría, Argentina

Cristina Bayón Departamento de Humanidades, Universidad Nacional del Sur, Bahía Blanca, Argentina

Juan Bautista Belardi CIT Santa Cruz, Consejo Nacional de Investigaciones Científicas y Técnicas (CONICET), Universidad Nacional de La Patagonia Austral, Unidad Académica Río Gallegos (UNPA-UARG), ICASUR, Rio Gallegos, Santa Cruz, Argentina

Pablo E. Bianchi IMHICIHU-CONICET, Buenos Aires, Argentina

Mariano Bonomo CONICET-División Arqueología, Facultad de Ciencias Naturales y Museo, Universidad Nacional de La Plata, La Plata, Argentina

Mariana Carballido Calatayud Instituto Nacional de Antropología y Pensamiento Latinoamericano (INAPL), Consejo Nacional de Investigaciones Científicas y Técnicas (CONICET), Universidad de Buenos Aires (UBA), Buenos Aires, Argentina

Natalia Carden INCUAPA-CONICET. Facultad de Ciencias Sociales, Universidad Nacional del Centro de la Provincia de Buenos, Tandil, Argentina

Gisela Cassiodoro INAPL, CONICET, Universidad de Buenos Aires (UBA), Buenos Aires, Argentina

Agustín Castillo Laboratorio de Paleoecología Humana, Facultad de Ciencias Exactas y Naturales, Universidad Nacional de Cuyo, Mendoza, Argentina

Silvina Castro Laboratorio de Paleoecología Humana, Facultad de Ciencias Exactas y Naturales, Universidad Nacional de Cuyo, Mendoza, Argentina

Natalia A. Cirigliano IMHICIHU-CONICET, Buenos Aires, Argentina

Valeria Cortegoso CONICET, Laboratorio de Paleoecología Humana, Facultad de Ciencias Exactas y Naturales, Universidad Nacional de Cuyo, Mendoza, Argentina

Juan Dellepiane Instituto Nacional de Antropología y Pensamiento Latinoamericano (INAPL), Consejo Nacional de Investigaciones Científicas y Técnicas (CONICET), Buenos Aires, Argentina

Paula D. Escosteguy CONICET— Universidad de Buenos Aires, Facultad de Filosofía y Letras, Instituto de Arqueología, Buenos Aires, Argentina

María Victoria Fernández CONICET, Instituto de Investigaciones en Diversidad Cultural y Procesos de Cambio, Universidad Nacional de Río Negro, Mendoza, Argentina

Pablo Marcelo Fernández Instituto Nacional de Antropología y Pensamiento Latinoamericano (INAPL), Consejo Nacional de Investigaciones Científicas y Técnicas (CONICET), Universidad de Buenos Aires (UBA), Buenos Aires, Argentina

Josefina Flores Coni Instituto Nacional de Antropología y Pensamiento Latinoamericano (INAPL), Consejo Nacional de Investigaciones Científicas y Técnicas (CONICET), Buenos Aires, Argentina

Fernando Franchetti Department of Anthropology, University of Pittsburgh, Pittsburgh, PA, USA

Nora V. Franco IMHICIHU-CONICET, Buenos Aires, Argentina;
Universidad de Buenos Aires, FFyL, Dpto. Cs. Antropológicas, Buenos Aires, Argentina

M. Magdalena Frère Facultad de Filosofía y Letras, Instituto de Arqueología, Universidad de Buenos Aires, Buenos Aires, Argentina

Romina Frontini CONICET, Departamento de Humanidades, Universidad Nacional del Sur, Bahía Blanca, Argentina

Raven Garvey Department of Anthropology, University of Michigan, Ann Arbor, MI, USA

Miguel Giardina CONICET/Instituto de Evolución, Ecología Histórica y Ambiente-Universidad Tecnológica Nacional, Facultad Regional San Rafael, Department of Anthropology, Museo de Historia Natural de San Rafael, Mendoza, Argentina

Brenda L. Gilio CIT Santa Cruz-CONICET, Río Gallegos, Argentina

Rafael Goñi INAPL, Universidad de Buenos Aires (UBA), Buenos Aires, Argentina

María Isabel González Facultad de Filosofía y Letras, Instituto de Arqueología, Universidad de Buenos Aires, Buenos Aires, Argentina

Florencia Gordón CONICET-FCNyM (UNLP), La Plata, Argentina

Guillermo Heider CONICET-Departamento de Geología, Universidad Nacional de San Luis, San Luis, Argentina

Darío Hermo División Arqueología, Museo de La Plata, Universidad Nacional de La Plata and CONICET, La Plata, Argentina

Cristian A. Kaufmann Instituto de Investigaciones Arqueológicas y Paleontológicas del Cuaternario Pampeano (INCUAPA-CONICET), Facultad de Ciencias Sociales, Universidad Nacional del Centro de la Provincia de Buenos Aires, Olavarría, Argentina

Virginia Lynch División Arqueología, Museo de La Plata, Universidad Nacional de La Plata, La Plata, Argentina

Lucía Magnin División Arqueología, Museo de La Plata, Universidad Nacional de La Plata and CONICET, La Plata, Argentina

Laura Marchionni División Arqueología, Museo de La Plata, Universidad Nacional de La Plata and CONICET, La Plata, Argentina

Flavia Carballo Marina ICASUR, UNPA-UARG, Rio Gallegos, Santa Cruz, Argentina

Erik Marsh CONICET, Laboratorio de Paleoecología Humana, Facultad de Ciencias Exactas y Naturales, Universidad Nacional de Cuyo, Mendoza, Argentina

Jorge G. Martínez Instituto Superior de Estudios Sociales (ISES) CONICET, Instituto de Arqueología y Museo, Universidad Nacional de Tucumán, San Miguel de Tucumán, Argentina

Matías E. Medina Consejo Nacional de Investigaciones Científicas y Técnicas (CONICET), División Arqueología, Facultad de Ciencias Naturales y Museo, Universidad Nacional de La Plata, La Plata, Argentina

Pablo G. Messineo Instituto de Investigaciones Arqueológicas y Paleontológicas del Cuaternario Pampeano (INCUAPA-CONICET), Facultad de Ciencias Sociales, Universidad Nacional del Centro de la Provincia de Buenos Aires, Olavarría, Argentina

Laura Miotti División Arqueología, Museo de La Plata, Universidad Nacional de La Plata and CONICET, La Plata, Argentina

Enrique Moreno Centro de Investigaciones y Transferencia Catamarca (CITCA— CONICET/UNCA), Escuela de Arqueología, Universidad Nacional de Catamarca (UNCA), San Fernando del Valle de Catamarca, Catamarca, Argentina

Bruno Moscardi FCNyM (UNLP), La Plata, Argentina

Bruno Mosquera División Arqueología, Museo de La Plata, Universidad Nacional de La Plata and CONICET, La Plata, Argentina

Clara Otaola CONICET/IDEVEA-UTN FRSR, Department of Anthropology, Museo de Historia Natural de San Rafael, Mendoza, Argentina

S. Ivan Perez CONICET-FCNyM (UNLP), Calle 60 y 122, La Plata, Argentina

Diego D. Rindel CONICET-INAPL, Buenos Aires, Argentina

Agustina Rughini CONICET, Laboratorio de Paleoecología Humana, Facultad de Ciencias Exactas y Naturales, Universidad Nacional de Cuyo, Mendoza, Argentina

Mónica C. Salemme CADIC-CONICET, Universidad Nacional de Tierra del Fuego, Antártida e Islas del Atlántico Sur, Ushuaia, Argentina

Enrique Terranova División Arqueología, Museo de La Plata, Universidad Nacional de La Plata and CONICET, La Plata, Argentina

Jorgelina Vargas Gariglio División Arqueología, Museo de La Plata, Universidad Nacional de La Plata, La Plata, Argentina

Rodrigo Vecchi CONICET, Universidad Nacional del Sur, Bahía Blanca, Argentina

Lucas Vetrisano IMHICIHU-CONICET, Buenos Aires, Argentina

Celeste Weitzel CONICET—Área de Arqueología y Antropología, Museo de Ciencias Naturales de Necochea, Necochea, Argentina

Lucía Yebra CONICET, Laboratorio de Paleoecología Humana, Facultad de Ciencias Exactas y Naturales, Universidad Nacional de Cuyo, Mendoza, Argentina

Chapter 1
Ancient Hunting Strategies of Wild Camelids Through the Study of Multiple Lines of Archaeological Evidences at Southern Argentine Puna

Enrique Moreno, Jorge G. Martínez, and Carlos A. Aschero

Abstract In recent decades, wild camelids hunting strategies have been a topic of interest for several research groups in Argentina's southern Puna in Northwestern Argentina. In this chapter, we present a synthesis of hunting strategies models that would have been implemented at Antofagasta de la Sierra (Catamarca, Argentina) in a long-lasting account that covers the entire Holocene. The models we will treat were defined for two discrete areas within this Puna environment: Quebrada Seca and the Antofalla ravine. For both areas, different hunting models were postulated based on the combination of a series of variables such as landscape features and weapon systems. They varied in time and space for both areas, although vicuñas were a common factor as hunting prey. Our interest here lies, then, in reflexively evaluating these models in order to form a theoretical, methodological, and technical basis for the study of pre-Hispanic hunting practices in the higher Andes environment.

Keywords Hunting practices · Weapons · Landscape · Antofagasta de la Sierra · Holocene · Northwestern Argentina

1.1 Introduction: About Hunting as a Practice

Before beginning our proposal on hunting strategies in the Puna of Catamarca Province, Argentina implemented through the Holocene, we believe it is necessary to think on what we understand by hunting and what these practices imply for the human populations that developed them. In this sense, it is reductionist to think that hunting involves only the killing of one or more animals by one or more people in order to obtain primary and secondary resources. It is clear that the significance of

---

E. Moreno (✉)
Centro de Investigaciones y Transferencia Catamarca (CITCA—CONICET/UNCA), Escuela de Arqueología, Universidad Nacional de Catamarca (UNCA), San Fernando del Valle de Catamarca, Catamarca, Argentina

J. G. Martínez · C. A. Aschero
Instituto Superior de Estudios Sociales (ISES) CONICET, Instituto de Arqueología y Museo, Universidad Nacional de Tucumán, San Miguel de Tucumán, Argentina

© Springer Nature Switzerland AG 2021
J. B. Belardi et al. (eds.), *Ancient Hunting Strategies in Southern South America*,
The Latin American Studies Book Series,
https://doi.org/10.1007/978-3-030-61187-3_1

this practice far exceeds this only dietary objective. Many authors have asked for the importance of hunting in different spheres of the social reproduction of human populations (Laughlin 1968; Binford 1988; Churchill 1993; Aschero and Martínez 2001; among others). Going further from the food supply, one of the main aspects surrounding hunting practices would be linked to the symbolic role generated by the action of killing wild animals, to the social hierarchy reached by the one who could obtain the prey and to the social implications that the collective hunting might have had. In the particular case of Southern Argentine Puna, the main prey would have been the vicuña (*Vicugna vicugna*), a wild animal that has a great capacity to identify and escape from potential predators in an environment high above sea level, where the hunters had simple weapons and some difficulties to obtain hiding places, given the absence of high vegetation capable of providing hideout and wide visibility. However, as we will see, these characteristics would not be so homogeneous and would also affect the actions of prey as well.

Thus, it is necessary to think of hunting in terms of these social implications as a relevant practice on the social and inter-group scale for strengthening relationship nets. Since to achieve success, every hunt needs to articulate several factors. These refer to (a) hunters knowledge about the behavior of potential prey, (b) tactical resources that offer the local environment characteristics, which include not only the relief and vegetation, but the action of winds, location relative to the position of the sun, among others; (c) operational or control relations between hunters and (d) the possibilities provided by the implementation of multiple technical devices, such as weapons or structures. These, including many other issues, such as premonitory dreams, an adequate calendar for hunting, social events involved before and/or after hunting, such as rites of passage, propitiatory rites for the success of hunting, requests for the successful reproduction of the prey, prior to the time of the female's calving, are relevant aspects for hunting practices.

For this work, in which we will focus on archaeological evidence, some of these aspects will not be specifically addressed but will be taken into account for the interpretations that may be reached. Some years ago, two of the authors raised the need to articulate multiple lines of archaeological evidence to study hunting strategies: the weapons systems, the particularities of the relief and climate, the ethology of prey and the social relations between hunters (Aschero and Martínez 2001).

Pointing out the importance of hunting as a social practice in the reproduction of human groups over time and the need for a comprehensive approach to understand hunting in archaeological research, in this chapter our main aim is to develop a theoretical-methodological contribution based on the case studied and articulating these different lines of evidence, to help to understand the importance and particularities of hunting strategies for pre-Hispanic populations through the Holocene in Argentine Puna.

1.2 Hunting Strategies and Its Relevance in Argentine Puna

Through the history of human occupation in the South-central Andes, the interaction between camelids and human populations was central in the social reproduction, in relation with the obtaining of a series of resources such as meat, leather, bone, tendons, wool, transport, etc. Among the strategies practiced by human populations in order to appropriate these animals (sensu Ingold 1987), hunting results the most important because of its realization in the long term of human occupation of the area, and also because of its relevance in different social, economic, political, and historical contexts. A multiplicity of investigations has provided information about these populations and the relevance of hunting in this long historical process which covers approximately the last 10,000 years. In this sense, these investigations have proposed that during the early and middle Holocene, human populations were characterized by an economy based in camelids and rodents hunting and in the exchange of vegetable resources from lower areas, principally the mesothermal valleys (Aschero 2000; Elkin 1996; Martínez 2003; Yacobaccio et al. 1997–1998). The archaeological investigations were able to advance in the characterization of hunting strategies, as well as on the settlement and mobility patterns of these groups. Among these studies it is the one carried on by Aschero and Martínez (2001) who assure that "the hunting of camelids was the principal subsistence activity, including during late moments under the full establishment of agricultural practice (although) hunting and gathering dominated the strategies of subsistence of most of the history of men in the Puna desert, until herdering and agriculture, as productive ways of subsistence, started to become preponderant in these economies" (Aschero and Martínez 2001: 216, author's translation. Also see Martínez 2003).

In the same way, Elkin (1996), analyzing the archaeofaunal remains of Quebrada Seca 3 (Antofagasta de la Sierra, Catamarca) shows that camelids were the principal resource of this zone in the Puna of Catamarca. This author proposes the relevance of hunting camelids without selecting ages nor sex of prey. An important conclusion she arrives at is that "the camelids populations of the Antofagasta de la Sierra basin seems to have supported hunting pressure through several millennia without the need of protecting the animal's reproduction rate, systematically preying over family groups, the most vulnerable part of the population" (Elkin 1996: 134–135, author's translation).

These authors, together with other investigations in the South-central Andes, have proposed the realization of camelids hunting, being a very important resource due to its caloric input as well as the use of secondary products. In this way the mobility of human populations would also have been related with the mobility strategies of troops of camelids in moments of climate changes, occupying lower or higher ecological levels (Fernández Distel 1974; Gambier 1981; Núñez 1983; Yacobaccio 1991; Yacobaccio et al. 1997–1998).

Around 5500 years BP, the process of domestication of plants and animals should have begun, which implies an important modification in economic, social, political, and religious contexts in the local populations. This period shows a progressive decrease in the importance of hunting camelids which Yacobaccio et al. (1997–1998) proposed as a process beginning with a hunting-gathering economy, passing through hunting-domesticating, hunting-herding until reaching a time of herding-hunting. This modification would be given in the predominant strategy that is defined as the one that determines the organizational structure over which different economic activities are planned and realized. This process implies a complexity of the hunting-gathering societies, characterized by aspects such as the reduced residence mobility, territorial behavior, high population density and presence of bigger groups of residents, intra-group inequalities, development of ritual practices as a form of social cohesion (Hocsman 2006; Yacobaccio 2001).

Around the start of the First millennium BC the agricultural-herding societies are definitively established, which conform the "Formative period" inside the chronology established by the regional archaeology (Olivera 2001). These societies, in Puna case, have been characterized as small populations dedicated to herding, with a differential importance of agriculture development and with the input of wild camelid hunting (*Vicugna vicugna* and *Lama guanicoe*). In this way the economic organization and therefore the reproduction strategies of human groups were based around the control of the herds, subjecting the other practices to the development of these activities (Yacobaccio 2001).

However, information obtained by archaeological investigations, show that this situation was more flexible, where there can be noted a diverse economical organization, where different economic strategies had a relevant importance on everyday life reproduction. Regarding agriculture, Quesada (2001, 2007) has developed an investigation in the Antofalla area, where he shows the agricultural development and the social scale of work associated with these practices, remarking the importance of this activity. On the other hand, investigations centered in the archaeofaunal remains have shown a relative preponderance of the exploitation of wild camelids, specifically vicuñas, compare to the already domesticated llamas (*Lama glama*). These are the cases, among others, of Tebenquiche Chico 1 (Haber 2006; Revuelta 2005), Quebrada Seca 3 (Elkin 1996) and Real Grande 1 (Olivera 1997), in the southern Puna (Catamarca) and Huachichocana III (Yacobaccio and Madero 1992) in the northern Puna (Jujuy). This allows us to reflect about the role of hunting of wild camelids in the agricultural-herding period, being an economy based on diversified economic strategies. In this historical context, the relevance of wild camelids, particularly vicuñas, started to modify, particularly because of the quality of its wool and its role in the regional articulation and the reproduction of social hierarchies.

Following this imaginary timeline, in the Inka period and according to what the historical chronicles show, the vicuñas would have recovered an important "economical-ritual" role by taking part of *chaku* celebrations in honor of the Inka (Puló 1998, 2000; Ratto 2003). This ritual consisted of the preparation of a great circle, in which a troop of vicuñas was entered and then they were hunted and the flesh and wool were given to the Inka. It seems that this practice had a strong control by the Inka state as it is shown in several chronicles and ethno-historical investigations (Cieza de León [1553] 1984; Murra 1978; Polo de Ondegardo [1571] 1990; Yacobaccio 2009). Later on, during the colonial period (XVI and XVII centuries), the vicuña would have turned in one of the principal resources to accomplish tribute payment by local populations due to its characteristics (possible to be changed for metals, raw material to be transformed into manufactures which could be placed in the market or object which would be accepted as "money of the earth") (Lema 2004; Yacobaccio et al. 2007). However, this is referred in the narrative construction of travellers of the zone from a deterministic view, where the unique economic option for local populations was the subsistence through the vicuña and it was not thought as a mechanism of articulation of the local societies with the emerging colonial markets (Haber and Lema 2006; Lema 2004; Moreno and Revuelta 2010).

Already in the Republican period (nineteenth century), the vicuña's hunting relevance would continue being central for the local populations, providing a resource which was possible to be exchanged for goods from other regions. Thus, the vicuña hunting of other species, would provide a surplus of resources even more important than agriculture. This activity supplied resources such as meat, wool and leather. However, the principal resource would have been the weave of the vicuña which would allow the exchange for other goods in places such as Cachi (Salta) or San Pedro de Atacama and Toconao (Chile) (Benedetti 2005). "*The commercial exchange consists in selling the leathers and wool of the vicuña, llama, sheep and goat leather, and there can be added the animal skins obtained from hunting… Other products which they exchanged for corn or flour are the woollens which they spin and knit by primitive methods and which are very appreciated by experts*" (Catalano 1930 in Benedetti 2005: 400, author's translation).

The materialization of vicuña hunting and its introduction into the European markets due to the fine quality of its wool, promoted the realization of an excessive hunt of these animals, causing the ban of hunting and marketing of vicuñas wool since approximately 60 years in the territory of the Province of Catamarca, Argentina, as well as in all the areas which own vicuñas in other countries of South America. These laws were established because of the claim of different areas because of the killing of vicuñas due to the high prices of the wool and the total lack of control of this practice (Moreno 2012; Puló 1998, 2000; Vilá 2006).

1.3 Antofagasta de la Sierra: Environmental Characteristics

The department of Antofagasta de la Sierra (Catamarca, Argentina) is located in the Southern Puna of Argentina above 3000 m a.s.l., and it is characterized by extreme aridity, large daily thermal amplitude, scarce watersheds and very low rainfall, so it is defined as a high altitude desert. This vision of the Puna environment assumed a scarce human population or conditions that implied difficulties for the development of life. However, we believe that the main problem of this vision is based on negating the variability of spaces with differential water availability, as oasis, from which desert spaces were managed as pathways of circulation and exploitation of mineral resources and where the temporal depth and growing social complexity has been a major axis in the reproduction of human populations along time.

This chapter will focus on two research areas of Antofagasta de la Sierra Department, whose data outline the basic nucleus of it. On one hand we have information from Quebrada Seca, in the micro-region of Antofagasta de la Sierra and on the other hand, from the Antofalla ravine, on the periphery of the homonymous "Salar" (i.e., a large salt lake) (Fig. 1.1).

Quebrada Seca is located 15 km east of Antofagasta de la Sierra village at ca. 4100 m a.s.l. and it is where the stratified archaeological site Quebrada Seca 3 (QS3) is located. It is a rocky cave that was interpreted as the central point of a settlement location, established by a limited space with a radius of 2.5 km in which different micro-environments are articulated: high altitude marshes, gullies with ignimbrite outcrops—with sporadic drains and shrubby vegetation typical of the rocky outcrops—that connect marshes with high plains in the relief of the glacis, with a steppe east-west slope and "pajonal" type vegetation. In this place (according to Ingold 2000) there are a set of interrelated sites inhabited at different times along

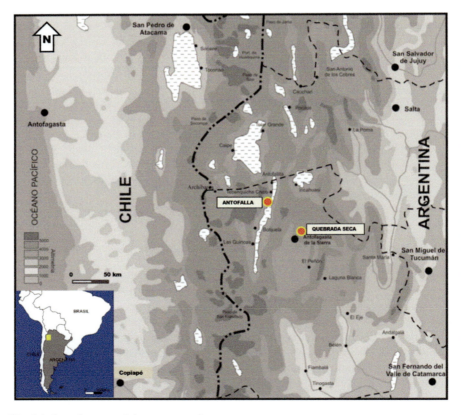

Fig. 1.1 Location map of the two research areas

the Holocene (Martínez 2003). It should be noted that due to the excellent conservation of archaeological material and the extensive time range it represents, QS3 is a very important site for understanding the human occupation of southern Puna in Argentina. Its stratification shows a remarkable sequence of occupations along the Holocene (Aschero et al. 1993–1994), spanning the period between ca. 9790 years BP and 2480 years BP (Aschero and Martínez 2001).

The Antofalla ravine is located in the northwestern sector of the department of Antofagasta de la Sierra, province of Catamarca, Argentina. It is one of the ravines that descends toward the Salar de Antofalla, following the water course that originates in two springs located at approximately 4100 and 3900 m a.s.l. and that in its lower part forms a dejection cone with an approximate height of 3400 m a.s.l., where it is lost in the salt flats. This particularity of the water regime forms a marsh landscape around the watercourse; the rest is arid. The Antofalla ravine has two well-marked sides, whose slopes are very variable, in some sectors they are steep, in others, quite soft. Nowadays, despite the location of the town of the same name in the lower part of the ravine and the use of several spaces for grazing lamas (*Lama glama*), sheep (*Ovis aries*) and donkeys (*Equus asinus*), vicuña herds can be observed living at some sectors of this ravine.

1.4 Knowing the Preys: Vicuñas

It is important, before entering into the models of hunting strategies, to make a brief comment on the main prey evidenced in the zooarchaeological record: vicuñas (Fig. 1.2). This emerges from the multiple works carried out in the micro-region of Antofagasta de la Sierra and Antofalla, denoting the dominance of this specie in the faunal remains of various archaeological contexts analyzed (Elkin 1996; Erramouspe et al. 2017; Grant 2017; Grant et al. 2017; Haber 2006; Mondini and Elkin 2014; Mondini et al. 2015; Moreno and Revuelta 2010; Olivera 1997; Revuelta 2005; Urquiza 2009; Urquiza and Aschero 2014).

The social organization of vicuñas is characterized by the existence of family groups, herds of single males and lone males. In this case, we will focus on the family groups, since it has been evidenced the utilization of animals of both sexes and different age groups which would predominate hunting on family groups (Elkin 1996). The family groups are defined by a dominant male or "*relincho*," who maintains and controls the territory, a variable number of adult females, young females older than one year and offspring of both sexes younger than one year (Bonacic 2005; Franklin 1982; Hoffman et al. 1983; Tomka 1992; Wheeler 2006). The dominant male is in charge of protecting the troop against possible dangers, initiating the escape if necessary, while the females and offspring graze. These animals have the capacity to escape at high speed and through steep slopes, so hunting for persecution would not be a viable option. The form of establishment and delimitation of territories is based on the formation of "*bosteaderos*," that is, common sites of defecations that mark the boundaries of the territory (Bonacic 2005; Tomka 1992; Wheeler 2006). Within this

Fig. 1.2 Vicuña's herd at Antofagasta de la Sierra

territory is included an elevated area which is used as a sleeping place, preferably taking advantage of rock shelters that provide some protection, and lower areas with pastures and a water source. His daily movement is routine, sleeping in high areas and descending during sunlight hours to graze and drink in rivers or marshes, returning at twilight to the rocks used as sleeping place (Franklin 1982; Haber 2003; Haber and Moreno 2018; Hoffman et al. 1983; Koford 1957; Tomka 1992). Because of the physiology of these animals, they must drink water every day, so this movement is performed unfailingly on a daily basis, and through paths that remain marked in the arid landscape because of their continuous walking. The ethological characteristics of vicuñas and their paths would show the need to prepare landscapes to stimulate encounters by the appropriation of topographic resources to perform hunting tactics. That is, they are animals that have a routine movement, relatively predictable, but that in turn perceive the predators through different senses (smell, sight, hearing), being able to quickly escape in front of almost any obstacle that shows up.

1.5 The Construction of Hunting Models at Southern Argentine Puna

1.5.1 Quebrada Seca Case

Research at Quebrada Seca (Fig. 1.3) allowed the construction of models involving changes along the early and middle Holocene in hunting strategies linked to the use of different spaces, the participation of a variable number of hunters, the use of hiding structures and the modification in weapon systems.

A first **model A** (Aschero and Martínez 2001) was proposed, which could be associated with the exploration phase of Puna toward the Pleistocene–Holocene transition. In this model a long-distance hunt is proposed, in open spaces such as pampas and plains, supported by the use of atlatl or spearthrower, as a powerful weapon system where the hunter has a stalking movement toward the prey. This approach would be given using natural hideouts and could have been a solitary hunt or a few hunters who would make their attack toward mainly passive prey. Atlatl would have counted on darts whose heads are triangular similar to the "pattern" of Tuina-Inca Cueva, which were recovered in the earliest layers of QS3 site within the range ca. 10,000–8660 years BP and were assigned to the Morphological Type QSA (Martínez 2003). This triangular without peduncle design denotes a clear recurrence

Fig. 1.3 General view of Quebrada Seca

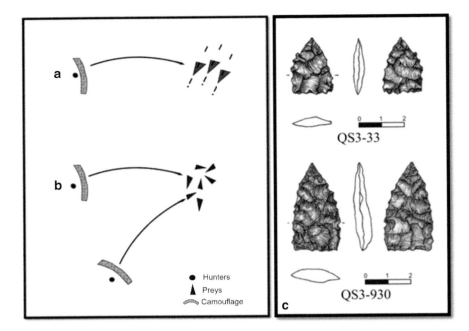

Fig. 1.4 Dynamic scheme of Model A. **a** Hunting with moving prey. **b** Approaching with camouflage and passive prey. **c** QSA Morphological Type of QS3 Projectile point (Hocsman et al. 2012)

of this pattern with early chronologies in both Andean slopes of the Puna, setting up a stability in its use under the same strategy for the period ca. 11,000–8500 years BP (Fig. 1.4).

Later on, between ca. 9000 and 7700 years BP, it is proposed the operation of another **model B** based on hunt by interception taking advantage of ravines or hollows with the visible paths used by vicuñas herds in whose springs preys were stalked. The projectile points associated with these moments are triangular with prominent peduncle and incoming fins, defined as Morphological Type QSB (Martínez 2003, 2007). This model is also based on the use of atlatl, and there would be a greater use of topographic characteristics, as well as the aggregation of more hunters who would launch their darts simultaneously to achieve success in the hunt. This model would constitute the antecedent of collective hunting techniques. It should be noted that in QS3 there is a greater redundancy of human occupation for this period (levels 2b14–2b11), evidenced by greater archaeological material density (Aschero et al. 1991, 1993–1994), which could indicate a greater number of people involved (Fig. 1.5).

For the same model, the variant of the use of short-range throwing spears is proposed associated with QSC Morphological Type projectile points recorded in QS3 for the period 7700–7200 years BP, and in both cases supports the alternative of driving vicuña herds into ravines that connect the lowland sectors with the open

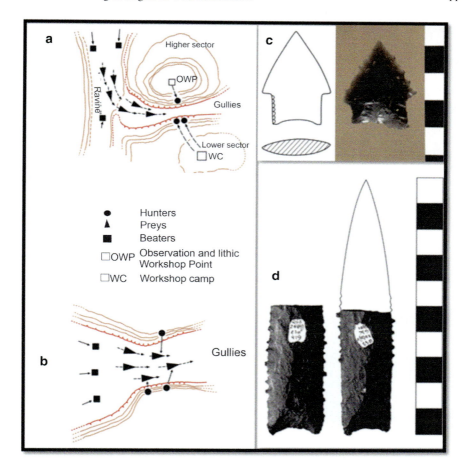

Fig. 1.5 Dynamic scheme of Model B. **a** Intercept hunting and use of atlatl associated with Morphological Type QSB. **b** Hunting by interception and use of throwing spear associated with Morphological Type QSC. **c** Morphological Type QSB of projectile tips of site QS3. **d** QSC Morphological Type of QS3 site projectile points

pampas. This would have led to a reduction in the hunting-prey distance and an increase in the effectiveness of shots. In addition, this hunting system which involves driving prey makes it possible to manage the time factor since, when the prey is grazing at the bottom of the plain or the ravines, it is hunter's decision to start the action without waiting for vicuñas to return by their paths to higher places.

With certain chronological and spatial overlap, a third **model C** alludes to hunting with the use of spears and the forced driving of prey toward the concentration of hiding structures, named hunting blinds. It would have started in the period of 7700–7200 years BP associated with the use of short-range spears with large-scale QSC morphological projectile points, where there would have been a simultaneous use of several hunting blinds by a greater number of hunters and beaters. Therefore, this model assumes a combination of natural and artificial features. Hunting blinds are small semicircular stone structures, about 2 m long and 70 cm high (Fig. 1.6). They are located at higher areas of landscape that give a better camouflage to the hunters as is the case with the concentration of the site Quebrada Seca 5 (QS5; Fig. 1.7). In this model, it is necessary to decrease distance between hunters and vicuñas, which is managed by beaters participation. The slope toward the hunting blinds in this case is ascending from west to east, and this same direction is taken by vicuña's herds that are being driven by the beaters from a gully that connects this sector of pampas with the marsh of Quebrada Seca. If this strategy was scheduled at dawn, the incidence of sun's rays could have been an extra help by decreasing the vision of vicuñas that would have the sun facing, which would increase hunters hiding behind hunting blinds.

These models show different hunting strategies, which varied over time, taking advantage of different sectors of the local landscape, occurring at Quebrada Seca

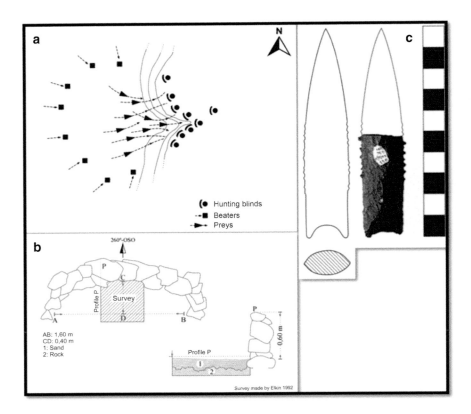

Fig. 1.6 Dynamic scheme of Model C. **a** Collective hunting with the use of spears, hunting blinds and beaters, associated with the Morphological Type QSC (case of the site QS5). **b** Plant and profile of a typical QS5 site hunting blind. **c** QSC Morphological Type of QS3 site projectile point

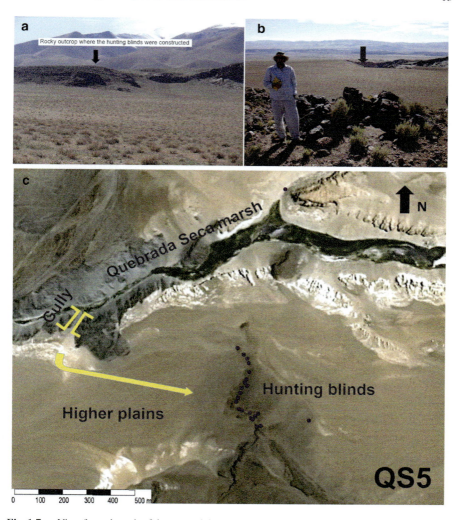

Fig. 1.7 a View from the exit of the vega-plain connecting gully towards the hunting blinds of QS5 (from west to east). **b** View from QS5 towards the lower part; the black arrow shows the access gully. **c** Movement direction of vicuña's herds towards QS5 hunting blinds concentration; small circles indicate the position of each structure

spring where the QS3 has played a gravitational role. Its function would have remained constant over time, being primarily a temporary residential base related to hunting, processing and consumption of vicuñas (Elkin 1996). The faunal evidence reveals a highly stable economic system throughout the sequence, in relation to exploited taxa, their relative economic importance, and the obtaining and processing characteristics.

One issue that could be suggested by the model of collective hunting is the repetition of predation on the same spaces through time. That means, the possibility of an over-killing by pressing on certain vicuña's herds. But there are four other ravines with high altitude marshes in which, although they are not completely surveyed, information about the existence of hunting blinds would imply a potential rotation of hunting places. This is the case of the nearby ravines of Ilanco, Miriguaca, Cacao, and Curuto. Survey carried out in a tributary ravine of Ilanco River at its northeast band, counted more than 10 hunting blinds that offered protection from the southwest winds. Unlike those of the QS5 site (Fig. 1.7), they showed a higher altitude due to a maintenance made by the contribution of smaller blocks on pre-existing structures and the presence of small projectile points assigned to the Formative and/or Later periods. Another survey carried out in a ravine on the side of Cacao ravine (Aschero et al. 2018) documented a couple of hunting blinds in the southern spring, called "Agua de las vicuñas". Here, unlike the previous one, there would have been no recorded maintenance. A third survey between Quebrada Seca and Real Grande, located a hill with hunting blinds dominating a gully with drainage toward Real Grande.

The information obtained by this survey, bring up the issue of the variation in the number of hunting blinds in each spring and the time of use and operation of them. There are reliable data on the use of hunting blinds by vicuñas hunters in Antofagasta de la Sierra at least until the 1960s. In that case, individual hunters with rifles using the old hunting blinds. Also the above mentioned near Ilanco ravine could have been recycled in late pre-Hispanic times but also for collective hunting. However, the number of structures in the same location also refers to a variation in the number of members of the collective attack. These isolated data already indicate a widespread use in which the old hunting blinds prepared in the Archaic could be maintained or recycled hundreds or thousands of years later. This is a pending issue in the ravines of the eastern band of the Punilla River: establishing relative chronologies based on the presence of lichens in the rocks used, variation in size between the base rocks and the summit of hunting blinds, heights reached by the walls, the dispersion of blocks at the foot of them and the association of morphological types of projectile points recovered at the periphery of structures (Fig. 1.8).

It is worth noting here the presence of a set of hunting blinds on the southeastern edge of Laguna Colorada, which is located on the west bank of Punilla River. These structures are associated with small lanceolate projectile points similar to those detected in Peñas Chicas 1.1 site (on the Las Pitas river) corresponding to the morphological type Peñas Chicas E (sensu Hocsman 2006). This morphological type is associated with chronologies of the range ca. 4800–2900 years BP within a wide area that takes the Argentine Puna and even the north of Chile (Núñez et al. 1999; Hocsman 2006), so we could link the use of these hunting blinds to the end of the middle Holocene and the beginning of the late Holocene. Over a block that is part of a hunting blinds was identified an engraving of the "sub-style of marks" of the modality Quebrada Seca, equal to that of the sites Punta de la Peña 4 a lower altitude allows to propose the use of hunting blinds associated with lagoon edges for chronologies of the late Archaic period.

1 Ancient Hunting Strategies of Wild Camelids …

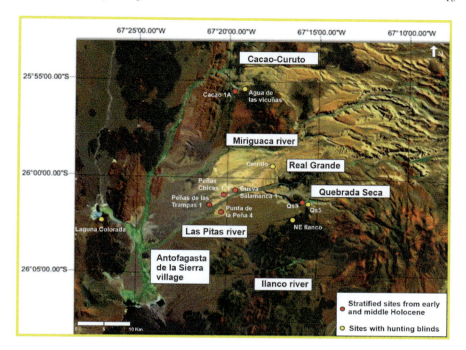

Fig. 1.8 Location of ravines and archaeological sites mentioned in the text

1.5.2 Antofalla Ravine

For the study of hunting strategies in this ravine, the interest was put in the articulation between landscape transformation, the different types of weapons used for this practice over time and the ethological characteristics of prey.

An intensive survey was carried out at Antofalla ravine (Fig. 1.9). It covered an area of approximately 40 km^2 (Moreno 2010), through parallel transects, separated every 40 m and carried out systematic sampling of 1 m^2 every 100 meters (Gianotti 2004; Haber 1999; Moreno 2010; Nance 1979). The identification and collection of projectile points was of particular interest. In the field, we took the geographical coordinates of each recording unit, the landscape characteristics and the association with other archaeological features and photographed the area (Moreno 2010).

The evidence recorded shows different cultural landscapes and historical moments (Haber 2006; Haber et al. 2002; Moreno 2010, 2018; Quesada 2001, 2007). Intensive survey, however, produced an important amount of information related to hunting strategies. The most relevant is the identification of a large number of hunting blinds, identified along the ravine. But, the defining feature for interpreting its functionality was based on spatial location, as they were in high sectors relative to near topography and, in many cases, associated in small sectors. These hiding structures were built with stone blocks of varying sizes and whose shape is in most cases in arc, although

Fig. 1.9 General view of Antofalla ravine

it can also be straight. They are formed by a simple wall with an average length of 1.5 m, being the average maximum height of 0.7 m (Fig. 1.10). We have recorded hunting blinds of different sizes and forms, but the principle is the same in all cases: to supply the hunter a hiding place of the prey, being located for it in strategic points in relation to the surrounding landscape. This protection or hiding place is related

1 Ancient Hunting Strategies of Wild Camelids …

Fig. 1.10 Hunting blinds registered at Antofalla ravine

to openings, steps or breakages of slopes, always located in elevated topographic positions. This gives a good hiding place to hunters and in addition they do not need to possess much height because when joining with the natural forms of the relief, the visual in relation to the ascending prey is reduced. A characteristic of these structures is that their construction and location in landscape, made them difficult to identify at a distance since they are confused with other rocks. These characteristics could avoid the "*relincho*" perceived danger of hunters stalking so easily.

Regarding this characteristic, the hunting strategy would focus on wait in hiding the movement through that place of vicuña herds as they ascended to the higher sectors, mainly related to the moment of return to the sleeping areas, located in rocky areas of the ravine. However, we also believe that it is very possible to involve beaters in order to drive animals to the position of hunters, similar to the **model C** proposed for Quebrada Seca. The number of hunting blinds identified in Antofalla is striking, as we recorded 503 structures throughout the space surveyed (Fig. 1.11). It also highlights that in some cases these structures are associated in small spaces with a number of up to 30 hunting blinds, but also isolated cases can be observed.

Beyond this diversity of associations and the number of structures of this type, the same constructive characteristic is repeated in every case, so we imagine that what could have varied is the participation of a variable number of hunters. Thus, as an example, we propose that a case (Moreno 2010, 2012) where 30 hunting blinds are associated could be clearly linked to the **model C** proposal described for Quebrada

Fig. 1.11 Distribution of hunting blinds throughout Antofalla ravine

1 Ancient Hunting Strategies of Wild Camelids …

Fig. 1.12 Path joining hunting blinds. The arrow indicates the position of another structure

Seca, where a large number of hunters would be hidden and beaters would direct herds to their position to initiate the attack. Another possible strategy, somewhat different or alternative, was observed in a sector of the western slope of Antofalla, where we identified several hunting blinds, which were joined by a path prepared by stone removal, as shown in Fig. 1.12. This path could be used for hunters to fast move between the different structures in order to achieve the most effective position against the potential prey(s). In this sense, it would be possible to think that a person could be in a position with good visibility indicating to the other participants in which position to place themselves according to the direction of herds ascending toward the higher sectors of the ravine.

The structures location referred above, together with the ethological characteristics of prey, makes it possible to define a hunting strategy linked to ambush in the elevated sectors, sheltered behind hunting blinds, waiting for animals passing close to them to carry out the attack. This situation would have occurred at dusk, when vicuñas were returning to the sleeping places (Haber and Moreno 2018; Moreno 2010). It is also likely the participation of beaters driving the animals to the places where hunting blinds are located, but this would imply the passage of the animals on the run, which could make it difficult to succeed in the attack (Moreno 2009).

However, the question related to the hunting landscape in Antofalla is related to its temporal depth, especially due to the possible association observed in some cases with **model C**, but also with some variants that do not relate directly to the models proposed for Quebrada Seca. From the architectural characteristics of the structures described above, it is impossible to define a temporality or a constructive history.

However, one potential line of evidence is the data provided by projectile points recovered from the systematic survey.

A total of 192 projectile points of which only 13 were complete were recovered at Antofalla ravine, without observing differential distributions in the landscape of complete or fractured specimens (Moreno 2010, 2011). Considering the objective of this work, we will focus on the relative chronological information that projectile points can provide. Other characteristics of these sets have already been described on other occasions (Moreno 2010, 2011). From the technological and morphological study of the specimens recovered in the survey, we constructed ten morphological types of projectile tips and four morphological specimens. This construction has two objectives: evaluate the different types of weapons used in the area, as well as their relative chronological allocation, through comparison with specimens obtained from contexts with radiocarbon dating (Moreno 2011). In Fig. 1.13, we present some of the projectile point designs identified at Antofalla ravine.

With this information, we contrast projectile point design with specimens with chronological associations, especially from Antofagasta de la Sierra (Hocsman 2006;

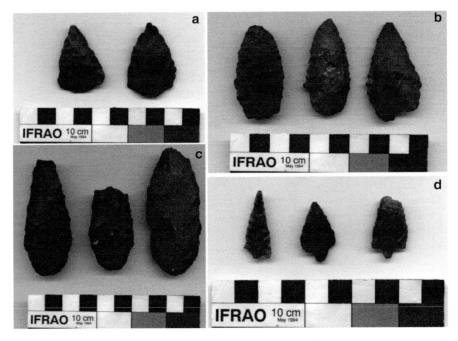

Fig. 1.13 Different types of projectile points are registered in Antofalla. **a** Specimens of projectile point assigned to atlatl darts and to specimens from QS3 and Tuina (Chile) corresponding to the early Holocene (Martínez 2003; Núñez 1983). **b** Specimens of projectile points assigned to throwing spears, corresponding to specimens placed around 6080 years BP in QS3 (Hocsman 2006). **c** Specimens of projectile point assigned to atlatl darts, corresponding to a design placed between 4200 and 3800 years BP (Hocsman 2006). **d** Specimens of projectile points assigned to bow and arrow and to the 1st millennium of the era (Escola 1987, 2000; Hocsman 2006; Moreno 2010)

1 Ancient Hunting Strategies of Wild Camelids …

Table 1.1 Chronological correlation of projectile points registered at Antofalla ravine

ID	Correlation	Chronology
Af-I	Peñas Chicas E	4150–3430 BP
Af-II	Quebrada Seca A - Tambillo-1	8600 BP
Af-III	X	X
Af-IV	Peñas Chicas C	4150–3430 BP
Af-V	X	X
Af-VI	Quebrada Seca F	4150–3430 BP
Af-VII	Peñas de la Cruz A	7270 BP
Af-VIII	Peñas Chicas A	4150–3430 BP
Af-IX	Similar designs at TC1, Casa Chavez Montículos, Chaschuil, Real Grande I, Tulan-54	1° Millennia b.C.
Af-X	X	X
Af-A	Quebrada Seca B	7350–3500 BP
Af-B	X	X
Af-C	X	X
Af-D	Peñas Chicas 4	4150–3430 BP

Martínez 2003) This comparison, presented in Table 1.1, allows us to observe the presence of projectile points, assigned to different historical moments, from 8600 years BP, to the 1st millennium of the Common Era. Similarly, we can observe the use of different weapon systems over time, with the predominant use of spears and atlatl darts for the early and middle Holocene, while these technologies would be replaced by bow and arrow toward the beginning of the Formative period (AF-IX) (Moreno 2010, 2011).

One of the objectives of this chronology is to analyze the spatial location of these projectile points in order to evaluate possible differences in the use of hunting spaces and therefore infer variations in hunting strategies. In particular, by this analysis we try to link some designs, especially AF-VII and Af-A, to limited spaces to strengthen the linkage with **model C**. However, as it can be seen in Fig. 1.14 there is no trend in the use of the landscape according to the temporality of the projectile points, but there is a recurrence of the same space. An important remark should be made here for the absence of projectile points chronologically assigned to the period between 7500 and 5000 years BP, which would correspond to the *Altithermal* period (Tchilinguirian 2009; Tchilinguirian and Morales 2013; Yacobaccio 2013). It is possible that during this moment this ravine was not used as a hunting space or perhaps with projectile points designs that could not be compared with designs located chronologically at other archaeological sites of Antofagasta de la Sierra. That is, that there could be designs typical of this ravine at that time, such as AF-III and AF-V that could not be correlated with designs of other researched spaces. However, this is a question that further research at Antofalla will allow us to contrast.

Fig. 1.14 Distributional map of projectile points at Antofalla ravine by its chronological correlation

In summary, the information obtained at Antofalla ravine allows us to understand it as a suitable space for hunting wild camelids, particularly vicuñas, since it presents the ecological characteristics selected by these animals, such as bedrock and wide pasture spaces and water. The daily movement made by vicuñas between these two spaces, in addition to other behaviors, was known by the hunters. Groups of hunters had, over time, weapons to kill these animals, which did not allow shooting from very long distances, as guns. To manage these characteristics, hunters took advantage of local landscape and through the construction of simple structures, they prepared a space that would facilitate the encounter with prey in close positions, thus increasing the possibility of success. The information from projectile points lets us to think of a recurrent use in the long historical term of these spaces, reproducing the knowledge possessed by hunters on the behavior of these prey. We believe that the strategy of ambush (Churchill 1993), would have been reproduced in time, developing in some cases the participation of beaters, especially in the case of spaces with many associated blinds and articulating the technical possibilities of the different types of weapons, the ethological characteristics of vicuñas and the preparation of a landscape aimed at expanding the chances of success. However, we also believe that it is necessary to advance with more research in the area to understand the patterns of occupation along the Holocene in this area and thus contribute to the correlation with models proposed for Quebrada Seca.

1.6 Discussion: Intersecting Knowledges

Throughout this chapter, we have presented a proposal on the construction of models of hunting strategies at Southern Argentine Puna, presenting a theoretical-methodological vision and some lines of evidence that we believe are essential to understand these practices. The articulation of multiple lines of evidence, allow us to understand and explain hunting as a particular and complex social phenomenon. In this sense, the first important source of information was the ethological characteristics of prey. For example, Laughlin (1968) argues that many groups of hunters spend more time and attention to understand animal behavior than in the improvement of hunting equipment or its use. In this particular case we focus on the vicuña and its general aspects related to the daily behavior and the creation of territories and groups of these animals. In general, what this information provides is the presence of a highly mobile prey, with great speed to escape and an important capacity to perceive danger. However, they make regular movements between the higher and more protected sectors, where they took refuge at night and the lower sectors, where the water and pastures areas were located. This feature gave hunters the possibility to anticipate routine movements and try to anticipate the possible escape of prey by attempting to initiate the attack by hunters.

But, to anticipate the movements of prey, there are some important factors used by hunters, trying to increase success chances. The first of these factors, that we evaluate, are weapons systems used by hunters to kill animals. And in the case of Puna, this aspect has a relevant regional context, since at regional scale very similar designs are observed on projectile points and weapons systems used over time. The contextual and chronological information focuses on the knowledge of the investigations developed in the micro-region of Antofagasta de la Sierra, and more specifically in Quebrada Seca 3. In this area, it was possible to identify a series of morphological designs and types of projectile tips that were located chronologically and that could be assigned to different weapon systems, where the throwing spears, atlatl darts and bow and arrow would have been a sort of evolutionary sequence of weapons used during the Holocene (Aschero and Martínez 2001).

This information allowed us to advance in the characterization of projectile points from other sectors and to evaluate their chronological depth. Thus, in Antofalla, it was possible to identify designs consistent to different historical moments and to the use of specific weapons systems (Moreno 2010, 2011). But in addition, in other places in the Argentine Puna, various researchers have identified some very similar designs that allow to think about shared knowledge at macro-regional scale (De Souza 2004; Hoguin 2014; Hoguin and Restifo 2012; Ratto 1994, 2003; Restifo 2013).

Another central factor considered to identify hunting strategies was landscape. In this sense, the documentation of environmental characteristics, the location of water and pastures, was relevant in this cases, and the way hunters had prepared the landscape to generate spaces that would promote the encounter and to avoid prey's escape. At Antofalla ravine it was possible to identify a large number of structures linked to the organization of what was called the "hunting landscape" where hunting blinds and other structures constituted a scenery produced for the encounter between hunters and prey, where the former attempted to minimize the possibilities to perceive danger and to initiate the escape of vicuñas. Not only the location of these structures, but also their constructive characteristics and their aggregation allow us to interpret different scenarios in which these encounters could have taken place. It is different the situation at Quebrada Seca, where surveys provided much less information about structures linked to hunting, although it does offer it in terms of the relevance of this practice over time, as shown by the excavation of Quebrada Seca 3 (Aschero et al. 1991; Elkin 1996; Martínez 2003, 2007; Moreno 2013). The role of the rugged natural topography as a resource was key and appropriately exploited, as mentioned above. It was possible to identify some associated hunting blinds, constituting a hunting area, which could have been used since ca. 7700 years BP, associated with the use of short-range throwing spears (Aschero and Martínez 2001).

Another relevant point that we have taken into account to interpret hunting strategies models at the Antofagasta de la Sierra Department is the aggregation of hunters. We could consider the participation of several people in this practice and in particular in the collective hunting proposed in **model C**. Therefore, for Quebrada Seca, a process of social aggregation was assumed as the hunting models became more complex, where the use of the associated hunting blinds involved the participation of several hunters, as well as beaters. In the case of Antofalla, it was interpreted that the participation of several hunters, beaters and even observers was very similar to the proposal of the **model C** for Quebrada Seca, although with some differences.

Now, the models proposed for Antofagasta de la Sierra, could be the keys to the social homogenization of the archaeological landscape after 10,000–9000 years BP. A central point is the incidence of co-participation involving collective hunting in a scenario of low demography and in a high altitude desert environment but with an endorheic basin where the flow of the Punilla River, with alternative water inputs from Cerro Galán, ensured permanent water for flora, fauna, and human life throughout the *Altithermal* period (Tchilinguirian 2009; Tchilinguirian and Morales 2013; Yacobaccio 2013). Such co-participation, in collective hunting organization, would have generated an instance of cooperation between families from different bands. A co-participation that not only involved people but also territories that, alternatively, had to be shared to avoid the above mentioned over-killing. A co-participation that opened up a fluid set of interactions between families and bands. But, in the period ca. 8000–5000 years BP characterized by adverse conditions of the *Altithermal* on the resources, it could have operated encouraging that co-participation as a positive response of social collective. Thus, we propose for that period, a scenario in which a shared social topography is generated—interactions, landscape, and resources—reinforced by all the other social components that collective hunting could bring together and that we mentioned above: propitiatory rituals, activation of delayed consumption of goods distributed among the families—production of charqui and forms of storage—and possibly temporary aggregations with increase of the exchange of goods, instruments, raw materials, information, and genes. In this sense, it is possible to think about an integrated socio-economic system that articulated bands and their territories-patches from the **model C** in the temporal trajectory followed by the hunting systems. A system that was able to achieve an efficient balance in the management of subsistence resources, capable of absorbing people coming from the disaggregation or fission of bands from the Salar de Atacama and the Salado River during the "archaeological silence" that affected that region (Núñez and Grosjean 1994; Núñez et al. 1999, Fig. 1.15). Some balance that showed no changes in the visual expressions of rock art throughout that time up to a possible greater demographic pressure than, around 5000 years BP, is reflected in the increase

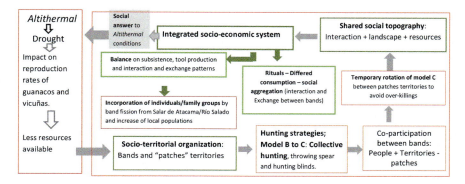

Fig. 1.15 Flow chart explaining the effects of collective hunting between 9000 and 5000 years BP

in grinding and a greater dependence on gathering resources until the appearance of the first domestic plants (Babot 2004, 2011). Thereby, only at 5000–6000 years BP began to change the social situation with a little more population from the lower basins (Salar de Atacama, Río Salado) or southern basins (El Peñón- Cerro Blanco) and the eruptions of the latter complicate the social panorama even more. From there, the process of transition to productive economies would begin, and these territorial dynamics would have made the possibility of continuing with communal hunts conflictive, modifying the forms of social aggregation. This process would have been experienced between 5000 and 3500 years BP as it is deeply described in various investigations in the area (Aschero and Hocsman 2011; Babot 2011; Aguirre and Rodríguez 2015). For this moment, in rock art also the change focuses on the appearance of the first human images but that is not linked to hunting scenes but with initial representations of the Lord (or Lady) of the animals and the role of the woman-female in the reproduction of domestic and wild animals. Thus, what is intended to emphasize is the importance that communal hunting models had in the establishment of social arrangements between local groups, where, in addition to the vicuña hunting, social networks were built and enhanced at the regional level.

The question to be asked here is if a similar picture could have been articulated in Antofalla. And here are some points that highlight important similarities that we want to revisit and that could be thought of as focal points for possible interactions in the past. A first topic, on which we commented earlier are the designs of the projectile points that show very clear similarities in Antofalla with those recorded at Quebrada Seca. But another important argument is the presence of obsidian projectile points from Ona source in Quebrada Seca. This obsidian source had a great importance at the regional level (Yacobaccio et al. 2004) and is located around 15 km from Antofalla, so it would surely have been an important resource for the people who inhabited this last ravine, but at the same time it is about 90 km from Quebrada Seca. This situation could imply some kind of knowledge among the people who lived in Quebrada Seca and Antofalla given the proximity of the latter with respect to the Ona source.

But also, we would like to state here that in Antofalla we have very little information about the human occupations during the early and middle Holocene, so we cannot, at first instance, transfer the models proposed for the micro-region of Antofagasta de la Sierra to this place. Focusing again on hunting strategies, there are some points that stand out for their differences between the two cases studied and that we believe provide criteria for thinking about regional differences around hunting characteristics. Assuming that the relief and location of water and pastures are central aspects of the mobility of vicuñas, the differences between the places where we focus research in Antofagasta de la Sierra, can be relevant. Quebrada Seca presents a relief marked by steep slopes with large blocks of ignimbrite that makes it impossible to connect with the high altitude plains by any sector, but only narrow paths can be used that allow this relationship. One space that could be used to link marshes and high altitude plains is where the most important set of hunting blinds was identified (QS5). In addition, water in this sector is restricted to two small springs, which vary in size at different times of the year, but which remain restricted and therefore water is not accessible throughout the ravine. On the contrary, Antofalla ravine presents a much more homogeneous landscape in relation to the characteristics of the slopes, being able to link marshes with high altitude plains, practically in all its extension and where water resource is permanent. This situation implies that, practically throughout the entire length of the ravine, it is possible to access from the low sectors, used by animals for feeding and drinking, to the elevated areas used as sleeping places. Therefore, it is possible that the spaces to materialize hunting are very different in both spaces and therefore also the hunting strategies potentially implemented. Clearly, the knowledge and choices of hunters, diminish the environmental differences from the activation of strategies, but there are some aspects, like the impossibility of climb slopes or the absence of pastures, that cannot be modify.

But also, in Antofalla, hunting blinds was registered in almost all of its extension and with variations in the number of structures and in the association with other structures and archaeological materials (Moreno 2010). At first glance, we could associate the **model C** proposed for Quebrada Seca with the characteristics of Antofalla, since the association of various hunting blinds is the most common situation. However, we must also consider that it was possible to activate other forms of hunting, perhaps individual or of very few participants in which hunters ambush vicuñas at dusk. In these cases, aspects such as winds and sunlight were managed to decrease the perception of danger by the "*relincho*." Also, the distribution along the ravine may be related to modifying hunting spaces over time and possibly the action of different groups of hunters, but using the same spaces and structures in the long historical sequence that show projectile point designs.

1.7 Final Remarks

Throughout this chapter, we have proposed and evaluated the articulation of several lines of archaeological evidence around hunting strategies implemented by human populations during the Holocene at Southern Argentine Puna. Based on the complexity of this practice and the need to understand various factors that give meaning to it, we focus on two study cases to evaluate these lines of evidence and to think about the similarities and differences between these places. It is clear that the aggregation of hunters and the different functions performed by each one involve important variations in the interaction between social groups that would have taken advantage of these moments for the establishment and reproduction of social networks at regional scale. This phenomenon, which for Quebrada Seca started around 7700 years BP, would have been the source of a social complexity phenomenon that allowed the origin of productive practices toward 5000 years BP. The hunting strategy that was implemented in Quebrada Seca with the aggregation of hunters responds to **Model C**, in which hunting blinds construction would also have played an important role for these populations. Hunting blinds are also the main territorial mark of hunting at Antofalla. 503 registered structures and almost 200 projectile points show the importance of this practice in this space. We could quickly link hunting practices here to **model C** and events linked to hunter aggregation. However, despite the information bias that we still have about human occupations during the early and middle Holocene, we believe that some alternatives could have been articulated in hunting strategies, some linked to that model, but also other ways of attacking, focusing mainly on taking advantage of the daily circulation of vicuñas between marshes and the rocks and thus be able to access nearby targets (Haber and Moreno 2018; Moreno 2010, 2011). Certainly, new evidence about local occupations during the early and middle Holocene in Antofalla could provide crucial information to complement and adjust this proposal.

Hunting wild camelids at Southern Argentine Puna meant much more than a way of acquiring faunal resources, since it implied a great number of social, technological and environmental features that shaped its image of the past, which, as research progresses, is more solidly defined.

Acknowledgements We would like to thank the editors of the volume for the invitation to participate in it. Also to reviewers for their comments on this chapter. We want to thank all the colleagues that participated in surveys at Antofalla and Quebrada Seca. Finally, to the people of Antofalla and Antofagasta de la Sierra, for letting us work on their territories.

References

Aguirre G, Rodríguez M (2015) Discusiones teóricas y metodológicas en torno a la transición entre la recolección y la agricultura incipiente en Antofagasta de la Sierra, Catamarca. Comechingonia 19(2):159–183

Aschero C (2000) El poblamiento del territorio. En Nueva Historia Argentina, Tomo I. Editorial Sudamericana, Buenos Aires

Aschero C, Elkin D, Pintar E (1991) Aprovechamiento de recursos faunísticos y producción lítica en el precerámico tardío. Un caso de estudio: Quebrada Seca 3 (Puna Meridional Argentina). Actas del XI Congreso Nacional de Arqueología Chilena Tomo II:101–114. Museo Nacional de Historia Natural, Santiago de Chile

Aschero C, Manzi L, Gómez A (1993–1994) Producción lítica y uso del espacio en el nivel 2b4 de Quebrada Seca 3. Relaciones de la Sociedad Argentina de Antropología XIX:191–214

Aschero C, Martínez J (2001) Técnicas de caza en Antofagasta de la Sierra, Puna meridional, Argentina. Relaciones de la Sociedad Argentina de Antropología XXVI:215–241

Aschero CA, Hocsman S (2011) Arqueología de las ocupaciones cazadoras- recolectoras de fines del Holoceno Medio de Antofagasta de la Sierra (Puna Meridional Argentina). Chungara 43(1):393–411

Aschero C, Bobillo F, Faundes W, Lund J, Olmos V (2018) Cacao 1.A: New data and questions about first South-Americans at Antofagasta de la Sierra, Argentina. XVIII° UISPP World Congress, París

Babot M (2004) Tecnología y utilización de artefactos de molienda en el Noroeste prehispánico. Unpublished doctoral thesis, Facultad de Ciencias Naturales e Instituto Miguel Lillo, Universidad Nacional de Tucumán

Babot M (2011) Cazadores-recolectores de los Andes Centro-Sur y procesamiento vegetal. Una discusión desde la Puna Meridional Argentina (ca. 7000-3200 años a.p.). Chungara 43(1):413–432

Benedetti A (2005) Un territorio andino para un país pampeano. Geografía histórica del Territorio de Los Andes (1900–1943). Unpublished doctoral thesis, Facultad de Filosofía y Letras, Universidad de Buenos Aires

Binford Lewis R (1988) En busca del pasado. Editorial Crítica, Barcelona

Bonacic C (2005) Vicuña ecology and management. Int Camelid Q 4(4):75–82. Rysko Pearson, Canada

Churchill S (1993) Weapon technology, prey size selection, and hunting methods in modern hunter-gatherers: implications for hunting in the Palaeolithic and Mesolithic (eds: Peterkin GL, Bricker HM, Mellars P). Archaeol Pap Am Anthropol Assoc 4:11–24

Cieza de León P [1553] (1984). La crónica del Perú. Edición de Manuel Ballesteros. Historia 16. Madrid

De Souza P (2004) Tecnologías de proyectil durante los períodos Arcaico y Formativo en el Loa Superior (Norte de Chile) a partir del análisis de puntas líticas. Chungara. Special Volume. Tomo I:61–76

Elkin D (1996) Arqueozoología de Quebrada Seca 3: indicadores de subsistencia temprana, en la Puna meridional argentina. Unpublished doctoral thesis, Facultad de Filosofía y Letras, Universidad de Buenos Aires

Erramouspe V, Urquiza S, Aschero C (2017) Manejo de camélidos durante el Formativo temprano en la Puna Seca de Jujuy (Argentina). Intersecciones en Antropología 18:295–303

Escola P (1987) Las puntas de proyectil del formativo en Puna y Quebradas de Acceso: un estudio tecno-tipológico de cuatro casos de análisis. Unpublished Graduation thesis, Facultad de Filosofía y Letras, Universidad de Buenos Aires

Escola P (2000) Tecnología lítica y sociedades agropastoriles tempranas. Unpublished doctoral thesis, Facultad de Filosofía y Letras, Universidad Nacional de Buenos Aires, Buenos Aires

Fernández Distel A (1974) Excavaciones arqueológicas en las cuevas de Huachichocana, departamento de Tumbaya, Prov. De Jujuy, Argentina. Relaciones de la Sociedad Argentina de Antropología VIII:101–134

Franklin W (1982) Biology, ecology, and relationship to man of the South American Camelids. In: Mares M, Genoways H (eds) Mammalian biology in South American. University of Pittsburgh Press, Pittsburgh, pp 457–490

Gambier M (1981) Asentamiento humano y transhumancia en los Andes Centrales argentino-chilenos. Publicaciones 9. Instituto de Investigaciones Arqueológicas y Museo, San Juan

Gianotti C (2004) La prospección como estrategia metodológica para el estudio del pasaje monumental en las tierras bajas uruguayas. In Arqueología Espacial 23–24, Arqueología espacial: Prospección, Coordinated by F. Burillo, pp 259–282

Grant J (2017) Of hunting and herding: isotopic evidence in wild and domesticated camelids from the Southern Argentine Puna (2120–420 years BP). J Archaeol Sci: Rep 11:29–37

Grant J, Mondini M, Panarello H (2017) Carbon and nitrogen isotopic ecology of holocene camelids in the Southern Puna (Antofagasta de la Sierra, Catamarca, Argentina): Archaeological and environmental implications. J Archaeol Sci: Rep 6:1–11

Haber A (1999) Informe de evaluación de impacto arqueológico de la fase de exploración de la reserva minera Antofalla Este. Centro Editor. Universidad Nacional de Catamarca

Haber A (2003) Hunting after Domestication. Paper presented at CHAGS 9. Edinburg

Haber A (2006) Una arqueología de los paisajes puneños. Domesticidad, interacción e identidad en Antofalla. Primer y segundo milenios d.C. Jorge Sarmiento Editor. Uni- versitas Libros, Córdoba

Haber A, Gastaldi M, Quesada M (2002) Arqueología industrial de un enclave minero salteño en Bolivia, mediados del siglo XIX. Actas de las XVIII Jornadas de Historia Económica. Mendoza

Haber A, Lema C (2006) La pura opinión de Vladimiro Weisser y la población indí- gena de Antofalla en la Colonia Temprana. Intersecciones en Antropología 7:179–191

Haber A, Moreno E (2018) Dos veces en la misma trampa. Notas de arqueología casi crepuscular. In: Flores Blanco L (ed) Lugares, monumentos y ancestros. Arqueología de paisajes andinos y lejanos. Avqui Ediciones, Lima, Perú, pp 311–328

Hocsman S (2006) Producción lítica, variabilidad y cambio en Antofagasta de la Sierra –ca. 5500–1500 AP-. Unpublished doctoral thesis, Facultad de Ciencias Naturales y Museo, Universidad Nacional de La Plata

Hocsman S, Martínez JG, Aschero CA, Calisaya AD (2012) Variability of triangular non-stemmed projectile points of early hunters-gatherers of the Argentinian Puna. In: Miotti L, Salemme, M, Flegenheimer N, Goebel T (eds) Southbound: late pleistocene peopling of Latin America. Special Edition Current Research in the Pleistocene. CFSFA, Texas A&M University, USA, pp 63–68

Hoffmann E, Otte K, Ponce C, Ríos M (1983). El manejo de la vicuña silvestre, Tomo II. Eschborn. Sociedad Alemana de Cooperación Técnica (GTZ)

Hoguin R (2014) Secuencia cronológica y tecnología lítica en la Puna seca y salada de los Andes Centro-Sur para el Holoceno temprano y medio a través del ejemplo de Susques. Relaciones de la Sociedad Argentina de Antropología XXXIX(2):333–364

Hoguin R, Restifo F (2012) Patterns of cultural transmission in the manufacture of projectile points: implications for the early settlements of the Argentine Puna. Current Research in the Pleistocene. Special Edition. Southbound: Late pleistocene peopling of Latin America, Texas, pp. 69–74

Ingold T (1987) The appropriation of nature: essays of human ecology and social relations. University of Iowa Press, Iowa City

Ingold T (ed) (2000) The perception of the environment: essays on livelihood, dwelling and skill. Routledge, Londres

Koford, C (1957) The vicuña and the puna. Ecol Monogr 27(2). Museum of Vertebral Zoology. University of California

Laughlin W (1968) An integrating biobehavior system and its evolutionary importance. In: Lee RB, De Vore I (eds), with the assistance of Nash J. Man The Hunter. Aldine Publishing Company, Chicago

Lema C (2004) Tebenquiche Chico en los siglos XVI y XVII. Unpublished degree thesis, Escuela de Antropología, Facultad de Humanidades y Artes, Universidad Nacional de Rosario

Martínez J (2003) Ocupaciones humanas tempranas y tecnología de caza en la microrregión de Antofagasta de la Sierra (10000–7000 AP). Unpublished doctoral thesis, Facultad de Ciencias Naturales e Instituto Miguel Lillo, Universidad Nacional de Tucumán

Martínez J (2007) Ocupaciones humanas tempranas y tecnología de caza en Antofagasta de la Sierra, Puna Meridional Argentina (10000–7000 AP) Cazadores- Recolectores del Cono Sur. Revista de Arqueología 2:129–150. Mar del Plata, Argentina

Mondini M, Elkin D (2014) Holocene hunter-gatherers in the Puna. Integrating bones and other zooarchaeological evidence in Antofagasta de la Sierra (Argentina). In: Pintar E (ed) Hunter-gatherers from a high-elevation desert. People of the Salt Puna, Northwest Argentina. Bar International Series 2641, pp 117–124

Mondini M, Marozzi A, Pintar E (2015) Interacciones entre humanos y animales en la Puna salada durante el Holoceno medio. El caso de Cueva Salamanca 1, Antofagasta de la Sierra, Catamarca. Arqueología 21(1):73–87

Moreno E (2009) El paisaje cazador en la quebrada de Antofalla. Antofagasta de la Sierra, Catamarca. La Zaranda de Ideas 5:101–120

Moreno E (2010) Arqueología de la caza de vicuñas en el área del Salar de Antofalla, Puna de Atacama. Una aproximación desde la arqueología del paisaje. Unpublished doctoral thesis, Facultad de Ciencias Naturales y Museo, Universidad Nacional de La Plata, Argentina

Moreno E (2011) Tecnología de caza en la quebrada de Antofalla. Revista del Museo de Antropología 4:17–32. Facultad de Filosofía y Humanidades, Universidad Nacional de Córdoba

Moreno E (2012) Naturaleza, cultura, desierto y dominación. In: Ayala P, Vilches F (eds) Teoría Arqueológica en Chile: Reflexionando en torno a nuestro quehacer disciplinario. Universidad Católica del Norte, Chile, pp 210–228

Moreno E (2013) Estrategias de caza y paisajes culturales en Antofagasta de la Sierra, Catamarca. Comechingonia 17(2):95–121

Moreno E (2018) Construcción, transformación y reproducción de paisajes campesinos. Aportes desde múltiples escalas. Arqueología 24(3) Dossier:79–100. Facultad de Filosofía y Letras, Universidad de Buenos Aires

Moreno E, Revuelta C (2010) La caza de vicuñas en Tebenquiche Chico (Dpto. Antofagasta de la Sierra, Catamarca). Un acercamiento de larga duración. Relaciones de la Sociedad Argentina de Antropología XXXV:171–194

Murra J (1978) La organización económica del estado Inka. Siglo XXI, México

Nance J (1979) Regional subsampling and statistical inference in forested habitats. Am Antiq 44(1):172–176

Núñez L (1983) Paleoindio y arcaico en Chile: Diversidad, secuencias y procesos. Cuicuilco, México

Núñez L, Grosjean M (1994) Cambio ambientales pleistoceno-holocénicos: ocupación humana y uso de recursos en la Puna de Atacama (norte de Chile). Estudios Atacameños 11:11–24

Núñez L, Grosjean M, Cartagena I (1999) Un ecorefugio oportunístico en la Puna de Atacama durante eventos áridos del Holoceno Medio. Estudios Atacameños 17:125–174

Olivera D (1997) La importancia del recurso Camelidae en la Puna de Atacama entre los 10.000 y 500 años A. P. Estudios Atacameños 14:29–41

Olivera D (2001) Sociedades agropastoriles tempranas: El formativo inferior del Noroeste Argentino. In: Berberian E, Nielsen A (eds) Historia Argentina Prehispánica. Brujas, Buenos Aires

Polo de Ondegardo. [1571] (1990). El mundo de los Incas. Edition by Laura González y Alicia Alonso. Historia 16. Madrid

Puló M (1998) La vicuña: el oro que camina por los andes. Andes. Antropología e historia 9:243–280

Puló M (2000) Desarrollo sustentable y la realidad social del NOA. Paper presented at 1o Congreso de Ambiente y Calidad de Vida, Facultad de Tecnología y Ciencias Aplicadas, Universidad Nacional de Catamarca

Quesada M (2001) Tecnología agrícola y producción campesina en la Puna de Atacama, I milenio d.C. Unpublished degree thesis, Escuela de Arqueología, Universidad Nacional de Catamarca

Quesada M (2007) Paisajes agrarios en el área de Antofalla. Procesos de trabajo y escalas sociales de la producción agrícola. Primer y Segundo milenio d.C. Unpublished doctoral thesis, Facultad de Ciencias Naturales y Museo, Universidad Nacional de La Plata

Ratto N (1994) Funcionalidad versus adscripción cultural: cabezales líticos de la margen norte del estrecho de Magallanes. In: Lanata J, Borrero L (eds) Arqueología de Cazadores-recolectores. Límites, casos y aperturas, Arqueología Contemporánea 5:105–120. Buenos Aires

Ratto N (2003) Estrategias de caza y propiedades del registro arqueológico en la Puna de Chaschuil (Departamento de Tinogasta, Catamarca, Argentina). Unpublished doctoral thesis, Facultad de Filosofía y Letras, Universidad de Buenos Aires

Restifo F (2013) Tecnología de caza durante el Holoceno temprano y medio en la Puna de la Provincia de Salta (República Argentina): patrones de variación y procesos de cambio. Comechingonia 17:59–84

Revuelta C (2005) Apropiación social y vicuñas. Análisis zooarqueológico de la unidad doméstica TC1. Oasis de Tebenquiche Chico – Primer milenio d.C. Unpublished degree thesis, Escuela de Arqueología, Universidad Nacional de Catamarca

Tchilinguirian P (2009) Paleoambientes Holocenos en la Puna Austral (27oS): Implicancias Geoarqueológicas. Unpublished doctoral thesis, Facultad de Ciencias Exactas y Naturales, Universidad de Buenos Aires

Tchilinguirian P, Morales MR (2013) Mid-holocene paleoenvironments in North-Western Argentina: main patterns and discrepancies. Quatern Int 307:14–23

Tomka S (1992) Vicuñas and Llamas: parallels in behavioral ecology and implications or the domestication of Andean Camelids. Hum Ecol 20(4):407–433

Urquiza S (2009) Arqueofaunas del Alero Punta de la Peña 4: Implicaciones para el Manejo del Recurso Camelidae en Antofagasta de la Sierra, Puna Meridional, Catamarca. Unpublished doctoral thesis, Universidad Nacional de Tucumán

Urquiza S, Aschero C (2014) Economía animal a lo largo del Holoceno en la Puna Austral Argentina. Alero Punta de la Peña 4. Cuadernos del Instituto Nacional de Antropología y Pensamiento Latinoamericano 1(2):86–112

Vilá B (ed) (2006) Investigación, conservación y manejo de vicuñas. Proyecto MACS. Universidad Nacional de Luján

Wheeler J (2006) Historia natural de la vicuña. In: Vilá (ed) Investigación, conservación y manejo de vicuñas. Proyecto MACS. Universidad Nacional de Luján, pp 25–36

Yacobaccio H (1991) Sistemas de asentamiento de cazadores-recolectores tempranos de los andes centro-sur. Unpublished doctoral thesis, Facultad de Filosofía y Letras, Universidad de Buenos Aires

Yacobaccio H (2001) Cazadores complejos y domesticación de camélidos. In: Mengoni G, Olivera D, Yacobaccio H (eds) El uso de los camélidos a través del tiempo. Ediciones del tridente, Buenos Aires, pp 261–282

Yacobaccio H (2009) The historical relationship between people and the Vicuña. In: Gordon I (ed) The Vicuña: the theory and practice of community based wildlife management. Springer Science + Business Media, pp 7–21

Yacobaccio H (2013) Towards a human ecology for the Middle Holocene in the Southern Puna. Quatern Int 307:24–30

Yacobaccio H, Madero C (1992) Zooarqueología de Huachichocana III (Jujuy, Argentina). Arqueología 2:149–188

Yacobaccio H, Madero C, Malmierca M, Reigadas M (1997–1998) Caza, domesticación y pastoreo de camélidos en la Puna Argentina. Relaciones de la Sociedad Argentina de Antropología XXII–XXIII:389–418

Yacobaccio H, Escola P, Pereyra F, Lazarri M, Glascock M (2004) Quest for ancient routes: obsidian sourcing research in Northwestern Argentina. J Archaeol Sci 31:193–204

Yacobaccio H, Killian L, Vilá B (2007) La explotación de la vicuña durante el período colonial (1535–1810). El negocio de los cueros y lanas de vicuña. Todo es Historia 483:16–21

Chapter 2
Tiny Arrow Points, Bone-Tipped Projectiles, and Foraging During the Late Prehispanic Period (Sierras of Córdoba, Argentina)

Matías E. Medina and Imanol Balena

Abstract This paper presents the techno-typological analysis carried out on the projectile points recovered from three Late Prehispanic Period archaeological sites (1500–360 year BP, Sierras of Córdoba, Argentina), in order to assess how the dynamic of the sociocultural process influenced the design of hunting and warfare weapons. Projectile points were described in techno-typological terms, classified in typological sub-groups and functionally assigned to arrow or atlatl dart point. The subgroup of tiny arrow points with short triangular-shaped blade, contracted stems and barbed shoulders dominate the assemblages. All of them were made of opal and chalcedony, a high-quality rock for tool knapping. Moreover, a subgroup of bone arrow points with triangular-shaped blade, straight stems, and barbed shoulders as well as other sub-groups of quartz unstemmed with a triangular-shaped blade and concave base or lanceolate-shaped dart points were also recognized. The diversity of projectile point-types and hafting methods identified on-sites, along with the extensive use of the bow, the selection of high-quality lithic raw material and the incorporation of bone-tipped projectiles, led to interpret that physical violence was not an uncommon behavior and that hunting was not a complementary subsistence activity, being the later integrated into a mixed foraging and cultivation economy where flexibility was one of its defining traits.

Keywords Sierras of Córdoba · Late Prehispanic Period · Projectile points · Weapon system · Niche breadth

2.1 Introduction

Projectile points collected from archaeological sites use to be the only elements remained from the weapon systems where they were hafted (Lyman et al. 2009). In general, projectile points belong to a composed artifact (bow, arrow, spear, and

---

M. E. Medina (✉) · I. Balena
Consejo Nacional de Investigaciones Científicas y Técnicas (CONICET), División Arqueología,
Facultad de Ciencias Naturales y Museo, Universidad Nacional de La Plata, La Plata, Argentina

© Springer Nature Switzerland AG 2021
J. B. Belardi et al. (eds.), *Ancient Hunting Strategies in Southern South America*,
The Latin American Studies Book Series,
https://doi.org/10.1007/978-3-030-61187-3_2

spear thrower) used for defense and attack, killing the prey or enemy by a massive hemorrhage (Christenson 1997; Hughes 1998; Loendorf et al. 2015). Even though the other elements of the weapon system were not preserved because they were made on sinew, cordage, wood, mastic or other biodegradable materials, projectile points or fragments thereof provide important clues about the characteristics and use of projectiles to which they were attached.

In the last decades, the study of projectile point technology has drawn a growing interest, standing out in Argentina the analysis on the functionality of projectile points, manufacture and maintenance processes, design and their relation within the hunting strategies and social organization (Aschero and Martínez 2001; Banegas et al. 2014; Castro 2017; Escola 1991, 2002, 2014; Hocsman 2010; Martínez and Bozzuto 2011; Moreno 2011; Ratto 1989, 2013; Restifo 2013; Sacur Silvestre et al. 2013; Vigna et al. 2014; Weitzel et al. 2014). Regarding Sierras of Córdoba (Argentina), lithic and bone projectile points were common artifacts in the Late Prehispanic Period (1500–360 BP) assemblages, being their presence striking not only by their relative abundance, but also by their wide range of morphological variation, indicating their key role on technological strategies. However, until recently archaeologists have largely approached to the analysis of projectile points using the assumption that measurable or morphological patterns among artifacts reflect differences in cultural or chronological aspects. Little attention has been paid to the functional characteristic of projectile point technology and the role that performance plays in morphological variation (Berberián 1984; González 1943; González and Crivelli 1978; Marcellino et al. 1967; Serrano 1945). The examples where hypotheses about the functionality of projectile points for hunting, warfare and their relation to regional resource structure were exceptional and have been suggested by ethnographic and experimental reconstruction (Pastor et al. 2005; Pautassi and Rivero 1999; Rivero and Recalde 2011).

In order to improve the discussion over the functional role of weapons types in late prehispanic groups, this paper presents the techno-typological analysis carried out on the flaked-stone and bone-tipped projectile points recovered from three archaeological sites from Sierras of Córdoba (Argentina) interpreted as semi-sedentary residential bases used by people with a mixed foraging and cultivation economy. The goal is to assess how the dynamic of the sociocultural process influenced the design of hunting and warfare weapons recovered on-sites. The study assumes that differences in design among projectile points are associated with intended use for hunting or for killing people, focusing the research on it. It is proposed that hunting and warfare differ fundamentally in that the former is undertaken to obtain meat, while the primarily intent of the latter is to kill or wound enemies. As result, different constraints exist for these two tasks. Hunting points were made to kill as rapidly as possible to avoid the effort of track the prey (Loendorf et al. 2015), something difficult when most of the land cover is characterized by xerophytic forest with shrubs and trees 15 m high (Giorgis et al. 2011). In contrast, warfare points were designed to maximize the probability that injury or death resulted, regardless how long this might take (Loendorf et al. 2015). Furthermore, the variability, standardized and uniform fashion of late prehispanic projectile points highlights the relevance of the

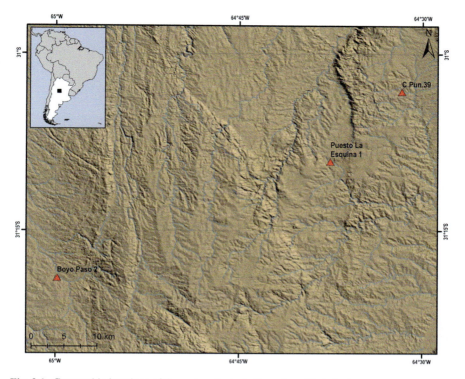

Fig. 2.1 Geographic locations of the archaeological sites referred to in text

study, especially to improve the understanding of the diet breadth and interpersonal violence in archaeological groups where the adoption of crop plants did not necessary lead to fully sedentary farming, a pattern commonly observed ethnographically but difficult to identify from the archaeological record.

2.2 Materials and Methods

The main characteristics of the sites Boyo Paso 2, C.Pun.39, and Puesto La Esquina 1 (Fig. 2.1) are in Table 2.1. The sites provided a total of 66 projectile points or fragments thereof. The identification of the raw materials used to make the tools was based on petrographic and faunal reference collections.[1] Morphological and

---

[1] Data regarding lithic raw material availability and quality came from Heider et al. (2015). Thus, quartz and chalcedony were considered as local raw materials available and located in immediately adjacent to the sites, even when the latter was low abundant compared to quartz, increasing its provision costs to flintknapping. Opal, conversely, come from primary and secondary sources located 100 km north to the sites. Consequently, it was defined as a non-local raw material.

Table 2.1 Main characteristics of Late Prehispanic Period open-air sites considered here (Sierras of Córdoba, Argentina)

Site	Localition	Chronology	Characteristics	Citation
C.Pun.39	1050 m asl, Punilla valley	854 ± 39 years BP 716 ± 39 years BP 525 ± 37 years BP	– Dense concentration of archaeological remains in a deposit of ca. 90 cm thick – Packed surface – Three statistically different radiocarbon dates from overlapping layers – High tool richness suggesting multiple activities, including farming and ritualized behaviors – 15 projectile points or fragments thereof – Primary burial – Evidences of caching (grinding tools, handstones, pigments, cores, large pottery vessels, etc.) – Crop and wild fruit remains – Bones of animals from different habitats – Spring–summer seasonal indicators – Palynological indicators of crops and anthropic disturbance	Balena et al. (2018); Medina (2010, 2015); Medina et al. (2014); Medina et al. (2017); Medina et al. (2009); Medina and Pastor (2012); Pastor et al. (2013)
Puesto La Esquina 1	1140 m asl, Pampa of Olaen	365 ± 38 years BP 362 ± 43 years BP	– Dense concentration of archaeological remains in a deposit of ca. 35 cm thick – Two statistically indistinguishable radiocarbon dates from overlapping layers – Firepit – High tool richness suggesting multiple activities, including farming – 7 projectile points or fragments thereof – Evidences of caching (handstones, pigments, cores, large pottery vessels, etc.) – Crop and wild fruit remains – Bones of animals from different habitats – Spring–summer seasonal indicators	Balena et al. (2018); Medina (2010, 2015); Medina et al. (2014); Medina and Pastor (2012)
Boyo Paso 2	1160 m asl, Salsacate valley	750 ± 70 years BP 866 ± 39 years BP, 870 ± 50 years BP, 878 ± 18 years BP, 970 ± 40 years BP, 1060 ± 50 years BP 1500 ± 80 years BP	– Dense concentration of archaeological remains in a deposit of ca. 60 cm thick – Two overlapping archaeological floors with three statistically indistinguishable radiocarbon dates – > 20 post-molds – Overlapping residential structures – Medium-sized semisubterranean feature – High tool richness suggesting multiple activities, including farming and ritualized behaviors – 44 projectile points or fragments thereof – Evidences of caching (grinding tools, handstones, pigments, cores, large pottery vessels, etc.) – Crop and wild fruit remains – Bones of animals from different habitats – Spring–summer seasonal indicators – Palynological indicators of crops and anthropic disturbance	Medina (2015); Medina et al. (2016); Medina et al. (2018); Medina et al. (2019)

metric analysis (maximum length, width and thickness) were undertaken following Aschero (1975, 1983), Hocsman (2010) and Knecht (1993). The study focused on complete or nearly complete projectile points that were classified in typological subgroups. However, some fragmented projectile points were also considered, mainly those attributes that were not affected by fragmentation. Moreover, the fractures were described and functionally interpreted following Weitzel et al. (2014).

The use and performance of projectile points as spear, dart, or arrow were assessed based on the gross weight (Fenenga 1953), allowing to interpret the social context of their use within the late prehispanic subsistence and mobility pattern. It was assumed that projectile points with a weight lighter than 4 gr were used on arrows, 4–20 gr on darts and bifaces with heavier weights than 20 gr on thrusting spear points, implying different ways of approaching to preys and socioeconomic organization. The discriminant analysis proposed by Shott (1997) was also used, being the maximum width the more important discriminating variable. The system of hafting and the size of the shaft were assessed by the morphology of the proximal end of the projectile point following Hocsman (2010) and Knecht (1993).

Finally, the performance of weaponry systems was analyzed by their capacity to wound vital organs, durability, distance range, accuracy, versatility and recovering possibilities, among others (Christenson 1997; Ellis 1997; Hughes 1998; Loendorf et al. 2015; Lyman et al. 2009; Ratto 1989). These categories were explored though the study of the design (Bleed 1986), artifacts frequency, raw material properties and delivery system.

2.3 Results

The assemblages documented a high variability of designs, which were classified in 7 sub-typological groups (Table 2.2, 2.3 and 2.4):

- *A.1.: Projectile point with short triangular-shaped blade (isosceles type), contracted stem and barbed shoulders*: The length varies between 27.77 and 15.92 mm (standard deviation 6.65 mm). They have a mean width of 12.70 mm, 3.77 mm thick and a mean weight of 0.85 gr. The section of the stems is biconvex, with a maximum width of 5.60 mm. They were shaped on opal and chalcedony flakes with a similar size of finished projectile points and without previous modification (Fig. 2.2a). Only two A.1. were made on quartz. The pieces show divergences in manufacture traces, mainly because some projectile points presented unifacial marginal retouching and other extended bifacial retouching, but always conserving the size and morphology standards (Fig. 2.2a). For example, BP2-pp2 and BP2-pp23 exhibited the marked curvature characteristically of flakes and show percussion bulbs or cortex. Other projectile points evidenced reactivation, but conserved the dimensions and morphology of the original design. 14 projectile points recorded signal of stress -i.e., impact fluted—related to their use as

Table 2.2 Main characteristics of the complete or nearly complete lithic projectile points recovered on-sites

Specimen number	Typological subgroup	Length (mm)	Width (mm)	Thickness (mm)	Weight (gr)	Stem width-thickness Module	Raw material	Type of fracture
BP2-pp1	A.1.	26.16	16	4.28	1.13	1.5	Chalcedony	–
BP2-pp2	A.1.	18.19	13.28	4.23	0.81	1.68	Chalcedony	Impact flute; Bending Fracture
BP2-pp3	A.1.	19.15	15.95	3.12	0.81	–	Chalcedony	Impact flute; Bending Fracture (stem)
BP2-pp4	A.1.	20.67	9.9	4.9	0.79	1.51	Chalcedony	–
BP2-pp6	A.1.	16.5	9	3.3	0.51	2.02	Chalcedony	–
BP2-pp7	A.1.	27.77	12.54	4.57	1.04	2.35	Chalcedony	–
BP2-pp9	A.1.	20.69	11.87	3	0.56	1.85	Opal	Bending Fracture
BP2-pp10	Preform	23.45	14.2	6.1	1.66	–	Chalcedony	Bending Fracture
BP2-pp11	Preform	29.5	13.5	4.71	1.53	–	Chalcedony	–
BP2-pp13	A.2.	44.7	18.89	3.36	0.71	1.84	Chalcedony	–
BP2-pp14	A.1.	24.65	13.23	4.3	0.88	1.93	Chalcedony	Impact flute
BP2-pp16	A.3.	12.84	10.74	2.85	0.32	1.33	Opal	Impact flute
BP2-pp22	A.1.	22.76	10.9	3.7	0.75	–	Chalcedony	Bending Fracture (stem and tip)
BP2-pp24	Preform	18.45	13.45	5.2	1.05	–	Chalcedony	–
BP2-pp28	A.1.	19.43	12.36	3.18	0.62	–	Undetermined	Bending Fracture (stem)
BP2-pp29	A.1.	16	10	2	0.26	–	Chalcedony	–

(continued)

Table 2.2 (continued)

Specimen number	Typological subgroup	Length (mm)	Width (mm)	Thickness (mm)	Weight (gr)	Stem width-thickness Module	Raw material	Type of fracture
BP2-pp34	Preform	20.15	14.5	6.82	1.63	–	Chalcedony	Bending Fracture
BP2-pp35	A.1.	25.2	16.5	5.45	1.86	2.2	Undetermined	–
BP2-pp36	B.2.	32.21	14.74	3.31	1.25	–	Chalcedony	–
BP2-pp37	A.1.	23.11	13.34	4.56	1.2	1.72	Quartz	Impact flute
BP2-pp38	A.1.	22.85	12.93	4.94	1.14	1.83	Chalcedony	Bending Fracture (tip)
BP2-pp39	A.1.	22.86	12.44	4.76	1.03	1.56	Quartz	–
BP2-pp42	A.2.	31	15.29	5.51	1.72	1.98	Chalcedony	–
BP2-pp43	A.2.	25.83	13	3.34	0.86	1.77	Chalcedony	Bending Fracture
BP2-pp44	A.3.	17.96	14.41	3.25	0.56	1.51	Chalcedony	–
PE1-pp1	C.1.	30.13	21.59	11.35	3.2	–	Undetermined	–
PE1-pp2	C.1.	56.14	24.26	12.13	10.8	–	Quartz	–
PE1-pp3	C.1.	40.68	22.73	10.16	5.1	–	Quartz	–
PE1-pp4	B.1.	36.65	27.23	5.66	6.5	–	Quartz	–
C.Pun.39-pp1	A.1.	24.16	17.21	4.28	0.9	1.5	Chalcedony	–
C.Pun.39-pp2	A.1.	15.92	12.73	2.86	0.54	1.88	Chalcedony	Bending Fracture (tip)
CP.un.39-pp3	A.1.	19.19	12	3.55	0.76	–	Chalcedony	Bending Fracture (stem and tip)
C.Pun.39-pp4	A.1.	23.20	11.58	3.80	0.86	1.71	Chalcedony	–

(continued)

Table 2.2 (continued)

Specimen number	Typological subgroup	Length (mm)	Width (mm)	Thickness (mm)	Weight (gr)	Stem width-thickness Module	Raw material	Type of fracture
C.Pun.39-pp5	A.1.	14.98	14.68	3.48	0.77	–	Chalcedony	Bending Fracture (stem and tip)
C.Pun.39-pp6	A.1.	18.84	14.71	3.22	0.85	2.01	Chalcedony	Bending Fracture
C.Pun.39-pp7	A.1.	12.45	11.73	3.07	0.37	–	Chalcedony	Bending Fracture (stem and tip)
C.Pun.39-pp8	A.1.	20.32	10.25	3.11	0.82	–	Undetermined	Bending Fracture (stem); Impact flute

Table 2.3 Main characteristics of the broken lithic projectile points recovered on-sites

Specimen number	Portion	Typological subgroup	Length (mm)	Width (mm)	Thickness (mm)	Weight (gr)	Raw Material	Type of fracture
BP2-pp5	Basal-mesial fragment	A.1.	11.2	13.12	3.45	0.38	Chalcedony	Bending Fracture; Spin-off fracture
BP2-pp8	Mesial fragment	A.1.	16.5	11.65	3.15	0.59	Chalcedony	Bending Fracture
BP2-pp12	Basal-mesial fragment	A.1.	27.77	13.32	4.16	0.91	Chalcedony	Bending Fracture (blade)
BP2-pp15	Mesial fragment	Undetermined	20.88	11.45	3.55	0.71	Chalcedony	Bending Fracture
BP2-pp17	Stem fragment	Undetermined	20.69	4	2.05	–	Chalcedony	Bending Fracture
BP2-pp18	Basal-mesial fragment	A.1.	23.45	13.5	3.62	0.44	Ópal	Bending Fracture (blade)
BP2-pp19	Mesial fragment	Undetermined	29.5	12.75	2.41	0.37	Undetermined	Bending Fracture
BP2-pp21	Basal-mesial fragment	A.1.	19.95	16.09	3	0.45	Undetermined	Bending Fracture; Spin-off fracture
BP2-pp23	Basal-mesial fragment	A.1.	44.7	9	2.25	0.23	Chalcedony	Bending Fracture (blade)
BP2-pp25	Basal-mesial fragment	B.1.	24.65	25	5.26	2.47	Quartz	Bending Fracture (blade); Spin-off fracture
BP2-pp26	Basal-mesial fragment	A.2.	16	15.3	2.1	0.34	Chalcedony	Bending Fracture (blade)

(continued)

Table 2.3 (continued)

Specimen number	Portion	Typological subgroup	Length (mm)	Width (mm)	Thickness (mm)	Weight (gr)	Raw Material	Type of fracture
BP2-pp27	Basal-mesial fragment	A.1.	12.84	15.65	3.78	0.65	Chalcedony	Bending Fracture (blade)
BP2-pp30	Basal-mesial fragment	A.1.	7	12.55	2.96	0.62	Chalcedony	Bending Fracture (blade)
BP2-pp31	Mesial fragment	Undetermined	11.1	13.71	3.3	0.6	Undetermined	Bending Fracture
BP2-pp32	Tip fragment	Undetermined	14.8	8.85	3.15	–	Chalcedony	Bending Fracture
BP2-pp33	Tip fragment	Undetermined	9	7.15	2.7	–	Chalcedony	Bending Fracture
BP2-pp41	Basal-mesial fragment	B.2.	12.24	14.45	4.43	–	Chalcedony	Bending Fracture (blade)
BP2-pp45	Tip fragment	Undetermined	8.68	7.1	1.81	–	Chalcedony	Bending Fracture
BP2-pp46	Tip fragment	Undetermined	15.54	7.68	4.52	–	Chalcedony	Bending Fracture
PE1-pp5	Tip fragment	Undetermined	11.1	8.16	3.45	–	Quartz	Bending Fracture
PE1-pp6	Mesial fragment	Undetermined	14.5	11.02	4.21	–	Quartz	Bending Fracture (blade)
PE1-pp7	Tip fragment	Undetermined	8.16	6.9	2.15	–	Chalcedony	Bending Fracture
C.Pun.39-pp9	Basal-mesial fragment	Undetermined	17.53	9.68	4.89	0.45	Chalcedony	Bending Fracture (tip and shoulder)
C.Pun.39-pp10	Tip fragment	Undetermined	7.2	6.5	2.54	–	Undetermined	Bending Fracture
C.Pun.39-pp11	Tip fragment	Undetermined	9.13	8.15	3.26	–	Chalcedony	Bending Fracture
C.Pun.39-pp12	Basal-mesial fragment	A.1.	21.16	16.23	5.01	0.57	Chalcedony	Bending Fracture (blade and stem); Spin-off fracture

(continued)

Table 2.3 (continued)

Specimen number	Portion	Typological subgroup	Length (mm)	Width (mm)	Thickness (mm)	Weight (gr)	Raw Material	Type of fracture
CPun39-pp13	Mesial fragment	Undetermined	13	10.13	3.98	–	Undetermined	Bending Fracture
C.Pun.39-pp14	Tip fragment	Undetermined	7.36	6.02	2.61	–	Undetermined	Bending Fracture
C.Pun3.9-pp15	Tip fragment	Undetermined	18.33	10.07	4.12	0.72	Chalcedony	Bending Fracture (blade)

Table 2.4 Main characteristics of the bone projectile points recovered on-sites (Typological subgroup D.1.)

Specimen number	Portion	Anatomic identification	Taxonomic identification	Observations
BP2-29	Fragment of the edge of the blade	long bone splinter	Macrovertebrate, sp. indet. (medium-large size)	The fragment is burned and has visible manufacture traces
BP2-56	Fragment of blade	long bone splinter	Macrovertebrate, sp. indet. (medium-large size)	The fragment is burned and has visible manufacture traces
BP2-78	Fragment of the edge of the blade	long bone splinter	Macrovertebrate, sp. indet. (medium-large size)	The fragment is burned and has visible manufacture traces
BP2-81	Fragment of a straight stem with a serrated edge	long bone splinter	Macrovertebrate, sp. indet. (medium-large size)	The fragment is burned and has visible manufacture traces
BP2-82	Fragment of a straight stem with a serrated edge	long bone splinter	Mammalia, sp. indet. (medium-large size)	The fragment has visible manufacture traces
C.Pun.39-1a, b, c and d	Nearly complete arrowpoint with triangular-shaped blade, barbed shoulders and straight stem with serrated edges	long bone splinter	Mammalia, sp. indet. (medium-large size)	The fragment is burned and has visible manufacture traces
C.Pun.39-2	Fragment of a straight stem with a serrated edge	long bone splinter	Macrovertebrate, sp. indet. (medium-large size)	The fragment has visible manufacture traces
C.Pun.39-3	Fragment of tip	long bone splinter	Mammalia, sp. indet. (medium-large size)	The fragment has visible manufacture traces
C.Pun.39-4	Fragment of a straight stem with a serrated edge	long bone splinter	Macrovertebrate, sp. indet. (medium-large size)	The fragment is burned and has visible manufacture traces

(continued)

Table 2.4 (continued)

Specimen number	Portion	Anatomic identification	Taxonomic identification	Observations
C.Pun.39-16	Fragment of a straight stem	long bone splinter	Macrovertebrate, sp. indet. (medium-large size)	The fragment is burned and has visible manufacture traces
PE1-1	Nearly complete arrowpoint with triangular-shaped blade, barbed shoulders and straight stem with serrated edges	long bone splinter	Mammalia, sp. indet. (medium-large size)	The fragment has visible manufacture traces and a possible impact breakage pattern
PE1-3	Fragment of a straight stem with a serrated edge	long bone splinter	Macrovertebrate, sp. indet. (medium-large size)	The fragment has visible manufacture traces
PE1-4	Fragment of a straight stem with a serrated edge	long bone splinter	Macrovertebrate, sp. indet. (medium-large size)	The fragment is burned and has visible manufacture traces
PE1-5a, b and c	Reassembled fragments of distal-medial portion of blade	long bone splinter	Macrovertebrate, sp. indet. (medium-large size)	The fragment is burned and has visible manufacture traces
PE1-6	Fragment of of distal-medial portion of blade	long bone splinter	Mammalia, sp. indet. (medium-large size)	The fragment is burned and has visible manufacture traces
PE1-15	Fragment of a straight stem	long bone splinter	Macrovertebrate, sp. indet. (medium-large size)	The fragment has visible manufacture traces
PE1-24	Fragment of a straight stem	long bone splinter	Macrovertebrate, sp. indet. (medium-large size)	The fragment is burned and has visible manufacture traces

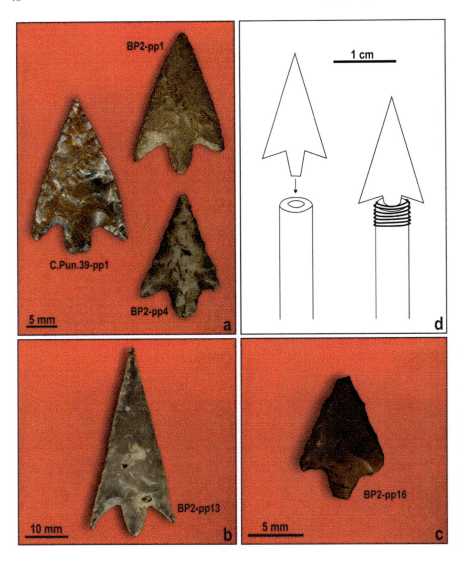

Fig. 2.2 Typological sub-groups of projectile points with triangular-shaped blade, contracted stems and barbed shoulders: (a) Typological subgroup A.1 from C.Pun.39 (C.Pun.39-pp1) and Boyo Paso 2 (BP2-pp1 and BP2-pp4); (b) Typological subgroup A.2 from Boyo Paso 2 (BP2-pp13); (c) Typological subgroup A.3. from Boyo Paso 2 (BP2-pp16); (d) Schematic model of the hafted method described in the text

projectile (sensu Weitzel et al. 2014). 4 pre-forms were included in this subgroup type. The amount of projectile points of this category is 32.

- *A.2.: Projectile points with long triangular-shaped blade (isosceles type), contracted stem and barbed shoulders*: the subgroup included two projectile points from Boyo Paso 2, that even when they look similar to A.1., they presented different characteristics (Fig. 2.2b). BP2-pp13 is 44.7 mm long, 18.89 mm wide, 3.36 mm thick and 1.93 gr in weight (Fig. 2.2b). The section of stem is biconvex, with a maximum width of 5.37 mm. The blade of BP2-pp26 was resharpened to fashion a drill, but it conserved the morphology of the stem and the maximum width of the barbs. The projectile points were fashioned on chalcedony flakes using extended bifacial thinning and extended bifacial retouching techniques.
- *A.3.: Projectile point with short triangular-shaped blade (equilateral type), contracted stem and barbed shoulder*: It is a tiny projectile point recovered on Boyo Paso 2 that was shaped by marginal and extended retouching on an opal flake which even presents the original curvature of the flake (Fig. 2.2c). The metric attributes are 12.84 mm long, 10.64 mm wide and 0.31 gr in weight. The stem has biconvex section and it is 3.61 mm wide. The tip shows a small impact fluted as a result of its use as a projectile.
- *B.1.: Large-sized non-stemmed projectile points with triangular-shaped blades (equilateral type) and concave base*: Two projectile points of this subgroup made on quartz were recovered on Puesto La Esquina 1 and Boyo Paso 2. PE1-pp4 is 36.65 mm long, 27.23 mm wide, 5.66 mm thick, and 6.5 gr in weight (Fig. 2.3a).

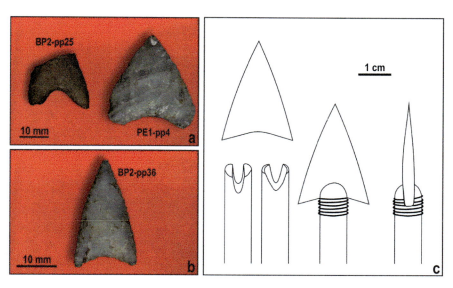

Fig. 2.3 Typological subgroup of non-stemmed projectile points with a triangular-shaped blade and concave base: (a) Typological subgroup B.1. from Boyo Paso 2 (BP2-pp25) and Puesto La Esquina 1 (PE1-pp4); (b) Typological subgroup B.2. from Boyo Paso 2 (BP2-36); (c) Schematic model of the hafted method described in the text

BP2-pp25 is a basal fragment with a stipulated length of 38 mm, 5.25 mm thick and 25 mm wide (Fig. 2.3a). The weight was estimated based on Shott (1997) formula: 4 gr. The points were manufactured on a medium-sized flake and shaped by extended bifacial retouching. BP2-pp25 also shows a bending fracture and a cone fracture which is initiated from the former, interpreted as impact caused fracture (Weitzel et al. 2014).

- *B.2: Small-sized non-stemmed projectile points with triangular-shaped blades (isosceles type) and concave bases*: Two projectile points were identified exclusively at Boyo Paso 2. They were fashioned on small chalcedony flakes shaped by bifacial thinning and extended bifacial retouching (Fig. 2.3b). The proximal ends also show basal thinning, presumably done to facilitate the hafting. BP2-pp36 is 32.21 mm long, 14.74 mm wide, 3.31 mm thick, and 1.25 gr in weight (Fig. 2.3b). BP2-pp41 is a basal-mesial fragment that presents a bending fracture and whose metric attributes are 12.24 mm long, 4.43 mm thick, 14.45 mm wide, and 0.96 gr in weight.
- *C.1.: Lanceolate-shaped projectile points:* They are three projectile points of this subgroup in Puesto La Esquina 1 made on quartz and an undetermined stone (Fig. 2.4a). Lanceolate-shaped projectiles tips were fashioned on medium-sized flakes shaped by bifacial thinning and marginal retouching. The basal ends are convergent convex. Mean metric structure was 42.32 mm long, 11.21 mm thick, 22.86 mm wide, and 6.37 gr in weight.
- *D.1.: Bone points with long triangular-shaped blade (isosceles type), straight or slightly contracted stems with serrated edges and barbed shoulders*: Two nearly

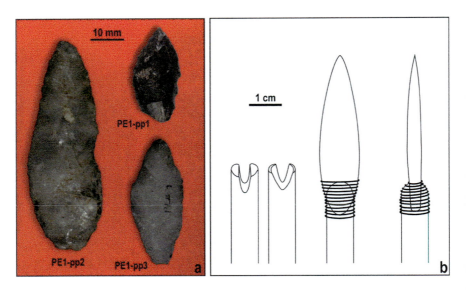

Fig. 2.4 Lanceolate-shaped projectile points (Typological subgroup C.1.): (a) Projectile points made on quartz (PE1-pp2 and PE1-pp3) and undeterminated rock (PE1-pp1) from Puesto La Esquina 1; (b) Schematic model of the hafted method described in the text

2 Tiny Arrow Points, Bone-Tipped Projectiles ...

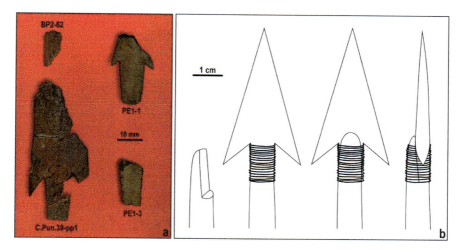

Fig. 2.5 Projectile points with triangular-shaped blade, straight stems and barbed shoulders (Subgroup D.1.): (a) Fragment of a stem from Boyo Paso 2 (BP2-86), nearly complete bone arrowpoint from C.Pun.39 (C.Pun.39-1), nearly complete bone arrowpoint (PE1-1) and a stem (PE1-3) from Puesto La Esquina 1 (b) Schematic model of the hafted method described in the text

complete projectile points and other small fragments were recovered on-sites, including 10 fragmented stems (Fig. 2.5a). They were assigned to a class of artifact relatively recurrent in late prehispanic assemblages, with a mean of 62.1 mm long, 14.6 mm wide, 2.6 thick, and y 2–4 gr in weight (Medina et al. 2014; Pastor et al. 2005; Pauttassi and Rivero 1999). The intense anthropic modification of the blank makes it difficult to identify the taxa and the body part selected to fashion the bone tips, which were roughly assigned to non-identified macrovertebrate elongated long bone splinters or to Mammalia sp. (medium-large size) at most. The fragments are burned and present longitudinal and oblique coarse striations suggesting that were shaped by abrasion with a coarse-grain material. Blades were more finely abraded to increase drag coefficient, reduce resistant and secure a deeper penetration on the rib cage of target. The bending fracture on PE1-1 (Fig. 2.5a) looks similar to the impact breakage pattern described by Knecht (1997), Cristiani (2008), and Petillon (2006).

The maximum width and gross weight of projectile tips suggest at least two weapon delivery systems to capture prey. The sub-groups A.1., A.2., A.3., B.2., and D.1. were hafted to a bow-and-arrow weapon delivery system, mainly because their light weight needs speed to increase their effectiveness and penetration capacity (Blitz 1988; Hughes 1998; Churchill 1993). Moreover, the stems of A.1., A.2., and A.3. indicate the utilization of light projectile shafts with a conical or cylindrical socket whittled out on the distal end to insert the tips and facilitate the quickly replace of the arrowhead once the costly shaft was recovered (Fig. 2.2d). The B.2. projectile points, conversely, were hafted using a simple U or V-shaped slot whittled out on distal end of the shafts (Fig. 2.3c). These modular designed arrows (sensu Bleed 1986), that is, hafted in such way that the point remains in the wound and the shaft could be recovered and easily brought to a functional state to be used again, coexisted with more complex hafting systems that involve shafts with a distal end whittled down to match a stem with a serrated edge to reduce the slippage of the ligature and bound the point firmly fastened to the shaft, as the bone arrow points classified as D.1. (Fig. 2.5b).

Unstemmed projectile points B.1. and C.1. share many characteristics with those projectile points from early archaic assemblages dated at ca. 4000–2000 AP (González and Crivelli 1978; Menghín and González 1954; Rivero 2009), where it is possible that tips were claimed. Projectile points B.1. have proximal ends relatively wide that were bounded to shafts with a size relatively larger than the previously considered ones, with a simple U or V-shaped slot (Fig. 2.3c), while C.1. were hafted with simple slot whittled out on the shafts and fastened with organic ligatures (Fig. 2.4b). The weight of these projectile points is compatible with spearthrower or atlatl-delivered system dart points, where these types of tips have an excellent performance, distance range, and accuracy (Pastor et al. 2005). Stone-tipped projectiles like the recently described lose less kinetic energy during long-distance shooting, have a high penetration power (Hutchings and Brüchert 1997) and can produce a more serious wound (Christenson 1997), being optimal for large-game hunting in open terrain. However, the accuracy of darts may be lower when compared to arrows due to its minor speed (Blitz 1988; Cattelain 1997; Churchill 1993; Hughes 1998; Pastor et al. 2005).

2.4 Discussion

The lithic and bone technology of Late Prehispanic Period is dominated by expediently used tools manufactured on local lithic raw material and the by-products of the faunal consumption, mostly according to immediate needs and discarded once the activities were finished (Balena et al. 2018; Medina et al. 2014; Pastor 2007; Rivero and Pastor 2004). However, the projectile points documented here are fashioned on raw material that requires a high provisioning and/or manufacture effort, showing that late prehispanic groups also elaborated costly, standardized and reliable tools for hunting and warfare.

The high relative abundance of the subgroup A.1. in late prehispanic assemblages (48.5%) suggests that these arrowtips were utilized on the day-to-day basis for hunting diverse animal preys, being the most used and discarded (Loendorf et al. 2015; Lyman et al. 2009; Politis et al. 2013). It is interpreted that these projectile points were primary accumulated through in situ repairing-related activities after hunting, where tips were replaced and the shaft were brought to a functional state for use again. Some of them could have entered in association with the body of prey, especially when projectile tips were not securely hafted to hang in the wound after the projectile shaft had fallen out or been removed. Once again, the advantage of this head loosely attached design is that the main shaft will often come away from the tip once it struck the prey, enabling hunters to recover the shaft and use it again, avoiding the implication of the costly work involved in its manufacture. However, it is striking the high frequency of lithic arrow-tips without severe damage. A possible explanation is related to site furniture behaviors, where artifacts that still had use life and pre-form were left on-sites in anticipation of being used when the sites were reoccupied (Medina et al. 2016).

The identification of unstemmed projectile points B.1. and C.1. can be seen as a reclaiming example (sensu Schiffer 1987), where late prehispanic people recovered these artifacts from early archaic sites and took them to their settlements where they were finally discarded. The absence on-sites of flakes of quartz indicating extended bifacial retouching, a common by-product of lithic debitage in archaic assemblages dated at ca. 4000–2000 BP (Rivero 2009), reinforces this argument. However, the recurrent recovering of these types of projectile points in late prehispanic sites would evidence that the spear thrower and the bow were simultaneously used to hunting large-game as guanaco (*Lama guanicoe*) or for small-animals, although the use of the former was in clear declination regarding the latter. Ethnohistoric records and atlatl hooks coexisting with arrow points within contemporary or early colonial societies from neighboring region, supports this assertion (see Sacur Silvestre et al. 2013; Swanton 1938). Moreover, it opens to question the widespread assumption that the bow and arrow completely replaced the spear thrower, even when bow duplicated the function and accuracy of spear thrower (Hughes 1998). However, the spear thrower has not been found yet in late prehispanic sites and the hypothesis requires further investigation, even though distal extremities of atlatl made of stone were recovered from Ongamira site ca. 3000 BP (Menghín and González 1954).

The sub-groups A.2. and D.1. was interpreted as weapons designed for using against people in warfare (Loendorf et al. 2015), although other arrowheads could have been used with the same purpose. Moreover, this should explain why they are recorded in low frequency in the late prehispanic deposits (Politis et al. 2013). The capacity of these tips to pierce the rib cage, heart and lung, adding barbed tangs that resist removal from the wound and securely hafted method for D.1., favor that if the projectile enters to the body of enemy it cannot be easily withdrawn from the wound, with the point attached to the arrow, creating a more serious internal hemorrhaging, also preventing the projectile from being fired in return (Christenson 1997; Hughes 1998; Loendorf et al. 2015). Even if warfare arrows were recovered from the enemy dead bodies and require reparation, the stems are likely to be attached because they were intentionally firmly fastened to the shaft. Thus, brought the arrow to functional state again requires transporting the projectile point to the camps and removing the ligatures of the hafting system using the heat of a domestic hearths, explaining the frequency of burned and isolated stems recovered on-sites. Ethnographic examples show that arrow points with similar characteristics to D.1. are used to hunt in forest environment, basically because once the arrow is in target it avoids the flight of the prey and increases the hemorrhage while the shaft gets caught on vegetation (Griffin 1997; Politis et al. 2013). However, the record of late prehispanic human skeletal remains with clear evidence of death caused by bone-tipped projectiles similar to the here described, reinforce this functional hypothesis (Pastor et al. 2012; González 1943; Fabra et al. 2015; Weyenbergh, 1880). Thus, the spread of weapons designed to warfare ca. 1500 BP indicates that during Late Prehispanic Period the interpersonal violence increased respect to previous archaic periods. The violence concern was also evidenced by rock-art with panels showing conflicts scenes and human figures carrying weapons (Pastor 2012; Rivero and Recalde 2011). The finding of human trophy-heads or headless bodies can be interpreted under the same criteria (Berberián 1984; González 1949; Paulotti 1943).

2.5 Conclusion

Most archaeological interpretations of the Sierras of Córdoba Late Prehispanic Period assumed that the adoption of farming ca. 1500 years BP quickly derived in a high reliance on domesticated plants and a sedentary way of life in year-round pit-house villages (Aparicio 1939; Berberián 1984; Canals Frau 1953; González 1943; Laguens and Bonnín 2009; Outes 1911; Serrano 1945). It was ignored that evolutionary change is not unidirectional and switching foraging by people who previously practiced cultivation was a common behavior in the past (Layton et al. 1991).

Fortunately, the archaeological interest in how late prehispanic people adjusted their foraging and mobility strategies to plant cultivation has increased over the last years, fielding a spectrum of farming and foraging strategies that discredited this rigid normative point of view. Now, the late prehispanic situation was at odds with the conventional wisdom about cultural evolution, and the replacement of foraging by farming anticipated in most culture evolution schemes did not occur in Sierras of Córdoba. For instance, the absence of evidence of year-round residences and the low investment in farming fields, as well as other archaeological indicators, supports this new model (Medina et al. 2014; Medina et al. 2016, 2018). Conversely, the evidence suggests that late prehispanic people developed a mixed foraging and cultivation economy, where flexibility was one of its defining traits (Medina et al. 2014). Late prehispanic hunting, for example, was centered about the pursuit of *L. guanicoe* plus small-game (Medina et al. 2019; Medina and Pastor 2012). Pottery, maize, and other crops farming were also extensively used, but within broad-spectrum foraging base looking forward to increasing the productivity per unit of time and space and included high residential mobility (Medina et al. 2016, 2018; Pastor et al. 2012). Thus, foraging for wild resources continued being an important subsistence activity, while farming was seasonally abandoned when most profitable wild resources were available in the landscape. The development of a diversified economy, in consequence, was accompanied by a high residential mobility, co-residential group fission–fusion mechanisms and the abandonment of crop field to forage, where the local resource abundance was weighed in term of the regional foraging potential (Medina et al. 2016; Pastor et al. 2012).

According to this model, late prehispanic villages as Boyo Paso 2, C.Pun.39, and Puesto La Esquina 1 reflect few extended family reoccupations during the growing and planting season to do on-site farming, harvesting wild fruits, and small-game hunting activities (Medina et al. 2014; Pastor et al 2012). When harvest and stored activities finished, co-residential groups dispersed across the landscape to forage resources that were distributed in heterogeneous fashion, collected information about their social-environment and maintained the socio-political fluidity upon which they depended. Therefore, the late prehispanic people made a seasonal and diversified use of the landscape, where social unit for food production, consumption, and landscape occupation was the nuclear family, which adjust settlement location, group size, or the mix of farming and foraging to changing circumstances (Medina et al. 2014; Pastor et al. 2012).

It is within this framework where the abundance and diversity of projectile points, along with the different hafting methods, the adoption of the bow, the selection of high-quality lithic raw material and the incorporation of bone-tipped projectiles, became the fundamental pillars to assess key aspects of the late prehispanic socio-cultural process related to economic and social intensification. Therefore, the results indicate that multiple strategies of design, manufacture, and performance of projectile points were emphasized through the Late Prehispanic Period, which is interpreted as an archaeological indicator that the exploitation of a wide range of vertebrates was not a complementary activity. Conversely, hunting played a key role in a mixed foraging and cultivation economy, which is also pointed out by the abundance of camelid, cervid, and small vertebrate bone remains with evidence of human consumption (Medina et al. 2019; Medina and Pastor 2012). The evidence shows that bow-delivered projectile points were crucial for shooting small-to-large game at different distances and cover structures, including dangerous animal as humans that are more difficult to kill and requires long-distance shooting, a situation consistent with a time period where subsistence activities were diversified and social tensions increased, with clear osteological evidences of physical violence. The arrow technology facilitated a broad-spectrum hunting base, but paradoxically it probably caused an increase of the importance of plant food because a large fraction of the meat easily available by bow hunting came from fat-poor small-game. Thus, caloric needs had to be offset by input of plant fat coming from wild or possible domesticated tubers and roots rich in carbohydrates, which have been well documented at several late prehispanic sites (Medina et al. 2018; Recalde and López 2017).

The use of bow-delivered projectiles also led to adjust the hunting or defense strategy to the size of the groups, encouraging the development of more independent family-based economic and political systems. That is, the bow-and-arrow technology allowed the hunters individually to kill preys without requiring the cooperation or mutual help of several hunters (Bettinger 2013), facilitating that minimal social unit colonized new farming lands or hunting territories. The existence of communal hunting events or co-residence was not precluded (Pastor et al. 2012), but when communal activities finished each family could develop their individual strategy without depending on the decisions of larger groups. On the other hand, the superiority of the bow as an offensive and defensive weapon created the opportunity for effective individual defense, increasing the political self-sufficiency of families and strictly limiting the authority to the short-term duration of cooperative activities or co-residence, being this interpretation consistent with the small autonomous kin-based groups described in early colonial documents (González Navarro 2009).

To conclude, one of the main properties resulting from the weaponry systems analysis is the diversity of projectile point designs and raw materials utilized in their manufacture. This at least shows the niche breadth during the Late Prehispanic Period and highlights the importance of minimizing the cost of failure in the capture of the prey they depended on. Results also outlined the importance of hunting among groups traditionally interpreted as sedentary farmers which, along with harvesting wild and domesticated plants, governed the pattern of seasonal movement. The multiple-available evidence suggests that late prehispanic people moved around the landscape to take advantage of both wild resources and domesticated as they became available, making difficult to estimate the reliance on cultivated plants over foraging. Thus, the evidence indicated that there is considerable fluidity across economic modes and the Late Prehispanic Period would constitute a model to interpret other archaeological cases during the Neolithic or Formative transition, where the boundaries between farming and foraging could have been fluid, but remained relatively invisible according to the existing terminology.

Acknowledgements We thank the financial support by the Secretaría de Ciencia y Técnica de la Universidad Nacional de La Plata (11/N885) and the Agencia Nacional de Promoción Científica y Tecnológica (PICT-201-0677). Our acknowledgement also extends to Robin Torrence, Lucía Yebra, Salomón Hocsman, Robert Bettinger, Diego Gobbo, Norma Ratto, and Patricia Escola, who provided professional advices, equipment and replied to our numerous requests to improve the original.

References

Aparicio F (1939) La Antigua Provincia de los Comechingones. In: Academia Nacional de la Historia (ed) Historia de la Nación Argentina I, Tiempos Prehistóricos y Protohistóricos. Editorial El Ateneo, Buenos Aires, pp 359–386

Aschero C (1975) Ensayo Para una Clasificación Morfológica de Artefactos Líticos Aplicada a Estudios Tipológicos Interpretativos. Informe inédito presentado al CONICET. Manuscrito, Buenos Aires.

Aschero C (1983) Ensayo para una Clasificación Morfológica de Artefactos Líticos. Apéndices A y B. Apunte inédito para la Cátedra de Ergología y Tecnología. Facultad de Filosofía y Letras, Universidad de Buenos Aires, Buenos Aires

Aschero C, Martínez G (2001) Técnicas de caza en Antofagasta de la Sierra, Puna Meridional Argentina. Relaciones de la Sociedad Argentina de Antropología 26:215–241

Balena I, Heider G, Medina M (2018) Tecnología lítica entre las sociedades del Período Prehispánico Tardío (Sierras de Córdoba, Argentina). Mundo de Antes 12(2), en prensa

Banegas A, Gómez Otero J, Goye S, Ratto N (2014) Cabezales líticos del Holoceno Tardío en Patagonia Meridional: diseños y asignación funcional. Magallania 42(2):155–174

Berberián E (1984) Potrero de Garay: Una entidad sociocultural tardía de la región serrana de la Provincia de Córdoba (Rep. Argentina). Comechingonia 4:71–138

Bettinger R (2013) Effects of the bow on social organization in Western North America. Evol Anthropol 22:118–123

Bleed P (1986) The optimal design of hunting weapons: maintainability or reliability. Am Antiq 51:737–747

Blitz J (1988) Adoption of the bow in prehistoric North America. North American Archaeologist 9(2):123–145

Canals Frau S (1953) Las Poblaciones Indígenas de la Argentina. Editorial Sudamericana, Buenos Aires

Castro S (2017) Tecnología de caza en la cuenca alta del río Las Taguas (San Juan, Argentina). Análisis morfológico de proyectiles líticos del sitio ARQ-18 (8.900–790 AP). Cuadernos del Instituto Nacional de Antropología y Pensamiento Latinoamericano 26(1):1–20

Cattelain P (1997) Hunting during the Upper Paleolithic: bow, spearthrower, or both? In: Knetch H (ed) Projectile Technology. Plenum Press, New York, pp 213–240

Christenson A (1997) Side-notched and unnotched arrow points. Assesing functional differences. In Knetch H (ed) Projectile technology. Plenum Press, New York, pp 131–142

Churchill S (1993) Weapon technology, prey size selection and hunting methods in modern hunter-gatherer: implications for hunting in the Paleolithic and Mesolithic. In: Peterkin G, Bricker H, Mellars P (ed) Hunting and animal exploitation in the later paleolithic and mesolithic of Eurasia. Archaeological Papers of the American Anthropological Association, New York, pp 11–24

Cristiani E (2008) Analisi funzionale dei manufatti in materia dura animale del Riparo Dalmeri (Altopiano della Marcesina, Trento). Prehistoria Alpina 43:259–287

Ellis C (1997) Factor influencing the use of stone projectile tips. An ethnographic perspective. In: Knetch H (ed) Projectile technology. Plenum Press, New York, pp 37–78

Escola P (1991) Puntas de proyectil de contextos formativos: acercamiento tecno-tipológico a través de cuatro casos de análisis. Actas del Congreso Nacional de Arqueología Chilena, Tomo 2. Museo Nacional de Historia Natural, Santiago de Chile, pp 175–184

Escola P (2002) Caza y pastoralismo: un reaseguro para la subsistencia. Relaciones de la Sociedad Argentina de Antropología 27:233–245

Escola P (2014) Proyectiles líticos en contexto de Arroyo Seco 2: algo más que una tecnología para la caza. In Politis G, Gutiérrez M, Scabuzzo C (eds) Estado Actual de las Investigaciones en el Sitio Arqueológico Arroyo Seco 2 (Partido de Tres Arroyos, Provincia de Buenos Aires, Argentina). Universidad Nacional de Centro de la Provincia de Buenos Aires, Tandil, pp 229–275

Fabra M, González C, Robin S (2015) Evidencias de violencia interpersonal en poblaciones del piedemonte y las llanuras de Córdoba (Argentina) a finales del Holoceno tardío. Runa 36:5–27

Fenenga F (1953) The weights of chipped stone points: a clue to their functions. Southwest J Anthropol 9(3):309–323

Giorgis M, Cingolani A, Chiarini F, Chiapella J, Barboza G, Ariza L, Morero L, Gurvich D, Tecco P, Subilis R, Cabido M (2011) Composición florística del Bosque Chaqueño Serrano de la provincia de Córdoba, Argentina. Kurtziana 36:9–43

González A (1943) Arqueología del yacimiento indígena de Villa Rumipal (Pcia. de Córdoba). Publicaciones del Instituto de Arqueología, Lingüística y Folklore IV. Universidad Nacional de Córdoba, Córdoba

González A (1949) Nota sobre la arqueología de Pampa de Olaen (Córdoba). Notas del Museo de La Plata. Tomo XIV. Antropología Nro 56:463–503

González Navarro C (2009) Autoridades étnicas en un contexto de desestructuración: Córdoba entre la fundación y la visita de Antonio Martines Luxan de Vargas. In: Bixio B, González Navarro C, Grana R, Iarza V (eds) Visita a las Encomiendas de Indios de Córdoba 1692–1693. Editorial Brujas, Córdoba, pp 63–114

González S, Crivelli E (1978) Excavaciones arqueológicas en el abrigo de Los Chelcos (Dpto. San Alberto. Córdoba). Relaciones de la Sociedad Argentina de Antropología 12:183–212

Griffin B (1997) Technology and variation in arrow design among the Agta of Northwestern Luzon. In: Knetch H (ed) Projectile Technology. Plenum Press, New York, pp 267–286

Heider G, Rivero D, Baldo E (2015) Rocas de uso arqueológico en Sierras Centrales. Fuentes de recursos líticos identificadas y potenciales en las provincias de Córdoba y San Luis, Argentina. Revista de Antropología del Museo de Entre Ríos 1(2):55–72

Hocsman S (2010) Cambios en las puntas de proyectil durante la transición de cazadores-recolectores a sociedades agropastoriles en Antofagasta de la Sierra (Puna Argentina). Arqueología 16:59–86

Hughes S (1998) Getting to the point: evolutionary change in prehistoric weaponry. J Archaeol Method Theory 5(4):345–408

Hutchings W, Brüchert L (1997) Spearthrower performance: ethnographic and experimental research. Antiquity 71:890–897

Knecht H (1993) Early upper paleolithic approaches to bone and antler projectile technology. In: Peterkin G, Bricker H, Mellars P (eds) Hunting and animal exploitation in the later paleolithic and mesolithic of Eurasia. Archaeological Papers of the American Anthropological Association, New York, pp 33–47

Knecht H (1997) Projectile points of bone, antler and stone. Experimental exploration of manufacture and use. In: Knecht H (ed) Projectile technology. Plenum Press, New York, pp 191–212

Laguens A, Bonnín M (2009) Sociedades Indígenas de las Sierras Centrales. Arqueología de Córdoba y San Luis. Editorial de la Universidad Nacional de Córdoba, Córdoba, Córdoba

Layton R, Foley R, Williams E (1991) The transition between hunting and gathering and the specialized husbandry of resources. Current Anthropology 32:255–274

Loendorf C, Simon L, Dybowski D, Woodson M, Plumlee R, Tiedens S, Withrow M (2015) Warfare and big game hunting: flaked-stone projectile points along the middle Gila River in Arizona. Antiquity 89:940–952

Lyman R, VanPool T, O´Brien M (2009) The diversity of North American projectile-point types, before and after the bow and arrow. J Anthropol Archaeol 28:1–13

Marcellino A, Berberián E, Pérez J (1967) El yacimiento arqueológico de Los Molinos (Dpto. Calamuchita, Córdoba). Publicaciones del Instituto de Antropología 26:1–68

Martínez J, Bozzuto D (eds) (2011) Armas Prehispánicas: Múltiples Enfoques para su Estudio en Sudamérica. Fundación de Historia Natural Felix de Azara, Buenos Aires

Medina M (2010) Tecnología cerámica, subsistencia y uso del Espacio en el tardío prehispánico de las Sierras de Córdoba (Argentina). Revista Werkén 13:305–322

Medina M (2015) Casas-pozo, Agujeros de Postes y Movilidad Residencial en el Período Prehispánico Tardío de las Sierras de Córdoba, Argentina. In: Salazar J (ed) Condiciones de Posibilidad de la Reproducción Social en Sociedades Prehispánicas y Coloniales Tempranas en las Sierras Pampeanas (República Argentina). Centro de Estudios Históricos "Prof. Carlos S.A. Segreti", Córdoba, pp 267–301

Medina M, Buc N, Pastor S (2014) Intensificación y dinámica ocupacional en el Periodo Prehispánico Tardío de las Sierras de Córdoba (Argentina): Una aproximación desde el registro artefactual óseo. Chungara 46(1):73–90

Medina M, Campos M, Ávila N, Soibelzon E, Fernandez F (2019) Animal food during the Late Prehispanic Period at Sierras of Córdoba (Argentina). A zooarchaeological view from Boyo Paso 2. Anthropozoologica (in press)

Medina M, Grill S, Fernández AL, López L (2017) Anthropogenic pollen, foraging and crops during Sierras of Córdoba Late Prehispanic Period (Argentina). The Holocene 27:1769–1780

Medina M, López L, Berberián E (2009) Agricultura y recolección en el Tardío Prehispánico de las Sierras de Córdoba (Argentina): el registro arqueobotánico de C.Pun. 39. Arqueología 15:217–230

Medina EL, López L, Buc N (2018) Bone tool and tuber processing: a multi-proxy approach at Boyo Paso 2, Argentina. Antiquity 92:1040–1055

Medina M, Pastor S (2012) Zooarqueología de Sitios Residenciales Tardíos de las Sierras de Córdoba (Argentina, ca. 1100–300 AP): Avances y Perspectivas. In: Acosta A, Loponte D, Mucciolo L (eds) Temas de Arqueología, Estudios Tafonómicos y Zooarqueológicos II. Instituto Nacional de Antropología y Pensamiento Latinoamericano, Buenos Aires, pp 45–66

Medina M, Pastor S, Recalde A (2016) The archaeological landscape of late prehispanic mixed foraging and cultivation economy (Sierras of Córdoba, Argentina). J Anthropol Archaeol 42:88–104

Menghín O, González A (1954). Excavaciones arqueológicas en el yacimiento de Ongamira, Córdoba (Rep. Arg.). Nota preliminar. Notas del Museo de La Plata, T XVII, Antropología N° 67. Universidad Nacional de La Plata, La Plata.

Moreno E (2011) Tecnología de caza en la Quebrada de Antofalla, Departamento Antofagasta de la Sierra, Catamarca. Revista del Museo de Antropología 4:17–32

Outes F (1911) Los tiempos prehistóricos y protohistóricos en la provincia de Córdoba. Revista del Museo de La Plata, Tomo VII (Segunda serie, Tomo IV), 261–374

Pastor S, Medina M, Berberián E (2013) Poblados, Casas y Maizales. Arqueología de los Sitios Residenciales Tardíos de las Sierras de Córdoba (ca.1100–300 AP), Argentina Central. Revista Española de Antropología Americana 43:31–55

Pastor S (2007) Arroyo Tala Cañada 1 (Valle de Salsacate). Espacio doméstico y productivo en el sector central de las Sierras de Córdoba (Argentina) durante el Período Prehispánico Tardío (1000–300 AP). Arqueología 14:41–74

Pastor S (2012) Arte rupestre, paisaje y tensión social: un caso de estudio en Córdoba, Argentina. Revista Chilena de Antropología 26:7–32

Pastor S, Medina M, Recalde A, López L, Berberián E (2012) Arqueología de la región montañosa central de Argentina. Avances en el conocimiento de la historia prehispánica tardía. Relaciones de la Sociedad Argentina de Antropología 37:89–112

Pastor S, Rivero D, Pautassi E (2005) Los sistemas de armas de las comunidades agroalfareras de Córdoba: una aproximación arqueológica y experimental. Actas del XIII Congreso Nacional de Arqueología Argentina, Tomo IV. Córdoba, pp 253–266

Paulotti O (1943) Tipos de inhumación de los antiguos habitantes de las fuentes del río Tercero (Dpto. de Calamuchita, Prov. De Córdoba). I Congreso de Historia Argentina del Norte y Centro, Tomo I. Córdoba, pp 239–266

Pautassi E, Rivero D (1999) La configuración de los sistemas de armas y su relación con la estructura de los recursos en la cuenca del río San Antonio (Dpto. de Punilla, Pcia. de Córdoba). Actas del XII Congreso Nacional de Arqueología Argentina, Tomo III. La Plata, pp 517–520

Petillon J (2006) Des Magdaleniens en Armes Technologie de Projectile en Bois de Cervide du Magdelenien Supereueur de la Grotte D´Isturitz (Pyrenees-Atantiques). Editions du Centre D´Etudes et de Documentation Archéologiques, Treignes.

Politis G, González Ruibal A, Hernando A, Beserra Coelho E (2013) Etno-arqueologia do descarte de flechas entre os Awá-Guajá da Floresta Amazônica brasileira. In: Hernando A, Beserra Coelho E (eds) Estudos sobre os Awá, Caçadores-Coletores em Transição. EDUFMA, São Luís-Maranhão, pp 131–154

Ratto N (1989) Eficacia funcional y técnicas de caza. Shincal 1:45–52

Ratto N (2013) Diversidad de tecnologías de caza en la Puna transicional de Chaschuil (Dpto. Tinogasta, Catamarca). Comechingonia 17(2):85–103

Recalde A, López L (2017) Las sociedades prehispánicas tardías en la región septentrional del centro de Argentina (Sierras del Norte, Córdoba). Avances a su conocimiento desde los recursos vegetales. Chungara 49(4):573–588

Restifo F (2013) Tecnología de caza durante el Holoceno Temprano y Medio en la Puna de la Provincia de Salta (República Argentina): patrones de variación y procesos de cambio. Comechingonia 17:59–84

Rivero D (2009) Ecología de Cazadores-Recolectores del Sector Central de las Sierras de Córdoba (Rep. Argentina). BAR, International Series 2007, Oxford

Rivero D, Pastor S (2004) Sistemas de producción lítica de las comunidades productoras de alimentos de las sierras de Córdoba. Análisis de tres conjuntos de la Pampa de Achala. In: Bechis M (ed) Terceras Jornadas de Arqueología Histórica y de Contacto del Centro Oeste de la Argentina y Seminario de Etnohistoria. Cuartas Jornadas de Arqueología y Etnohistoria del Centro Oeste del país. Universidad Nacional de Río IV, Río IV, pp 67–78

Rivero D, Recalde A (2011) El uso del arco en la guerra durante el Prehispánico tardío de las Sierras de Córdoba. In: Martínez J, Bozzuto D (eds) Armas Prehispánicas: Múltiples Enfoques para su Estudio en Sudamérica. Fundación de Historia Natural Felix de Azara, Buenos Aires, pp 151–171

Sacur Silvestre R, Buc N, Acosta A, Loponte D (2013) Estrategias de captura de presas y sistemas de armas de los cazadores-recolectores que habitaron el Humedal del Paraná Inferior: una aproximación experimental y arqueológica. Comechingonia 17:27–57

Schiffer M (1987) Formation process of the archaeological records. University of New Mexico Press, Albuquerque

Serrano A (1945) Los Comechingones. Serie Aborígenes Argentinos I. Instituto de Arqueología, Lingüística y Folklore de la Universidad Nacional de Córdoba, Córdoba

Shott M (1997) Stones and shafts redux: the metric discrimination of chipped-stone dart and arrow points. Am Antiq 62(1):86–101

Swanton J (1938) Historic use of the spear-throw in Southwestern North America. Am Antiq 3(4):356–358

Vigna M, González I, Weitzel C (2014) Los cabezales líticos de la microrregión del río Salado bonaerense, Argentina. Diseños e historias de vida. Intersecciones en Antropología 15:55–69

Weitzel C, Flegenheimer N, Colombo M (2014) Breakage patterns on fishtail projectile points: experimental and archaeological cases. Ethnoarchaeology 6(2):81–102

Weyenbergh H (1880) Alt-indianische werkzeuge, pfeilspitzen u. dgl. Verhandlungen der Berliner Gesselschaft für Anthropologie, Ethnologie und Urgeschichte XII:366–374

Chapter 3
Assessing Strategies for Coypu Hunting and Use in the Salado River Depression (Buenos Aires Province, Argentina)

María Isabel González, Paula D. Escosteguy, Mónica C. Salemme, M. Magdalena Frère, Celeste Weitzel, and Rodrigo Vecchi

Abstract Coypu (*Myocastor coypus*) was intensively exploited during the Late Holocene in different areas of the Pampean Region and the Northeast of Argentina. This species was one of the most important faunal resources for the hunter-gatherer-fishers that inhabited the Salado River Depression (Buenos Aires Province). In this area, coypu was exploited for meat and marrow consumption, and its fur was also well appreciated. As a resource available in lakes and ponds near the base camps, organizing special hunting parties to obtain this prey would not have been necessary. In this contribution, we analyze the capture and hunting strategies, handling, and consumption of coypu, using data from zooarchaeological studies, experimental archaeology, ethnoarchaeology, lithic weapons, and the pottery employed for its processing. Even though the capture of coypu would have been possible using only a stick, and without other sophisticated tools, evidence from the Salado Depression suggests past hunters would have also used arrows and/or bola stones.

Keywords *Myocastor coypus* · Archaeofauna · Lithic weapons · Late Holocene · Current hunters

---

M. I. González · M. M. Frère
Facultad de Filosofía y Letras, Instituto de Arqueología, Universidad de Buenos Aires, Buenos Aires, Argentina

P. D. Escosteguy (✉)
CONICET—Universidad de Buenos Aires, Facultad de Filosofía y Letras, Instituto de Arqueología, Buenos Aires, Argentina
e-mail: pdescosteguy@uba.ar

M. C. Salemme
CADIC-CONICET, Universidad Nacional de Tierra del Fuego, Antártida e Islas del Atlántico Sur, Ushuaia, Argentina

C. Weitzel
CONICET—Área de Arqueología y Antropología, Museo de Ciencias Naturales de Necochea, Necochea, Argentina

R. Vecchi
CONICET, Universidad Nacional del Sur, Bahía Blanca, Argentina

© Springer Nature Switzerland AG 2021
J. B. Belardi et al. (eds.), *Ancient Hunting Strategies in Southern South America*,
The Latin American Studies Book Series,
https://doi.org/10.1007/978-3-030-61187-3_3

3.1 Introduction

The presence of small and medium-sized animals in archaeological contexts from the Pampean Region, has been discussed for decades regarding its role in site formation processes, as environmental proxies, and as a resource for pre-Hispanic societies, among other issues (González 2005; Acosta and Sartori 2011; Salemme et al. 2012; see discussion in Frontini and Escosteguy 2015; Day Pilaría 2018; among others). In this context, medium-sized rodents are of special interest due to their importance as potential disturbance agents in archaeological sites, and to their economic contribution in the past (Lloveras et al. 2009; Acosta and Sartori 2011; Quintana and Mazzanti 2011; Santini 2011; León and Bonomo 2011; Escosteguy et al. 2012; among others). Traditionally, capture strategies, handling, and the possible final products were analyzed using methods originally developed for big game (Salemme et al. 2012). Several works have shown that even when these methods are useful, they usually require some adjustments according to prey sizes, and to the potential modes of use of their byproducts (Quintana and Mazzanti 2011). This contribution focuses on coypu (*Myocastor coypus*), a medium-sized rodent that inhabits wetland environments. The abundance of coypu in a landscape with streams, rivers, and fresh water shallow lakes is strongly related to the high water availability, rather than to seasonality (Bó et al. 2006).

Archaeological research shows that coypu was intensively exploited in the past in different areas of Argentina, especially in the Pampean and Northeast Regions (Acosta 2005; Balbarrey et al. 2010; Acosta and Sartori 2011; León and Bonomo 2011; Santini 2011; Escosteguy et al. 2012; Aldazábal et al. 2017; Day Pilaría 2018). Its exploitation has also been reported in freshwater environments in Patagonia (Svoboda and Moreno 2018).

In the past, coypu was highly and immediately available in the Salado Depression, especially during the Late Holocene (Fig. 3.1), as evidenced in the archaeological assemblages (González 2005; Escosteguy et al. 2012, 2015). The hunter-gatherer-fishers societies settled near the lower basin of the Salado River, and its streams and shallow lakes. They used a variety of animal resources, with special emphasis on small aquatic and terrestrial fauna. In the last years, we used several lines of evidence to study the strategies and possible weapons for capturing and hunting coypu, the ways of processing coypu to use its meat and fur, and the use of bones for tool manufacture (González 2005; Escosteguy et al. 2012, 2017a, b, c; Vigna et al. 2014; Vecchi and González 2018).

Our main goal in this paper is to present a comprehensive assessment of the strategies and techniques employed for capturing and using coypu, and the relationships that the human groups could have established with this rodent. In order to understand the ways of life of the human groups that inhabited the Salado Depression, and their interaction and use of this species, we used information gathered through zooarchaeological, lithic, ceramic, and actualistic studies (experiments and ethnoarchaeology), and from documentary sources from the sixteenth to nineteenth centuries.

3 Assessing Strategies for Coypu Hunting and Use …

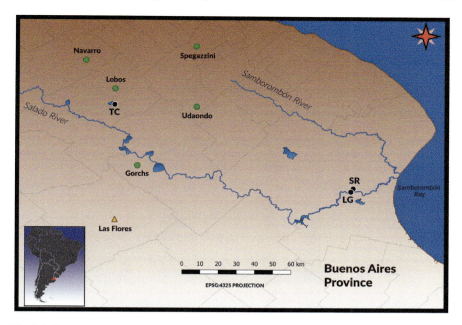

Fig. 3.1 Study area. Ref.: black circles: analyzed localities; green circles: localities of the interviews with *nutrieros* (coypu hunters); triangle: locality of the hunting party

According to González (2005), the cultural development in the micro-region was linked to the Samborombón and Salado Rivers, and the surrounding interconnected shallow lakes. This model is based on data obtained in the archaeological project of the Salado River lower basin (Salado Depression sub-area), which encompasses the study of sites located in the sector shown in Fig. 3.1. For this contribution, we considered the assemblages with coypu remains and with evidence of technologies that would have potentially been used for its capture and consumption. These assemblages were recovered at several sites located at San Ramón archaeological locality (SR4, SR5, SR7), La Guillerma archaeological locality (LG1, LG4, LG5, LGÑ), and the Techo Colorado site (TC).

The chronological sequence for the study area is based on radiocarbon dates obtained from charcoal, coypu, deer and fish bones, human teeth and organic residues recovered from pottery fragments. This sequence shows continuous recurrent occupations in the area since 750 years BC until recent years before European contact (Frère et al. 2016). Three of the radiocarbon dates obtained from coypu bones correspond to an interval between 690 and 1148 AD (2 sigmas), and are consistent with the chronology of the area (Fig. 3.2), and with a moment of high human population density in the micro-region (Frère et al. 2016). Recently, we obtained a new radiocarbon date from human remains—with no associated context—recovered in 1910 by Florentino Ameghino at El Siasgo stream, located on the left bank of the Salado river, between San Miguel del Monte and General Paz districts, near the small village

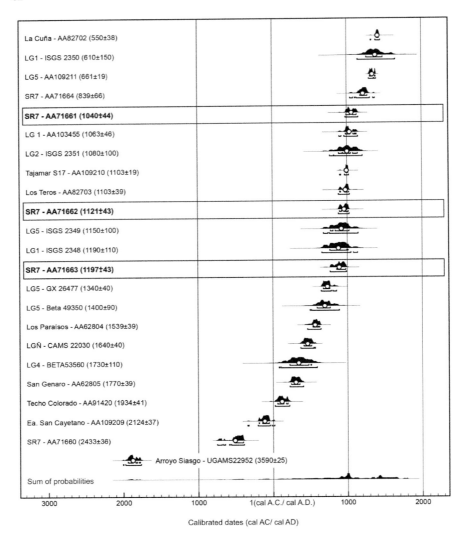

Fig. 3.2 Radiocarbon chronology for the study area (modified from Frère et al. 2016)

of Villanueva (Escosteguy et al. 2017a). This date, which evidence human occupations since at least 3590 ± 25 years BP (UGAMS22952) (Fig. 3.2), or 1976–1768 cal BC, is the earliest for the Salado Depression at the moment.

3.2 Natural Environment

The dominant vegetation in the Salado Depression is the steppe or the pseudo-steppe with grasses; but there are also grasslands, psammophyte and halophyte steppes, gallery forests, and several types of hydrophilic plants (Gómez and Toresani 1998). Native plant resources include *tala* woods (*Celtis tala*) and its associated species (Morello 2006): grasses, vines, bushes, and trees, like *coronillo* (*Scutia buxifolia*), *sombra de toro* (*Jodina rhombifolia*), *aromo* (*Acadia caven*), and *molle* (*Schinus longifolius*) (Haene 2006; González and Frère 2009).

In these woods, some of which are located on low hills near the lakes and rivers of the area, like the Samborombón and Salado Rivers, fauna corresponds to the Pampasic domain (Ringuelet 1961). These animals include Pampean deer (*Ozotoceros bezoarticus*)—currently inhabiting a more restricted area to the east—, marsh deer (*Blastocerus dichotomus*), which occasionally enters this area of Buenos Aires province, and several species of rodents like coypu (*M. coypus*), capybara or *carpincho* (*Hydrochaeris hydrochaeris*), *tucu-tucu* (*Ctenomys* sp.) and several types of armadillos. In the Salado River basin, there are also many birds (ducks, herons, swans, and coots, among others) and fish species (López et al. 2001).

3.2.1 Myocastor coypus *(Molina 1782)*

Myocastor coypus is an herbivorous rodent native of South America. It inhabits large areas of Argentina, Chile, Bolivia, Uruguay, and Paraguay (Bó et al. 2006). Adults usually average 5 kg in weight (Fig. 3.3a), and they breed two or three times a year, giving birth to an average of 6 offspring *per* time. The coypu lives in territorial groups composed of several adult and subadult females, a dominant male, several adult, and subadult males, and juveniles (Guichón et al. 2003). After they reach sexual maturity, males disperse over long distances. The coypu lives in semi aquatic habitats and it spends most of its life in the water, near ponds and rivers. Its distribution depends on the quality, quantity, and availability of food, water, and shelter (Fig. 3.3b–d). However, these rodents have a high tolerance to a variety of climatic and hydrological conditions, and a high dispersion and colonization ability (Bó et al. 2006).

In Argentina, coypu was captured for fur trade until the early 2000s (Bó et al. 2006). Its fur is unique, and has three types of hair: the primary or protective fur is 7–8 cm long; the next secondary layer has more hair, which gives fur its primary yellowish and dark brown coloration of the species. Finally, the short undercoat—known as "*felpa*"—, is a lush dark gray hair. These different layers confer impermeability and resistance to cold temperatures. Even though coypu meat is protein-rich and low in fat and cholesterol (Curto and Castellino 2006), it is not commercialized on a large scale, but it is consumed by the rural population.

Fig. 3.3 a-b *Myocastor coypus* (Photos: Gustavo Porini). **c** Coypu burrows along a creek cliff. **d** Coypu nest (Photo: Marcelo Canevari)

3.3 Methodological Aspects

In this section, we present a synthesis of the methods used in this contribution. The details of the different analyses were published in previous papers.

The archaeofaunal analysis included the anatomical and taxonomic identification, using reference atlas and comparative collections. Quantification and abundance estimations were made using NISP, %NISP, and MNI. The evidence of anthropic exploitation considered for coypu was cut marks, thermal alterations and fresh fractures (Lyman 1994; Mengoni Goñalons 1999 and references cited therein; see also Escosteguy et al. 2012).

Regarding weapons, we analyze lithic projectile points and bola stones. The lithic projectile point's technological and morphological analyses were made following the proposals of Aschero (1975, 1983). The functional or delivery system classification was carried out using several methods, including those proposed by Fenenga (1953), Hughes (1998), Ratto (2003), and Shott (1997). For the bola stones analysis, we used the proposal of Vecchi (2010, 2011), which considers raw material and morphometric attributes (diameter, weight, morphology, and condition). The finishing of the artifact (pecked or grounded) and the presence/absence, width, and depth of the channel or "waist" were also considered.

Pottery macroscopic analyses were made following different methods (Rice 1987; Balfet et al. 1992; Rye 1994; Orton et al. 1997; among others). Organic residues absorbed in the fabric of ceramic sherds were studied with a gas chromatograph at the Universidad Nacional del Sur (Frère et al. 2010). Stable isotopes ($\delta^{13}C$ and $\delta^{15}N$) extracted from burnt residue deposits adhering to the sherd surface were processed at the Instituto Nacional de Geología Isotópica (INGEIS-CONICET-Universidad de Buenos Aires) (González and Frère 2017).

Actualistic studies included interviews with current coypu hunters, participant observation in a hunting party, and in the subsequent skinning and butchering of coypu with experimental lithic flakes and tools (Escosteguy and Vigna 2010; Escosteguy 2014). Finally, we analyzed documentary sources written between the 16th and 19th centuries, to gain information on the use of coypu after the arrival of Europeans to the region (Escosteguy 2013), and on the different uses of bola stones (Vecchi 2010).

3.4 The Exploitation of Coypu in the Salado River Depression

3.4.1 The Archaeofaunal Record

Over the last 30 years, we carried out different analyses of faunal assemblages from five archaeological sites of the Salado River Depression (for more detail, see González 2005; Escosteguy et al. 2012, 2017b, c). Data show an intensive use of different species, especially small game, being coypu the most frequently used, suggesting its economic importance in the past.

A summary of the archaeofaunal remains recovered at the archaeological sites selected for this paper is shown in Fig. 3.4, which displays the %NISP of the taxa recorded in each assemblage. Coypu was identified in three of the five sites of La Guillerma archaeological locality, and in the sites SR7, and TC. It exhibits high frequencies at LG5 = 46.24%, LG4 = 77.77%, and SR7 = 77.47%, and lower frequencies at LG1 = 21.92% and TC (%NISP = 5.16). The MNI shows the highest frequencies at LG1 ($N = 15$) and LG5 ($N = 25$); while they are much lower at LG4 ($N = 2$), SR7 ($N = 3$), and TC ($N = 1$).

Evidence of human exploitation was identified in three sites (Table 3.1), and were identified on skull bones (mandible, Fig. 3.5), and on postcranial bones (scapula, humerus, ilium, ischium, femur, tibia, metapodials, and phalanges). Also, at LG1, LG4, and LG5 there are fresh fractures, and evidence of flaking in humerus, ulna, femur, tibia, and metatarsals. At LG1 a metatarsal with technological marks was interpreted as a bone bead (Escosteguy et al. 2017b, p. 72, Fig. 2b). It has straight, transverse, and regular fractures with oblique fracture surfaces; other associated features are cut marks, small flake scars on the fracture margins, and polish. Coypu incisors would have also been expediently used for pottery decoration. Experiments with pottery replicas showed that coypu teeth could have served to make "*banderitas*" (little flags), a decoration characterized by steeped marks of three sub-rectangular dashes (see Escosteguy et al. 2017b, p. 82, Fig. 8). Bones recovered at SR7 and TC

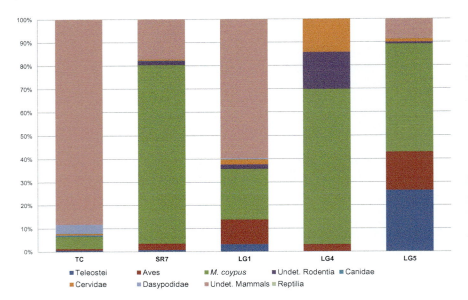

Fig. 3.4 %NISP of taxa recorded in the sites of the Salado Depression. TC: NISP = 153; SR7: NISP = 1527; LG1: NISP = 2486; LG4: NISP = 73; LG5: NISP = 6049

Table 3.1 Evidence of coypu exploitation

Site	%NISP		
	Cut marks	Burnt bones	Fresh fractures[a]
TC (NISP = 8)	–	25	–
SR7 (NISP = 1183)	–	1.93	–
LG1 (NISP = 545)	1.10	10	0.91
LG4 (NISP = 42)	2.38	–	2.38
LG5 (NISP = 2797)	0.71	1.82	0.21

[a]It includes fractures and associated features such as flake scars. TC = Techo Colorado; SR7 = San Ramón 7; LG1 = La Guillerma 1; LG4 = La Guillerma 4; LG5 = La Guillerma 5

have no evidence of cut marks or fresh fractures. Specimens with signs of thermal alteration were identified at LG1, LG5, SR7, and TC, with an overall low frequency; the exception is the specimens from TC where the 25% recorded is biased by the small size of the sample. At SR7, we recorded burnt and calcined teeth and limb distal elements.

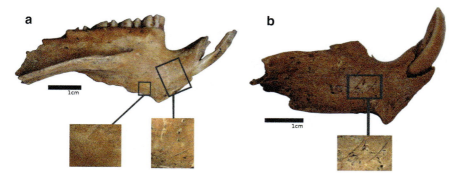

Fig. 3.5 Cut marks on hemi-mandibles from LG5

Mammals are the most diverse class, and they include deer (*B. dichotomus* and *O. bezoarticus*), small carnivores like the Pampean fox –*L. gymnocercus*–, undetermined armadillos, and small rodents (guinea pig or *cuis* –*Cavia aperea*–, tucu-tucu –*Ctenomys* sp.–, among others). Medium and small size species are abundant in the assemblages. Among fish, catfish (*Rhamdia sapo*), tiger fish (*Hoplias malabaricus*), mullet (*Mugil* sp.) and black drum (*Pogonias cromis*) were identified. Small birds, like *E. elegans*, *Fulica* sp., and other undetermined Anatidae are also predominant (González 2005; González et al. 2016) (Fig. 3.4).

3.4.2 Lithic Weapons: Projectile Points and Bola Stones

One way of knowing hunting strategies in past societies is by studying their weaponry. Since the organic portions of weapons are rarely preserved, usually the fragmentary stone components are the only evidence to make inferences (Shott 1997; Erlandson et al. 2014). In this contribution, we assess the projectile points and bola stones recovered in different sites of the study area, by revisiting previous studies (González 2005; Vecchi 2010; Vigna et al. 2014; Vecchi and González 2018), and adding new data.

Sixteen lithic projectile points were recovered from excavation and from surface contexts in five different sites: SR7 ($N = 8$), SR5 ($N = 1$), LG1 ($N = 3$), LGÑ ($N = 1$), and TC ($N = 3$) (Table 3.2, Fig. 3.1). A thorough analysis of most of these points was presented in a previous study (Vigna et al. 2014). In the Salado Depression, lithic resources were absent and all the lithic raw materials had to be transported from at least 150 km away (González 2005). As shown in Table 3.2, projectile points were more frequently manufactured using Sierras Bayas Group orthoquartzite ($N = 10$; 62.5%), followed by phtanite ($N = 3$; 18.75%), and silicified limestone ($N = 3$; 18.75%). Most of them are broken (62.5%), others show minor fractures at the tip (12.5%), and some are whole (25%). Two points show evidence of maintenance

Table 3.2 Projectile point sample from the Salado Depression. Ref: LG: La Guillerma; LGÑ: La Guillerma Ñandú; SR: San Ramón; TC: Techo Colorado

	Description	Raw material	Condition	Fracture type
LG 225	Small triangular stemless/bifacial/maintained	Orthoquartzite	Minor fracture	Bending (tip)
LGÑ sup	Small triangular stemless/bifacial	Orthoquartzite	Whole	
SR7 4	Blade fragment/bifacial	Orthoquartzite	Broken	Bending
SR7 C5b 76	Blade fragment/bifacial	Phtanite	Broken	Bending
SR7 A	Medium triangular stemless/bifacial	Phtanite	Whole	
SR7 2	Small triangular stemless/bifacial	Orthoquartzite	Minor fracture	Bending
LG 125	Small triangular stemless/bifacial/maintained	Orthoquartzite	Whole	
LG1 53 + 51	Small triangular stemless/bifacial	Orthoquartzite	Broken/Complete	Bending + impact at the tip
SR7 C5b 81	Small triangular stemless basal fragment/bifacial	Orthoquartzite	Broken	Bending
SR7 5	Blade fragment/bifacial	Phtanite	Broken	Impact burination + compressive
SR7 22a	Blade fragment/bifacial	Orthoquartzite	Broken	Bending
TC 1	Blade fragment/bifacial	Silicified limestone	Broken	Bending
SR5 4	Small triangular stemless basal fragment/bifacial	Orthoquartzite	Broken	Compressive
TC	Small triangular stemless/bifacial	Silicified limestone	Whole	
TC S6	Blade fragment/bifacial	Silicified limestone	Broken	Bending
SR7 0-10	Small triangular stemless basal fragment/bifacial	Orthoquartzite	Broken	Compressive

and repair (Table 3.2, Fig. 3.6 c), and other two have impact fractures at the tip. In 10 points we were able to identify the triangular stemless design (Vigna et al. 2014) (Fig. 3.6a, d, f, g). Nine are small triangular points, which appear by the Late Holocene in the Pampean Region, and are considered to be associated with the introduction of the bow and arrow (Politis and Madrid 2001). The remaining point is a medium-sized triangular stemless point (Fig. 3.6h). These latter points are recorded in sites dated to the Middle Holocene in the Pampean Region (Politis and Madrid 2001; Politis et al. 2014).

3 Assessing Strategies for Coypu Hunting and Use …

Fig. 3.6 Lithic weapons examples. A-G: arrow points; H: dart point; I-L:bola stones recovered at I La Guillerma 1. J San Ramón 4. K and L Casamayou private collection

Several researchers have proposed different methods to distinguish between dart and arrow points, developed mainly for stemmed points (Fenenga 1953; Thomas 1978; Shott 1997; Hughes 1998; Ratto 2003; Hildebrandt and King 2012). Here, we used those proposals that allowed us classifying stemless points, including basal fragments (Fenenga 1953; Shott 1997; Hughes 1998; Ratto 2003), in order to infer the weapons systems that were in use in the Salado Depression. Fenenga (1953) used weight to distinguish between small (arrow) and large (dart) point classes and established a maximum threshold of 3.5 g for arrow points and a minimum threshold of 4.5 g for darts. Hughes (1998) and Shott (1997) developed different formulas where the raw values of our stone points can be replaced. Hughes (1998) primary variables for delivery systems distinction are: mass (g), cross-sectional area (1/2 thickness x width), and perimeter (4s, where $s = (1/2 \text{ width})^2 + (1/2 \text{ thickness})^2$). Given values for each attribute allow distinguishing between thrusting spear, flight spear, dart, and arrow (Hughes 1998, p. 374, Table IX). Shott (1997) developed classification functions based on previous work by Thomas (1978). We selected the functions that use one (base width) (Shott 1997) and two (base width and thickness) (Shott 1997) variables because they allowed us to classify most of the stone tips, and according to Shott (1997), the one and two variables formulas might be the most important for prediction. Finally, Ratto (2003) considers several variables to distinguish between arrows, thrusting spears, and throwing spears: reinforcement, which is based on width and thickness; aerodynamic, based on cross-section and outline symmetry; penetration, based on tip angle; and hafting, based on base width (Ratto 2003, see pp. 87–91).

We were able to analyze most of the proposed variables in ten points (Table 3.3), and they were classified into different projectile delivery systems (Table 3.4). The results obtained using the different methods seem to agree (Table 3.4): most of the points ($N = 9$) in these contexts of the Salado Depression are arrows, except for the middle-sized point classified as a dart point (Fig. 3.6h). This last specimen is chronologically associated with the Middle Holocene in the Pampean Region. The presence of this point and the new dates from El Siasgo might evidence a Middle Holocene occupation in an area traditionally considered as first occupied during the Late Holocene times (González 2005; Vigna et al. 2014; Escosteguy et al. 2017a); it is also possible that this point was reclaimed from another area and transported to the Salado Depression.

The bola stones ($N = 27$; Table 3.5) were recovered during excavations and from surface contexts in several sites (LG1, LG5, SR4, and SR7), and others were found in local private collections (Casamayou collection —CSY—; González 2005; Vecchi and González 2018). Spheroids and spheroidal forms are the most frequent. Despite the high breakage index of the stone balls, a higher frequency of specimens with diameters between 55 and 69 mm (with sizes between 44 and 73 mm), and weights averaging 200–300 g (with specimens between 174 and 500 g) is clear. Like all the lithic artifacts in the sites of the area, bola stones were manufactured from long distance-rocks, mainly Balcarce Formation orthoquartzites (37%), and diabase (30%). Many stone balls (58%) exhibit a channel or "waist" (Fig. 3.6a–d), which was the main way of fastening the balls, probably with leather or sinew cords. Identified channels are wide (between 8 and 17 mm), and shallow (between 1 and 4 mm in depth) (Vecchi 2011; Vecchi and González 2018).

3.4.3 Pottery

All the archaeological sites in the Salado Depression were places of pottery manufacture (González 2005). Potters used coiling and modeling to make vessels. Using different lines of evidence (profile analyses, refitting, experimental archaeology, and bibliographic review) we were able to identify five vessel shapes, being open vessels of medium and small size the most frequent. The preferred surface treatment was smoothing; polishing, engobe, and red paint were less used. Main decoration techniques were incision and impression, which were used to display a variety of motifs. According to the potsherd's shapes, the thickness of the walls, the damage on the surface of some fragments, shape reconstructions, and experimental studies with replicas, we suggested that the ceramic containers were appropriate for cooking, storage, and/or food and drink service (González et al. 2012; González and Frère 2009, 2017).

Several archaeometric studies on potsherds were carried out in order to know the diet of the human groups that inhabited the area. Fatty acids analyses allowed us to determine that some pots were used in meat consumption, according to the lipid proportions and the presence of cholesterol. In some particular cases, the percentage

Table 3.3 Variables recorded with each classification method

	Reinforcement (Ratto 2003)	Aerodynamic (Ratto 2010)	Haft (Ratto 2010)	Penetration (Ratto 2010)	Weight (g)	Base Width (mm)	Thickness (mm)	Tip cross-section (cm2) (Hughes 1998)	Perimeterr (cm) (Hughes 1998)
SR 7 sup A	0.36	low	imperfect	>10 mm	>45°	11.35	27	8.1	1.09	7.94
SR7 sup 2	0.2	low	normal	>10 mm	<45°	0.98	12.3	2.2	0.1353	1.56
SR7 C5b 81	0.13	very low	perfect	>10 mm	(<45°)		14.4	1.9	0.1368	2.1
SR5 24	0.37	low	perfect	>10 mm	(>45°)		16.5	5.7	0.47	3.04
LGÑ sup	0.25	low	perfect	>10 mm	>45°	0.85	16.3	2.6	0.212	2.71
LGI 125	0.25	low	imperfect	>10 mm	>45°	0.66	12.5	3.1	0.193	1.656
LGI 225	0.36	low	perfect	>10 mm	>45°	0.62	12.5	3.9	0.243	1.71
LGI 53 + 51	0.25	low	perfect	>10 mm	<45°	1.9	15.8	3.2	0.252	2.60
TC	0.28	low	normal	>10 mm	>45°	2.84	18	5.1	0.46	3.5
SR7 0-10	0.3	low	perfect	>10 mm	(<45°)		12	3	0.18	1.53

Table 3.4 Functional classification of projectile points

	Fenega (1953)	Hughes (1998)	Shott (1997) Two variables	Shott (1997) One variable	Ratto (2003)
SR 7 sup A	Dart	Flight spear/dart	Dart	Dart	Throwing spear/dart
SR7 sup 2	Arrow	Arrow	Arrow	Arrow	Arrow
SR7 C5b 81		Arrow	Arrow	Arrow	Arrow
SR5 24		Arrow	Arrow	Arrow	Arrow
LGÑ sup	Arrow	Arrow	Arrow	Arrow	Arrow
LG1 125	Arrow	Arrow	Arrow	Arrow	Undetermined (due to maintenance)
LG1 225	Arrow	Arrow	Arrow	Arrow	Arrow
LG1 53 + 51	Arrow	Arrow	Arrow	Arrow	Arrow
TC	Arrow	Arrow	Arrow	Arrow	Undetermined (due to maintenance)
SR7 0-10		Arrow	Arrow	Arrow	Arrow

Table 3.5 Bola stones from archaeological sites and private collections of the Salado River Depression. Ref: LG: La Guillerma; LGÑ: La Guillerma Ñandú; SR: San Ramón; CSY: Casamayou private collection

Site/Collection	Whole	Fragments	Preform	With channel	Total
LG1	2	3	–	1	5
LG5	–	1	–	1	1
SR4	–	3	2	1	5
SR7	–	1	–	1	1
CSY	14	1	–	10	15
Total	16	9	2	15	27

of saturated fatty acids and the relation between them, along with the good preservation of polyunsaturated fatty acids, suggested the consumption of meat of a small or medium-sized herbivore—probably coypu. There is also a set of potsherds with long-chain polyunsaturated fatty acids of the n3 and n6 series, which suggests they were used for fish processing (Frère et al. 2010). Finally, stable isotopes analysis showed that these pots were probably used for food preparation that included proteins of continental aquatic animals (González and Frère 2017).

3.4.4 Actualistic Studies

We carried out a project with current coypu hunters or *nutrieros,* and other people involved in hunting activities, which included interviews, participant observation in a coypu hunting party, and participant observation of the experimental processing and handling of coypu carcasses (Escosteguy 2014; Escosteguy and Vigna 2010).

We conducted 31 interviews in different localities of the Salado River area, and nearby wetlands (Fig. 3.1). The interviews were designed to record (1) use of space, (2) capture methods, (3) the *nutrieros* knowledge about biology and behavior of coypu, (4) carcass processing, (5) meat preparation and consumption, (6) and the use of offspring as pets, among other issues detailed in Escosteguy (2014). Also, we observed a hunting party that took place at Las Flores locality (Buenos Aires); during this experience we recorded the placement and removal of traps, and the subsequent butchering of the prey. Three experimental butchering events were observed, and during each event we recorded: prey weight, processing stages, and gestures, among other data. Coypu bones resulting from the butchering were then cleaned at the lab to analyze fractures and cut marks. The details of this research were published in Escosteguy (2014) and Escosteguy and Vigna (2010).

Nutrieros recognize different landscape elements that determine the selection of a given capture strategy and its associated specific gear. Hunting/trapping territories are always linked to water bodies, but the capture strategy will vary if it is a pond or shallow lake (permanent or temporary), a stream, or a river with or without cliffs (Escosteguy 2014). Coypu hunters noted that coypu stays longer at ponds and lakes, thus being the more appropriate environments for placing traps. Cliffs are favorable features for coypu to burrow and place their nests. In this case, *nutrieros* may place traps in the burrow opening, wait for the animals and kill them with a blow to the head, or they may use wire to catch them and take them out. Other signs considered by the hunters to choose the hunting location were the presence of burrows, paths, and coypu feces (Escosteguy 2014). During the hunting party, steel traps were placed in a location with such evidence, and the next morning a juvenile specimen (of about 2 kg) was found trapped and alive, and then killed with a blow to the head using a stick (see Escosteguy 2014, p. 151; Figs. 1a, b).

Currently, the usual hunting method is the use of foothold or body traps, but *nutrieros* also mentioned the use of hunting dogs, snares, slingshots, flash blinding or dazzling of the prey, and guns. Hunting with dogs is usually used during droughts, when coypu gather in the scarce water bodies, providing the *nutrieros* with many prey in a single event.

Nutrieros have deep knowledge about the biology and behavior of coypu. They know the mating, pregnancy, and lactation periods, the periods of offspring birth, male behavior during mating periods, females behavior during nursing, feeding habits, and responses to risk. All this knowledge is key for selecting specific capture strategies. For example, a *nutriero* can know if there are offspring inside a nest, and can anticipate the response of that mother facing a risk situation.

On several occasions, informants mentioned the practice of keeping coypu offspring as pets. We could observe a coypu couple with their offspring, living at one of the *nutrieros'* homes. Another informant rescued two offspring after their mother was captured. A juvenile coypu was rescued and taken to a dairy farmer's home, where they fed it with milk and vegetables, until it became familiar with humans and became a pet living inside the family house. Once coypu reach maturity, they usually become unfriendly, and they are returned to the fields.

We observed three events of butchering and handling of coypu carcasses, which provided information about the different stages in the skinning and butchering sequence (Escosteguy and Vigna 2010). These activities were carried out using lithic experimental tools and flakes, manufactured like those recovered in the sites of the Salado Depression. In all three events, the skin was removed as a sack: whole, and from the legs to the head. The operator´s ability was essential, and those with better skills or expertise finished faster (in less than 30 min), and produced less damage (fractures and cut marks) to the bones.

The analysis of the experimental bone assemblage allowed us associating specific cut marks with different activities like skinning (on the distal ends of the limbs, and on the skull bones), and dislocation (on long bones ends and/or on articular surfaces). Fractures were recorded on skull bones (as a consequence of the blows to the head), mandible and maxilla (as a result of the breakage of incisors), and incisors, which were broken to prevent skin damage during its removal. We observed that being coypu a medium-sized prey, operators could use their hands to avoid making specific cuts (Escosteguy and Vigna 2010).

3.4.5 Documentary Sources

Many documentary sources (traveler's chronicles, missionary's diaries, government documents) provided information on the use and availability of coypu (for more details see Escosteguy 2013). Even though not all of these sources refer to our study area, they contain data from nearby related areas.

Different travelers of the sixteenth and seventeenth centuries mention the abundance of coypu, and the use of its fur to make coats. Ulrico Schmidl ([1534/1554] 1903) mentions this use among the *querandíes* aboriginals settled near Buenos Aires. Written documents left by Jesuit missionaries during the eighteenth century describe the appearance, behavior, distribution, and abundance of coypu. They also mention the consumption of coypu meat, and the processing and use of furs (sometimes painted) as coats. Thomas Falkner ([1774/1746] 1974), who was a missionary in the south of the Salado River, also mentions the use of coypu hide to make tents and shelters (see Escosteguy 2013).

Documentary sources of travelers and chroniclers of the sixteenth to nineteenth centuries (for more details see Vecchi 2010) along with the ethnographic record, provided information on the use of bola stones (*boleadoras*), and the animals hunted with this weapon. These sources (Sánchez Labrador [1772] 1936, p. 172; Musters

[1869–1870] 1964, p. 131; among others) describe its uses in warfare and hunting. There are different types of bola stones, and they were used to hunt a variety of animals, including mammals of all sizes, and big, medium, and small birds. With big sized animals (like guanaco, deer, and rhea), bola stones were mainly used as long-range weapons that were thrown to the animals entangling their legs. They were also used as short distance maces, to hit or kill the prey, especially when the animals were in a disadvantaged position to escape (see Vecchi 2010).

Coypu hunting was controlled by the Buenos Aires government since 1820, with an order signed by Governor Martín Rodríguez, banning this activity. By the end of the nineteenth century, coypu furs were circulating in extensive trade networks in which both indigenous and Hispanic groups participated (for more details see Escosteguy 2013).

3.5 Discussion

In the last decade, we studied the procurement, processing, and consumption of coypu using different methods. The information gathered using these different lines of evidence, allows us to make some inferences about the strategies that could have been used in the past for capturing and using this rodent.

The coypu characterizes for its high population density, usually concentrated and highly localized in specific sectors of the landscape (water bodies); it is highly predictable, with low riskiness, and a somewhat small size. This makes coypu a low cost prey in terms of search, capture, and transport. For the hunter-gatherer-fishers groups of the Salado Depression, coypu was available in the aquatic environments near the campsites, where any member of the group could capture them, without special trips or specialized gear, making coypu a high energy return resource (Santini 2011).

In the studied sites, the archaeofaunal analysis showed high diversity and taxonomic abundance, with intensive use of medium-sized and small fauna, including birds, freshwater fishes, and rodents of different sizes, with an emphasis on coypu. Coypu remains exhibit high %NISP and MNI frequencies in the five assemblages analyzed in this contribution. *M. coypus* bone remains exhibit cut marks, intentional fractures, fire exposure, and technological traits. These anthropic evidence present low frequencies, and this trend is also observed in other assemblages with coypu or other small size taxa remains (Acosta 2005; Acosta and Sartori 2011; Escosteguy et al. 2012; Day Pilaría 2018; among others). There are also examples from sites of the Humid Chaco and the Paraná River alluvial plains, where anthropic accumulations of coypu remains are numerous and the record of anthropic modifications is low (see Acosta 2005; Santini 2011; Sartori et al. 2014). The low frequency of cut marks and anthropic fractures may be related with the methods for skinning, processing and/or cooking this prey by boiling, neither of which would require, for example, cutting and removing flesh. The presence of potsherds from containers of different sizes, and the identification of fatty acids of a small or medium herbivore, probably coypu, from some pottery fragments (González et al. 2012) could support the boiling hypothesis. Other evidence, like bone remains with thermal alterations (especially distal elements and teeth) may indicate roasting (Escosteguy et al. 2012). The low frequency of cut marks associated with skinning may be a result of the skill of the operator, as mentioned above.

Perishable materials are rarely preserved in the Salado Depression, but the use of fur has been proposed based on the presence of bone needles that could have been used for sewing hides to make tents, clothes, or other leather implements (González 2005; Escosteguy et al. 2012, 2017c). Coypu fur is soft and delicate, and easy to sew or pierce with those bone needles or awls (Escosteguy et al. 2017c). Jesuit missionaries also mention that coypu fur could have been painted (see Escosteguy 2013). The presence in the studied sites of mineral pigments (iron oxide) transported from the Tandilia Ranges located more than 200 km away from the Salado Depression, was considered to propose hide and pottery painting (González 2005).

Historical documentary sources also provided information about coypu exploitation throughout several centuries, its hunting environments, and its different uses (Escosteguy 2013). Some data collected from the documentary sources were corroborated in our work with the *nutrieros,* an experience that was informative about different hunting and capturing strategies, that can be achieved without specialized technologies, using simple sticks, as mentioned ahead.

At least two weapon systems coexisted in the Salado Depression during the Late Holocene: bow and arrow, and bola stones (González 2005; González et al. 2006; Vigna et al. 2014). The only dart point identified is traditionally associated with the Middle Holocene in the Pampean Region, and it could have been reclaimed from other areas during raw material procurement. The bow and arrow have several advantages to be used in the environments of the Salado Depression. It requires a small movement range, so it can be used in woods and dense forests, but is also highly effective in open environments, due to its long-distance range, high speed, and accuracy (Hughes 1998; Shott 1993; Tomka 2013; Whittaker 2013; Yu 2006). Arrows could be used to obtain most of the faunal resources identified in the faunal assemblages, from large mammals like *O. bezoarticus,* and *B. dichotomus* (Tomka 2013) to small aquatic and terrestrial birds, fish, reptiles, and rodents like coypu (Vigna et al. 2014; for fishing examples White and Roth 2009).

Bola stones or *boleadoras* are highly versatile, and as the bow and arrow, could be effective both in open spaces, woodlands, and forests, as they could be used to reduce mobility, to hit the animals from a distance, or as short-range maces (Vecchi 2011). Shallow and wide channels identified in most of the stone balls might be evidence of a particular fastening method, using thick leather cords to avoid short term damage and decay produced by aquatic and wetter environments. As we already mentioned, it was used for hunting a wide range of species, like guanaco, deer, rhea, and probably also coypu. Considering coypu ethology and the high fragmentation index recorded in skull bones (Escosteguy et al. 2012, 2015), we suggest that bola stones could have been used as maces for coypu hunting.

Both of these weapon systems could have been used along with other technologies like traps or sticks, to obtain the available faunal resources. The work with current coypu hunters showed that sticks could be used as maces, also producing a high number of broken skulls. The use of nets of perishable materials was also proposed for the Salado Depression, based on the presence of different species of fish, and fishing net weights made of stone and clay (González 2005; Vecchi and González 2018). Nets could also have been used to capture coypu, as mentioned by Santini (2011) for sites in the Chaco region, in Northeastern Argentina. After the animal was trapped, it was killed with a blow to the head. The selection of a particular weapon was influenced by ethology (for example, burrowing habits), and by the topographical traits of the environment (streams or shallow lakes).

The inhabitants of the Salado Depression employed different methods of food preparation using a variety of animals. Fatty acids and stable isotope analyses showed that vessels of different shapes and sizes were used to prepare foods with proteins of continental aquatic animals, which include coypu meat (Frère et al. 2010; González and Frère 2017). Current *nutrieros* provided information about the preparation and cooking of coypu meat in stews, casseroles, or simply by boiling in pots, which enhances the flavor of the meat (Salemme et al. 2012; Escosteguy et al. 2012, 2015; Escosteguy 2014).

3.6 Final Comments

In sum, the analysis of the strategies for hunting, capturing, and exploiting coypu using different lines of evidence, allowed us to assess the role of this prey in the lives of the hunter-gatherer-fishers groups of the Salado Depression, in the Humid Pampas, and also to deepen those inferences related to the presence of small and medium-sized animals in archaeological contexts. Coypu was an abundant and available resource throughout the year in the wetlands of the studied area. Its immediate availability and the technologies for its capture would not have required special trips. It could have been hunted with both of the identified weapon systems, and also captured with other technologies, and even with simple tools. Even though the anthropic modifications on coypu bones have low frequencies, there are also other lines of evidence for its consumption and use (pottery and fatty acid analysis). Finally, the experience with current hunters evidenced that even when coypu is a wild species, people established different relationships with these animals, like the rescue of orphan offspring to be raised as pets. So, coypu probably familiarizes easily with humans. As discussed in Escosteguy (2014), the same thing could have happened in the past, transcending the predator–prey relationship.

Acknowledgements This research was supported by PICT 2015 0272, PICT 2016 0368, and UBACyT 2018 20020170100525BA. Thanks to the coypu hunters (*nutrieros*) that helped us with their knowledge and were involved in the experiments. Olivia Sokol drew the map in Figs. 3.1 and 3.4; Teresa Capdevielle edited Figs. 3.3 and 3.5. Gustavo Porini and Marcelo Canevari kindly authorized the use of their photographs. Two anonymous reviewers made useful comments that helped us to improve this chapter. The authors are the only responsible for the arguments discussed in this paper.

References

Acosta A (2005) Zooarqueología de cazadores-recolectores del extremo nororiental de la provincia de Buenos Aires (humedal del río Paraná inferior, Región Pampeana, Argentina). Unpublished doctoral thesis, Universidad Nacional de La Plata, La Plata

Acosta A, Sartori J (2011) Explotación de Myocastor coypus en el extremo meridional de la Cuenca del Plata durante el Holoceno tardío. Revista de Arqueología 24(2):10–30

Aldazábal V, Eugenio E, Silveira M (2017) Nuevos datos sobre la subsistencia de los cazadores recolectores del sitio "Divisadero Monte 6" (partido de General Lavalle, provincia de Buenos Aires). Cuadernos de Antropología 18:105–120

Aschero C (1975) Ensayo para una Clasificación Morfológica de Artefactos Líticos aplicada a Estudios Tipológicos Comparativos. Unpublished report to CONICET, Buenos Aires

Aschero C (1983) Ensayo para una Clasificación Morfológica de Artefactos Líticos aplicada a Estudios Tipológicos Comparativos. Apéndices A-C. Unpublished report, Cátedra de Ergología y Tecnología, Facultad de Filosofía y Humanidades, Universidad de Buenos Aires, Buenos Aires

Balbarrey G, Lamenza G, Santini M, De Feo C, Salceda S, Calandra H (2010) Espacio social y territorialidad de Sociedades Prehispánicas del Chaco Húmedo Argentino. Folia Histórica del Nordeste 18:137–150

Balfet H, Fauvet Berthelot MF, Monzón S (1992) Normas para la descripción de vasijas cerámicas. Centre d´Etudes Mexicaines et Centramericaines, México

Bó R, Porini G, Corriale MJ, Arias S (2006) Proyecto Nutria. Estudios ecológicos básicos para el manejo sustentable de Myocastor coypus en la Argentina. In: Bolkovic ML, Ramadori D (eds) Manejo de Fauna Silvestre en la Argentina. Programa de Uso Sustentable. Dirección de Fauna Silvestre, Secretaría de ambiente y Desarrollo Sustentable, Buenos Aires, pp 93–104

Curto E, Castellino R (2006) Coipo o nutria. In: Bucher E (ed) Bañados del río Dulce y Laguna Mar Chiquita (Córdoba, Argentina). Academia Nacional de Ciencias de Córdoba, Córdoba, pp 285–293

Day Pilaría F (2018) Gestión de los recursos faunísticos en sociedades cazadoras, recolectoras y pescadoras. Análisis arqueozoológico en sitios del litoral del Río de la Plata (partidos de Magdalena y Punta Indio, provincia de Buenos Aires). Unpublished PhD thesis, Universidad Nacional de La Plata, La Plata

Erlandson J, Watts J, Jew N (2014) Darts, arrows, and archaeologists: distinguishing dart and arrow points in the archaeological record. Am Antiq 79:162–169

Escosteguy P (2013) El uso de fuentes documentales y etnográficas para la interpretación del registro arqueofaunístico de coipo. Revista de Arqueología Histórica Argentina y Latinoamericana 7:41–65

Escosteguy P (2014) Estudios etnoarqueológicos con cazadores de coipo de Argentina. Revista Antípoda 20:145–165. https://doi.org/10.7440/antipoda20.2014.07

Escosteguy P, Vigna M (2010) Experimentación en el procesamiento de Myocastor coypus. In: Berón M, Luna L, Bonomo M, Montalvo C, Aranda C, Carrera Aizpitarte M (eds) Mamül Mapu: pasado y presente desde la arqueología pampeana, T. I. Editorial Libros del Espinillo, Ayacucho, pp 293–307

Escosteguy P, Salemme M, González MI (2012) Myocastor coypus ("coipo", Rodentia, Mammalia) como recurso en los humedales de la Pampa bonaerense: patrones de explotación. Revista del Museo de Antropología 5:13–30

Escosteguy P, González MI, Frère M (2015) Nuevos datos sobre fauna menor de la Depresión del Río Salado (Provincia de Buenos Aires, Argentina): el caso de San Ramón 7. Archaeofauna. Int J Archaeozoology 24:295–313

Escosteguy P, Scabuzzo C, González MI (2017a) Análisis bioarqueológico de los restos de Arroyo Siasgo, (supuesto Homo caputinclinatus de Ameghino 1910). Revista Argentina de Antropología biológica 19(2):4. https://doi.org/10.17139/raab.2017.0019.02.04

Escosteguy P, Rivas González M, Fiel MV, Vigna M (2017b) A orillas de la laguna de Lobos: el sitio Techo Colorado (microrregión del río Salado Bonaerense). Comechingonia. Revista de Arqueología 21(2):15–45

Escosteguy P, Salemme M, González MI (2017c) Tecnología ósea en la Depresión del río Salado (provincia de Buenos Aires). Arqueología 23(3):65–90

Falkner T. [1744/1746] (1974). Descripción de la Patagonia y de las partes contiguas de la América del Sur. Hachette, Buenos Aires

Fenenga F (1953) The weights of chipped stone points: a clue to their functions. Southwest J Anthropol 9:309–323

Frère MM, González MI, Constenla D, Bayón C (2010) Experimentación con recursos actuales mediante el empleo de análisis químicos. In: Berón M, Luna L, Bonomo M, Montalvo C, Aranda C, Carrera Aizpitarte M (eds) Mamül Mapu: pasado y presente desde la arqueología pampeana, t. I. Editorial Libros del Espinillo, Ayacucho, pp 65–76

Frère MM, González MI, Greco C (2016) Continuity in the use of shallow sites of the Salado river basin in the Pampean Region, Argentina. Radiocarbon 58(4):921–933

Frontini R, Escosteguy P (2015) El rol de los pequeños animales en los estudios arqueofaunísticos de Argentina. Archaeofauna. Int J Archaeozoology 24:67–85

Gómez, SE, Toresani N (1998) Pampas. In: Canevari P, Blanco D, Bucher E, Castro G, Davidson I (eds) Los humedales de la Argentina. Clasificación, situación actual, conservación y legislación. Wetlands International, SRNYDS, Buenos Aires, 97–114

González MI (2005) Arqueología de alfareros, cazadores y pescadores pampeanos. Sociedad Argentina de Antropología, Buenos Aires

González MI, Frère MM (2009) Talares y Paisaje Fluvial Bonaerense: Arqueología del Río Salado. Intersecciones en Antropología 10:249–266

González MI, Frère MM (2017) Análisis de isótopos estables en cerámica arqueológica del río Salado Bonaerense). Comechingonia. Revista de Arqueología 21(2):13–41

González MI, Frère MM, Escosteguy P (2006) El Sitio San Ramón 7. Curso Inferior del río Salado, provincia de Buenos Aires. Relaciones de la Sociedad Argentina de Antropología XXXI:187–204

González MI, Frère MM, Frontini R (2012) Formas de ollas de cerámica pampeana y consumo de alimentos. In: Babot P, Pazzarelli F, Marschoff M (eds) Las manos en la masa. Arqueologías y antropologías de la alimentación en Suramérica. Universidad Nacional de Córdoba, Museo de Antropología UNC, Instituto Superior de Estudios Sociales UNT, Córdoba, pp 405–424

González MI, Escosteguy P, Frère M (2016) Estudio ictioarqueológico y la presencia de corvina negra en La Guillerma 5 (Depresión del río Salado, provincia de Buenos Aires). III Encuentro Latinoamericano de Zooarqueología, Aracajú, Brasil

Guichón ML, Doncaster P, Cassini M (2003) Population structure of coypus (Myocastor coypus) in their region of origin and comparison with introduced populations. J Zool 261:265–272. https://doi.org/10.1017/S0952836903004187

Haene E (2006) Caracterización y conservación del talar bonaerense. In: Mérida E, Athor J (eds) Talares bonaerenses y su conservación. Fundación de Historia Natural Félix de Azara, Buenos Aires, pp 46–70

Hildebrandt W, King J (2012) Distinguishing between darts and arrows in the archaeological record: implications for technological change in the American West. Am Antiq 77:789–799

Hughes S (1998) Getting to the point: evolutionary change in prehistoric weaponry. J Archaeol Method Theory 1:345–406

León DC, Bonomo M (2011) Índice de rendimiento económico de coipo (Myocastor coypus). In: II Congreso Nacional de Zooarqueología Argentina, Libro de Resúmenes, 48. Universidad Nacional del Centro de la Provincia de Buenos Aires, Olavarría

Lloveras L, Moreno-García M, Nadal J (2009) Butchery, cooking and human consumption marks on rabbit (Oryctolagus cuniculus) bones: an experimental study. J Taphon 7(2–3):179–201

López HL, Baigún C, Iwaszkiw J, Delfino R, Padin O (2001) La Cuenca del Salado: Uso y posibilidades de sus recursos pesqueros. Editorial de la Universidad de La Plata, La Plata

Lyman RL (1994) Vertebrate taphonomy. Cambridge University Press, Cambridge

Mengoni Goñalons G (1999) Cazadores de guanacos de la estepa patagónica. Sociedad Argentina de Antropología, Buenos Aires

Morello J (2006) Acciones urbanas y conservación de Talares: un marco de negociación. In: Mérida E, Athor J (eds) Talares bonaerenses y su conservación. Fundación de Historia Natural Félix de Azara, Buenos Aires, pp 16–20

Musters GC [1869–1870] (1964) Vida entre los patagones. Un año de excursiones por tierras no frecuentadas, desde el Estrecho de Magallanes hasta el Río Negro. Ediciones Solar/Hachette, Buenos Aires, Argentina

Orton C, Tyers P, Vince A (1997) La cerámica en arqueología. Crítica, Barcelona

Politis G, Madrid P (2001) Arqueología Pampeana: Estado Actual y Perspectivas. In: Berberián E, Nielsen A (eds) Historia Argentina Prehispánica, t. 2. Editorial Brujas, Córdoba, pp 737–814

Politis G, Gutiérrez M, Scabuzzo C (eds) (2014) Estado actual de las investigaciones en el sitio arqueológico Arroyo Seco 2 (partido de Tres Arroyos, provincia de Buenos Aires, Argentina). INCUAPA-UNICEN, Buenos Aires

Quintana C, Mazzanti D (2011) Las vizcachas pampeanas (Lagostomus maximus, Rodentia) en la subsistencia indígena del Holoceno tardío de las Sierras de Tandilia Oriental (Argentina). Lat Am Antiq 2:253–270

Ratto N (2003) Estrategias de Caza y Propiedades del Registro Arqueológico en la Puna de Chaschuil (Departamento Tinogasta, Catamarca). Unpublished doctoral thesis, Facultad de Filosofía y Letras, Universidad de Buenos Aires, Buenos Aires

Rice P (1987) Pottery analysis: a sourcebook. University of Chicago Press, Chicago

Ringuelet R (1961) Rasgos fundamentales de la zoogeografía de la Argentina. Physis 22(63):151–170

Rye O (1994) Pottery technology: principles and reconstruction. Manuals on archaeology 4, Taraxacum, Washington, DC

Salemme M, Escosteguy P, Frontini R (2012) La fauna de porte menor en sitios arqueológicos de la región pampeana, Argentina. Agente disturbador vs. recurso económico. Archaeofauna. Int J Archaeozoology 21:163–185

Sánchez Labrador J [1772] (1936) Los indios Pampas-Puelches-Patagones. Editorial Viau y Zona, Buenos Aires

Santini M (2011) Aprovechamiento de Myocastor coypus (Rodentia, Caviomorpha) en sitios del Chaco Húmedo argentino durante el Holoceno tardío. Intersecciones en Antropología 12:195–205

Sartori J, Colasurdo MB, Santiago F (2014) Zooarchaeology in the Paraná River floodplain: GIS implementation at a regional scale. J Anthropol Archaeol 2(2):77–106

Schmidl U [1534/54] (1903) Viaje al Río de La Plata. Biblioteca Virtual Cervantes. http://www.cer vantesvirtual.com. Accessed 1 june 2008

Shott M (1993) Spears, darts, and arrows: late woodland hunting techniques in the Upper Ohio Valley. Am Antiq 58:425–443

Shott M (1997) Stones and shafts redux: the metric discrimination of chipped-stone dart and arrow points. Am Antiq 62:86–101

Svoboda A, Moreno E (2018) Peces y coipos: zooarqueología del sitio Valle Hermoso 4 (lago Colhué Huapi, Chubut). Revista del Museo de Antropología 11(1):85–98

Thomas DH (1978) Arrowheads and atlatl darts: how the stones got the shaft. Am Antiq 43:461–472

Tomka S (2013) The adoption of the bow and arrow: a model based on experimental performance characteristics. Am Antiq 78:553–569

Vecchi R (2010) Bolas de boleadora en los grupos cazadores-recolectores de la pampa bonaerense. Unpublished doctoral thesis, Facultad de Filosofía y Letras, Universidad de Buenos Aires, Buenos Aires

Vecchi R (2011) Bolas de boleadora del curso inferior del río Salado: Análisis de procedencia de materias primas. In: Martínez JB, BozzutoD (eds) Armas prehispánicas: múltiples enfoques para su estudio en Sudamérica. Fundación de Historia Natural Félix Azara, Buenos Aires, pp 195–204

Vecchi R, González MI (2018) Artefactos formatizados por picado, abrasión, pulido y modificados por uso en la depresión del Río Salado, Provincia de Buenos Aires. Argentina. Revista del Museo de Antropología 11(2):85–100

Vigna M, González MI, Weitzel C (2014) Los cabezales líticos de la microrregión del río Salado bonaerense, Argentina. Diseños e historias de vida. Intersecciones en Antropología 15(1):55–69

Whittaker JC (2013) Comparing atlatls and bows: accuracy and learning curve. Ethnoarchaeology 5(2):100–111. https://doi.org/10.1179/1944289013Z.0000000009

White E, Roth BJ (2009) Fish traps on ancient shores: exploring the function of Lake Cahuilla fish traps. J Calif Gt Basin Anthropol 29(2):183–194

Yu PL (2006) From atlatl to bow and arrow: implicating projectile technology in changing systems of hunter-gatherers mobility. In: Sellet F, Greaves R, Yu PL (eds) Archaeology and ethnoarchaeology of mobility. University Press of Florida, Gainesville, pp 201–220

Chapter 4
Guanaco Hunting Strategies in the Southeastern Pampas During the Late Holocene

Cristian A. Kaufmann, María C. Álvarez, Pablo G. Messineo, María P. Barros, Mariano Bonomo, and Guillermo Heider

Abstract In this chapter we discuss the strategies used by hunter-gatherers to capture guanaco (*Lama guanicoe*) in the southeastern Pampas during the Late Holocene (ca. 3500 to 500 ^{14}C years BP). We summarize the analysis of different evidence (e.g., mortality and skeletal part profiles, sex structure, weapons systems) obtained from four archaeological sites; three associated with the initial Late Holocene (ca. 3400–1700 ^{14}C years BP; Calera, Nutria Mansa 1, and Empalme Querandíes 1) and one with the final Late Holocene (ca. 1300–800 ^{14}C years BP; Hangar). Results indicate that during the initial Late Holocene, the guanaco hunting tactics were focused on family groups and troops of males. At this time, bola stones were more frequently used as thrown weapons. On the other hand, during the final Late Holocene, there is a significant quantity of small triangular projectile points linked with the use of bow and arrow, indicating a change in the Pampas weapon systems. The landscape geomorphology in which some of the archaeological sites are located allows us to suggest the use of active traps during the Late Holocene. River junctions and dune ridges were places where it would have been possible to enclose the principal prey of pre-Hispanic indigenous populations that inhabited the Pampas for millennia.

Keywords Pampa grasslands · Artiodactyls · Weapon systems · Active traps

---

C. A. Kaufmann (✉) · M. C. Álvarez · P. G. Messineo · M. P. Barros
Instituto de Investigaciones Arqueológicas y Paleontológicas del Cuaternario Pampeano
(INCUAPA-CONICET), Facultad de Ciencias Sociales, Universidad Nacional del Centro de la
Provincia de Buenos Aires, Olavarría, Argentina
e-mail: ckaufman@soc.unicen.edu.ar

M. Bonomo
CONICET-División Arqueología, Facultad de Ciencias Naturales y Museo, Universidad Nacional
de La Plata, La Plata, Argentina

G. Heider
CONICET-Departamento de Geología, Universidad Nacional de San Luis, San Luis, Argentina

© Springer Nature Switzerland AG 2021
J. B. Belardi et al. (eds.), *Ancient Hunting Strategies in Southern South America*,
The Latin American Studies Book Series,
https://doi.org/10.1007/978-3-030-61187-3_4

4.1 Introduction

For thousands of years, many indigenous societies of South America obtained their food primarily from hunting and gathering. These human groups relied on a deep traditional knowledge of the environment, the resources available there, and the hunting techniques used to obtain them. The South American archaeology and ethnography show they used different weapons for hunting, such as spears, shuttles, bow and arrow, bola stones, slings, and blowguns, as well as ties, nets, and other traps (Métraux 1949). The early traces of humans in the Pampa grasslands of Argentina date back to ca. 12,200 ^{14}C years BP. From the Late Pleistocene up to the Spanish Conquest in the sixteenth century, hunter-gatherer groups occupied, at least continuously, the southeastern area of the Pampas (Flegenheimer 2004; Martínez 2006; Mazzanti 2007; Politis 2008; Martínez et al. 2015, among others). These societies maintained for millennia a hunter way of life based on wild animals. In spite of occupying one of the most fertile lands in the world, the indigenous populations did not adopt the agriculture, widely spread across South America (Bonomo 2013a).

Throughout the Holocene, the guanaco (*Lama guanicoe*) was the main prey hunted by indigenous societies. The Pampas deer (*Ozotoceros bezoarticus*), the Greater rhea (*Rhea americana*), the armadillos (Dasypodidae and Chamyphoridae), and the plains vizcacha (*Lagostomus maximus*) were secondary resources. Other animals, such as some birds, rodents, and carnivores were occasionally exploited, although not necessarily as food. During the Late Holocene a process of diversification and intensification in the pre-Hispanic diet was proposed for the Pampa grasslands (Quintana and Mazzanti 2001; Martínez and Gutiérrez 2004), but in some areas the guanaco still was the main food resource. However, while the remains of this camelid have been recorded in most archaeological sites of the southeastern Pampas, there are not models addressing the strategies and tactics of its procurement and this aspect is only occasionally mentioned (e.g., Politis and Salemme 1990; Kaufmann 2009; Álvarez et al. 2017). An important previous study was conducted by Madrazo (1979) who differentiated Pampean indigenous societies according to the main prey exploited, guanaco in the south and Pampas deer in the north of the Salado river, both hunted to long-distance with bola stones.

The objective of this chapter is to discuss the guanaco hunting strategies in the southeastern Pampas and its changes during the Late Holocene. We present the analysis of different lines of evidence: mortality and skeletal part profiles, sex structure, and weapon systems. The evidence was obtained from four archaeological sites associated with two temporal sets: three of them with the initial Late Holocene (3400–1700 ^{14}C years BP; Calera, Nutria Mansa 1, and Empalme Querandíes 1 archaeological sites) and one with the final Late Holocene (1300–800 ^{14}C years BP; Hangar archaeological site) (Fig. 4.1). In the discussion, we include the information from other archaeological sites of the southeastern Pampas (e.g., Cueva Tixi, Paso Otero 3, Quequén Salado 1, Claromecó 1, Cueva El Abra, Lobería 1, Amalia 3, and Alero Curicó) to compare our results and have a better knowledge about the hunting strategies and the weapon systems used by hunter-gatherer groups.

4 Guanaco Hunting Strategies in the Southeastern …

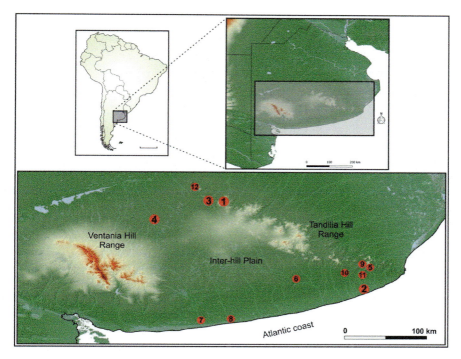

Fig. 4.1 Location of the study area and the main archaeological sites mentioned in this chapter. (1) Calera; (2) Nutria Mansa 1; (3) Empalme Querandíes 1; (4) Hangar; (5) Cueva Tixi; (6) Paso Otero 3; (7) Quequén Salado 1; (8) Claromecó 1; (9) Cueva el Abra; (10) Lobería 1; (11) Amalia 3; (12) Alero Curicó

Hunting strategies include encounter techniques, prey selection, and the organization of human groups (Churchill 1993; see also Métraux 1949; Gusinde 1986; Marean 1997; Musters 1997; Arenas 2003, Claraz 2008, among others). The obtaining of the prey can combine different actions such as driving or intercepting animals and using passive (e.g., sticky traps) or active (e.g., natural geoforms) traps. The main techniques recorded for American hunter-gatherer groups are described below.

- Stalking. Animals are surprised through ambushes in certain places of the landscape, such as obligated passages (e.g., a mountain pass) or frequented places (e.g., shallow lakes with drinkable water). The hunters can wait for the animals positioned behind natural or artificial features.
- Approximation. Animals are observed without being noticed and thus their escape is prevented. It is necessary to have a detailed knowledge about prey ethology, surrounding landscape, and to consider the wind and smell, among other things. This technique could be favored by the use of camouflage, decoys, bait, and other devices that prevent animals from perceiving human presence.

- Persecution. Animals are persecuted until they are located at a distance in which the hunter's weapon is effective, or they are chased, sometimes for days, until they are totally exhausted and vulnerable. To shorten the distance to the prey, the hunter can be helped by domestic animals such as horses or dogs.
- Passive traps. Hunters can use, for example, loops on trails that are regularly frequented by animals. Another option is the construction of pits in closer proximity to burrows or water sources where the animals live or go daily. The traps used by tactical methods can be mobile, as in the case of some nets held by people. The effective application of this last technique requires much knowledge about the prey ethology.
- Active traps. Include geomorphological features of the landscape such as ravines, watercourses, shallow lakes, marshes and dunes, as well as the use of artificial constructions (e.g., corrals) or a combination of both. The key to this strategy is to slow down or limit the escape of the animals and give the hunters effective shooting opportunities. This type of hunting may require a certain degree of planning and organization, especially when it involves artificial modifications of the landscape or the cooperation of a significant number of people.
- Burning. It consists of making a circle of fire in areas that have abundant grasses. Several hunters can bet around the fire while waiting for the stampede of animals to kill them. Once the fire is over, an inspection is made of the burned area to collect the animals that have died in the event.

The strategies for animal obtaining are a continuum between specialized hunting—i.e., the choice of a very limited number of prey in relation to the available species—to general hunting—i.e., a wide choice of the species considered edible. Foragers can vary seasonally or occasionally the prey choosing from a specialist to a generalist hunting (Marean 1997). Regarding the organizational hunting techniques, this can include a single or several individuals, a cooperative with hunters acting together, or a communal involvement of all group or band members hunting together (Driver 1995). A classic example of Tehuelche cooperative hunting is described in Claraz's (2008:85) travel to Chubut in 1865–1866. The place named Yamnago was used as a natural trap for the guanaco groups that descended from the mountains to drink water in a small lake. There was a low elevation where the hunters were hidden to look out for the herds. One man could surround the place without being seen and scare the guanacos to where the other hunters were waiting with their bola stones. The communal hunting technique should not necessarily involve a specialized hunting (Marean 1997), but it requires all hunters to participate in a previously conceived plan (Driver 1995). Following Politis and Angrizani (2008), communal hunting in tropical foragers (Nukak, Hoti, and Awa-Guajá) is planned in advance and includes more people from different families or segments of the band, and women take part in the hunting event.

4.2 Environmental and Ecological Characteristics of the Area

The Pampa grassland is an extensive plain located in the eastern portion of Argentina. The native vegetation is medium-height grasslands, with perennial and annual grasses (mainly of the genus *Stipa*, *Piptochaetium*, and *Poa*), with scattered shrubs (e.g., *Colletia paradoxa* and *Dodonaea viscosa*; Soriano 1992). At present, this landscape is modified considerably by agricultural and livestock activities (López Castro 2017). The climate of the Pampas is temperate (14–20 °C annual average) with average annual rainfall of 1000 mm (Burgos 1968; Prieto 2000). However, during different moments of the Late Pleistocene and Holocene a cold and dry climate prevailed, that was interspersed with warmer and wetter pulses (Tonni et al. 1999). Although sea levels also varied, flooding or exposing large areas of habitable plains, during the Late Holocene the coastline remained at its relative current height (Isla 1995).

In relation with the animal species in the Pampa grassland, the artiodactyls guanaco and Pampas deer predominated in the past. Other species characteristic of the Pampas are cougar (*Puma concolor*), Pampas fox (*Lycalopex gymnocercus*), Geoffroy's Cat (*Leopardus geoffroyi*), hairy armadillo (*Chaetophractus villosus*), hog-nosed armadillo (*Dasypus hybridus*), plains vizcacha, wild cavy (*Cavia* sp.), tuco-tuco (*Ctenomys* sp.), white-eared opossum (*Didelphys albiventris*), Greater rhea, as well as several small-sized birds, reptiles, and fish (Cabrera and Willink 1980).

The southeast area of the Pampas comprises a wide flat to slightly undulating surface landscape. This area is only interrupted by two major orographic systems: Tandilia Hill Range, located in the central and eastern Buenos Aires province, and Ventania Hill Range, located in the southwest (Fig. 4.1). Extensive primary outcrops and secondary deposits are located in both ranges and in some fluvial valleys, such as fine-grained orthoquartzite from the Sierras Bayas Group, chert from the Cerro Largo Formation, rhyolite and metaquartzite from La Mascota Formation, and igneous and metamorphic rocks from the crystalline basement (Bayón et al. 2006; Colombo 2011; Catella et al. 2013; Messineo and Barros 2015; Vecchi 2016, among others).

The hydrographic system is constituted by fluvial courses with an irregular regime, according to rainfall, that comes from Tandilia and Ventania and high plains and flow into the ocean. The Atlantic coast has rocky points of Tandilia outcrops, active cliffs, and mainly a continuous dune chain along 340 km with 4–3.5 km of maximum width (Fig. 4.1). Coastal cobbles and pebbles are deposited on the Pampas beaches and have mainly a volcanic origin—basalts, andesites, rhyolites, among others—elliptical shapes and sizes minor than 10 cm (Bonomo 2005). Our research in the southeast sector was carried out mainly in the plain between Tandilia and Ventania Hill Ranges at different distances from the Atlantic coast, and in the northwestern sector of Tandilia. All the archaeological sites correspond to open-air sites and they are located near watercourses.

4.3 Characterisctis of Guanaco (*Lama Guanicoe*)

The guanaco was the base of the subsistence for the hunter-gatherers that inhabited the Pampas during the Holocene. Hunter-gatherers used its meat, skin, bones, fat, and stomach stones (Politis and Pedrotta 2006). The guanaco is a camelid native of South America, and is one of the largest wild artiodactyls in the region. Currently, it is distributed in a wide range of habitats, from northern Peru to central Chile, and across the Argentinean and Chilean Patagonia (Franklin 2011). Guanacos are diurnal and grazers, but also feed on tree and shrub foliage. Adult individuals weigh between 88 and 120 kg (Franklin 1983; Fritz 1985).

Guanaco populations were reported to be both sedentary and migratory. Their social organization, based on a polygamous mating system, is central to understand the hunting strategies used by hunter-gatherers in the past. During the breeding season, three basic social units can be found: Family groups, solitary males, and non-reproductive male. The family group is territorial and is the basic social unit. It is integrated by a territorial male and several females, with offspring less than 15 months old. Solitary males (>15 months old) are individuals that were expelled from the family group. These animals can remain alone, join other family groups, or join male herds. Male groups are non-territorial and are mainly composed of individuals (6 to 167 animals) of various ages (Franklin 1983, 2011; Bank et al. 2003).

4.4 Materials and Methods

4.4.1 Archaeological Sites

4.4.1.1 Calera

This site is located at 36°58'56"S and 60°14'24"W, in a high valley in the northwestern sector of Tandilia Hill Range (Fig. 4.1). Archaeological materials were distributed along a surface that was perturbed during construction works carried out in a factory (7.5 m^2). Subsequently, an excavation of 6.5 m^2 was conducted at this site. Calera has been interpreted as an exceptional context constituted by offerings and ceremonial trash deposited in pits related to ritual origin, probably produced as the result of several ceremonies performed during band aggregation periods in the Late Holocene, between ca. 3400 and 1750 ^{14}C years BP (Politis et al. 2005). The ceremonial functionality was assigned on the basis of the quantity and variety of archaeological material related to the ideational sphere (e.g., a carved plaque, a polished axe, a shell bead, an engraved stomach stone, and potsherds with figurative motifs). Moreover, there was an unusual representation of carnivores (e.g., the extinct South American fox *Duscycyon avus*), as well as resources coming from other areas of the region (e.g., seashells, mineral pigments, some lithic tools, and ceramic motifs), and a complex spatial arrangement (e.g., intentional excavated pits, slab levels that separate occupation events, faunal assemblages delimited by stones, and an accumulation of guanaco skulls).

The faunal assemblage of Calera has a high integrity and an excellent preservation. There are skeletal parts from at least 22 different species with evidence of human exploitation (Table 4.1; Kaufmann and Álvarez 2007; Álvarez 2009; Scheifler 2014). In regard to the weapon systems, we recovered three complete triangular projectile points, 12 bola stones, and one preform of bola stone (Table 4.1; Barros and Messineo 2007; Matarrese 2015). Most of the bola stones are fractured ($n = 9$) and only two present grooves. The projectile points were made on chert ($n = 2$) and orthoquartzite ($n = 1$), while the bola stones were manufactured on different types of granites ($n = 9$), quartzite ($n = 2$), porphyritic rock with reddish minerals ($n = 1$), and chert ($n = 1$).

4.4.1.2 Nutria Mansa 1

This archaeological site is located at 38°24′54.2″S and 58°15′50.1″W, on the left bank of the Nutria Mansa creek, 3.5 km in a straight line to the Atlantic coast (Fig. 4.1). An excavation of 23 m^2 was conducted at this site. Three AMS radiocarbon dates show that the human occupations of the Lower Component occurred between ca. 3000 and 2700 ^{14}C years BP (Bonomo 2005). The settlement was placed on the margins of a permanent water source by hunter-gatherers who carried out multiple activities, including primary and secondary guanacos processing and consumption (Table 4.1). In addition, Pampas deer, armadillos (Dasypodidae, *Chaetophractus villosus, Zaedyus pichiy,* and *Dasypus hybridus*), canids (*Lycalopex gymnocercus, Dusicyon avus, Chrysocyon brachyurus*), felids (*Panthera onca*), mephitids (*Conepatus* sp.), rodents (e.g., *Lagostomus* sp., *Myocastor coypus, Galea musteloides,* Sigmodontinae) and otariids (Otariidae), were recorded.

In regard to technology, some of the guanaco bones were used as tools and two white shark (*Carcharodon carcharias*) teeth into pendants. Other activities carried out on the settlement were the initial reduction of coastal cobbles and pebbles and cores for obtaining blanks, the manufacture of various types of tools (scrapers, sidescrapers, drills, knives, and other unifacial flake tools), and the retouching and maintenance of their edges. Finally, it is important to mention the absence of projectile points and the presence of seven bola stones and two bolas pre-forms with and without equatorial groove (Table 4.1; Bonomo 2005). They were manufactured with granites of the black-white, green-white and blue-gray varieties, as well as with coarse-grained quartzite (Matarrese 2015). In addition, in the surface assemblage recovered in the Nutria Mansa archaeological locality, 28 bola stones were recorded.

Table 4.1 Chronology, exploited species, and weapon systems recorded in the archaeological sites analyzed

Site	^{14}C dates	Faunal with evidence of exploitation	Projectile points	Bola stones	References
Calera	3390 ± 170 3160 ± 320 3008 ± 46 3005 ± 66 2272 ± 51 2232 ± 55 2075 ± 44 1748 ± 42	*Lama guanicoe* *Ozotoceros bezoarticus* *Lycalopex gymnocercus* *Rhea americana* *Chaetophractus villosus* *Zaedyus pichiy* *Dasypus hybridus* *Holochilus brasiliensis* *Dolichotis patagonum* *Necromys* sp. *Reithrodon auritus* *Ctenomys* sp. *Anas platalea* *Dendrocygna viduata* *Fulica armillata* *Vanellus* cf. *Vanellus chilensis* *Asio* cf. *Asio flammeus* *Eudromia* cf. *Eudromia formosa* *Nothura* cf. *Nothura darwinni* *Rhynchotus rufescens* *Dendrocygna* sp. *Fulica* cf. *Fulica leucoptera*	3	12	Politis et al. 2005; Kaufmann and Álvarez 2007; Scheifler 2014
Nutria Mansa 1	3080 ± 100 2920 ± 110 2705 ± 66	*Lama guanicoe* *Ozotoceros bezoarticus* Dasipodidae *Zaedyus pichiy* *Lagostomus* sp. *Carcharodon carcharias*	0	9	Bonomo 2005
Empalme Querandíes 1	3095 ± 50 2816 ± 49 2050 ± 62	*Lama guanicoe* *Ozotoceros bezoarticus* *Myocastor coypus* *Lagostomus maximus* *Chaetophractus villosus* *Zaedyus pichiy* *Dasypus hybridus* *Tolypeutes matacus* *Rhea americana*	2	4	Messineo et al. 2013
Hangar	1335 ± 30 835 ± 30	*Lama guanicoe* *Ozotoceros bezoarticus* *Lagostomus maximus*	38	3	Barros et al. 2018

4.4.1.3 Empalme Querandíes 1

This site is located at 37°0′22.57″S and 60°22′39.28″W, in the left margin of the Tapalqué creek (Fig. 4.1). An excavation of 8 m^2 was conducted at this site. Three AMS radiocarbon dates show that the occupations occurred at the beginning of the

Late Holocene, between ca. 3100 and 2000 ^{14}C years BP (Table 4.1). The excavated sector of the Empalme Querandíes 1 site could represent a very small portion of a larger base camp situated on the margin of a palustrine or swampy environment associated with the old flood plain of the Tapalqué creek (Messineo et al. 2013). One particularity of this site is the presence of two spatially separated bone piles with an anthropogenic origin, which are composed of complete guanaco bones. Also, several lithic tools were recovered inside these accumulations (Álvarez et al. 2017).

Faunal analyses indicate that the guanaco, the Pampas deer, the Greater rhea, coypu (*Myocastor coypus*), plains vizcacha, and four armadillo species were part of the diet (Table 4.1). Moreover, bone remains of the first two species were also used as raw material to manufacture tools. Related to the weapon systems, we recovered four bola stones of granite, one small triangular projectile point and a fragmented point pre-form on chert, and one arrow point manufactured on bone (Table 4.1; Messineo et al. 2013; Colantonio et al. 2016).

4.4.1.4 Hangar

This site is located at 37°14′37.40″S and 61°14′5.04″W, on a small hill in the Salado creek (Fig. 4.1). Two AMS radiocarbon dates place the site at the end of the Late Holocene, between ca. 1300 and 700 ^{14}C years BP (Table 4.1). Materials recovered from this site come both from superficial (11,750 m^2) and buried deposits (11 m^2). Most remains correspond to non-decorated potsherds, faunal and human specimens, and lithic artifacts. Hangar site would have functioned as a base camp where the manufacture, replacement, and conditioning of the weapons took place, together with the butchery of different prey (Barros et al. 2018).

The faunal remains recovered in Hangar correspond to several species, being the guanaco the most abundant. Other taxa present in the site are Greater rhea, plains vizcacha, Pampas deer, and Canidae. Butchery evidence, such as cut marks and anthropic fractures, were recorded for artiodactyls and plains vizcacha (Table 4.1). Hangar faunal assemblage has not been studied yet. However, the remains are scarce and the preservation is poor. In relation to the weapon systems, 38 projectile points were recovered at Hangar. Twenty-two of them were made on chert, seven on orthoquartzite from the Sierras Bayas Group, five on silicified limestone, two on rhyolite, one on chalcedony, and one on flint. Also, three bola stones were recovered (Table 4.1); two of them were made on diabase and one on metaquartzite.

4.4.2 Methodology

In order to construct guanaco mortality profiles and sex structure, we analyzed the total teeth remains from the sites with this type of material: Calera, Nutria Mansa 1, and Empalme Querandíes 1. We assigned an age to the dental series (mandibles) and isolated diagnostic teeth (Pd4/M3) considering the sequence of eruption, development, and wear of guanaco teeth proposed by Kaufmann (2009). We represented the site age structures by using a triangular graph or ternary diagram as originally proposed by Stiner (1994). With this method, specimens are assigned to one of these age classes: juvenile (0–2 years old), adult (2–7 years), and senile (more than 7 years). The proportions of individuals in each class are plotted on the graph. Bootstrapping the age class data allows to account for sample size and approximate confidence intervals around age structure data points on the triangular graph. We constructed the ternary graph by using software provided by Weaver et al. (2011) with 95% confidence intervals. We followed the proposal by Discamps and Costamagno (2015); who developed a species-specific way to rezone ternary graphs. Additionally, we compared the archaeological results with actualistic data of a guanaco living population from Torres del Paine (Fritz 1985).

We estimated the time of the year in which the sites were occupied. For this, we considered the development and wear of the newborns dP4 in their first year of life together with the guanaco birthing date. The determination of the sex structure was made through the analyses of the canine teeth that were inside the mandibles/maxilla or isolated. We made the sexual discrimination by considering the following metric variables: canine total length, canine root length, canine mesiodistal diameter, and canine buccolingual diameter. These variables were measured with a digital caliper. The sex was assigned to each specimen by using the range of values offered by Kaufmann (2009).

We calculated the guanaco Minimum Number of Individuals (MNI) (Grayson 1984; Klein and Cruz-Uribe 1984), considering the most commonly occurring kind of skeletal element (Lyman 2008). The skeletal part profiles included the quantification of Minimum Number of Elements (MNE) and Minimum Animal Units (MAU and %MAU) (Binford 1978; Klein and Cruz-Uribe 1984). MNE is the minimum number of skeletal elements necessary to account for the specimens understudy, while MAU is the MNE standardized by the number of times the skeletal portion occurs in a complete skeleton. MAU values are normed by dividing the greatest MAU in an assemblage and multiplying each resulting value by 100 (%MAU) (Lyman 2008). Skeletal part profiles were compared with the guanaco Meat Utility Index (MUI) developed by Borrero (1990) through Spearman's rho correlations.

Lithic projectile points considered in this chapter ($n = 42$) were studied by using a techno-typological perspective (Aschero 1975, 1983). We considered different variables such as raw material, condition (broken or complete), relative dimension (length, width, and thickness), width-thickness ratio, weight, and technical series. Different proposals allow estimating the projectile points function. These were made based on experimental, ethnographic, and historical information (Thomas 1978; Shott 1997; Hughes 1998; Ratto 2003, among others). In this article we followed the Shott's (1997) proposal for one variable in which the classification function for dart is 1.40 (shoulder width) -16.85, and for arrow is 0.89 (shoulder width) -7.22 (see discussion in Martínez 2003). This is one of the most accepted methods for discriminating between different projectile propulsion systems (Okumura and Araujo 2015). However, it is important to note that there is an overlap between the measurements

4 Guanaco Hunting Strategies in the Southeastern …

of darts and arrow points and, in some particular cases, Shott's formulae was not the most successful for distinguishing both types of projectile points (Railey 2010). However, this is a useful starting point for this discussion because most of the studied projectile points are broken ($n = 28$; 65.1%) and in this function it is possible to consider both complete and broken points (if the bases are present). On the contrary, other methodological proposals can only be applied to complete items (Ratto 2003).

4.5 Results

4.5.1 Mortality Profiles

4.5.1.1 Calera

Forty-three hemi-mandibles, 42 hemi-maxilla, two incisive series, and 780 isolated teeth were recovered in this site. Besides, we recorded 588 fragments of enamel, roots, and cusps. The MNI obtained by considering together the hemi-mandibles and the isolated teeth (45 dP4 and 34 M3) is 58 in 14 m^2. The profile obtained from the hemi-mandibles indicates a higher frequency of adult individuals, between 3 and 5 years old, although the juveniles are also abundant (Fig. 4.2). The results of the Calera mortality profile falls in the juvenile-adult-senile (JAS) sector (Fig. 4.3), which represents a living population. The confidence area also covers almost only the JAS profile type.

The metric analysis of the canine teeth was conducted on 113 specimens. From these, 13 were in the mandible/maxilla alveoli (associated with dental series) and 100 were isolated. Considering the metric range of the guanaco canines, we determined that 53 (46.9%) correspond to males, 51 (45.1%) to females, six (5.3%) are undetermined, and three (2.7%) were juveniles and therefore sex could not be determined. The analysis of the dP4 shows different ages represented in the sample. Forty-four percent of the pieces were assigned to individuals between 0–15 days, 21% between 15 days–3 months, and 35% between 6–19 months. These data indicate that an important percentage of guanacos were killed at the end of the spring and, in less proportion, between the summer and the fall.

4.5.1.2 Nutria Mansa 1

Fifty-seven hemi-mandibles, 27 hemi-maxilla, and 358 isolated guanaco teeth were recovered. Also, we determined 1620 fragments of enamel, roots, and cusps. The MNI obtained by considering together the hemi-mandibles and the isolated teeth (20 dP4 and 31 M3) is also high: 60 in the 23 m^2 excavated. The profile constructed from the hemi-mandibles indicates a high frequency of adult individuals, between 5 and 7 years old (Fig. 4.2). The results of the Nutria Mansa 1 profile falls in the

Fig. 4.2 Guanaco mortality profiles based on MNI obtained from hemimandibles

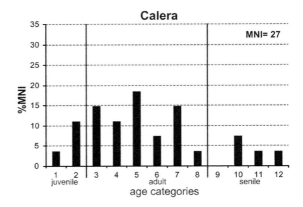
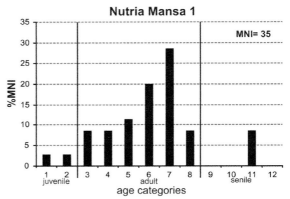
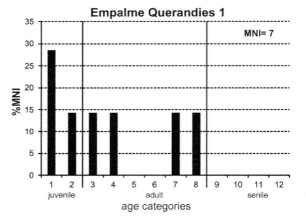

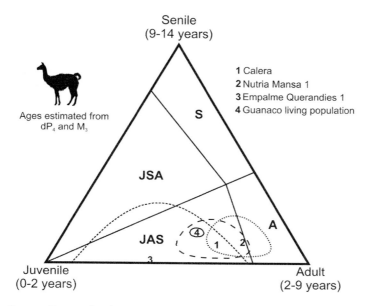

Fig. 4.3 Ternary diagram showing guanaco mortality profiles based on MNI (dP4 and M3) and an actual living population as a reference. Diagram divisions correspond to those proposed by Discamps and Costamagno (2015): JSA: Juvenile-Senile-Adult; JAS: Juvenile-Adult-Senile; A: Adult; S: Senile. Circles around the numbers represent approximate 95% confidence intervals

JAS sector, which represents a living population structure (Fig. 4.3). However, it is located on the boundary with the sector dominated by prime adults. The confidence area covers both types of age structures.

The metric analysis of the canine teeth was conducted on 31 specimens. From these, eight were in the mandible/maxilla alveoli (associated with dental series) and 23 were isolated. Considering the metric range of the guanaco canines, we determined that 23 (74%) correspond to males, three (10%) to females, and five (16%) are undetermined. The analysis of the dP4 shows different ages represented in the analyzed sample. Thirty-five percent of the pieces were assigned to individuals between 0–15 days, 45% between 15 days–3 months, and 15% between 6–19 months. These data indicate that most of the guanacos were killed between the end of the spring and the summer.

4.5.1.3 Empalme Querandíes 1

Eleven hemi-mandibles, five hemi-maxilla, and 26 isolated teeth were recovered on this site. Moreover, we recorded 106 fragments of enamel, roots, and cusps. The MNI obtained by considering together the hemi-mandibles and the isolated teeth (2 dP4 and 1 M3) is 10 in the 8 m² excavated. The profile obtained from the hemi-mandibles indicates a higher frequency of juvenile individuals, although it is important to consider that this sample is small (Fig. 4.2). The results of the Empalme Querandíes 1 mortality profile falls in the JAS sector (Fig. 4.3), which represents a living population. The confidence area also covers almost only the JAS profile type.

Isolated canines were not recorded in Empalme Querandíes1 site. When present, these teeth were inside the alveoli ($n = 7$) and could not be measured. Qualitative observations made on a skull with its mandible indicate that these elements correspond to a male. The analysis of the dP4 shows different ages represented in the sample. Twenty-five percent of the pieces were assigned to individuals between 0–15 days, 37.5% between 3–6 months, and 37.5% between 6–19 months. Although the sample is small, the data indicate that guanacos were hunted during the four seasons of the year.

4.5.2 Representation of Guanaco Skeletal Parts

4.5.2.1 Calera

Guanaco skeletal profiles were analyzed for four of the features identified in Calera. In pit 4 there was a MNE of 152 and a MNI of 5. The higher values were for the scapula (Fig. 4.4a). The correlation with the MUI was positive and significant ($r_s = 0.6$; $p = 0.001$). In pit 2, we determined a MNE of 625 and a MNI of 13. The higher %MAU values were obtained for the sacrum and the shaft of the femur (Fig. 4.4b). The correlation with the MUI was positive and non-significant but close to being statistically significant ($r_s = 0.4$; $p = 0.052$). In the upper levels of pit 1, we determined a MNE of 284 and a MNI of 7. The higher %MAU values were for the innominate (Fig. 4.4c). The correlation with the MUI was positive and significant ($r_s = 0.7$; $p < 0.01$). In the lower levels of pit 1, it was determined a MNE of 110 and a MNI of 3. The higher values of %MAU were also obtained for the innominate (Fig. 4.4d). Results of the correlation between %MAU and MUI show positive and significant values ($r_s = 0.09$; $p = 0.7$). In general, in Calera site the most represented skeletal units are those with higher nutritional value.

4.5.2.2 Nutria Mansa 1

In this site, a large amount of guanaco bone remains was recovered (MNE $= 1572$; MNI $= 28$). Moreover, a bone accumulation or bone pile was identified. This feature was almost exclusively composed of guanaco bones (MNE $= 150$; MNI $= 8$). Both assemblages were integrated by a wide variety of skeletal units, among which the most abundant were the long bones (Fig. 4.4e, f). The correlation with the MUI was positive but the result had no statistical significance both for the bone pile ($r_s = 0.09$; $p = 0.6$) and for the rest of the faunal assemblage ($r_s = 0.002$; $p = 0.9$). In

4 Guanaco Hunting Strategies in the Southeastern …

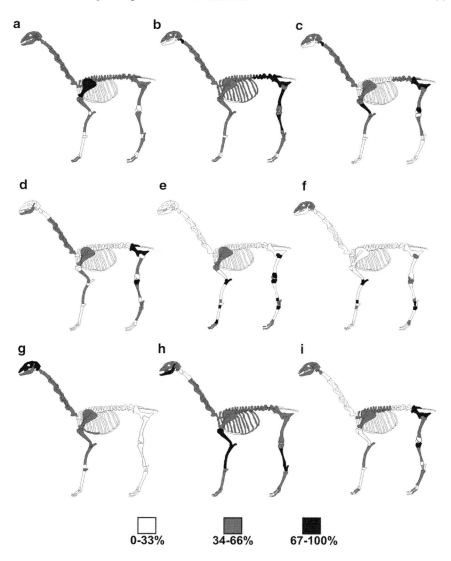

Fig. 4.4 %MAU of the guanaco skeletal profile from the archaeological sites. (a) Calera pit 4; (b) Calera pit 2; (c) Calera, pit 1 upper levels; (d) Calera pit 1 lower levels; (e) Nutria Mansa 1 bone pile; (f) Nutria Mansa 1, general assemblage; (g) Empalme Querandíes 1 bone pile 1; (h) Empalme Querandíes 1 bone pile 2; (i) Empalme Querandíes 1 general assemblage

Nutria Mansa 1 site, there is no selection of specific skeletal units in relation with its nutritional values.

4.5.2.3 Empalme Querandíes 1

Two bone piles were identified in this site, both of them integrated by guanaco bone remains. In the bone pile 1 we determined a MNE of 45 and a MNI of 5. The higher %MAU values correspond to the skull and the forelimb, while the axial skeleton has low %MAU values and the hind limb is practically absent (Fig. 4.4g). The correlation with MUI indicated a significant and positive result ($r_s = 0.5$; $p = 0.01$). In bone pile 2 we determined a MNE of 266 and a MNI of 4. All the skeletal units were well represented but the long bones had the higher %MAU values (Fig. 4.4h). The correlation with MUI was negative and the result had no statistical significance ($r_s = -0.180$; $p = 0.4$). For the rest of the faunal assemblage, the MNE was 277 and the MNI of 9. The %MAU was obtained for the proximal end of tibia, innominate, sacrum, and skull (Fig. 4.4i). The correlation with MUI was positive and significant ($r_s = 0.1$; $p = 0.5$). Most skeletal parts are represented in this site.

4.5.3 Projectile Point Types

The dimensions of the pieces, as well as the raw materials and possible weapon systems are presented in Table 4.2. All the lithic projectile points are triangular and stemless (Fig. 4.5). In general, the pressure technique was used for making thinner points and regular and parallel retouch are observed in the piece edges; only one specimen presents denticulate edges. The contours of the bases are straight ($n = 13$; 35.1%), convex ($n = 12$; 32.4%), concave ($n = 11$; 29.7%), and undifferentiated ($n = 1$; 2.7%) (Table 4.2; Fig. 4.5). The technical treatment of the bases shows that nine of them were thinned by retouch. In the other cases, the blanks, mainly flakes, have no technological modifications, suggesting no special manufacture of the projectile bases. In this case, there is a previous selection of blanks with the suitable shape and dimensions.

There are some differences in the production sequence of projectile points for each raw material. While most of the chert could have entered to the settlements in the form of cores and blanks, the transport of natural nodules cannot be discarded. In Calera, Empalme Querandíes 1, and Hangar sites, we recognized the entire lithic reduction sequence on chert (Barros and Messineo 2007; Colantonio et al. 2016; Barros et al. 2018), but some projectile points in Hangar could have entered broken to be replaced at the camp, as it is evidenced by the presence of 12 fractured basal fragments (Table 4.2; Fig. 4.5) some of which were reactivated while they were hafted. Projectile points in these sites are small (eight of the points are less than 25 mm); in general are thin (between 1.8 and 4 mm) and to a lesser extent, thick (between 6.6 and 8 mm of thickness). Results on the study of the weapon system

Table 4.2 Results for the lithic projectile points. References: NA = not applicable; UN = undifferentiated; SBG = Sierras Bayas Group; EQ1 = Empalme Querandíes 1; C = Calera; H = Hangar. The measurements of the fractured pieces are indicated in brackets

ID #	Raw material	State	Length in mm	Width in mm	Thickness in mm	Weight in gm	Section	Base	Function (sensu Shott 1997)
FCS.EQ1.2621	Chert	Complete	16	14	2.5	–	Complete	Concave	Arrow
FCS.C.376	Chert	Complete	36	12	3	–	Complete	Concave	Arrow
FCS.C.693	Chert	Complete	40	22	8	–	Complete	Convex	Dart
FCS.C.436	Orthoquartzite SBG	Complete	38	23	8	–	Complete	Straight	Dart
FCS.H.1	Rhyolite	Broken	(14)	19	4	1	Base	Concave	Dart
FCS.H.2	Rhyolite	Broken	(42)	23	7	7.3	Base + blade	Concave	Dart
FCS.H.4	Orthoquartzite SBG	Broken	(33)	20	9	7.2	Base + blade	Straight	Dart
FCS.H.5	Orthoquartzite SBG	Complete	39	31	8	8.1	Complete	Convex	Dart
FCS.H.6	Orthoquartzite SBG	Complete	27	17	5	2	Complete	Concave	Arrow
FCS.H.7	Orthoquartzite SBG	Complete	21	15	2	0.9	Complete	Straight	Arrow
FCS.H.8	Orthoquartzite SBG	Broken	(30)	27	5	5.3	Base + blade	Straight	Dart
FCS.H.9	Orthoquartzite SBG	Broken	(13)	16	3	0.7	Base	Straight	Arrow
FCS.H.10	Orthoquartzite SBG	Broken	(23)	15	4	1.6	Base + blade	Straight	Arrow
FCS.H.11	Silex	Broken	(10)	(11)	2	0.3	Base	UN	N/A
FCS.H.12	Silicified limestone	Broken	(10)	(9)	2	0.3	Blade	N/A	N/A
FCS.H.13	Silicified limestone	Broken	(24)	21	4.5	2.4	Base + blade	Concave	Dart
FCS.H.15	Silicified limestone	Broken	(16)	14	3	0.8	Base + blade	Convex	Arrow
FCS.H.39	Silicified limestone	Broken	(18)	13	3	0.7	Base + blade	Concave	Arrow
FCS.H.1547	Silicified limestone	Broken	(17)	15	3.7	0.9	Tip + blade	N/A	N/A
FCS.H.25	Chalcedony	Broken	(20)	16	4	1.5	Base	Convex	Arrow
FCS.H.14	Chert	Complete	24	15	4	1.1	Complete	Straight	Arrow
FCS.H.16	Chert	Broken	(9)	9.5	2.5	0.3	Base	Straight	Arrow

(continued)

Table 4.2 (continued)

ID #	Raw material	State	Length in mm	Width in mm	Thickness in mm	Weight in gm	Section	Base	Function (sensu Shott 1997)
FCS.H.18	Chert	Broken	(8)	17	2	0.4	Base	Convex	Arrow
FCS.H.19	Chert	Broken	(30)	19	6	4.1	Base + blade	Straight	Arrow
FCS.H.20	Chert	Broken	(14)	10	2	0.4	Base + blade	Concave	Arrow
FCS.H.21	Chert	Broken	(19)	16	3	1.2	Base + blade	Convex	Arrow
FCS.H.22	Chert	Broken	(20)	16	3	1	Base + blade	Straight	Arrow
FCS.H.23	Chert	Broken	(12)	14	2.5	0.5	Base	Straight	Arrow
FCS.H.24	Chert	Complete	17	13	2.5	0.5	Complete	Concave	Arrow
FCS.H.26	Chert	Complete	23	17	5	1.6	Complete	Concave	Arrow
FCS.H.27	Chert	Complete	17	12	2	0.5	Complete	Convex	Arrow
FCS.H.28	Chert	Complete	22	12	2	0.8	Complete	Convex	Arrow
FCS.H.29	Chert	Broken	(12)	(8)	1	0.1	Tip	N/A	N/A
FCS.H.30	Chert	Broken	(10)	13	2	0.4	Base	Straight	Arrow
FCS.H.33	Chert	Broken	(11)	12	2	0.4	Base	Concave	Arrow
FCS.H.34	Chert	Complete	12	11	2	0.5	Complete	Convex	Arrow
FCS.H.40	Chert	Broken	(11)	11	1.8	0.3	Base	Straight	Arrow
FCS.H.1542	Chert	Broken	(45.2)	(23.5)	6.7	6.4	Tip + blade	N/A	N/A
FCS.H.1543	Chert	Broken	(16.2)	11	2.8	0.5	Base + blade	Convex	Arrow
FCS.H.1544	Chert	Broken	(20.3)	13	3.4	1.4	Base + blade	Convex	Arrow
FCS.H.1545	Chert	Broken	(16.9)	(14)	3.2	0.6	Tip + blade	N/A	N/A
FCS.H.1546	Chert	Complete	20.3	17.5	2.7	0.1	Complete	Convex	Arrow

Fig. 4.5 Stemless triangular projectile points of Hangar site. Points that were assigned to darts (upper half) and arrows (lower half). See details in Table 4.2

indicate that 21 chert projectile points were related to the use of bow and arrow and only one case of Calera site was assigned to a dart (Table 4.2).

In the case of orthoquartzite from the Sierras Bayas Group, it is observed that a large part of the operational sequence for making these points is represented in the Hangar and Calera sites. As in the case of chert, some points would have entered fractured to Hangar (Fig. 4.5) to be replaced by new ones or could have been transported inside the hunted animal carcasses (Barros et al. 2018: Figure 6). Three of the complete projectile points are medium size (more than 25 mm in length) and they were manufactured on thick flakes (Table 4.2). One complete projectile point is small and thin (2 mm of thickness). In this sense, there is no standardization in the point's production for the orthoquartzite from the Sierras Bayas Group. Two different weapon systems were recognized for this lithic raw material: darts in Hangar ($n = 3$) and Calera ($n = 1$), and arrow points in Hangar ($n = 4$) (Table 4.2).

In the case of silicified limestone (the third more frequent rock for making points in the Hangar site), some points could have been manufactured on the settlement as we recovered items (e.g., flakes and tools) related to different stages of the production sequence. On the contrary, in rhyolite, chalcedony, and flint the final stages of the projectile points manufacture are not recorded in this site. All these points are broken (Table 4.2). For this reason, we propose that these projectile points were carried to the settlement to be re-sharpened or replaced by others. In the case of the weapon system, two silicified limestone points correspond to arrows and one to a dart (Fig. 4.5), one chalcedony point is an arrow, and two rhyolite points are darts (Table 4.2; Fig. 4.5). The differences in the thicknesses are due to the raw materials and weapon systems, thinner in flint (2 mm), silicified limestone (between 2 and 4.5 mm), chalcedony (4 mm), and thicker in rhyolite (between 4 and 7 mm).

In different Pampean sites there is evidence of the use of bone as raw material. Most of these tools could be related with butchering and knapping activities. However, in Empalme Querandíes 1 site there is a projectile point manufactured on an undetermined bone. According to the measures of this item, it corresponds to an arrow point, which could have been used in hunting activities (Messineo et al. 2013: Figure 3). These items are almost absent in the southeastern Pampas, but are frequent in Central Argentina (provinces of Córdoba, Santiago del Estero, and San Luis) and, in a lesser extent, in the Paraná Delta and in the North area of the Pampas (Pastor et al. 2005; Bonomo 2013b). The use of bone as a raw material for making projectile points would not be a common behavior in the southern Pampas and this isolated item could have been obtained through exchange.

4.6 Discussion

4.6.1 Trends for the Initial Late Holocene

During the initial Late Holocene (3400–1700 ^{14}C years BP) there is a prevalence of throwing weapon systems such as bola stones (85.2%). Also, there is evidence (e.g., Empalme Querandíes 1 and Calera) that darts or spears and arrows were used at that time, but their relative frequency is low (Table 4.2). These artifacts were made on raw materials from the outcrops located in the Tandilia and Ventania Hill Ranges, near to the sites (Fig. 4.1). The results of the mortality profiles indicate that guanaco hunting was mainly oriented to living populations (JAS structure), with a tendency toward adult individuals in the case of Nutria Mansa 1. We consider that the recurrent target would have been the family group because this social unit has a territorial behavior, which facilitates a pre-hunt planning through cooperative or communal strategies. Moreover, in all the sites there is evidence of newborn guanacos, which were highly valued not only for the meat, but also for the quality of their skin (Claraz 2008). In addition, the significant percentage of males in at least two of the analyzed samples (Nutria Mansa 1 and Calera) could indicate that male troops were also a common target. Male troops are non-territorial but are usually integrated by several animals, which would allow the obtaining of many individuals during cooperative or communal hunting; or that one or several guanaco individuals were obtained in a single hunting episode in daily foraging trips.

The skeletal part profiles show the representation of both axial and appendicular bone elements. For some assemblages, such as Nutria Mansa 1 and Empalme Querandíes 1, the guanacos were transported relatively complete from the killing site to the base-camp. In this sense, both types of sites should have been close to each other (Bonomo 2005; Álvarez et al. 2017). In the case of Calera, there is a better representation of those skeletal parts with high meat utility values. It is important to consider that this is a ritual context, an aspect that could have influenced the selection of the skeletal parts. Assemblages resulting from rituals or ceremonial trash are usually characterized by an important frequency of high-ranked elements because the best parts of the animals are selected (e.g., Kelly 2001; Pauketat et al. 2002).

Empalme Querandíes 1 and Nutria Mansa 1 present bone piles with complete guanaco bones. These types of accumulations are recorded in the second half of the Middle Holocene and in the initial Late Holocene (between ca. 4800 and 2000 ^{14}C years BP) in the Tandilia Hill Range (Cueva Tixi; Quintana and Mazzanti 2001) and in the plains of the Quequén Grande River (Paso Otero 3; Martínez 2006). It is during this period when the diet becomes strongly focused on guanaco in the southeastern Pampas (Quintana and Mazzanti 2001; Martínez and Gutiérrez 2004; Frontini 2013; Álvarez 2014). It has been proposed that the presence of bone piles could be related with guanaco cooperative hunting and the use of active traps near the basecamps (Kaufmann 2009; Álvarez et al. 2017). The places of the landscape selected to implement this type of strategy are rooted in the hunter's knowledge of prey biology and behavior (Frison 2004). In many opportunities, the topographic features of the landscape are combined with artificial constructions to increase the effectiveness of the hunting tactics. These structures are recorded in different parts of Argentine. For example, in the high Pampas of the Argentinean Northwest region, some stone macrostructures have been identified (Ratto and Orgaz 2002–2004). These are simple stonewalls less than 30 cm high that could have also functioned as landscape markers. These places were used in the *chakus* or communal hunting events where several camelids were obtained. This technique includes driving the animals from the high to plain and open spaces, where they are enclosed in a huge human circle and then killed by the use of bola stones. People used cords to enclose and drive the animals (Ratto and Orgaz 2002–2004). Other types of structures are the hunting blinds or *parapetos* that are usually recorded in the Patagonia and were used for guanaco hunting (e.g., Belardi et al. 2017; Mange et al. 2019). These stone structures are semielliptical and were regularly used in ambush hunting strategies, particularly in the Late Holocene (Goñi et al. 2016; Belardi et al. 2017).

During the initial Late Holocene in the southeastern Pampas there is no record of hunting structures. However, we do not discard that some of them could have been made on the same perishable materials (wood and skin). On the other hand, the observation of the landscape geomorphology in which the sites are located allows us to suggest the use of active traps. In this region with lower relief, shallow lakes, rivers and streams would be places where it would have been possible to enclose the prey. Although rivers and streams have many sections that are suitable for this purpose, the confluence of two water courses (*rinconadas* in Spanish) has the best conditions to corral and hunt many animals together. These places would constitute excellent hunting fields that could have been used on a recurrent basis throughout the Holocene. Many Pampean archaeological sites are located near or in *rinconadas* of rivers and streams. In relation to our case study, Empalme Querandíes 1 is located inside a *rinconada* formed by two water courses, the Tapalqué creek and a minor tributary (Fig. 4.6a). Likewise, Nutria Mansa 1 is also located near the intersection of the Nutria Mansa creek, and the coastal dunes that would have constituted a natural barrier that facilitated the animal hunting.

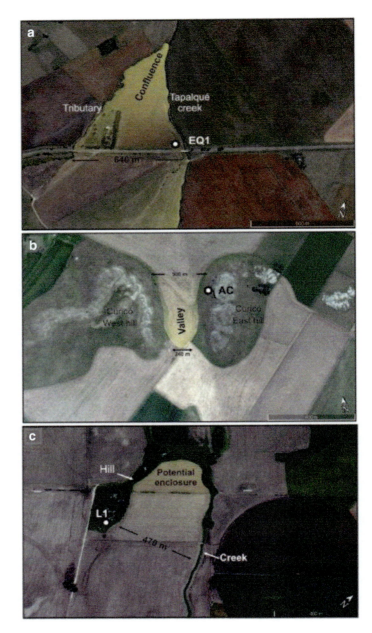

Fig. 4.6 Examples of active traps associated with archaeological sites mentioned in this chapter. (a) Empalme Querandíes 1; (b) Alero Curicó; (c) Lobería 1

Darts and spears as well as bola stones are recorded since the early peopling of the Pampas. In the initial Late Holocene the environment of the Pampas was more arid and there was a lower level of plant cover that favored the guanaco hunting in open spaces with bola stones. These weapons are effective in open places and especially in strategies involving corralling, such as human encircling. In addition, bola stones have not only been associated with the obtaining of guanaco, but also with Greater rhea, Pampas deer, sea lions, fur seals, foxes, cougar, and were used in the war (Sánchez Labrador 1936; González 1953; Musters 1997; Vecchi 2016). These weapon systems, together with the presence of guanaco bone piles in this period, suggest the use of active traps and the hunting in open places, but also could be related with the use of cooperative tactics. These strategies would have been used mainly during the spring and the summer, because of the presence of newborn guanacos with high-quality skins.

4.6.2 Trends for the Final Late Holocene

This period differs from the previous one. At Hangar site, the recorded weapon systems for the final Late Holocene (1300–700 ^{14}C years BP) show a predominance of small projectile points associated with the use of the bow and arrow. Also, there is evidence that darts and bolas were used, but with a lower frequency (Table 4.2). Most of the projectile points and also bola stones were made on raw materials from the Pampean grasslands (orthoquartzite and chert from Tandilia and rhyolite from Ventania; Fig. 4.1), but five projectile points of the Hangar site were manufactured on silicified limestone, a rock that comes from the xerophytic woodland of the Pampas, about 500 km away from the site. The analyses conducted on the lithic sample of Hangar indicated that most of the points would have been used as arrows and a very lower percentage as darts. Other archaeological sites corresponding to this period are Quequén Salado 1 (1000–320 ^{14}C years BP; Fig. 4.1; Madrid et al. 2002) and Claromecó 1 (ca. 800 ^{14}C years BP; Bonomo et al. 2008), both located near the Atlantic coast. In these sites, there are small stemless triangular projectile points with concave and straight bases manufactured with coastal cobbles and pebbles and a calcareous bola stone in Quequén Salado 1. On the other hand, at the eastern end of the Tandilia Hill Range (Mazzanti et al. 2010), there are sites with occupations corresponding to the final Late Holocene that present a large number of projectile points: Cueva El Abra ($n = 137$), Lobería 1 ($n = 202$), Cueva Tixi ($n = 21$), and Amalia 3 ($n = 8$) (Fig. 4.1). In addition, in some of these sites (e.g., Cueva El Abra, Amalia 2, 4, and 5) the bola stones have a low frequency (Bonnat et al. 2019). The studies carried out on these materials indicate the coexistence of at least three weapon systems: bola stones, darts or spears, and bow and arrow (Mazzanti et al. 2010). Most of the points that could be measured are associated with the last one (Valverde and Martucci 2004). Another site with a large number of points is Alero Curicó (ca. 412–190 ^{14}C years BP), which is situated at the Sierras de Curicó archaeological locality, at the western end of the Tandilia Hill Range (Fig. 4.1; Madrid et al. 2000). Among the findings of this site, there are 32 small stemless triangular projectile points. The morphological characteristics and sizes were associated with the use of the bow and arrow. Besides, two apical fragments of points of larger dimensions were related with the use of darts and spears (Pedrotta 2005).

For the final late Holocene we do not have information about the mortality profiles and in general, faunal data are scarce for the southeastern Pampas. Some exceptions are Claromecó 1, with dates of ca. 800 ^{14}C years BP, and Quequén Salado 1 sites (Fig. 4.1). In both assemblages, guanaco bone remains were recorded, and in Claromecó 1 there are individuals of different ages that include newborns, juveniles, and adults (Bonomo et al. 2008). On the other hand, in the sites of the eastern end of the Tandilia Hill Range, there is evidence that during this period, the diet included a higher frequency of small species such as Tegu lizard (*Salvator merianae*), rodents, armadillos, and birds (Mazzanti et al. 2010; Quintana and Mazzanti 2014). There was a decrease in the appropriation of large prey and a diversification of small ones. According to these authors, changes in the diet could have been related with changes in the weapon systems.

Beyond faunal information, there are some structures and features in the landscape that are associated with the sites and allow us to propose some ideas about the hunting tactics. The Tandilia Hill Range, adjacent to the plains, constituted geomorphological features that could have been used as active traps during the final Late Holocene and also before. Sites and archaeological localities such as Alero Curicó, Cueva El Abra, Cueva Tixi, and Amalia 3 (Mazzanti 2006; Valverde and Martucci 2004; Mazzanti et al. 2010), are located in high sectors of the landscape that are favorable to prey sighting and to corral animals like the guanaco in the valley bottoms. For example, the case of the Sierras de Curicó archaeological locality presents several items to discuss aspects related to guanaco hunting. This locality, with human occupations for the final Late Holocene presents a favorable geomorphological scenario to implement active hunting tactics; using natural features of the landscape to corral the guanacos and put them at a distance in which the weapons, mainly the bow and arrow system, were efficient. The Curicó East and West hills are separated by a small valley of 500 m wide at the North and 250 m at the South (Fig. 4.6b; Madrid et al. 2000; Pedrotta 2005). At the bottom of this small valley there was a water source that could have attracted different mammals such as guanacos (periodic drinkers; Puig 1986). In this locality, six rock structures have been identified. Two of them are located at high altitudes with very good visibility to the adjacent plains (Pedrotta 2005), and these structures could have functioned as viewing sites, since from them it is possible to observe the location and movement of potential prey. Two other structures are located on the slope of the hill. Their function is not clear and it is not discarded that these were used as hunting blinds, although their shape is closed and different to the structures that have been recorded in Patagonia. In the case of Lobería 1 site, this place could have also functioned as a hunting field. There, the junction between a creek and some isolated rocks could have functioned as a suitable place for the obtaining of guanacos (Fig. 4.6c).

Spears and darts, bola stones, bow and arrows are the main weapon systems identified in this research. This archaeological evidence coincided with the first descriptions of the indigenous weapons by the Europeans that arrived to La Plata River in the first half of XVIth century (e.g., Fernández de Oviedo y Valdés 1851–1855; Ramírez, in Madero 1902). Spears are weapons that are used at distances no greater than 10 m, that is, a maximum approach of hunters to the prey is needed. According to different authors, the shooting range with bola stones can reach between 25 and 64 m (González 1953; Musters 1997). The use of bow and arrow give more precision, speed, and distance. For example, Gusinde (1986) mentions that the Selk´nam and Haush from Tierra del Fuego could reach up to 170 m distance with the bow. Métraux (1949) indicates that the Guayakí could reach a target at 91 m. Métraux (1949) and Lane (1959) synthesize the information on the efficiency of the indigenous arrows but they mention that they do not exceed 30 m. However, the penetration of the dart is better, specifically for large prey. Then, unless accompanied by changes in hunting strategies (e.g., corralling), the bow and arrow is not as effective for large prey, although it is for medium and small. Maintaining the dart and bola stones systems and adding bow and arrows allowed a more flexible strategy against demographic changes of large animals (Tomka 2013). In this context, the bow and arrow weapon system was advantageous because it allows more precision and speed shooting, as well as a greater distance to the prey. Also, the bow and arrow have been demonstrated to suit longer trip times, more shots per trip, and targeting of small prey (Yu 2006). Individual hunting would have been easier with this kind of weapon, although it could have been combined with cooperative strategies.

4.7 Conclusion

We identified three major weapon systems used during the Late Holocene in the southeastern Pampas: bola stones, spears and darts, and bow and arrows. These weapons were recovered in all the sites presented here, both for the initial (Calera, Nutria Mansa 1, and Empalme Querandíes 1) and final Late Holocene (Hangar). One of the changes that are observed between the initial and the final moments of this period is a predominance of bola stones in the initial stage and an extended use of the arrows toward later moments. This indicates not only changes in the weapon systems but also in the subsistence, mobility, and social relationships of the Pampas groups in the moments previous to the Spanish Conquest. The hunting strategies mentioned in this chapter have been documented historically and archaeologically for the Pampas. Moreover, many of these places and weapon systems (e.g., bola stones) continued being used by indigenous and *gauchos* in historical moments, even after the introduction of the horse (González 1953; Sánchez Labrador 1936; Ferrer and Pedrotta 2006). Finally, traditional knowledge and practices related to landscape use are central elements when discussing hunting strategies. We hope that the future studies allow us to discuss these topics in greater depth.

Acknowledgements Financial support for this project was granted by the Agencia Nacional de Promoción Científica y Tecnológica (PICT 2008-0430, 2014-2070, 2015-0235, 2015-2777, and 2017-1969) and Universidad Nacional de La Plata (11/N885). The INCUAPA-CONICET provided institutional support.

References

Álvarez MC (2009) Análisis de los restos faunísticos del sitio Calera (Sierras Bayas, partido de Olavarría). Un aporte a su funcionalidad a través del estudio de los mamíferos. Relaciones de la Sociedad Argentina de Antropología 34:53–73

Álvarez MC (2014) Subsistence patterns during the Holocene in the Interserrana area (pampean region, Argentina): evaluating intensification in resource exploitation. J Anthropol Archaeol 34:54–65. https://doi.org/10.1016/j.aa.2014.01.0030378-4165

Álvarez MC, Messineo PG, Kaufmann CA (2017) Guanaco bone piles from the Pampas region (Argentina) and its implications for hunter-gatherers subsistence. Hunter Gatherer Research 3(2):289–321. https://doi.org/10.3828/hgr.2017.14

Arenas P (2003) Etnografía y alimentación entre los Toba-Ñachilamole#ek y Wichí-Lhuku'tas del Chaco Central (Argentina). Latín Grafica S. R. L, Buenos Aires

Aschero CA (1975) Ensayo para una clasificación morfológica de artefactos líticos. Informe presentado al CONICET (Unpublished manuscript).

Aschero CA (1983) Registro de códigos para atributos descriptivos aplicados a artefactos líticos. Informe presentado al CONICET (Unpublished manuscript).

Bank MS, Sarno RJ, Franklin WL (2003) Spatial distribution of guanaco mating sites in southern Chile: conservation implications. Biol Cons 112:427–434. https://doi.org/10.1016/s0006-320 7(02)00342-7

Barros MP, Messineo PG (2007) Producción lítica en el sitio Calera (Sierras Bayas, Región Pampeana). In: Bayón C, Pupio A, González MI, Flegenheimer N, Frère M (eds) Arqueología en las Pampas, Tomo II. Sociedad Argentina de Antropología, Buenos Aires, pp 721–744

Barros MP, Heider G, Álvarez MC, Kaufmann C, Bellinzoni J (2018) First results of the hunter-gatherer weapon system studies in the middle basin of the Salado creek (Pampas Region, Argentina). J Lithic Stud 5(2). https://doi.org/10.2218/jls.2785

Bayón C, Flegenheimer N, Pupio A (2006) Planes sociales en el abastecimiento y traslado de roca en la Pampa Bonaerense en el Holoceno temprano y tardío. Relaciones de la Sociedad Argentina de Antropología XXXI:19–45

Belardi JB, Carballo Marina F, Madrid P, Barrientos G, Campan P (2017) Late Holocene guanaco hunting grounds in southern Patagonia: blinds, tactics and differential landscape use. Antiquity 91(357):718–731. https://doi.org/10.15184/aqy.2017.20

Binford L (1978) Nunamiut etnoarchaeology. Academic Press, New York

Bonnat FG, Mazzanti DL, Donadei Corada JP, Quintana CA (2019) Análisis comparativo de los sistemas de armas arrojadizas en la secuencia arqueológica de Tandilia oriental (Buenos Aires, Argentina). In: Laguens A, Bonnin M, Marconetto B (Comp) XX Congreso Nacional de Arqueología Argentina: 50 años de Arqueologías. Universidad Nacional de Córdoba, Córdoba, pp 1435–1438

Bonomo M (2005) Costeando las Llanuras. Arqueología del Litoral Marítimo Pampeano. Colección de Tesis Doctorales. Sociedad Argentina de Antropología, Buenos Aires

Bonomo M (2013a) Comentario 3 en "Sedentarismos y complejidad prehispánicos en América del Sur" de Tom Dillehay. Intersecciones en Antropología 14:58–60

Bonomo M (2013b) Reanálisis de la colección de Samuel Lothrop procedente del Delta del Paraná. Relaciones de la Sociedad Argentina de Antropología 38(1):169–198

Bonomo M, León DC, Turnes L, Apolinaire E (2008) Nuevas investigaciones sobre la ocupación prehispánica de la costa pampeana en el Holoceno tardío: el sitio arqueológico Claromecó 1 (partido de Tres Arroyos, provincia de Buenos Aires). Intersecciones en Antropología 9:25–41

Borrero LA (1990) Fuego-Patagonian bone assemblages and the problem of communal guanaco hunting. In: Davis LB, Reeves BO (eds) Hunter of the recent past. Unwin Hyman, London, pp 373–399

Burgos JJ (1968) El clima de la provincia de Buenos Aires en relación con la vegetación natural y el suelo. In: Cabrera AL (ed) Flora de la Provincia de Buenos Aires. Colección Científica del INTA, Buenos Aires, pp 33–99

Cabrera AL, Willink AW (1980) Biogeografía de América Latina. Serie de Biología. Monografía Nro. 13. Secretaría General de la Organización de los Estados Americanos. Programa Regional de Desarrollo Científico y Tecnológico. Washington, DC.

Catella L, Manassero M, Moirano J, Oliva F (2013) Nuevos aportes al estudio del aprovisionamiento de cuarcita en la Región Pampeana, Argentina. Cuadernos del Instituto Nacional de Antropología y Pensamiento Latinoamericano-Series Especiales 1(2):200–215

Churchill SC (1993) Weapon technology, prey size selection, and hunting methods in modern hunter-gatherers, implications for hunting in the Palaeolithic and Mesolithic. Archaeol Pap Am Anthropol Assoc 4:11–24. https://doi.org/10.1525/ap3a.1993.4.1.11

Claraz G (2008) Viaje al río Chubut. Aspectos naturalísticos y etnológicos (1865–1866). Continente, Buenos Aires

Colantonio MJ, Pal N, Messineo PG (2016) Análisis de las prácticas de producción y uso de los materiales líticos del sitio Empalme Querandíes 1 (cuenca superior del Arroyo Tapalqué, Región Pampeana). Arqueología 22(2):243–268

Colombo M (2011) El área de abastecimiento de las ortocuarcitas del grupo Sierras Bayas y las posibles técnicas para su obtención entre los cazadores y recolectores pampeanos. Intersecciones en Antropología 12:155–166

Discamps E, Costamagno S (2015) Improving mortality profile analysis in zooarchaeology: a revised zoning for ternary diagrams. J Archaeol Sci 58:62–76. https://doi.org/10.1016/j.jas.2015.03.021

Driver, JC (1995) Social hunting and multiple predations. In: Campana DV (ed) Before farming: hunter-gatherer society and subsistence. MASCA research papers in science and archaeology. University of Pennsylvania Press, Pennsylvania, pp 23–38

Fernández de Oviedo y Valdés G (1851–1855) [1546–1547] Historia general y natural de las Indias, Islas y Tierra Firme del Mar Océano, Libro XXIII. Guarania, Asunción del Paraguay

Ferrer E, Pedrotta V (2006) Los corrales de piedra: comercio y asentamientos aborígenes en las sierras de Tandil, Azul y Olavarría. Crecer Ediciones, Tandil

Flegenheimer N (2004) Las ocupaciones de la transición Pleistoceno-Holoceno: una visión sobre las investigaciones en los últimos 20 años en la Región pampeana. In: Beovide L, Barreto I, Curbelo C (eds) Actas del X Congreso Nacional de Arqueología Uruguaya. CD, Montevideo, pp 26–29

Franklin WF (1983) Contrasting socioecologies of South America's wild camelids: the vicuña and the guanaco. In: Mares MA, Genoways NN (eds) Mammalian biology in South America, vol 6. Special publication series. University of Pittsburgh, Pittsburgh, pp 573–629

Franklin WL (2011) Family Camelide (Camels). In: Wilson DE, Mittermeier RA (eds) Handbook of the mammals of the world, vol 2. Hoofed mammals. Lynx Ediciones, Barcelona, pp 206–246

Frison GC (2004) Survival by hunting: human predators and animal prey. University of California Press, Berkeley

Fritz M (1985) Population dynamics and preliminary estimates of the harvestatibility of the Patagonian Guanaco. Unpublished Master's thesis. Iowa State University, Iowa

Frontini R (2013) Aprovechamiento faunístico en entornos acuáticos del sudoeste bonaerense durante el Holoceno (6900–700 años AP). Relaciones de la Sociedad Argentina de Antropología XXXVIII(2):493–519

González AR (1953) La boleadora. Sus áreas de dispersión y tipos. Revista del Museo de la Universidad Eva Perón 4(NS):133–292

Goñi RA, Cassiodoro G, Flores Coni J, Dellepiane JM, Agnolín A, Guichon R (2016) Estrategias de caza y movilidad: parapetos del sitio K116 (meseta del Strobel, Santa Cruz). In: Mena F (ed) Arqueología de la Patagonia: de Mar a Mar. Ediciones CIEP, Ñire Negro Ediciones, Andros Impresores, Santiago, pp 441–449

Grayson DK (1984) Quantitative zooarchaeology: Topics in the analysis of archaeological Faunas. Academic Press, Orlando

Gusinde M (1986) Los indios de Tierra del Fuego, 1. CAEA-CONICET, Buenos Aires

Hughes SS (1998) Getting to the point: evolutionary change in prehistoric weaponry. J Archaeol Method Theory 5:345–408. https://doi.org/10.1007/BF02428421

Isla FI (1995) Holocene coastal evolution in Buenos Aires Province, Argentina. Quaternary of South America and Antarctic Peninsula 11:297–321

Kaufmann CA (2009) Estructura de Edad y Sexo en Lama guanicoe (Guanaco). Estudios Actualísticos y Arqueológicos en Pampa y Patagonia. Sociedad Argentina de Antropología, Buenos Aires

Kaufmann CA, Álvarez MC (2007) La arqueofauna del sitio Calera (Sierras Bayas, Región Pampeana): un abordaje a los aspectos rituales del descarte de huesos de animales. In: Bayón C, Pupio A, González MI, Flegenheimer N, Frère M (eds) Arqueología en las Pampas, Tomo II. Sociedad Argentina de Antropología, Buenos Aires, pp 745–764

Kelly L (2001) A case of ritual feasting at the Cahia site. In: Dietler M, Hayden B (eds) Feasts. Archaeological and ethnographic perspectives on food, politics, and power. Smithsonian Institution Press, Washington, DC, pp 334–367

Klein R, Cruz-Uribe K (1984) The analysis of animal bones from archaeological sites. Chicago University Press, Chicago

Lane F (1959) Arcos e flechas dos índios kaingáng do estado de São Paulo. Revista do Museu Paulista 11:71–97

López Castro N (2017) Transformaciones sociales en el agro pampeano en las últimas décadas: concentración, persistencia de la producción familiar y su potencial aporte a un nuevo modelo de desarrollo. In: De Martinelli G, Moreno M (eds) Agronegocios en la Región Pampeana: Tensiones por la Imposición de un Modelo Concentrador. Universidad Nacional de Quilmes, Bernal, pp 259–289

Lyman RL (2008) Quantitative paleozoology. Cambridge Manuals in Archaeology, Cambridge University Press, Cambridge

Madero E (1902) Historia del Puerto de Buenos Aires. La Nación, Buenos Aires

Madrazo G (1979) Los cazadores a larga distancia de la Región Pampeana. Prehistoria Bonaerense, 12–67

Madrid P, Politis GG, March R, Bonomo M (2002) Arqueología microrregional en el sudeste de la Región Pampeana Argentina: el curso del río Quequén Salado. Relaciones de la Sociedad Argentina de Antropología 27:327–355

Madrid P, Politis GG, Poiré D (2000) Pinturas rupestres y estructuras de piedra en las Sierras de Curicó (extremo noroccidental de Tandilia, Región Pampeana. Intersecciones en Antropología 1:35–53

Mange E, Serna A, Miotti L, Vargas Gariglio J, Béguelin M, Prates L (2019) Ocupaciones prehispánicas en las zonas áridas del centro y sur de Río Negro. In: Prates L, Mange E, Serna A (Eds) Los Pueblos Nómades de Río Negro. Fondo Editorial Rionegrino, Viedma (in press)

Marean CW (1997) Hunter-gatherer foraging strategies in tropical grasslands: Model building and testing in the East African Middle and Later Stone Age. J Anthropol Archaeol 16:189–225

Martínez G (2006) Arqueología del curso medio del río Quequén Grande: estado actual y aportes a la arqueología de la región pampeana. Relaciones de la Sociedad Argentina de Antropología XXXI:249–275

Martínez G, Gutiérrez MA (2004) Tendencias en la explotación humana de la fauna durante el Pleistoceno final y Holoceno en la Región Pampeana (Argentina). In Mengoni Goñalons G (ed) Zooarchaeology of South America. BAR international series 1298, Oxford, pp 81–98

Martínez G, Prates L, Flensborg G, Stoessel L, Alcaráz AP, Bayala P (2015) Radiocarbon trends in the Pampean region (Argentina). Biases and demographic patterns during the final Late Pleistocene and Holocene. Quatern Int 356:89–110. https://doi.org/10.1016/j.quaint.2014.09.056

Martínez JG (2003) Ocupaciones humanas tempranas y tecnología de caza en la microrregión de Antofagasta de la Sierra (10000–7000 AP). Unpublished Doctoral thesis. Universidad Nacional de Tucumán, San Miguel de Tucumán

Matarrese A (2015) Tecnología lítica entre los cazadores-recolectores pampeanos: los artefactos formatizados por picado y abrasión y modificados por uso en el área Interserrana Bonaerense. Unpublished Doctoral thesis. Universidad Nacional de La Plata, La Plata

Mazzanti DL (2006) La constitución de territorios sociales durante el Holoceno tardío. El caso de las sierras de Tandilia, Argentina. Relaciones de la Sociedad Argentina de Antropología XXXI:277–300

Mazzanti DL (2007) Arqueología de las relaciones interétnicas posconquista en las sierras de Tandilia. Unpublished Doctoral thesis. Universidad de Buenos Aires, Buenos Aires

Mazzanti DL, Colobig MM, Zucol FA, Martínez GA, Porto López J, Brea M, Passeggi E, Soria JL, Quintana C, Puente V (2010) Investigaciones arqueológicas en el sitio 1 de la Localidad Lobería I. In: Berón MA, Luna L, Bonomo M, Montalvo C, Aranda C, Carrera Aizpitarte M (eds) Mamül Mapu. Pasado y Presente desde la Arqueología Pampeana, Tomo II. Libros del Espinillo, Ayacucho, pp 99–114

Messineo PG, Álvarez MC, Favier Dubois C, Steffan P, Colantonio MJ (2013) Estado de avance de las investigaciones arqueológicas en el sitio Empalme Querandíes 1 (centro de la subregión Pampa Húmeda, provincia de Buenos Aires). Comechingonia, Revista de Arqueología 17:123–148

Messineo PG, Barros MP (2015) Lithic raw materials and modes of exploitation in quarries and workshops from the center of the Pampean grassland of Argentina. Lithic Technol 40(1):3–20

Métraux A (1949) Weapons. In: Steward J (ed) Handbook of South American Indians, Bull. 143, vol 5. Smithsonian Institution, Bureau of American Ethnology, Washington, DC, pp 229–263

Musters GC (1997) Vida entre los Patagones. El Elefante Blanco, Buenos Aires

Okumura MM, Araujo AGM (2015) Contributions to the dart versus arrow debate: New data from Holocene projectile points from Southeastern and Southern Brazil. Anais da Academia Brasileira de Ciências 87(4):2349–2373

Pastor S, Pautassi E, Rivero D (2005) Los sistemas de armas de las comunidades agroalfareras de Córdoba: una aproximación arqueológica y experimental. Actas del XIII Congreso Nacional de Arqueología Argentina, Tomo IV. Córdoba, pp 253–265

Pauketat TR, Kelly LS, Fritz GJ, Lopinot NH, Elias S, Hargrave E (2002) The residues of feasting and public ritual at Early Cahokia. Am Antiq 67(2):257–279

Pedrotta V (2005) Las sociedades indígenas de la provincia de Buenos Aires entre los siglos XVI y XIX. Unpublished PhD's thesis. Universidad Nacional de La Plata, La Plata

Politis GG (2008) The Pampas and Campos of South America. In: Silverman H, Isbell WH (eds) The handbook of South American archaeology. Springer, New York, pp 235–260

Politis GG, Angrizani R (2008) Communal hunting, butchering and sharing patterns among the Tropical Forest hunter-gatherers of South America. Lessons for archaeology. Paper presented at the World Archaeological Congress, Dublin

Politis GG, Messineo PG, Kaufmann CA, Barros MP, Álvarez MC, Di Prado V, Scalice R (2005) Persistencia ritual entre cazadores-recolectores de la llanura pampeana. Boletín de Arqueología PUCP 9:67–90

Politis GG, Pedrotta V (2006) Recursos faunísticos de subsistencia en el Este de la región pampeana durante el Holoceno tardío: el caso del guanaco (*Lama guanicoe*). Relaciones de la Sociedad Argentina de Antropología XXXI:301–336

Politis GG, Salemme M (1990) Pre-hispanic mammal exploitation and hunting strategies in the eastern Pampas subregion of Argentina. In: Davis L, Reeves B (eds) Hunters of the recent past one world archaeology 15. One World Archaeology Series, Unwin Hyman, London, pp 353–372

Prieto A (2000) Vegetational history of the late glacial-Holocene transition in the grasslands of Eastern Argentina. Palaeogeogr Palaeoclimatol Palaeoecol 157:167–188. https://doi.org/10.1016/S0031-0182(99)00163-7

Puig S (1986) Ecología poblacional del guanaco (*Lama guanicoe*, Camelidae, Artiodactyla) en la Reserva Provincial de La Payunia (Mendoza). Unpublished Doctoral thesis. Universidad de Buenos Aires, Buenos Aires

Quintana CA, Mazzanti DL (2001) Selección y aprovechamiento de recursos faunísticos. In: Mazzanti DL, Quintana CA (eds) Cueva Tixi: Cazadores y Recolectores de las Sierras de Tandilia Oriental. 1 Geología, Paleontología y Zooarqueología. Laboratorio de Arqueología, UNMdP, Mar del Plata, pp 181–209.

Quintana CA, Mazzanti DL (2014) La emergencia de la diversificación de la caza en las sierras de Tandilia oriental durante el Holoceno Tardío final. Comechingonia, Revista de Arqueología 18:41–64

Railey JA (2010) Reduced mobility or the bow and arrow? Another look at "expedient" technologies and sedentism. Am Antiq 75(2):259–286

Ratto N (2003) Estrategias de caza y propiedades del registro arqueológico en la Puna de Chaschuil (Departamento de Tinogasta, Catamarca, Argentina). Unpublished Doctoral thesis. Universidad de Buenos Aires, Buenos Aires.

Ratto N, Orgaz M (2002–2004) Cacería comunal de camélidos en los Andes: el caso de las macroestructuras La Lampaya y El Matambre en Cazadero Grande (Chaschuil, dpto. Tinogasta, Catamarca, Argentina). Arqueología 12:75–97

Sánchez Labrador J (1936) Los Indios Pampas, Puelches, Patagones. Viau y Zona, Buenos Aires

Scheifler NA (2014) Zooarqueología de los pequeños vertebrados del sitio Calera (cuenca superior del Arroyo Tapalqué, provincia de Buenos Aires). Aprovechamiento humano, depredación por aves rapaces y acción hídrica. Relaciones de la Sociedad Argentina de Antropología XXXIX(1):145–173

Shott MJ (1997) Stones and shafts redux: the metric discrimination of chipped-stone dart and arrow points. Am Antiq 62:86–101

Soriano A (1992) Río de La Plata grasslands. In: Coupland RT (ed) Ecosystems of the world. Natural grasslands. Elsevier, Amsterdam, 367–407

Stiner MC (1994) Honor among thieves: A zooarchaeological study of neanderthal ecology. Princeton University Press, Princeton

Thomas DH (1978) Arrowheads and atlatl darts: how the stones got the shaft. Am Antiq 43:461–472

Tomka SA (2013) The adoption of the bow and arrow: a model based on experimental performance characteristics. Am Antiq 78(3):553–569

Tonni EP, Cione AL, Figini AJ (1999) Predominance of arid climates indicated by mammals in the pampas of Argentina during the Late Pleistocene and Holocene. Palaeogeography, Palaeoclimatology, Palaeoecology 147:257–281. https://doi.org/10.1016/S0031-0182(98)00140-0

Valverde F, Martucci M (2004) Estudio tecno-tipológico de las puntas de proyectil del sitio Cueva El Abra (provincia de Buenos Aires). In: Martínez G, Gutiérrez M, Curtoni R, Berón M, Madrid P (eds) Aproximaciones Contemporáneas a la Arqueología Pampeana. Universidad Nacional del Centro de la Provincia de Buenos Aires, Olavarría, pp 419–434

Vecchi R (2016) Materias primas líticas de bolas de boleadora del sector bonaerense de la región Pampeana. Relaciones de la Sociedad Argentina de Antropología XLI(1):191–215

Weaver TD, Boyko RH, Steele TE (2011) Cross-platform program for likelihood-based statistical comparisons of mortality profiles on a triangular graph. J Archaeol Sci 38:2420–2423

Yu PL (2006) From atlatl to bow and arrow. Implicating projectile technology in changing systems of Hunter-gatherer mobility. In: Seller F, Greaves R, Yu PL (eds) Archaeology and ethnoarchaeology of mobility. University Press of Florida, Florida, pp 201–220

Chapter 5
Fish Capture Strategies in Atlantic Littoral of Monte Hermoso District (Pampean Region Argentina) During Middle Holocene

Romina Frontini, Cristina Bayón, and Rodrigo Vecchi

Abstract Pampean hunter-gatherers marine fish capture strategies during the Middle Holocene are analyzed based on fish remains, lithic technology, paleoenvironmental reconstructions and fish ethology. Barrio Las Dunas site and El Americano II site archaeofaunistic record evidence of the exploitation of estuarine-dependent fish species: *Pogonias cromis* and *Micropogonias furnieri*. Lithic assemblages comprise scarce lithic weights corresponding to net weights and line weights that evidence the use of two fishing gears. It is concluded that the study sector was a hunter-gatherers preferential place for marine resource acquisition due to its palaeoenvironmental conditions.

Keywords Fishing · Middle Holocene · Hunter gatherers · *Pogonias cromis* · *Micropogonias furnieri* · Lithic weights · Atlantic coast

5.1 Introduction

In the Pampa region, the earliest evidence of Atlantic coastal resources exploitation is recorded in a restricted area of 4 km in the Monte Hermoso district, Southwestern Buenos Aires Province. Four archaeological sites dated to the middle Holocene (sensu Walker et al. 2012) were identified therein: La Olla site (Bayón and Politis 2014; León et al. 2017); Monte Hermoso 1 site (Bayón and Politis 1996; Bayón et al. 2011; Politis et al. 2009), Barrio Las Dunas site (Bayón et al. 2012), El Americano II site (Frontini et al. 2019a; Frontini and Bayón 2017; Vecchi et al. 2014). These sites yielded evidence of the supply of immediately available raw materials and the exploitation of sea fauna including Otariids, Cetaceans, fish and invertebrates. Among vertebrates, Otariids were the preferential prey exploited (León et al. 2017);

R. Frontini (✉) · R. Vecchi
CONICET, Departamento de Humanidades, Universidad Nacional del Sur, Bahía Blanca, Argentina

C. Bayón
Departamento de Humanidades, Universidad Nacional del Sur, Bahía Blanca, Argentina

© Springer Nature Switzerland AG 2021
J. B. Belardi et al. (eds.), *Ancient Hunting Strategies in Southern South America*,
The Latin American Studies Book Series,
https://doi.org/10.1007/978-3-030-61187-3_5

but fish comprised a relevant portion of the diet of hunter-gatherers (Bayón et al. 2012; Frontini and Bayón 2017). Isotopic information from human remains from Monte Hermoso 1 site, also provided evidence toward the significant consumption of marine resources (Politis et al. 2009).

The capture of marine fish is an unpredictable activity, due to the low visibility of the prey and the changing ocean conditions (Acheson 1981). Fishing gear is not a simple adaptation of the terrestrial equipment, but specific technology has been developed for fish capture (Von Brandt 2005). Fish capture requires particular abilities and expert knowledge. Expert knowledge includes how to operate and maintain the equipment and also a comprehensive understanding of ethology, reproductive cycle, predators, feeding behavior, habitats and migration behavior from fish (Acheson 1981, Morales Muñiz 2008). Finally, a familiarity with the ocean is required (Acheson 1981; Von Brandt 2005; Morales Muñiz 2008; Wheeler and Jones 1989).

The aim of this paper is to analyze Pampean hunter-gatherers marine fish capture strategies during the Middle Holocene. Different lines of evidence will be assessed, including fish remains, lithic technology, paleoenvironmental reconstructions and fish ethology.

5.2 Study Sector: Monte Hermoso District

5.2.1 Environmental Settings

The coast of Monte Hermoso district (Buenos Aires Province, Argentina) (Fig. 5.1) presents sandy beaches of *ca.* 270 m width (Cavallotto 2008; Fernández et al. 2003). The beaches suffer from direct wave action that is characterized by a mesotidal regime with semidiurnal tides with a mean amplitude of 2.40 m (Servicio de Hidrografía Naval 2019). Toward the continent there are mobile and semi-fixed sand dunes that form the Southern Sand Barrier (sensu Isla et al. 2001). The climate is temperate, with warm summers, cold winters and moderate autumns and springs (Campo et al. 2004). Environmentally, the study area is a broad transitional zone where ecotonal flora and fauna converge. Wildlife biodiversity in the past was higher, and included *Lama guanicoe* (guanaco), *Ozotoceros bezoarticus* (Pampas deer), *Pseudalopex* sp., *Dolichotis patachonica*, *Conepatus* sp., *Lagostomus maximus*, among many others (Deschamps 2005). Phytogeographically, the southwest of Buenos Aires Province corresponds to the intersection of the Southern District of the Pampean Province with the District of Caldén of the Province of Espinal, forming a large transitional area (Cabrera 1968).

Shoreline was affected by regressions and transgressions of sea due to fluctuations of sea level along time (Cavallotto 2008; Fernández et al. 2003). The current coast was established at ca. 4000 years BP (Aramayo et al. 2005; Quattrocchio et al. 2008) while the sand dunes were formed earlier, by the middle Holocene (Blasi et al. 2013; Isla et al. 2001; Quattrocchio et al. 2008).

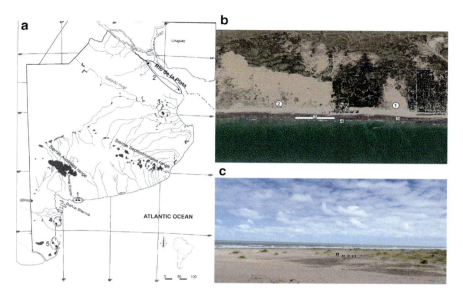

Fig. 5.1 Location map with sites mentioned in the paper. **a** Buenos Aires Province; 1 = Study sector; 2 = Río de la Plata Estuary sector; 3 = Salado River Depression sector; 4 = Río Colorado sector; 5 = Bahía San Blas sector. **b** Aerial view of Monte Hermoso district; 1 = Barrio Las Dunas archaeological site; 2 = El Americano II archaeological site; 3 = Monte Hermoso 1 archaeological site; 4 = La Olla archaeological site; 5 = El Cangrejal paleontological site. **c** Landscape view of El Americano II site

5.2.2 Fish Species Composition

The fish species in the Atlantic littoral from Buenos Aires province correspond to Argentine Zoogeographical province (Balech and Ehrlich 2008). It is characterized by warm and temperate water from Brazilian currents that flow up to meet with the Malvinas current, in the convergence of subtropical and subantarctic. It can be divided into two districts: the Uruguayan district to the north, and the Río Negro District to the south. The limit of both occurs at 38° South (Díaz de Astarloa 2016), and the studied sites are in this limit.

At present, study sector is inhabited by fish species with the ability to adapt to a wide range of salinity, temperature and depth including *Acanthistius patachonicus* (patagonian sea bass), *Anchoa marinii* (anchovy), *Galeorhinus galeus* (school shark), *Micropogonias furnieri* (white croaker), *Pogonias cromis* (black drum), *Mugil liza* (grey mullet), *Mustelus schmitti* (narrownose smooth hound), *Myliobatis goodei* (southern eagle ray), *Paralichthys patagonicus* (Patagonian flounder), *Paralichthys orbignyanus* (mire flounder), *Porichthys porosissimus* (toad fish), *Odontesthes simitti* (silver side), among many others (Díaz de Astarloa 2016).

Currently, both artisanal fisheries and sport fishing are relevant in Monte Hermoso. Small-scale fisheries have a key role as an economic activity for vulnerable social sectors, including 200 families that own *ca.* 100 fishing vessels (Barbero et al. 2017). The artisanal fishermen of Monte Hermoso have their origins in the 1940s driven mainly by shark fishing (Lascano 1989). Sport fishing is usually performed from the sandy beach.

5.3 Materials and Methods

The archaeological faunal and technological remains included in this study come from Barrio Las Dunas site (BLD; 38° 59´ S - 61° 20´ W) and El Americano II site (EAII; 38° 59´ S - 61° 22´ W) (Fig. 5.1); that were previously reported (Bayón et al. 2012; Frontini and Bayón 2017; Frontini et al. 2019b; Vecchi et al. 2014). These sites are located in the first line of sand dunes from the Atlantic littoral in Monte Hermoso resort and are at a distance of *ca.* 3 km from one another (Fig. 5.1) (Bayón et al. 2012; Frontini et al. 2019b; Vecchi et al. 2014). Both sites are surface assemblages that were left exposed due to sand dune erosion (Bayón et al. 2012; Vecchi et al. 2014). EAII comprises also an assemblage that comes from an excavated area of consolidated sands. Calibrated radiocarbon dates from Barrio Las Dunas site and El Americano II site suggest contemporaneous occupations between 7700 and 7500 years BP (Bayón et al. 2012; Frontini and Bayón 2017; Vecchi et al. 2014). Two radiocarbon dates on *Pogonias cromis* yielded 7561 to 7714 calibrated years BP (BLD lab code: AA93961; d13C 12.7%; Bayón et al. 2012) and 7674 to 7513 calibrated years BP (EAII lab code: AA111718: BP d13C-13.5%o; this work). They provided taxon dates that allowed to confirm the antiquity of fish exploitation in the study area. BLD and EAII were interpreted as multiple activities sites where Otariids and marine fish were butchered and processed for consumption and where stone tools were manufactured and used.

Barrio Las Dunas archaeofaunistic assemblage comprises 994 specimens, including Otariids (*Arctocephalus australis* and *Otaria flavescens*) and fish (%NISP 79%) with evidence of human butchering (Bayón et al. 2012). The site yielded 912 artifacts including tools, cores and flakes (Bayón et al. 2012). Lithic assemblage is composed of 35 tools, 62 cores, 789 flakes, 18 pecked stone and 8 nodules. Chipped and grinding artifacts are present but flaked artifacts are more abundant. Diverse raw materials were used although basandesite rocks and chert are more abundant (81%) followed by quartzite rocks (14%), and orthoquartzite from the Sierras Bayas Group (Bayón et al. 2012).

El Americano II archaeofaunistic assemblage comprises 1599 specimens, including terrestrial mammals (*Lama guanicoe*), marine mammals (*Arctocephalus australis* and *Otaria flavescens*) and fish. Fish remains 30% of the total assemblage. The site yielded 7288 artifacts, including 56 tools, 289 cores, 6611 flakes/debris, 282 nodules and 50 indeterminate fragments. Raw materials in order of frequency are represented by basandesite (65%), quartzite rocks (23%), chert (3.5%), muddy sandstone (2.2%). Toolstones were used both for chipped and pecking/grinding tools and different raw materials were chosen for each technology (Vecchi 2011).

Middle Holocene hunter-gatherers fishing strategies will be assessed considering:

1. *Fish remains*: Taxonomic identification of fish remains were performed using reference collections hosted at Departamento de Humanidades, Universidad Nacional del Sur (Bahía Blanca, Argentina) and at Fundación Azara—Universidad Maimónides (Buenos Aires, Argentina). Quantification units included Number of Identified Specimens per Taxon (NISP); Minimum Number of Skeletal Elements (MNE); Minimum Number of Individuals (MNI) (Grayson 1984; Klein and Cruz Uribe 1984; Lyman 2008). In order to estimate fish size, published morphometric estimation models for represented species were used (Volpedo 2001). Whenever there was not a model, estimation of fish size was assessed by comparisons to reference collections.

2. *Lithic Technology*: The technological and typological classification proposed by Aschero (1975, 1983) and Aschero and Hocsman (2004) was followed. Tools, cores, flakes, debris, nodules were the artifactual categories considered. Processes of lithic production were analyzed according to artifact type. Fragmentation stages, presence/absence of cortex and lithometric features such as length, width and thickness were recorded. We also consider raw material use taking into account regional lithic resources, raw material availability, provenience and transport distances (Bayón et al. 2006, Catella et al. 2013; Flegenheimer et al. 2015; Messineo and Barros 2015).

3. *Palaeoenvironmental characteristics* of the study area for the middle Holocene will be assessed based on published information (Aramayo et al. 2005; Blasi et al. 2013; Cuadrado and Blasi 2017; Quattrocchio et al. 2008) considering the following topics: location, chronology; proxy and interpretation.

4. *Fish species biological information*: Fish species represented in archaeological assemblages provide key information about capture strategies because size, behavior and habitat of fish are limiting factors of the kinds of technological strategies that can be used for capture (Belcher 1994; Butler 1994; Coutts 1975). Ethology and biology of fish species was synthetized based on published data considering habitat, feeding and reproduction habits and modern capture techniques used for each.

5.4 Results

5.4.1 Fish Remains

Barrio Las Dunas site yielded a total of 780 marine fish identified specimens. The ichthyofaunal assemblage shows a low taxonomic diversity as only Sciaenidae family was identified. The best represented species is *Pogonias cromis* (black drum) (Table 5.1). Anatomical elements represented comprised mainly vertebrae, fins, and pterygiophores (Table 5.2 and Fig. 5.2a, c). While scarce cranial elements were represented, neither otoliths nor scales were recovered. MNI was 6 and it was obtained based on the first pterygiophore from the anal fin. The size of black drum was estimated based on comparisons to individuals from the reference collection with known

Table 5.1 NISP, %NISP, MNE and MNI of the fish assemblages from Barrio Las Dunas site and El Americano II site (excavated and surface assemblages)

Taxa	BLD				EAII							
					Excavated assemblage				Surface assemblage			
	NISP	%NISP	MNE	MNI	NISP	%NISP	MNE	MNI	NISP	%NISP	MNE	MNI
Teleostei	211	27.05	n/a	n/a	129	38.17	n/a	n/a	47	33.10	40	n/a
Sciaenidae*	0	0.00	0	0	57	16.86	n/a	n/a	20	14.08	15	n/a
*Pogonias cromis**	568	72.82	416	6	103	30.47	100	3	33	23.24	32	1
*Micropogonias funieri**	1	0.13	1	1	40	11.83	35	9	37	26.06	30	2
Mugil sp.	0	0.00	0	0	9	2.66	9	1	0	0.00		0
Gennidens barbus	0	0.00	0	0	0	0.00	0	0	1	0.70	1	1
Odontesthes sp.	0	0.00	0	0	0	0.00	0	0	2	1.41	2	1
Myliobatidae	0	0.00	0	0	0	0.00	0	0	2	1.41	2	1
Total	**780**			**7**	**338**			**13**	**142**			**6**

References: * = show the species with evidence of human butchering; n/a = not applicable

Table 5.2 *Pogonias cromis* and *Micropogonias furnieri* anatomical element representation in Barrio Las Dunas site (BLD) and in El Americano II site (EAII)

Anatomical element	Pogonias cromis						Micropogonias furnieri					
	BLD		EA II				BLD		EAII			
			Exc.		Surf.				Exc.		Surf.	
	NISP	NME	NISP	NME	NISP	NME	NISP	MNE	NISP	MNE	NISP	MNE
Supraoccipital	0	0	3	3	0	0	0	0	0	0	0	0
Basioccipital	0	0	2	2	1	1	0	0	9	9	3	3
Epioccipital	0	0	0	0	0	0	0	0	1	1	0	0
Parasphenoid	0	0	0	0	1	1	0	0	0	0	0	0
Upper pharyngeal bone	0	0	1	1	2	2	0	0	2	2	0	0
Lower pharyngeal bone	0	0	1	1	2	2	1	1	2	2	0	0
Pharyngeal bone	14	5	1	1	0	0	0	0	5	2	0	0
Pharyngeal teeth	215	215	0	0	8	0	0	0	0	0	0	0
Premaxilla	1	1	0	0	0	0	0	0	0	0	1	1
Dentary	0	0	0	0	0	0	0	0	0	0	1	1
Otolith	0	0	0	0	0	0	0	0	0	0	1	1
Opercular	14	4	0	0	0	0	0	0	0	0	1	1
Quadrate	1	1	0	0	0	0	0	0	0	0	0	0
Suborbital	2	2	0	0	0	0	0	0	0	0	0	0
Hyomandibular	0	0	4	4	0	0	0	0	0	0	0	0
Cleithrum	0	0	1	1	1	1	0	0	1	1	0	0
Urohyal	0	0	0	0	1	1	0	0	0	0	0	0
Ceratohyal	0	0	4	4	0	0	0	0	0	0	0	0

(continued)

Table 5.2 (continued)

Anatomical element	Pogonias cromis						Micropogonias furnieri					
	BLD		EA II				BLD		EAII			
			Exc.		Surf.				Exc.		Surf.	
	NISP	NME	NISP	NME	NISP	NME	NISP	MNE	NISP	MNE	NISP	MNE
Epihyal	0	0	2	2	0	0	0	0	0	0	0	0
Coracoids	0	0	0	0	0	0	0	0	1	1	0	0
Ribs	13	7	0	0	0	0	0	0	0	0	0	0
Branchiostegal ray	0	0	0	0	0	0	0	0	1	1	0	0
Atlas	0	0	0	0	1	1	0	0	0	0	2	2
1st precaudal vertebra	0	0	2	2	1	1	0	0	1	1	4	3
2nd precaudal vertebra	0	0	1	1	0	0	0	0	0	0	0	0
Precaudal vertebra	3	3	6	6	5	5	0	0	3	3	12	10
Caudal vertebra	4	4	2	2	0	0	0	0	4	4	12	9
Penultimate vertebra	0	0	2	2	0	0	0	0	0	0	0	0
Vertebra (indeterminate)	15	15	5	3	5	4	0	0	10	8	0	0
Undifferentiated spines	138	80	0	0	0	0	0	0	0	0	0	0
Hypural	0	0	6	6	0	0	0	0	0	0	0	0
1st pterygiophore from dorsal fin	6	6	0	0	0	0	0	0	0	0	0	0
1st pterygiophore from anal fin	4	4	1	1	0	1	0	0	0	0	0	0

(continued)

Table 5.2 (continued)

Anatomical element	Pogonias cromis						Micropogonias furnieri					
	BLD		EA II				BLD		EAII			
			Exc.		Surf.				Exc.		Surf.	
	NISP	NME	NISP	NME	NISP	NME	NISP	MNE	NISP	MNE	NISP	MNE
Pterygiophore	35	30	1	1	1	1	0	0	0	0	0	0
Fin ray	69	35	5	6	1	2	0	0	0	0	0	0
1st anal fin ray	0	0	2	1	3	3	0	0	0	0	0	0
1st dorsal fin ray	4	4	0	0	0	0	0	0	0	0	0	0
Scales	0	0	51	51	1	1	0	0	0	0	0	0
TOTAL	538	416	103	101	34	26	1	1	40	35	37	31

References: Exc. = excavated assemblage; Surf. = surface assemblage

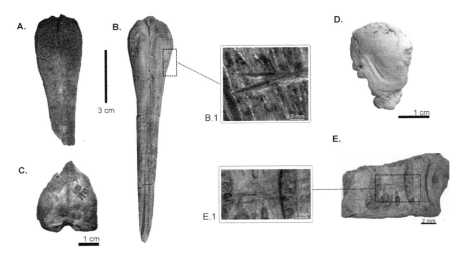

Fig. 5.2 Archaeological fish remains from BLD and EAII sites. **a** = BLD/1895 *Pogonias cromis* first pterygiophore of the anal fin; **b** = EAII-509/13, *Pogonias cromis* pterygiophore first pterygiophore of the anal fin with cut marks (detail at b.1); **c** = BLD/1924, *Pogonias cromis* first spine of the second dorsal fin; **d** = EAII-224/16, *Micropogonias furnieri* otolith; **e** = EAII-110/16, *Micropogonias furnieri* vertebra with cut marks (detail at e.1)

weight at death. It was inferred that archaeological individuals weighed between 15 and 20 kg (Bayón et al. 2012; Sergio Bogan, Fundación Félix Azara, Universidad Maimónides, 2011, personal communication). Cut marks were registered in the lower section of two fin rays and were interpreted as primary butchering (Bayón et al. 2012; Stewart and Gifford-González 1994). The 27% of specimens showed thermal alteration; it affected vertebrae, rays, pharyngeal plate, pterygiophores and ribs (Bayón et al. 2012).

Ichthyofaunal assemblage from El Americano II site comprises 480 remains representing Sciaenidae, Mugilidae, Myliobatidae, Ariidae and Atherinopsidae families (Table 5.1). In the excavated assemblage, *Pogonias cromis* (black drum) and *Micropogonias furnieri* (white croaker) are the best represented species. Also, low anatomical representation of *Mugil* sp. was registered (Table 5.1). *Pogonias cromis* specimens include cranial and postcranial anatomical elements (Table 5.2). Also, cycloids scales are abundant in the assemblage ($N = 51$). Analysis on seasonality and age at death of individuals based on scales were not possible due to their fragmented edges. The MNI obtained for *Pogonias cromis* is 3 and it was estimated based on three left hyomandibular and three left ceratohyal. *Micropogonias furnieri* anatomical elements include vertebrae, basioccipital and cleithrum; the best represented element is basioccipital; based on it the MNI was estimated in 9. Regarding anthropic evidences cut marks were registered in the lower sector of a 1st pterygiophore of the anal fin of black drum (EAII 509/13), that was interpreted as consequence of primary butchering (following Stewart and Gifford-González 1994) (Fig. 5.2b.1).

In the surface assemblage marine fish representation includes five taxa (Table 5.1); *Pogonias cromis* and *Micropogonias furnieri* are the best represented. Black drum anatomical elements include pharyngeal plates, precaudal and caudal vertebrae, urohyal, first pterygiophore of anal fin and rays (Table 5.2). MNI obtained was 1. White croaker anatomical elements include basioccipital, premaxilla, dentary, otolith, cleithrum, first precaudal vertebrae, caudal and precaudal vertebrae (Table 5.2); the MNI of 3 was estimated based on basioccipital. White croaker size was estimated based on the size of the otolith (EAII 224/16; Fig. 5.2d) following the morphometric model proposed by Volpedo (2001). The obtained Total Length is 43 cm. Cut marks were registered in Sciaenidae and *Micropogonias furnieri*. A Sciaenidae fin ray (EAII 24/16) and a spine (EAII 23/16) show cut marks interpreted as primary butchering. A white croaker vertebra (EAII 110/16; Fig. 5.2e.1) shows two cut marks placed transversely to the vertebra centrum; they are interpreted as derived from primary butchering.

The other fish Families are represented in a very low proportion with a maximum of 2 anatomical elements each (Table 5.1). Neither *Gennidens barbus*, *Odonthestes* sp. nor Myliobatidae specimens show evidence of human butchering.

5.4.2 Lithic Technology

In this section only the artefacts related to fishing technology will be analyzed. The surface assemblage from EAII site, yielded three stone tools related to fishing gear. EAII/6256 (Fig. 5.3a) is a quartzite fluvial cobble with subrectangular shape and four notches located on the long sides of the pebble, at opposite sides; it presents a cortex in both faces. Its length is 125 mm, its width is 64 mm, its thickness is 43 mm and its weight is 648 g. It has been interpreted as a lithic weight. EAII/6280 (Fig. 5.3b) is a flat chert pebble with rounded trapezoidal shape. It was modified by bipolar technique forming a concave platform and shoulders. Notches are chipped on the short sides. It is 36 mm long, 43 mm wide, 18 mm thick and it weighs 23 g. As in the previous one, we propose it was a lithic weight. EAII/6295 (Fig. 5.3c) is a flat chert pebble with rounded rectangular shape. It was chipped by bipolar technique and notches are flaked on the short sides, besides a partial groove was carved in a pebble face. Its length is 35.88 mm, its width is 24.4 mm, its thickness is 18 mm and its weight is 23 g. Based on morphological similarities with elements found in coastal contexts of other regions (see discussion below) we propose that it was a lithic weight.

BLD site yielded two relevant stone tools for this study: artifact BLD/418 is a quartzite cobble with rounded cube shape; cortex is present. Two notches on opposite sides were flaked and natural depressions of the surface were aligned. Its length is 98 mm, its width 80 mm, its thickness 43 mm and its weight is 515 g. It is a multiple functional artifact: anvil, handstone and we also propose it was used as a lithic weight (Fig. 5.3d). The tool BLD/781 is a complete, triangular, stemless medium

Fig. 5.3 Lithic weights were recovered in El Americano II site and in Barrio Las Dunas site. A = EAII/6256; B = EAII/6280; C = EAII/6295; D = BLD/418

size projectile point retouched bifacially in a flake of chert. Its length is 36 mm, its width is 43 mm, its thickness is 18 mm and its weight is 6 g.

5.4.3 Palaeoenvironmental Background of Study Area

Several palaeoenvironmental analyses were carried out in the study sector, using different proxies (Aramayo et al. 2005; Blasi et al. 2013; Cuadrado and Blasi 2017; Fontana 2004; Quattrocchio et al. 2008; Zavala et al. 1992). Table 5.3 shows a

5 Fish Capture Strategies in Atlantic Littoral …

Table 5.3 Synthesis of palaeoenvironmental reconstructions from the study sector for the middle Holocene

Site name/location	Calibrated radiocarbon years BP	Proxies	Palaeoenvironmental inference
El Cangrejal Palaeontological site (38° 59´ S; 61° 19´ W)	7288–7515 7637–7796	Paleontological remains: remnants and burrows of crab *Chasmagnathus granulata* Dana Ostracods and diatoms species. Sediments	Transitional palaeoenvironment, either estuarine or lagoon (Aramayo et al. 2005)
La Olla 1-4 archaeological site (38° 59´ S; 61° 21´ W)	7936–7672 7618–7155	Stratigraphic and sedimentological analysis (LO4)	Tidal flat associated with an estuary (Blasi et al. 2013)
		Pollen and Diatoms (LO1)	Halophytic plant community in a coastal environment (Fontana 2004)
Monte Hermoso 1 archaeological site (38° 59´ S; 61° 20´ to 61° 21´ W)	7530–7667 7203–7425	Sediments	Interdunal lakes with some marine influence (Zavala et al. 1992) Presence of microbial matts (Cuadrado and Blasi 2017)
		Pollen	Psammophytic herbaceous plan community (characteristic of coastal dunes) Interdune ponds with a slight marine influence. Local humid conditions (Quattrochio et al. 2008)

synthesis of available palaeoenvironmental reconstructions. For the period of first human occupations (from *ca.* 7900 calibrated years BP), the different studies are coincident in that a palaeo-estuary was developed in the sector. It is worth mentioning that El Cangrejal palaeontological site (Fig. 5.1), distant *ca.* 300 m from BLD archaeological site toward the South, evidence of a transitional environment either estuarine or lagoon (Aramayo et al. 2005). Also, La Olla 4 site sedimentological analyses yielded a sub-tidal environment, with embrionary dunes located toward the continent (Blasi et al. 2013). La Olla site is located 1000 m from El Americano II site (Fig. 5.1).

5.4.4 Fish Species Biological Information

Pogonias cromis (black drum) and *Micropogonias furnieri* (white croaker) belong to Sciaenidae Family (Nelson 2006). The Sciaenidae Family joins 70 genera with about 270 species. It comprises carnivora fish, widely distributed in warm coastal waters from the Atlantic and Pacific Oceans. Most Sciaenidae fish inhabit open sandy and muddy seabeds (Militelli et al. 2013; Nelson 2006).

Black drum is the largest member of the Sciaenidae family. It is distributed along the western Atlantic coast from the Bay of Fundy, Canada (44° North), to San Matías gulf, Argentina (42° South) (Nelson 2006; Urteaga and Perrotta 2001). Black drum can quickly adapt to a wide range of salinities and usually inhabits sandy and muddy beds in coastal waters, especially in areas with large river runoffs. Juveniles often enter estuaries. The average total length is 50 cm, with a maximum informed total length of 170 cm. The maximum weight recorded is 51.3 kg (Urteaga and Perrotta 2001). It is a long-living species, with low natural mortality rates (Urteaga and Perrotta 2001). It feeds mainly on crustaceans, mollusks and small fish. Feeding behavior of black drum includes the ingestion and crushing of crabs and other prey with its robust pharyngeal teeth. Also, it is usual that, while looking for food, black drums "stand on heads" waving their caudal fins aloft, making them visible for some distance (Cate and Evans 1994). This behavior was observed in Monte Hermoso resort in the early 1950s and was used by modern fishermen to locate black drums (Natalia Sánchez, Director of the Museo de Ciencias Naturales de Monte Hermoso V. Di Martino, personal communication, 2018).

White croaker inhabits Southeast Atlantic Ocean, from Veracruz, Mexico (19° North) to San Jorge Gulf, Argentina (47° South) (Cousseau and Perrotta 2013). It is an estuarine spawner associated with the bottom salinity front (Carozza et al. 1997; Cousseau and Perrotta 2013; Militelli et al. 2013). Its average total length varies between 30 and 50 cm; the maximum Total Length registered in the Bonaerian coast is 63 cm. The average weight is 5 kg (Cousseau and Perrotta 2013). It is a long-living species, with a maximum age of 39 years old. It shows a generalist-opportunistic feeding behavior. It feeds on bottom organisms by sediment biting or burrowing (Hozbor and García de la Rosa 2000). Its diet includes polychaetes, bivalves, snails and shrimps; in a lesser extent, it also feeds of small fish as anchovy (*Anchoa marinii*; *Engraulis anchoita*) (Cousseau and Perrotta 2013; Figuereido and Vieria 1998).

5.5 Discussion

In order to analyze fish exploitation strategies during the Middle Holocene in Pampean region, we assume that some capture techniques and fishing gears would have been more appropriate than others for the capture of certain fish species due to the behavior of fish species and the environmental conditions. The behavioral characteristics of fish species include the social habits (gregarious *vs.* solitary), migration habits, reproductive habits and feeding behaviors. These aspects would condition the availability of the resource, the catch quantity and the seasonality of obtention, among others. Environments are directly related to fish species habitats; also, daily or seasonal fluctuations (i.e. tidal; storms) might have had a great influence in the visibility and predictability of the resource. Capture strategies include the use of technological implements specially designed for fish capture as well as versatile tools and may include weapons and facilities (sensu Oswalt 1976). Regarding weapons, which function is to kill the prey, they comprise leisters, spears, arrows and bows and harpoons. These weapons for aquatic resources generally have tips with multiple barbs for holding the fish during capture, making it difficult to pull itself out and escape. Facilities used for obtaining food in aquatic environments include weirs, basket traps, blinds, lures, poisons, nets and lines among many others (Oswalt 1976). Facilities differentiate from weapons in that they are aimed to reduce the prey movement rather than to kill it. Thus, the capture risks are reduced and also it is possible to acquire several individuals at the same time (Oswalt 1976).

In Barrio Las Dunas site and El Americano II site fish capture is evidenced by fish remains and scant lithic artefacts related to fish capture strategies. *Pogonias cromis* and *Micropogonias furnieri* are the two fish species that show clear evidence of human processing (i.e. cut marks and burning); both species are estuarine-dependent, that is to say they spend part of their lives in estuarine environments, for breeding or feeding. In BLD site black drum is the only fish species represented, while in EAII site, white croaker predominates. Regarding the abundance of fish species in the analyzed sites, the obtained MNI for *Pogonias cromis* is higher in BLD site ($n = 6$) than in EAII site (NMI $= 4$). *Micropogonias furnieri* is highly represented in EAII site, by an estimated MNI of 9 in excavated assemblage and an MNI of 3 individuals in the surface assemblage; in BLD site only one anatomical element was recovered representing an MNI of one individual.

Palaeoenvironmental conditions inferred along the study area for the period of the sites occupation (see Table 5.3) allow to propose that the study sector would have been a suitable scenario for black drum and white croaker capture. At 300 m. southern Barrio Las Dunas site, based on the presence of paleo-crab borrows and crab remains, the existence of a palaeo-estuary was inferred (Aramayo et al. 2005). During the middle Holocene, the availability of *Pogonias cromis* in this sector was probably related to the feeding habits of this species that includes crabs. The black drums feeding behavior of "standing on heads" could have been used by huntergatherers to locate them. The predominance of this species in the BLD assemblage is interpreted as directly related to its availability in this sector.

Toward 1000 m southeastern from El Americano II site, in La Olla 4 site, palaeoenvironmental analysis identified a sector of a tidal flat that was connected to an early/mid-Holocene estuary (Blasi et al. 2013: 1557; Table 3). The tidal flat formed in protected sectors with absence of strong wave action and with measurable tidal range; in estuaries it was subjected to fluctuations in the salinity. It constituted a transitional zone between the land and the sea, where the sea biotic elements predominated (Reise 1985). There was a high biomass of invertebrates and benthic microalgae were important; these elements offered ample food for fish, especially juveniles that in this environment were safe from their marine predators (Reise 1985). Generally, a wide diversity of fish species inhabits tidal flats; regarding Sciaenidae, during the spawning period, there are dense aggregations of adult individuals in shallow, nearshore water. According to the paleoenvironment inference, this sector would constitute a preferential area for the capture of fish.

The estimated Total Length of a white croaker individual from EAII based on an otolith is 43 cm. Taken into account that the first maturity period is established from 33 cm TL for this species (Macchi et al. 1996), archaeological specimens correspond to an adult individual. Its capture could have been related to the reproductive behavior of this species that breeds along a wide strip of coastline, in shallow waters and grouped in dense schools in certain seasons. In the study sector, the breeding period extends from spring to summer (September to March); being a predictable and vulnerable resource at this time of the year (Carozza et al. 2004).

The low representation of fish individuals in the archaeofaunal assemblages could be related to taphonomic effects or to human action. Detailed taphonomic studies evidence the low integrity of the BLD and EAII assemblages, considering the high dynamic of the deposition environment (sand dunes) (Frontini et al. 2019a). Nevertheless, different taphonomic effects prevailed in each assemblage. For BLD site, based on the high fragmentation and on the prevalence of advance weathering stages (stage 3 and 4) it was inferred that the archaefaunistic assemblages suffered from long-time exposition or re-expositions in sand dunes surface (Frontini et al. 2019a). In EAII site, the most represented taphonomic effect is sand abrasion, affecting 70% of fish assemblage (Frontini et al. 2019b). Signs of subaerial affectation show low stages (stage 1–2). Based on the low weathering stages represented, and on the recovery of *Pogonias cromis* vertebrae in anatomical position, it was proposed a fast burial of archaeological assemblage, allowing a good preservation including small fish anatomical elements (Frontini et al. 2019a, b). Also, this situation could be linked to the higher diversity of fish assemblage compared with BLD sites. According to these taphonomic effects, that may have produced a bias in the original anthropic assemblages, no accurate inferences on fish catch quantity could be discussed (Colley 1987).

Regarding lithic technology five artifacts are relevant for discussing fish capture strategies. In the analyzed archaeological assemblages a solely lithic projectile point (BLD 781) was recovered. Morphological features suggest that it would not have been appropriate for fish capture as it lacks barbs. In BLD and EAII based on their shape and on the presence of a notch or groove, four tools were defined as stone weights. According to the morphology and the position of the notches, they can be associated with different fishing gears (Torres 2009). Artifacts EAII 6256 and BLD 418 weight *ca.* 500 g each, and show notches knapped on the longest side that create a niche (depression) in each side of the pebbles; these features would be suitable for cord or rope accommodation. Based on these attributes they were interpreted as net weights. Artifacts EAII 6280 and EAII 6295 were manufactured on small pebbles; their weight is *ca.* 20 g. They present notches on the short side of the pebble that were flaked by bipolar technique. They were interpreted as line weights. These four artifacts are simple regarding their morphological and technological features but provide indirect evidence of the use of two different fishing gears: nets and lines, that are complex artifacts, sensu Oswalt (1976).

Fishing nets are formed by several techno-units including the net, net weights and handles (Oswalt 1976). The manufacture and the use of fishing nets may require the investment of high energy and in some cases the joint work of several people; the proper location for its use are open sandy beaches (Morales Muñiz 2008; Torres 2009). Ethnographic records show that nets are manufactured on perishable materials, including vegetable fibers, human hair, whale barbs and animal tendons (Morales Muñiz 2008; Oswalt 1976; Torres 2007). Regarding net weights, its weight and shape can vary according to the type of net (length, width, shape) and also according to their position in the net (Torres 2007); usually narrow cobbles were selected; with a weight that ranges between 300 and 1000 g. (Torres 2007). In the study case, the weight and thickness from analyzed nets weights are in the estimated mean range for this stone tool (Torres 2007). The tidal flat inferred in the nearby El Americano II site would have been a suitable location for fishing net use. Fishing nets capture multiple individuals and in the present are usually used to capture gregarious fish species, such as *Sciaenidae*. Current capture techniques for *Pogonias cromis* and *Micropogonias furnieri* correspond to trawl nets (Carozza et al. 1997).

Fishing lines are formed by different techno-units, including the line and a small weight; it can also include a bait (Oswalt 1976). The manufacture and use of fishing lines requires low technical investment and it can be operated by a solely individual (Torres 2007). It has a high versatility as it can be used in open beaches and rocky shores, allowing it to capture a great diversity of fish species (Morales Muñiz 2008; Torres 2007). Line weights are usually small, with a range of weight between 20 g. and 243 gr. Generally, narrow cobbles are selected for line weights manufacture (Torres 2007). Fishing lines are used to capture one individual at a time. Current fishing gear for white croakers includes fishing lines (Cousseau and Perrotta 2013).

Raw materials used in the lithic archaeological weights evidence the use of different rocks that were available at different distances from the archaeological sites. In Humid Pampa Subregion lithic resources are localized in Sierras Australes Range, Sierras Septentrionales Range, along the Atlantic coast and in small outcrops in the plains (Bayón et al. 1999; Bonomo 2005; Colombo 2011, 2013; Flegenheimer et al. 2015; Messineo and Barros 2015). In the neighboring sector of BLD site and EAII site pebbles and cobbles of Basandesite, Basalt, Rhyolite and Chert are available in the Atlantic coast (Bayón et al. 2012; Bonomo 2005, 2011; Frontini and Bayón 2017). Fluvial cobbles and pebbles of quartzite and quartz rocks are available in secondary deposits of the Sauce Grande River, within 20 km around the sites. Quartzites, Quartz, Rhyolite and Muddy Sandstone are available in the Sierras Australes Range within 60–100 km around sites (Bayón et al. 1999; Catella et al. 2013, Oliva and Barrientos 1988, Oliva and Moirano 1994). Finally Sierras Bayas Group Orthoquartzite (SBGO), Balcarce Formation Orthoquartzite (BFO), Chert, Silicified dolomite, Granite and Diabase were available at Sierras Septentrionales Range (Tandilia Range) within 350 km around sites (Colombo 2011, 2013; Flegenheimer et al. 2015; Messineo and Barros 2015; Vecchi 2011, among others) (Fig. 5.1). The raw materials used for lithic weights comprise a quartzite cobble obtained at

18 km from the site, a BFO artifact transported for 300 km, locally available raw materials available in the adjacent coast. This is concordant with different strategies applied in the acquisition of raw materials for other stone tools from sites (Bayón et al. 2012; Vecchi et al. 2014).

In synthesis, fish capture strategies in the Atlantic littoral from Southwestern Buenos Aires province during the middle Holocene include the capture of estuarine-dependent fish species using at least two fishing gears: nets and lines. Palaeoenvironmental conditions of this sector were accurate for marine resource acquisition.

The archaeological information of our study sector constitutes the evidence of the earliest fish capture strategies of hunter-gatherers in the Humid Pampa region. On the bases of the presence of cranial and postcranial bones from black drum and white croaker; it is proposed that fish individuals were transported whole to the sand dunes, where they were processed (Bayón et al. 2012; Frontini and Bayón 2017) Cut marks and thermal alteration suggest that butchering and cooking of fish occurred in the neighboring area of the capture location.

In Northern Patagonia region, evidence of middle Holocene marine fish exploitation is more intense (Cardillo et al. 2015; Favier Dubois and Scartascini 2012; Gómez Otero et al. 2014; Scartascini et al. 2009; Scartascini 2014). The archaeological remains include fish otoliths and bones, lithic weights and also weirs (Cardillo et al. 2015; Gómez Otero et al. 2014).

For the late Holocene the number of archaeological sites in Pampa region with evidence of capture and consumption of marine fish increased. The evidence from Salado River Depression shows the exploitation of *Pogonias cromis* together with the exploitation of fresh-water fish and other small-sized resources (González 2005; González et al. 2016). Capture technology includes net weights (González 2005). In the Río de la Plata Estuary there are around 5 archaeological sites with evidence of *Pogonias cromis* exploitation (Day Pilaría 2018; Paleo et al. 2002). It was proposed that the obtention of marine fish included the exploitation of mass death of this species (Politis and León 2010). In the Colorado River, the human exploitation of *Micropogonias furnieri* and *Pogonias cromis* is registered in the San Antonio site and in El Tigre site (Martínez 2017); for both sites, the lack of specific technology for fish capture was informed (Martínez 2017).

5.6 Conclusions

In the Pampean region, marine resources were relevant during the Middle Holocene, especially pinnipeds, and in less proportion, fish. The Monte Hermoso littoral was especially attractive to hunter-gatherers, due to the availability of marine resources including fish and tool stones. In the study case, the particular palaeoenvironmental conditions during the middle Holocene would have been the key attraction for fishing; this activity was performed with different fishing gear. Although the archaeological record is limited, the multidisciplinary approach yielded novel knowledge about ancient hunter-gatherers fish capture strategies.

Acknowledgements We are grateful to the Museo Municipal de Ciencias Naturales de Monte Hermoso V. Di Martino and the park rangers from the Reserva Natural Pehuén co-Monte Hermoso for permanent help in fieldwork. Mónica Salemme, Paula Escosteguy and Clara Scabuzzo read the first version of the manuscript and made valuable comments on it. Two anonymous reviewers made valuable comments that helped to improve the manuscript. Sergio Bogan from Fundación Félix Azara helped with taxonomic identification. The research was funded by grants Préstamo BID PICT 2015-0272; 2016-0368; PGI SECYT-UNS 24/I 266; PIP-112-201301-00362.

References

Acheson JM (1981) Anthropology of fishing. Annu Rev Anthropol 10:275–315

Aramayo SA, Gutierrez Tellez B, Schillizzi RA (2005) Sedimentologic and paleontologic study of the southeast coast of Buenos Aires province, Argentina: A late Pleistocene Holocene paleoenvironmental reconstruction. J S Am Earth Sci 20:65–71

Aschero C (1975) Ensayo para una Clasificación Morfológica de Artefactos Líticos aplicada a Estudios Tipológicos Comparativos. Informe presentado al CONICET, Buenos Aires

Aschero C (1983) Ensayo para una Clasificación Morfológica de Artefactos Líticos aplicada a Estudios Tipológicos Comparativos. Apéndices A-C. Buenos Aires: Cátedra de Ergología y Tecnología, Facultad de Filosofía y Humanidades, Universidad de Buenos Aires, unpublished

Aschero C, Hocsman S (2004) Revisando cuestiones tipológicas en torno a la clasificación de artefactos bifaciales. In: Acosta A, Loponte D, Ramos M (eds) Análisis lítico. Universidad Nacional de Luján, Luján, pp 7–25

Balech E, Ehrlich MD (2008) Esquema biogeográfico del Mar Argentino. Revista de Investigación y Desarrollo Pesquero 19:45–75

Barbero A, Noceti B, Cattáneo C (2017) Interacciones, conflictos y nuevas formas de gobernanza en el estuario de Bahía Blanca-Monte Hermoso. Presentation at XXXI ALAS Congress, Uruguay

Bayón C, Flegenheimer N, Pupio A (1999) Dime cómo eres y te diré de dónde vienes: la procedencia de rocas cuarcíticas en la Región Pampeana. Relaciones de la Sociedad Argentina de Antropología XXIV:187–232

Bayón C, Flegenheimer N, Pupio A (2006) Planes sociales en el abastecimiento y traslado de roca en la pampa bonaerense en el Holoceno temprano y tardío. Relaciones de la Sociedad Argentina de Antropología XXXI:19–45

Bayón C, Frontini R, Vecchi R (2012) Middle Holocene settlements on coastal dunes, southwest Buenos Aires Province, Argentina. Quatern Int 256:54–61

Bayón C, Manera T, Politis G, Aramayo S (2011) Following the tracks of the first South Americans. Evolution Education and Outreach 4:205–217

Bayón C, Politis G (1996) Estado actual de las investigaciones en el sitio Monte Hermoso 1, Provincia de Buenos Aires. Arqueología 6:83–115

Bayón C, Politis G (2014) The inter-tidal zone site of La Olla: early-middle Holocene human adaptation on the Pampean Coast of Argentina. In: Evans AM, Flatman JC, Flemming NC (eds) Prehistoric archaeology on the continental shelf. Springer, New York, pp 115–130

Belcher W (1994) Multiple approaches towards the reconstruction of fishing technology: net making and the Indus Valley Tradition. In: Kenoyer JM (ed) From sumer to Melluha: Contributions to the archaeology of Southwest and South Asia in Memory of George F. Dales. University of Wisconsin, Department of Anthropology, Madison, pp 129–142

Blasi A, Politis G, Bayón C (2013) Palaeoenvironmental reconstruction of La Olla, a Holocene archaeological site in the Pampean coast (Argentina). J Archaeol Sci 40:1554–1567

Bonomo M (2005) Costeando las llanuras: arqueología del litoral marítimo pampeano. Sociedad Argentina de Antropología, Buenos Aires

Bonomo M (2011) The use of the space in the Pampean Atlantic Coast and the adjacent plains (Argentina, South America): a comparative view. In: Bicho NF, Haws JA, Davis LG (eds) Trekking the shore: changing coastlines and antiquity of coastal settlement. Springer, New York, pp 333–353

Butler V (1994) Fish feeding behaviour and fish capture: the case for variation in Lapita fishing strategies. Archaeol Ocean 29(2):81–90

Cabrera A (1968) Vegetación de la provincia de Buenos Aires. Flora de la provincia de Buenos Aires. Colección científica 4(1):101–120

Campo AM, Capelli A, Diez P (2004) El clima del Suroeste bonaerense. EdiUNS, Bahía Blanca

Cardillo M, Scartascini F, Zangrando F (2015) Combining morphological and metric variations in the study of design and functionality in stone weights: a comparative approach from continental and insular Patagonia, Argentina. J Archaeol Sci Rep 4:578–587

Carozza CR, Cotrina CP, Cousseau MB (1997) Corvina Rubia. Informe Técnico del INIDEP 15:53–79

Carozza C, Lasta C, Ruarte C (2004) Corvina Rubia (Micropogonias furnieri). El mar argentino y sus recursos pesqueros 4:255–270

Cate AS, Evans I (1994) Taphonomic significance of the biomechanical fragmentation of live molluscan shell material by a bottom-feeding fish (Pogonias cromis) in Texas coastal bays. Palaios 9:254–274

Catella L, Manassero M, Moirano J, Oliva F (2013) Nuevos aportes al estudio del aprovisionamiento de cuarcita en la Región Pampeana, Argentina. Cuadernos del Instituto Nacional de Antropología y Pensamiento Latinoamericano (Series Especiales) 1(2):200–215

Cavallotto JL (2008) Geología y geomorfología de los ambientes costeros y marinos. Atlas de Sensibilidad Ambiental de la Costa y el Mar Argentino. http://atlas.ambiente.gov.ar/tematicas/mt_01/geologia.htm. Accessed 10 April 2011

Colley SM (1987) Fishing for Facts. Can We Reconstruct Fishing Methods from Archaeological Evidence? Australian Archaeology 24(1):16–26.

Colombo M (2011) El área de abastecimiento de las ortocuarcitas del grupo Sierras Bayas y las posibles técnicas para su obtención entre los cazadores y recolectores pampeanos. Intersecciones en Antropología 12:231–243

Colombo M (2013) Los cazadores recolectores pampeanos y sus rocas. La obtención de materias primas líticas vista desde las canteras arqueológicas del centro de Tandilia. La Plata: Facultad de Ciencias Naturales y museo, Universidad Nacional de La Plata, unpublished doctoral thesis

Cousseau B, Perrotta RG (2013) Peces marinos de Argentina Biología, distribución, pesca. Instituto Nacional de Investigación y Desarrollo Pesquero, Mar del Plata

Coutts PJF (1975) Marine fishing in archaeological perspective: techniques for determining fishing strategies. In: Casteel RW, Quimby GI (eds) Maritime adaptations of the Pacific. Mouton Press, The Hague, pp 265–306

Cuadrado DG, Blasi AM (2017) Reconocimiento de actividad microbiana en ambientes silicoclásticos actuales y en paleoambientes. Estudio comparativo para el establecimiento de análogos. Lat Am J Sedimentol Basin Anal 24(2):39–73

Day Pilaría F (2018) Gestión de los recursos faunísticos en sociedades cazadoras, recolectoras y pescadoras. Análisis arqueozoológico en sitios del litoral del Río de la Plata (partidos de Magdalena y Punta Indio, provincia de Buenos Aires). Facultad de Ciencias Naturales y Museo, Universidad Nacional de La Plata (La Plata, Argentina), unpublished doctoral thesis

Deschamps C (2005) Late Cenozoic mammal bio-chronostratigraphy in southwestern Buenos Aires Province, Argentina. Ameghiniana 42(4):733–750

Díaz de Astarloa JM (2016). Peces Marinos de la Costa Bonaerense. In: Athor J, Celsi C (eds) La Costa Atlántica de Buenos Aires Naturaleza y Patrimonio Cultural, Vázquez Mazzini, Buenos Aires, pp 399–431

Favier Dubois CM, Scartascini F (2012) Intensive fishery scenarios on the North Patagonian coast (Río Negro, Argentina) during the Mid-Holocene. Quatern Int 256(1):62–70

Fernández E, Caló J, Marcos A, Aldacou H (2003) Interrelación de los ambientes eólico y marino a través del análisis textural y mineralógico de las arenas de Monte Hermoso, Argentina. Revista Asociación Argentina de Sedimentología 10:151–161

Figuereido GM, Vieria JP (1998) Cronologia alimentar e dieta da corvina, *Micropogonias furnieri*, no estuário da Lagoa dos Patos, RS, Brasil. Atlântica 20:55–72

Flegenheimer N, Mazzia N, Weitzel C (2015) Landscape and rocks in the East-Central portion of the Tandilia range (Buenos Aires Province, Argentina). PaleoAmerica 1(2):163–180

Fontana S (2004) Holocene vegetation history and palaeoenvironmental conditions on the temperate Atlantic coast of Argentina, as inferred from multi-proxy lacustrine records. J Paleolimnol 34(4):445–469

Frontini R, Bayón C (2017) Use of marine resources (fauna and tool stones) in the southwest of Buenos Aires Province (Argentina) during the Middle and Late Holocene. In Mondini M, Muñoz AS, Fernández PM (eds), Zooarchaeology in the Neotropics: environmental diversity and human-animal interactions, Springer, New York, pp 25–46

Frontini R, Vecchi R, Bayón C (2019a) Procesos de formación de sitios del Holoceno Medio en el Litoral Atlántico Bonaerense. Implicancias para la reconstrucción de la subsistencia. V Congreso Nacional de Zooarqueología Argentina. Catamarca. Libro de resúmenes. Universidad Nacional de Catamarca, pp 86–87

Frontini R, Fernández-Jalvo Y, Pesquero-Fernández MD, Vecchi, RJ (2019b) Abrasion in archaeological fish bones from sand dunes: an experimental approach. Archaeol Anthropol Sci. https://doi.org/10.1007/s12520-019-00834-3

Gómez Otero J, Schuster V, Svoboda A (2014) Fish and plants: the "hidden" resources in the archaeological record of the North-central Patagonian coast (Argentina). Quatern Int 373:72–81

González MI (2005) Arqueología de alfareros, cazadores y pescadores pampeanos. Sociedad Argentina de Antropología, Buenos Aires

González MI, Escosteguy P, Frère MM (2016) Estudio ictioarqueológico y la presencia de corvina negra en La Guillerma 5 (Depresión del río Salado, provincia de Buenos Aires). Ponencia presentada en el III Encuentro Latinoamericano de Zooarqueología. Aracajú, Brasil

Grayson D (1984) Quantitativezooarchaeology: Topics in the analysis of archaeological faunas. Academic Press, Orlando

Hozbor NM, García de la Rosa SB (2000) Alimentación de juveniles de corvina rubia (Micropogonias furnieri) en la Laguna Costera Mar Chiquita (Buenos Aires, Argentina). Frente Marítimo 18:59–70

Isla FI, Cortizo L, Turno Orellano H (2001) Dinámica y Evolución de las Barreras Medanosas, Provincia de Buenos Aires, Argentina. Revista Brasileira de Geomorfologia 2:73–83

Klein R, Cruz-Uribe K (1984) The Analysis of Animal Bones from Archaeological Sites. Chicago University Press, Chicago

Lascano OJ (1989) Cien años de pesca costera en la Argentina. Informe FAO.INIDEP, Mar del Plata

León C, Gutiérrez MA, Politis G, Bayón MC (2017) Análisis faunístico del sitio arqueológico La Olla (Sectores 3 y 4), Costa Sudoeste del Litoral Atlántico Bonaerense. Relaciones de la Sociedad Argentina de Antropología XLII(1):107–131

Lyman RL (2008) Quantitative paleozoology. Cambridge University Press: United Kingdom

Macchi G, Acha ME, Lasta C (1996) Desove y fecundidad de la corvina rubia (*Micropogonias furnieri*) Desmarest, 1923 del estuario del Río de La Plata, Argentina. Boletín del Instituto Español de Oceanografía 12(2):99–113

Martínez G (ed) (2017) Arqueología de Cazadores-recolectores del curso inferior del Río Colorado (Provincia de Buenos Aires). Aportes al conocimiento de las ocupaciones humanas Pampeano-Patagónicas. INCUAPA-CONICET-UNICEN, Olavarría

Messineo PG, Barros MP (2015) Lithic raw materials and modes of exploitation in quarries and workshops from the center of the Pampean grassland of Argentina. Lithic Technology 40(1):3–20

Militelli MI, Rodríguez KA, Cortés F, Macchi GJ (2013) Influencia de los factores ambientales en el desove de los esciénidos en la zona costera de Buenos Aires, Argentina. Ciencias Marinas 39(1):55–68

Morales Muñiz A (2008) De los peces a las redes: las artes de pesca desde una perspectiva arqueoictiológica. Archaeobios 2:40–63

Nelson LS (2006) Fishes of the world. Wiley, New York

Oliva F, Barrientos G (1988) Laguna de Puan: Un potencial sitio de aprovisionamiento de materia prima lítica. In: Resúmenes de las ponencias científicas presentadas al IX Congreso Nacional de Arqueología Argentina. Instituto de Ciencias Antropológicas, Facultad de Filosofía y Letras, Universidad de Buenos Aires, Buenos Aires, pp 46–47

Oliva F, Moirano J (1994) Primer informe sobre aprovisionamiento primario de riolita en Sa. de la Ventana. In: Berón M, Politis G (eds), Arqueología Pampeana en la década de los '90. Museo de Historia Natural de San Rafael Mendoza/INCUAPA, San Rafael, pp 137–146

Oswalt WH (1976) An anthropological analysis of food-getting technology. Wiley, New York and London

Paleo MC, Paez MM, Pérez Meroni M (2002) Condiciones ambientales y ocupación humana durante el Holoceno tardío en el litoral fluvial bonaerense. In: Mazzanti DL, Berón M, Oliva F (eds) Del Mar a los Salitrales. Diez mil años de Historia Pampeana en el Umbral del Tercer Milenio. Universidad Nacional de Mar del Plata—SAA, Mar del Plata-Buenos Aires, pp 365–376

Politis G, León DC (2010) Patrones adaptativos de los cazadores-recolectores-pescadores de la margen occidental del Paraná Inferior-Plata. In: Cocco G, Feuillet Terzaghi MR (eds) Arqueología de cazadores-recolectores en la Cuenca del Plata. Centro de Estudios Hispanoamericanos, Santa Fé, pp 63–86

Politis G, Scabuzzo C, Tykot R (2009) An approach to pre-hispanic diets in the pampas during the early/middle Holocene. Int J Osteoarchaeol 19:266–280

Quattrocchio ME, Borromei AM, Deschanps CM, Grill SC, Zavala CA (2008) Landscape evolution and climate changes in the Late Pleistocene -Holocene, southern Pampa (Argentina): evidence from palynology, mammals and sedimentology. Quatern Int 181:123–138

Reise K (1985) Tidal flat ecology: an experimental approach to species interactions. Springer-Verlag, Berlin and New York

Scartascini, FL (2014) Arqueología de la pesca en la costa rionegrina. Patagonia Argentina. Facultad de Filosofía y Letras, Universidad de Buenos Aires (Buenos Aires, Argentina), unpublished doctoral thesis

Scartascini FL, Charo M, Volpedo A (2009) Caracterización de las estrategias de obtención de recursos ícticos a partir del análisis de otolitos. El caso de la costa norte del Golfo San Matías. In: Salemme M, Santiago F, Álvarez M, Piana E, Vázquez M, Mansur E (eds) Arqueología de Patagonia: una mirada desde el último confín. Utopías, Ushuaia, pp 845–852

Servicio de Hidrografía Naval (2019) Tablas de Marea. Departamento de Artes Gráficas del Servicio de Hidrografía Naval, Buenos Aires

Stewart KM, Gifford-González D (1994) An Ethnoarchaeological contribution to identifying hominid fish processing sites. J Archaeol Sci 21:237–248

Torres JA (2007) ¿Redes o líneas de pesca? El problema de la asignación morfofuncional de lo pesos líticos y sus implicancias en las tácticas de pesca de los grupos del extremo austral de Sudamérica. Magallania 35(1):53–70

Torres JA (2009) La pesca entre los cazadores recolectores terrestres de la Isla Grande de Tierra del Fuego, desde la prehistoria a tiempos etnográficos. Magallania 37(2):109–138

Urteaga JR, Perrotta RG (2001) Estudio preliminar de la edad, el crecimiento, área de distribución y pesca de la corvina negra, Pogonias cromis, en el litoral de la provincia de Buenos Aires. Informe Técnico del INIDEP, Buenos Aires

Vecchi R (2011). Bolas de boleadora en los grupos cazadores-recolectores de la pampa bonaerense. Buenos Aires: Facultad de Filosofía y Letras, Universidad de Buenos Aires, unpublished doctoral thesis

Vecchi R, Frontini R, Bayón C (2014) *Ocupaciones en las dunas del litoral atlántico del Sudoeste bonaerense: el sitio El Americano II*. Ponencia presentada en el VII Congreso de Arqueología de la Región Pampeana Argentina. Rosario, Argentina

Volpedo A (2001) *Estudio de la morfometría de las sagittae en poblaciones de sciaenidos marinos de aguas cálidas del Perú y aguas templado-frías de Argentina*. La Plata: Facultad de Ciencias Naturales y museo, Universidad Nacional de La Plata, unpublished doctoral thesis

Von Brandt A (2005) Fish catching methods of the world. Wiley-Blackwell, London

Walker MJ, Berkelhammer CM, Björck S, Cwynar LC, Fisher DA, Long AJ, Lowe JJ, Newnham RM, Rasmussen SO, Weiss H (2012) Formal subdivision of the Holocene Series/Epoch: a Discussion Paper by a Working Group of INTIMATE (Integration of ice-core, marine and terrestrial records) and the Subcommission on Quaternary Stratigraphy (International Commission on stratigraphy). J Quat Sci 27(7):649–659

Wheeler A, Jones AKG (1989) Fishes. Cambridge University Press, Cambridge

Zavala C, Grill S, Martínez D, Ortiz H, González R (1992) Análisis paleoambiental de depósitos cuaternarios. Sitio Paleoicnológico Monte Hermoso I, Provincia de Buenos Aires. In: Actas de las Terceras Jornadas Geológicas Bonaerenses. La Plata, pp 31–37

Chapter 6
The Introduction of the Bow and Arrow Across South America's Southern Threshold Between Food-Producing Societies and Hunter-Gatherers

Silvina Castro, Lucía Yebra, Valeria Cortegoso, Erik Marsh, Agustín Castillo, Agustina Rughini, María Victoria Fernández, and Raven Garvey

Abstract This study presents a discriminant analysis of projectile points ($n = 44$) from late Holocene contexts (~3100–400 cal BP) in the Argentine Andes (29–37° S). About two thousand years ago, the groups that inhabited the regions north and south of 34° S began divergent cultural histories. To the north, groups developed mixed economies that included domestic plants and animals. To the south, Patagonian hunters maintained their nomadic lifestyle until European contact. This study explores the geographic vectors and pace of the initial spread of the bow and arrow, if the bow replaced or coexisted with other weapon systems, and how these trends differed north and south of 34° S. We use Shott's formula to metrically distinguish darts and arrows. Current data suggest that the bow was an innovation in the central Andes that rapidly spread south along the Andes to around 29° S at 3500–3000 cal BP. At this point, the tempo slowed dramatically. It was adopted by groups at 32° S around 1300 cal BP. At 37° S it arrived shortly after 1000 cal BP. Over the next two to three centuries, it was rapidly adopted by more sedentary food-producing groups north of 34° S as well as more mobile hunter-gatherers to the south. There is no evidence the bow was ever abandoned once adopted, and except in the case of Patagonia, it seems to have replaced previous weapon systems. This speaks to its versatility regardless of ecology, economic system, or cultural preferences.

S. Castro (✉) · A. Castillo
Laboratorio de Paleoecología Humana, Facultad de Ciencias Exactas y Naturales, Universidad Nacional de Cuyo, Mendoza, Argentina

L. Yebra · V. Cortegoso · E. Marsh · A. Rughini
CONICET, Laboratorio de Paleoecología Humana, Facultad de Ciencias Exactas y Naturales, Universidad Nacional de Cuyo, Mendoza, Argentina

M. V. Fernández
CONICET, Instituto de Investigaciones en Diversidad Cultural y Procesos de Cambio, Universidad Nacional de Río Negro, Mendoza, Argentina

R. Garvey
Department of Anthropology, University of Michigan, Ann Arbor, MI, USA

© Springer Nature Switzerland AG 2021
J. B. Belardi et al. (eds.), *Ancient Hunting Strategies in Southern South America*,
The Latin American Studies Book Series,
https://doi.org/10.1007/978-3-030-61187-3_6

Keywords Projectile points · Bow and arrows · Weapon system · Argentine Andes

6.1 Introduction

Technological innovation has been a perennial topic in anthropological theory since the twentieth century, which has seen debate on the conditions that create innovation, the degree to which it spreads, and the possibility of independent invention. Many arguments have been based on theoretical assumptions and not strictly on material evidence. These proposals focus on the human capacity for innovation in general and can be baised against specific groups for innovation. These generalities are then projected onto the potential spread of technological characteristics. The earliest evolutionary schemes were based on inflection points in technological innovation: the bow and arrow are specifically one of the key elements that marks the step to the highest level of barbarism (Morgan 1877).

Lemonnier (1992: 6) explains that addressing technological possibilities tracks the conditions of change and continuity in material culture, whether due to endogenous invention or external borrowing. He argues that borrowing is very common in human history while endogenous innovation remain one of the most disconcerting questions in anthropology. Even though archaeologists infrequently deal with innovation explicitly, assumptions about technological knowledge underlie all explanations of technological change (Schiffer and Skibo 1987: 596).

Cultural ecology was the first broadly conceived attempt to explore the relationship between society, technology, and environment. This body of knowledge provided foundations for understanding the historical dimension of technological knowledge (Bettinger 1991; Richerson 1977) as well as demographic and evolutionary approaches to understanding and explaining technological change (Kelly 1995; Smith et al. 2014). Explaining behavioral shifts remains a challenge and the most important theoretical advances are accompanied by transdisciplinary perspectives: "encompassing theories are essential for understanding evolutionary processes, selection pressures, human development, and shared perceptions, tendencies, and strategies across societies" (Fuentes and Wiessner 2016: 3).

In both the Old and New Worlds, the Mesolithic and Archaic periods not only represent major changes in technology, but also set the stage for domestication; hence the emergence of these technological changes is central to our understanding of cultural change (Hayden 1981: 519). One of these major innovations was the bow and arrow, a recurrent hunting system that often co-occurs with a more diverse resource base. Its adoption and widespread use are tied to environmental conditions, demography, and economy that are broadly part of economic intensification that immediately precedes the Neolithic (Eerkens 1998).

In South America, there was a regional shift from foraging to agropastoralism ~3540–3120 cal BP in the Lake Titicaca Basin (Marsh 2015) as well as other parts of the central Andes. This change included the region's earliest use of ceramics and widespread use of the bow and arrow, though the earliest arrows are from contexts just prior to this shift (Klink and Aldenderfer 2005: 54). At this time, arrows are also found much farther south in northern Chile and Argentina (De Souza 2011; Hocsman 2010; Oliszewski et al. 2018; Ratto 2003). In contrast, in southern South America, Patagonian hunter-gatherers used spears throughout prehistory. They added bows to their hunting repertoire just a few centuries prior to European contact (Banegas et al. 2014; Charlin and González-José 2018). Here we use this continental-scale framework to assess changes in weapon systems along the southern Andes.

This paper presents a spatial and chronological analysis of latitudinal bands in the Andes that include that southernmost food-producing economies and northern-most hunter-gatherers at Spanish contact. In central western Argentina, ethnohistoric records describe an agropastoral economy for the sedentary Huarpes who lived north of the Diamante River (34° S) and the hunter-gatherer nomadic Puelches, among other groups, to the south (Michieli 1978, 1994; Prieto 1989; among others). The process that led to this scenario may have started two thousand years ago, when we have the earliest evidence for increasingly less mobile hunter-gatherers who used pottery (Durán et al. 2006; Marsh 2017). At Spanish contact, groups both north and south of 34° S used the bow and arrow but did not develop similar economies. Hence this is a case of the same weapon system being adopted by groups with divergent culture histories.

Archaeological research in the last decade has shown that the incorporation of domestic plants and animals did not follow simple temporal or geographic trajectories. For example, pottery was present as early as 2200 cal BP but there is no evidence that other elements of the "Neolithic package" accompanied this new technology (Marsh 2017). Isotopic and demographic changes suggest complex and fluid scenarios that require higher resolution chronologies (Barberena et al. 2017; Gil et al. 2009, 2014, 2018; Llano et al. 2017). For this reason, we track the introduction of the bow with artifacts closely associated with radiocarbon dates.

This study of the introduction of bow and arrow technology is part of a larger project that uses biogeography to understand the biological and cultural history in various regions in the southern Andes (Barberena 2013; Cortegoso et al. 2014). The Andes are the main topographic feature in the region and structure environmental variability on both sides of the mountains, along the continent's Arid Diagonal (de Porras and Maldonado 2018; Rojo et al. 2012; Zárate 2002). This major ecological barrier runs southward from the Atacama Desert in northern Chile and crosses the Andes in Mendoza into Patagonia in central and southern Argentina.

One way to contribute to this globally relevant topic is to refine the spatial and temporal distribution of the bow and arrow in the southern Andes. The goal of this paper is to present new, standardized data on the small but growing body of projectile points identified as arrow points that are reliably associated with radiocarbon dates (Castro et al. 2018). We use associated radiocarbon dates to build a chronology of the earliest introduction of the bow at a series of sites located between 29 and 37° S for ~3100–400 cal BP. This information can be used to evaluate the consequences of adopting this new weapon system on subsistence patterns and its synchronicity with other innovations in the region. Even though the literature emphasizes that hunting was a persistent activity throughout the late Holocene, the adoption of the bow and arrow could have had profound changes in the social and economic organization. This is the first research project in the region to approach this major technological change on a large spatial and temporal scale. This paper explores the geographic vectors and pace of the initial spread of the bow and arrow, its replacement or coexistence with other weapon systems, and how these trends differed north and south of 34° S.

6.2 Background

The bow and arrow is present in archaeological and ethnographic records from around the world in highly diverse environments, from the Arctic to deserts to jungles (Cattelain 1997). In most regions, the transition from using the atlatl and dart to the bow and arrow was a major shift that completely replaced atlatls, because the bow offers many advantages to hunters (Railey 2010). In North America, this change was associated with substantial social and economic changes (Bingham et al. 2013; Rorabaugh 2018). Group composition changes and the spread of the bow and arrow are generally associated with increasing complexity in sociopolitical organization and interaction (Simms 1994). In other regions, the bow was instead tied to groups breaking apart, since it permitted smaller family groups to be self-sufficient (Bettinger 2013). Hence the introduction of this revolutionary technology does not necessarily lead down paths toward social complexity. Groups may use the same technology in different ways and incorporate it into social and economic systems differently.

In South America, there are a variety of hypotheses for the replacement of one weapon system by another, but these are largely unable to explain late prehistoric cases where atlatls and darts persisted despite the bow and arrow having become widespread in neighboring regions (Cardillo and Alberti 2015; De Souza 2011; Owen 1998; Scheinsohn 2016). Part of this variability can be explained by migration, contact between groups, the form of cultural transmission, and learning new technologies.

In archaeology in general and especially in the Andes, the bow and arrow continues to be thought of as a major technological innovation associated with the beginning of economic diversification as well as more complex sociopolitical organization (Chamussy 2014; Kennett et al. 2013; Klink and Aldenderfer 2005). In terms of Andean economies from the last few millennia, the present paper study's area includes the southernmost example of this major shift, which was associated with increasingly broad diets. This highlights how this technology has the potential to modify some socioeconomic variables based on local ecological conditions. Generally speaking, understanding how people design weapons systems can inform us about how they use material culture to adapt to their natural and social environment (Eerkens 2003). The results presented below are discussed based on environmental and demographic trends, which are very different north and south of 34° S.

The study area was occupied by hunter-gatherers as early as the Pleistocene–Holocene transition. Evidence of these early populations extends to the eastern side of the Andes in areas where glaciers were retreating (Castro et al. 2013; García 2003;

García and Lagiglia 1998–1999; Marsh et al. 2016). Hunting and gathering was the only economic lifeway on either side of the Andes until that last two millennia of the Holocene (Méndez et al. 2015; Neme and Gil 2009). Around two thousand years ago, environmental changes and growing populations created the conditions for divergent histories north and south (Lagiglia 2001; Morales et al. 2009). To the north, groups had mixed economies that incorporated domestic plants and animals, following the central Andean pattern. To the south, Patagonian hunters maintained their nomadic lifestyle until European contact. The spatial limit was around the Diamante River, a major river flowing to the east out of the Andes, which might have been a buffer area where these two types of societies interacted (Durán et al. 2006). Archaeological data in this area from the last two thousand years reflects a complex mosaic of societies that depended to varying degrees on hunting, gathering, and horticulture (Llano et al. 2017). This transitional area was dynamic and there is evidence for complementary strategies and increasing evidence for the circulation of goods north and south of this river basin (Durán 2000; Nami et al. 2015; Cortegoso et al. 2019).

A series of technological innovations is associated with the major shift around two thousand years ago: horticulture, agriculture, pit houses, earth ovens for baking, and the earliest ceramics (Marsh 2017). The other key change at around this time was probably the bow and arrow (Durán et al. 2006), although it has not been investigated in detail. This weapon system is mentioned in early ethnographic accounts of the Huarpes in Mendoza. Metraux (1929: 13) describes a range of prey that were hunted with bows as tall as a man and arrows slightly longer than 80 cm with chert points. The only archaeological bow from Mendoza is 1073 mm in length (Lagiglia 1975), but its date is unknown. Longer bows shoot faster and more accurately (Bartram 1997: 340). Throughout the Americas, the only type of bow was the straight bow (Cattelain 1997). By European contact, bows had been adopted throughout the study area.

We recently conducted the first metric study of projectile points over a large region in the Argentine Andes (29–34° S), based on points associated with radiocarbon dates with medians spanning 3080–470 cal BP (Castro et al. 2018). This preliminary study established a baseline to be contrasted with larger samples from other regions. This paper builds on that baseline and incorporates projectile points from farther south at 37° S. The results allow us to begin to explore broad regional trends in the initial adoption and spread of the bow and arrow and the variable speeds with which it was adopted in different areas as well as possible vectors such as migrants, bows and arrows themselves, or the idea. Its spread may well have been tied to other contemporary interactions, for example, the trade networks that facilitated the movement of obsidian from southern Mendoza hundreds of kilometers from its source, as far north as 32° S (Cortegoso et al. 2019).

6.3 Environmental Setting

The study area includes high-altitude environments in the provinces of San Juan, Mendoza, and Neuquén (Fig. 6.1). The climate is arid to semiarid with summer

Fig. 6.1 Map of archaeological sites with projectile points. At the time of Spanish contact, the Diamante River (34° S) was reported to be the limit between sedentary food-producing groups and nomadic hunter-gatherers

rains in the valleys and winter snow in the mountains. The gradient of precipitation is irregular and decreases to the north, though in general annual rainfall is around 250 mm (Cabrera 1971). Mountain wetlands or *vegas* are very important because they offer rich summer pastures, especially for guanacos (*Lama guanicoe*), the largest mammals and most important prey in the Andes. In the northern and central part of the study area, lithic raw materials are principally chert and rhyolite; in the southern area, there is good availability of obsidian (Castro et al. 2014; Cortegoso et al. 2017; Cortegoso 2008; Durán et al. 2012).

Part of the study area falls within the Arid Diagonal, one of South America's major biogeographic barriers (de Porras and Maldonado 2018). In general, this area has low and unpredictable precipitation. The Southern Hemisphere Westerlies bring strong rains to the western side of the Andes and snow to the high Andes during the winter. During the summer, rains reach the eastern side of the Andes from systems originating in the Atlantic Ocean, around the equator, and off the Patagonia coast. During the warmer months, glaciers and snow melt create lush conditions in the mountains and in some valleys, which have microclimates during other parts of the year. Few of these higher areas can be occupied year-round because of winter snowfall. In the lowlands, permanent water is only available in the rivers flowing out of the Andes, creating a desert environment punctuated by linear east–west oases.

6.4 Sites and Phases

The projectile points analyzed in this study ($n = 44$) are from six sites (Table 6.1) at 29, 32, 34, and 37° S. The sample does not include many points because of strict inclusion criteria. We excluded points without associated radiocarbon dates as well as points with evidence that they had been reused as non-projectile tools or otherwise modified, which would have obscured the original dimensions.

The northernmost sites are the rock shelter Arq-18 and the surface site Arq-5 in the Las Taguas River valley (29° S, San Juan province). Occupations associated with projectile points in this study have median calibrated dates between 3080 and 510 cal BP (Lucero et al. 2017). By the occupation dated to 3080 cal BP, material patterns suggest longer stays at this high-mountain valley with domestic llamas (Lama glama) and continued evidence of hunting and gathering (Castro et al. 2013).

Moving south, Agua de la Cueva (AGC) is a rock shelter from the Precordillera highlands (32° S, Mendoza province). At Agua de la Cueva and other nearby sites, there is consistent evidence for mixed economies in occupations dated between 1500 and 470 cal BP, however, only the Uspallata valley has a climate suitable for year-round occupation (Castro and Yebra 2018; Durán and García 1989; Frigolé and Gasco 2016).

At 34° S, there are two sites on the shores of the alpine lake Laguna del Diamante (LD) (Mendoza province), S2-E1 and S4-E1, where informal stone structures are associated with three dates between 1280 and 680 cal BP. These groups were

Table 6.1 Archaeological sites, dates, and phases associated with projectile points. Dates calibrated with SHCal13 (Hogg et al. 2013) and rounded by 10 years. In the text, we refer to calibrated medians but do not disregard the error ranges

Site—Latitude—Altitude	Context	Number of pieces	Laboratory Code	^{14}C age	Median cal BP	95% probability range	Phase	Reference
Arq-18 (29° S, 3750 masl)	C-I (outside rock shelter)	4	LP-1748	2980 ± 70	3080	3340–2870	1	Cortegoso et al. (2014)
			LP-1851	2300 ± 60	2230	2380–2090	1	
			LP-1842	1900 ± 70	1780	2000–1600	1	
			LP-2094	1750 ± 60	1600	1810–1430	1	
			LP-2085	1540 ± 60	1380	1530–1300	1	
	C-I (inside rock shelter)	1	LP-2098	790 ± 60	690	790–560	2	
Arq-5 (29° S, 3750 masl)	Stratum 2	5	LP-1987	510 ± 60	510	630–320	3	
AGC (32° S, 2990 masl)	Stratum 5 (CJ-5)	5	LP-1621	1330 ± 60	1200	1300–1070	2	see Castro and Yebra (2018)
			LP-1627	1220 ± 70	1090	1270–950	2	
	Stratum 6 (CJ-6)	3	LP-2994	780 ± 50	700	750–560	2	
			LP-2950	600 ± 60	550	660–500	2	
	Stratum 7 (CJ-7)	5	AC-1563	470 ± 80	470	630–300	3	
LD-S2-E1 (34° S, 3300 masl)	Stratum 2-3	1	LP-1400	1410 ± 40	1280	1350–1180	2	Durán et al. 2006)
LD-S4-E1 (34° S, 3300 masl)	C-III	3	LP-1043	1100 ± 40	960	1070–900	2	
	C-II	8	AA-58290	782 ± 35	680	740–570	2	
Cueva Yagui (37° S, 1371 masl)	C-1	9	D-AMS 018772	1133 ± 54	1000	1180–910	2	Romero Villanueva et al. (2019)

seasonally mobile and there is evidence of ceramics, domestic plants, and domestic animals (Durán et al. 2006).

The southernmost site, Cueva Yagui, is located at 37° S (Neuquén province). The occupation of site began in the early Holocene, prior to a mid-Holocene hiatus, and more intensive year-round occupations began around one thousand years ago (Romero Villanueva et al. 2019).

We organized the dates into three phases: 3080–1360 cal BP, 1280–550 cal BP, and 550–400 cal BP. These phases are delimited by four inflection points of significant change in the regional culture history: (1) around three thousand years ago, when pastoralists first left an unambiguous material pattern in the northern area, (2) around two thousand years ago, roughly contemporaneous with the earliest ceramics, (3) shortly following 1500 cal BP, when pastoralism and horticulture became more common in the central area at 32° S, (4) 550 cal BP, when the Inca empire arrived in the northern and central area, and (5) European contact ~400 cal BP.

6.5 Methods

There is a long history of research on quantitative methods for distinguishing darts and arrows through the study of lithic projectiles, based on metric variables, weight, and aerodynamics (Bradbury 1997; Fenenga 1953; Hildebrandt and King 2012; Ratto 2003; Shott 1997; Thomas 1978; among others). So far, there is not a consensus on which variables or method is best; the appropriate index and variables seem to vary by region. This type of analysis assumes that spears are large and heavy, arrows are small and light, and darts are of intermediate size and weight (Hutchings 1997). However, experimental work indicates that small projectile points can be used to tip atlatls, spears, or harpoons, and they may have been used in aquatic hunting and fishing (Erlandson et al. 2014). Therefore, discriminant analyses should be used cautiously and interpreted with an eye toward the possibility of regional variation (Erlandson et al. 2014; Martínez 2007).

In this paper we use Shott's proposal (1997) since it is the most widely applied means of metrically distinguishing darts and arrows. Building on Thomas (1978), Shott added the variable shoulder width, which he found to be the most discriminating variable in his ethnographic collection. His classification functions are:

Dart: 1.40 × (shoulder or maximum width)—16.85
Arrow: 0.89 × (shoulder or maximum width)—7.22

The width of a single point is inputted into both equations and the one with the higher value is the correct classification. In the comparative sample, this function identified 92.4% arrows and 76.9% darts, which were more variable. This single-variable function was preferable to multivariable functions. Shott's study uses mostly stemmed points to determine shoulder width. The current study uses both stemmed and non-stemmed points, which do not have a shoulder. For non-stemmed points, we use the maximum width, following Shott (1993: 431).

6.6 Results

Shott's single-variable function separated the samples into two clear groups (Fig. 6.2). Of the total sample, 39 (89%) were identified as arrows and five (11%) as darts (Table 6.2 and 6.3).

Phase 1 (3080–1360 cal BP) comprises four points from the northernmost site, Arq-18 (29° S). Three arrows and one dart were identified (Table 6.2). The earliest arrow is from the layer just above the oldest date, 3080 cal BP (LP-1748). Two of these arrow points are smaller than points from layers deposited by possible transitional herders in lower levels (Castro 2017). The only point identified as a dart is from level 3, which was deposited between 1780 (level 5) and 1380 cal BP (level 2) (Cortegoso 2014). This is the latest dart registered at Arq-18 and in the upper Las Taguas River basin.

Phase 2 (1280–550 cal BP) comprises 30 points from five sites at all four latitudes (Table 6.3). Twenty-six points were identified as arrows (87%) and four as darts

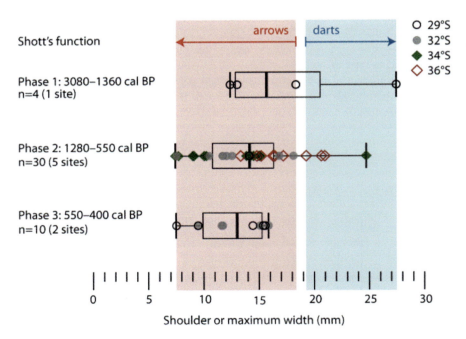

Fig. 6.2 Measurements and Shott's function for projectile points. The central value of the box plots is the median, the box edges are the 25th and 75th percentiles, and the whiskers extend to the minimum and maximum values

6 The Introduction of the Bow and Arrow Across …

Table 6.2 Measurements and function scores for projectile points from phase 1 (3080–1360 cal BP). The shaded box indicates the higher value of Shott's function and hence the dart or arrow classification

Point		Site	Context (Unit—sector—level)	Shoulder(*) or maximum width (mm)	Shott's dart function	Shott's arrow function	Morphology
Number	Reference Fig. 6.3						
1	–	Arq-18 (C-I/outside)	A-NO-10	12.36	0.45	3.78	Non stemmed (oval)
2	b		S2-6	18.36	8.85	9.12	Non stemmed (triangular)
3	c		A-NE-3	13.03	1.39	4.37	Non stemmed (oval)
4	a		B-NO-3	27.38	21.48	17.14	Non stemmed (triangular)

Table 6.3 Measurements and function scores for projectile points from phase 2 (1280–550 cal BP). The shaded box indicates the higher value of Shott's function and hence the dart or arrow classification

Point		Site	Context (Unit—sector—level)	Shoulder(*) or maximum width (mm)	Shott's dart function	Shott's arrow function	Morphology
Number	Reference Fig. 6.3						
9	d	Arq-18 (C-I/inside)	S3-5	14.14*	2.940	5.36	Stemmed (triangular)
10	–	AGC (stratum 5)	B-NE-34	10.5	−2.15	2.12	Non Stemmed (triangular)
11	–		A-SE-27	12.12*	0.11	3.56	Stemmed (triangular)
12	–		A-NO-25	18.12*	8.51	8.90	Stemmed (triangular)
13	–		B-NE-24	7.56	−6.26	−0.49	Non stemmed (triangular)
14	g		A-NE-24	12.57*	0.74	3.96	Stemmed (triangular)
15	–	AGC (stratum 6)	A-SE-18	11.77	−0.37	3.25	Non stemmed (undetermined)
16	h		A-SO-19	11.74	−0.41	3.22	Non stemmed (triangular)
17	–		A-NE-21	16.82	6.69	7.74	Non stemmed (triangular)
18	–	LD-S2-E1	E1.1-NO	15.08	4.26	6.20	Non stemmed (triangular)

(continued)

Table 6.3 (continued)

Point		Site	Context (Unit—sector—level)	Shoulder(*) or maximum width (mm)	Shott's dart function	Shott's arrow function	Morphology
Number	Reference Fig. 6.3						
19	–	LD-S4-E1 (C-II)	B-4	9.04	−4.19	0.82	Non stemmed (triangular)
20	n		C-4	7.68	−6.09	−0.38	Non stemmed (triangular)
21	–		C-5	15	4.15	6.13	Stemmed (triangular)
22	–		A-SE-5	7.41	−6.47	−0.62	Non stemmed (triangular)
23	–		A-SE-6	14.49	3.43	5.67	Non stemmed (undetermined)
24	–		B-SO-5	10.24	−2.51	1.89	Stemmed (oval)
25	–		C-4	9.03	−4.20	0.81	Non stemmed (undetermined)
26	l		C-4	24.69	17.71	14.75	Non stemmed (triangular)
27	–	LD-S4-E1 (C-III)	B-SE-8	14.19	3.01	5.40	Non stemmed (triangular)
28	m		C-8	9.98	−2.87	1.66	Non stemmed (triangular)
29	–		C-NO-8	13.85	2.54	5.10	Non stemmed (triangular)
40	–	Cueva Yagui	C1, nivel 1	15.18	4.40	6.29	Non stemmed (triangular)
41	–		C1, nivel 2	16.31	5.98	7.29	Non stemmed (triangular)
42	–		C1, nivel 2	14.78	3.84	5.93	Non stemmed (triangular)
43	–		C1, nivel 3	20.64	12.04	11.14	Non stemmed (triangular)
44	–		C1, nivel 3	13.39	1.89	4.69	Non stemmed (triangular)
45	q		C1, nivel 3	16.4	6.11	7.37	Non stemmed (triangular)
46	o		C1, nivel 5	20.98	12.52	11.45	Non stemmed (triangular)
47	–		C1, nivel 5	17.21	7.24	8.09	Non stemmed (oval)
48	p		C1, nivel 6	19.31	10.18	9.96	Non stemmed (triangular)

(13%). Arrows are present at all sites. The arrow point from Arq-18 is associated with a date of 690 cal BP. At AGC, eight arrow points are from contexts dated between 1200 and 550 cal BP. The arrow point from LD-S2-E1 (34° S) is from a level dated to 1280 cal BP. At the neighboring site LD-S4-E1, ten points were identified from levels dated 960 and 680 cal BP. Finally, at Cueva Yagui (37° S), six arrow points are from level above and later than 1000 cal BP. This same context includes three darts. The only other dart from this phase is from LD-S4-E1 (34° S) and is associated with the date of 680 cal BP.

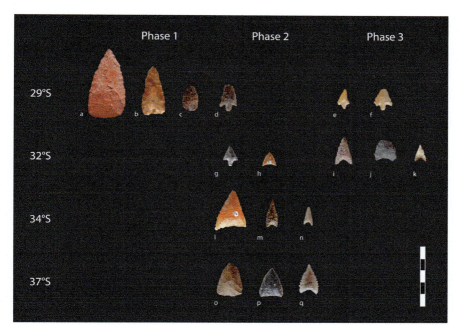

Fig. 6.3 Photographs of selected points ordered by latitude and phase. See Table 1 for details of each lettered point. Scale bar measures 5 cm

Phase 3 (550–400 cal BP) comprises 10 points from Arq-5 (29° S) and AGC (32° S). All points were identified as arrows, confirming the sustained pattern in phase 2 with improved chronological control (Table 6.4).

6.7 Discussion

This study builds on an earlier one, which included sites between 29° S and 34° S (Castro et al. 2018). The results led us to discussions of (1) the origin and spread of the earliest bow and arrows at each latitude, (2) associations between the bow and arrow and patterns in subsistence, settlement, and mobility, and (3) the bow's replacement of other weapon systems or the coexistence of multiple systems. In this paper, we add data from Cueva Yagui (37° S) to re-evaluate these trends farther south and to make larger-scale hypotheses to be tested as new data come to light.

1. The origin and spread of the earliest bow and arrows

The earliest record of arrows is in the northernmost part of the study area (29° S), which supports the idea that this technology was introduced from north to south, even though the sample is small. Farther north at 16–26° S, highland sites have arrow points around 3500–3000 cal BP or slightly prior (De Souza 2004; Hocsman

Table 6.4 Measurements and function scores for projectile points from phase 3 (550–400 cal BP). The shaded box indicates the higher value of Shott's function and hence the dart or arrow classification

Point		Site	Context (Unit—sector—level)	Shoulder(*) or maximum width (mm)	Shott's dart function	Shott's arrow function	Morphology
Number	Reference Fig 6.3						
30	–	Arq-5 (surface)	5	11.64*	−0.55	3.13	Stemmed (oval)
31	–		1	11.72*	−0.44	3.21	Stemmed (triangular)
32	–		6	15.78	5.24	6.82	Non stemmed (undetermined)
33	e		2	9.43*	−3.64	1.17	Stemmed (triangular)
34	f		Structure 1	15.12*	4.31	6.23	Stemmed (triangular)
35	–	Agua de la Cueva (stratum 7)	B-SO-15	7.5	−6.35	−0.54	Non stemmed (triangular)
36	–		B-NO-14	15.58*	4.96	6.64	Stemmed (triangular)
37	k		B-NE-14	9.42	−3.66	1.16	Non stemmed (triangular)
38	j		B-SE-14	14.42	3.33	5.61	Non stemmed (undetermined)
39	i		B-SE-12	15.39	4.69	6.47	Non stemmed (triangular)

2010; Oliszewski et al. 2018). The earliest arrow point in this study is from 29° S in a context deposited just after 3080 cal BP. This suggests a spread of this technology along a large part of the Andes, perhaps within a few centuries. South of 29° S, there is a temporal discontinuity, as the earliest arrows for 32° and 34° S are at 1200 and 1280 cal BP, which suggests a roughly simultaneous adoption in these two areas. In the southern area at 37° S, the arrows points were recovered from and above the level dated to 1000 cal BP.

Along a large part of the Andes, it seems the bow spread south to ~29° S rather quickly, south of which the tempo slowed. This could be because the herders using bows in this region had a stable east–west annual mobility circuit. In addition, there are long distances between high-altitude microclimates suitable for herding as well as the slow demographic growth of mobile human and camelid populations. These factors may help explain how this technology did not spread to 32° S for close to two millennia. Once bows were adopted farther south, they appeared at 32°, 34°, and 37° S, within a few centuries, a notable acceleration.

It seems likely that this innovation was borrowed in a down-the-line fashion along the Andes. In support of this and against the possibility of independent invention within the southern Andes, all ethnographic and archaeological bows follow the same design: simple straight bows. Additionally, current data show a coherent geographic pattern of north to south in progressively later contexts. This is what we would expect in a scenario of technological borrowing between Andean hunters, though this needs to be refined with future data.

2. The association between the bow and arrow and subsistence and mobility patterns

The introduction of the bow and arrow has been correlated with subsistence and settlement changes, social complexity, storage, exchange, and other technological transformations such as the predominance of expedient technologies (Eerkens 2003; Railey 2010). However, these transformations do not necessarily occur at the same time. Some of these changes may have taken place in response to others (Eerkens 2003).

At 29° S, there is evidence of domestic camelid bones, implying herding activities and transhumant mobility as early as 5810 cal BP (Castro 2018; Castro et al. 2013; Gasco 2014). The use of the bow in phase 1 (3080–1360 cal BP) seems to have been later and perhaps in response to the development of transhumant mobility patterns that are evident following a long hiatus in the occupation of the site during the arid mid-Holocene (Marsh et al. 2016: 71). At this time the faunal data show that hunters had incorporated birds into the diet, including the large Andean goose (*Chleoephaga melanoptera*) (see Gasco 2014: 184, Table 4). The addition of birds may correlate with the introduction of the bow and arrow. Compared to the atlatl and thrown spear, it is a more flexible weapon system that can be used effectively with a larger range of prey, especially smaller prey like birds (Ratto 2003).

At 32° S, subsistence and settlement shifts began around 2200–2100 cal BP with the earliest ceramics (Marsh 2017) but did not intensify until after 1500 cal BP (Cortegoso 2006; Durán et al. 2012; Neme 2002). These shifts are coeval with the dominant presence of arrows in the later part of phase 1 (3080–1360 cal BP) and especially phase 2 (1280–550 cal BP). The bow was adopted as part of a suite of broader shifts such as economic intensification, reduction in mobility, pottery production, and long-distance contacts (Cortegoso et al. 2019; Frigolé and Gasco 2016). This broadly follows the pattern of changes that took place in the Lake Titicaca Basin around 3500 cal BP (Marsh 2015), but in the southern Andes there was no suite of Neolithic material—current evidence suggests pottery was in use a millennium before the bow.

With demographic growth, the adoption of the bow and arrow would have been an efficient strategy since it would have led to hunting prey of a wider size range (23–230 kg) and shorter hunting times (Churchill 1993; Tomka 2013). At 34° and 37° S, groups quickly adopted the bow after 1300 cal BP but never abandoned the atlatl. They seem to have added this new weapon system and new prey and tactics to existing ones, as diet breadth increased around this time (Neme 2007), but they did not stop hunting with atlatls nor become sedentary. It is possible that the bow allowed them to make longer stays at larger residential base camps, for example, Cueva Yagui. The projectile points from this site are associated with ceramics and other material that suggest a much more intensive occupation than is evident in earlier levels. Unlike groups north of 34° S, they only adopted the bow but not domestic plants and animals. The reason for this may be ecological—the growing season is significantly shorter and less predictable. Despite this, demography was increasing at the time, an important concomitant change with the spread of the bow into Patagonia.

3. The bow's replacement of other weapon systems or the coexistence of multiple systems

The presence of a dart at 29° S during phase 1 (3080–1360 cal BP) suggests continuity in the use of atlatls and/or spears after the initial adoption of the bow and arrow. However, in phases 2 and 3, darts are absent. Darts are also absent at 32° S, which do not reflect hunting practices. This suggests that the bow had replaced spear-based weapon systems, without the notable exception of darts found as grave goods, over a large area. At 34° S, 11 of the 12 points were identified as arrows. The single dart (point 26) is from a level dated to 680 cal BP. It is possible that this dart was left by Patagonia hunters who occupied the area during the summer (Durán et al. 2006). At 37° S, darts were most common, 3 out of 9 total points, and all postdate 1000 cal BP.

Beginning around 1280 cal BP, all darts are from 34 and 37° S, probably made and used by Patagonian hunters. In this region, darts persisted and coexisted with the bow and arrow following initial adoption. These data are consistent with studies from other areas of Patagonia that indicate darts were used until a few centuries prior to European contact (Banegas et al. 2014; Charlin and González-José 2018). In contrast, at 29° and 32° S, groups with more diversified economies and reduced mobility abandoned atlatls and darts. After 1280 cal BP, the bow had replaced the atlatl for hunting and perhaps violent conflict; however, the atlatl and darts are known from late-period burial contexts and iconography (see Chamussy 2014; De Souza 2011; Nami et al. 2015; Owen 1998).

6.8   Conclusion

This comparative study includes six sites over a large region, which allows us to begin outlining the introduction of the bow and arrow in the southern Andes, between 29 and 37° S. In the northern part of the study area (29° S), the bow and arrow was first used shortly after 3080 cal BP. During phase 1, both darts and arrows were present, but the sample size is very limited. At 32° and 34° S, the bow and arrow was not used until 1280 cal BP and it replaced atlatls and darts. At 37° S, this hunting technology arrived shortly after 1000 cal BP and darts coexisted with arrows until Spanish contact. The clearest pattern in the dataset is the dominant presence of arrows after 1280 cal BP at 29–34° S. These arrows are associated with demographic growth, reduced mobility, low-level food production, and herding economies, following similar trends in other regions.

These data allow us to begin to sketch out a large-scale narrative that needs to be modified and evaluated with larger data sets. Current data suggest that the bow was an innovation from the central Andes that rapidly spread south along the Andes to around 29° S at 3500–3000 cal BP. At this point, the tempo slowed dramatically. It was not adopted by groups at 32° S until after 1300 cal BP. Over the next two to three centuries, it was rapidly adopted by more sedentary food-producing groups north of 34° S as well as more mobile hunter-gatherers to the south. Because it was incorporated by groups with very different economies spread over a biogeographically diverse area, its effectiveness and versatility must have been clear to ancient hunters. This had important ramifications in all groups, but not evenly. North of 34° S, the various advantages it offers larger, less mobile groups led to a complete replacement of previous hunting systems. South of 34° S, it allowed hunter-gatherers greater diversity in hunting tactics, prey, and reduced mobility in a few key microclimates. In this area, the bow did not replace the atlatl but became an additional tool available to hunters.

There is no evidence the bow was ever abandoned once adopted, and except in the case of Patagonia, it seems to have replaced previous weapon systems. This speaks to its versatility regardless of biogeographic area, economic system, or cultural preferences. As such an effective innovation, it was likely borrowed by successive groups in contact with each other along the Andes, making it a notable example of technological borrowing (Lemonnier 1992). The specific social contacts and ecological settings where this borrowing took place likely conditioned the alternating pluses of rapid spread to 29° S, very slow to 32° S, and then rapid again to at least 37° S and probably the rest of Patagonia. This narrative is based on a skeleton framework of data so far, but we think it is productive to begin to put these pieces together into a big-picture perspective. It can serve as a broad continental-scale research question that can be a useful way for regionally specific data to be more effectively integrated as well as encourage researchers to more carefully assess Andean projectile points and evaluate how specific regions follow or diverge from this narrative. Beyond regional research, this instance of borrowing a highly effective technological innovation can be compared to the spread of the bow in other parts of the world, including North America, where the chronology is roughly comparable.

References

Banegas A, Goye S, Ratto N (2014) Cabezales líticos del holoceno tardío en patagonia meridional: diseños y asignación funcional. Magallania 42(2):155–174

Barberena R (2013) Biogeografía, competencia y demarcación simbólica del espacio: modelo arqueológico para el norte de Neuquén. Intersecciones en Antropología 14:367–381

Barberena R, Durán V, Novellino P, Winocur D, Benítez A, Tessone A, Quiroga MN, Marsh E, Gasco A, Cortegoso V, Lucero G, Llano C, Knudson KJ (2017) Scale of human mobility in the southern Andes (Argentina and Chile): a new framework based on strontium isotopes. Am J Phys Anthropol 164:305–320

Bartram LE (1997) A comparison of Kua (Botswana) and Hadza (Tanzania) bow and arrow hunting. In: Projectile technology. Springer, Boston, MA, pp 321–343

Bettinger RL (1991) Hunter-gatherers: archaeological and evolutionary theory. In: Interdisciplinary contributions to archaeology. Plenum Press, New York

Bettinger RL (2013) Effects of the bow on social organization in western North America. Evol Anthropol: Issues, News, Rev 22(3):118–123

Bettinger RL, Eerkens JW (1999) Point typologies, cultural transmission, and the spread of the bow-and-arrow technology in the prehistoric Great Basin. Am Antiq 64:231–242

Bingham PM, Souza J, Blitz JH (2013) Introduction: social complexity and the bow in the prehistoric North American record. Evol Anthropol: Issues, News, Rev 22(3):81–88

Bradbury AP (1997) The bow and arrow in the Eastern Woodlands: evidence for an archaic origin. North Am Archaeol 18:207–233

Cabrera AL (1971) Fitogeografía de la República Argentina. Boletín de la Sociedad Argentina de Botánica 14:1–50

Cardillo M, Alberti J (2015) The evolution of projectile points and technical systems: a case from Northern Patagonian coast (Argentina). J Archaeol Sci, Rep 2:612–623

Castro S (2017) Tecnología de caza en la cuenca alta del río de Las Taguas (San Juan, Argentina). Análisis morfológico de proyectiles líticos del sitio Arq-18 (8.900–790 años AP). Cuadernos del Instituto Nacional de Antropología y Pensamiento Latinoamericano 26(1):1–20

Castro S (2018) Cazadores-recolectores y pastores en los Andes (San Juan, Argentina): cambios en la organización tecnológica durante el Holoceno. Arqueología 24(1):103–125

Castro S, Gasco A, Lucero G, Cortegoso V (2013) Mid-Holocene hunters and herders of southern cordillera, Northwestern Argentina. Quatern Int 307:96–104

Castro S, Lucero G, Cortegoso V, Winocur D (2014) Fuentes de aprovisionamiento de materia prima y sistemas de producción lítica en Los Andes (Noroeste de San Juan, Argentina). Relaciones de La Sociedad Argentina de Antropología 39(2):365–386

Castro S, Yebra L (2018) Ocupación tardía de la precordillera de Mendoza: organización tecnológica en Agua de la Cueva Sector Norte (ca. 1700–500 años cal. AP). Anales de Arqueología y Etnología de la Facultad de Filosofía y Letras. Universidad Nacional de Cuyo 73(1):7–40

Castro S, Yebra L, Marsh E, Cortegoso V, Lucero G (2018) The introduction of the bow and arrow in the Argentine Andes (29–34o S): A preliminary metric approximation. J Lithic Stud 5(2) (in press)

Cattelain P (1997) Hunting during the Upper Paleolithic: bow, spearthrower, or both? In: Knetch H (ed) Projectile technology. Plenum Press, pp 213–240

Chamussy V (2014) Estudio sobre armas de guerra y caza en el área centro-andina. descripción y uso de las armas de estocada y de tajo. Arqueología y Sociedad, Museo de Arqueología y Antropología de la Universidad Nacional Mayor de San Marcos 27:297–338

Charlin J, González-José R (2018) Nesting an ethnographic analogy through geometric morphometrics: a comparison between ethnographic arrows and archaeological projectile points from Late Holocene Fuego-Patagonia. J Anthropol Archaeol 51:159–172

Churchill S (1993) Weapon technology, prey size selection and hunting methods in modern hunter-gatherer: implications for hunting in the Paleolithic and Mesolithic. In: Peterkin GL, Bricker H, Mellars P (eds) Hunting and animal exploitation in the later Paleolithic and Mesolithic of Eurasia. Archaeological Papers of the American Anthropological Association, New York

Cortegoso V (2006) Comunidades agrícolas en el Valle de Potrerillos (NO de Mendoza) durante el Holoceno tardío: organización de la tecnología y vivienda. Intersecciones en Antropología 7:77–94

Cortegoso V (2008) Disponibilidad de recursos líticos en el Noroeste de Mendoza: cambios en la organización tecnológica en la cuenca del río Blanco. Cazadores-Recolectores del Cono Sur. Revista de Arqueología 3:95–112

Cortegoso V (2014) Valle de Las Taguas ARQ-18 Estratigrafía, secuencia temporal y ocupaciones humanas. In: Cortegoso V, Durán V, Gasco A (eds) Arqueología de ambientes de altura de Mendoza y San Juan (Argentina). EDIUNC, Mendoza, pp 209–242

Cortegoso V, Durán V, Gasco A (2014) Arqueología de Ambientes de Altura de Mendoza y San Juan (Argentina). EDIUNC, Mendoza

Cortegoso V, Lucero G, Castro S, Winocur D (2017) Bosques fósiles y tecnología humana: la explotación de materias primas líticas en el Bosque de Darwin, Paramillos (Argentina). Am Antiq 28(3):317–336

6 The Introduction of the Bow and Arrow Across … 155

Cortegoso V, Yebra L, Castro S, Durán V (2019) La presencia de obsidiana en contextos arqueológicos del Norte de Mendoza: interacciones humanas en una región andina sin fuentes volcánicas. Intersecciones en Antropología. En prensa

De Porras ME, Maldonado A (2018) Metodologías y avances de la palinología del Cuaternario Tardío a lo largo de la Diagonal Árida Sudamericana. Publicación Electrónica de la Asociación Paleontológica Argentina 18(2):18–38

De Souza P (2004) Tecnologias de proyectil durante los períodos Arcaico y Formativo en el Loa Superior (Norte de Chile): a partir del análisis de puntas líticas. Chungara Revista de Antropología Chilena 36:61–76

De Souza P (2011) Sistemas de proyectiles y cambio social durante el tránsito Arcaico tardío-Formativo temprano de la Puna de Atacama. In: Hubert A, González J, Pereira M (eds) Temporalidad, Interacción y Dinamismo Cultural, la Búsqueda del Hombre: Homenaje al Profesor Lautaro Núñez Atencio. Universidad Católica del Norte, Ediciones Universitarias, Antofagasta, pp 201–246

Durán V (2000) Poblaciones Indígenas de Malargüe. Su arqueología e historia. CEIDER, Mendoza

Durán V, De Francesco A, Cortegoso V, Neme G, Cornejo L, Bocci M (2012) Caracterización y procedencia de obsidianas de sitios arqueológicos del centro oeste de Argentina y centro de Chile con metodología no destructiva por fluorescencia de rayos X (XRF)=Non-destructive X-ray flurorescence (XRF) characterization and sourc. Intersecciones en Antropología 13:423–437

Durán V, García C (1989) Ocupaciones agro-alfareras en el sitio Agua de la Cueva—sector norte (NO de Mendoza). Revista de Estudios Regionales 3:29–69

Durán V, Neme G, Cortegoso V, Gil A (2006) Arqueología del Área Natural Protegida Laguna del Diamante (Mendoza, Argentina). In: Durán V, Cortegoso V (eds) Arqueología y Ambiente de Áreas Naturales Protegidas de la Provincia de Mendoza. Anales de Arqueología y Etnología. Tomo 61, Mendoza, Argentina, pp 81–134

Eerkens JW (1998) Reliable and maintainable technologies: Artifact Standardization and the Early to Later Mesolithic transition in Northern England. Lithic Technol 23(1):42–53

Eerkens JW (2003) Sedentism, storage, and the intensification of small seeds: prehistoric developments in owens valley California. North American Archaeologist 24(4):281–309

Erlandson JM, Watts JL, Jew NP (2014) Darts, arrows, and archaeologists: distinguishing dart and arrow points in the archaeological record. Am Antiq 79(1):162–169

Fenenga F (1953) The weights of chipped stone points: a clue to their functions. Southwest J Anthropol 9:309–323

Frigolé C, Gasco A (2016) Potters and herders at the southern edge of the Andean world: risk management and mobility in Northwestern Mendoza, Argentina. Quaternary Internacional 422:152–162

Fuentes A, Wiessner P (2016) Reintegrating anthropology: from inside out: an introduction to supplement 13. Curr Anthropol 57(13):S3–S12

García A (2003) La ocupación temprana de los Andes Centrales Argentinos (ca. 11.000–8.000 años C14 AP). Relaciones de la Sociedad Argentina de Antropología 28:153–165

García A, Lagiglia H (1998–1999) Avances en el estudio del registro pleistocénico tardío de la Gruta del Indio (Mendoza). Cuadernos del Instituto Nacional de Antropología y Pensamiento Latinoamericano 18:167–174

Gasco A (2014) Las arqueofaunas del alero ARQ-18 (San Juan, Argentina): aprovechamiento de camélidos silvestres y dompesticos durante el Holoceno medio y tardío. In: Cortegoso V, Durán V, Gasco A (eds) Arqueología de ambientes de altura de Mendoza y San Juan (Argentina). Colección Encuentros no 3. EDIUNC, Mendoza, pp 171–202

Gil A, Neme G, Tykot R, Novellino P, Cortegoso V, Durán V (2009) Stable isotopes and maize consumption in Central Western Argentina. International Journal of Osteoarchaeology 19:215–236

Gil A, Giardina M, Neme G, Ugan A (2014) Demografía humana e incorporación de cultígenos en el centro occidente argentino: explorando tendencias en las fechas radiocarbónicas. Revista Española de Antropología Americana 44(2):523–553

Gil A, Menéndez L, Atencio J, Peralta E, Neme G, Ugan A (2018) Estrategias humanas, estabilidad y cambio en la frontera agrícola Suramericana. Lat Am Antiq 29(1):6–26

Hayden B (1981) Research and development in the Stone Age: technological transitions among hunter-gatherers. Curr Anthropol 22:519–2872

Hildebrandt WR, King JH (2012) Distinguishing between darts and arrows in the archaeological record: implications for technological change in the American West. Am Antiq 77:789–799

Hocsman S (2010) Cambios en las puntas de proyectil durante la transición de cazadores-recolectores a sociedades agro-pastoriles en Antofagasta de la Sierra (Puna Argentina). Arqueología 16:59–86

Hogg AG, Hua Q, Blackwell PG, Niu M, Buck CE, Guilderson TP, Heaton TJ, Palmer JG, Reimer PJ, Reimer RW (2013) SHCal13 southern hemisphere calibration, 0e50,000 cal yr BP. Radiocarbon 55:1889–1903

Hutchings WK (1997) The Paleoindian fluted point: dart or spear armature? The identification of Paleoindian delivery technology through the analysis of lithic fracture velocity. Simon Fraser University, British Columbia, Canadá

Kelly RL (1995) The foraging spectrum. Diversity in Hunter Gatherers lifeways. Smithonian Institution Press, Washington

Kennett DJ, Lambert PM, Johnson JR, Brendan JC (2013) Sociopolitical effects of bow and arrow technology in prehistoric coastal California. Evol Anthropol: Issues, News, Rev 22(3):124–132

Klink C, Aldenderfer M (2005) A projectile point chronology for the south-central Andean highlands. In: Stanish C, Cohen AB, Aldenderfer MS (eds) Advances in Titicaca Basin archaeology. Cotsen Institute of Archaeology, University of California, Los Ángeles, pp 25–54

Lagiglia H (1975) Descubrimiento del primer arco indígena de Mendoza. Revista Del Museo de Historia Natural II(4):147

Lagiglia H (2001) Los orígenes de la agricultura en Argentina. In: Berberian R, Nielsen A (eds) Argentina Prehistórica. Brujas, Córdoba, pp 41–81

Lemonnier P (1992) Elements for an anthropology of technology. Anthropological papers. Museum of Anthropology, University of Michigan 88:1–24

Llano C, Cortegoso V, Marsh E (2017) Small-scale horticultural production at the continental limit of Andean cultural development: a contribution from archaeobotany. Darwiniana 5(2):109–125

Lucero G, Castro S, Cortegoso V (2017) Tecnología lítica de cazadores y pastores andinos: cambios y continuidades en la explotación de recursos líticos durante el Holoceno en el NO de San Juan. Revista del Museo de Antropología, Suplemento Especial 1:65–74

Marsh E (2015) The emergence of agropastoralism: Accelerated ecocultural change on the Andean altiplano, ~3540–120 cal BP. Environ Archaeol 20:13–29

Marsh E (2017) La fecha de la cerámica más temprana en los Andes Sur. Una perspectiva macroregional mediante modelos Bayesianos. Revista del Museo de Antropología, Suplemento Especial 1:83–94

Marsh E, Cortegoso V, Castro S (2016) Hunter-gatherer mobility decisions and synchronous climate change in the Southern Andes: the Early and Middle Holocene occupations of ARQ-18, San Juan, Argentina (29.5° S). Quat Int 422:66–80

Martínez JG (2007) Ocupaciones humanas tempranas y tecnológicas de caza en Antofagasta de La Sierra, Puna meridional argentina (10000–7000 AP). Cazadores-Recolectores del Cono Sur. Revista de Arqueología 2:129–150

Méndez C, Gil A, Neme G, Nuevo Delaunay A, Cortegoso V, Huidobro C, Durán V, Maldonado A (2015) Mid Holocene radiocarbon ages in the Subtropical Andes (~29°–35° S), climatic change and implications for human space organization. Quat Int 30:1–12

Metraux A (1929) Contribución ala etnografía y arqueología de la Provincia de Mendoza. Revista de la Junta de Estudios Históricos de Mendoza VI 15–16:1–66

Michieli CT (1978) Los puelches. Publicaciones 4. Universidad Nacional de San Juan, Facultad de Filosofía, Humanidades y Artes, Instituto de Investigaciones Arqueológicas y Museo

Michieli CT (1994) Antigua historia de Cuyo. Ansilta Editora, San Juan

Morales M, Barberena R, Belardi JB, Borrero L, Cortegoso V, Durán V, Guerci A, Goñi R, Gil A, Neme G, Yacobaccio H, Zárate M (2009) Reviewing human-environment interactions in arid regions of southern South America during the past 3000 years. Palaeogeogr Palaeoclimatol Palaeoecol 281(3–4):283–295

Morgan LH (1877) Ancient society; or, researches in the lines of human progress from savagery, through barbarism to civilization. H. Holt

Nami H, Durán V, Cortegoso V, Giesso M (2015) Análisis morfológico-experimental y por fluorescencia de Rayos X de las puntas de proyectil de obsidiana de un ajuar del Periodo Agropecuario Tardío del NO de Mendoza. Boletín de la Sociedad Chilena de Arqueología 45:7–37

Neme G (2002) Arqueología del alto valle del río Atuel: modelos, problemas y perspectivas en el estudio de las regiones de altura del sur de Mendoza. In: Gil A, Neme G (eds) Entre Montañas y Desiertos: Arqueología del Sur de Mendoza. Sociedad Argentina de Antropología, Buenos Aires, pp 65–84

Neme G (2007) Cazadores-recolectores de altura en los Andes meridionales: el alto valle del río Atuel. BAR International Series 1951

Neme G, Gil A (2009) Human occupation and increasing Mid-Holocene Aridity: Southern Andean perspectives. Curr Anthropol 50:149–163

Oliszewski N, Martínez JG, Arreguez GA, Gramajo Bühler CM, Naharro ME (2018) La transición vista desde los valles intermontanos del Noroeste Argentino: nuevos datos de la Quebrada de los Corrales (El Infiernillo, Tucumán, Argentina). Chungara Revista de Antropologia Chilena 50:71–86

Owen B (1998) Bows and Spearthrowers in southern Peru and northern Chile: evidence, dating, and why it matters. In: 63rd annual meeting of the society for American archaeology. Seattle, WA

Prieto M (1989) La frontera meridional mendocina durante los siglos XVI y XVII. Xama 2:117–132

Railey JA (2010) Reduced mobility or the bow and arrow? Another look ar "expedient" technologies and sedentism. Am Antiq 75(2):259–286

Ratto N (2003) Estrategias de caza y propiedades del registro arqueológico en la Puna de Chaschuil (Departamento Tinogasta, Catamarca). Tesis Doctoral Inédita, Universidad de Buenos Aires

Richerson PJ (1977) Ecology and human ecology: a comparison of theories in the biological and social sciences. Am Ethnol 4(1):1–26

Romero Villanueva G, Barberena R, Rughini A, Garvey R, Acuña L (2019) Cueva Yagui (norte del Neuquén): evidencias arqueológicas e implicancias regionales para Patagonia septentrional. Ms

Rojo LD, Mehl AE, Paez MM, Zárate MA (2012) Mid- to Late Holocene pollen and alluvial record of the arid Andean piedmont between 33° and 34° S, Mendoza, Argentina: Inferences about floodplain evolution. J Arid Environ 77:110–122

Rorabaugh AN (2018) Hunting social networks on the Salish Sea before and after the bow and arrow. J Archaeol Sci: Rep 23:842–843

Scheinsohn V (2016) A hook on Patagonia: spearthrowers, bone hooks, and grips from Patagonia. Cuadernos del Instituto Nacional de Antropología y Pensamiento Latinoamericano, Series Especiales 3(2):88–102

Schiffer MB, Skibo J (1987) Theory and experiment in the study of technological change. Curr Anthropol 28(1):595–622

Shott MJ (1993) Spears, darts and arrows: late woodland hunting techniques in the Upper Ohio Valley. Am Antiq 58(3):425–443

Shott MJ (1997) Stones and shaft redux: the metric discrimination of chipped-stone dart and arrow points. Am Antiq 62:86–102

Smith LM, Garvey R, Carlson ES (2014) Hunter-gatherer subsistence variation and intensification. In: Smith C (ed) Encyclopedia of global archaeology. Springer, New York, pp 3578–3586

Simms SR (1994) Farmers and foragers in the Late Holocene eastern Great Basin. In: The 24th Great Basin Anthropological Conference, Elko, NV

Thomas DH (1978) Arrowheads and atlatl darts: how the stones got the shaft. Am Antiq 43:461–472

Tomka SA (2013) The adoption of the bow and arrow: a model based on experimental characteristics. Am Antiq 78(3):553–569

Zárate MA (2002) Los ambientes del Tardiglacial y Holoceno en Mendoza. In: Gil A, Neme G (eds) Entre montañas y desiertos: arqueología del sur de Mendoza. Sociedad Argentina de Antropología, Buenos Aires, pp 9–42

Chapter 7
Hunting, Butchering and Consumption of Rheidae in the South of South America: An Actualistic Study

Miguel Giardina, Clara Otaola, and Fernando Franchetti

Abstract Ethnographic studies and ethnohistoric literature from the south of South America showed strong interest in Rheas (*Rhea americana* and *Rhea pennata*) consumption. The Chronicles from numerous explorers of the nineteenth century mentioned different aspects of the exploitation of these birds by Native American people from South America, as well as by rural populations from the Pampa and Patagonia regions at the beginning of twentieth century. In this chapter we show the traditional techniques of hunting, butchering and consumption of these birds. The information belongs to direct observations and interviews to ranchers from rural areas of southern Mendoza, Argentina.

Keywords Rheas · Hunting · Actualistic study · Pampa and Patagonia

7.1 Introduction

Traditional uses of fauna are a very important topic to understand central aspects of Conservation Biology and the evolution of human/fauna relationship (Wolverton 2013). Rheas had an important role in the life of people that inhabited and currently reside in the meridional half of the South of the South American continent (del Papa and Moro 2017; Frontini and Picasso 2010; Medina et al. 2011; Miotti 1998; Moreno 2018; Prates and Acosta Hospitaleche 2010; Salemme and Miotti 1998). Prehispanic iconography, historical references, and actual use of these birds by creoles people supports this idea (Álvarez and Heider 2019; Beerbohm 2004; Claraz 1988; Guinnard 2006; Salemme and Frontini 2011; Musters 1997). However, like other ratite species in the world, the archaeological record suggests a rare use of this animal during

---

M. Giardina (✉) · C. Otaola
CONICET/Instituto de Evolución, Ecología Histórica y Ambiente-Universidad Tecnológica Nacional, Facultad Regional San Rafael, Department of Anthropology, Museo de Historia Natural de San Rafael, Mendoza, Argentina
e-mail: mgiardina@mendoza-conicet.gob.ar

F. Franchetti
Department of Anthropology, University of Pittsburgh, Pittsburgh, PA, USA

© Springer Nature Switzerland AG 2021
J. B. Belardi et al. (eds.), *Ancient Hunting Strategies in Southern South America*,
The Latin American Studies Book Series,
https://doi.org/10.1007/978-3-030-61187-3_7

most of the Holocene (Garvey et al. 2011; Giardina 2010a, b; Janz et al. 2009; Nagaoka 2005; O'Connell 2000). The poor evidence of these birds in archaeological sites had been attributed to difficulties of the hunting this prey and problems of the conservation of bones due to taphonomic process (Belardi 1999; Cruz and Elkin 2003; Fernández 2000).

In this chapter we provide the frame of reference from surveying of "*puesteros*"— goat ranchers which live in the rural landscape. The aim is to generate information about hunting and consumption strategies over Rheas by the "*puesteros*".

The main objective is to synthesize the information about the use of this specific resource in South America from an ethnoarchaeological perspective. We present qualitative data from direct observations and conversation to the "*puesteros*" to generate a corpus of knowledge complementary for zooarchaeological investigations.

7.2 Methodology

In this case study, we /conversate with/ "*puesteros*" from rural areas of North Patagonia. These conversations point out to understand the importance of these birds in human subsistence and other aspects of the social life as well as the formation of the archaeological record.

On the other hand, we conducted a direct observation of a communal hunting event of Rheas called "*boleadas*"—a name that derives from the use of "*bolas*" (weapons made by leather cords and stone balls) during the hunt (Fig. 7.1). The animal acquisition, the butchering techniques and the discard of the carcasses, was of special interest in this observation.

During the fieldwork, it was possible to participate in different ways to prepare and cook the Rheas. Specifically, the "*chaya en bolsa*", which is a traditional dish, also described in the narratives of the first chroniclers regarding the native people from this region (Agüero Blanch 1967; Embon 1950; Musters 1997).

7.3 Study Area

The area for this study is southern Mendoza Province, northern Patagonia. This area is dominated by the Pacific and Atlantic Anticyclone and corresponds to Altoandina, Patagonia and Monte phytogeographic provinces (Cabrera 1976; Roig et al. 2000). In this region, Rheas habit only the piedmont and the lowlands, not the highlands (Tambussi and Acosta Hospitaleche 2002). The piedmont represents an ecotone between the Monte and Patagonian phytogeographic provinces. In this area average temperatures in summer are 22 °C and in winter 5 °C. The lowlands are dominated by Monte phytogeography characterized by mean temperatures of 15 °C, the maximum average temperature reaching 37 °C.

7 Hunting, Butchering and Consumption of Rheidae …

Fig. 7.1 *"Boleadoras"*: typical bolas in South America for hunting Rheas

7.4 The "Puesteros"

The "*Puesteros*" are local shepherds that inhabit rural areas with an economy based in herding goats, cows, horses, and sheep. They sell their goods to visitors and when possible, travel to the city to sell their products and buy supplies. Generally, the "*Puestos*" (houses, usually next to a corral, a water stream, and trees) are occupied by small family groups. In some cases, the "*puestos*" can be composed by a larger group, depending on the water availability and the quality of grasses. Younger generations who have access to formal education are moving to the city and finding professional jobs, and not returning to their homes in the country land.

Most of the "*puestos*" do not have basic services such as water, light, sewers, or gas; they depend on the resources available from the natural environment (Bocco de Abeyá 1988; Otaola et al. 2016). The water is obtained at wells, springs, creeks, rivers, and temporal accumulations from rains and snow precipitations. The heat for their houses and the fire for cooking depend almost exclusively on the use of wood acquired from the surroundings of their "house".

The "*puesteros*" families have a quite solitaire way of life, far from other people. However, occasionally they meet to celebrate special dates such as Easter, local saint's festivity, weddings, and the fifteen years old birthdays of the daughters. They also gather when some job requires the help of several "*puesteros*", such as gathering and branding cattle, an activity that requires several people. These are very active social events, where all kinds of activities like eating, dancing, playing music, and storytelling takes place. One of the most important meetings is the one where communal Rhea hunting takes place (Agüero Blanch 1969–1970; Bocco de Abeyá 1988). In the last decades, the laws that forbid the capture of native animals (National Law N° 22,421 and Provincial Law N° 4602), imposed expensive fines on people that hunt these animals, limiting the hunting for subsistence of "*puesteros*". Usually, these activities match with the school break. Children go to shelter-schools in which they stay for 15 days, while the remaining 15 days of the month they stay at the houses. It is important for teenagers to participate in this activity, because they learn many of the tasks done in the field from the talks with the adults and by doing them.

7.5 Observations and Oral Stories from Rural People

7.5.1 Hunting

The hunt of Rheas by the "*boleadas*" is a constant practice which follows the same traditional activities in each encounter. The "*boleadas*" starts with the gathering of 10–30 people in a pre established place, usually during 3–4 days. Neighbors, friends, nuclear and extended family sensu Bocco de Abeyá (1988), travel from the city located at 130 km distance (Fig. 7.2). The first activity is to find a place to camp and to make a "*real*"—this is a circular structure made with stones and without a roof,

7 Hunting, Butchering and Consumption of Rheidae ...

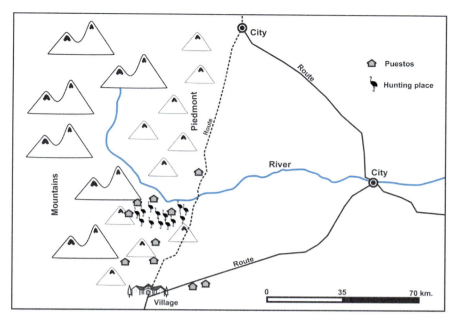

Fig. 7.2 Schematic map with the localization of the hunting and the distance to main cities and villages

which works as a refuge for cold and wind. Everyone provides their equipment and dogs. Once the "*real*" has been built, they organize their beds and the preparation of food for dinner. In the meantime, there are intense conversations and storytelling until the sun goes down. At the same time, the older people repair and make "*boleadoras*". The following day, the people wake up early, ride their horses and decide where they would locate the capture fence. People who live nearby arrive directly from their "*puestos*" to the meeting. The "*puestero*" that organizes the "*boleada*" does not fit any age or status rank, but usually is the one who called everyone to the gathering. This "*puestero*" makes the final choice of where to commence the hunt, after discussing different locations with the other participants.

The observed hunt lasted three days; several "*boleadas*" had been recorded during these days, with different amounts of hunters, dogs, and travel distances. Not all the "*boleadas*" were successful (see Table 7.1).

The hunters chose a place where they would enclose the Rheas making a "human fence" riding their horses, one next to the other in a large circle of varied size (7.5–11.5 km circle perimeter). The minimum number of people necessary to make the communal hunting is around 10–15 people, but if more people participate, they will make a larger circle. Since the beginning of the hunt, the hunters are paying close attention to any traces of Rheas prints on the ground.

Commonly the location chosen is a geoform in the landscape well known by the presence of Rheas. At the beginning, after all the participants arrive at the chosen

164   M. Giardina et al.

Table 7.1 It summarizes the observations made in the hunting place

		First Boleada	Second Boleada	Third Boleada	Fourth Quarter Boleada	Fifth Boleada	Sixth Boleada
People	"*Puesteros*" adults over 50 years old	0	4	4	4	0	4
	"*Puesteros*" adults between 18 at 50 years old	3	12	12	12	8	12
	"*Puesteros*" Young between 10 at 17 years old.	4	10	10	10	8	10
	Foreign people	3	7	7	7	0	3
Dogs		no	30	30	30	15	30
Distance traveled (km)		6	8.21	2.38	2.16	*	9.5
Circle perimeter (km)		9.3	11.5	7.57	8.35	*	8.8
Area (km^2)		3.88	7.83	4.15	4.81	*	5.75
Distance between hunters (m)		530	359	236	260	*	314
Catch		no	no	no	no	1 Rheas	1 Rheas
Remark		Traces are observed and one of the participants says he observes 3 Rheas, and then when we return they observe more traces of an Rhea	Traces are observed and there are participants who try to capture, but they fail.	Tracs are observed and there are participants who try to capture, chase after them with dogs but fail to catch.		They observe about 10 Rheas, the majority of the members launch the boleros, but they get to capture 1 prey thanks to the help of the dogs.	Another Rheas is chased, they try to beat him but you don't catch him, he was followed only by a hunter and his two pairs of boleadoras

*Data not available

7 Hunting, Butchering and Consumption of Rheidae ...

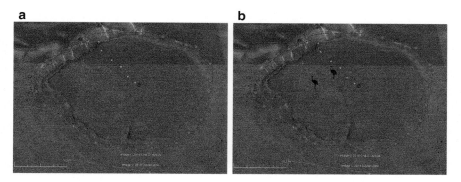

Fig. 7.3 Localization of the sixth "*boleada*" **a** The yellow dots mark the trajectory of the observer and the blue dots mark the position of the hunters. **b** The red arrows are marking the direction where the animal tries to escape while the circle closes

place, they form the circle, placing each other at equidistance according to the number of hunters and the size of the circle (see Table 7.1). The hunters explained that the circle starts to close when one of them stays in front of the rest of the group. At the moment someone sees the Rhea, he makes signals to the rest of the group in order to take position surrounding him, leaving about 250–500 m between each individual, and in this way, the circle stretches further more. Then, they move toward the center of the circle, closing it, waiting for some Rheas to stand up. When a Rhea is visible, two of the hunters ride into the "human fence", carrying their "*boleadoras*" and give origin to the hunting.

Figure 7.3a shows the hunters located in the margins of the chosen geoform. When the circle closes, all the hunters begin to ride toward the center, the Rheas that are locked up, begin to run to the outskirts and it is at that moment when two or three hunters try to capture them (Fig. 7.3b).

In the observation, the "*puesteros*" said that the hunt many times fails. Usually the prey escapes, especially if the "*boleadoras*" did not reach the neck of the animal. Two "*puesteros*" chased the animal; one of them helps the other to throw the "*boleadoras*". If the prey was not caught in a first attempt, the second hunter/ can make another shot. When the first "*boleadora*" screwed in the animal neck, or around the body, the animal fell down. In that moment, the hunter waits until the animal stands up again and throws a second "*boleadora*". Before killing the animal, they check if it is in a good nutritional shape and if it has the desired size. Finally, the animal is killed by twisting its neck.

An interesting thing we note is that if the hunters throw the "*boleadoras*" and the animal is not caught, they continue pursuing the prey and throw another pair of "*boleadoras*" that they carry with them. After the hunting act is finished, the hunters go back to the area of persecution and try to find the first "*boleadora*" he throws, but many times they do not find them again. This has direct implications for the archaeological record since we can expect to find bolas in places where the "*boleada*" occurred.

Fig. 7.4 Two "*puesteros*" butcher the Rhea while the others look around them

In the exact place where the Rhea was captured, they twist its neck to kill it. They also fracture the tarsometatarsus and consume the raw marrow; this bone is discarded in the hunting place. However, the rest of the leg (phalanges especially) are attached to the skin of the animal, and these are transferred to the place of processing and consumption (Fig. 7.4).

From the economic perspective, all the body is used. Moreover, the "*puesteros*" use sub products like feathers, which had been an important good for exchange in historic and prehistoric times. Also, the skin from the neck is used to make tobacco containers and as a "*salero*" (salt shaker). The rest of the bones can also be used to make a wide variety of tools (i.e., handle of knives).

Once the hunt has been completed, all the participants gather around the animal, (Fig. 7.4). Then, the hunted animal is loaded on the hunter's horse and they return to the "*real or puestos*".

After the hunt, the animal is completely transported to the "*real*", where they take out the feathers. If they eat the complete animal in the "*real*", they take out all the feathers. If they only consume a portion of the animal, they will take out the feathers from the portion that is going to be consumed. In this case, they will continue taking out the feathers in their "*puesto*".

The preferred portion is the "*picana*", which is the upper part of the pelvic region, the section with larger amounts of grease and meat (Fig. 7.5). This part can have approximately 4200 grams of meat and grease (Giardina 2006, 2018).

When the animal is consumed in the "*puesto*", the only anatomical parts left in the hunting site are the viscera and the broken tarsometatarsus. In the observation made, the "*puestero*" leaves only the tarsometatarsus from the animal, carrying with him all the phalanges of the leg attached to the leather. When they decide to eat the entire animal in the hunting place, they meet in one of the "*reales*", gather some

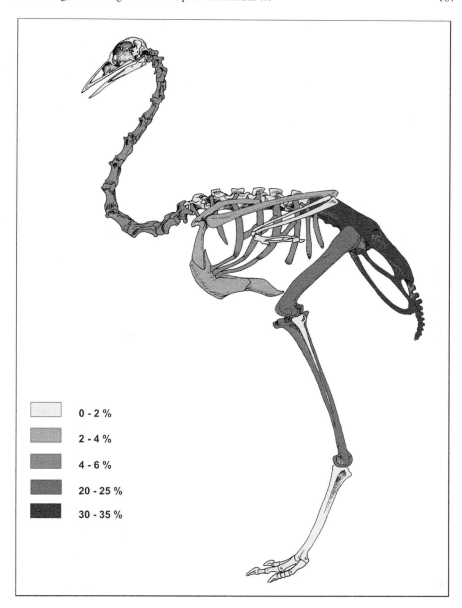

Fig. 7.5 Meat and grease index distribution

wood and start the preparations for cooking the prey. If there are a lot of people, they make more "*reales*"; each real can provide refuge for 5–6 people each.

Table 7.1 summarizes the observations made, number of participants, the age of the participants, the average kilometers traveled, the average distance between the hunters once the circle was formed and the perimeter of the circle, and the presence and number of dogs that helped hunting.

Finally, the observations suggested that the hunt is a difficult and very dangerous task for hunters, since they often fall from the horses while galloping and chasing the Rheas when, for example, the horse stumbles on the caves of some rodents.

7.5.2 Processing and Consumption

During the observed "*boleada*", the principal way to cook the Rheas was in the "house", where the family lives. The most traditional way of preparing the Rheas is the "*chaya en bolsa*". There are mentions of this kind of preparation in the first publications about the ways of life of the "*puesteros*" by Agüero Blanch (1969–1970); as well as in chronicles of the first explorers that visited the meridional portion of the South American continent (Musters 1997; Claraz 1988).

In our observations, it was possible to record similar proceedings to those observed by Agüero Blanch (1969–1970). After the eviscerated pluck of the animal, all the skin was taken out from the body of the animal. This task started with the extraction of the lower members (in this case, only the femur and tibiotarsus were present). Once the extremities were taken out, the axial skeleton was also separated from the skin leaving only the head attached to it. While the "*puestero*" is defleshing, generally with the help of some of the commensals, the other members of the family peel and chop vegetables (garlic, squash, onions, and potatoes). Some of these vegetables (squash and potatoes) are pre-cooked before putting them into the skin-bag where the cooking is going to take place.

In the task of taking out the skin, they disaggregated three anatomical units: first, the posterior members (femur and tibiotarsus); second, the pelvis with lumbar and cervical vertebrae, the ribs, the sternum, the scapula and coracoid; third, the head, which is attached to the skin of the neck and the anterior members (Fig. 7.6). During the disarticulation of the animal, the grease of the waist and the sternum is still attached to the skin, which can be removed easily from the meat if it was kept in a fresh place.

For the "*Chaya en bolsa*", only the meat from the posterior extremities was used, the rest of the animal was left for making a "*chaya*" in the pot or another dish. With the meat of the posterior extremities, they can also make a preparation similar to the slim steak and the defleshed bones can be used to make another food. Different kinds of spices were added to the meat and vegetables, such as cumin, salt, pepper, sweet paprika and crushed red pepper.

For the "*Chaya en bolsa*" the "*puestero*" gathered about 10 rocks the size of a chicken egg, which were heated in the fire. Another rock, relatively thin and plane

7 Hunting, Butchering and Consumption of Rheidae …

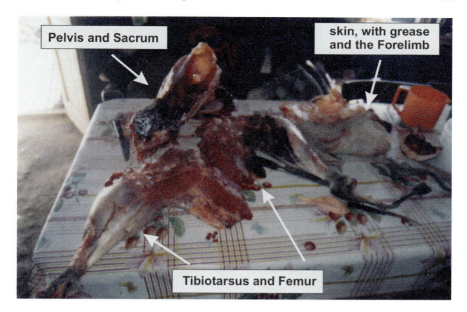

Fig. 7.6 Primary butchering of the prey

of a larger size was also heated. The bag made with the skin of the animal was then placed on top.

The bag only has two openings: in one of the legs, and the other between the other leg and the cut in which the animal was eviscerated. This last cut is larger, because all the vegetables and meat were put inside using this hole. In the boundary of this hole, small incisions were made, and the bag was sewed with a rawhide cord. When the bag was ready, the spices were incorporated into the hole. It is important to mention that the bag had the wings in the original location, including the complete bones, the meat, the grease, and the skin (Fig. 7.7).

Then, the "*puestero*" made a knot in the neck and prepared four sticks made by debarked wood of a similar size, around 15 cm, which have a sharp point. He locked the knot with two of these sticks to avoid the knots to untie during the coking. Then he made another knot in the smaller hole which was in the other leg. When the bag is ready, they put it in a kind of table made with stones near the fire. They placed the bag, the spiced meat, the vegetables, and a jar with hot red wine. Then, they started to take out the small rocks and they surrounded them with the slices of meat. They put these rocks inside the bag, a helper closed the bag with it hands to avoid the steam to get out of it. When half of the bag is full with rocks and meat, they added the vegetables and then continued to add more rocks and meat. Once all the meat and vegetables are in the bag, they pour wine, close the opening, and they put the two crossed sticks to reinforce the knot. They put two rocks in the hot coal and over these two rocks, a larger and plane rock where the bag is placed. Then, more hot coal was added under this rock and surrounding it. The cooking took at least one hour; during

Fig. 7.7 Cooking of the "*Chaya en Bolsa*"

this time the "*puestero*" turns the bag to let the heat cook the bag evenly. When the bag started to increase the heat, one of the openings was untied to let the steam out of the bag. After some time, the liquids and juices were poured in a jar from which all the guests share and drink. This liquid had melted grease, wine, and all the juices from the meat. To avoid the "*chaya*" to cool off, they put a cloth over it. During the cooking, the skin of the "*chaya*" started to break, and some juice dropped over the stone. When all the skin was roasted, they put the bag over a tray and carry it to the table. Once it was on the table, they cut the bag in pieces and served a piece of meat, vegetables and a piece of the skin which had abundant grease. Then, they poured with a ladle more juice. The preparation of one animal with this recipe is enough to feed between 10 and 15 people.

7.6 Discussion

Prichard (2003) observed in the Tehuelches society that the hunting of Rheas did not differ from the hunting of other animals of similar importance like the guanaco. Our direct observations and the information from historic sources showed both the economic and social importance of Rheas. The wide spatial distribution of these birds made them an ubiquitous resource, complemented with the collection of eggs. This highlights that Rheas are hunted during special events, related to the congregation of people, such as parties (e.g. birthdays, weddings, Christian celebrations, among others) or tasks related with the herds, like marking and vaccination of the animals. During these parties it was evident that the hunting of the Rhea is a highly anticipated social activity during the year. Throughout this activity, people share information regarding the quality of the fields in different localities, the frequency of rains and problems with predators such as puma and foxes. It is quite common during these meetings, while the complete family is present, to have the opportunity to establish new relationships like dating partners and fiancés.

In all the conversations the "*puesteros*" mention the preoccupation of the conservation of the species and the proper practices that allow protecting them. For example, the selection of the animals being hunted, those which are not fat enough are left behind as well as the exclusive election of males. This election intends to protect the females to promote the safety of the eggs. They also do not hunt during spring when the males are hatching the eggs. If the male gets up it will no longer take care of his eggs and the future offspring would be lost, the hatching begins the first days of September and extends until November (Bruning 1974; Drenowatz et al. 1995; Reboreda and Fernández 1997).

The seasonality involved in the hunt of Rheas, takes place during autumn and winter (March–July). According to the information provided by the "*puesteros*", these are the months in which they have less work with their livestock. It is also a moment in which the animals have a more abundant grease reserve, a fact confirmed by the economic utility index (Giardina 2006). It has been estimated that in autumn, *Rhea pennata* had around 2700 grams of grease, which is equivalent to 20% of the exploitable resources of the animal (Giardina 2006). On the other hand, the chronicles mentioned the great importance that the hunt of Rheas had to obtain and consume grease by the native populations (Musters 1997).

When historical and present sources are compared, they show a great similitude regarding the practices used for hunting Rheas. Even though nowadays this hunting is made using horses, the ethnohistoric information mentions that human groups from southern Patagonia used the same technique of rounding the birds in a circle without horses (Guinnard 2006). This suggests that this technique could have been used in prehispanic times, before the introduction of horses.

The information generated from this work and from historic sources indicates that for the hunting of Rheas they still used "*boleadoras*" instead of fire guns. This reinforces the argument that Rheas hunting have a high social value, that involved around 15/30 people and it is related with meetings and parties. Dogs are also important participants in the hunts, improving the capacity of pursuit and capture of Rheas.

7.7 Final Remarks

In this chapter, we present the way in which people from northern Patagonia obtain and consume Rheas, using information from interviews to local people, direct observations in the field and data provided by historic sources.

During our observations, Rheas were preferred over other wild animals of the region. The grease seems to be the main attraction of this prey, as chronicles and local people mention (Agüero Blanch 1970). However, the feathers, skin, and bones are mentioned as important sub products obtained from these birds. In addition, the eggs are a great source of energy and kilocalories they provide, but also due to the behavior of Rheas, that generate nests with a dozen of eggs, which are easy to gather (Giardina et al. 2013).

The places selected to hunt are commonly related to geoforms, which are known to the "*puesteros*". These are recurring places to hunt Rheas. In relation to the observations made directly in the hunt, the night when they arrive at the "*puesto*" or "*real*", they rearrange the "*boleadoras*" that have been broken and make new "*boleadoras*" if anyone has lost them. This is the moment, in which everybody comments what happened during the day and many stories became part of their shared memory for future story-telling.

The hunting of these animals was made during autumn and winter, when herding activities are reduced and Rheas have the greatest reserve of grease in the year. Speed and danger are two characteristics that make it difficult to capture Rheas. The hunting technique seems to remain without modifications and perhaps similar to the practice that could have been performed by pedestrian groups (Guinnard 2006). The challenges during hunting may have implied that Rheas did not have an important role in the diet of prehistoric populations. Only in particular moments, when different bands aggregate, the communal hunting could have taken place. Therefore, the presence of Rheas in the archaeological record would be very occasional.

On the other hand, the chronicles of the first explorers point out the importance of Rheas in the diet of the ethnographic groups. However, we must consider that this evidence corresponds to the period after the incorporation of the horse. It is just after the incorporation of the horse that meat and especially grease from this resource became important. Ethnohistoric, ethnographic and ethnoarchaeological data are crucial to study the continuity and changes in Rheas' hunting. At this point, we can infer that before the incorporation of the horse, due to the ethological characteristics of the animal, the exploitation was mainly related to eggs acquisition.

We propose as an hypothesis that the incorporation of horses and dogs may have improved the chances to capture Rheas—making its consumption more frequent after the Spaniards invasion. In Alero Puesto Carrasco site the Rheas record shows an important increase for the last 300 years, being one of the sites with the greatest presence of these birds (Giardina 2010b, c). More post-Spanish zooarchaeological records will improve our capability to test that hypothesis.

References

Agüero Blanch V (1967) Supervivencia aborigen en la alimentación, en el Departamento de Malargüe, (Mendoza). Anales de Arqueología y Etnología 22:93–100

Agüero Blanch V (1969–1970) Malargüe Pueblo trashumante. *Anales de Arqueología y Etnología* 24–25:209–223

Agüero Blanch V (1970) La caza ritual del guanaco y del avestruz. Boletín de Antropología 3:103–121

Álvarez MC, Heider G (2019) Conocimiento tradicional y sus implicancias para la caza de jabalí y ñandú en comunidades campesinas del sur de la provincia de San Luis, Argentina. Revista Etnobiología 17(1):5–17

Beerbohm J (2004) *Vagando por la Patagonia. La vida entre los cazadores de ñandúes y un motín en Punta arenas. Agosto 1877–Noviembre 1877*, edition. Zagier and Urruty, Ushuaia

Belardi J (1999) Hay choiques en la terraza. Información tafonómica y primeras implicaciones arqueo faunísticas para Patagonia. Arqueología 9:163–187

Bocco de Abeyá A (1988) Contribución al conocimiento del espacio social pastoral de subsistencia. Estudio de caso: los puesteros trashumantes del departamento de Malargüe, Mendoza. Cuadernos de Antropología Social 1:79–96

Bruning D (1974) Social structure and reproductive behavior of the Greater Rhea. *Living Bird* 13:251–294

Cabrera A (1976) Regiones fitogeográficas argentinas. Enciclopedia Argentina de Agricultura y Jardinería. ACME, Buenos Aires

Claraz J (1988) *Diario de viaje de exploración al Chubut 1865–1866*, edition. Marymar, Buenos Aires

Cruz I, Elkin D (2003) Structural bone density of the lesser Rhea (*Pterocnemia pennata*) (Aves: Rheidae). Taphonomic and archaeological implications. J Archaeol Sci 30:37–44

del Papa L, Moro L (2017) Representación diferencial de partes esqueletales de Rhea americana en el sitio Beltrán Onofre Banegas-Lami Hernández del Chaco seco (Santiago del Estero). Revista del Museo de Antropología 10:7–18

Drenowatz C, Sales J, Sarasqueta D, Weilbrenner A (1995) History & geography. In: Drenowatz C (ed) The ratite encyclopedia: ostrich, emu, rhea. Ratite Records Incorporated, San Antonio, TX, pp 3–30

Embon A (1950) Fuentes Históricas con Noticias Etnográficas y Arqueológicas del Indígena Patagón (AoeniKenk). Unpublished Doctoral Dissertation, Facultad de Humanidades y Ciencia de la Educación, Universidad Nacional de la Plata

Fernández P (2000) Rendido a tus pies: acerca de la composición anatómica de los conjuntos arqueo faunísticos con restos de Rheiformes de Pampa y Patagonia. In: Belardi J, Carballo F, Espinosa S (eds) Desde el País de los Gigantes, Perspectivas arqueológicas en Patagonia. UNPA, Río Gallegos, pp 572–586

Frontini R, Picasso M (2010) Aprovechamiento de *Rhea americana* en la localidad arqueológica El Guanaco. In: Gutiérrez M, De Nigris M, Fernández P, Giardina M, Gil A, Izeta A, Neme G, Yacobaccio H (eds) Zooarqueología a principios del siglo XXI. Ediciones del Espinillo, Buenos Aires, pp 563–574

Garvey J, Cochrane B, Field J, Boney C (2011) Modern emu (*Dromaiusnovaehollandiae*) butchery, economic utility and analogues for the Australian archaeological record. Environ Archaeol 16(2):97–112. https://doi.org/10.1179/174963111X13110803260840

Giardina M (2006) Anatomía económica de Rheidae. Intersecciones en Antropología 7:263–276

Giardina M (2010a) El aprovechamiento de la avifauna entre las sociedades cazadoras recolectoras del sur de Mendoza: un enfoque arqueozoológico. Unpublished Doctoral Dissertation, Facultad de Ciencias Naturales y Museo, Universidad Nacional de la Plata

Giardina M (2010b) Human exploitation of Rheidae in North Patagonia, Argentina (South America). In: Prummel W, Zeiler J, Brinkhuizen D (eds) Birds in Archaeology. Groningen Archaeological Studies, Barkhuis, pp 97–102

Giardina M (2010c) Registro zooarqueológico en el Alero Puesto Carrasco: un aporte para discutir la explotación de rheidos en Nordpatagonia. In: Gutiérrez M, De Nigris M, Fernández P, Giardina M, Gil A, Izeta A, Neme G, Yacobaccio H (eds) Zooarqueología a principios del siglo XXI. Ediciones del Espinillo, Buenos Aires, pp 133–143

Giardina M, Neme G, Gil A (2013) Rheidae egg human exploitation and stable isotopes: trends from West Central Argentina. Int J Osteoarchaeol. https://doi.org/10.1002/oa.2346

Giardina M (2018) Economic anatomy of Rheidae and its implication for the archeological record. Archaeol Anthropol Sci. https://doi.org/10.1007/s12520-018-0659-x

Guinnard A (2006) *Tres años entre los patagones: apasionado relato de un francés cautivo en la Patagonia (1856–1859)*, edition Continente, Buenos Aires

Janz L, Elston R, Burr G (2009) Dating North Asian surface assemblages with ostrich eggshell: implications for palaeoecology and extirpation. J Archaeol Sci 36:1982–1989

Miotti L (1998) Zooarqueología de la Meseta Central de Santa Cruz, Un enfoque de las estrategias adaptativas aborígenes y los paleoambientes. Museo Municipal de Historia Natural, San Rafael, Mendoza

Medina M, Pastor S, Apolinaire E, Turnes L (2011) Late Holocene subsistence and social integration in sierras of Córdoba (Argentina): the South-American ostrich eggshells evidence. J Archaeol Sci 38:2071–2078

Moreno F (2018) Aprovechamiento de ñandú (*Rhea americana*) en la prehistoria del sudeste uruguayo. Archaeofauna 27:83–92

Musters G (1997) Vida entre los Patagones. Un Año de excursiones por tierras no frecuentadas desde el Estrecho de Magallanes hasta Río Negro, edition. El Elefante Blanco, Buenos Aires

Nagaoka L (2005) Declining foraging efficiency and moa carcass exploitation in southern New Zealand. J Archaeol Sci 32:1328–1338

O'Connell J (2000) An emu hunt. In: Anderson A, Murray T (eds) Australian archaeologist: collected papers in honor of Jim Allen. Coombs Academic Publishing, The Australian National University, Canberra, pp 172–181

Otaola C, Giardina M, Fry M, Neme G, Wolverton S (2016) Zooarqueología y Tafonomía en pastores actuales del Sur de Mendoza. Intersecciones en Antropología 17:121–127

Prates L, Acosta Hospitaleche C (2010) Las aves de sitios arqueológicos del Holoceno tardío de Norpatagonia, Argentina. Los sitios Negro Muerto y Angostura 1 (Río Negro). Archaeofauna 19:7–18

Prichard H (2003) En el Corazón de la Patagonia, en busca del últimomilodón, septiembre 1990–Mayo 1991, edition. Zagier and Urruty, Ushuaia

Reboreda J, Fernández G (1997) The effect of sex and group size on individual vigilance in the greater rhea, Rhea americana. Ethology 103:198–207

Roig F, Martínez Carretero E, Méndez E (2000) Mapa de vegetación de la Provincia de Mendoza (eds: Abraham ME, Rodríguez Martínez F). Recursos y problemas ambientales de zonas áridas CRICYT, Mendoza, p 10

Salemme M, Miotti L (1998) The status of Rheids in Patagonia: environmental approach and economic interpretation during the late Pleistocene/early Holocene transition. In: 8 International Conference of Archaeozoology. ICAZ, Abstracts: 249. Victoria (Canadá)

Salemme M, Frontini R (2011) The exploitation of Rheidae in Pampa and Patagonia (Argentina) as recorded by chroniclers, naturalists, and voyagers. J Anthropol Archaeol 30:473–483

Tambussi C, Acosta Hospitaleche C (2002) Reidos (Aves) Cuaternarios de Argentina: inferencias paleoambientales. Ameghiniana 39:95–102

Wolverton S (2013) Interdisciplinarity in an era of rapid environmental change. Ethnobiol Lett 5:21–25

Chapter 8
The Role of Small Prey in Human Populations of Northwest Patagonia and Its Implications

Diego D. Rindel, Florencia Gordón, Bruno Moscardi, and S. Ivan Perez

Abstract The prehistoric rise in the consumption of small prey has traditionally been explained by archaeologist as the result of diet intensification under situations of demographic pressure. However, alternative explanations have been proposed, such as processes of niche differentiation, nutritional decisions that increase reproductive success or processes of complementarity between resources. In particular, studies of Nutritional Ecology, which focuses on the reproductive advantages of the consumption of all the essential nutrients to the human life, rather than the energy return rate per se, provides an alternative explanation for changes in the consumption of small prey. In this study we examine the role of this prey—which includes dasipodids (i.e., piche and peludo), mollusks, birds, small carnivores, rodents, and fish—in the diet of Northwestern Patagonian prehistoric populations, considering different demographic scenarios for the human populations and their most common prey, guanaco. We use zooarchaeological and stable isotope data to describe dietary patterns and changes, and consider the available ethnohistorical information for the exploitation of these resources in the area. Finally, we gather nutritional and socioethological data of the fauna from the region and discuss some of the applications and assumptions of prey choice models. We suggest that the role of small prey in human diets in Northwest Patagonia was more important along the Holocene than what is traditionally held and was complementary to the consumption of guanaco in terms of availability and nutritional content and in the costs of obtaining and processing.

Keywords Northwest Patagonia · Hunter-gatherers · Diet breadth models · Nutritional Ecology

---

D. D. Rindel (✉)
CONICET-INAPL, 3 de febrero 1370, Capital Federal, Buenos Aires, Argentina

F. Gordón · S. I. Perez
CONICET-FCNyM (UNLP), Calle 60 y 122, La Plata, Argentina

B. Moscardi
FCNyM (UNLP), Calle 60 y 122, La Plata, Argentina

© Springer Nature Switzerland AG 2021
J. B. Belardi et al. (eds.), *Ancient Hunting Strategies in Southern South America*,
The Latin American Studies Book Series,
https://doi.org/10.1007/978-3-030-61187-3_8

8.1 Introduction

From a human behavioral ecology perspective, changes in human diet can be explained as a result of the operation of different variables, such as environmental changes (Meltzer 1999; Wolverton 2005), demographic changes in predators and/or prey, different socio-cultural processes (e.g., differences in foraging goals between women and men; Zeanah 2004), costly signaling (Bliege Bird et al. 2001), among others. However, from this perspective, small prey were usually considered as "marginal" (Davidson 1976, 1989; Simms 1987). In this sense, when they enter in the diet of human populations, were typically explained as a response to conditions of population growth and/or demographic stress (Binford 1968; Flannery 1969; Stiner et al. 2000; Stiner 2001; among others). This explanation is based on formal Diet breadth models that predict that the order of selection of the resources during their search by hunters is carried out to maximize the energy rate in foraging (Mac Arthur and Pianka 1966; Hawkes and O'Connell 1992). According to these models, prey are randomly distributed in the territory, have a fixed amount of energy and required a fixed time to hunt, process, and consume. These variables are the constraints that influence the hunter's decisions, which theoretically will tend to choose high ranked species, which optimize the handling cost/energy return ratio (Kelly 2013). Therefore, the general expectation of these models is that, if processes of increase in population density (i.e., population packing sensu Binford 2001) occurred, human groups would deplete the preferred prey, resulting in the introduction of more species in the diet (Stiner et al. 2000). Alternatively, Nutritional Ecology models focus on the reproductive benefits of the consumption of vital essential nutrients, suggesting that some nutrient-rich resources, such as small prey, at all times have an important role in the human diet (Hockett and Haws 2003; Haws and Hockett 2004).

Northwest Patagonia is an ideal region to study the importance of the consumption of small prey by human groups and their temporal and spatial changes in relation to human population increase and nutritional demands. Several works, based on molecular data, estimated a positive trend for a sustained increase in the size of human populations through the Holocene (Perez et al. 2016, 2017; Bernal et al. 2018). The population growth rate would have accelerated after 7000–6000 years BP. Likewise, the statistical analysis of the frequency and distribution of radiocarbon dates led to similar demographic trends (Barberena et al. 2015; Perez et al. 2016, 2017; Bernal et al. 2018). Particularly, the demographic curves based on radiocarbon data show that, although the populations would have increased during the Holocene, this increase would have occurred in an accelerated way after 3000 years BP to reach its maximum size around 500 years BP. In this sense, it is worth mentioning the detection of sites with a high frequency of buried individuals, particularly in the North of Neuquén, which are chronologically located at the beginning of the late Holocene, in particular Hermanos Lazcano (Della Negra et al. 2014) and Aquihuecó sites (Della Negra and Novellino 2005; Perez et al. 2009; Gordón et al. 2019a). This region also displays large changes in human diet through the Late Pleistocene-Holocene. Rindel (2017) identified a general tendency for Neuquén toward a decrease in the number of consumed species, starting after the extinction of megafauna. This work indicates a high faunal diversity in the beginning of the sequence of El Trébol site—in the end of Late Pleistocene—and a decrease in the number of species in the sites of the Early Holocene that decreases again toward the Middle Holocene and continues decreasing toward the Late Holocene. More importantly, the consumption of guanaco (*Lama guanicoe*, frequently considered as the main prey of hunter-gatherers of the region) relative to other species shows that the contribution of this species to the human diet grows over time, according with the expectation of the demographic trend inferred with molecular data (Metcalf et al. 2016; Moscardi et al. 2020). The guanaco is the most ubiquitously represented species in almost all sites in the region (Rindel 2017), being the main prey in North Neuquén, where the diet was composed in more than 80% by *Rhea* and *Lama guanicoe* (Gordón et al. 2018). In this context it is interesting to remark that the guanaco presents a very lean meat that probably does not cover many basic nutritional requirements (Rindel 2013).

Interestingly, molecular studies of current and ancient guanaco populations suggest a recent origin of *Lama guanicoe guanicoe*, the subspecies from Patagonia, a demographic and geographic expansion of this subspecies along a north-south axis, and a recolonization of Southern Patagonia from northern populations between 8000 and 10,000 years BP (Metcalf et al. 2016; Moscardi et al. 2020). Particularly, Metcalf et al. (2016) have indicated that guanaco mitochondrial DNA samples dated before 10,000 years BP differ from the current guanaco populations, especially those from Southern Patagonia. Moreover, the low molecular diversity of the current *L. guanicoe guanicoe* specimens suggests that this subspecies experiences a recent demographic growth, probably after 5000 years BP, with all mtDNA lineages coalescing in the Holocene (Marín et al. 2013; Moscardi et al. 2020). Therefore, the guanaco and human demographic histories appear to display a similar trend in Patagonia, suggesting a significant relationship between both (Moscardi et al. 2020; Perez et al. 2017; Bernal et al. 2018), and probably explaining in part the increase in human population density in the region along the Holocene.

In this context, it is remarkable that since the beginning of the human peopling in Northwest Patagonia (12,500 cal. years BP), a moment characterized by low population density (Perez et al. 2016), small prey constituted part of the human diet (Rindel 2017). However, the temporal and regional changes in the role of small prey in human populations of Northwest Patagonia and its relationships with human demography have not yet been explored and discussed in depth. On the basis of previous studies and following important regional differences in consumption of resources and human demography (Fernández and Panarello 2001; Neme et al. 2013; Gil et al. 2014a; Bernal et al. 2016; Gordón et al. 2018, 2019b), we divide the region into three different areas (South Mendoza, North Neuquén, and South Neuquén; Fig. 8.1). Specifically, we analyze the importance and the changes in the contribution of small fauna in the diet of the human groups from the different areas of Northwest Patagonia and related them to processes of human and guanaco demographic growth during the Holocene. We discuss if demographic pressure and/or niche differentiation processes, nutritional decisions that grant greater reproductive success, and processes of complementarity between resources, could be important

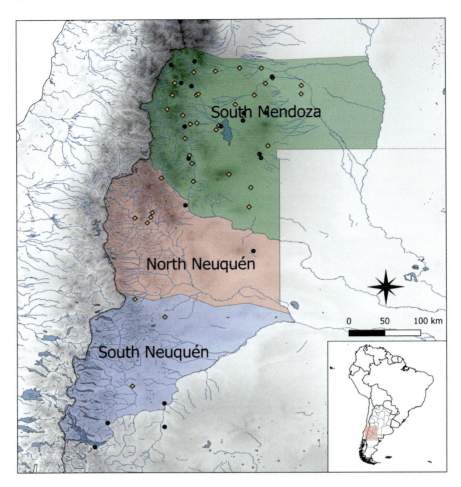

Fig. 8.1 Map of the study area. References: Provenance of samples. yellow diamonds: human stable isotopes; black circles: zooarchaeological samples

to explain the patterns of small fauna consumption through the Holocene. In order to explore these subjects, we used several lines of evidence to investigate diet changes in the region. First, we study the main trends in human diet at temporal and spatial scales by analyzing zooarchaeological data by area, starting from 15,000 years BP. To explore dietary patterns in human populations of the last 4300 years, we complemented the zooarchaeological data with stable isotope analysis. Secondly, we explore the ethnohistorical literature to search about the importance of the consumption of small fauna for hunter-gatherer populations of the region in historical times. Finally, to reconstruct the hunter-gatherers predatory behavior, we gather and analyze nutritional yield and socio-ethological data of the different consumed species in the region. The results are integrated and discussed from a traditional perspective (i.e., formal

Diet breadth models) to be then reconsidered from a Nutritional Ecology point of view. This framework gives us tools for interpreting why in some specific areas and moments small fauna were incorporated to the diet of human groups.

8.2 Archaeological and Ethnohistorical Lines of Evidence

8.2.1 Zooarchaeological Data to Describe Spatial and Temporal Diet Changes

In order to explore the changes in the faunal component of the diet of human prehistoric populations over time, we defined three areas, as follow: South Mendoza (SMza—the area between the Barrancas-Colorado river and the Diamante river and Atuel river-Llancanelo lagoon system), North Neuquén (NNqn—the area between the Barrancas-Colorado river and the 38th parallel south) and South Neuquén (SNqn—the area between the 38th parallel south and the southern province limit). We also include in the last area two sites located in the Rio Negro province in order to cover the complete temporal sequence of zooarchaeological data. We analyzed zooarchaeological assemblages previously published and dated between the Late Pleistocene and historical times from several sites in Northwest Patagonia. Only sites with large sample size, long occupational sequences and adequate chronological control were included. Most samples were previously taphonomically analyzed and represent unambiguous evidence of human consumption. An exception is the assemblage corresponding to El Trébol site, which was not analyzed from a taphonomic perspective. However, the species included in this assemblage also present evidence of anthropic processing (Lezcano et al. 2010). As a whole, 47 assemblages belonging to 34 sites were analyzed, 28 from South Mendoza (Otaola et al. 2012; Neme and Gil 2009), 2 from North Neuquén (Barberena et al. 2015, Bernal et al. 2018; Rindel 2017) and 4 from South Neuquén subregions (Bernal et al. 2018; Cordero 2010; Lezcano et al. 2010; Rindel 2017) (Fig. 8.1 and Table 8.1). It is worth mentioning that there is no evidence for South Mendoza for the period 15,000–9000, there are no samples for North Neuquén in the periods 9000–7000 and 7000–5000, while South Neuquén presents occupations in all periods. The total sample corresponds to 16,208 specimens that were determined taxonomically; among them 9623 correspond to guanaco (*L. guanicoe*) (Table 8.1). For the following analyses and based on their calibrated dates, this sample was divided into periods that are sufficiently long to have a relatively homogenous sample and small enough to define changes in the diet on a relevant scale (Table 8.1). Since these periods were unequal in length, a correction factor was applied by dividing each period by its number of years. In the study region, in addition to large fauna such as the cervidae (*Hippocamelus bisulcus* and *Ozotoceros bezoarticus*), guanacos (*Lama guanicoe*), and rheids (*Rhea americana* and *Rhea pennata*), were exploited small preys such as dasipodids (*Chaetoprhactus villosus* and *Zaedyus pichiy*), fish (*Odonthesthes* sp. and *Percichtys trucha*), aquatic

Table 8.1 Taxa per area and period (NISP). References: SMza: 9000–7000: Arroyo Malo 3 (9-7,5) and El Manzano Unit D; 7000–5000: Arroyo El Desecho 4 and Arroyo Malo 3 (7.5-5); 5000–2000: Arroyo Malo 3 (5-2,2), Cueva Palulo, Cueva Luna, Cueva Arroyo Colorado Unidad 1, Cueva Arroyo Colorado Unidad 1, Llancanelo 17, Llancanelo 22, Llancanelo 50, Panchino, Arroyo Malo 3 (<2200), Laguna El Sosneado 3, El Manzano units ABC and Alero Puesto Carrasco; 2000–0: La Olla, La Corredera, La Peligrosa, Rincón del Atuel 1, Agua de los Caballos, Ojo de Agua, Laguna Diamante, El Indígeno, Puesto Ortubia 1, El Bosquecillo 5, Los Leones 5, Los Leones 3, Arroyo Malo 1 and Los Peuquenes (Neme and Gil 2009 for Arroyo Malo 3 site) (Otaola et al. 2012 for the rest of sites). NNqn: 15,000–9000: Cueva Huenul component 2 (Barberena et al. 2015); 5000–2000: Cueva Ruka units 2/3 (Bernal et al. 2018); 2000–0: Cueva Ruka unit 1 (Bernal et al. 2018), Cueva Huenul component 4 (Barberena et al. 2015). SNqn: 15,000–9000: El Trébol (levels 5 and 7D-Early Holocene) (Lezcano et al. 2010), Epullán Grande stratum 7 and Traful 1 Initial Occupations (Cordero 2010); 9000–7000: Traful 1 component 1, Epullán Grande stratum 106, Traful 1 component IIA (Cordero 2010); 7000–5000: El Trébol (levels 1, 7A, 7B and 7C-Middle Holocene) (Lezcano et al. 2010); 5000–2000: Traful 1 component IIB (Cordero 2010); 2000–0: Cueva y Paredón Loncomán lower, middle and upper levels (Cordero 2010), El Trébol (levels 1, 2, 3 and 4-Ceramic) (Lezcano et al. 2010). *Fragments of eggs

TAXA	SMza NISP				NNqn NISP			SNqn NISP				
	9000–7000	7000–5000	5000–2000	2000–0	15000–9000	5000–2000	0–2000	15000–9000	9000–7000	7000–5000	5000–2000	2000–0
Lama guanicoe	53	11	1604	349	24	98	229	1033	2510	151	260	3300
Hippocamelus bisulcus								129	2	56	9	2
Cervidae (*Ozotoceros bezoarticus*)			2					16		2		
Lycalopex culpaeus						6		61	13	56	1	21
Lycalopex griseus								127	20	1	1	32
Dusycion avus?								5				
Conepatus chinga								62				66

(continued)

Table 8.1 (continued)

TAXA	SMza NISP				NNqn NISP			SNqn NISP				
	9000–7000	7000–5000	5000–2000	2000–0	15000–9000	5000–2000	0–2000	15000–9000	9000–7000	7000–5000	5000–2000	2000–0
Galictis cuja												1
Lyncodon patagonicus												1
Oncifelis sp.								2		3		4
Puma concolor												8
Dolichotis patagonum			1	2								
Microcavia australis			1									
Myocastor coipus	2											
Lagidium viscacia							1	9	100	5	5	30
Chaetophractus villosus	9		69					343	29	7	1	275
Zaedyus pichiy			39	3				14		24		426

(continued)

Table 8.1 (continued)

TAXA	SMza NISP				NNqn NISP			SNqn NISP				
	9000–7000	7000–5000	5000–2000	2000–0	15000–9000	5000–2000	0–2000	15000–9000	9000–7000	7000–5000	5000–2000	2000–0
Dasipodidae indet.	41	1	73	748	9	51	2	1		5		343
Rheidae Indet.	3*		41*	9*	*	*		*	*	*		
Rhea pennata	1		28	1		4	1	70	21			65
Rhea americana				5								
Mylodon								242		49		
Xenartha	1											
Bird Indet. (big)	55		1			2	8	48	13	45		40
Bird Indet.(medium)			6*	32								
Tinamidae Indet.				5*								
Eudromia elegans				4								
Anseriforme Indet.				1								
Anatidae Indet.			1	31								
Anas sp.			3	6								
Anas platalea				1								

(continued)

8 The Role of Small Prey in Human Populations …

Table 8.1 (continued)

TAXA	SMza NISP				NNqn NISP			SNqn NISP				
	9000–7000	7000–5000	5000–2000	2000–0	15000–9000	5000–2000	0–2000	15000–9000	9000–7000	7000–5000	5000–2000	2000–0
Anas georgica			1									
Anas specularoides				2								
Choephaga melanoptera				1								
Rallidae Indet.			1	5								
Charadriiformes Indet.				2								
Attigisgayi				1								
Scolopacidae Indet.			1									
Bird Indet. small		1	16									
Zenaida auriculata				1								
Passeriformes Indet.			22	2								
Suboscine Indet.				1								

(continued)

Table 8.1 (continued)

TAXA	SMza NISP				NNqn NISP			SNqn NISP				
	9000–7000	7000–5000	5000–2000	2000–0	15000–9000	5000–2000	0–2000	15000–9000	9000–7000	7000–5000	5000–2000	2000–0
Osteichthyes Indet.												
Actinopterygii												
Fish Indet.		648		37	1			29	3	176		8
Perciformes (*Percichtys trucha*)			2	57								
Atheriniformes (*Odonthesthes hatcheri*)			486	4								
Chilinia sp.												8
Diplodon sp.								3	11	491	14	448
Subtotal species/genus	165	13	3046	1310	34	161	241	2076	2722	1071	291	5078
NTAXA	6	3	12	18	3	5	5	16	10	12	7	17

birds (*Anas* sp. among others), flightless birds (*Eudromia elegans*, among others), flyng birds (*Zenaida auriculata*, among others), mollusks (*Diplodon* sp.), carnivores (felids, canids, and mustelids), and several species of rodents (varying in size from maras-*Dolichotis patagonum*- to tucu-tucu -*Ctenomys* sp.) (Table 8.1). There is also evidence of the consumption of eggs (mostly Rheidae) in the three areas analyzed and in most periods (Table 8.1). Temporal changes in species diversity and the relative contribution of guanaco to human diet were explored, plotting different variables of interest against the mean age of each stratum. The strata were constructed from calibrated dates, using the program calib 7.0.4 and the calibration curve for the southern hemisphere "shcal13."

Changes in species diversity over time provide the most direct estimate of the impact of ecological disturbances on human population dynamics. So, for assessing temporal changes in diversity, the number of species (NTAXA; Grayson and Delpech 1998) for different temporal strata from each archaeological site was obtained. Additionally, the Shannon Diversity Index (Shannon 1948; based on NISP values) was calculated for each temporal stratum, which allows us to measure the relative proportion of each species to the total sample (Grayson 1984). Third, proportional changes in the primary prey exploited by humans in Patagonia (guanaco, *Lama guanicoe*) were estimated. The relative frequency of guanaco over other faunal species using the NISP guanaco/NTAXA index (Grayson and Delpech 1998) was measured for each temporal stratum. Additionally, the contribution of small prey was estimated using NISPsmall-prey/NTAXA index. It is worth nothing that the values of these last two indexes (i.e., NISPg/NTAXA and NISPsp/NTAXA) were standardized by turning them into proportions, dividing the total value of each period of every region by the sum of the NISP/NTAXA values of that region. Figure 8.2a displays the temporal changes in NTAXA in South Mendoza (SMza), North Neuquén (NNqn) and South Neuquén (SNqn). In all analyzed regions, there is a general trend toward an increase in the number of exploited taxa (NTAXA) throughout the Holocene, which increases particularly faster during the Late Holocene. In SMza there in a downward trend in the 7000–5000 years BP period, followed by a subsequent increase. In the case of NNqn, a low number of species is detected until 6000 years BP and a constant increase is observed from this moment on, in a similar way to that observed for the two other areas. In SNqn there is an increase in the number of exploited taxa since the Pleistocene-Holocene transition until about 5000 BP, followed by a downward trend toward 5000-2000 period, and a steady increase until recent times. We want to highlight the general similarity between SMza and SNqn, with a relatively large number of used taxa in both regions from 5000 calib years BP onwards. Figure 8.2b shows the changes in Shannon Diversity Index over time in the three considered areas. In SMza a high diversity peak is detected in the Early Holocene, followed by a decrease in the Middle Holocene, and then an increase in the Late Holocene. The SNqn curve shows a relatively large diversity for the Pleistocene-Holocene transition, a decrease in the Early Holocene, an increase in Middle Holocene following by an abrupt decrease of the index in the 5000–2000 year period, and an increase again in last 2000 years AP. Finally, in NNqn, high values are only observed for the

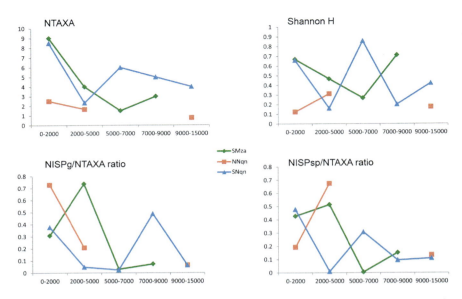

Fig. 8.2 Zooarchaeological patterns in the study area based on: **a** NTAXA. **b** Shannon (H) diversity index. **c** NISP guanaco/NTAXA ratio. **d** NISP small prey/NTAXA ratio. Since intervals are unequal in length, a correction factor was applied by dividing each period by the number of years represented

index in the Late Holocene, though we have to take into account that the periods 9000–7000 and 7000–5000 are not represented.

Figure 8.2c shows the NISPg/NTAXA Index, which measures the relative contribution of guanaco in the diet. SMza shows a relatively low contribution of guanaco in the diet until the Middle Holocene, at which point the proportion of this camelid increases significantly, although it is lower in the last 2000 years than in previous moments. SNqn shows a relatively different pattern: the contribution of the guanaco is relatively low at moments of the transition Pleistocene-Holocene, increases in the Early Holocene (9000–7000 BP), decreases in the Middle Holocene (7000–5000 years BP) and increases steadily from this last period until historical times. In NNqn there is an increase of this index from 5000 to 2000 calib. years BP. Figure 8.2d in turn shows the NISPsmall-prey/NTAXA depicting the relative frequency of small prey over the other species. The main trend, although with fluctuations, is toward an increase in the consumption frequency of these prey through the Holocene. Particularly, SNqn and SMza shows relatively high values in the last two periods, the former displaying a constant increase since the end of the Middle Holocene, and the latter showing a lesser decrease from that time. Interestingly, NNqn shows an important decrease during the same period, which contrasts with the synchronic rise in guanaco consumption in this area.

In summary, the main trends for all regions are an increase in the number of taxa throughout the Holocene, including small prey, with a pattern of diversity in U form, where high diversity is observed in the Pleistocene–Early Holocene and toward late

8 The Role of Small Prey in Human Populations ...

times of occupation (last 5000 years BP, with particular emphasis in the period 5000–3000), and finally, a fluctuating but greater role for the guanaco starting from the last 5000 years BP.

8.2.2 Stable Isotope Data to Explore Mean Diet in Each Subregion

The zooarchaeological line of evidence is complemented by an independent one; stable isotopes analysis of human remains. The chronological resolution of the available human remains sample specifically covers the last 4300 years, allowing us to model which species were included in the diet and, especially, in what percentage. We analyzed isotopic values of δ^{13}C and δ^{15}N from bone collagen of 88 adult individuals of both sexes belonging to prehistoric populations from Mendoza and Neuquén (Fernández and Panarello 2001; Gil et al. 2011; Gordón et al. 2013, 2018; Salgán al. 2012). Individuals were determined as adults on the basis of two criteria: the obliteration of the spheno-basilar suture and eruption of the third molar (Buikstra and Ubelaker 1994). The studied individuals also were grouped in the three samples corresponding to geographical areas SMza ($N = 53$), NNqn ($N = 26$) and SNqn ($N = 9$). The samples come from archaeological sites dated between $ca.$ 4000 and 200 calibrated years before present (cal. BP) (Bernal et al. 2016; Gil et al. 2011, 2014a, b; Gordón et al. 2018).

To estimate the mean contribution of resources to human diets, an isotopic ecology was constructed using 288 δ^{13}C and δ^{15}N values of plants and animals, current and archaeological, from Mendoza (SMza) and Neuquén (NNqn and SNqn) (Boeck et al. 2005; Gil et al. 2006, 2009, 2011, 2016; Giardina et al. 2014; Fernández et al. 2016; Barberena et al. 2018; Gordón et al. 2018; Otaola et al. 2019). Based on this previous archaeological evidence about the prehistoric diets in Mendoza and Neuquén, the resources were grouped in six categories: (1) Large herbivores (*Rhea* and *Lama*); (2) Small herbivore mammals (Rodents); (3) Carnivore-omnivore mammals (dasipodids, small felids and canids); (4) Birds; (5) C3 plants and (6) *Araucaria* (Table 8.2). These categories were generated considering the existence of archaeological evidence that

Table 8.2 Mean δ^{13}C and δ^{13}N and SD for different resources in study area

	Mean δ^{13}C	SD δ^{13}C	Mean δ^{15}N	SD δ^{15}N	N
Small mammals	−18.63	2.97	4.32	1.98	92
Large herbivores	−19.62	1.32	5.21	0.99	79
Birds	−14.03	3.39	9.68	2.09	46
C3 plants	−23.65	1.70	8.26	5.29	7
Carnivore-omnivore mammals	−17.53	1.43	7.03	1.740	64
Araucaria	−24.23	0.35	1.35	1.693	13

suggest the contribution of these resources to the diets of the populations inhabiting the regions studied. Moreover, resources exhibiting similar isotopic values were pooled within the same group (Gordón et al. 2018). The three studied areas encompass a similar diversity of available wild resources, partly because they display the same three phytogeographical regions (Patagonica, Monte and Altoandina). Sampling of isotope data for some resources is not exhaustive across areas, but available data suggest that isospace variation among sources is not substantial across Neuquén and South of Mendoza.

Bayesian mixing model implemented in MixSIAR GUI for R (Stock and Semmens 2013) was applied to analyze the proportional contribution of different sources to the diet of the consumers (i.e., individuals) using δ^{13}C and δ^{15}N values. The method takes into account Markov chain Monte Carlo (MCMC) algorithms to generate a posterior probability distribution of the diet proportions in each population. We established populations as a random effect and used the default parameters for MCMC, corresponding to the "very long" option. It is a method that considers uncertainty linked to multiple resources, fractionation values and isotope signatures (Parnell et al. 2013; Stock and Semmens 2013). We take this factor into account using the aforementioned categories of resource and isotope fractionation values for the different resources (for animals $\Delta 13$C 1.0 ± 0.3/ $\Delta 15$ N 4.0 ± 1.0 and for C3 plants and Araucaria: $\Delta 13$C 3.9 ± 1.4/ $\Delta 15$ N 2.2 ± 0.3 for C3). Based on experimental and comparative studies, fractionation values were defined (Hare et al. 1991; Bocherens and Drucker 2003). In this sense, in previous studies it has been shown that obtained results are more consistent in this way than if a single value is used for all resources (Bernal et al. 2016; Gordón et al. 2018). In order to correct Suess effect, $+1\%_0$ was added to the δ^{13}C values.

Geographical pattern indicates that SMza values are located around small fauna, particularly carnivores/omnivores (Fig. 8.3). In this sense, Table 8.3 shows that birds and small herbivores mammals explain 56.4% of the diet, while big herbivores contribute in a 15%. In the same table it is observed that vegetables and carnivores-omnivores mammals represent a minor contribution. In the case of NNqn, the greatest contribution is given for large herbivores, and then, but in a high proportion too, carnivores-omnivores mammals and *Araucaria* (Table 8.3). These three kinds of resources represent more than the 80% of the total diet (Table 8.3). Finally, in the SNqn, diet is mostly represented (more than 60%) by *Araucaria*. Then, the 10% of the diet is explained by the consumption of small fauna, represented by birds (Table 8.3). The rest of the resources are present in very low proportions (Fig. 8.3, Table 8.3). The increase of isotopic and radiocarbon data will allow us to delineate not only the spatial pattern but also the temporal one. These results indicate a good fit with faunal data for the last 5000 years, indicating a variable presence of small prey, being especially important in SMza.

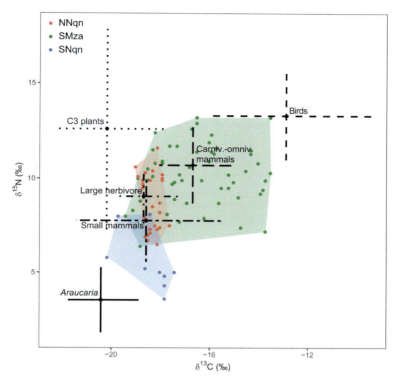

Fig. 8.3 Isospace plot of δ^{13}C and δ^{15}N for the resources and consumers grouped by geographical areas

Table 8.3 Mean dietary proportion for the studied human population by region. The dietary proportions are inferred using the Bayesian method implemented in MixSIAR. References: **Highly important. *Relatively important. +Marginally significant

	Large herbivores	C3 plants	Small mammals	Birds	Carnivore-omnivore mammals	Araucaria
SMza	0.155*	0.055	0.165*	0.399**	0.105+	0.12+
NNqn	0.362**	0.087	0.055	0.051	0.236**	0.209**
SNqn	0.068	0.026	0.078	0.108+	0.095	0.625**

8.2.3 Ethnohistorical Data

Following a chronological perspective, one kind of independent and complementary record to the archaeological data is the ethnohistorical information available for Patagonian region. In the reports of travelers to Patagonia, which began with the Hispanic-Indian contact in the sixteenth century, there are many references not only to the consumption of certain animal species, but also about the techniques used for their exploitation. Likewise, there are mentions of the differential nutritional contributions of the prey. In this section, we present a synthesis of the recovered ethnohistorical information from the review of these sources.

The ethnohistorical data provide a clear picture of the use of resources by Patagonia's historical groups, including the Northwest Patagonian ones. This data provides knowledge of the types of exploited prey, who obtained and consumed these items and what were the reasons given for their use in a living system. With this in mind, we review historical sources of travelers and explorers from north and south Patagonia to explore the mean regional diet during the contact of the Patagonian aborigines with the first Spanish travelers. Therefore, in order to study which animals were obtained, what was the objective of their capture, and if there was a differential procurement and consumption of these resources by specific segments of the population, the following variables were selected: presence of consumption of small prey, what species were selected, preference of animals with fat, presence of storage, evidence of egg consumption and differential procurement, and consumption of small prey by women and children.

In ethnographic and ethnohistorical literature there are numerous references to the procurement and consumption of alternative animals to the guanaco, mostly referring to small prey. The use of ñandú is frequently mentioned, even identifying this animal as preferred to the guanaco (Guinnard 1961; Bourne 1998; Priegue 1971; Claraz 1988; Musters 1997; Lista 1998; Onelli 1998; Prichard 2003). Likewise, the consumption of piche was favored due to the great amount of fat that it possessed (Moreno 1969; Priegue 1971; Lista 1998; D'Orbigny 1999; Aguerre 2000). Other animals often mentioned are skunk (Schmid 1964; Bourne 1998) and puma (Schmid 1964; Musters 1997). Particularly, is indicated in North Patagonia the obtaining of "hares," that is, mara patagónica (*Dolichotis patagonum*) (Priegue 1971; Claraz 1988; Lista 1998), as well as "mice" (Pigafetta 1963). Both in the coast and in the interior the consumption of birds is often mentioned (Viedma 1972; Priegue 1971; Lista 1998; Aguerre 2000). An interesting point is the abundant mention of the exploitation of eggs, especially those of ñandú (Guinnard 1961; Priegue 1971; Musters 1997; Lista 1998; Aguerre 2000). Toward the middle of the seventeenth century, domestic animals began to be included in the diet. The sources frequently mention the consumption of fat horsemeat (Guinnard 1961; Schmid 1964; de la Cruz 1969; Moreno 1969; Claraz 1988; Bourne 1998; Meinrado Hux 1998; D'Orbigny 1999; Aguerre 2000) and cattle (Claraz 1988; D'Orbigny 1999).

Interestingly, the sources point out to the addition of fats from piche, choique, and other animals to the guanaco meat or jerky to make it more palatable (Schmid 1964; Musters 1997; Aguerre 2000). The case is similar to that of domestic animals, since meat and especially horse fat and bovid fat were consumed in large quantities due to its resemblance to ñandú meat (Claraz 1988) and its fat was mixed with meat or jerky of wild species (Aguerre 2000).

Unlike meat, used for immediate consumption (with the possible exception of charqui), fat was stored in leather bags that were transported from camp to camp (Claraz 1988; Musters 1997; Bourne 1998; Lista 1998; Onelli 1998). The long bones of the different prey were also stored with a view to their subsequent processing in order to obtain the prized medullar fat (Claraz 1988; Musters 1997; Aguerre 2000). It was also used as a cooking product, that is, for frying (de la Cruz 1969; Musters 1997; Bridges and Briano 2000; Lista 1998). Finally, it is mentioned in the sources that in the consumption of these small prey all group participated, but there are repeated references to preferential consumption by women, children, and babies (Guinnard 1961; Musters 1997; D'Orbigny 1999). The absence of farinaceous foods in the diet of the aborigines is indicated as an explanation for the consumption of fat and meat with fat (Musters 1997).

In summary, the ethnohistorical data indicate that many resources of small fauna were exploited in all Patagonian region, including the studied areas in the north-western of the region. In most cases, the reasons given for their use were a complementarity of nutrients, given that they provided resources that were not present in large quantities in the guanaco, especially fat. Also, this complementarity was also temporary, given that some of these nutrients where susceptible to storage. It is important to note that the sources suggest that the rapid acceptance of domestic animals (horse, cow and sheep) in Patagonia could have been due to the fact that they provided nutrients that were present in small quantities in traditional aboriginal diets. Finally, several of the sources reviewed indicate that the acquisition and especially the consumption of these resources of small fauna were destined preferentially to certain segments of the population: women and children.

8.3 Socio-Ethological and Nutritional Parameters of the Consumed Prey in the Study Area

Considering the previous data and results, we could now turn our attention to the socio-ecological characteristics and to investigate the nutritional traits of the resource base of populations from Northwest Patagonia. This section presents some anatomical, socio-ecological and behavioral characteristics of the animals that have formed the resource base and represent the nutritional information of the consumed species. These data are presented due to the importance of these different aspects in order to evaluate human predatory behavior. As Foley (1983) has emphasized, it is important to use neo-ecological data systematically in conjunction with zooarchaeological analyzes. According to this author, the anatomy, ecology and behavior of the prey can be characterized in terms of a series of attributes that may be of importance to the predator. Similarly, the requirements and priorities of the predator can be formally described and related to the characteristics of the prey. From this approach it is possible to specify the links in the chain of inference between the structure of the archaeological record and the prehistoric hunting techniques, and in this way to reconstruct the human predatory behavior based on the attributes of the prey. To fulfill this goal, we turn to Scheifler (2019) who obtained from the bibliography values of live weight and Kcal/kg, optimal condition and differential availability throughout the annual cycle, period of main activity along the day and the character

Table 8.4 Live weight, energetic return and socio-ethological characteristics of the exploited resources in the study area, modified from Scheiffler 2019

Taxa	Weight	Yield		Optimal condition	Social organization	Activity patterns
		Kcal/kg	Kcal/indiv.			
Guanaco	80–120	990	59,400	Summer-Autumn	Solitary and Gregarious	Diurnal
Huemul	40–90	1095	28743,75	Summer-Autumn	Solitary and Gregarious	Diurnal
Ñandu	25–40	1980	21235,5	Autumn-winter	Solitary and Gregarious	Diurnal
Mara	7–9	1141	3742,48	Spring-Summer	Gregarious	Diurnal
Vizcacha	5–9	1141	4632,46	Spring-Summer	Gregarious	Nocturnal
Armadillos	1–3	1290	1935	Autumn-Winter	Solitary	Diurnal-crepuscular
Aquatic birds	0.5–3	1230	1506,75	Autumn-Winter	Solitary and Gregarious	Diurnal
Flightless birds	0.5–1	1275	7172	Autumn-Winter	Solitary and Gregarious	Diurnal
Flyng birds	0.5–1	1275	7172	Autumn-Winter	Solitary and Gregarious	Diurnal-nocturnal
Tuco-tucos and cuises	0.5–1	1095	615,94	Spring-Summer	Gregarious	Diurnal-crepuscular
Cricetids	<0.5	1095	410,62	Spring-Summer	Solitary	Nocturnal

of the sociability for different exploited taxa (Table 8.4). Finally, we recorded the values of essential nutrients, vitamins, mineral content and fatty acid composition of the different exploited animals (Table 8.5). It has been observed that all the variables previously reviewed influence human and animal predatory behavior in the present (Frison 2004; Hockett and Haws 2003), and very probably have operated in the same way in the past (Frison 2004; Foley 1983; Binford 1978).

It is evident that during the year the period of better nutritional condition of many of these alternative resources occurs in moments of low nutritional guanaco condition (Table 8.4). In this sense, the ñandú, mara, vizcacha, armadillos, and birds are in optimal conditions in autumn, winter, and early spring, that is, in the most difficult periods to overcome in the Patagonian interior. In the same way, many of these resources are presented in large quantities and have a gregarious social structure, so they are available in higher densities in the environment, and have the moments of major activity, that is, they are easier to obtain, during moments of less activity of large ungulates. Also, as can be seen, there are large differences between big game (guanaco and huemul) and small prey in energetic returns. First, in terms of weight, the guanaco is clearly separated from the rest of the consumed resources, which explains the importance of this ungulate in the diet of hunter-gatherer populations in the area. However, when considering the yield in kilocalories per kilogram, it is evident that large ungulates have lower values than the rest of species.

Table 8.5 Nutritional contents of exploited faunal resources in the study area. References: (1) Barros et al. 2003; (2) De Arellano et al. 1993; (3) Fellenberg et al. 2016; (4) Polidori et al. 2007a; (5) Polidori et al. 2007b; (6) Hoffman 2008; (7) Saadoun and Cabrera 2008; (8) Acuña Reyes 2013; (9) Closa and de Landeta 2008; (10) Schmitt Hebbel et al. 1992; (11) Bressani 1977; (12) Navarro et al. 2001; (13) Navarro et al. 2003; (14) USDA https://fdc.nal.usda.gov/fdc-app.html#food-details/337073/nutrients; (15) González et al. 2004; (16) Saadoun et al. 2014; (17) Sitio argentino de producción animal http://www.produccion-animal.com.ar/produccion_aves/producciones_avicolas_alternativas/29-Caracteristicas_Carne_Pato; (18) USDA https://fdc.nal.usda.gov/fdc-app.html#food-details/169905/nutrients; (19) USDA https://fdc.nal.usda.gov/fdc-app.html#food-details/337414/nutrients; (20) Menchú et al. 1996; (21) USDA https://fdc.nal.usda.gov/fdc-app.html#food-details/173855/nutrients; (22) Salvá et al. 2009; (23) Antonio et al. 2007; (24) Echalar et al. 1998

TAXA	Essential Nutrient			Minerals									
	Energy (kcal)	Fat (g)	Protein (g)	Ca (mg)	Fe (mg)	K (mg)	Cu (mg)	Zn (mg)	Se (mg)	Mg (mg)	P (mg)	Mn (mg)	Na (mg)
Guanaco (L. guanicoe)	99	1.02 (15)	20.9 (7)	11.6(5)	3.26 (5)	447.1 (5)	0.101 (22)	4.44 (5)		28.4 (5)	379.4 (5)	0.015 (22)	105.6 (5)
Deer (O. Bezoarticus/H. Bisulcus)	109.5–120 (21)	2.06–2.42 (21)	22.96 (21)	5 (21)	3.4 (21)	318 (21)	0.253 (21)	2.09 (21)	9.7 (21)	23 (21)	202 (21)	0.041 (21)	51 (21)
Vizcacha (2) (L. maximus)	129.22	3.74	23.87	11.58 (2)	2.57–2.43 (2)	232.00 (2)					133.10 (2)		143.00 (2)
Southern vizcacha (3)L. viscacia)	131.3	6.1	19.1		13.76 (24)	3.54 (23)				1.12 (23)	8.06 (23)		
Guinea pig (3) (C. porcelus)	151.4	7.8	20.3	13.56 (16)	1.18 (16)	240 (16)					89.6 (16)		210 (16)
Coipo (3) (M. coypus)	108.2	2.2	22.1	5.9	2.4								74
Dasipodidae	129.0–172 (11)	5.4 (11)	29 (11)	16 (14)	1.2 (14)	394 (14)	0.056	3	12.9	27	133		222

(continued)

Table 8.5 (continued)

TAXA	Essential Nutrient			Minerals									
	Energy (kcal)	Fat (g)	Protein (g)	Ca (mg)	Fe (mg)	K (mg)	Cu (mg)	Zn (mg)	Se (mg)	Mg (mg)	P (mg)	Mn (mg)	Na (mg)
Ñandu (1) (R. americana)	112.4	1.2	22.9	1.89	320	257	141	1465	82	15	384	11.3	63.7
Choique (1) (R. pennata)	104.8	1.3	22.1										
Ñandu (egg) (12)	165.64	24.76	24.3	3.25	0.11	5.15							
Choique (egg) (13)	195,88	39.54	29.28	1.83 (13)	0.10 (13)	1.78 (13)	0.03 (13)	0.055 (13)		1.13 (13)			8.50 (13)
Aquatic birds	227 (17)	1.72 (17)	18.10 (17)	14 (17)	2.50 (17)	270 (17)	0.24 (17)	1.80 (17)	12.40 (17)	22 (17)	196 (17)	0.05 (17)	38 (17)
Flightless birds	226 (19)	14.04 (19)	25 (19)	15 (19)	4.41 (19)	215 (19)	0.59 (19)	3.09 (19)	21.7 (19)	22 (19)	278 (19)		214 (19)
Flyng birds	213 (18)	13 (18)	23.9 (18)	17 (18)	5.91 (18)	256 (18)	0.763 (18)	3.83 (18)	20.1 (18)	26 (18)	332 (18)		57 (18)
Fish (O. hatcheri)	77 (9)	1.7 (8)	18.7 (8)	20 (9)	1.90 (9)	256 (9)					311 (19)		68 (19)

TAXA	Fatty acid composition			Noncaloric									
	Cholesterol (mgrs.)	SFA	MUFA	PUFA	C (mg)	Thiamin (mg)	Riboflavin (mg)	Niacin (mg)	B-6 (mg)	B-12 (mg)	A (IU)	Folate (mg)	D (mcg)	E (mg)
Guanaco (L. guanicoe)	27.2 (7)	47.7 (7)	30.6 (7)	12.4 (7)							0.17 (22)			0.31 (22)
Deer (O. Bezoarticus/H. Bisulcus)	85 (21)	45.45 (21)	32.05 (21)	22.48 (21)	0 (21)	0.22 (21)	0.48 (21)	6.37 (21)	0.37 (21)	6.31 (21)	0 (21)	4 (21)		0.2 (21)

(continued)

Table 8.5 (continued)

TAXA	Fatty acid composition				Noncaloric									
	Cholesterol (mgrs.)	SFA	MUFA	PUFA	C (mg)	Thiamin (mg)	Riboflavin (mg)	Niacin (mg)	B-6 (mg)	B-12 (mg)	A (IU)	Folate (mg)	D (mcg)	E (mg)
Vizcacha (2) (L. maximus)	50 (2)	37.7 (2)	62.29 (2)		9.9									
Southern vizcacha (3)L. viscacia	64.40 (24)	21.42 (3)	34.0 (3)	40.20 (3)										
Guinea pig (3) (C. porcelus)	60 (16)	33.44 (3)	15.44 (3)	50.67 (3)										
Coipo (3) (M. coypus)	71.5–72.05 (7)	40 (7)	32.4 (7)	27.6 (7)	0.8						3.2			
Dasipodidae	77 (14)	35.62 (14)	46.85 (14)	17.52 (14)	0	0.309	0.139	4.192	0.416	0.7	0	6	0	0.38
Ñandu (1) (R. americana)	59.0 (7)	32.8 (7)	26.8 (7)	39.7 (7)										
Choique (1) (R. pennata)	55.0 (7)	33.3 (7)	32.2 (7)	33.6 (7)										
Ñandu (egg) (12)	18–21	30.9	40.54	28.55										
Choique (egg) (13)	27.93–39.91	27.06	43.6	29.34										
Aquatic birds	76 (17)	36.14 (17)	49.96 (17)	13.88 (17)	0			3.50 (17)	0.33 (17)	1.80 (17)	24 (17)	25 (17)	0 (17)	0.70 (17)

(continued)

Table 8.5 (continued)

TAXA	Fatty acid composition				Noncaloric									
	Cholesterol (mgrs.)	SFA	MUFA	PUFA	C (mg)	Thiamin (mg)	Riboflavin (mg)	Niacin (mg)	B-6 (mg)	B-12 (mg)	A (IU)	Folate (mg)	D (mcg)	E (mg)
Flightless birds	86 (19)	32.06 (19)	39.66 (19)	28.27 (19)	2.3 (19)	0,219 (19)	0.299 (19)	7,887 (19)	0.617 (19)	0.36 (19)	70 (19)	6 (19)	0.2 (19)	0.7 (19)
Flyng birds	116 (18)	31.29 (18)	45.80 (18)	22.90 (18)	2.9 (18)	0.28 (18)	0.35 (18)	7.6 (18)	0.57 (18)	0.41 (18)	95 (18)	6 (18)	7 (18)	0.06 (18)
Fish (O. hatcheri)	11.15 (10)	30 (8)	22–44 (8)	26–48 (8)	0 (19)	0.01 (19)	0.05 (19)	4.50 (19)						

Table 8.5 presents values of energetic return characteristics that influence the selection of prey by human populations. A cautionary note should be mentioned when considering this dataset. Some of the local species used by man do not have nutritional content values available (e.g., *Hippocamelus bisulcus/Ozotoceros bezoarticus*). Where possible, values of related taxa were used for which there was data (e.g., *Odocoileus virginianus*). In the case of certain categories (Flyng, aquatic and flightless birds) we use available values for a particular species (wild pigeon, wild duck, and wild quail), respectively. We also consider values of some species that came from commercial hatcheries (chinchilla) or domestic species (llama and alpaca). Many of these factors demonstrably have an influence on the nutritional content of the animals analyzed, which is why we believe that our values do not express detailed differences between wild and domestic populations but different orders of magnitude in the nutritional content between small fauna and big mammals. Taking this limitations into account, it is evident that the content of some essential macro and micronutrients (i.e., fats, vitamin C, B-6, B-12, A, D, folates, calcium, iron, and potassium) is considerably higher in the flesh of small prey than in the case of the great ungulates. Particularly relevant to the discussion presented here are fats. On average, fats produce approximately 9.3 kilocalories per gram compared to 3.79 kilocalories per gram of carbohydrates or 3.12 kilocalories per gram of protein (Curtis and Barnes 1993). They are also more efficient in the energy storage process than any other type of molecule (Curtis and Barnes 1993). On the other hand, small amounts of certain types of fat are required for the normal functioning of the body, the so-called essential fatty acids. They also provide the vehicle for certain lipid-soluble proteins such as vitamins A, D, E, and K. Finally, these improve the taste of foods, produce satiety and are especially important in the neurological development of children (Eaton 1992; Jenike 2001). Fat in the diet can come from a number of sources. An especially important source of this resource is the animal carcasses, especially terrestrial and marine mammals and birds (Outram 2001; Haws and Hockett 2004). It has been calculated that the fat requirements in an optimal diet are approximately 50–70 grams of fat per day per person (Bunn and Ezzo 1993). However, the meat of wild animals usually has a lower fat content than that of domestic animals (Eaton 1992; Mengoni Goñalons 1996; Jenike 2001). Particularly acute is this issue in the case of the large ungulates of the study area. Guanaco and huemul meat are especially lean, even when compared with other wild species (Rindel 2013). This is true even when considering the contribution of different tissues to the total body weight of both species. In this regard, both ungulates have no subcutaneous fat, and a very small amount of intramuscular fat and bone marrow (Belardi and Gómez Otero 1998; González et al. 2004). This invites us to consider alternative sources of these resources.

8.4 Discussing the Role of Small Prey in the Diets of Northwestern Prehistoric Populatons

The results obtained from multiple lines of evidence suggest that the patterns of consumption of small prey in Northwest Patagonia varied through time and space. However, in the areas considered in this study, these resources were consumed throughout the Holocene and regardless of the density of human populations. In this context, we choose to investigate the role of small prey, taking as framework the data provided by the demographic characteristics of the human populations and their main prey, the guanaco. In this sense, the data of the summed probability distributions of radiocarbon dates indicate an increase in human populations throughout the Holocene, while the molecular evidence obtained from mitochondrial DNA confirms this pattern and allows an estimate of the human population size throughout the studied period (Perez et al. 2016, 2017). Consistent with this pattern, the mitochondrial DNA data for the guanaco also shows a trend toward sustained population growth throughout the Holocene (Moscardi et al. 2020). The zooarchaeological information, which shows the species that were effectively part of the human diet throughout the process of settlement of the area, indicates an increase in the consumption of guanaco through the Holocene, especially in Neuquén. Particularly during the last 2000 years, the consumption of large herbivores (i.e., guanaco) increased, in line with the population growth curve of this ungulate. Along with this general trend toward a greater incorporation of guanaco into the diet, there is also a tendency toward a variable incorporation of small prey fauna throughout the Holocene. This brings little support for the notion that the consumption of small fauna was due to situations of imbalance between human populatons and their main resource, because both populations grows along the Holocene. That is to say, humans did not consume smaller prey due to the depletion of food staples. Probably, the human population increase was fuelled by the guanaco, whose populations accompanied human population growth.

The isotopic data of human remains, meanwhile, are in accordance with these trends, and make it possible to detail the pattern of the last 5000 years BP, contributing percentages of consumed species, and modeling the inclusion of plant resources and indicating which small prey resources were consumed preferentially. The isotopic results show that in NNqn the diet was mainly based in the consumption of large herbivores with some contribution of small fauna. It is interesting to note that this predominance of guanaco in the diet contrast with SMza and SNqn, also in agreement with zooarchaeological data, and that NNqn was where the human population increase was the least significant (Gil et al. 2014a; Gordón et al. 2019b). In SMza the diet was the most varied being primarily composed of birds and small mammals, while large herbivores occupy the third place. Finally, in SNqn *Araucaria* was the main food with low contribution of the other resources, especially birds and small fauna. The dietary patterns observed in the isotopic analyses generally agree with the zooarchaeological results, suggesting a well-established pattern of dietary changes in the region.

In this context, the problem with Diet breadth models, at least in their archeological applications, is their insensitivity to other variables than body size. Characteristically, other physical and behavioral differences of prey animals are neglected in the analyses. Even when en masse collecting may upset the ranking between small and large prey, in general the consumption of small resources implies higher costs of obtaining and lower rates of energy return. Within this context, we must seek the explanation of the inclusion of small prey in other aspects that go beyond body size. We think that Nutritional Ecology, a perspective that focuses on the reproductive benefits of the essential nutrients vital to human diet rather than the energy return rate per se (Hockett and Haws 2003; Haws and Hockett 2004) could potentially help to clarify the role of these resources and provides an alternative explanation to the heavy emphasis of Diet breadth models in body size and net nutrient yields. From this perspective, the consumption of small prey, which was sustained in Northwest Patagonia during the Holocene, would be a nutritional choice more than a result of hunting pressure on the main resource (i.e., guanaco) and its subsequent incorporation as "marginal resources."

The isotopic and zooarchaeological data for the region allows us to defend the idea of diets with a high intake of proteins provided by large herbivores, in the order of between 20 and 50%. The problem with this type of diet is that proteins are not metabolized easily. If the body depends on proteins to obtain its energy, the amino acids that compose them are synthesized to fulfill these requirements instead of fulfilling their normal function of replacing the body's proteins. Its consumption in large quantities, therefore, leads to severe metabolic disorders and death if not complemented by other sources of energy (protein poisoning, see for example Binford 1978; Speth 1983, 1987, 1991; Speth and Spielmann 1983; Borrero 1991). It is important to mention that this "threshold" in the content of proteins in the diet, which was mentioned that it could be of the order of 50%, can in fact be much lower in the case of pregnant women. Speth (1991) has pointed out that high levels of protein in the diet can have highly deleterious effects on the development of the fetus. The problem is further complicated in arid environments where the restricted water availability limits the ability to consume protein-rich foods. In this case, the elimination of urea cannot be sustained via the formation of urine, which can lead to uraemic poisoning because the capacity of the liver to synthesize urea is exceeded (Speth 1991). Carbohydrates are the best to reverse this process, but in environments such as Northwest Patagonia they are not abundant and their supply is seasonal. Therefore, an adequate amount of fat in the diet is essential. At this point, it is important to note that the small prey fauna provides nutrients that big game does not have. This is especially important in the case of fats, which, as macronutrients, constitute a limitation to the growth of the human population in areas such as the Patagonian interior. Not only do they provide elements and nutrients that the resources that formed the basis of the diet do not possess, but they are also available at times when the major resources do not, both daily and throughout the annual cycle, and at high densities. The ethnographic and ethnohistorical literature supports what has been said, explicitly indicating the complementary use of these resources with respect to the main prey, the guanaco, basically complementing what the guanaco does not offer: fats and other macro and micronutrients. They also can be stored, and usually are obtained and consumed by other social segments such as women and children.

As it was mentioned in the introduction, there are different causal mechanisms that have been used to explain changes in human diets over time within the framework of human behavioral ecology. In this work, we chose to analyze these changes considering different demographic scenarios of human groups and the main prey, the guanaco. In this regard, it is unlikely that situations of resource stress due to population growth explain the observed patterns. As indicated, although human populations showed a sustained increase over time, the populations of the main hunted resource, the guanaco, also increase in a similar way. Although beyond the objectives of this work, we believe that a future agenda should consider the extent to which this was accompanied by changes in hunting strategies and/or greater intensity in the use of this species. On the other hand, the inclusion of small prey could be a factor that has contributed to processes of differentiation of the niche exploited by human populations. Again, this does not seem to be the case in the study region. In this regard, even with major fluctuations throughout the Holocene, what is observed is the inclusion of resources of small prey and plants, but within a strong contribution in the diet of large prey. The presence of domesticated animal and plant resources is a very late and insignificant contribution in the diets of the study area until historical moments. As previously discussed, the small fauna resources are different in terms of their ethology, density, availability throughout the annual cycle, and nutritional content with respect to large ungulates. This allows for the possibility of a complementary use of these species, offering resources that are not immediately available, especially in times of low environmental productivity such as winter and early spring, when the main prey is in their worst condition. Therefore, studies that allow evaluating the seasonality of occupations should be emphasized in future work. The Patagonian interior environment can be characterized as seasonal, arid, with low productivity, and plant diversity, and very lean large ungulates. The ethnographic literature indicates that scarcity of fat is a limitation for human life, but small prey allows us to overcome this limitation by providing resources that the main prey does not possess and at times of the year where the severity of the environment is accentuated. Over time, they have possibly allowed and sustained the population growth observed in the study area. This, ultimately, provides a link between the complementarity of resources, nutritional decisions that in the long term provide greater reproductive success and population growth, situations such as those described for the study region. The incorporation into the diet of macro and micronutrients that are not provided by the main resources is a decisive factor when explaining the population growth. In this regard, nutrition is the key to the normal development of the brain in childhood. Among the minerals that are key elements for the normal development of children are iron, copper, zinc, and selenium, as well as an adequate amount of fatty acids, particularly the polyunsaturates (Cunnane 2005). As we showed in Table 8.4, many of the resources that we collectively refer to as "small prey" possesses high values of these nutrients, of which the guanaco lacks. In this way, we propose that there is a direct link between their inclusion in the diet and the possibility of greater reproductive success, which in the long term results in population increase.

It is interesting to link these results with the comparison between our study region with another region that presents marked differences in the availability of alternative resources to the guanaco: Southern Patagonia. In a recent paper (Perez et al. 2017), we observed significant differences in population size between Southern and Northern Patagonia. Those results indicate that Northern Patagonia populations were an order of magnitude greater than those of the south. On the other hand, the exploitation of resources in Southern Patagonia seems to have been strongly based on the consumption of the guanaco, with a very scarce contribution from small prey, becoming relevant only during the last 2000 years BP (Bernal et al. 2018). As noted previously, in Northern Patagonia, those resources were used from the very beginning of human occupation and throughout the entire settlement process. This supports the previously indicated notion about the link between these small prey resources as facilitators of population growth.

8.5 Conclusion

Small prey enters the diet as resources that complement the heavy consumption on guanaco meat. As such, they make it possible to overcome the limitations to human population growth presented by the ecosystems of the Patagonian interior, as they allow the incorporation of nutrients that large ungulates in the area provide scarcely or directly do not possess, and at certain times of the year when the latter are in low condition. This possibly explains the difference in demographic trends observed in different parts of Patagonia, where the north (which has these complementary resources in abundance) has a population of an order of magnitude greater than the south (which has them in small quantity). That is to say, under an ecological difference, the early incorporation of these resources, which were available in the north, is explained in front of a shortage of these in the south, which generates a lower population density throughout the Holocene.

Acknowledgements We want to thank the editors of the book for their invitation to participate in it and the reviewers who made valuable comments that greatly improved the text. We also thank Lic. Redondo Caamaño and Lic. Della Negra of the Dirección Provincial de Áreas Naturales Protegidas and of the Dirección Provincial de Patrimonio Cultural of Neuquén province. This work was carried out in the framework of projects PIP-729 (Consejo Nacional de Investigaciones Científicas y Técnicas) and PICT-2134 (Agencia de Promoción Científica y Tecnológica).

References

Acuña Reyes MJ (2013) Peces de cultivo, composición, comparación con carnes de consumo habitual. Ventajas del consumo de pescados. Diaeta 31(143):26–30
Aguerre AM (2000) Las vidas de Pati en la toldería tehuelche y el después. Buenos Aires (FFYL-UBA)

Antonio S, Velho J, Carvalho P, Backes A, Sánchez L, Velho I (2007) Body composition prediction and net macroelements requirements (*Chinchilla lanigera*). Ciência e Agrotecnologia 31(2):548–553

Barberena R, Borrazzo K, Rughini A, Romero G, Pompei P, Llano C, de Porras E, Durán V, Stern C, Re A, Estrella D, Forasiepi A, Fernández F, Chidiak M, Acuña L, Gasco A, Quiroga M (2015) Perspectivas arqueológicas para Patagonia septentrional: sitio Cueva Huenul 1 (provincia del Neuquén, Argentina). Magallania 43(1):1–27

Barberena R, Tessone A, Quiroga MN, Gordón F, Llano C, Gasco A, Paiva J, Ugan A (2018) Guanacos y ecología isotópica en el norte del Neuquén: El registro de Cueva Huenul 1. Revista del Museo de Antropología 11(1):7–14

Barros A, Iturralde JJ, Ibarlucea A (2003) Manual de cortes de ñandú (Rhea americana) y subproductos. Dirección de Servicios Técnicos a la Cadena Agroindustrial. Instituto Nacional de Carnes, Uruguay

Belardi JB, Gómez Otero J (1998) Anatomía Económica del Huemul (Hippocamelus bisulcus): una contribución a la interpretación de las evidencias arqueológicas de su aprovechamiento en Patagonia. Anales del Instituto de Patagonia, Sección Ciencias Históricas 26:195–207

Bernal V, Gonzalez P, Gordón F, Perez SI (2016) Exploring dietary patterns in the southernmost limit of pre-Hispanic agriculture in America by using Bayesian stable isotope mixing models. Curr Anthropol 57:230–239

Bernal V, Perez SI, Postillone MB, Rindel DD (2018). Hunter-Gatherer persistence and demography in Patagonia (southern South America): the impact of ecological changes during the Pleistocene and Holocene. In: Temple D, Stojanowski C (eds) Hunter-Gatherer resilience in bioarchaeological perspective, Chapter 3, SBEA Series. Cambridge University Press, pp 47–64

Binford LR (1968) Post-pleistocene adaptations. In: Binford SR, Binford LR (eds) New perspectives in archaeology. Aldine, Chicago, pp 313–341

Binford LR (1978) Nunamiut Ethnoarchaeology. Academic Press, New York

Binford LR (2001) Constructing frames of reference. An analytical method for archaeological theory building using hunter-gatherer and environmental data sets. University of California Press, Berkeley

Bliege Bird R, Smith EA, Bird DW (2001) The hunting handicap: costly signaling in male foraging strategies. Behav Ecol Sociobiol 50:9–19

Bocherens H, Drucker D (2003) Trophic level isotopic enrichments for carbon and nitrogen in collagen: case studies from recent and ancient terrestrial ecosystems. Int J Osteoarchaeol 13:46–53

Boeck P, Paulino L, Oyarzún C, van Cleemput O, Godoy R (2005) Soil δ15 patterns in old-growth forests of southern Chile as integrator for N-cycling. Isot Environ Health Stud 41(3):249–259

Borrero LA (1991) Los selk´nam. Su evolución cultural. Ed. Búsqueda del Ayllu, Concepción del Uruguay

Bourne BF (1998) Cautivo en la Patagonia. Ed. Emecé, Buenos Aires

Bressani R (1977) Función de las especies de animales menores en la nutrición y producción de alimentos. Boletín de la Oficina Sanitaria Panamericana 1: 206–215

Bridges EL, Briano MM (2000) El último confín de la tierra. Buenos Aires, Editorial Sudamericana

Buikstra J, Ubelaker D (1994) Standards for data collection from human skeletal remains. Arkansas Archaeological Survey Research Series 44, Fayetteville

Bunn HT, Ezzo JA (1993) Hunting and scavenging by plio-pleistocene hominids: Nutritional constraints, archaeological patterns and behavioral implications. J Archaeol Sci 20:365–398

Claraz S (1988) Diario de Viaje de Exploración al Chubut 1865–1866. Ed. Marymar, Buenos Aires

Cunnane SC (2005) Survival of the fattest: the key to human brain evolution. World Scientific, Hackensack

Curtis H, Barnes S (1993) Biología. Ed. Médica Panamericana, Buenos Aires

Cordero A (2010) Explotación animal en el Holoceno del noroeste de la Patagonia argentina. Cambios climáticos y transformaciones del comportamiento humano: una primera aproximación. Thesis doctoral, Facultad de Filosofía y Letras, Universidad de Buenos Aires. MS

Closa S, de Landeta M (2008). Tabla de composición de alimentos Universidad Nacional de Lujan, Argentina. http://www.unlu.edu.ar/~argenfood/-Pejerrey

Davidson I (1976) Les Mallaetes and Mondúver: the economy of a human group in prehistoric Spain. In: Sieveking G, Longworth JK, Wilson KE (eds) Problems in economic and social archaeology. Duckworth, London, pp 483–499

Davidson I (1989) La Economía del Final del Paleolítico en la España Oriental. Serie de Trabajos Varios, Valencia, Servicio de Investigación Prehistórica, Diputación Provincial de Valencia, Serie de Trabajos Varios, 85

De Arellano ML, Luco JM, Fernández S, Micalizzi Y, Fisetti M, Lucero JB, Mucciarelli S (1993) Mountain chinchilla (Lagostomus maximus maximus Blainv) meat. Biological value. Archivos latinoamericanos de nutrición 43(3):254–257

de La Cruz L (1969) Viaje desde el fuerte de Ballenar hasta Buenos Aires. En Colección de Obras y Documentos relativos a la historia antigua y moderna de las Provincias del Río de la Plata. Editado por Pedro de Angelis, tomo II. Editorial Plus Ultra, Buenos Aires, pp 9–491

Della Negra CE, Novellino PS (2005) "Aquihuecó": un cementerio arqueológico, en el Norte de la Patagonia, Valle del Curi Leuvú-Neuquén, Argentina. Magallania (Punta Arenas) 33(2):165–172

Della Negra C, Novellino P, Gordón F, Vázquez R, Béguelin M, González P, Bernal V (2014) Áreas de entierro en cazadores-recolectores del Noroeste de Patagonia: sitio Hermanos Lazcano (Chos Malal, Neuquén). Runa 35(2):5–19

D´Orbigny A (1999) Viaje por la América meridional II. Editorial Emecé

Eaton SB (1992) Humans, lipids and evolution. Lipids 27:814–820

Echalar S, Jiménez M, Ramón A (1998) Valor nutritivo y aceptabilidad de la carne de chinchilla. Archivos latinoamericanos de nutrición 48(1):77–81

Fellenberg A, Cawley AM, Peña I (2016) Nutritional value of chinchilla meat and its agroindustrial derivatives. Carpathian J Food Sci & Technol 8(2):22–29

Fernández C, Panarello H (2001) Cazadores recolectores del Holoceno Medio y Superior de la Cueva Haichol, región cordillerana central del Neuquén, Republica Argentina. Relaciones de la Sociedad Argentina de Antropología 26:9–30

Fernández FJ, Gil A, Ugan A, Neme G (2016) Ecological conditions and isotopic diet (13C and 15N) of Holocene caviomorph rodents in northern Patagonia. J Arid Environ 127:44–52

Flannery KV (1969) Origins and ecological effects of early domestication in Iran and the Near East. In: Ucko PJ, Dimbleby GW (eds) The domestication and exploitation of plants and animals. Aldine, Chicago, pp 73–100

Foley, R. (1983). Modeling hunting strategies and inferring predator behavior from prey attributes. In: Clutton-Brock J, Grigson C (eds) Animals and archaeology I: Hunters and their prey. BAR International Series 163. Oxford, pp 63–76

Frison G (2004) Survival by hunting: prehistoric human predators and animal prey. University of California Press, Berkeley

Giardina M, Corbat M, Otaola C, Salgán L, Ugan A, Neme G, Gil A (2014) Recursos y dietas humanas en Laguna Llancanelo (Mendoza, Nordpatagonia): una discusión isotópica del registro arqueológico. Magallania (Punta Arenas) 42(1):111–131

Gil A, Tykot R, Neme G, Shelnut N (2006) Maize on the frontier: isotopic and macrobotanical data from central-western Argentina. In: Staller JE, Tykot R, Benz B (eds) Histories of maize: multidisciplinary approaches to the prehistory, biogeography, domestication, and evolution of maize. Academic Press, New York, pp 199–214

Gil AF, Neme GA, Tykot RH, Novellino P, Cortegoso V, Durán V (2009) Stable isotopes and maize consumption in central western Argentina. Int J Osteoarchaeol 19(2):215–236

Gil AF, Neme GA, Tykot RH (2011) Stable isotopes and human diet in central western Argentina. J Archaeol Sci 38(7):1395–1404

Gil A, Giardina MA, Neme G, & Ugan A (2014a) Demografía humana e incorporación de cultígenos en el centro occidente argentino: explorando tendencias en las fechas radiocarbónicas. Revista Española de Antropología Americana 44: 523–553

Gil A, Villalba R, Ugan A, Cortegoso V, Neme G, Michieli C, Novellino P, Durán V (2014b) Isotopic evidence on human bone for declining maize consumption during the Little Ice Age in central western Argentina. Journal of Archaeological Science 49: 113–227

Gil AF, Ugan A, Otaola C, Neme G, Giardina M, Menéndez L (2016) Variation in camelid $\delta13C$ and $\delta15N$ values in relation to geography and climate: Holocene patterns and archaeological implications in central western Argentina. J Archaeol Sci 66:7–20

González F, Smulders FJM, Paulsen P, Skewes O, Konig HE (2004) Anatomical investigations on meat cuts of guanacos (Lama guanicoe, Muller, 1776) and chemical composition of selected muscles. Wiener Tierarztliche Monatsschrift 91(3):77–84

Gordón F, Béguelin M, Vázquez R, Cobos V, Pucciarelli H, Bernal, V. (2013) El "Hombre Fósil de Mata Molle" (Pcia. de Neuquén, Patagonia Argentina): cronología y variación craneofacial en el contexto patagónico y sudamericano. Revista Argentina de Antropología Biológica 15(1): 77–89

Gordón F, Perez SI, Hajduk A, Lezcano M, Bernal V (2018) Dietary patterns in human populations from northwest Patagonia during Holocene: an approach using Binford's frames of reference and Bayesian isotope mixing models. Archaeol Anthropol Sci 10(6):1347–1358

Gordón F, Beguelin M, Novellino P, Archuby F (2019a) Inferencias paleodemográficas en el noroeste de Patagonia a partir del sitio Aquihuecó, Provincia del Neuquén, Argentina. Enviado a Chungara. Revista de Antropología Chilena. En prensa

Gordón F, Beguelin M, Rindel D, Della Negra C, Hajduk A, Vázquez R, Cobos V, Perez SI, Bernal V (2019b). Estructura espacial y dinámica temporal de la ocupación humana de Neuquén (Patagonia Argentina) durante el Pleistoceno final-Holoceno. Send to InterSecciones en Antropología. In press

Grayson DK (1984) Quantitative zooarchaeology. Academic Press, Orlando

Grayson DK, Delpech F (1998) Changing diet breadth in the early Upper Paleolithic of southwestern France. J Archaeol Sci 25:1119–1129

Guinnard AM (1961) Tres años de cautividad entre los patagones. Editorial Universitaria de Buenos Aires

Hare PE, Fogel ML, Stafford TW Jr, Mitchell AD, Hoering TC (1991) The isotopic composition of carbon and nitrogen in individual amino acids isolated from modern and fossil proteins. J Archaeol Sci 18:277–292

Hawkes K, O´Connell J (1992) On optimal foraging models and subsistence transitions. Curr Anthropol 33: 63–66

Haws JA, Hockett BS (2004) Theoretical perspectives on the dietary role of small animals in human evolution. In *Petits animaux et sociétés humaines. Du complément alimentaire aux ressources utilitaires*, Editado por J. P. Brugal y J. Hesse. XXIV Rencontres Internationales d´Archaeologie et d´Histoire d´Antibes, Antibes, Francia, 173–184

Hockett B, Haws J (2003) Nutritional ecology and diachronic trends in Paleolithic diet and health. Evol Anthropol: Issues, News, Rev 12(5):211–216

Hoffman LC (2008) The yield and nutritional value of meat from African ungulates, Camelidae, rodents, ratites and reptiles. Meat Sci 80(1):94–100

Jenike MR (2001) Nutritional ecology: diet, physical activity and body size. In: Panter-Brick C, Layton RH, Rowly Conwy P (eds) Hunter-gatherers: An interdisciplinary perspective. The Biosocial Simposium Series. University of Cambridge, Cambridge

Kelly, R.L. (2013). The Lifeways of Hunter-Gatherers. The foraging spectrum, 2nd edn. Cambridge University Press, Cambridge

Lezcano MJ, Hajduk A, Albornoz AM (2010) El menú a la carta en el bosque ¿entrada o plato fuerte?: una perspectiva comparada desde la zooarqueología del sitio El Trébol (lago Nahuel Huapi, Pcia. de Río Negro). In: Gutiérrez M, De Nigris M, Fernández P, Giardina M, Gil A, et al. (eds) Zooarqueología a principios del siglo XXI: aportes teóricos, metodológicos y casos de estudio. Buenos Aires, Ediciones del Espinillo, pp 243–257

Lista R (1998) Obras. Volúmenes 1 y 2. Editorial Confluencia, Buenos Aires. República Argentina

MacArthur RH, Pianka ER (1966) On optimal use of a patchy environment. Am Nat 100:603–609

Marín JC, González BA, Poulin E, Casey CS, Johnson WE (2013) The influence of the arid Andean high plateau on the phylogeography and population genetics of guanaco (*Lama guanicoe*) in South America. Mol Ecol 22:463–482

Meinrado Hux P (1998) Memorias del ex cautivo Santiago Avendaño. Ediciones El Elefante Blanco, Buenos Aires

Meltzer DJ (1999) Human responses to middle Holocene (Altithermal) climates on the North American Great Plains. Quat Res 52(3):404–416

Menchú MT, Méndez H, Barrera MA, Ortega L (1996) Tabla de composición de alimentos de Centroamérica. Organización Panamericana de la Salud

Mengoni Goñalons, G.L. (1996). La domesticación de los camélidos sudamericanos y su anatomía económica. In: Elkin DC, Madero CM, Mengoni Goñalons GL, Olivera DE, Reigadas MC, Yacobaccio HD (eds) Zooarqueología de Camélidos 2, Grupo Zooarqueología de Camélidos, Buenos Aires, pp 33–45

Metcalf JL, Turney C, Barnett R, Martin F, Bray SC, Vilstrup JT, Orlando L, Salas-Gismondi R, Loponte D, Medina M, De Nigris M, Civalero T, Fernández P, Gasco A, Durán V, Seymour K, Otaola C, Gil A, Paunero R, Prevosti F, Bradshaw C, Wheeler J, Borrero L, Austin J, Cooper A (2016) Synergistic roles of climate warming and human occupation in Patagonian megafaunal extinctions during the Last Deglaciation. Sci Adv 2(6):e1501682

Moreno FP (1969) Viaje a la Patagonia Austral. 1876–1877. Ediciones Solar - Hachette, Buenos Aires

Moscardi B, Rindel DD, Perez SI (2020) Human diet evolution in Patagonia was driven by the expansion of Lama guanicoe after megafaunal extinctions. J Archaeol Sci 115:105098

Musters GC (1997) *Vida entre los patagones*. Un año de excursiones por tierras no frecuentadas desde el Estrecho de Magallanes hasta el Río Negro. Ediciones El Elefante Blanco, Buenos Aires, Argentina

Navarro JL, López ML, Maestri DM, Labuckas DO (2001) Physical characteristics and chemical composition of Greater Rhea (*Rhea americana*) eggs from wild and captive populations. Br Poult Sci 42(5):658–662

Navarro JL, Barri FR, Maestri DM, Labuckas DO, Martella MB (2003) Physical characteristics and chemical composition of Lesser Rhea (*Pterocnemia pennata*) eggs from farmed populations. Br Poult Sci 44(4):586–590

Neme G, Gil A (2009) Human occupation and increasing mid-Holocene aridity: Southern Andean perspectives. Curr Anthropol 50(1):149–163

Neme G, Gil A, Otaola C, Giardina M (2013) Resource exploitation and human mobility: trends in the archaeofaunal and isotopic record from central Western Argentina. Int J Osteoarchaeol 25(6):866–876

Onelli, C. (1998). Trepando los Andes. Editorial Elefante Blanco

Otaola C, Giardina M, Corbat M, Fernández FJ (2012) Zooarqueología en el Sur de Mendoza: Integrando perspectivas zooarqueológicas en un marco biogeográfico. In: Gil A, Neme G (eds) Paleobiogeografía en el Sur de Mendoza. Sociedad Argentina de Antropología, Buenos Aires

Otaola C, Giardina MA, Franchetti FR (2019) Human biogeography and faunal exploitation in Diamante river Basin, Central Western Argentina. Int J Osteoarchaeol 29(1):134–143

Outram AK (2001) A new approach to identifying Bone Marrow and Grease exploitation: why the "indeterminate" fragments should not be ignored. J Archaeol Sci 28:401–410

Parnell AC, Phillips DL, Bearhop S, Semmens BX, Ward EJ, Moore JW, Jackson AL, Grey J, Kelly DJ, Inger R (2013) Bayesian stable isotope mixing models. Environmetrics 24:387–399

Perez SI, Della Negra C, Novellino P, González P, Bernal V, Cuneo E, Hajduk A (2009) Deformaciones artificiales del cráneo en cazadores-recolectores del Holoceno medio-tardío del noroeste de Patagonia. Magallania (Punta Arenas) 37(2):77–90

Perez SI, Postillone MB, Rindel D, Gobbo D, Gonzalez PN, Bernal V (2016) Peopling time, spatial occupation and demography of Late Pleistocene-Holocene human population from Patagonia. Quat Int 425:214–223. https://doi.org/10.1016/j.quaint.2016.05.004

Perez SI, Postillone MB, Rindel D (2017) Domestication and human demographic history in South America. Am J Phys Anthropol 163:44–52. https://doi.org/10.1002/ajpa.23176

Pigafetta A (1963) Primer viaje en torno del globo. Editorial Espasa-Calpe, Madrid

Polidori P, Renieri C, Antonini M, Passamonti P, Pucciarelli F (2007a) Meat fatty acid composition of llama (*Lama glama*) reared in the Andean highlands. Meat Sci 75(2): 356–358

Polidori P, Antonini M, Torres D, Beghelli D, Renieri C (2007b) Tenderness evaluation and mineral levels of llama (*Lama glama*) and alpaca (*Lama pacos*) meat. Meat Sci 77(4): 599–601

Prichard HH (2003) En el Corazón de la Patagonia. Editorial Zagier y Urruty, Ushuaia, Argentina

Priegue CN (1971) La información etnográfica de los patagones del siglo XVIII. Tres documentos inéditos de la expedición Malaspina 1789–1794. Textos comentados. Cuadernos del Sur. Universidad Nacional del Sur, Bahía Blanca

Rindel DD (2013). Marcos de referencia y frecuencia de partes esqueletarias de guanaco en sitios de Patagonia meridional: el caso del Índice de Médula Insaturada. In: Zangrando AF, Barberena R, Gil A, Neme G, Giardina M, Luna L, Otaola C, Paulides S, Salgán L, Tivoli A (eds) Tendencias teórico-metodológicas y casos de estudio en la arqueología de Patagonia. Museo de Historia Natural de San Rafael, SAA e INAPL, pp 515–522

Rindel DD (2017) Explorando la variabilidad en el registro zooarqueológico de la provincia del Neuquén: tendencias cronológicas y patrones de uso antrópico. In: Gordón F, Barberena R, Bernal V (eds) El poblamiento humano del norte del Neuquén: estado actual del conocimiento y perspectivas. Aspha Ediciones, pp 101–122

Saadoun A, Cabrera MC (2008) A review of the nutritional content and technological parameters of indigenous sources of meat in South America. Meat Sci 80(3):570–581

Saadoun A, Cabrera MC, Terevinto A, del Puerto M (2014) Why not a piece of meat of rhea, nutria, yacare, or vicugna for dinner? Anim Front 4(4):25–32

Salgán L, Tucker H, Luna L, Aranda CM, Gil A (2012) Estudios arqueológicos y bioarqueológicos en la cuenca media del río Malargüe (provincia de Mendoza): El sitio Bajada de las Tropas 1. Relaciones de la Sociedad Argentina de Antropología 37:113–135

Salvá BK, Zumalacárregui JM, Figueira AC, Osorio MT, Mateo J (2009) Nutrient composition and technological quality of meat from alpacas reared in Peru. Meat Sci 82(4):450–455

Scheifler N (2019) Ecología y subsistencia de los cazadores-recolectores en el campo de dunas del centro pampeano. Sociedad Argentina de Antropología, Buenos Aires

Schmid T (1964) Misionando por la Patagonia Austral 1868–1866. Usos y Costumbres de los Indios Patagones. Academia Nacional de la Historia. Colección cronistas y viajeros del Río de la Plata, tomo I

Schmidt Hebbel HI, Pennacchiotti Monti L, Masson Salaué, Mella Rojas MA (1992) Tabla de composición química de alimentos chilenos. http://repositorio.uchile.cl/handle/2250/121427

Shannon CE (1948) A mathematical theory of communication. AT&T Tech J 27:379–423

Simms SR (1987) Behavioral ecology and hunter-gatherer foraging: an example from the Great Basin. BAR International Series 381, Oxford

Sitio argentino de producción animal (2019) http://www.produccion-animal.com.ar/produccion_a ves/producciones_avicolas_alternativas/29-Caracteristicas_Carne_Pato

Speth JD (1983) Bison kills and bone counts. University of Chicago Press, Chicago

Speth JD (1987) Early hominid subsistence strategies in seasonal habitats. J Archaeol Sci 14:13–29

Speth JD (1991) Protein selection and avoidance strategies of contemporary and ancestral foragers: unresolved issues. Philos Trans R Soc Lond B 334:265–270

Speth JD, Spielmann KA (1983) Energy source, protein metabolism, and hunter-gatherer subsistence strategies. J Anthropol Archaeol 2:1–31

Stiner MC (2001) Thirty years on the "Broad Spectrum Revolution" and Paleolithic demography. Proc Natl Acad Sci 98:6993–6996

Stiner MC, Munro ND, Surovell TA (2000) The tortoise and the hare: small-game use, the Broad Spectrum Revolution and Paleolithic demography. Curr Anthropol 41:39–73

Stock BC, Semmens BX (2013) MixSIAR GUI User Manual, version 1.0. http://conserver.iugo-cafe.org/user/brice.semmens/MixSIAR

USDA https://fdc.nal.usda.gov/fdc-app.html#/food-details/337073/nutrients
USDA https://fdc.nal.usda.gov/fdc-app.html#/food-details/169905/nutrients
USDA https://fdc.nal.usda.gov/fdc-app.html#/food-details/337414/nutrients
USDA https://fdc.nal.usda.gov/fdc-app.html#/food-details/173855/nutrients
Viedma A (1972) Descripción de la costa meridional del sur llamada vulgarmente patagonica. En Colección de Obras y Documentos relativos a la historia antigua y moderna de las Provincias del Río de la Plata. Editado por Pedro de Angelis, tomo VIII. Editorial Plus Ultra, Buenos Aires, pp 937–966
Wolverton S (2005) The effects of the hypsithermal on prehistoric foraging efficiency in Missouri. Am Antiq 70(1):91–106
Zeanah DW (2004) Sexual division of labor and central place foraging: a model for the Carson Desert of 1739 Western Nevada. J Anthropol Archaeol 23:1–32

Chapter 9
Hunting Techniques Along the Rain Shadow Gradient in North-Central Patagonia, Argentina

Mariana Carballido Calatayud and Pablo Marcelo Fernández

Abstract The forest and the steppe of North-Central Patagonia (Argentina) are contiguous yet contrasting environments that have been connected throughout their peopling history. Human occupation began in the early Holocene, became more regular ca. 3500 years BP, and has increased since 2200–1700 years BP. Beyond this general picture, the nature of the relationship between forest and steppe over time is a matter of debate. To better our understanding of the human use of both environments, where assessed and investigated various hunting techniques employed over the last 3500 years, a central activity for hunter-gatherer societies. First, we modeled hunting techniques combining ecology, size, and behavior of prey, ethnographic, historical, and archaeological data, and the environmental settings (topography and vegetation). Then, we evaluated the models using weapon lithic technology and the zooarchaeological records recovered from archaeological sites located in both the forest (Cholila, Epuyén, and Manso) and the steppe (Piedra Parada area) and dated to the last 3500 years. The analysis showed that in both environments the ungulates of medium to large sizes were the main prey (huemul, *Hippocamelus bisulcus*, and guanaco, *Lama guanicoe*). They were captured near the sites, in hunting events involving few animals. In the forest, small huemul social groups were hunted by 'encounter' technique mainly with bows and arrows. This weapon system would have enabled more recurrent and/or longer stays in the forest. In the steppe, the 'approach' method was the most used technique to hunt guanacos and lesser rheas (choique, *Pterocnemia pennata*). These animals could be captured in high productive wetlands (*mallines*) using mainly throwing weapons, and handheld weapons to a lesser extent. Our results reinforce the idea that by the end of the peopling process of both environments, distinctive traits had developed beyond the existing networks of interaction.

Keywords Hunter gatherer · Bow and arrow · Spears · Andean forest · Steppe

---

M. Carballido Calatayud (✉) · P. M. Fernández
Instituto Nacional de Antropología y Pensamiento Latinoamericano (INAPL), Consejo Nacional de Investigaciones Científicas y Técnicas (CONICET), Universidad de Buenos Aires (UBA), Buenos Aires, Argentina

© Springer Nature Switzerland AG 2021
J. B. Belardi et al. (eds.), *Ancient Hunting Strategies in Southern South America*,
The Latin American Studies Book Series,
https://doi.org/10.1007/978-3-030-61187-3_9

9.1 Introduction

Patagonia was populated through a slow and heterogeneous process of occupation that prioritized the best-ranked areas according to the resources they offered (Barberena et al. 2015; Borrero 1994–1995; Borrero et al. 2013). Thus, it is not until the Late Holocene that environments traditionally considered marginal, like the arid hinterland, the high plateaus, and the forest, were effectively occupied. Regular human presence in these environments was the result of the gradual demographic expansion throughout the Holocene that reached its maximum at 1000 years cal BP (Pérez et al. 2016). In agreement with this general model, the forest and steppe of North-Central Argentine Patagonia (between latitudes 41° 30′S and 42° 30′S) show an increase in human occupation from 3500 years BP (Bellelli and Guráieb 2019; Fernández et al. 2013).[1] These contiguous environments were inhabited by groups that shared ideological (rock art style), and technological traits (same raw materials, and characteristics of lithic and ceramic technology) (Bellelli et al. 2003, 2006, 2008, 2018; Fernández et al. 2011; Marconetto 2002; Pérez de Micou 2002a; Podestá and Tropea 2010; Podestá et al. 2019). The similarities were attributed to groups that first used forest and steppe complementarity (Bellelli et al. 2003). Later, around 1700 years BP, hunter-gatherer groups occupied the forest more assiduously and/or intensively (Fernández et al. 2013; Fernández and Tessone 2014). This way of inhabiting the forest resulted in specific strategies for its exploitation, and even prompted the emergence of a local rock art style, named as *Modalidad del Ámbito Boscoso Lacustre* [MALB] (Albornoz and Cúneo 2000; Podestá et al. 2007). In the steppe, a similar process is observed where human presence began increasing from 2300 years BP, accompanied by the development of a local rock art variant, and by the use of raw materials from the forest (*Nothofagus* sp. wood, and the *Chusquea culeou* bamboo cane) (Bellelli and Guráieb 2019). Under this new context, the continuity of social networks could explain the evidence of shared cultural traits between the forest and the steppe.

To deepen our knowledge on the human use of these environments, in this paper we developed a comparative study of hunting techniques in the forest and the steppe of North-Central Patagonia. In Argentine Patagonia, the interest on hunting practices is longstanding (Gradin 1959–1960; Vignatti 1947), but only a few decades ago archaeologist started to integrate multiple lines of evidence in the study of this behavior (Belardi and Goñi 2006; Belardi et al. 2013, 2017; Cassiodoro et al. 2014; Goñi et al. 2014, 2016; Miotti et al. 2016; Ratto 1992; Santiago and Salemme 2016). Most of these researches were developed in the steppe, and were focused on guanaco (*Lama guanicoe*) and the role of blinds as part of the technology for hunting (Belardi and Goñi 2006; Belardi et al. 2013, 2017; Cassiodoro et al. 2014; Goñi et al. 2014, 2016; Miotti et al. 2016). In contrast, fewer papers explored techniques employed to hunt in the forest or to obtain other ungulates in this environment (Alunni 2018;

---

[1] In the study area, the relationship between forest and steppe dates back to the Early and Middle Holocene, before human presence increased in both environments (Bellelli et al. 2018; Fernández et al. 2019).

Borrero 1985; Carballido Calatayud and Fernández 2013; Fernández and Carballido Calatayud 2015; Pérez and Batres 2008; Ratto 2003). However, there are no comparative studies between hunting techniques used in the Andean forest and the steppe. These environments represent the extremes of the strong gradient of precipitations registered in Patagonia (Paruelo et al. 1998), characterized by biotic and abiotic differences that allow us exploring the weight of well-established hunting constraints, such as topography, plant coverage and faunal resource structure (Aschero and Martínez 2001; Binford 2001; Bird et al. 2005; Churchill 1993; Hutchings and Brüchert 1997; Peterson 1998; Shott 1993) to the ways people obtain mobile prey. In the forest, the combined effect of dense vegetation and rough terrain severely limited hunter-gatherer pedestrian mobility, and water and wood availability contrasted with the scarcity of edible plants and large to medium-sized animals. On the contrary, the steppe had abundant large to medium-sized preys, but humans were dependent on the strongly localized water sources and the scarcity of firewood.

To accomplish our objective, we modeled three hunting scenarios based on information about plant coverage and topography; the ethology and the characteristics of the prey, and ethnographical and historical data. Then, the models were tested on archaeological data from sites located in the forest (Manso, Epuyén, and Cholila localities) and steppe (Piedra Parada area), focusing on the lithic point technology and the zooarchaeological assemblages (Fig. 9.1). Finally, we developed a comparative analysis between the forest and steppe hunting techniques.

9.2 Environments

In this study, we focused on the forest and steppe environments located between latitudes 41° 30′S and 42° 30′S, on the eastern slope of the Andes. As we noted before, precipitations decrease from West to East according to the rain shadow effect resulting from the presence of the Andean Cordillera, acting as a barrier for the humid air masses coming from the Pacific Ocean (Paruelo et al. 1998). Because of this steep gradient, the forest occupies a narrow strip of 30–50 km wide on the western side of the Andes. Precipitation ranges between an annual rate of 2000 mm near the border with Chile, to an annual rate of 800/700 mm close to the forest/steppe ecotone. Precipitation is highest in winter and the mean annual temperature ranges from 4 to 8 °C (Marchetti and Prudkin 1982; Paruelo et al. 1998). In the study area, forests cover a glacial modified landscape with deep lakes, V-shaped valleys with low altitude (350–600 m a.s.l.), and moraines and mountain ranges up to 2200 m a.s.l. A mixed forest of *Nothofagus* sp.—and *Austrocedrus chilensis* with grassland patches predominates. Towards the forest-steppe ecotone, *Austrocedrus chilensis* becomes more important (Bernades 1981; Marchetti and Prudkin 1982).

The Piedra Parada area is located on the steppe. There, the principal landform is the drainage system of the Chubut River in its middle course with extremely arid conditions (138 mm annual precipitations). Temperatures range between 17 °C in January to 3 °C in July (Aschero et al. 1983; León et al. 1998). This narrow (3 km

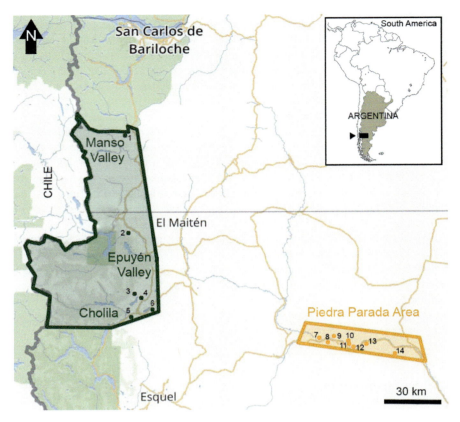

Fig. 9.1 Location of the study areas and archaeological sites analyzed of forest (shaded in green) and steppe (shaded in orange) of North-Central Patagonia (Argentina). Sites references: 1 Paredón Lanfré and Población Anticura, 2 Risco de Azócar 1, 3 Los Guanacos 3, 4 Juncal de Calderón 1, 5 Cerro Pintado, Lili 2, 7 Barda Blanca 4 and 5, 8 Angostura Blanca, 9 Campo Cerda 1 and 2, 10 Campo Moncada 1 and 2, 12 Piedra Parada 11, 13 Campo Nassif 1 and 14 Bajada del Tigre 3 and Mallín Blanco

wide) river valley is located at 400 m a.s.l. and connects with higher sectors (800 m a.s.l.) through canyons. The dominant plant formation is the shrub-steppe but there are very important areas of wetlands (locally known as *mallines*) near the river, as well as shallow lakes and wetlands composed of dense Gramineae grasslands in the highest areas (Aschero et al. 1983; León et al. 1998).

9.3 Forest and Steppe Preys

In order to build the hunting models, ecology, behavior, abundance, habitat selection, social groups' composition, and anti-predator behavior of animals were considered. The models took into account the main prey that would have been captured primarily for food, as well as for leathers, tendons, feathers, and bones. Ordered by live weight, the largest prey is the guanaco (100–120 kg), the intermediate prey is the huemul (60–100 kg), and the smallest prey is the choique (17–25 kg). Nowadays, the huemul (*Hippocamelus bisulcus*) is a cervid that only inhabits the forest. The guanaco (*Lama guanicoe*), a South American camelid, and the lesser rhea or choique (*Pterocnemia pennata*), a flightless bird, both mainly inhabit the steppe, and are also found in the forest-steppe ecotone (Daciuk 1978; Franklin 1983; Serret 2001).

9.3.1 Guanaco

The guanaco is the largest terrestrial vertebrate of Patagonia and mainly lives in the steppe although it also inhabits the forest in Tierra del Fuego, where it seeks refuge during the winter (Montes et al. 2000; Raedeke 1978). The guanaco's social structure is formed of family groups (7–16 individuals), male groups (20–50 individuals) and solo males (Franklin 1983). The family groups are territorial, and the male defends the essential food resources for the females (Raedeke 1978; Franklin 1983; Merino 1986). Some populations move seasonally or use different altitudes throughout the year. These migrations may be related to the snow cover, the absence of forage in winter or the possibility of improving forage conditions by alternating sites (Franklin 1983; Montes et al. 2000; Ortega and Franklin 1988; Puig et al. 2003). Guanaco anti-predatory behavior is related to the puma (*Puma concolor*), its main threat (Taraborelli et al. 2012). Its defense strategy combines surveillance, flight and alarm vocalizations (Donadio and Buskirk 2006; Taraborelli et al. 2012; Young and Franklin 2004). In family groups, the females remain alert trying to reduce the risk of predation, while the males' surveillance has as main objective to keep other guanacos out of their territory. However, this behavior also works for detecting predators. In non-territorial groups, such as male groups or mixed groups, surveillance is more relaxed, and the main strategy is grouping (Marino 2012; Taraborelli et al. 2012).

9.3.2 Huemul

Huemul ecology and distribution have been affected by habitat loss and hunting pressures since the European colonization (Povilitis 1978; Serret 2001; among others). Nowadays, the huemul is restricted to forested mountain areas of difficult access, but in the past, the forest-steppe ecotone would have been its optimal habitat (Serret

2001). The social structure of this cervid comprises solitary male, female with or without fawn/yearlings, and family groups—up to four individuals (male, female, fawn, and yearling). Additionally, there are transient social forms, such as mixed groups (more than four individuals from both sexes and different ages during the fall/winter), yearling, and pair of yearlings, corresponding to individuals that were expelled from their birth group (Garay et al. 2016; Povilitis 1978; Serret 2001). The family group usually remains in the same area, and its home range is about 3–4 km^2 (Garay et al. 2016; Gill et al. 2008). Most huemul populations move seasonally, downslope in winter (500–800 m a.s.l.) and upslope in summer (1000–1400 m a.s.l., Gill et al. 2008; Povilitis 1978, 1983; Serret 2001), but some remain year-round above 1400 m a.s.l. (Galende et al. 2005). Like the guanaco, the huemul's main predator is the puma. The anti-predator behavior of this cervid is related to its distance with the potential predator (Povilitis 1978). When the huemul detects an observer, it usually remains motionless, looking directly at the intruder. Then, if the distance is less than 34 m, the huemul will make for an abrupt escape. An intermediate distance (77 m average) generates slow and cautious movements to go unnoticed and avoid an attack. If the distance is more than 190 m, the animal simply walks away or cautiously resumes the activity before the alarm. Topographic features will serve to hide it from the intruder's view, but it can also use the vegetation cover to obstruct eye contact. With the arrival of the Europeans with firearms, horses, and dogs, immobility was turned inadequate, and topography and vegetation cover became the best resources for survival (Povilitis 1978). Because of this behavior, the huemul was viewed as an easy target by late nineteenth and early twentieth century travelers (Díaz 2000). However, despite being easy to wound with firearms, huemules can flee at full speed and even with a gunshot wound can cross rivers to distance themselves from the aggressor (Skottsberg 1911). The huemul is a very good swimmer and its dense fur facilitates its flotation. Thus, flight through lakes and waterways is a common tactic of their anti-predatory behavior (Moreno and Pastore 1998; Serret 2001).

9.3.3 Choique

The lesser rhea or choique is a medium-sized flightless bird, endemic to shrub steppes and semi-deserts of Argentine Patagonia and southern Chile. In these arid lands it is patchily distributed in high productivity wetland areas or *mallines* (Bellis et al. 2006; Daciuk 1978). The choique has suffered a marked population decline over recent decades, mainly as a result of livestock production and overhunting (Pedrana et al. 2011). During the reproduction and breeding season, groups of 15–40 individuals are observed, distributed in four types: solo males, females (2–15) with one or two males, large groups of birds less than one-year-old (more than 40) with some 'non-reproductive' adults, and males with its chicks. The male is responsible for hatching the eggs, and with its chicks forms a group that stays together during the summer and the following winter. These families represent the core of the large winter group (more than 100 birds) (Bruning 1974; Daciuk 1978). The speed and ability to stop and suddenly change direction while running are its main defense mechanism (Martella et al. 1995). Hence, the open and flat lands favor the 'watch-and-run' anti-predator strategy (Bruning 1974).

9.4 Hunting Techniques Data from Historical and Ethnographical Sources

Most of the data on hunting techniques utilized in Patagonia in the past were recorded in societies that had already incorporated the horse into their hunting practices (Bourne 1853; Furlong 1912; Musters 1871; Perea 1989; Prichard 1910; among others). In northern Patagonia, the use of the horse for hunting dates back at least to the beginning of the seventeenth century (Florez de León 1992). Prior to this, there is practically no data on pedestrian hunting, except for a brief mention of a member of the Magellan's expedition who in 1520 reached the Atlantic coast of Patagonia (Pigafetta 1874 [1536]). However, in Tierra del Fuego pedestrian hunting practices lasted until the early twentieth century. These activities were depicted in detail by travelers and ethnographers (see reviews in Borrero 2013; Ratto 2003; Santiago and Salemme 2016), and we will use this information to model hunting techniques.[2] Below, we present the data from the historical sources that were viewed ordered by species.

9.4.1 Guanaco

Pigafetta's early mention of a hunting technique pointed out the use of juvenile guanacos as bait to attract adult animals that were killed with bows and arrows by hunters hidden in the bushes (Pigafetta 1874 [1536]: 51). This 'approach' hunting technique (sensu Churchill 1993) contrasts significantly with the eighteenth and nineteenth century chronicles of continental Patagonia. In these sources the tactics are based on the use of horses, generally involving numerous hunters and the use of

---

[2]In this paper we follow the classification of hunting techniques proposed by Churchill (1993: 16). They comprise disadvantage, that 'includes any technique [also drives animal into a handicapped position in which the weapon was applied] that limits the escape of an animal or exploits an animal naturally disadvantaged to gain time or access so that a weapon can be employed'; ambush that 'involves instances in which hunters wait in hiding, whether behind man-made blinds or natural features, for animals to pass within effective range of their weapons. Drives were considered ambushing if the intent was to force animals past concealed hunters'; approach that 'includes stalking free-moving animals to within effective weapon range. Luring of animals was also included in this category'; pursuit that 'entails chasing an animal to overtake it and place the hunter within effective weapon range or to exhaust and thus disadvantage it. Pursuit may involve domesticated animals such as horses to close the distance between the hunter and prey or dogs to keep the animal moving until exhaustion', and encounter that 'refers to hunting in which animals are taken, either jumped from the bush or spotted in trees, as they are encountered'.

bolas, fire, and dogs ('disadvantage' technique, sensu Churchill 1993). Furthermore, in these hunting events, several types of prey were usually obtained at the same time (guanacos, choiques, foxes, and pumas).

The Yámana canoers observed in the early nineteenth century hunted guanacos using a 'disadvantage' technique (sensu Churchill 1993). In winter, when the animals moved down the slopes toward the seacoast, the deep snow would prevent their escape, thus allowing the hunters and their dogs to surround and kill them easily (Fitz-Roy 1839: 186). At other times of the year, the Yámana hunted guanacos using the 'ambush' technique (sensu Churchill 1993). The hunters hid themselves in the forest paths usually used by these animals and would 'sometimes get them by laying in wait and shooting them with arrows, or by getting into a tree near a track, and spearing them as they pass beneath the branches' (Fitz-Roy 1839: 187). The Selknam, pedestrian hunters, used a similar technique to capture guanacos in the forest, by using dogs and/or beaters to drive the animals toward ambushed archers. Furlong (1912) recorded another variant of the 'ambush' technique in the early twentieth century. The guanacos were rounded up and driven between two lines of hunters, which gradually converged toward a narrow runway where the bowmen's pits were located. Guanacos were slaughtered in the vicinity of the bowmen's pits. Usually, a valley was chosen for the drive, but it could also occur between two small rivers (Furlong 1912:9). Another alternative consisted in driving guanacos through the open lands between patches of dense woods. Hunters often approached them disguised with guanaco skins and gradually drove them to the meadows. As guanacos passed through narrow spaces between the trees, they certainly became an easy prey to the arrows of the concealed hunter (Furlong 1912: 11). Nevertheless, Lothrop (1928: 81) rejected the notion that the Selknam ever came in sufficient numbers to execute the drives and he also wondered how the pits were dug in the frozen ground during the winter. This author describes another variant of the ambush hunting technique during the moving of the residential camp. While women and children followed the bottom of the valleys, some men kept on higher land on either side. They, acting as beaters, startled the guanacos which fled to the heights where the hunters were waiting for them (Lothrop 1928: 81). However, solitary hunting would have been the most frequent strategy for pedestrian hunters ('pursuit' technique, sensu Churchill 1993). A lone hunter could head out in any direction at random. When dogs discovered a trail, they followed it, and the hunter approached the guanaco in a concealed manner, and when at about 20–30 meters shot an arrow toward the animal's neck (Gusinde 1982: 251). In summary, according to these historical and ethnographic records, the guanaco was hunted using the 'ambush', 'disadvantage', and/or 'pursuit' approaches, using bows, arrows and spears, and with the help of dogs and baits.

9.4.2 Huemul

The information on huemul hunting techniques in historical and ethnographical sources is scarce. Data was compiled by Norma Díaz (2000: 8–10) and refers almost exclusively to canoers groups in southern Chile, restricting its application in the cases discussed in this paper. In canals and fjords, these groups used a 'disadvantage' technique (sensu Churchill 1993) driving the huemules into the sea and using harpoons for hunting them from their canoes (Bird 1946: 61; Emperaire 1955: 201). Emperaire also points out that when hunted in the mountain, the huemul is cornered with dogs and killed by a blow to the head or beaten with rocks (Emperaire 1955: 201). De Córdova (1788: 340) and Fitz-Roy (1839: 141) also mentioned the use of dogs in hunting huemul. Finally, for the early twentieth century' in the Neuquén province, indigenous people used the lasso to capture huemules (Perea 1989: 40).

9.4.3 Choique

As reported as early as 1869, 'the arrival of Europeans in South America has very considerably modified the manner of living amongst the Patagonians' (Hutchinson 1869: 321). This statement is reflected by examining historical references to choique hunting. Unlike the guanaco, there are no early accounts prior to the horse being integrated within hunting practices. As we noted, equestrian hunting particularly if it involves several hunters—can result in the simultaneous capture of guanacos and choiques and, occasionally, pumas and foxes. According to Musters' description (1871: 72–73), couples of riders accompanied by dogs spread themselves out in a crescent, lighting fires at intervals to mark their track, eventually forming a circle and narrowing its radius. The game ran from the advancing party, and when the circle was closed and tightened, the animals were attacked with the bolas ('disadvantage' technique, sensu Churchill 1993). Other nineteenth and early twentieth century chroniclers and ethnographers describe this same 'disadvantage' technique of hunting, performed either by indigenous groups or by Creole and European hunters (Bourne 1853:113, D'Orbigny 1839–1843: 193–194; Guinard 1868: 120; Perea 1989; Prichard 1910: 32–33). Musters (1871: 128) also reported two other choiques' hunting techniques by disadvantage, both employed in the winter season. The first one consisted of driving the birds 'into the water, where, their legs getting numbed with cold, they are drifted to the shore by the current, and easily captured, being unable to move'. The second was used in snowy weather, as the eyes of these birds are affected by the glare of the white snow, and their snow-saturated plumage becomes heavier, facilitating their capture.

9.5 Hunting Models

The three following hunting scenarios (Into the forest, Forest-steppe ecotone, and Steppe) were modeled using the information previously outlined about plant coverage, topography, prey's characteristics, and ethnographic and historical data (Aschero and Martínez 2001; Churchill 1993; Marean 1997).

9.5.1 Into the Forest

We proposed hunting models for guanacos and huemuls due to their different characteristics and behavior. For guanacos, we use the information from Tierra del Fuego since there is no data on these animals from the forest of North-Central Patagonia. As guanacos' behavior is spatially and temporally predictable, we proposed the use of an 'ambush' hunting technique. The recurrent use of trails by territorial guanaco family groups would have allowed hunters hidden by the dense vegetation to intercept the animals on their way. Ambush could also have been used to hunt mixed groups of males and females formed during the winter. These large groups could have been located in open sectors of the forest (Borrero 1985: 270). Another variant of an 'ambush' technique could have included driving animals to hunters hidden in the forest. Besides, the 'encounter' hunting technique could have been employed on non-territorial guanacos' social groups, such as male groups. The weapon systems employed for all these hunting techniques would have included throwing weapons, such as spears (with and without thrower), and bows and arrows.

In the forest, the huemul would have been hunted mainly through the 'encounter' technique' because its location is only predictable on a wide spatial scale. During winter, the huemul is found in valleys and areas protected from snow, below 700 m a.s.l, while in summer it is usually found between 1000 and 1200 m a.s.l. Due to the small size of the social groups, hunting events would have yielded few prey. However, during the rutting season the more numerous social groups and the smaller home range would have allowed more animals to be captured. The importance of water bodies on the huemul's anti-predatory behavior would have prompted the use of a 'disadvantage' hunting technique. The animals would be frightened away and, on their way to a lake or river, they would be shot by hidden hunters on the shore. It is expected that, like the guanaco, the huemul was hunted using throwing weapons, facilitated by the use of open areas and the immobilizing anti-predator behavior. Also, the concealment of hunters must have been very important to get the animals within the effective range of weapons. In the case of populations not accustomed to humans, it would have been possible to approach the animal and kill it with handheld weapons or even with heavy items with no archaeological visibility, such as sticks and stones.

9.5.2 Forest-Steppe Ecotone

In the forest-steppe ecotone, only guanacos and huemuls are recorded. These animals would have been captured with the same hunting techniques ('ambush', 'disadvantage', and 'encounter') and the same weapons as those used in the forest, although the reduced vegetation cover would have also facilitated the use of bolas. The main difference with the inner forest is the higher abundance of ungulates. Guanaco family groups are larger than in the forest (Franklin 1983; Merino 1986), while huemules would tend to group in larger numbers as an anti-predation strategy (Frid 1994; Povilitis 1978). In both cases, the risk of loss is expected to decrease due to the greater abundance of prey and the fact that many animals could be obtained by hunting events. The differences in predictability between both ungulate species would be similar to those proposed for the forest, with the guanaco family groups being the easiest to locate.

9.5.3 Steppe

The 'approach' hunting technique (including luring animals such as those mentioned by Pigafetta 1874 [1536]) would have been used to hunt guanacos and choiques in wetlands (*mallines*), where these animals' food resources are concentrated. The 'approach' hunting technique could also have been used to capture male choiques during hatching, which has the additional benefit of collecting the eggs. Another hunting technique that would have been used in the ravines to capture guanacos during their seasonal movement (summer upslope and winter downslope) was through the 'ambush' technique. The guanacos could also have been driven into the ravines at any time of the year. Bounded between the rock walls and with only one escape route, they would have been intercepted by hidden hunters. Before the adoption of the horse, the 'ambush' hunting technique with a drive must have demanded a large number of hunters to catch choiques. Because of the bird's flight pattern—high speed and suddenly change of direction—a narrow circle with many shooters was required to maximize their effectiveness. Besides, and without an association with a specific topography, guanacos and solitary choiques would have been hunted by the 'encounter' technique. All the above techniques would have used throwing weapons, such as spears, bows and arrows, and bolas. In other sectors of Patagonia, ambush in blinds (*parapetos*) was a very frequent technique for the summer guanaco hunting at the high plateaus (Belardi et al. 2017; Flores Coni et al., this volume, Goñi et al. 2016; Lynch et al. 2020; Miotti et al. 2016). Future research on Piedra Parada highlands will allow evaluation of whether this technique took place in the study area.

In all three hunting scenarios we do not rule out the use of dogs as a complement to hunting techniques, although their importance in pre-European times is not clear. The few remains of domestic canids found in the Pampas and Patagonia date from the last thousand years, come almost exclusively from funerary contexts and have been interpreted as individual exchange goods (Acosta et al. 2011; Prates et al. 2010a, b). This scarcity contrasts with historical chronicles that mention the use of numerous dogs for hunting (Bourne 1853; D'Orbigny 1839–1843; Gallardo 1910; Guinard 1868; Musters 1871; Prichard 1910).

9.6 Archaeological Data

The two forest hunting models were assessed using mostly lithic points and bone remains from stratified rock-shelters (Paredón Lanfré, Población Anticura, Risco de Azócar 1, and Cerro Pintado). The open-air surface sites Los Guanacos 3, Juncal de Calderón 1, and Lili 2 only provided one point each. Radiocarbon dates of stratified sites span from 3350 to 280 years BP (Table 9.1). The open-air surface sites are not dated, but have traits like lithic raw material, grinding stones and end scrapers morphology, that suggest they belong to the same period (Bellelli et al. 2003; Carballido Calatayud 2009). Regarding the precipitation gradient, the sites located in sectors with more than 1200 mm of annual precipitation were used to assess the model Into the forest (Paredón Lanfré, Población Anticura, and Risco de Azócar 1). Cerro Pintado and the open-air surface (716 mm annual) were employed to assess both Into the forest and the Forest-steppe ecotone hunting models. The steppe zooarchaeological and lithic points data mostly comes from the stratified rock shelter sites Angostura Blanca, Campo Cerda 1, Piedra Parada 1, Campo Moncada 1, Campo Moncada 2, and Campo Nassif 1, that are dated between 3350 and 450 years BP (Table 9.1). The open-air surface sites Barda Blanca 4 and 5, Campo Cerda 2, Piedra Parada 11, Mallín Blanco, and Bajada del Tigre 3 presented lithic assemblages but no bones.[3] These sites are not dated, but Barda Blanca Médanos, a site near Barda Blanca 4, has a radiocarbon date of 1320 ± 60 years BP (Bellelli and Guráieb 2019). We assume that the open-air sites have occupations within the same time range as the rock shelter sites, although we do not rule out older materials. Archaeological evidence recovered from both types of loci was used to contrast the Steppe hunting model.

Both forest and steppe stratified rock shelter and open-air surface sites have evidence of multiple activities. In rock-shelters, discard and resharpening of lithic points, as well as food consumption and the use of leather, bones, and tendons from preys, were identified (Aschero et al. 1983; Bellelli 1994, 2005; Bellelli et al. 2003; Carballido Calatayud 2009; Carballido Calatayud and Fernández 2013; Fernández 2010; Fernández et al. 2011; Marchione and Bellelli 2013; Onetto 1986–1987; Pérez de Micou 1979–1982, 1987; Podestá et al. 2007). At surface sites, bones were not preserved, and lithic points were reduced in number due to non-archaeological collectors/amateurs' action. Therefore, the interpretation of the activities developed in these types of sites in both environments is limited.

---

[3] A resident of the Piedra Parada area has a collection of archaeological materials including bolas. Unfortunately, we did not have access to her collection and, although the material was studied decades ago, the results were never reported.

9 Hunting Techniques Along the Rain Shadow …

Table 9.1 Chronology of the forest and steppe contexts analyzed

Site	Analysis unit	Chronology (yrs. BP)	Reference
Forest			
Paredón Lanfre (PL)	Single (palimpsest)	330 ± 50 470 ± 70 490 ± 60 790 ± 60 930 ± 60 1030 ± 70 1450 ± 70 1480 ± 70 1500 ± 60 1570 ± 60	Bellelli et al. (2007) and Fernández et al. (2010a, 2013)
Población Anticura (PA)	Historical Times (PA HsT)	280 ± 40 300 ± 50 400 ± 70	Fernández et al. (2010a, 2013)
	Final Late Holocene (PA FLH)	480 ± 70 530 ± 50 550 ± 50 590 ± 50 660 ± 50 690 ± 60 700 ± 60 710 ± 70 810 ± 50 1150 ± 60 1420 ± 70 1550 ± 30	Fernández et al. (2010a, 2013)
	Initial Late Holocene (PA ILH)	2270 ± 80 2530 ± 60 2660 ± 80 2960 ± 25 3180 ± 30 3350 ± 100	Fernández et al. (2010a, 2013)
Risco de Azócar 1 (RA1)	Single (palimpsest)	820 ± 60 1200 + 60 1250 ± 70 1330 ± 70 1600 + 90 1690 ± 60	Podestá et al. (2007)
Cerro Pintado (CP)	Single (palimpsest)	680 ± 60 1100 ± 60 1120 ± 60 1870 ± 80	Bellelli et al. (2003)
Steppe			
Angostura Blanca (AB)	Test pit	450 ± 110 2960 ± 60	Bellelli (2005)

(continued)

Table 9.1 (continued)

Site	Analysis unit	Chronology (yrs. BP)	Reference
Campo Cerda 1 (CCe1)	Unit 2-3 (CCe1 2-3)	580 ± 60	Bellelli (1994)
	Unit 5 (CCe1 5)	1715 ± 70 1870 ± 50 1910 ± 80 2050 ± 110 2850 ± 50	Bellelli (1994) and Bellelli (2000–2002)
Piedra Parada 1 (PP1)	Single (palimpsest)	1330 ± 50	Pérez de Micou (1979–1982)
Campo Moncada 2 (CM2)	Unit 0-2b (CM2 0-2b)	780 ± 60 860 ± 80	Nacuzzi (1987)
	Unit 2c (CM2 2c)	1750 ± 80 3350 ± 90	Pérez de Micou (1987) and Pérez de Micou (2002b)
Campo Nassif 1 (CN1)	Single (palimpsest)	480 ± 75	Onetto (1986–1987)

9.7 Analytical Methods

9.7.1 Lithic Points

The analysis of the lithic points included metric (length, width, thickness, weight, angles, etc.) and technical variables, such as the shape and direction of the flakes and their extension on the faces of the piece (Aschero 1975, 1983). Also, the points were evaluated in search of resharpening (reactivation without change of function) and/or recycling (a change in function) evidence. The minimal number of points was calculated by considering the section represented (body, stem, or base), the existence of refittings, and the raw material (Carballido Calatayud and Fernández 2013). Each fragment analyzed belonged to a different piece, 91 lithic points in total. The lithic points functional assignment followed the model developed by Ratto (1994, 2003), based on ethnographic and archaeological information from Southern Patagonia. This model takes into account (a) the reinforcement surface, (b) the aerodynamics, (c) the penetration, and (d) the hafting (Ratto 1994, 2003). The first (a) includes the ratio between the maximum thickness and the width in that same sector (MT/W) and the toughness of the rock.[4] The MT/W values range from 1 to 0 and form an ordinal scale: 1 to 0.8 very high, 0.79 to 0.6 high, 0.59 to 0.4 medium, 0.39 to 0.2 low, and

---

[4]The raw material identification was based on macroscopic comparison with rocks determined by petrographic thin sections (Carballido Calatayud 1999, 2009). These identifications considered the color, brightness, texture, type, and size of the crystals included and the presence of other heterogeneities like impurities, fissures or alterations. To overcome the lack of specific studies on the toughness of the analyzed points' raw materials, values calculated for Patagonian rocks of comparable origin and characteristics were used (Banegas et al. 2014; Ratto and Nestiero 1994).

9 Hunting Techniques Along the Rain Shadow …   223

0.19 to 0 very low. The second (b) combines the cross-section of the piece, body contour and the length and width of the body, to create a qualitative classification of point aerodynamics (perfect, normal, imperfect and non-aerodynamic). The third (c) considers the tip section (> or < 1 mm^2) and angle (> or < 45°). The fourth (d) combines width, length, and thickness of the stem or base (Banegas et al. 2014; Ratto 1994, 2003, 2013). According to the model, an arrow point has low MT/W ratio, low or medium toughness, perfect or normal aerodynamic, tip section $\leq$ 1 mm^2, tip angle $\leq$ 45°, and $\leq$ 10 mm stem or base width. A spear point has medium, high or very high MT/W ratio, high toughness, imperfect or non-aerodynamic, tip section between >1 and $\leq$ 1.5 mm^2, tip angle $\geq$ 45°, and $\geq$ 10 mm stem or base width. Hand-held point has low MT/W ratio, low or medium toughness, non-aerodynamic, tip section between >1 and $\leq$ 1.5 mm^2, tip angle $\geq$ 45°, and $\geq$ 10 mm stem or base width (Ratto 2003, 2013).

As shown by previous studies, the best sample to evaluate the model is complete, not resharpened and/or not recycled points (Banegas et al. 2014; González-José and Charlin 2012; Shott 1997). One limitation to estimate the penetration variable is the breakage or slight modification of the very fragile tip even in the non-resharpened or non-recycled points (Banegas et al. 2014; Fernández and Carballido Calatayud 2015). In the fragmented points, we measured all possible variables to be identified and fragments were assigned functionally if at least three of the model variables could be calculated. Finally, aerodynamics and penetration could not be measured in the Campo Nassif 1 sample (steppe). Those variables were not taken into account 20 years ago, when these projectile points were analyzed for the first time. Because they are currently missing, we were not able to re-analyze the assemblage.

Also, because of its relevance, we plotted the stem or base width to explore differences and similarities between points of each environment. The stem/base width is key to distinguishing between weapons systems because of its direct link to the type of hafting (Thomas 1978; Ratto 1991, 2003; Shott 1997). Indeed, it is insusceptible to the resharpening effects (Banegas et al. 2014; Franco et al. 2009; Ratto 1991; Shott 1997). Here, we follow Patagonian ethnographic data that shows a 10 mm width of the stem or base is an adequate limit to discriminate between arrows vs. spearheads or handheld points (Ratto 1991; Ratto and Marconetto 2011).

9.7.2 Bone Assemblages

The detailed methodology of the zooarchaeological analysis and the complete data of the faunal assemblages recovered from each site can be found in the following published works for the forest data (Andrade and Fernández 2017; Fernández 2008; Fernández and Fernández 2019) and for the steppe data (Fernández 2008, 2010). Based on this information, we considered the estimated number of preys represented in each archaeological context, the age of individuals, the skeletal parts profiles, and the butchery evidence (cut and percussion marks) as relevant data to contrast hunting technique models. Osteology manuals (Altamirano Enciso 1983; Pacheco Torres et al. 1986) and comparative skeletal collections housed at the *Instituto Nacional de Antropología y Pensamiento Latinoamericano* (INAPL, Buenos Aires, Argentina) were used for the anatomical and taxonomic identification. We employed the NISP (number of identified specimens) and the MNI (minimum number of individuals) to quantify the species representation. Here, the MNI considers both the side of paired bones (left or right) and the epiphyseal fusion stages. Both measures (NISP and MNI) are estimates of taxonomic abundances and do not represent the actual number of prey hunted in the past (Lyman 2019). It is used as a very rough proxy to differentiate contexts with few animals represented (estimated) and those with a large number of preys (categorized as massive hunting, see Borrero 2013 and Santiago and Salemme 2016 for the discussion of this topic in Patagonia). Age estimates were based on epiphyseal fusion following guanacos Kaufmann (2009) and huemuls Fernández (2010) studies. These authors identified a group of early fused bones (newborns, 0–12 months) and a late fused group (adults to senile, 36–48 months), generating an approximate age structure.

Anatomical diversity was estimated by MNE (minimal number of elements), calculated following the Mengoni Goñalons (1999) procedure: counting bone diagnostic zones, considering diaphyseal fragments, and long bones and symmetrical elements of the skeleton. Minimal anatomical units (MAU) were calculated based on MNE, and the anatomical abundance was presented through %MAU graphs. Bone modifications were initially examined with the naked eye, followed by inspection under a 10x hand lens. To resolve questions about particular specimens, a binocular zoom magnifier up to 16x, was used. The analysis took into account the influence of the general taphonomic process (Lyman 1994) and regional accumulation and preservation characteristics (Borrero 2001; Borrero and Muñoz 1999; Fernández and Forlano 2009; Fernández et al. 2010b).

9.8 Results

9.8.1 Lithic Points

The forest sample comprises 44 points, highly fragmented so that only nine are complete (Table 9.2, Fig. 9.2). We applied the functional assignment model to complete ($N = 9$), almost complete[5] (one ear lost, $N = 2$), and one fragmented point. Two arrowheads, two spearheads, and one handheld point (Table 9.3) were identified. The remaining ($N = 7$) was classified as ambiguous because they combine attributes of two or three types of weapons (Table 9.3). In four cases, the non-assignment is due to resharpening or recycling that modified the body-size relationships (Table 9.3). At the steppe sites, 47 points were recovered, and only a third of them are complete ($N = 16$, Table 9.2; Fig. 9.3). We applied the functional assignment model to seven

---

[5]We considered fragmented points if we can measure three of the four functional assignment model's variables.

Table 9.2 Details of the lithic points from the forest and steppe contexts

Environment	Site	Analysis unit	Item code	Raw Material	Part	Resharpening/recycled	Length	Width	Thickness	Stem or base width	Tip section	Tip angle (degree)
Forest	PL	S(P)	PL 220	Silex	Bs	–	–	–	–	16	–	–
	PL	S(P)	PL 297	Silex	C	Rs	17.5	10	3	5	1.5	50
	PL	S(P)	PL 235	Silex	C	Rc	31	15	3.5	7	1	52
	PL	S(P)	PL 180	Silex	Bd frg (Tl)	–	–	–	–	–	–	–
	PL	S(P)	PL 260	Obsidian	Bd frg (Tl)	Rs	–	–	–	–	–	–
	PL	S(P)	PL 337bis	Silex	Bd frg	–	–	–	–	–	–	–
	PL	S(P)	PL 495	Silex	St or Bs	–	–	–	–	7	–	–
	PL	S(P)	PL 514	Translucid Silex	Bd (Tb)	–	–	–	–	–	–	–
	PA	HsT	PA 2	Indeterminate	St + Bd frg	–	–	–	–	7	–	–
	PA	HsT	PA 908	Translucid Silex	C	–	24	12	3	6.5	1	46
	PA	HsT	PA 909	Silex	Bd frg	–	–	–	–	–	1.5	58
	PA	HsT	PA 9	Silex	Bd (Tl)	–	–	–	–	–	–	–
	PA	HsT	PA 100	Translucid Silex	C	Rs	12.5	10	3	9	2	59

(continued)

Table 9.2 (continued)

Environment	Site	Analysis unit	Item code	Raw Material	Part	Resharpening/recycled	Length	Width	Thickness	Stem or base width	Tip section	Tip angle (degree)
	PA	HsT	PA 29	Translucid Silex	AC (Tl)	–	–	–	–	7.5	–	–
	PA	HsT	PA 36	Silex	Bd frg	–	–	–	–	–	1.5	61
	PA	HsT	PA 974	Basalt	C	Rs	16	10.5	3	6.5	0.5	43
	PA	HsT	PA 43	Silex	St frg	–	–	–	–	–	–	–
	PA	HsT	PA 25	Translucid Silex	C	–	11	9	1.5	5	1.5	61
	PA	HsT	PA 889	Translucid Silex	St frg	–	–	–	–	–	–	–
	RA1	S(P)	RA1 148	Silex	AC (Tl)	–	–	–	–	8.5	–	–
	RA1	S(P)	RA1 166	Silex	C (Tb)	Rc	20	14	3.5	7.5	–	–
	RA1	S(P)	RA1 161	Silex	C (Tb)	Rs	39.5	19	7.5	13	–	–
	CP	S(P)	CP 2	Silex	Bd frg	–	–	–	–	–	1.5	43
	CP	S(P)	CP 3	Silex	Bd frg (Tl)	–	–	–	–	–	–	–
	CP	S(P)	CP 112	Indeterminate	St + Bd frg	–	–	–	–	7	–	–

(continued)

9 Hunting Techniques Along the Rain Shadow …

Table 9.2 (continued)

Environment	Site	Analysis unit	Item code	Raw Material	Part	Resharpening/recycled	Length	Width	Thickness	Stem or base width	Tip section	Tip angle (degree)
	CP	S(P)	CP 9	Translucid Silex	St + Bd frg	Rs	–	–	–	6	–	–
	CP	S(P)	CP 17	Silex	St + Bd frg	Rs	–	–	–	8.5	–	–
	CP	S(P)	CP 28	Translucid Silex	Bd frg	–	–	–	–	–	–	–
	CP	S(P)	CP 48	Indeterminate	Bd frg	Rs	–	–	–	–	–	–
	CP	S(P)	CP 66	Translucid Silex	Bd frg (Tl)	Rc	–	–	–	–	–	–
	CP	S(P)	CP 84	Obsidian	Bs	–	–	–	–	13	–	–
	CP	S(P)	CP 121	Translucid Silex	Bd frg	–	–	–	–	–	1	38
	CP	S(P)	CP 122	Indeterminate	Bd frg (Tl)	–	–	–	–	–	–	–
	CP	S(P)	CP 143	Silex	St + Bd frg	–	–	–	–	8.5	–	–
	CP	S(P)	CP 144	Translucid Silex	Bd frg	–	–	–	–	–	1	40
	CP	S(P)	CP 145	Silex	Bd frg (Tb)	Rs	–	–	–	–	–	–
	CP	S(P)	CP 150	Translucid Silex	Bd frg	–	–	–	–	–	1	36

(continued)

Table 9.2 (continued)

Environment	Site	Analysis unit	Item code	Raw Material	Part	Resharpening/recycled	Length	Width	Thickness	Stem or base width	Tip section	Tip angle (degree)
	CP	S(P)	CP 258	Silex	Bs	–	–	–	–	12	–	–
	CP	S(P)	CP 219	Silex	Bd frg	–	–	–	–	–	1	36
	CP	S(P)	CP 273	Translucid Silex	St	–	–	–	–	6	–	–
	CP	S(P)	CP 247	Translucid Silex	Bd frg	–	–	–	–	–	1	39
	LG3	S	LG3 2	Basalt	C	Rs	35	18	6	15.5	1.5	49
	JC1	S	JC1 4	Limolite	Bd frg	–	–	–	–	–	–	–
	LI2	S	LL2 1	Silex	St frg+ Bd frg (TI)	–	–	–	–	–	–	–
Steppe	AB	TP	AB 260	Limolite	Bd (TI)	–	–	15	4.5	–	–	–
	AB	TP	AB 255	Silex	Bd (TI)	–	–	16	4	–	–	–
	AB	TP	AB	Translucent silex	C	Rs	29	14	3	8	1	30
	CCe1	U 2-3	CCe1 77	Silex	AC (TI)	Rc	27	19	6	13.5	–	–
	CCe1	U 2-3	CCe1 63	Silex	AC (TI)	–	19	10.5	2.5	4	–	–
	CCe1	U 2-3	CCe1 1	Limolite	AC (TI)	Rc & Rs	48	27	6	15	–	–

(continued)

9 Hunting Techniques Along the Rain Shadow … 229

Table 9.2 (continued)

Environment	Site	Analysis unit	Item code	Raw Material	Part	Resharpening/recycled	Length	Width	Thickness	Stem or base width	Tip section	Tip angle (degree)
	CCe1	U 2-3	CCe1 62	Translucent silex	AC (Tl)	Rc & Rs	20	11	2	7	–	–
	PP1	S(P)	PP1 10	Limolite	C	Rc	29	15	3	8	1	30
	CM1	S	CM1 1	Silex	Bd frg	–	–	–	–	–	–	–
	CM2	U 0-2b	CM2 826	Limolite	C	Rs	56.5	30	9	19	1.5	50
	CM2	U 0-2b	CM2 126	Limolite	C (Tb)	Rc & Rs	26	20.5	7	15	–	–
	CM2	U 0-2b	CM2 98	Limolite	AC (1 El and Tb)	Rs	33	–	7	16	–	–
	CM2	U 0-2b	CM2 64	Translucid Silex	St + Bd	–	–	–	–	12	–	–
	CM2	U 0-2b	CM2 234	Andesite	Bs + Bd frg	–	–	–	–	15	–	–
	CM2	U 0-2b	CM2 235	Tuff	Bd frg	–	–	–	–	–	–	–
	CM2	U 0-2b	CM2 102	Limolite	AC (Tl)	Rc & Rs	29	27	6	12	–	–
	CM2	U 0-2b	CM2 797	Limolite	St + Bd frg	Rc & Rs	–	–	–	16	–	–

(continued)

Table 9.2 (continued)

Environment	Site	Analysis unit	Item code	Raw Material	Part	Resharpening/recycled	Length	Width	Thickness	Stem or base width	Tip section	Tip angle (degree)
	CM2	U 0-2b	CM2 4/101	Tuff	C (Tb)	Rc & Rs	25	19	5.5	14	–	–
	CM2	U 0-2b	CM2 799	Obsidian	Bd frg	–	–	–	–	–	1	39
	CM2	U 0-2b	CM2 384	Rhyolite	C (Tb)	Rc & Rs	22	17	6	14.5	–	–
	CM2	U 0-2b	CM2 124	Tuff	St + Bd	–	–	25.5	6	13.5	–	–
	CM2	U 0-2b	CM2 811	Limolite	Bs + Bd	–	–	32	9	21	–	–
	CM2	U 2c	CM2 367	Silex	Bs + Bd	–	–	21	13	18	–	–
	CN1	S(P)	CN1 29b	Translucent silex	St + Bd	Rs	–	20	7.5	14.5	–	–
	CN1	S(P)	CN1 166	Tuff	C	–	27	22	5	13	n/d	n/d
	CN1	S(P)	CN1 157b	Obsidian	Bd frg	–	–	–	–	–	n/d	n/d
	CN1	S(P)	CN1 27b	Limolite	C	Rs	55	37	9	14	n/d	n/d
	CN1	S(P)	CN1 53	Rhyolite	Bd (Tl)	–	–	–	–	–	–	–

(continued)

Table 9.2 (continued)

Environment	Site	Analysis unit	Item code	Raw Material	Part	Resharpening/recycled	Length	Width	Thickness	Stem or base width	Tip section	Tip angle (degree)
	CN1	S(P)	CN1 910	Indeterminate	Bd (Tl)	Rc	–	–	–	–	–	–
	CN1	S(P)	CN1 121	Limolite	C	Rs	51	21	6	14	n/d	n/d
	CN1	S(P)	CN1 43	Translucent silex	C	–	26	15	3	6	n/d	n/d
	CN1	S(P)	CN1 257	Silex	AC (1 El)	–	28.5	13.5	4	7	n/d	n/d
	CN1	S(P)	CN1 28	Limolite	C	–	33	18	6	17	n/d	n/d
	CN1	S(P)	CN1 30	Translucent silex	C	–	38.5	22	6	18	n/d	n/d
	CN1	S(P)	CN1 31	Limolite	C	Rs	18	9	3	8	n/d	n/d
	CN1	S(P)	CN1 2	Rhyolite	C	–	31	11	2.5	7	n/d	n/d
	CN1	S(P)	CN1 192	Indeterminate	Bd (Tl)	–	–	–	–	–	–	–
	CN1	S(P)	CN1 113	Limolite	St frg	–	–	–	–	7	–	–
	BB4	S	SUP A2/1	Silex	C	Rs	27	16	5	13	2	48
	BB4	S	SUP 21/15 1	Limolite	Bs	Rs	–	–	–	15	–	–

(continued)

Table 9.2 (continued)

Environment	Site	Analysis unit	Item code	Raw Material	Part	Resharpening/recycled	Length	Width	Thickness	Stem or base width	Tip section	Tip angle (degree)
	BB4	S	SUP 13	Silex	AC (Tl)	Rs	45.5	33	7	18	–	–
	BB5	S	SUP 1	Silex	AC (Tl)	Rs	42	23	7	16.5	–	–
	CCe2	S	U177/1	Translucent silex	AC (1 El)	–	40	23	6	15	1.5	40
	CCe2	S	U177/2	Silex	Bd frg (Tl)	–	–	25	5	–	–	–
	PP11	S	PP11 1	Translucent silex	C	Rs	53	25	8	13.5	1	41
	MB	S	MB 1	Translucent silex	Bs	–	–	–	–	19	–	–
	BT3	S	BT3 37/1	Silex	AC (1 El)	Rs	44	17.5	6	12.5	1.5	38

Note All dimensions in mm

References

Sites: PL: Paredón Lanfré; PA: Población Anticura; RA1: Risco de Azócar 1; LG3: Los Guanacos 3; JC1: Juncal de Calderón 1; Ll2: Lili 2; AB: Angostura Blanca; CCe1: Campo Cerda 1; PP1: Piedra Parada 1; CM1: Campo Moncada 1; CM2: Campo Moncada 2; CN1: Campo Nassif 1; BB4: Barda Blanca 4; BB5: Barda Blanca 5; CCe2: Campo Cerda 2; PP11: Piedra Parada 11; MB: Mallín Blanco; BT3: Bajada del Tigre 3

AC: Almost complete; Bd: Body; Bs: Base; C: Complete; El: Ear lost; Frg: Fragment; n/d: No data; Rc: Recycled; Rs: Resharpened; St: Stem; Tb: Tip blunt; Tl: Tip lost

Analysis Units: HsT: Historical times; S: Single; S(P): Single (Palimpsest); TP: Test Pit; U 0-2b: Unit 0-2b; U2c: Unit 2c; U 2-3: Unit 2-3; U 5: Unit 5

Fig. 9.2 Lithic points from the forest. Body fragments (A, B), stem (C), base (D), recycled point (E), resharpened points (F, G), stemmed points (H, I, J), unstemmed point (K, L)

complete and ten almost complete points (three with one ear lost and seven with tip lost, Table 9.3). As already noted, we had to rule out eight complete points from the CN1 site because of the lack of aerodynamics and penetration data. Also, CM2 384 was not considered as its intense resharpening and reactivation prevented aerodynamics calculations. From the 17 points analyzed, four arrows and seven handheld points were identified (Table 9.3). The six remaining were classified as ambiguous and all of them have body-size relationships modified by resharpening or recycling (Table 9.3). Therefore, due to the model's requirements and both samples characteristics (high fragmentation, re-sharpening, and recycling) we could only assign 11% of the points recovered to the forest and 23% to the steppe. At the forest sites, the three types of weapons are represented in similar proportions while at the steppe handheld points are more frequent than arrows, and spears were not clearly identified.

To partially avoid the effects of fragmentation, resharpening, and recycling, we measured the width of the stem or base in both samples ($N = 58$, 64% of total points). From the forest sites, we tallied 21 complete and fragmented points (48% of the total

Table 9.3 Metric variables and functional assignment of lithic points from forest and steppe contexts

Environment	Site	Analysis unit	Item code	Rc/Rs	Reinforcement surface		AE	Penetration		Hafting	Functional assignment
					MT/W	T		Tip section	Tip angle (degree)		
Forest	Complete										
	PL	S(P)	PL 297	Rs	H	L	N	1.5	50	5	Ambiguous
	PL	S(P)	PL 235	Rc	M	L	NA	1	52	7	Ambiguous
	PA	HsT	PA 908	–	M	L	NA	1	46	6.5	Ambiguous
	PA	HsT	PA 100	Rs	M	L	N	2	59	9	Ambiguous
	PA	HsT	PA 974	Rs	M	M	N	0.5	43	6.5	Arrow
	PA	HsT	PA 25	–	L	L	N	1.5	61	5	Ambiguous
	RA1	S(P)	RA1 166	Rc	H	L	NA	– *	– *	7.5	Ambiguous
	RA1	S(P)	RA1 161	Rs	VH	L	NA	– *	– *	13	Spear
	LG3	S	LG3 2	Rs	L	M	NA	1.5	49	14	Hand-held point
	Almost Complete (tip lost)										
	PA	HsT	PA 29	–	–	L	NA	–	–	7.5	Ambiguous
	RA1	S(P)	RA1 148	–	–	L	N	–	–	8.5	Arrow
	Body										
	PA	HsT	PA 36	–	–	L	NA	1.5	61	–	Spear
Steppe	Complete										
	AB	TP	AB	Rs	M	L	N	1	30	8	Arrow

(continued)

Table 9.3 (continued)

Environment	Site	Analysis unit	Item code	Rc/Rs	Reinforcement surface		AE	Penetration		Hafting	Functional assignment
					MT/W	T		Tip section	Tip angle (degree)		
	PP1	S(P)	PP1 10	Rc	L	M	N	1	30	8	Arrow
	CM2	U 0-2b	CM2 826	Rs	L	M	NA	1.5	50	19	Hand-held point
	CM2	U 0-2b	CM2 126	Rc & Rs	L	M	N	–*	–*	15	Ambiguous
	CM2	U 0-2b	CM2 4/101	Rc & Rs	L	M	NA	–*	–*	14	Hand-held point
	BB4	S	BB4 SUP A2/1	Rs	L	L	P	2	48	13	Ambiguous
	PP11	S	PP11 1	Rs	L	L	NA	1	41	13.5	Ambiguous
Almost Complete (one ear lost)											
	CM2	U 0-2b	CM2 98	Rs	L	M	NA	–*	–*	16	Hand-held point
	CCe2	S	U177/1	–	L	L	1	1.5	40	15	Hand-held point
	BT3	S	BT3 37/1	Rs	L	L	1	1.5	38	12.5	Ambiguous
Almost Complete (tip lost)											
	CCe1	U 2-3	CCe1 77	Rc	L	L	N	–	–	13.5	Ambiguous

(continued)

Table 9.3 (continued)

Environment	Site	Analysis unit	Item code	Rc/Rs	Reinforcement surface		AE	Penetration		Hafting	Functional assignment
					MT/W	T		Tip section	Tip angle (degree)		
	CCe1	U 2-3	CCe1 63	–	L	L	N	–	–	4	Arrow
	CCe1	U 2-3	CCe1 1	Rc & Rs	L	M	NA	–	–	15	Hand-held point
	CCe1	U 2-3	CCe1 62	Rc & Rs	L	L	N	–	–	7	Arrow
	CM2	U 0-2b	CM2 102	Rc & Rs	VL	M	N	–	–	12	Ambiguous
	BB4	S	SUP 13	Rs	VL	L	NA	–	–	18	Hand-held point
	BB5	S	SUP 1	Rs	L	L	NA	–	–	16.5	Hand-held point

Note All dimensions in mm

*Tip blunt

References

Rs/Rc: Rc: Recycled; Rs: Resharpened

AE: Aerodynamics. P: Perfect; N: Normal, NP: non-perfect; NA: non-aerodynamic

MT/W: Ratio maximum thickness and width (data source in Table 9.2) in ordinal scale: VH: Very high; H: High; M: Medium; L: Low; VL: Very low

T: Toughness in ordinal scale: L: Low; M: Medium

Sites and Analysis Units Codes from Table 9.2

9 Hunting Techniques Along the Rain Shadow ...

Fig. 9.3 Lithic points from the steppe. Fragmented points: base + body (A), base (B), stem + body (C), body (D), recycled points (E, G), resharpened points (F, H), unstemmed point (I), stemmed point (J, K, L). In the point L the sinew employed for hafting can be observed

forest sample) recording a minimum value of five mm and a maximum of 16 mm, with a median of 7.5 mm (Table 9.4 and Fig. 9.4). Using the criteria of ≤ 10 mm stem or base width for differentiating arrowheads from other weapons, we identified 16 arrows and five points belonging to spears or handheld weapon types. The stem or base width allows the identification of a more considerable proportion of cases (48% vs. 13%) than the functional assignment model and shows arrows' predominance among the points from the forest. Additionally, to explore the width and hafting type association we plotted separately stemmed and unstemmed points (Fig. 9.4). The former ($N = 16$) have a stem width ranging 5–9 mm, a median of 7 mm, and one

Table 9.4 Descriptive statistics of the points from the forest and steppe contexts

	Forest	Steppe
N	21	37
Min	5	4
Max	16	21
Sum	180.5	490
Mean	8.595238	13.24324
Standard error	0.6819257	0.6930645
Variance	9.765476	17.77252
Standard deviation	3.124976	4.215747
Median	7.5	14
25 percentil	6.5	10
75 percentil	10.5	16
Skewness	1.103165	−0.4739096
Kurtosis	0.2019807	−0.5151156
Geometric mean	8.128661	12.43294
Coefficient of variation	36.35706	31.83319

Note All dimensions in mm

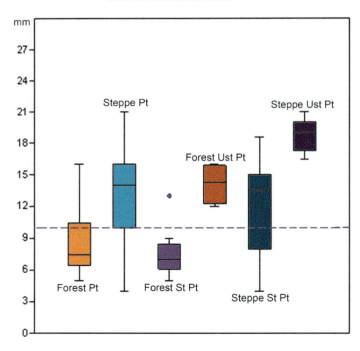

Fig. 9.4 Stem and base width of lithic points. References: Forest Pt and Steppe Pt: total samples from forest and steppe. Forest St Pt and Steppe Ust Pt: forest stemmed and unstemmed points. Steppe St Pt and Steppe Ust Pt: steppe stemmed and unstemmed points

outlier of 13 mm. The four unstemmed points possess bases between 12 and 16 mm, with a median of 14.25 mm (Fig. 9.4). As the Kruskal-Wallis test for equal medians shows, there is a significant difference between sample medians of stemmed and unstemmed forest points (H (χ^2) = 8.306, p = 0.003778), so it can be said that they belong to different populations. In the steppe sample, we could measure 37 complete and fragmented points (79% of steppe sample). In this assemblage, the stem or base width ranged between 4 and 21 mm, with a median of 14 mm (Table 9.4 and Fig. 9.4). Twenty nine points are wider than 10 mm, showing that arrows are not so frequent. On the other hand, the stemmed points are more common (N = 32) and less wide (4–18.5 mm, median 13.5 mm) than the five unstemmed points recognized (16.5–21 mm, median 18.5 mm). As seen for the forest sample, stemmed and unstemmed points from the steppe belong to two different populations (Kruskal-Wallis test, H (χ^2) = 11.25, p = 0.0007689).

9.8.2 Zooarchaeology

At the forest sites, 525 huemul and 17 guanaco bones were recovered, with a minimum number of 14 and two individuals, respectively (Table 9.5). The NISP

Table 9.5 Number of specimens identified (NISP) and minimum number of individuals (MNI) of huemul (*Hippocamelus bisulcus*), guanaco (*Lama guanicoe*), and lesser rhea (*Rhea* sp.) by analyzed unit Sites and Analysis Units Codes from Table 9.2

	Hippocamelus bisulcus		Lama guanicoe		Rhea sp.	
	NISP	MNI	NISP	MNI	NISP	MNI
Forest						
PL	22	1	–	–	–	–
PA HsT	208	5	–	–	–	–
PA FLH	115	2	1	1	–	–
PA ILH	49	2	–	–	–	–
RA1	20	1	–	–	–	–
CP	111	3	16	1	–	–
Subtotal	525	14	17	2	–	–
Steppe						
CCe1 2-3	–	–	243	4	42	2
CCe1 5	–	–	305	4	9	2
PP1	–	–	273	6	5	1
CM2 0-2b	–	–	167	2	8	1
CM2 2c	–	–	83	3	7	1
CN1	–	–	119	3	7	1
Subtotal	–	–	1190	22	78	8

variability between sites is influenced by bone preservation. The lowest values are observed at sites located on flood plains (PL and RA1), which have more intense geomorphological dynamics than sites situated on valley slopes (PA and CP). Furthermore, on these sites, sedimentation is associated with chronological resolution and bone preservation, as it can be seen from the comparison between CP palimpsest (NISP = 127), and PA's three occupation periods (NISP: 373). In the same way, guanaco bones are recorded in PA FLH and CP while huemul is present in all units studied (Table 9.5). The ungulates' representation is linked to the huemul and guanaco's spatial distribution. Cerro Pintado (CP), located near the forest-steppe ecotone, has evidence of in situ guanaco consumption (Fernández 2010). On the contrary, the only guanaco bone recovered inside the forest—a metapodial distal fragment from PA FLH unit—would have been transported to the site still attached to the skin (Fernández and Carballido Calatayud 2015). The MNI per analysis unit is low, except in PA HsT (Table 9.5). Although this may be explained by poor preservation, no massive accumulations have been identified, even in the units with the best preserved bones. Huemul fawns were recorded in PA HsT (two individuals), PA FLH, and PL units (one individual in each), but the absence of fawn in other units may be due to the preservation conditions already indicated. The bias against the representation of the youngest individuals affected by taphonomic processes was observed in other ungulate study case (González et al. 2012). Diversity of skeletal parts is conditioned by the size of the bone assemblage; hence it does not make sense to evaluate this in NISP <50 assemblages. The bone assemblages >100 huemul specimens (PA HsT, PA FLH, and CP), have elements of the entire skeleton, although the appendicular skeleton predominates (Fig. 9.5). This suggests that animals were brought back to the site relatively whole, and that they were hunted in nearby areas. The cut and percussion marks are related to different stages of the huemul's slaughter sequence, the most important being marrow extraction from long bones. Also, the first steps of the reduction of huemul carcasses took place in CP. In this site, guanaco bones indicate long bones marrow extraction (Carballido Calatayud and Fernández 2013; Fernández and Carballido Calatayud 2015).

At the steppe sites, 1190 guanaco and 78 lesser rhea bones were recovered, with a minimum number of 22 and eight individuals, respectively (Table 9.5). The guanaco's NISP varies less sharply than for the forest sites, probably due to the very similar micro-environment bone deposition at the steppe sites. Based on the bone fusion timings, newborns (up to 12 months) and adults (over 36–48 months) were identified in all assemblages except in CCe1 2-3, with no newborns. This data supports the predation on guanaco family groups. The guanaco skeletal parts in assemblages with NISP >100 (all contexts except CM2 2c) suggest that animals entered relatively complete into the sites (Fig. 9.6), and were hunted in the surroundings. The diversity of skeletal parts (Fig. 9.6), the percentage of specimens with butchering marks (from 20 to 59% NISP, median 38%), the more relative importance of cut marks, and the high amount of intentionally broken bones indicate that the bone assemblages represent the final stage of processing the guanacos' carcasses (Fernández 2008, 2010).

9 Hunting Techniques Along the Rain Shadow ...

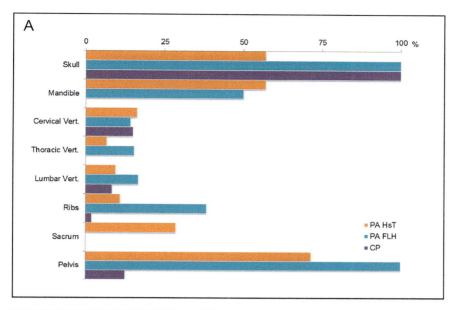

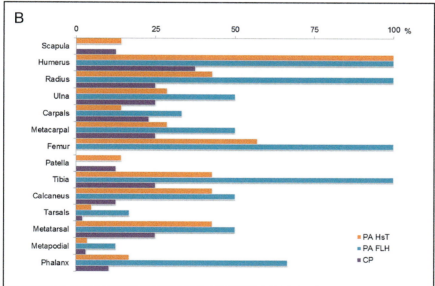

Fig. 9.5 Huemul skeletal part profiles (%MAU). **a** axial, **b** appendicular. Only analysis units with NISP >100 are charted

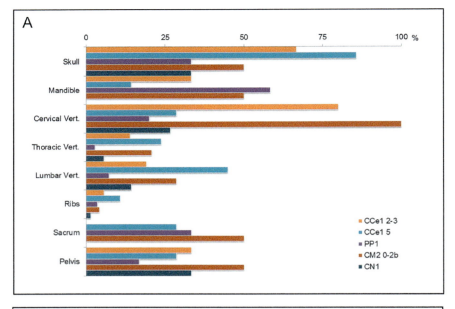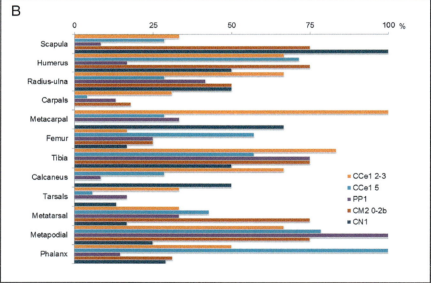

Fig. 9.6 Guanaco skeletal part profiles (%MAU). **a** axial, **b** appendicular

9 Hunting Techniques Along the Rain Shadow … 243

Small amount and low variety of choique elements in Piedra Parada assemblages (Table 9.5 and Fig. 9.7) are common to most contexts from the Patagonia and Pampa regions, and their meaning has been the subject of intense debate (Belardi 1999; Cruz

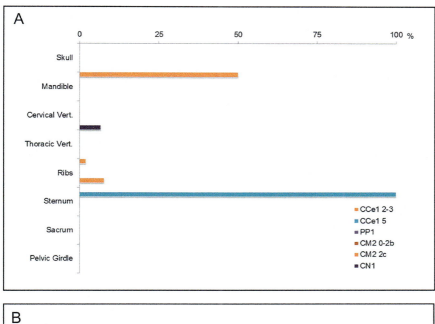

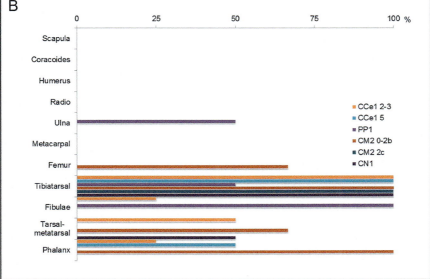

Fig. 9.7 Lesser rhea skeletal part profiles (%MAU). **a** axial, **b** appendicular

and Elkin 2003; Fernández 2000; Fernández et al. 2001; Frontini and Picasso 2010; Miotti and Salemme 1999; Moreno 2018; among others). The scarcity of choique remains was attributed to the difficulties of hunting them before the introduction of the horse (Fernández 2000, 2008, 2010; Giardina 2006). But the almost exclusive representation of the hind limbs has been interpreted as a result of the differential preservation linked to bone mineral density (Cruz and Elkin 2003; Fernández et al. 2001) and its relationship with attritional processes such as carnivore activity and weathering (Belardi 1999; Cruz 1999, 2007, 2015; Cruz and Muñoz 2020). This pattern could also show selective human transport determined by the economic anatomy of these birds (Giardina 2006) as well as by the distribution of non-food products such as leather, feathers, and tendons (Fernández 2008, 2010). Hence, this lack of consensus strongly limits the use of skeletal part profiles as the only source for discussing the selective transport of these birds. In the Piedra Parada case, the combination of skeletal parts and butchering marks informs on the products used, mainly bone marrow and meat, tendons and bones employed as raw material (Fernández 2008). Egg-shell fragments associated with all the bone assemblages were also recovered, indicating their consumption.[6] Finally, only adults are identified except one juvenile element (determined by its size) recovered in the CCe1 5 unit.

9.9 Contrasting the Models

The analysis of the lithic and bone assemblages allows testing our hypothesis regarding the hunting practices carried out in North-Central Patagonia forest and steppe during the last 3500 years. We proposed two general models for guanaco and huemul hunting in the forest, Into the forest and Forest-steppe ecotone. Evidence of guanaco exploitation was only recorded in CP, the forest site closest to the ecotone. It is difficult to interpret the technique used for hunting guanacos due to the small number of bone specimens recovered at CP (NISP = 16, MNI = 1). Both models proposed the capture of guanacos through ambush on trails, or over mixed guanaco groups at open sectors of the forest, or by the encounter of non-territorial groups. Although we cannot establish the technique used for hunting the guanaco, this animal appears to have been exploited opportunistically, in the sense of Jaksić (1989). That is, a species is hunted in the same proportion as it is available over time and space. By contrast to Tierra del Fuego, there is no record of this species inhabiting the forest of continental Patagonia, and currently, guanacos have been observed about 15–20 km from CP, toward the steppe. On the other hand, all the forest archaeological sites provided evidence of huemul exploitation. The skeletal parts profiles showed that animals were brought back relatively whole to the sites, and that huemul was hunted in the nearby area. Even though dense vegetation and its influence on human mobility should encourage selective transport, there was no evidence of that. The low MNI per

---

[6]In the CCe1 site, one choique egg-shell fragment presents an engraved geometric motif (Bellelli 1994).

assemblage suggest hunters predated on solitary animals and/or small social groups of huemul. There was no data to support the exploitation of large social groups like those that occur during the rutting season. Additionally, the record of fawns suggests the predation over family groups or females with their yearling. Both 'encounter' and 'disadvantage' hunting techniques, proposed by Into the forest model could have taken place. We consider the first technique, that refers to hunting in which animals are taken as they are encountered (Churchill 1993), as the most probably used. We founded this assumption on the low density and the spatial distribution of huemul, only predictable in a coarse-grained scale. However, the employment of the 'disadvantage' technique cannot be discarded, especially at the sites placed near river shores (Paredón Lanfré, Risco de Azócar 1, and Cerro Pintado).

Following the functional assignment model, the presence of arrowheads, spearheads, and handheld points was identified in fairly similar proportions. However, as we have already pointed out, the requirements of the model limit its application to samples with significant fragmentation, resharpening, and reactivation, such as those discussed here. The study of the stem/base width confirmed the presence of these types but indicated the arrows' predominance and that only 24% of the stems/bases were spears or perhaps handheld points. The dominance of the bow and arrow for hunting in the forest can be explained by the advantages it offers (Bergman et al. 1988; Tomka 2013). It allows a greater effective range, increases stealth by avoiding or delaying prey alert (Cattelain 1997; Hames 1979; Hughes 1998), and allows for more shooting positions and requires less space to be operated (Bergman et al. 1988; Yu 2006). Bows and arrows also allow for several shots in a brief period of time (Hughes 1998; Shott 1993) with projectiles that are easily transported (Bergman et al. 1988; Greaves 1997; Hughes 1998) and are convenient for search situations that can be prolonged due to the dispersal of the prey (Churchill 1993).

In the steppe, zooarchaeological information suggests the concurrent exploitation of guanacos and choiques in the same place. In the Piedra Parada area, herbivore's food resources are concentrated in the *mallines*, the most likely locations for hunting territorial guanaco family groups by approaching. The guanaco age classes support these social groups' predation, and the anatomical data shows the absence of selective transport. The latter suggests that guanacos were hunted in the nearby vicinity of the rock-shelters. Indeed, *mallines* and temporary lagoons are located between the Chubut River and the slopes where the studied archaeological sites can be found. These wetlands are also the habitat of the choiques, also captured by approach hunting techniques. The remains of this flightless bird are present in all bone assemblages, indicating that they were repeatedly selected as prey. This hunting technique could also have been used to capture hatching males, a hypothesis partially founded on the eggshells recorded in all archaeological sites. Nevertheless, the low abundance of choique is probably showing the challenge of its pedestrian capture.

The 'approach' hunting technique, as well the other techniques proposed by the Steppe hunting model, involves the use of throwing weapons, such as spears and bows and arrows to hunt guanacos and choiques.[7] The functional assignment model applied allowed us to recognize four arrows and seven handheld points. The absence of spears, whose use has been widely recorded in the steppe environment of Patagonia, is noteworthy (Banegas et al. 2014; Cardillo and Alberti 2015; González-José and Charlin 2012; Lynch et al. 2020; Ratto 1994; among others). It is possible that throwing weapons are masked among the handheld points due to resharpening and recycling. All but one of these points have modified body proportions, a key trait discriminating them from spears. Furthermore, handheld weapons have been recorded in other steppe archaeological contexts, but they never represent the most abundant type (Banegas et al. 2014; González-José and Charlin 2012; Ratto 1994). Consequently, in this case we believe their frequency is overestimated. Beyond its frequency, the presence of a handheld point with unmodified body size indicates the use of a hunting technique with a thrusting weapon. Just as functional assignment results showed, the stem/base width data establishes the prevalence of spears and/or handheld weapons (78%) over arrows.

9.10 Hunting Techniques Comparison

Our assessment of the proposed hunting models indicates that the main prey were the huemul and guanaco, the only medium to large sized ungulates available in the interior of continental Patagonia. These animals, as well as the choique, were captured in hunting events where few individuals were obtained nearby the archaeological sites. In both the forest and the steppe, the main weapons employed were the bow and arrow, and the spear. The most important determinants in the selection of prey and methods of capture were the animals' spatial distribution and abundance. In the forest, hunting was focused on huemul small social groups, and in the steppe, it was centered on guanaco family groups. We consider that in the forest, the most likely used hunting technique was 'encounter' (huemul) while the 'approach' technique (guanaco and choique) was the most utilized in the steppe.

As in other regions of Patagonia, in both environments we observed the coexistence of diverse types of weapons (Banegas et al. 2014; Cardillo and Alberti 2015; González-José and Charlin 2012; Lynch et al. 2020; Ratto 1994). However, we detected a significant difference in the relative frequency of arrows—determined by the width of the stem—in each environment: in the forest, they represent 76% of the sample assemblage and in the steppe, 22%. We previously pointed out the advantages of the bow and arrow. We think these benefits are more significant in the forest, where the weapons used for hunting must compensate for the scarcity/dispersion of prey and the density of vegetation. Indeed, the forest cover adversely impacts traffic, prey sighting and the hunter's stealth. Thus, bow and arrow technology allowed more efficient hunting in places where other weapon systems had limited performance. At

---

[7] As we pointed out, *bolas* were recovered in the area and could have been used for hunting on foot or horseback.

this point, we can question if the widespread employment of the bow and arrow made it possible to occupy the forest of North-Central Patagonia in an assiduous and/or more permanent way. In the study area, we observed a convergence in the chronology of arrowheads (the last 1800 years BP, Table 9.1) and this pattern of forest use. It is not possible to determine whether the variation in weapons accompanied the change in forest usage by human groups over time because of the absence of lithic points in the only earlier context analyzed (PA ILH, Table 9.1).

In the Piedra Parada area, arrowheads are not only less frequent but come from two contexts dated to the final late Holocene[8] (CCe1 2-3 and CN1, 580–480 years BP, Table 9.1). In the steppe, the reasons we invoked to explain the predominance of arrows in the forest are less significant. The guanaco is more abundant and predictable than the huemul, and the steppe vegetation does not limit the use of different weapon systems. Likewise, the use of spears precedes the adoption of the bow and arrow. When the latter appeared, they were employed alongside preexisting weapon systems, but the arrowhead points never exceeded one-third of the point assemblages (Banegas et al. 2014; Cardillo and Alberti 2015; González-José and Charlin 2012; Lynch et al. 2020; Ratto 1994). This suggests the bow and arrow did not represent a substantial advantage over the weapon systems in use.

Besides, the study of the hafting section dimensions revealed that the forest points are smaller than the steppe ones (Fig. 9.4). In the case of the stemmed points, we attributed the difference to the prevalent use of bow and arrow in the forest (Kruskal-Wallis test, $H(\chi^2) = 14.48, p = 0.0001354$). However, differences between unstemmed points from each environment cannot be attributed to the propulsion system (Kruskal-Wallis test, $H(\chi^2) = 6, p = 0.0139$). All the bases are larger than 10 mm, and therefore assignable to spears or handheld weapons. Consequently, the difference in size between forest and steppe unstemmed points could be due to variations in the availability of raw materials, the use of different hunting techniques, or the influence of cultural decisions, or all these combined.

9.11 Final Words

Here, we proposed to deepen our knowledge of the human use of forest and steppe of North-Central Patagonia in the last 3500 years. The comparative study of hunting techniques, allowed us to recreate how hunter-gatherers combined technology and social practices to obtain their main staples in each environment. The modeling of three hunting scenarios provided us with the opportunity to assess constraints on hunting practices, like topography, vegetation cover and faunal resources structure. It also allowed us to understand the decisions taken regarding these conditions. For example, hunting with bows and arrows to ensure ungulate supply would have been a

---

[8] Another arrowhead comes from the AB archaeological site, dated between 2900 and 450 years BP (Table 9.1). This point is not attributed to a provenance level precluding its precise chronological assignment.

key decision to enable longer and more recurrent stays in the forest. Conversely, the bow and arrow did not seem to represent an advantage for the exploitation of steppe resources. There, guanacos and choiques were already being hunted with weapons whose efficiency had been established long ago. Another distinctive element is the narrower width of the hafting section in the forest points. In the stemmed points, this would be an effect of the most widely used weapon system in the forest. However, this reason cannot be invoked in the case of the unstemmed points. This characteristic, along with the hunting practices and the local rock art style, represents distinctive features of the forest inhabitants of the study area during the final Late Holocene. We are aware that new evidence could broaden our knowledge on these societies. The ongoing research programs in both study areas will improve this picture, especially in the steppe, with the addition of the bolas to widen our understanding of hunting technique. Equally, more extensive research in higher altitude sectors could provide information about techniques currently still unrecorded, like the use of blinds or the development of massive hunting events.

Acknowledgements This article is rooted in the research we have been carrying out with our colleagues for two decades in the forest of the Río Negro and Chubut provinces. The Piedra Parada area has a longer research history and we are indebted to those who started the work there in the late 1970s. Also, we are grateful for the support and friendship of the people of Cholila, Epuyén, El Manso, and Piedra Parada. We are also especially thankful to Cristina Bellelli, our mentor and teacher, who encouraged the continuation of the work through time in both study areas. Ophélie Lebrasseur and Gabriela Guráieb kindly revised the translation and their comments and suggestions improved the manuscript considerably. Ana Forlano made the figures that illustrate the article, many thanks for her work. We also thank the valuable suggestions of the two anonymous reviewers that enhanced the manuscript. The research program is supported by the National Council of Scientific and Technical Research (PIP CONICET 907), and the National Agency of Scientific and Technological Promotion (PICT 2017-0525).

References

Acosta A, Loponte D, García Esponda C (2011) Primer registro de perro doméstico prehispánico *(Canis familiaris)* entre los grupos cazadores recolectores del Humedal de Paraná inferior (Argentina). Antípoda 13:175–199

Albornoz A, Cúneo E (2000) Análisis comparativo de sitios con pictografías en ambientes lacustres boscosos de Patagonia septentrional: lagos Lácar y Nahuel Huapi (provincias del Neuquén y de Río Negro). In: Podestá MM, de Hoyos M (eds) Arte en las Rocas. Arte rupestre, menhires y piedras de colores en Argentina. Sociedad Argentina de Antropología y Asociación de Amigos del Instituto Nacional de Antropología y Pensamiento Latinoamericano, Buenos Aires, pp 163–174

Altamirano Enciso A (1983) Guía Osteológica de los Cérvidos Andinos. Universidad Nacional Mayor de San Juan Marcos, Lima

Alunni D (2018) Estrategias de aprovisionamiento de guanacos y uso del bosque Magallánico por cazadores-recolectores costeros. Revista del Museo de Antropología 11(2):7–22

Andrade A, Fernández P (2017) Rodent consumption by hunter-gatherers in north Patagonian Andean forests (Argentina): insights from the small vertebrate taphonomic analysis of two late Holocene archaeological sites. J Archaeol Sci Rep 11:390–399

Aschero C (1975) Ensayo para una clasificación morfológica de artefactos líticos aplicada a estudios tipológicos comparativos. Unpublished internal report, CONICET

Aschero CA (1983) Ensayo para una clasificación morfológica de artefactos líticos. Apéndice A y B. Manuscrito en archivo de la Cátedra de Ergología y Tecnología. Facultad de Filosofía y Letras, UBA

Aschero CA, Pérez de Micou C, Onetto M, Bellelli C, Nacuzzi L, Fisher A (1983) Arqueología del Chubut. El Valle de Piedra Parada. Dirección Provincial de Cultura del Chubut, Rawson

Aschero CA, Martínez J (2001) Técnicas de caza en Antofagasta de la Sierra, Puna meridional, Argentina. Relaciones de la Sociedad Argentina de Antropología XXVI:215–241

Banegas A, Gómez Otero J, Goye S, Ratto N (2014) Cabezales líticos del Holoceno tardío en Patagonia meridional: diseños y asignación funcional. Magallania 42(2):155–174. https://doi.org/10.4067/S0718-22442014000200009

Barberena R, Prates L, Eugenia de Porras M (2015) The human occupation of northwestern Patagonia (Argentina): paleoecological and chronological trends. Quatern Int 356:111–126. https://doi.org/10.1016/j.quaint.2014.09.055

Belardi JB (1999) Hay choiques en la terraza. Información tafonómica y primeras implicaciones arqueofaunísticas para Patagonia. Arqueología 9:163–185

Belardi JB, Carballo Marina F, Madrid P, Barrientos G, Campan P (2017) Late Holocene guanaco (*Lama guanicoe*) hunting grounds in Southern Patagonia: blinds, tactics and landscape use. Antiquity 91(357):718–731. http://doi.org/10.15184/aqy.2017.20

Belardi JB, Espinosa S, Barrientos G, Carballo Marina F, Re A, Campan P, Súnico A, Guichón F (2013) Las mesetas de San Adolfo y Cardiel Chico: estrategias de movilidad y tácticas de caza de guanacos en el SO de Santa Cruz. In: Zangrando F, Barberena R, Gil A, Neme G, Giardina M, Luna L, Otaola C, Paulides L, Salgan L, Tívoli A (eds) Tendencias teórico-metodológicas y casos de estudio en la arqueología de Patagonia. Museo de Historia Natural de San Rafael, Sociedad Argentina de Antropología e Instituto Nacional de Antropología y Pensamiento Latinoamericano, Buenos Aires, pp 261–270

Belardi JB, Goñi RA (2006) Representaciones rupestres y convergencia poblacional durante momentos tardíos en Santa Cruz. El caso de la meseta del Strobel. In: Fiore D, Podestá MM (eds) *Tramas en la Piedra. Producción y usos del arte rupestre*. WAC-SAA y Asociación Amigos del INAPL, Buenos Aires, pp 85–94

Bellelli, C (1994) El sitio Campo Cerda 1. Comunicaciones. Actas y Memorias del XI Congreso Nacional de Arqueología Argentina. Revista del Museo de Historia Natural de San Rafael 14 (1/4):285–287

Bellelli C (2000–2002) Dataciones por AMS de artefactos realizados con técnicas cesteras en Campo Cerda 1 (valle de Piedra Parada, Chubut). Cuadernos del Instituto Nacional de Antropología y Pensamiento Latinoamericano 19: 660–662

Bellelli C (2005) A la sombra de Don Segundo. Una cantera-taller en el valle de Piedra Parada. Intersecciones en Antropología 6:75–92

Bellelli C, Carballido Calatayud M, Fernández P, Scheinsohn V (2003) El pasado entre las hojas. Nueva información arqueológica del noroeste de la provincia de Chubut. Argentina Werken 4:25–42

Bellelli C, Carballido Calatayud M, Fernández M, Scheinsohn V (2007) Investigaciones arqueológicas en el valle del río Manso inferior (provincia. de Río Negro). Pacarina, Revista de Arqueología y Etnografía Americana, volumen especial del XVI Congreso Nacional de Arqueología Argentina Tomo III:309–314

Bellelli C, Carballido Calatayud M, Stern C (2018) Obsidianas en el bosque: determinación geoquímica de artefactos arqueológicos del S-O de Río Negro y N-O de Chubut (Patagonia argentina). Chungara, Revista de Antropología Chilena 50(2):201–216. https://doi.org/10.4067/S0717-73562018005000601

Bellelli C, Guráieb AG (2019) Reevaluación cronológica de la secuencia arqueológica del curso medio del río Chubut (área Piedra Parada). In: Gómez Otero J, Svoboda A, Banegas A (eds)

Arqueología de la Pata gonia: el pasado en las arenas. IDEAUS-CONICET, Puerto Madryn, pp 259–270

Bellelli C, Xavier Pereyra F, Carballido M (2006) Obsidian localization and circulation in northwestern Patagonia (Argentina): sources and archaeological record. In: Maggetti M, Messiga B (eds) Geomaterials in cultural heritage, special publications 257. Geological Society, London, pp 241–255

Bellelli C, Scheinsohn V, Podestá M (2008) Arqueología de pasos cordilleranos: un caso de estudio en Patagonia norte durante el Holoceno tardío. Boletín del Museo Chileno de Arte Precolombino 13(2):37–55

Bellis L, Navarro J, Vignolo P, Martella M (2006) Habitat preferences of—lesser rheas in Argentine Patagonia. Biodivers Conserv 15:3065–3075. https://doi.org/10.1007/s10531-005-5398-5

Bergman C, McEwen E, Miller R (1988) Experimental archery: projectile velocities and comparison of bow performances. Antiquity 62:658–670. https://doi.org/10.1017/S0003598X00075050

Bernades A (1981) Chubut. Atlas Total de la República Argentina. In: Atlas Físico de laRepública Argentina. Centro Editor de América Latina, Buenos Aires, pp 148–153

Binford L (2001) Constructing frames of reference. An analytical method for archaeological theory building using ethnographic and environmental data sets. University of California Press, California

Bird D, Bliege Bird R, Parker C (2005) Aboriginal burning regimes and hunting strategies in Australia's Western Desert. Hum Ecol 33(4):443–464. https://doi.org/10.1007/s10745-005-5155-0

Bird J (1946) The Alacalufes. In: Steward J (ed) Handbook of South American Indians, vol 1. Smithsonian Institution, Washington, DC, pp 55–80

Borrero LA (1985) La economía prehistórica de los habitantes del norte de la Isla Grande de Tierra del Fuego. Unpublished doctoral thesis, Facultad de Filosofía y Letras, Universidad de Buenos Aires. Ms

Borrero LA (1994–1995) Arqueología de la Patagonia. Palimpsesto. Revista de Arqueoogía 4:9–70

Borrero LA (2001) Regional taphonomy: background noise and the integrity of the archaeological record. In: Kuznar L (ed) Ethnoarchaeology of Andean South America. Contributions to archaeological method and theory, ethnoarchaeological, Series 4. International Monographs in Prehistory, Ann Arbor, pp 243–254

Borrero LA (2013) Estrategias de caza en Fuego-Patagonia. Comechingonia. Revista de Arqueología 17:11–26

Borrero LA, Muñoz SA (1999) Tafonomía en el bosque patagónico. Implicaciones para el estudio de su explotación y uso por poblaciones humanas de cazadores- recolectores. In: Soplando en el Viento. In: Actas de las III Jornadas de Arqueología de la Patagonia. Instituto Nacional de Antropología y Pensamiento Latinoamericano y Universidad Nacional del Comahue, Neuquén-Buenos Aires, pp 43–56

Borrero LA, Prevosti F, Martin F (2013) Ranked habitats and the process of human colonization of South America. Quatern Int 305:1–4. https://doi.org/10.1016/j.quaint.2013.06.013

Bourne BF (1853) Captive in Patagonia; or life among the giants, a personal narrative. Lothrop & Co, Boston

Bruning D (1974) Social structure and reproductive behavior in the Greater Rhea. The Living Bird 13:251–294

Carballido Calatayud M (1999) Análisis del material lítico del valle de Piedra Parada (Pcia. de Chubut). Tendencias en la organización de la tecnología lítica de los últimos 2000 años. Dissertation, University of Buenos Aires

Carballido Calatayud M (2009) Evaluación del registro lítico de superficie en la localidad de Cholila (Chubut): un problema nada superficial. In: Salemme M, Santiago F, Álvarez M, Vázquez M, Estela Mansur M (eds) Arqueología de la Patagonia. Una mirada desde el último confín. Editorial Utopías, Ushuaia, pp 315–326

Carballido Calatayud M, Fernández PM (2013) La caza de ungulados en el bosque de Patagonia. Aportes desde la localidad de Cholila (Chubut, Argentina). Relaciones de la Sociedad Argentina de Antropología XXXVIII(1):59–82

Cardillo M, Alberti J (2015) The evolution of projectile points and technical systems: a case from Northern Patagonian coast (Argentina). J Archaeol Sci Rep 2:612–623. https://doi.org/10.1016/j.jasrep.2014.11.005

Cassiodoro G, Re A, Rindel D (2014) Estrategias de caza en espacios altos de Patagonia meridional durante el Holoceno tardío: evidencia arqueofaunística, tecnológica y rupestre. In: Cassiodoro G, Re A, Rindel D (eds) Integración de diferentes líneas de evidencia en la arqueología argentina. Aspha, Ciudad Autónoma de Buenos Aires, pp 113–137

Cattelain P (1997) Hunting during the Upper Paleolithic: bow, spear thrower, or both? In: Knecht H (ed) Projectile technology. Plenum Press, New York, pp 213–240

Churchill S (1993) Weapon technology, prey size selection, and hunting methods in modern hunter-gatherers: implications for hunting in the Palaeolithic and Mesolithic. Archaeol Pap Am Anthropol Assoc 4(1):11–24

Cruz I (1999) Estepa y bosque: paisajes actuales y tafonomía en el NO de la provincia de Santa Cruz. In: Soplando en el viento. Actas de las III Jornadas de Arqueología de la Patagonia. Universidad Nacional del Comahue—Instituto Nacional de Antropología y Pensamiento Latinoamericano, Neuquén-Buenos Aires, pp 303–317

Cruz I (2007) The recent bones of the Río Gallegos Basin (Santa Cruz, Argentina) and their preservation potential. In: Gutiérrez MA, Miotti L, Barrientos G, Mengoni Goñalons G, Salemme M (eds) Taphonomy and archaeozoology in Argentina. British Archaeological Reports, Oxford, pp 161–170

Cruz I (2015) Las investigaciones sobre preservación de huesos de aves y mamíferos en Patagonia (Argentina). Archaeofauna 24:189–204

Cruz I, Elkin D (2003) Structural bone density of the Lesser Rhea (*Pterocnemia pennata*) (Aves: Rheidae). Taphonomic and archaeological implications. J Archaeol Sci 30:33–47. https://doi.org/10.1006/jasc.2001.0826

Cruz I, Muñoz S (2020) Between space and time. Naturalist taphonomic observations of lesser rhea (*Rhea pennata pennata*) remains in southern Patagonia and its archaeological implications. J Archaeol Sci Rep 31:102290. https://doi.org/10.1016/j.jasrep.2020.102290

D'Orbigny A (1839–1843) Voyage dans l'Amérique Méridionale (Le Brésil, la République Orientale de l'Uruguay, la République Argentine, la Patagonie, la République du Chili, la République de Bolivia, la République du Pérou). Tome Deuxiéme. P. Bertrand éditeur, Paris

Daciuk J (1978) Notas faunísticas y bioecológicas de Península de Valdés y Patagonia. XXIII. Estudio bioecológico y etológico general del ñandú petiso patagónico y de los tinámidos de Península de Valdés, Chubut, Argentina. Physis, Sección C 38(95):69–85

De Córdova A (1788) Relación del último viaje al estrecho de Magallanes de la fragata de S.M. Santa María de la Cabeza en los años de 1785 y 1786. Extracto de todos los anteriores desde su descubrimiento impresos y MSS y noticia de los habitantes, suelo, clima y producciones del estrecho. Trabajada por orden del rey, atribuido a Vargas Ponce y publicado en Madrid por Viuda de Ibarra

Díaz N (2000) El huemul (*Hippocamelus bisulcus* Molina, 1782): Una perspectiva histórica. In: Díaz N, Smith-Flueck JA (eds) El Huemul Patagónico. Un misterioso cérvido al borde de la extinción. L.O.L.A., Monografía N° 3, Buenos Aires, pp 1–32

Donadio E, Buskirk SW (2006) Flight behavior of guanacos and vicunas in areas of western Argentina with and without poaching. Biol Cons 127:139–145. https://doi.org/10.1016/j.biocon.2005.08.004

Emperaire J (1955) Les Nomades de la Mer. Gallimard, Paris

Fernández PM (2000) Rendido a tus pies: acerca de la composición anatómica de los conjuntos arqueofaunísticos con restos de Rheiformes de Pampa y Patagonia. In: Desde el país de los gigantes. Perspectivas arqueológicas en Patagonia, Tomo II. UNPA, Río Gallegos, pp 573–586

Fernández PM (2008) Taphonomy and zooarchaeology in the Neotropics: a view from north-western Patagonian forest and steppe. Quatern Int 180:63–74. https://doi.org/10.1016/j.quaint.2007.08.012

Fernández PM (2010) Cazadores y presas. 3500 años de interacción entre seres humanos y animales en el noroeste de Chubut. Fundación de Historia Natural Félix de Azara, Buenos Aires

Fernández PM, Fernández M (2019) Interacciones entre los seres humanos y los carnívoros en el bosque de Patagonia centro-septentrional a lo largo del Holoceno. Cuadernos del Instituto Nacional de Antropología y Pensamiento Latinoamericano - Series Especiales 7(2):110–116

Fernández PM, Forlano A (2009) Tafonomía, arqueología y conservación de especies silvestres: el caso de los huemules (*Hippocamelus bisulcus*) de Lago La Plata (Chubut). In: Salemme M, Santiago F, Álvarez M, Piana E, Vázquez M, Estela Mansur M (eds) Arqueología de Patagonia: una mirada desde el último confín, Tomo 2. Editorial Utopías, Ushuaia, pp 743–758

Fernández PM, Tessone G (2014) Modos de ocupación del bosque patagónico de la vertiente oriental de los andes: aportes desde la ecología isotópica. Revista Chilena de Antropología 30:83–89. https://doi.org/10.5354/0719-1472.2015.36274

Fernández PM, Cruz I, Elkin D (2001) Densidad mineral ósea de *Pterocnemia pennata* (Aves: Rheidae). Una herramienta para evaluar frecuencias anatómicas en sitios arqueológicos. Relaciones de la Sociedad Argentina de Antropología 26:243–260

Fernández PM, Bellelli C, Carballido Calatayud M, Podestá M, Vasini A (2010a) Primeros resultados de las investigaciones arqueológicas en el sitio Población Anticura (Río Negro, Argentina). In: Bárcena R, Chiavazza H (eds) Arqueología Argentina en el Bicentenario de la Revolución de Mayo, Tomo V, 1895–1900. Facultad de Filosofía y Letras-Universidad Nacional de Cuyo e Instituto de Ciencias Humanas, Sociales y Ambientales (INCIHUSA)-CONICET, Mendoza

Fernández PM, Cruz I, Forlano A (2010b) Sitio 37: una madriguera de carnívoro en el norte de la Patagonia Andina (Cholila, Provincia de Chubut, Argentina). In: Gutiérrez Ma, De Nigris M, Fernández PM, Giardina M, Gil A, Izeta A, Neme G, Yacobaccio HD (eds) Zooarqueología a principios del siglo XXI: aportes teóricos, metodológicos y casos de estudio. Ediciones del Espinillo, Buenos Aires, pp 409–417

Fernández PM, Carballido Calatayud M, Bellelli C, Podestá M, Scheinsohn V (2011) Marcas en la piedra, huellas en la tierra. El poblamiento del bosque del suroeste de Río Negro-noroeste de Chubut. In: Valverde S, Maragliano G, Impemba M, Trentini F (eds) Procesos históricos, transformaciones sociales y construcciones de fronteras. Aproximaciones a las relaciones interétnicas (Estudios sobre Norpatagonia, Argentina y Labrador, Canadá). Facultad de Filosofía y Letras, Universidad de Buenos Aires, Buenos Aires, pp 195–221

Fernández PM, Carballido Calatayud M, Bellelli C, Podestá M (2013). Tiempo de cazadores. Cronología de las ocupaciones humanas en el valle del río Manso inferior (Río Negro). In: Zangrando F, Barberena R, Gil A, Neme G, Giardina M, Luna L, Otaola C, Paulides L, Salgan L, Tívoli A (eds) Tendencias teórico-metodológicas y casos de estudio en la arqueología de Patagonia. Museo de Historia Natural de San Rafael, Sociedad Argentina de Antropología e Instituto Nacional de Antropología y Pensamiento Latinoamericano, Buenos Aires, pp 167–175

Fernández PM, Carballido Calatayud M (2015) Armas y presas: técnicas de caza en el interior del bosque patagónico. Relaciones de la Sociedad Argentina de Antropología 40(1):279–301

Fernández PM, Carballido Calatayud M, Bellelli C, Tchilinguirián P, Leonardt S, Fernández M (2019) Nuevos datos sobre el poblamiento inicial del bosque del centro-norte de Patagonia, Argentina. Lat Am Antiq 30(2):300–317. https://doi.org/10.1017/laq.2019.13

Fitz-Roy R (1839) Narrative of the surveying voyages of his Majesty's Ships Adventure and Beagle between the years 1826 and 1836, describing their examination of the Southern Shores of South America, and the Beagle's circumnavigation of the globe. In: Volume II: Proceedings of the Second Expedition, 1831–1836, Under the Command of Captain Robert Fitz- Roy, R. N. Published by H. Colburn, London

Flores Coni J, Dellepiane J, Cassiodoro G, Goñi R, Agnolin A (this volume) Technological strategies and guaranteed return: hunting blinds and patagonic plateaus

Florez de León D (1992) Florez de León, Diego "Memorial". Publicación del Museo de la Patagonia F. P. Moreno, Bariloche

Franco N, Castro A, Cardillo M, Charlin J (2009) La importancia de las variables morfológicas, métricas y de microdesgaste para evaluar las diferencias en diseños de puntas de proyectil bifaciales pedunculadas: un ejemplo del sur de Patagonia continental. Magallania 37(1):99–112. https://doi.org/10.4067/S0718-22442009000100008

Franklin W (1983) Contrasting socioecologies of South America's wild camelids: the vicuña and the guanaco. In: Eisemberg J, Kleinman D (eds) Advances in the study of mammalian behavior. American Society of Mammologist, Special Publication 7, Shippensburg, pp 573–629

Frid A (1994) Observations on habitat use and social organization of a huemul (*Hippocamelus bisulcus*) coastal population in Chile. Biol Conserv 67(1):13–19. https://doi.org/10.1016/0006-3207(94)90003-5

Frontini R, Picasso M (2010) Aprovechamiento de *Rhea americana* en la localidad arqueológica El Guanaco. In: Amelia Gutiérrez M, De Nigris M, Fernández PM, Giardina M, Gil A, Izeta A, Neme G, Yacobaccio H (eds) Zooarqueología a principios del siglo. Ediciones del Espinillo, Buenos Aires, pp 563–574

Furlong C (1912) Hunting the guanaco. The Outing Magazine LXI(1):3–20

Galende G, Ramilo E, Beati A (2005) Diet of Huemul deer (*Hippocamelus bisulcus*) in Nahuel Huapi National Park, Argentina. Stud Neotrop Fauna Environ 40(1):1–5. https://doi.org/10.1080/01650520400000822

Gallardo C (1910) Los Onas. CABAUT y Cia. Editores, Buenos Aires

Garay G, Ortega I, Guineo O (2016) Social ecology of the huemul at Torres del Paine National Park, Chile. Anales del Instituto de la Patagonia 44(1):25–38. https://doi.org/10.4067/S0718-686X2016000100003

Giardina M (2006) Anatomía económica de Rheidae. Intersecciones en Antropología 7:263–276

Gill R, Saucedo Gálvez C, Aldridge D, Morgan G (2008) Ranging behaviour of huemul in relation to habitat and landscape. J Zool 247:254–260. https://doi.org/10.1111/j.1469-7998.2007.00378.x

González-José R, Charlin J (2012) Relative importance of modularity and other morphological attributes on different types of lithic point weapons: assessing functional variations. PLoS One 7(10):e48009. https://doi.org/10.1371/journal.pone.0048009

González M, Clara Álvarez M, Massigoge A, Amelia Gutiérrez M, Kaufmann C (2012) Differential bone survivorship and ontogenetic development in Gua-naco (*Lama guanicoe*). Int J Osteoarchaeol 22(5):523–536. https://doi.org/10.1002/oa.1271

Goñi R, Re A, Bautista Belardi J, Flores Coni J, Guichón F (2014) Un lugar muy particular. Caza, convergencia de poblaciones y circulación de información en la Meseta del Strobel. In: Goñi R, Bautista Belardi J, Cassiodoro G, Re A (eds) Arqueología de las cuencas de los lagos Cardiel y Strobel: poblamiento humano y paleoambientes en Patagonia. Aspha, Ciudad Autónoma de Buenos Aires, pp 155–185

Goñi R, Cassiodoro G, Flores Coni J, Dellepiane J, Agnolin A, Guichón Fernández R (2016) Estrategias de caza y movilidad. Parapetos del sitio K116 (Meseta del Strobel, Santa Cruz). In: Mena F (ed) Arqueología de Patagonia: de Mar a Mar. Ediciones CIEP/ Ñire Negro, Santiago, pp 441–449

Gradin C (1959–1960) Tres informaciones referentes a la meseta del Lago Strobel (Provincia de Santa Cruz, Argentina). Acta Praehistorica III/IV:144–149

Greaves R (1997) Hunting and multifunctional use of bows and arrows: ethnoarchaeology of technological organization among Pumé hunters of Venezuela. In: Knecht H (ed) Projectile technology. Plenum Press, New York, pp 287–320. https://doi.org/10.13140/2.1.3212.5446

Guinard A (1868) Trois Ans'*esclavage chez les Patagons*. P. Briez Imprimerie, Abbeville

Gusinde M (1982) Los indios de Tierra del Fuego. Los Selk'nam, Tomo I (2). Centro Argentino de Etnología Americana, CONICET, Buenos Aires

Hames R (1979) A comparison of the efficiencies of the shotgun and the bow in neotropical forest hunting. Hum Ecol 7(3):219–252. https://doi.org/10.1007/BF00889493

Hughes S (1998) Getting to the point: evolutionary change in prehistoric weaponry. J Archaeol Method Theory 5(4):345–408. https://doi.org/10.1007/BF02428421

Hutchings WK, Brüchert L (1997) Spearthrower performance: ethnographic and ex-perimental research. Antiquity 71:890–897. https://doi.org/10.1017/S0003598X0008580X

Hutchinson TJ (1869) The Tehuelche Indians of Patagonia. Trans Ethnol Soc London 7:313–325

Jaksić F (1989) Opportunism vs. selectivity among carnivorous predators that eat mammalian prey: a statistical test of hypotheses. Oikos 56:427–430. https://doi.org/10.2307/3565630

Kaufmann C (2009) Estructura de edad y sexo en Lama guanicoe (guanaco). Estudios actualísticos y arqueológicos en Pampa y Patagonia. Sociedad Argentina de Antropología, Buenos Aires

León R, Bran D, Collado M, Paruelo J, Soriano A (1998) Grandes unidades de vegetación de la Patagonia extra andina. Ecología Austral 8:125–144

Lothrop SK (1928) The Indians of Tierra del Fuego. Museum of the American Indian. Haye Foundation, New York

Lyman R (1994) Vertebrate Taphonomy. Cambridge University Press, Cambridge

Lyman R (2019) A critical review of four efforts to resurrect MNI in zooarchaeology. J Archaeol Method Theory 26:52–87. https://doi.org/10.1007/s10816-018-9365-3

Lynch V, Hermo D, Miotti L (2020) Ocupaciones humanas del Holoceno tardío y tecnologías de caza en la localidad arqueológica Laguna Azul (meseta de Somuncurá, Río Negro, Argentina). Boletim do Museu Paraense Emílio Goeldi. Ciências Humanas 15(1):e20190088. https://doi.org/10.1590/2178-2547-bgoeldi-2019-0088

Marchetti B, Prudkin N (1982) Los biomas. Atlas Total de la República Argentina 2: Atlas Físico. CEAL, Buenos Aires, pp 420–449

Marchione P, Bellelli C (2013) El trabajo del cuero entre los cazadores- recolectores de la Patagonia centro-septentrional. Campo Moncada 2 (valle medio del río Chubut). Relaciones de la Sociedad Argentina de Antropología XXXVIII(1):223–246

Marconetto B (2002) Análisis de los vestigios de combustión de los sitios Aleros Don Santiago y Campo Moncada. In: Pérez de Micou C (ed) Plantas y cazadores en Patagonia. FFyL, UBA, Buenos Aires, pp 33–53

Marean CW (1997) Hunter-gatherer foraging strategies in tropical grasslands: model building and testing in the East African Middle and Later Stone Age. J Anthropol Archaeol 16:189–225. https://doi.org/10.1006/jaar.1997.0309

Marino A (2012) Indirect measures of reproductive effort in a resource-defense polygynous ungulate: territorial defense by male guanacos. J Ethol 30:83–91. https://doi.org/10.1007/s10164-011-0299-4

Martella M, Renison D, Navarro J (1995) Vigilance in the greater rhea: effects of vegetation height and group size. J Field Ornithol 66(2):215–220

Mengoni Goñalons GL (1999) Cazadores de guanacos de la estepa patagónica. Colección Tesis Doctorales, Sociedad Argentina de Antropología, Buenos Aires

Merino M (1986) Algunos aspectos de la ecología del guanaco (Lama guanicoe) en el área de Caleta Policarpo. Península Mitre. Informe preliminar para el Programa Extremo Oriental del Archipiélago Fueguino, Proyecto Biología de Camélidos. Ms

Miotti L, Terranova E, Blanco R, Marchionni L, Hermo D, Magnin L (2016) Entre basaltos y lagunas: las estructuras de piedra de la meseta de Somuncurá. Apuntes para la reflexión de los patrones de movilidad de los cazadores-recolectores. In: Mena F (ed) Arqueología de Patagonia: de Mar a Mar. Ediciones CIEP/ Ñire Negro, Santiago, pp 256–296

Miotti L, Salemme M (1999) Biodiversity, taxonomic richness and specialists-generalists during Late Pleistocene/Early Holocene times in Pampa and Patagonia (Argentina, Southern South America). Quatern Int 53(54):53–68. https://doi.org/10.1016/S1040-6182(98)00007-X

Montes C, Alfredo de Lamo D, Zavatti J (2000) Distribución de abundancias de guanaco (*Lama guanicoe*) en los distintos ambientes de Tierra del Fuego, Argentina. Mastozoología Neotropical 7(1):23–31

Moreno D, Pastore H (1998) Estudios y conservación del huemul en el Valle Esperanza, Provincia de Chubut. Boletín Técnico No 40. Fundación Vida Silvestre Argentina, Buenos Aires

Moreno F (2018) Aprovechamiento de ñandú (*Rhea americana*) en la prehistoria del sudeste uruguayo. Archaeofauna. Int J Archaeozoology 27:83–92. https://doi.org/10.15366/archaeofa una2018.27.005

Musters GC (1871) At home with the Patagonians. A year's wanderings over untrodden ground from the Straits of Magellan to the Rio Negro. John Murray, Albemarle Street, London

Nacuzzi L (1987) Una hipótesis etnohistórica aplicada a sitios de Patagonia Central y Septentrional. In: Comunicaciones de las Primeras Jornadas de Arqueología de la Patagonia. Dirección de Cultura de la Provincia, Rawson, pp 179–184

Onetto M (1986–1987) Nuevos resultados de las investigaciones en Campo Nassif 1. Valle de Piedra Parada, Provincia del Chubut. Relaciones de la Sociedad Argentina de Antropología 17(1):95–121

Ortega I, Franklin W (1988) Feeding habitat utilization and preference by guanaco male groups in the Chilean Patagonia. Revista Chilena de Historia Natural 61:209–216

Pacheco Torres V, Altamirano Enciso A, Guerra Porras E (1986) The osteology of South American camelids. Archaeological research tools, vol 3. Institute of Archaeology, University of California, Los Angeles

Paruelo J, Beltrán A, Jobbagy E, Sala O, Golluscio R (1998) The climate of Patagonia: general patterns and controls on biotic processes. Ecología Austral 8:85–101

Pedrana J, Bustamante J, Travaini A, Rodríguez A, Zapata S, Zanón Martínez JI, Procopio D (2011) Environmental factors influencing the distribution of the Lesser Rhea (*Rhea pennata pennata*) in southern Patagonia. Emu 111:350–359. https://doi.org/10.1071/MU11007

Perea E (1989). Y Félix Manquel dijo… Fundación Ameghino, Viedma

Pérez A, Batres D (2008) Los otros cazadores. Explotación de cérvidos en la Localidad Arqueológica Meliquina, Parque Nacional Lanín, República Argentina. In: Díez JC (ed) Zooarqueología hoy. Encuentros Hispano-Argentinos. Universidad de Burgos, Burgos, pp 89–107

Pérez SI, Bárbara Postillone M, Rindel D, Gobbo D, González PN, Bernal V (2016) Peopling time, spatial occupation and demography of Late Pleistocene–Holocene human population from Patagonia. Quatern Int 425:214–223. https://doi.org/10.1016/j.quaint.2016.05.004

Pérez de Micou C (1979–1982) Sitio Piedra Parada 1 (PP1), Departamento de Languiñeo, Provincia de Chubut (República Argentina). Cuadernos del Instituto Nacional de Antropología 9:97–111

Pérez de Micou, C (1987) Aprovechamiento de la flora local en los sitios Campo Nassif 1 y Piedra Parada 1. Depto. Languiñeo. Chubut. In: Comunicaciones. Primeras Jornadas de Arqueología de la Patagonia. Dirección de Cultura del Chubut, Rawson, pp 235–241

Pérez de Micou C (2002a) Del bosque a la estepa. La caña coligüe, visibilidad arqueológica de una materia prima vegetal. In: Plantas y cazadores en Patagonia. FFyL, UBA, Buenos Aires, pp 65–87

Pérez de Micou C (2002b) Tecnología cestera en Patagonia. Fechando artefactos. In: Pérez de Micou C (ed) Plantas y cazadores en Patagonia. FFyL, UBA, Buenos Aires, pp 55–63

Peterson J (1998) The Natufian hunting conundrum: spears, atlatls, or bows? Musculo skeletal and armature evidence. Int J Osteoarchaeol 8:378–389. https://doi.org/10.1002/(SICI)1099-1212(199 8090)8:5%3c378:AID-OA436%3e3.0.CO;2-I

Pigafetta A (1874) The first voyage round the world, by Magellan. With notes and an introduction, by Lord H. Edward John Stanley. Printed for the Hakluyt Society, London

Podestá M, Bellelli C, Fernández P, Scheinsohn V, Carballido Calatayud M, Forlano A, Marchione P, Tropea E, Vasini A, Alberti J, Gallo M, Moscovici Vernieri G (2007) Arqueología del valle del río Epuyén (El Hoyo, Chubut, Patagonia argentina). In: Morello F, Martinic M, Prieto A, Bahamonde G (eds) Arqueología de Fuego-Patagonia. Levantando piedras, desenterrando huesos… y develando arcanos. Centro de Estudios del Cuaternario de Fuego, Patagonia y Antártica (CEQUA). Centro de Estudios del Hombre Austral- Instituto de la Patagonia - Universidad de Magallanes, Punta Arenas, pp 427–442

Podestá M, Romero Villanueva G, Bellelli C, Forlano A, Caracotche S (2019) Gran Paredón de Azcona (Provincia de Río Negro, Patagonia): puesta al día en la documentación de sus pinturas rupestres (1955–2015). Revista Sociedades de Paisajes Áridos y Semi-Áridos XII(T.2):177–197

Podestá M, Tropea E (2010) Expresiones del arte rupestre tardío en el ecotono bosque-estepa (Comarca Andina del Paralelo 42°. Patagonia). In: Oliva F, de Grandis N, Rodríguez J (eds) Arqueología Argentina en los inicios de un Nuevo Siglo, Tomo 3. Laborde Libros Editor, Rosario, pp 555–571

Povilitis A (1978) The Chilean Huemul project—a case history (1975–76). In: The IUCN Threatened Deer, Part I: Threatened Deer Programme 2. Endangered, vulnerable and rare species under continuing pressure. IUCN, Switzerland, pp 109–128

Povilitis A (1983) Social Organization and mating strategy of the Huemul (*Hippocamelus bisulcus*). Journal of Mammalogy 64(1):156–158

Prates L, Berón M, Prevosti F (2010a) Los perros prehispánicos del Cono Sur. Tendencias y nuevos registros. In: Berón M, Luna L, Bonomo M, Montalvo C, Aranda C, Carrera Aizpitarte M (eds) Mamüel Mapu: pasado y presente desde la arqueología pampeana. Editorial Libros del Espinillo, Buenos Aires, pp 215–228

Prates L, Prevosti F, Berón M (2010b) First records of prehispanic dogs in Southern South America (Pampa-Patagonia, Argentina). Curr Anthropol 51(2):273–280. https://doi.org/10.1086/650166

Prichard H (1910) Hunting camps in wood and wilderness. T. Nelson, London

Puig S, Ferraris G, Superina M, Videla F (2003) Distribución de densidades de guanacos (*Lama guanicoe*) en el norte de la Reserva La Payunia y su área de influencia (Mendoza, Argentina). Multequina 12:37–48

Raedeke K (1978) El guanaco de Magallanes, Chile. Su distribución y biología. Publicación Técnica 4 Ministerio de Agricultura. CONAF, Chile

Ratto N (1991) Análisis funcional de las puntas de proyectil líticas de sitios del sudeste de a Isla Grande de Tierra del Fuego. Arqueología 1:151–175

Ratto N (1992) Técnicas de caza prehistórica en ambiente de Patagonia (Tierra del Fuego – Argentina). Palimpsesto. Revista de Arqueología 1:37–49

Ratto N (1994) Funcionalidad vs. adscripción cultural: cabezales líticos de la margen norte del Estrecho de Magallanes. Arqueología Contemporánea 5:105–120

Ratto N (2003) Estrategias de caza y propiedades del registro arqueológico en la Puna de Chaschuil (Departamento Tinogasta, Catamarca). Unpublished doctoral thesis, Universidad de Buenos Aires—Facultad de Filosofía y Letras. web page http://cambiocultural.homestead.com/ratto.html

Ratto N (2013) Diversidad de tecnologías de caza en la puna transicional de Chaschuil (Dpto. Tinogasta, Catamarca). Comechingonia. Revista de Arqueología 17(1): 85–103

Ratto N, Marconetto B (2011) Proyectiles en acción, 20 años después... Diseños de astiles fueguinos de colecciones etnográficas. In: Martínez J, Bozzuto D (comp.) Armas prehispánicas: múltiples enfoques para su estudio en Sudamérica. Fundación Félix de Azara, Buenos Aires

Ratto N, Nestiero O (1994) Ensayos cuantitativos sobre rocas para determinar sus propiedades físico mecánicas de las rocas: sus implicancias arqueológicas. Actas y Memorias del XI Congreso Nacional de Arqueología Argentina (Resúmenes). Revista del Museo de Historia Natural de San Rafael XIII(1–4):368–371

Santiago F, Salemme M (2016) Guanaco hunting strategies in the northern plains of Tierra del Fuego, Argentina. J Anthropol Archaeol 43:110–127. https://doi.org/10.1016/j.jaa.2016.07.002

Serret A (2001) El huemul. Fantasma de la Patagonia. Zagier & Urruty Publications, Ushuaia

Skottsberg C (1911) The wilds of Patagonia. Edward Arnold, London

Shott M (1993) Spears, darts, and arrows: Late Woodland hunting techniques in the Upper Ohio Valley. American Antiquity 58(3):425–443. https://doi.org/10.2307/28105

Shott M (1997) Stones and shafts redux: the metric discrimination of chipped-stone dart and arrow points. American Antiquity 62(1):86–101. https://doi.org/10.2307/282380

Taraborelli P, Gregorio P, Moreno P, Novaro A, Carmanchahi P (2012) Cooperative vigilance: the guanaco's (*Lama guanicoe*) key antipredator mechanism. Behavioural Processes 91:82–89. https://doi.org/10.1016/j.beproc.2012.06.002

Thomas DH (1978) Arrowheads and atlatl darts: how the stones got the shaft. Am Antiq 43(3):461–472. https://doi.org/10.2307/279405

Tomka SA (2013) The adoption of the bow and arrow: a model based on experimental performance characteristics. Am Antiq 78(3):553–569. https://doi.org/10.7183/0002-7316.78.3.553

Vignatti MA (1947) Contribuciones al conocimiento de la paleopatología argentina. XII. Vértebra de huemul flechada. Notas del Museo de La Plata T. XII Antropología 47:69–77

Young JK, Franklin W (2004) Activity budget patterns in family-group and solitary territorial male guanacos. Revista Chilena de Historia Natural 77:617–625

Yu P-L (2006) From atlatl to bow and arrow. Implicating projectile technology in changing systems of Hunter-Gatherers mobility. In: Sellet F, Greaves R, Yu P-L (eds) Archaeology and ethnoarchaeology of mobility. University Press of Florida, Gainesville, pp 201–220

Chapter 10
Changes and Continuities of Hunting Practices from the Late Pleistocene to the Late Holocene Among Nomadic Societies of the Patagonian Plateaus

Laura Miotti, Laura Marchionni, Darío Hermo, Enrique Terranova, Lucía Magnin, Virginia Lynch, Bruno Mosquera, Jorgelina Vargas Gariglio, and Natalia Carden

Abstract The research developed from different lines of evidence in the central plateau of Santa Cruz and the Somuncurá plateau of Río Negro, provides information for approaching the hunting strategies carried out by hunter-gatherer societies who inhabited these massifs in the past. The information about both regions results from the analysis of archaeofauna, lithic technology, rock art, stone structures, special topographies and archaeological landscapes. In this work we introduce a summary of the progress achieved so far, from which we have managed to define patterns related to the hunting strategies developed in these Patagonian plateaus, and their variations along time. The results we discuss show changes in hunting strategies, linked to the incorporation of new technologies. While a close encounter strategy is proposed for the Pleistocene-Holocene transition and early Holocene, distance hunting strategies seem to become more relevant towards the mid and late Holocene. This change suggests that the tactics deployed over time tended to incorporate more social actors cooperating in hunting events.

Keywords Pleistocene/Holocene · Patagonian plateaus · Weapons · Hunting blinds · Rock art

---

L. Miotti (✉) · L. Marchionni · D. Hermo · E. Terranova · L. Magnin · B. Mosquera
División Arqueología, Museo de La Plata, Universidad Nacional de La Plata and CONICET, La Plata, Argentina

V. Lynch · J. Vargas Gariglio
División Arqueología, Museo de La Plata, Universidad Nacional de La Plata, La Plata, Argentina

N. Carden
INCUAPA-CONICET. Facultad de Ciencias Sociales, Universidad Nacional del Centro de la Provincia de Buenos, Tandil, Argentina

© Springer Nature Switzerland AG 2021
J. B. Belardi et al. (eds.), *Ancient Hunting Strategies in Southern South America*,
The Latin American Studies Book Series,
https://doi.org/10.1007/978-3-030-61187-3_10

The first painters were hunters whose lives, as everybody else's in the tribe, depended on their close knowledge of animals. Yet the act of painting was not the same as the act of hunting: the relation between the two was magical…we do know that painting was used to confirm a magical "companionship" between prey and hunter or, to put it more abstractly, between the existent and human ingenuity.

John Berger 2001: 21[1]

10.1 Introduction

From the early colonization of the Patagonian plateaus until well into the twentieth century, the hunter-gatherer peoples hunted guanacos to a very great extent, and complemented their consumption with other animals, such as birds, armadillos and sea fauna. The hunting practices of the Tehuelche Indians are well represented in chronicles and ethnographic works; however, these descriptions generally refer to collective hunts on horseback. Chronicles describing the hunting activities of pedestrian hunters from the Patagonian continental sector are very scarce, and they mainly refer to individual hunting (Pigafetta [1519–1522] 1986). Thus, the ethnographic and ethnohistorical perspective presents only a late stage of these societies. Even at this stage, the archaeological materiality is elusive. From the seventeenth century up to the present, there is no archaeological evidence supporting guanaco appropriation by the collective action of hunters on horseback. The closest data, so far, come from late Holocene sites in northern Tierra del Fuego (Borrero 2013; Legoupil 2011; Santiago and Salemme 2010, 2016), where the collective hunts took place among pedestrian societies (Bridges 1978; Gallardo 1910; Furlong 1912; among many others). However, Borrero et al. (1985) arrived at a different conclusion from their research in Bloque Errático 1 site, north Tierra del Fuego. In this small rockshelter, they found scarce archaeological evidence of hunting and butchering events of no more than two guanacos. The authors interpreted this record as the result of solitary hunts from 785 ± 120 RYBP (GR8846G). When comparing with other archaeofaunal contexts of continental Patagonia, they stated …"*In our opinion, this gap* [the absence of archaeological evidence of kill and butchering sites in Patagonia] *is because the ancient Patagonians lacked collective hunting techniques*" (Borrero et al. 1985: 273). However, more archaeological information is currently available for testing the hypothesis of highly sophisticated collective hunting strategies throughout the hunter-gatherer occupation of Patagonia (Dellepiane 2019; Dellepiane and Cassiodoro 2019; Flores Coni 2019; Goñi 2010; Santiago and Salemme 2010, 2016).

This work arose from the attempt to expand our ideas about the strategies and tactics developed in the Patagonian plateaus for hunting herd animals as guanacos (*Lama guanicoe*). These were the main prey throughout the human settlement in those regions. Their meat, fat and marrow constituted an important source of nourishment for human subsistence, and their hide, tendons and bones were used to make tools, clothes and dwellings. Beyond these economic aspects, guanaco hunting in the past

---

[1] berger, john. 2004. The Shape of a Pocket. Vintage, New York

had a symbolic dimension, which was strongly expressed in rock art (Aschero 1996, 2018; Aschero and Isasmendi 2018; Carden 2008; Casamiquela 1981; Miotti and Carden 2007; Paunero et al. 2005; Podestá et al. 1995; Re 2016, 2017; Schobinger and Gradin 1985; among others). For 12,000 years, the lifestyle of the people from extra-Andean Patagonia was based on hunting and gathering. Without doubt, guanaco was the favourite prey for human consumption, and the most represented one in the archaeological contexts. However, many aspects related to the procurement of these camelids, i.e. their complementary preys, the ways of structuring domestic spaces and logistic activities, as well as the weapons that were used, changed throughout time (Belardi et al. 2018; Borrero 2001; Goñi 2010; Mengoni-Goñalons 1999; Miotti and Salemme 1999; among others). In that sense, the general purpose of this work is to present archaeological, contextual and landscape information for arguing the dynamics of change in hunting strategies, both temporally and spatially.

We understand a hunting strategy as a set of actions, resources and techniques applied to develop a previously established plan of catching animals for numerous social uses. In these terms, and limiting the objective to the supply of gregarious animals as guanacos, it is expected that a strategy should change in a society according to the needs of the group at different times of the year, the animal condition, the number of hunters and the land characteristics (Borrero 2013; Kelly 1995). On the other hand, we consider tactics as the methods and ways of carrying out the plan; in this case, stalking and ambushing guanacos in the collective hunting strategies developed in special places of the Patagonian plateaus. Tactics are closely connected to changes introduced in the four main factors of a strategy: hunters, prey, weapons and landscapes. On this basis, the specific objectives of our work are: (1) to summarize our progress in the study of hunting strategies from different lines of evidence and (2) to discuss the variability of strategies and tactics developed throughout the Holocene for seeking prey in the Patagonian plateaus. Within the local and regional scales (Delcourt and Delcourt 1988), some of the questions we aim to approach are: Why are we finding design variation in lithic projectile points when hunting is specialized on a main resource? What archaeological markers are useful for recognizing hunting fields? How do we recognize archaeological markers that reflect changes in hunting strategies and/or tactics? We consider that these questions can provide us with elements for defining hunting strategies more clearly and exploring their continuity or discontinuity throughout time and space.

10.2 Archaeological and Ethnographic Models of Large Ungulate Hunting

The tactics developed in a hunting strategy vary according to its factors: humans, prey, weapons and organized landscape. In this work, we will refer to the collective hunting strategy for catching guanacos and other large animals in the interior aquatic environments of Patagonia (Miotti 2010a, b). Based on the archaeological expectation that collective hunts should leave more evidence than individual hunts (Kelly 1995; Legoupil 2011), we review the ethnographic information about these kind of practices in order to test it against the material record of the analyzed sites. In collective/co-operative hunts, the weapon system employed may be the same as the individual hunting weapon systems (spear, bow and arrow or bola stones, known as "boleadoras"), but their archaeological expectation is different. Whereas the material record in the latter is expected to be elusive (Borrero et al. 1985), collective hunts imply a larger archaeological signal, with concentrated archaeofaunal abundance resulting from communal human action (Churchill 1993).

Some models developed in Argentina provide information about different strategies for capturing large gregarious animals and define the archaeological markers for identifying them (Aschero and Martínez 2001; Belardi et al. 2017; Legoupil 2011). Two of these works, related to the late Holocene, propose hunting practices involving the construction of stone structures as hunting blinds. Aschero and Martínez (2001) offer great detail about the different "strategies" that could be inferred from the archaeological record of dry puna landscapes with scarce vegetation and wide fauna visibility. On the other hand, Belardi et al. (2017) model different hunting tactics by stalking through hunting blinds, in which variability would be expressed by the arrangement of these structures in the vast plateaus. A third model was proposed by Legoupil (2011) on the basis of chronicles about the collective hunting practices of the Selk'nam people (Furlong 1912; Gallardo 1910; among many others). It describes the tactics of enclosing guanaco herds using topographic and vegetation features, through which the beaters led the prey to a "shooting" place where hidden archers waited. This information only agrees in certain points with the archaeological record (Borrero 2013; Santiago and Salemme 2010, 2016), but it is persuasive as regards human cooperation and the use of landforms and special vegetation formations for capturing guanaco herds. It is noteworthy that the archaeological and ethnographic cases that the author considered correspond to pedestrian hunter-gatherers from Tierra del Fuego (Legoupil 2011). This example reinforces the idea of systematizing the study of the landscape is key to interpret the archaeological evidence of weapons and archaeofaunas in specific loci. Other models of tactics involved in collective/cooperative hunts, including stalking, guidance, enclosing and ambush of large ungulates, were also proposed for other contexts from archaeology and ethno-archaeology; and a chronological span from Pleistocene to modern times (Binford 1991; Bonomo 2005; Brink 2008; Frison and Todd 1987; Meltzer et al. 2002; Speth 1983). Most of them suggest the use of special landforms, i.e. ravines, gullies, parabolic dunes and confluences of streams, as "traps", driving lanes and natural corrals for enclosing bison (Carlson and Bement 2013; Churchill 1993; Davis 1987; Frison 1982; Frison and Todd 1987; Speth 1983; among many others). These collective hunting strategies have also been widely documented in the rocky deserts of the Near East, where driving lanes and corrals were built by stacking stones. The use of some of those *kites* dates back to 7000 years b.c. (Holzer et al. 2010). However, in Patagonia, the archaeological information on driving lanes and enclosing structures is elusive. The study of these collective tactics requires scanning landscapes in search of diagnostic evidence of slaughter and butchering events, which allow inferring cooperation, planning, stalking and ambush. Geological and vegetational features (Bonomo 2005; Furlong 1912; Santiago and Salemme 2016), as well as rock art, are other relevant indicators for analyzing the relationships between hunters, prey and places (Aschero and Isasmendi 2018; Carden 2008; Miotti et al. 1999, 2004, 2010; Re 2016, 2017).

10.3 Factors Approached in the Studied Cases

The different factors of a hunt strategy can be approached from a relational framework that considers materialities and attitudes. In this work we include:

1. Hunters. The appropriation of gregarious animals is very different from hunting animals of solitary habits. Although cooperation of hunting parties through the assistance of two or more hunters is necessary for both sorts of prey, human decision will depend on several reasons, such as skill, availability of prey in different seasons, social fusion and social fission of hunters (Kelly 1995). Indicators of these decisions may be found in rock art's subject matter, in the spatial arrangement of artificial and natural stone structures (i.e. hunting blinds, grand isolate blocks and parabolic dunes) and in the archaeological assemblages, especially on weapons. Furthermore, it is important to consider the location of these evidences, which may seem random at first glance.
2. The ethological characteristics of prey. Guanacos (*Lama guanicoe*) are camelids present in all the archaeological cases analyzed. This gregarious and territorial species is sympatric with other camelids and mutualist with rheids, which are flightless and gregarious birds. They have been available in the extra-Andean Patagonian ecosystem since the late Pleistocene.
3. Weapons. The lithic projectile points were designed for a specific weapon system—hand weapon, throwing distance weapon, with or without atlatl-. These systems imply tactics that range from capture by approach, where the hunter-prey are a few centimetres distant, as in the use of hand weapons, to distance capture, where the hunter-prey are separated by distances of several metres, as in the use of throwing weapons (Churchill 1993).
4. The topography. In the hunting landscape, water and shelter are prey attractors, and basins are topographic traps for driving fauna. Furthermore, stone structures (natural and artificial), as well as the distances and intervisibility between structures and animal trails, conform this hunting landscape.

In this work, these factors are evaluated and compared on the basis of the available archaeological information of the Deseado Massif and the Somuncurá plateau. The evidence from the former comes from Piedra Museo and La Primavera localities (Fig. 10.1g), while the data from the latter corresponds to Laguna Azul locality and the Yamnago complex, which includes Los Dos Amigos (LDA), Tromen Niyeu and Toco Luan (Fig. 10.1e). These sites are situated in relation to the lagoons of the

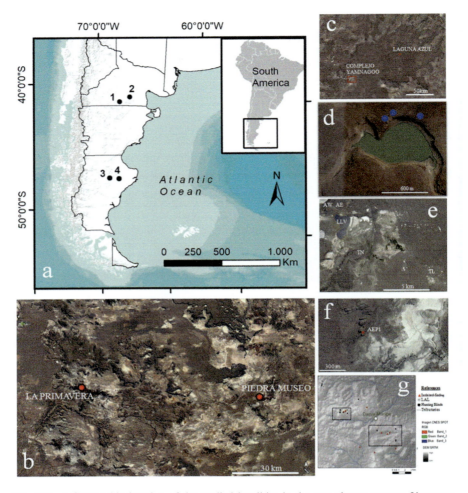

Fig. 10.1 **a** Geographic location of the studied localities in the two plateau sectors: Yamnago complex (1) and Laguna Azul (2) in Somuncurá; La Primavera (3) and Piedra Museo (4) in the Deseado Massif; **b** Detail of the archaeological localities in the Deseado Massif; **c** Detail of the archaeological localities in Somuncurá plateau; **d** Sectors with hunting blinds at Laguna Azul (blue dots); **e** Sites at the Yamnago complex; **f** Rocky outcrops and palaeolake at AEP-1; **g** Cueva Maripe site and Alta Primavera

nineteenth-century hunt complex known as Yamnago (Claraz 1988). The archaeological evidence from both sectors spans from the Pleistocene/Holocene transition to the late Holocene (Table 10.1).

Table 10.1 Summary of the archaeological evidence

Chronological periods	Locality	Site/archaeological component	Weapons	Prey	Rock Art	Stone structures	Topography
Pleistocene /Holocene transition c. 12-10 ky BP to Early Holocene c. 9.9-8 ky BP	Piedra Museo	AEP-1 SU 6 (c. 11-10.5 ky BP)	—	*Lama guanicoe Lama gracilis Hippidion saldiasi Mylodon* sp. Rhea sp.	Hand stencils?	—	Outcrop at border of paleolagoon. Several large boulders and rockshelters
		AEP-1 SU 4/5 (c. 10.5-9.2 ky BP)	2 fragments of FTP Spear/Pike	*Lama guanicoe Lama gracilis* Rhea sp.	Hand stencils?	—	
	Los Dos Amigos	Amigo Oeste On surface	131 FTP (complete and broken)	—	—	—	Butte opposite lagoon
	La Primavera	Cueva Maripe Component 1 (c. 9.5-8 ky BP)	2 unstemmed points	*Lama guanicoe*	Hand stencils	—	Cave in bottom of canyon (wetland)
Middle Holocene c. 7.9-3.5 ky BP	Piedra Museo	AEP-1 SU 2 (c. 7.7-7.4 ky BP)	8 triangular unstemmed points, 1 rhomboidal point (darts)	*Lama guanicoe* Rhea sp.	Hand stencils, dotted alignments	—	Outcrop at border of paleolagoon Several large boulders and rockshelters
	La Primavera	Cueva Maripe Component 2 (c. 7.7- 4.1 ky BP)	4 unstemmed points (dart) 3 bola stones	*Lama guanicoe* Rhea sp.	Hand stencils	—	Cave in bottom of canyon (wetland)

(continued)

Table 10.1 (continued)

Chronological periods	Locality	Site/archaeological component	Weapons	Prey	Rock Art	Stone structures	Topography
Late Holocene c. 3.6-0.13 ky BP	La Primavera	Cueva Maripe Component 3 (c. 3.6-1 ky BP)	2 stemmed points (bow and arrow)	*Lama guanicoe*	Hand stencils, dotted alignments completing previous scenes (zoomorphic figures and circles)	—	
	La Primavera	Cueva Mora (c. 3.6 ky BP)	—	*Lama guanicoe*	Circles, lines and dots	—	Rockshelter in creek slope
Late Holocene c. 3.6-0.13 ky BP	La Primavera	Alta Primavera /Las Mercedes. On surface	7 bolas 16 stemmed/unstemmed (bow and arrow) 1 unstemmed (dart)	—	—	15 hunting blinds	Upper slope at high pampa
	Laguna Azul	Laguna Azul Hunting blind 3 (c. 1.9-1.7 ky BP)	19 leaf points (dart/spear) 6 stemmed (bow and arrow), 1 unstemmed point	*Lama guanicoe*	Rectilinear geometric figures, axes	91 stone structures in two sectors at lagoon border	High pampa lagoon border
	Yamnago complex	Toco Luan Hunting blind 5 On surface	1 unstemmed point	*Lama guanicoe*	—	5 hunting blinds	Lagoon border in floodplain of temporary arroyo
		Los Cuatro Aleros (c. 1 ky BP)	2 points	*Zaedyus pichiy* *Rhea sp.*	—	—	Rockshelters at lagoon border

(continued)

Table 10.1 (continued)

Chronological periods	Locality	Site/archaeological component	Weapons	Prey	Rock Art	Stone structures	Topography
		El Pantano (c. 0.2 ky BP)	3 points	*Lama guanicoe* *Equus* *Ovis aries* *Zaedyus pichiy* Rhea *sp.*	—	—	Open air site at lagoon border
		El Manantial Tapera Isidoro (c. 0.13 ky BP)	7 points	*Lama guanicoe* Rhea sp.	—	—	Lagoon border in floodplain of temporary arroyo
		Tromen Niyeu Plateau	—	—	—	6 hunting blinds	Plateau Edge

10.4 Patagonian Landscapes and The Studied Localities

Extra-Andean Patagonia, apparently homogeneous, actually presents a wide range of environments and resources. It is assumed that, as nowadays, there were also significant regional ecological differences in the past. At least two major ecological regions are recognized, the steppe and the forest; each with its own subset of topographic and climatic conditions, soil types, precipitations and wind regimes, grass species associations and faunal communities that create a mosaic steppe with forest islands.

Within the steppe, the Deseado Massif of Santa Cruz province is a volcanic plate, which is an independent geologic block with a specific environment (De Giusto et al. 1980). Towards the west, the basaltic plateau is crosscut by deep ravines, which transform into temporary and shallow creeks to the east. Interior drainage basins ("bajos") and shallow lagoons are very frequent; volcanic cones and tuff formations produce a hilly landscape that interrupts the monotonous plateau of Patagonian steppe.

The Somuncurá plateau is a volcanic massif that reaches 1000 m a.s.l. in the middle of Río Negro province (Fig. 10.1). The landscape is characterized by plateaus cross cut by erosive processes of the Pliocene-Quaternary (Guarido 1998; Remesal et al. 2001), whith their base levels in the local endorheic basins. This topography, together with the availability of groundwater emerging as spring water, configures small ponds and/or salinizing lagoons. In these water reserves, which are limited by high plateaus and surrounding hills, the humidity and grass concentration is greater than in the extra basin zones, which are usually higher on the basaltic plateau, and lack shelter from the strong and permanent winds of the region.

10.5 The Evidence in the Deseado Massif

10.5.1 Piedra Museo Locality

Piedra Museo (PM) is located in the northeast of the Deseado Massif, Santa Cruz province (Fig. 10.1b and f). It corresponds to the lower endorheic basin of the Elhornia Creek. Several open air sites and rockshelters have been found in this locality across the creek that flows to Laguna Grande. AEP-1 site is a rock shelter situated about 50 metres from the margin of a currently dry "bajo" (paleo-shallow lake), which is an enclosed basin and a real attractor of animals and human beings (Fig. 10.2a). At present, the rural workers "puesteros" hunt guanacos and ñandúes (*Rhea pennata*) in an area of the paleo-shallow lake bank, near the spring waters.

Two broad occupational moments have been inferred for AEP-1; the first one towards the Pleistocene/Holocene transition (ca. 11,000 RYBP) and the second towards the middle Holocene (ca. 7500 RYBP). Within the oldest component, the stratigraphic unit (SU 6) presents evidence that suggests the use of this place for hunting and butchering megafauna and camelids, as well as the modern fauna of guanacos and rheids (Marchionni 2013; Marchionni and Vázquez 2012; Miotti 1996;

Fig. 10.2 a AEP-1 site at Piedra Museo locality; **b** Fish tail point (FTP) fragments from SU4/5; **c** Projectile points from SU2; **d** Engraved boulder from AEP-1

Miotti et al. 1999; Salemme and Miotti 1998). The second occupational pulse is registered in SU 4/5, dated back to the period between 10,500–9290 RYBP. This assemblage provides evidence of hunting events (bone piles) and butchering, mainly of guanaco, with a low record of Pleistocene species (Marchionni 2013; Miotti et al. 1999; Miotti and Salemme 2004). Although the technological assemblages of both units (SU6 and SU4/5) resemble in the prevalence of unifacial artifacts, bifacial objects are present in the second occupation (SU4/5), including two fragments of fishtail projectile points (FTP) (Fig. 10.2b; Cattáneo 2002; Lynch 2016; Miotti 1995). The mid-Holocene occupations (ca. 7700-7400 RYBP) were recorded in the upper component of the site (SU2). During this period, numerous activities were carried out in residential occupations, where the guanaco was the main faunal resource (Marchionni 2013; Marchionni et al. 2010; Miotti and Marchionni 2011). The mid-Holocene lithic assemblages present grater artifact variability than the previous occupations. In these assemblages, artifacts show an increase of bifaciality (Cattáneo 2002; Hermo 2016) and the designs of the projectile points are more diverse than in the earlier components (Hermo et al. 2017; Fig. 10.2c). In Piedra Museo, rocky structures used as hunting blinds have not been recorded, so far. However, the spatial distribution of the outcrops and the grand isolated blocks on the lagoon banks could have been suitable for hiding.

In correspondence with the occupational redundancy inferred in AEP-1, there is a recurrent signalling of the place by means of rock art. The most common painted motifs are the hand stencils on the walls and ceilings of AEP-1 and Cueva Grande (CG), located less than 100 m from the former site. The presence of pigments and a painted slab in the oldest layers of AEP-1, suggests that the painting activities could have started in the Pleistocene/Holocene transition, when the place was used for hunting and butchering animals. Nevertheless, the chronological relationship of the painting events with the archaeological components needs to be more accurately defined (Carden 2020). Another kind of rock art expression, petroglyphs, have been registered on the horizontal surfaces of large boulders, which are the remains of ancient roof fall events in the interior of both rockshelters. The engraved repertoire consists of lines, circles and complex curvilinear labyrinths, as well as bird, guanaco, feline and horse footprints, sometimes arranged in trails. Human handprints and footprints are also present in Cueva Grande (Carden 2008; Fig. 10.2d). The position of the engraved boulder of AEP-1 above the top layer suggests that it collapsed from the ceiling after the middle Holocene human occupation, dated between ca. 7700 and 7400 years BP and interpreted as a locus of multiple activities. Therefore, the production of petroglyphs may correspond to the end of the middle Holocene or, most likely according to the regional background, to the late Holocene (Miotti and Carden 2007). Considering the scarce late Holocene evidence in AEP-1 in comparison to the middle Holocene and Pleistocene/Holocene transition occupations, it is possible that both rockshelters were specially used for ritual activities linked to the production of petroglyphs, while other activities (i.e. residential, cinegetic) were carried out nearby (Carden 2008). The large concentration of animal footprints and trails in the engraved boulders is relevant if it is considered that this place was used from early moments for ambushing, driving and capturing prey.

10.5.2 La Primavera Locality

La Primavera is 80 km west of Piedra Museo, in the Deseado Massif (Fig. 10.1b and g). Its topography is characterized by extensive plains with a gentle east regional slope and terrain elevations ranging between 400 and 900 m. a. s. l, cross cut by numerous temporary streams and canyons.

Cueva Maripe is the main site of the locality. It is a large cave where domestic activities have been recorded throughout the entire archaeological sequence (Miotti et al. 2007; Fig. 10.3a). Three occupational components were defined through radiocarbon dating (Miotti et al. 2014a). Component 1 corresponds to the Pleistocene-Holocene transition and the early Holocene (between ca. 9500 and 7000 RYBP). In these assemblages, there is no record of extinct species, and guanacos correspond to the main utilized resource, with a greater emphasis on the selection of appendicular portions (Marchionni 2013). The technological context of this component consists of unifacial artifacts associated to triangular non-stemmed projectile points (Fig. 10.3b and c) (Hermo 2008; Hermo and Lynch 2017; Lynch 2016). Component 2 corresponds to the mid-Holocene (between 7700 and 4100 RYBP). Guanaco is

Fig. 10.3 La Primavera: **a** Cueva Maripe site and environmental context; **b** and **c** Unstemmed triangular projectile points from Component 1; **d** Bola stones from Component 2; **e** Stone structures from Alta Primavera

still the main resource in that period, although there is a trend towards more intensive processing (García Añino 2018). This situation, together with the presence of rheid eggshells, is probably related to the seasonal occupation of the site and a more intense hunting of guanaco herds in times of environmental stress (García Añino and Mosquera 2014; Marchionni 2013, 2016; Miotti 2012). Regarding lithic technology, four projectile points were recorded among the mid-Holocene lithic artifacts (Fig. 10.3b, c and d). Bola stones ($n = 3$) are incorporated as new weapons for the development of new strategies for obtaining resources (Hermo 2008; Hermo and Lynch 2017). Radiocarbon dating places the occupations of Component 3 in the late Holocene (ca. 3600-1000 RYBP). The lithic assemblages show that blades were the basic blanks for manufacturing different typological groups (Hermo 2008; Hermo and Lynch 2017; Lynch 2016). There is a trend towards the design of artifacts smaller than those of the previous periods (Hermo 2008). Two projectile points were recovered from this component; the presence of bone retouchers could be linked to the technological change observed in the lithic assemblage and to the development of specific activities in particular sectors of the site (Marchionni 2013; Miotti and Marchionni 2013, 2014). For this moment, guanacos are still the main hunted prey. The trend towards intensification on guanaco hunting and a grater processing of this resource observed for the mid-Holocene, increases in this period (García Añino 2018; Marchionni 2013; Miotti 2012).

The archaeological record of other sectors of La Primavera locality complements the evidence from Cueva Maripe. Together, they suggest an occupational redundancy of different microenvironments (i.e. canyon, slopes and high pampas) throughout the Holocene for developing hunting practices. At Alta Primavera and Las Mercedes localities (Table 10.1; Fig. 10.1g), stone structures assignable to hunting blinds are present (Magnin 2010; Magnin et al. 2015). Fifteen structures of this kind have been registered; generally oriented towards the wind direction. They present semicircular or straight morphologies, and some of them are intervisible (Figs. 10.3e, 10.4a and b). In the surface, artifacts associated to these structures, large and small stemmed projectile points, non-stemmed projectile points and bola stones outstand (Magnin et al. 2015). Based on the techno-morphological analysis of the projectiles recorded in La Primavera, at least three weapon systems were determined: bola stones (boleadoras), bow and arrow and dart/spear.[2] While the dart/spear system may have been used during the early and mid-Holocene (Hermo 2016), the bolas are present in contexts from the mid and late Holocene, and the emergence of the bow and arrow is recorded from the late Holocene. The presence of relatively large projectile points, associated with spear systems, has been recorded only on the surface; therefore, it has not been able to determine the chronology of the use of these weapons.

The presence of pigments in the stratigraphic contexts of Cueva Maripe suggests that the cave was painted since the beginning of the site's occupation. Among the rock art motifs recorded in this site, hand stencils are predominant. Two panels depict possible hunting scenes with quadruped zoomorphic figures related to circles and

---

[2]Given that in many archaeological cases it is not possible to distinguish dart points from spear points, we prefer to use the term "dart/spear".

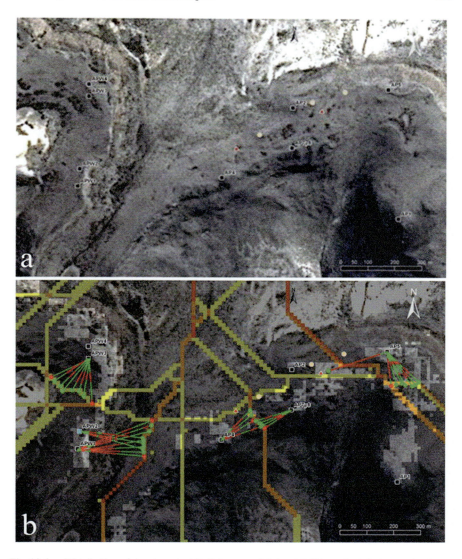

Fig. 10.4 **a** Distribution of structures in Alta Primavera; **b** Intervisibility analysis between structures and between structures and paths

dotted alignments (Carden 2008). Circles may represent water springs or lagoons frequented by animals, while the lines of dots could be figuring the animals' trails or their enclosing by people (Fig. 10.5a–c). The superimpositions and the different preservation of motifs show that the dotted alignments were added later to the circles and animals, completing and modifying the previous scene. The association between quadrupeds and circles is repeated in Los Ventisqueros locality, near La Primavera.

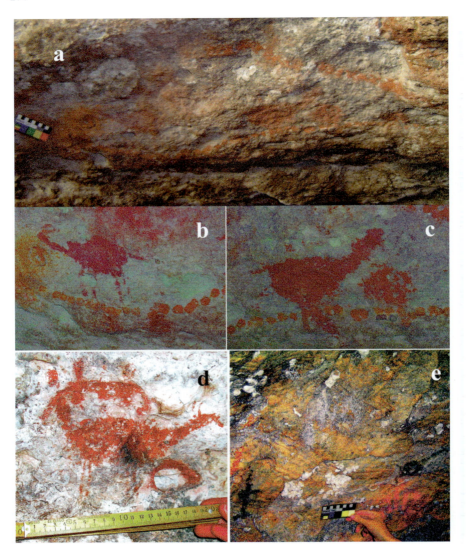

Fig. 10.5 **a** Rock art panel n° 7, Cueva Maripe; **b** and **c** Details of Panel 7, Cueva Maripe: zoomorphic figures (interpreted as guanacos) related to circles and dotted alignments. D Stretch lre scale 15; **d** Los Ventisqueros: zoomorphic figure (guanaco) related to painted hole and a dragged finger motif. D Stretch lrd scale 15; **e** Cueva 1, Cañadón de la Víbora: individual hunting scene. D Stretch lbk scale 15

In this case, the circular figures (shallow lakes?) were achieved by painting the borders and interior of natural hollows within a rockshelter (Fig. 10.5d). The only representation of a hunting scene including humans was recorded in Cueva 1 of Cañadón de la Víbora; it depicts an individual pursuing a guanaco (Fig. 10.5e). Although we have no contextual elements for assessing the chronology of these images, the better preservation of the dotted alignments from panel 7 of Cueva Maripe compared to the underlying motifs', suggests that they are relatively recent, from which we assign them to the late Holocene (Table 10.1). However, the age of the previous zoomorphic figures remains unknown. If the dotted lines represent the enclosing of guanacos or guanaco trails, it would be reasonable and congruent with the hunting tactics inferred for this period.

10.6 Evidence in the Somuncura Plateau

10.6.1 Yamnago Complex

This environment of flooding plains, located in the low basin of the Talagapa stream, varies according to the rainy or dry periods, which have an impact in the extent of Laguna de Las Vacas and the wetland sectors around Cerro Los Dos Amigos (LDA) (Fig. 10.1c and e). This sector is referred to as the "Yamnago Hunting Complex" by the chroniclers of the Nineteenth century (Claraz 1988). It consists of three different archaeological localities, the oldest of which is Los Dos Amigos (Fig. 10.1e). The evidence of the archaeological site Amigo Oeste (AW) has been interpreted as a locus for replacing weapon lithic heads, where more than 100 fragments of fishtail projectile points were probably deposited during the Pleistocene/Holocene transition (Miotti and Terranova 2015; Miotti et al. 2010; Terranova 2013). South East from LDA, the small Toco Luan lagoon (Fig. 10.1e) was identified in historic times as a guanaco collective hunting place (Boschín and Del Castillo Bernal 2005; Claraz 1988; Miotti and Terranova 2015; Miotti et al. 2004b; Terranova 2013). Five semicircular stone structures were recorded in this locality, near the NNE bank of the dry lake (Fig. 10.6a–c). Numerous faunal remains in an advanced stage of weathering were recorded in these stone structures. Among them, it was possible to identify the presence of guanaco's long bones and a fragment of a projectile point.

The Tromen Niyeu plateau stands out in the Yamnago hunting complex; six stone structures (of annular shapes and simple piles) were found in its northern end (Fig. 10.5d; Miotti et al. 2004). This plateau offers a wide panoramic view of the entire Yamnago complex, since the wetland can be seen to the East, including localities Toco Luan to the SE and Los Dos Amigos to the NW (Fig. 10.6d). At the foothills of the Tromen Niyeu plateau, towards Laguna de las Vacas, there are archaeological concentrations and sites (i.e. Los Cuatro Aleros, El Pantano and El Manantial/Tapera de Isidoro, Table 10.1) evidencing hunting activities during the late Holocene.

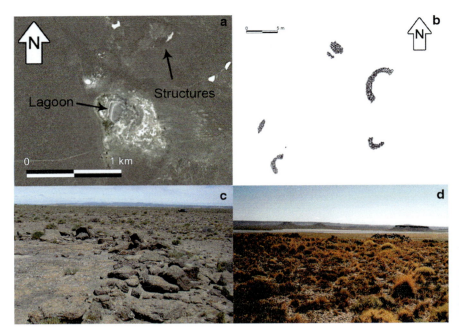

Fig. 10.6 Yamnago Complex: **a** Toco Luan locality; **b** Stone structure from Toco Luan; **c** Stone structure from Tromen Niyeu plateau; **d** Panoramic view of "bajo" from Tromen Niyeu plateau

10.6.2 Los Dos Amigos: The Gate of the Yamnago Complex

The most conspicuous feature in the Yamnago complex is Los Dos Amigos hill. It is a volcanic landform reworked into two hills by aeolic action, located on the northern bank of Laguna de Las Vacas, the baseline level of the Talagapa basin. Both relictual elevations were called Amigo Oeste (AW) and Amigo Este (AE) according to their geographic orientation. Thus, Los Dos Amigos (LDA) locality comprises Los Dos Amigos hill, the Talagapa basin and its adjacent plain (Hermo and Terranova 2012; Miotti 2010c; Miotti et al. 2009) (Figs. 10.1e and 10.7a).

These landforms are particularly visible from several kilometres away; on the other hand, the landscape can be widely observed in all directions from their summits. Due to their position in front of Laguna de Las Vacas and the vast adjacent grassland plain, they constitute a strategic place for controlling faunal resources and human movements. The lithic assemblage was assigned to the Pleistocene-Holocene transition; it includes numerous fishtail projectile points (FPT), most of which are fractured, as well as bifacial and discoidal stones (Fig. 10.7b). All the lithic materials were recovered on surface in Amigo Oeste (AW) site; there is no record of faunal remains (Hermo and Terranova 2012; Hermo et al. 2013; Lynch et al. 2017; Miotti and Terranova 2015; Terranova 2013; Terranova and Lynch 2017).

Fig. 10.7 Los Dos Amigos: **a** View of the locality including the two buttes and the lagoon; **b** Fishtail projectile points

10.6.3 Laguna Azul Locality

Laguna Azul (LA) is one among several shallow lakes of the eastern sector of the Somuncurá plateau (Fig. 10.1c and d). The archaeological evidence was found in different points of this lacustrine basin, located in an endorheic "bajo" (shallow depression) on the basaltic plateau. Due to the presence of water in the temporary shallow lake of this wetland "bajo" environment, birds and mammals are abundant and varied (Fig. 10.8a). The most outstanding anthropic modification of this landscape is constituted by different stone structures built from basaltic rocks. They were interpreted as hunting blinds and dwellings (Fig. 10.8b) (Miotti et al. 2014b, 2016). Together with other lakes of the area, LA evidences the circulation of people and goods in the Somuncurá massif during the Late Holocene (Gradin 1971; Lynch and

Fig. 10.8 Laguna Azul: **a** Landscape; **b** Stone structures; **c** Lanceolate points; **d** Stemmed points

Terranova 2019; Lynch et al. 2018; Miotti 2010c; Miotti et al. 2014b, 2016, Vargas Gariglio et al. 2019).

The stone structures, particularly those of semicircular morphology ($n = 24/91$), are located in different sectors close to the plateau edge. So far, some of them have been interpreted as residential bases, whereas those distant from the dwelling sector and closer to the basaltic walls may be related to hunting activities: stalking and hunting, shelter and control (Lynch and Terranova 2019; Lynch et al. 2018; Miotti et al. 2014b, 2016; Vargas Gariglio et al. 2019). Their temporal assignment corresponds to the late Holocene, since c. 2000 RYBP (Miotti et al. 2014b, 2016), a moment for which an increase of human frequency and density in the area is inferred (Barrientos and Pérez 2004).

In the domestic sector there is a high frequency of lithic artifacts, including grinding tools (hands and mortars on surface and stratigraphy), archaeofaunal remains and pottery (Lynch and Terranova 2017, 2019; Lynch et al. 2018; Miotti et al. 2014b, 2016; Vargas Gariglio et al. 2019). The weapons recorded in the dwelling sector are 19 lanceolate projectile points assigned to dart/spear projectiles (Fig. 10.8c), six stemmed projectile points related to the bow and arrow (Fig. 10.8d), and a triangular non-stemmed projectile point that could not be linked to any specific weapon system yet (Lynch et al. 2019).

The faunal remains analyzed so far come from one of the excavated hunting blinds (LA-P3) and correspond to 25 bone specimens, 15 were assigned to *Lama guanicoe*. The remaining bones were referred to mammalians because of their high fragmentation. The rock art recorded in the dry shallow lake gullies includes rectilinear geometric figures painted in red, among which axes are outstanding. Geometric motifs are also represented in the portable art (blocks and lithic plaquettes) (Blanco 2015, Blanco et al. 2013; Lynch et al. 2018; Vargas Gariglio et al. 2019). Table 10.1 summarizes the selected factors and characteristics for outlining the hunting strategies developed throughout time in the different localities of both plateau sectors.

10.7 Hunting Strategies in the Archaeological Sites

In this section, the results obtained from the different analytical lines are compared in order to evaluate the hunting techniques developed in the different studied contexts. The archaeological cases correspond to different chronologies and places. The differences are consistent with the variability of the archaeological record and topographic setting. The archaeofaunal information confirms that guanacos were the main resource throughout all the hunter-gatherer occupation. Therefore, the analytical approaches applied provide a general idea of the different hunting tactics that could have been at stake according to changes that occurred in any of the four factors mentioned above: hunters, prey, weapons and landscapes. Hereafter, we introduce our interpretation of the hunting strategies developed during the different occupational moments:

1. Pleistocene-Holocene transition/early Holocene

The rocky outcrop of Piedra Museo could have contributed to the tactic of driving animals towards the lagoon, where hunters could stalk hidden between the "outcrops and boulders" at its bank. They may have waited for guanacos while they drank water until being full, knowing that these animals drink only once a day (Cajal 1989). These animals' behaviour was surely widely known by hunter-gatherers, who would have quietly waited until the animals left the water source feeling heavy because of the liquid volume consumed, which made running difficult. In this situation, hunters would have approached the shallow lake bank with darts/spears, thrusting their projectiles to the swamped animals. During the period represented in the Lower Component of AEP-1 site, the favourite prey were gregarious animals (i.e. camelids, American horses), though they also killed xenarthrans, as *Mylodon*. However, we lack information about the behaviour of these big edentates in relation to water. Certainly, they were slow animals of several tons, so it is safe to infer the use of spears for hunting these animals, probably making them swamp in the nearby paleolake. Yet, there is no clear archaeological signal in AEP-1 indicating the slaughter and processing of these animals at the paleolake banks. The only inference that can be drawn is that some animal parts could have been butchered at the site, which implies an occasional use of this site. Nevertheless, for Piedra Museo, as well as for the Yamnago dry lakes, it is expected that the swamping of guanacos, extinct camelids, horses and ñandúes could have been an important tactic, regarding the sympatric and mutualist behaviours of these animals and the hand weapons and darts (FTP) used at this early period. Therefore, it is highly likely that the hunting strategy involved the bogging down and close approach (Table 10.2).

The swamping tactic is described in detail for guanaco collective hunts of the nineteenth century in the Yamnago complex (Claraz 1988). In this sense, and even though we lack zooarchaeological evidence of the different preys, such as we have for AEP-1, we can assume that the same tactic was used in Los Dos Amigos locality. The link between AEP-1 and AW is given by the use of the same sort of weapons: FTPs. Variability has been observed in the sizes of the FTPs from AEP-1 and AW (Flegenheimer and Weitzel 2017), which could be related to different weapon systems (Hermo et al. 2017, 2018). However, the landscape settings, ontologies (Laguens and Alberti 2019) and material culture are akin; consequently, the links with animals could have been very similar. Thus, AW site is understood as a key place for sighting animals and people from the top of the hill. The hunting plan would have been carried out by hunters hidden on the shallow lake bank for ambushing guanacos after they drank water. The massive disposal of fragmented FPTs in AW does not only suggest that the summit was a sighting and projectile replacement place, but also that it could have been a votive place where the broken FPTs were ritually "offered" to the hill through routinized practices related to the accomplished hunts (Miotti and Terranova 2015 and references quoted therein). We need further research in order to find an archaeological context near the shallow lake, with evidence of animal hunting and processing.

Finally, no hunting blind structures have been recorded in the mentioned localities, and this strengthens the idea of the landscape as a favourable scenario for prey stalking and hunting. In the case of Cueva Maripe, the archaeological evidence is different from the previous cases because, it is interpreted, from the beginning of the occupation, as a site of multiple activities (domestic space) to which preys were brought from hunting places. Since the preys were transported quite complete, a short distance to the hunt stations is inferred (Marchionni 2013). For this reason, we consider that the topography near Cueva Maripe (Table 10.1), unlike Piedra Museo and Los Dos Amigos, does not suggest favourable scenarios for hunting planning. However, the archaeological evidence supports hunting techniques from throwing weapon systems as darts (Table 10.1; Fig. 10.3b and c). The cave's rock art reinforces the idea of guanaco hunting through the representation of animals enclosed in dotted lines, which may have represented human hunting fences (Carden 2020; Fig. 10.5a).

When comparing the available information concerning the early moments of the human occupation in both plateaus (Deseado Massif and Somuncura), it allows inferring a hunting strategy characterized by close approach, driving and swamping of

Table 10.2 Interpretations about hunting strategies

Chronology	Sector/Locality	Landscape/topography	Stone structures	Weapon Systems	Fauna	Rock Art	Hunt tactics	Strategies
Pleistocene/Holocene Transition to Early Holocene 8 ky BP	Los Dos Amigos	plains around lagoon, butte with panoramic view	no	atlatl	no data	no	bogging and close approach	individual and collective
	Piedra Museo, Lower Component, Cueva Maripe, Component 1	low hills around lagoon, corridor between outcrops connecting plateau and bajo	no	spear, dart/atlatl and pike	generalized hunting focused on guanaco, complemented by megafauna	yes	driving /ambush, bogging and close approach	individual and collective
Middle Holocene 3.5 ky BP	Piedra Museo, Upper Component	low hills around lagoon, corridor between outcrops connecting plateau and bajo	no	spear, dart/atlatl	focused on guanaco	yes	driving, ambush and cornering	collective
	Cueva Maripe, Component 2	high pampas and canyons	yes	bola stones, spear, dart/atlatl,	focused on guanaco	yes	driving, ambush and cornering	individual and collective
Late Holocene	Laguna Azul, Toco Luan, Cueva Maripe Component 3, Alta Primavera/Las Mercedes	high pampas, canyon edge and lagoon border	yes	bola stones, spear, dart/atlatl, bow and arrow	focused on guanaco	yes	driving, ambush and cornering	individual and collective

gregarious animals (Table 10.2). This involves a deep knowledge of both, the "attractor" places and prey behaviour. It also implies the logistical use of special topographies as natural traps. This idea is related to the hunting models developed for large ungulate hunting since the end of Pleistocene in various places of North America and the Near East, where the topography played a main role in planning the driving and capture of animals (Frison and Todd 1987; Haynes 1993; Hershkovitz et al. 1987; Holzer et al. 2010).

2. Middle Holocene

The only two sites with chronologies for this period are AEP-1 of Piedra Museo and Cueva Maripe of La Primavera, both in the Deseado plateau, Santa Cruz. These contexts evidence multiple activities; however, they provide valuable clues for discussing aspects of the hunting strategies used (Marchionni 2013; Marchionni et al. 2019).

For Piedra Museo, strategies similar to those of the Pleistocene/Holocene transition could have continued in this period, with an important role of the landscape in the driving and stalking of hunt animals. The great difference for these middle Holocene occupations is that guanacos and ñandúes were the main prey. They continue grazing in the paleolake basin and its spring waters at present. This suggests that the paleolake was a place of natural animal circulation, where hunters stalked hidden on the banks and carried out the killing using darts with non-stemmed triangular projectile points (Fig. 10.2c). The increase of ñandú remains in the mid-Holocene component of AEP-1 implies that they were hunted together with guanacos, using the same weapon systems. It is worth remembering that guanacos and ñandúes share the same niche and it is usual to see both herds together. In reference to lithic technology, the presence of non-stemmed triangular projectile points marks a change in hunting technologies with respect to the occupations with FTPs. This change is an argument in favour of the specialization on guanaco and ñandú once the large Pleistocene mammals were no longer available. Finally, we conclude that the topographic trap with the outcrops and the lagoon as component parts was a tactic tool used since the oldest occupations. The animal footprints and trails (i.e. guanacos and birds) represented in the petroglyphs of Piedra Museo support its continued use as a hunting field during the late Holocene (see Fig. 10.2d). They also imply that, beyond the importance that Piedra Museo had in the long term for hunter-gatherer subsistence, it was a key place in the construction of a shared memory through daily, ritual and symbolic motivations.

Unlike Piedra Museo, in Cueva Maripe the capture with bolas is inferred in addition to the projectile hunt (Table 10.1; Fig. 10.3d). This suggests a more deliberate use of the first mentioned weapon in open and flat sectors as the close high pampas on the top of La Primavera canyon. In adition, even though bolas represent a technological innovation for trapping running prey, this does not imply the abandonment of other weapon systems that could also have been used for killing animals (i.e. pikes, darts). For this period in Cueva Maripe, the main prey is still the guanaco; however, the presence of ñandú bones and eggshells in these assemblages positions this species as a potential complementary prey (Table 10.1).

3. Late Holocene

For moments later than 3000 years BP, we find abundant evidence of hunting tactics in both plateau sectors. Whereas the Deseado Massif record comes exclusively from La Primavera locality, in Somuncurá it comes from the Yamnago complex and Laguna Azul locality (Table 10.1).

In the sector of Alta Primavera, in addition to the bola stones that are dated to the mid-Holocene in Cueva Maripe, small projectile points indicates the incorporation of a new weapon technology: the bow and arrow. Nevertheless, in this sector, non-stemmed triangular projectile points corresponding to darts were also found. They are similar to those from components 1 and 2 of Cueva Maripe and from the stratigraphic survey of Cueva Mora. The main prey, which is still guanaco, is registered in both stratified sites, and are assigned to late chronologies (Table 10.1).

Another relevant aspect of the latest moments in the locality is the construction of hunting blinds in strategic parts of the animal trails, as was recorded in association to Alta Primavera (Figs. 10.3e and 10.4a). According to the models proposed by Aschero and Martínez (2001) and Belardi et al. (2017), these hunting blinds organized the hunting strategy in key spots of the landscape, where it was possible to intercept the movements of guanacos from and towards the low areas of the canyon. The intervisibility between the Alta Primavera structures (Fig. 10.4b) is a clear signal of hunting by stalking between two or more hunters.

The studies carried out in La Primavera allow assuming three possible hunting tactics (Magnin et al. 2015): (1) the use of natural animal circulation paths from an individual position of observation and wait; (2) a similar tactic using more than one waiting position and (3) collective hunting in open spaces or high pampas with bola stones or with bow and arrow (Table 10.2).

In Somuncurá, the use of *bajos* and the construction of hunting blinds on the plateau edges were frequent during the late Holocene. This pattern is found both in landscapes of the high pampas, as Laguna Azul, and in the Yamnago complex. While in the former the hunting blinds are associated with shallow lake banks, in Yamnago they are on hillocks and plateaus related to the wetland of the Talagapa basin (Tables 10.1 and 10.2). In both cases, these structures are associated with special topographies that enhance the conditions for hunting by stalk. As in the Deseado plateau, the intervisibility of the hunting blinds and their location were strategic for the development of cooperative hunting.

For the late Holocene, in the analyzed localities (Table 10.1), as in other Patagonian plateaus (Dellepiane 2019; Dellepiane and Cassiodoro 2019; Flores Coni 2019; Goñi 2010), the presence of these kinds of structures is standardized for the collective hunts of gregarious animals. The zooarchaeological information from Laguna Azul and Toco Luan evidences that guanacos were the favourite prey in the Somuncurá plateau, complemented by rheids and other smaller species (Table 10.1). As regards weapons, in all the studied sites projectile points corresponding to dart/spear and bow and arrow systems were recovered. These technologies are associated to bolas and, as in the Deseado Massif, they support the coexistence of different weapon systems that, could be oriented to the capture of the same resource.

On the basis of these results, the layout of hunting blinds on shallow lake borders and its correlation with the use of throwing weapons, suggest a strategy of collective hunting by driving animals from the *bajo* to the high pampa, so that hunters stalking in hunting blinds could intercept them. In this strategy, it is also necessary to consider the cooperation of "beaters", who drove the animals from the bottom of the lakes towards the plateau edges. The summary of our interpretations for the different moments of the hunter-gatherer occupation in both study areas is shown in Table 10.2.

10.8 Discussion and Conclusions

If we consider the four main factors for hunting gregarious animals in the Patagonian plateaus, it appears that the positive topographies from the interior aquatic environments (i.e. bajos with shallow lakes and canyons) must have been essential for planning hunts. Hunting blinds were built as hiding structures for the development of collective hunts in open pampas without natural outcrops. Although these stone structures are a recurrent architectural features during the late Holocene, other kinds of hiding structures made with perishable materials as camouflage (i.e. branches, leather, etc.) should not be disregarded. Bushes are scarce in the rocky pampas of the Deseado and Somuncurá plateaus, so the construction of such structures must have required the use of materials brought from the lowlands.

The main technological changes occurred in the mid-Holocene, when bola stones where first used, and in the late Holocene, with the introduction of the bow and arrow (Matarrese 2015). However, neither of these weapon systems excluded the use of the dart/spear for approach hunting. Even though it implied a greater risk, it complemented the other systems by providing the "final stroke" to the already wounded prey.

Some of the natural features of the plateau landscapes, as well as rock art, had a significant hunting agency, since they marked the beginning of the strategy with favourable routines, and closed the strategy through gratitude routines (Andrew and Owoc 2010; Boivin and Owoc 2004). The petroglyphs of Piedra Museo, the paintings of La Primavera and the FTPs on the summit of AW, are the material correlates of these kinds of practices in the landscape. Hills, water sources, mineral outcrops and rock art were immersed in social networks and symbolically active (Taçón 2004). The process of the hunter-gatherer landscape construction began with the first human occupations of Patagonia and increased during the late Holocene, in conjunction with a demographic growth and a more frequent rock art production. This change is linked to more intense social relationships among hunter-gatherers, implying long distance mobility circuits and exchanges (Carden et al. 2018; Miotti 2008). Through their recurrent location on basaltic walls surrounding water sources, petroglyphs marked places in hunter-gatherer territories. The intervisibility of rock art sites through hills suggests that these positive features signalled the paths that connected them (Carden 2008; Miotti et al. 1999).

The studies carried out so far in the two plateau sectors from different lines of evidence, allowed us proposing changes in the collective hunting strategies developed throughout different moments of the hunter-gatherer occupation. The incorporation of new weapon systems and hunting blinds towards the late Holocene marks the most significant change in terms of the productivity of the collective hunts. The bow and arrow, aided by stone structures from which hunters could control herds without being seen, allowed thrusting projectiles through longer distances than by bogging with spear/darts, in which the hunter-prey distances had to be short (Churchill 1993). This suggests that there was a deliberate intention to create artificial scenarios that improved the driving of prey towards infallible ambushes. At the same time, we understand that the existence of artificially built hunting landscapes before the late Holocene could have involved perishable materials. Beyond this possibility, we recognize a series of concrete changes in human decisions as regards how to materialize and mark these places.

To summarize the variations in hunting strategies from the Pleistocene-Holocene transition to the late Holocene, we propose the following conclusions to be tested against future evidence:

1. At the Pleistocene-Holocene transition, from c. 11,000 years BP, spears or hand pikes were meant for a close approach hunt, while spears, pike points or darts with atlatl were used for hunting at short distance.
2. At the mid-Holocene, from c. 7000 years BP, other throwing projectiles, as bola stones, were incorporated; however, the use of spears and darts continued.
3. Towards the late Holocene, c. 2000 years BP, a new system, bow and arrow, appeared, which allowed hunting at longer distances (dozens of metres). Nonetheless, the use of the two previous systems remained in use.

In short, the technological innovations did not exclude the use of previous weapons. This tendency may be explained by the structure of the landscapes and the relevance of certain topographies in the organization of hunting strategies. Furthermore, the creation of artificial landscapes with stone structures and the spatial distribution of hunting parties, improved prey observation, driving and capture, and prevented hunters from being seen. Hunting blinds are more abundant in wide plains with high visibility (i.e. Laguna Azul, Yamnago complex and Alta Primavera). However, it is also possible that animals could have been driven towards archers with the aid of topography, considering that these stone structures are usually on the plateau edges where guanacos' ascend and descend trails are found.

Acknowledgements An oral version of this paper was presented at the Los Reyunos workshop, Mendoza 2018. Funds from The Consejo Nacional de Investigaciones Científicas (CONICET), PIP 0153 and PICT 2015-0102 (Agencia Nacional de Promoción Científica y Tecnológica) supported different aspects of our research. We are grateful to the organizers of the workshop for their kind invitation to participate in this volume.

References

Andrew J, Owoc N (2010) The malice of inanimate objects: material agency. In: Hicks D, Beudry M (eds) The Oxford handbook of material culture studies. Oxford University Press, 11:333–351

Aschero C (1996) A dónde van esos guanacos? In: Gómez Otero J (ed) Arqueología, sólo Patagonia. CONPAT-CONICET, Puerto Madryn, pp 153–162

Aschero C, Isasmendi M (2018) Arte rupestre y demarcación territorial: el caso del grupo estilístico B1 en el área Río Pinturas (Santa Cruz, Argentina). Revista del Museo de La Plata, 3(1):112–131

Aschero C, Martínez J (2001) Técnicas de caza en Antofagasta de la Sierra, Puna Meridional Argentina. Relaciones de la Sociedad Argentina de Antropología XXVI:215–241

Barrientos G, Pérez SI (2004) La expansión y dispersión de poblaciones del norte de Patagonia durante el Holoceno tardío: evidencia arqueológica y modelo explicativo. In: Civalero MT, Fernández P, Guráieb G (comp) Contra viento y marea. Arqueología de Patagonia, Instituto Nacional de Antropología y Pensamiento Latinoamericano y Sociedad Argentina de Antropología, Buenos Aires, pp 179–195

Belardi J, Bozzuto D, Fernández P, Moreno E, Neme G (2018) Ancient hunting strategies in Argentina. I Taller Estrategias y tácticas de procuramiento de presas en el pasado: su discusión a partir de la integración de distintas líneas de evidencia. Libro de resúmenes. Editorial: Universidad Nacional de la Patagonia Austral, Río Gallegos

Belardi J, Marina F, Madrid P, Barrientos G, Campan P (2017) Late Holocene guanaco hunting grounds in southern Patagonia: nlinds, tactics and differential landscape use. Antiquity 91(357):718–731. https://doi.org/10.15184/aqy.2017.20

Binford L (1991) A corporate Caribou hunt. Documenting the archaeology of past lifeways. Arct J Archaeol 33(1): 33–43

Blanco RV (2015) El arte rupestre en los macizos del Deseado y Somuncurá: la producción de grabados y pinturas entre cazadores-recolectores desde el Holoceno Medio. Unpublished doctoral thesis. Facultad de Ciencias Naturales y Museo- Universidad Nacional de La Plata, La Plata. MS

Blanco RV, Miotti L, Carden N (2013) Arte rupestre en la meseta de Somuncurá: las manifestaciones a escala microrregional. Revista Mundo de Antes 8:83–103

Bonomo M (2005) Costeando las llanuras: Arqueología del litoral marítimo pampeano. Sociedad Argentina de Antropología, Buenos Aires

Boivin S, Owoc M (eds) (2004) Soils, tones and symbols: cultural perceptions of the mineral world. UCL Press, London

Borrero LA (2001) El Poblamiento de la Patagonia. Toldos, milodones y volcanes. Emecé Editores, Buenos Aires

Borrero LA (2013) Estrategias de caza en Fuego-Patagonia. Comechingonia 17:11–26

Borrero L, Casiraghi M, Yacobaccio H (1985) First Guanaco-processing site in Southern South America. Curr Anthropol 26(2):273–276

Bridges EL (1978) El último confín de la tierra. Marymar, Buenos Aires

Brink JW (2008) Imagining head-smashed-in: aboriginal buffalo hunting on the northern plains. AU Press, Athabasca University, Edmonton

Boschín MT, Del Castillo Bernal F (2005) El Yamnago: del registro histórico al registro arqueológico. Revista Española de Antropología Americana 35:99–116

Cajal J (1989) Uso de hábitat por vicuñas y guanacos en la Reserva San Guillermo, Argentina. Vida Silvestre Neotropical 2:21–31

Carden N (2008) Imágenes a través del tiempo. Arte rupestre y construcción social del paisaje en la Meseta Central de Santa Cruz. Sociedad Argentina de Antropología, Colección Tesis Doctorales. Buenos Aires, Argentina

Carden N (2020) Piedra Museo's rock art: new questions for old images. In: Miotti L, Salemme M, Hermo D (eds) Archaeology of Piedra Museo locality. An open window to the early peopling of Patagonia. Springer, In press

Carden N, Miotti L, Blanco R (2018) Nuevos datos sobre las pinturas rupestres de Los Toldos: bases para un enfoque comparativo en Patagonia meridional. Lat Am Antiq 29(2):293–310. https://doi.org/10.1017/laq.2017.83

Carlson K, Bement R (2013) Organization of bison hunting at the Pleistocene/Holocene transition on the Plains of North America. Quat Int 297:93–99

Casamiquela R (1981) El arte rupestre de la Patagonia. Siringa Libros, Neuquén

Cattáneo R (2002) Una Aproximación a la Organización de la Tecnología Lítica entre los Cazadores-Recolectores del Holoceno Medio/Pleistoceno Final en la Patagonia Austral (Argentina). Unpublished doctoral thesis. Facultad de Ciencias Naturales-Universidad Nacional de La Plata, La Plata. MS

Churchill S (1993) Weapon technology, prey size selection, and hunting methods in modern hunter-gatherers: implications for hunting in the Paleolithic and Mesolithic. In: Peterkin GL, Bricker H, Mellars PA (eds) Hunting and animal exploitation in the later Paleolithic and Mesolithic of Eurasia. American Anthropological Association, Washington, DC, pp 11–24

Claraz J (1988) Diario de viaje de exploración al Chubut, 1865–1866. Ediciones Marymar, Buenos Aires

Davis S (1987) La arqueología de los animales. Ediciones Bellaterra, S.A. España

De Giusto J, Di Persia C, Pezzi E (1980) Nesocratón del Deseado. Geología Regional Argentina 2:1389–1462

Delcourt HR, Delcourt PA (1988) Quaternary landscape ecology: relevant scales in space and time. Landsc Ecol2 (1): 23–44

Dellepiane J (2019) Poblamiento y uso del espacio de sectores mesetarios del centro-oeste de Santa Cruz durante el Holoceno tardío. Una aproximación zooarqueológica. Unpublished doctoral. thesis. Facultad de Filosofía y Letras- Universidad de Buenos Aires. MS

Dellepiane J, Cassiodoro G (2019)¿Estructuras de caza o campamentos temporales? Registro arqueológico de parapetos del sitio Cerro Pampa 6 (Santa Cruz). In: Gómez Otero J, Svoboda A, Banegas A (eds), Arqueología de la Patagonia: el pasado en las arenas. Instituto de Diversidad y Evolución Austral, Puerto Madryn, pp 361–372

Flegenheimer N, Weitzel C (2017) Fishtail points from the Pampas of South America: their variability and life histories. J Anthropol Archaeol 45:142–156

Flores Coni J (2019) Poblamiento humano y uso del espacio en la meseta del Strobel (provincia de Santa Cruz). Un análisis sobre la variabilidad tecnológica durante el Holoceno. Ph.D. thesis. Facultad de Filosofía y Letras-Universidad de Buenos Aires. MS

Frison G (1982) Paleo-Indian winter subsistence strategies on the High Plains. Smithson Contrib Anthropol 30:193–201

Frison G, Todd L (1987) The horner site: the type site of the cody cultural complex. Academic Press, New York

Furlong CW (1912) Hunting the Guanaco. The Outing Magazine, Vol. LXI, n.1:3–20

Gallardo C (1910) Los Onas. Cabaut y Cía editores, Buenos Aires, Chile

García Añino E (2018) Estrategias de consumo de grandes mamíferos a lo largo del Holoceno entre los cazadores-recolectores de la meseta central de Santa Cruz. Unpublished doctoral thesis. Facultad de Ciencias Naturales y Museo- Universidad Nacional de La Plata.MS. http://sedici.unlp.edu.ar/handle/10915/71185

García Añino E, Mosquera B (2014) Resultado preliminar del análisis zooarqueológico de los hallazgos recuperados en zaranda en el sitio Cueva Maripe, Santa Cruz (Argentina). In: Castro Esnal A, Funes ML, Grosso M, Kuperszmit N, Murgo A, Romero G (eds) Entre Pasados y Presentes IV: Estudios Contemporáneos en Ciencias Antropológicas. Asociación Amigos del Instituto Nacional de Antropología, Buenos Aires, pp 446–460

Goñi R (2010) Cambio climático y poblamiento humano durante el Holoceno tardío en Patagonia meridional. Una perspectiva arqueológica. Unpublished doctoral thesis. Facultad de Filosofía y Letras- Universidad de Buenos Aires. MS

Gradin C (1971) Parapetos habitacionales en la meseta Somuncurá. Provincia de Río Negro. Relaciones de la Sociedad Argentina de Antropología V 2:171–185

Guarido J (1998) Unidad Geográfica Meseta de Somuncura. In: Masera R (comp) La Meseta Patagónica del Somuncura. Un horizonte en movimiento. Secretaría de Estado de Acción social de Río Negro. Segunda edición revisada y ampliada Viedma, pp 57–74

Haynes VC (1993) Clovis-Folsom geochronology and climatic change. In: Soffer O, Praslov ND (eds) From Kostenki to Clovis, Upper Paleolithic-Paleo- Indian adaptations. Plenum Press, New York, pp 219–249

Hermo DO (2008) Los cambios en la circulación de las materias primas líticas en ambientes mesetarios de Patagonia. Una aproximación para la construcción de los paisajes arqueológicos de las sociedades cazadoras-recolectoras. Unpublished doctoral thesis. Facultad de Ciencias Naturales y Museo- Universidad Nacional de La Plata. MS

Hermo DO (2016) Variabilidad morfológica y cronología en puntas triangulares apedunculadas del Macizo del Deseado (provincia de Santa Cruz). Actas del XIX Congreso Nacional de Arqueología Argentina, San Miguel de Tucumán, Argentina, pp 2132–2134

Hermo DO, Lynch V (2017) Análisis de la tecnología lítica del sitio Cueva Maripe (Santa Cruz, Argentina). Revista Española de Antropología Americana 47:69–90

Hermo D, Miotti L, Terranova E (2018) Explorando cadenas operativas y sistemas de armas en puntas cola de pescado de Patagonia argentina. 9 Simposio Internacional El Hombre Temprano en América "La gente y sus lugares", Necochea, pp 105–107

Hermo DO, Terranova ED (2012) Formal variability in Fishtail Projectile Points of Amigo Oeste archaeological site, Plateau (Río Negro, Argentina). In: Miotti L, Salemme M, Flegenheimer N, Goebel T (eds) Southbound late Pleistocene Peopling of Latin America, special edition current research in the Pleistocene. Center for the Study of First Americans (CSFA), Texas A&M University, pp 121–127

Hermo DO, Terranova ED, Miotti LL (2017) Technological decisions in Fishtail points from Patagonian contexts: a comparative overview. 11th Symposium on Knappable materials: from tools to stone tools. In: Alberti J, Borrazzo K, Buscaglia S, Castro Esnal A, Elías A, Franco N (comp) IMHICIHU - Instituto Multidisciplinario de Historia y Ciencias Humanas, Ciudad Autónoma de Buenos Aires, pp 122

Hermo DO, Terranova ED, Marchionni L, Magnin L, Mosquera B, Miotti L (2013) Piedras o litos discoidales en Norpatagonia: evidencias en la meseta de Somuncurá (Río Negro, Argentina). Intersecciones en Antropología 14(3–4):507–513

Hershkovitz I, Ben-David Y, Arensburg B, Goren A, Pichasov A (1987) Rock engravings in southern Sinai. In: Gvirtzman G, Shmueli A, Gardos Y, Beit-Arieh I, Harel M (eds) Sinai, vol 1. Defence Ministry, Tel Aviv, pp 605–616 (in Hebrew)

Holzer A, Avner U, Porat N, Horwitz LK (2010) Desert kites in the Negev desert and northeast Sinai: their function, chronology and ecology. J Arid Environ 74:806–817

Kelly R (1995) The foraging spectrum: diversity in hunter-gatherer lifeways. Smithsonian Institution Press

Laguens AG, Alberti B (2019) Habitando espacios vacíos. Cuerpos, paisajes y ontologías en el poblamiento inicial del centro de Argentina. Revista Del Museo De Antropología 12(2): 55–66

Legoupil D (2011) Guanaco hunting among the Selk'nam of Tierra del Fuego: portraceability of temporary halt and versatility of the kill site. In: Bon F, Costamagno S, Valdeyron N (eds) Hunting camps in prehistory: current archaeological approaches. Proceedings of the International Symposium, University Toulouse II, Le Mirail. Palethnology 3: 21–40

Lynch V (2016) Estudio Comparativo de la Producción y Uso de Artefactos Líticos en el Macizo del Deseado (Santa Cruz, Argentina). British Archaeological Report. International Series (S2816). UK

Lynch V, Terranova E (2017) Lithic micro-wear analysis of Late Holocene tools from Laguna Azul locality (Somuncurá plateau, Rio Negro, Argentina). 11th International Symposium on knappable materials: from tool-stone to stone tools. IMHICIHU, Buenos Aires

Lynch V, Terranova E (2019) A traceological approach to the use of Laguna Azul during the Late Holocene (from ca. 2000 years BP) in Nor-Patagonia, Argentina. Archaeol Anthropol Sci 11:4157–4169. https://doi.org/10.1007/s12520-019-00806-7

Lynch V, Terranova E, Vargas J (2017) Estudios funcionales en sitios de superficie, el caso de Amigo Oeste (AW) en la meseta de Somuncurá (Rio Negro, Argentina). Revista Museo de La Plata 2(1):10–12

Lynch V, Vargas Gariglio J, Terranova ED (2018) Engraved stone plaquettes from the North Patagonian area (Somuncurá plateau, Río Negro, Argentina) and the use of different microscopic techniques for their analysis. World Archaeol. https://doi.org/10.1080/00438243.2018.1542340

Lynch V, Vargas Gariglio J, Salgado E (2019) Aproximación experimental a la tecnología de caza identificada en el parapeto 3 del sitio Laguna Azul (macizo de Somuncurá, Río Negro, Argentina). In: Bonnin M, Laguens A, Marconetto MB (copm) Libro de resúmenes del XX Congreso Nacional de Arqueología Argentina, Universidad Nacional de Córdoba, Argentina, pp 807–811

Magnin L (2010) Distribuciones arqueológicas en la meseta central de Santa Cruz. Implicancias para los estudios de uso del espacio y movilidad de sociedades cazadoras recolectoras. Unpublished doctoral thesis. Facultad de Ciencias Naturales y Museo- Universidad Nacional de La Plata MS. http://sedici.unlp.edu.ar/handle/10915/24773

Magnin L, Hermo D, Weitzel C (2015) Estrategias de caza en la localidad arqueológica de La Primavera, Santa Cruz (Argentina). Análisis de visibilidad y accesibilidad mediante SIG. In: González H, Sepúlveda M (comp), Libro de las Actas del XIX Congreso Nacional de Arqueología Chilena. Ediciones Universidad de Tarapacá y Sociedad Chilena de arqueología, pp 63–67

Marchionni L (2013) Comparación de las distintas historias tafonómicas en conjuntos zooarqueológicos provenientes de la Meseta Central de la provincia de Santa Cruz. Unpublished doctoral thesis. Facultad de Ciencias Naturales y Museo- Universidad Nacional de La Plata. MS

Marchionni L (2016) Variabilidad tafonómica en conjuntos tempranos del Macizo del Deseado (Santa Cruz, Argentina). Revista Arqueología 22:163–189

Marchionni L, Vázquez M (2012) New data on exploited Pleistocene fauna at Piedra Museo (Central Plateau of Santa Cruz province, Argentina). In: Miotti L, Salemme M, Flegenheimer N, Goebel T (eds) Southbound: Late Pleistocene peopling of Latin America. Current research in the Pleistocene, Center for the Study of the First Americans. Texas A&M University, Texas, pp 139–142

Marchionni L, García Añino E, Miotti L (2019) La fracturación de huesos largos durante el Holoceno medio en el Macizo del Deseado. Implicancias para el estudio del aprovechamiento de los guanacos. Comechingonia 21(2): 81–110

Marchionni L, Miotti L, Mosquera B (2010) El uso de la fauna entre el Pleistoceno final y el Holoceno medio en la Patagonia extra-andina. In: Gutiérrez M, De Nigris M, Fernández P, Giardina M, Gil A, Izeta A, Neme G, Yacobaccio H (eds) Zooarqueología a principios del siglo XXI: Aportes Teórico, metodológicos y casos de estudio. Ediciones del Espinillo, Buenos Aires, pp 259–272

Matarrese A (2015) Tecnología lítica entre los cazadores-recolectores pampeanos: los artefactos formatizados por picado y abrasión y modificados por uso en el área Interserrana Bonaerense. Unpublished doctoral thesis. Facultad de Ciencias Naturales y Museo- Universidad Nacional de La Plata. MS

Meltzer DJ, Todd LC, Holliday VT (2002) The folsom (paleoindian) type site: past investigations, current studies. Am Antiq 67:5–36

Mengoni Goñalons G (1999) Cazadores de guanacos de la estepa patagónica. Sociedad Argentina de Antropología, colección Tesis Doctorales, Buenos Aires

Miotti L (1995) Piedra Museo locality: a special place in the new world. Curr Res Pleistocene 12:37–40

Miotti L (1996) Piedra Museo (Santa Cruz): nuevos datos para el debate de la ocupación Pleistocénica en Patagonia. In: Gómez Otero J (ed) Arqueología, sólo Patagonia. Publicación Secretaría de Cultura de Chubut-CONICET, Puerto Madryn, pp 27–38

Miotti L (2008) Household and sacred landscapes among Holocene hunter gatherers of Patagonia's Central Plateau. Before Farming 3:5–44

Miotti L (2010a) El rol del litoral marítimo y los ríos en la colonización humana de Patagonia desde finales de la Edad del Hielo. Una historia de más de 11.000 años. In: Masera R, Lew J (eds)

Los Ríos Mesetarios Norpatagónicos: Aguas Generosas del Ande al Atlántico, serie Las Mesetas Patagónicas. Fundación Ameghino, Río Negro, Argentina, pp 95–193

Miotti L (2010b) Cuevas y abrigos rocosos: nudos de las redes sociales entre los cazadores recolectores del Macizo del Deseado, Patagonia extra-andina. In: Jiménez JC, Serrano C, González A, Aguilar F (eds) III Simposio Internacional. El Hombre Temprano en América. UNAM- Instituto de Investigaciones Antropológicas-INAH, México, pp 147–174

Miotti L (2010c) La señal arqueológica de colonización finipleistocénica y la continuidad ocupacional en la meseta de Somuncurá, Provincia de Río Negro, Argentina. In: Bárcena JR, Chiavazza H (eds) Actas del XVII Congreso Nacional de Arqueología Argentina, Arqueología Argentina en el Bicentenario de la Revolución de Mayo. Universidad Nacional de Cuyo, Mendoza, Tomo V, pp 1853–1859

Miotti L (2012) El uso de los recursos faunísticos entre los cazadores-recolectores de Patagonia: tendencias espacio/temporales de las estrategias durante el Holoceno. La Potenciación de los recursos entre los cazadores-recolectores de Patagonia. Factores, Procesos e implicancias arqueológicas. Archaeofauna 21:137–160

Miotti L, Carden N (2007) The relationships between rock art and archaeofaunas in the Central Patagonian Plateau. In: Gutiérrez M, Miotti L, Barrientos G, MengoniGoñalons G, Salemme M (eds) Taphonomy and archaeology in Argentina. BAR International Series, Manchester, pp 203–218

Miotti L, Marchionni L (2011) Archaeofauna At Middle Holocene In Aep-1 Rockshelter, Santa Cruz, Argentina. Taphonomic implications. Quat Int 245:148–158

Miotti L, Marchionni L (2013) Beyond stones: bone as raw material for tools in Central plateau of Santa Cruz, Argentinian Patagonia. In: Choyke A, O'Connor S (eds) From these bare bones: raw materials and the study of worked osseous objects. Oxbow Books, London, pp 116–126

Miotti L, Marchionni L (2014) Autopodios de guanacos en sitios arqueológicos: equifinalidad entre lo palatable y lo preservado. Revista Chilena de Arqueología 29(1):122–129

Miotti L, Salemme M (1999) Biodiversity, taxonomic richness and generalist-specialists economical systems in Pampa and Patagonia Regions, Southern South America. Quat Int 53–54:53–68

Miotti L, Salemme M (2004) Poblamiento, movilidad y territorios entre las sociedades cazadoras-recolectoras de Patagonia: cambios desde la transición Pleistoceno/Holoceno al Holoceno medio. Complutum 15:177–206

Miotti L, Terranova E (2015) A hill plenty of points in terra incognita from Patagonia: Notes and reflections for discussing the way and tempo of the initial peopling. PaleoAmerica 11(2):181–196

Miotti L, Hermo D, Terranova E (2010) Fishtail points, first evidence of late pleistocenic hunter-gatherers in Somuncurá plateau (Rio Negro province, Argentina). Curr Res Pleistocene 29:23–25

Miotti L, Vázquez M, Hermo D (1999) Piedra Museo. Un yamnagoo pleistocénico de los colonizadores de la Meseta de Santa Cruz. El estudio de la arqueofauna. In: Goñi (ed) Soplando en el viento III Jornadas de Arqueología de la Patagonia. Bariloche, pp 113–136

Miotti L, Blanco R, Terranova E, Hermo D, Mosquera B (2009) Paisajes y cazadores-recolectores. Localidades arqueológicas de Plan Luan y cuenca inferior del arroyo Talagapa. In: Salemme M, Santiago F, Álvarez M, Piana E, Vázquez M, Mansur ME (eds) Arqueología de Patagonia: una Mirada desde el Último Confín. Ushuaia, Editorial Utopías, pp 265–280

Miotti L, Marchionni L, Mosquera B, Hermo D, Ceraso A (2014a) Fechados radiocarbónicos y delimitación temporal de los conjuntos arqueológicos de Cueva Maripe, Santa Cruz (Argentina). Relaciones 39(2):509–537

Miotti L, Salemme M, Hermo D, Magnin L, Rabassa J (2004) Yamnago 137 años después: otro lenguaje para la misma región. In: Civalero MT, Fernández P, Guraieb A (Comp) Contra Viento y Marea: Arqueología de Patagonia. Instituto Nacional de Antropología y Pensamiento Latinoamericano y Sociedad Argentina de Antropología, Buenos Aires, pp 775–796

Miotti L, Blanco R, Terranova E, Marchionni L, Hermo D, Mosquera B (2014b) La naturaleza de la observación: evidencias arqueológicas en Somuncurá (Río Negro). In: Cassiodoro G, Rindel D, Re A (eds)Integración de Diferentes Líneas de Evidencia en Arqueología Argentina, Editorial Aspha, Buenos Aires, pp 73–91

Miotti L, Terranova E, Blanco R, Marchionni L, Hermo D, Magnin L (2016) Entre basaltos y lagunas: las estructuras de piedra de la meseta de Somuncurá. Apuntes para la reflexión de los patrones de movilidad de los cazadores-recolectores. Arqueología de la Patagonia: de Mar a Mar. Ediciones CIEP / Ñire Negro Ediciones, Santiago de Chile, pp 256–266

Miotti L, Salemme M, Hermo D, Magnín L, Carden N, Mosquera B, Terranova E, Marchionni L (2007) Resolución e integridad arqueológica en la Cueva Maripe (Santa Cruz, Argentina). In: Morello F, Martinic M, Prieto A, Bahamonde G (eds) Arqueología de Fuego-Patagonia. Levantando piedras, desenterrando huesos. y develando arcanos. CEQUA, Pta. Arenas, Chile, pp 555–569

Paunero RS, Frank A, Skarbun F, Rosales G, Zapata G, Cueto M, Paunero MF, Martínez DG, López R, Lunazzi N, Del Giorgio M (2005) Arte rupestre en Estancia La María, Meseta Central de Santa Cruz: sectorización y contextos arqueológicos. Relaciones de la Sociedad Argentina de Antropología 30:147–168

Pigafetta A (1986) Primer viaje alrededor del globo. Ediciones Orbis, Barcelona

Podestá M, Paunero R, Rolandi D (1995) El Arte Rupestre de la Argentina Indígena. Patagonia. Union Académique Internationale-Corpus Antiquitatum Americanun Argentina VI. Academia Nacional de la Historia. Buenos Aires

Re A (2016) Las escenas de caza del Holoceno tardío en Patagonia centro-meridional. In: Mena F (ed) Arqueología de la Patagonia: de mar a mar. Ediciones CIEP, Santiago de Chile, pp 486–495

Re A (2017) Grabados de guanacos en la Patagonia austral. Intersecciones en Antropología 18(2):135–147

Remesal M, Salani F, Franchi M, Ardolino A (2001) Hoja Geológica 4169-IV, Maquinchao. Provincia de Río Negro. Instituto de Geología y Recursos Minerales, Servicio Geológico Minero Argentino, Buenos Aires. Boletín 312:1–72

Salemme M, Miotti L (1998) The status of Rheids in Patagonia: environmental approach and economic interpretation at the Transition Late Pleistocene/Early Holocene. 8th ICAZ, International Council of Archaeozoology. Victoria, Canadá, p 16

Santiago F, Salemme M (2010) A Guanaco kill site in Tierra del Fuego, Argentina. The case of Las Vueltas 1. Before Farming 2:1–17

Santiago F, Salemme M (2016) Guanaco hunting strategies in the northern plains of Tierra del Fuego, Argentina. J Anthropol Archaeol 43:110–127

Schobinger J, Gradín C (1985) Arte rupestre de la Argentina. Cazadores patagónicos y agricultores andinos. Editorial Encuentro, Madrid, España, p 99

Speth JD (1983) Bison Kills and bone counts: decision making by ancient hunters. University of Chicago Press, Chicago, Londres

Taçón P (2004) Ochre, clay, stone and art: the symbolic importance of minerals as life-force among aboriginal peoples of Northern and Central Australia. In: Boivin N, Owoc M (eds) Soils, stones, and symbols: cultural perceptions of the mineral world. UCL Press, London, pp 31–40

Terranova ED (2013) Arqueología de la Cuenca del Arroyo Talagapa, Meseta de Somuncurá (Provincia de Río Negro). Unpublished doctoral thesis. Facultad de Ciencias Naturales y Museo –Universidad Nacional de La Plata. MS.http://hdl.handle.net/10915/35034

Terranova ED, Lynch V (2017) Estudio tecnológico y funcional de artefactos formatizados del sitio Amigo Oeste (AW), Meseta de Somuncurá (Río Negro, Argentina)

Vargas Garilio J, Terranova E, Lynch V (2019) Estudio preliminar del parapeto 3 de Laguna Azul, Meseta de Somuncurá (Río Negro, Argentina). In: Gómez Otero J; Svoboda A, Benegas A (eds) Arqueología de Patagonia: El pasado entre las arenas. Instituto de Diversidad y Evolución Austral, Puerto Madryn, pp 443–454

Chapter 11
Technological Strategies and Guaranteed Return: Hunting Blinds and Patagonian Plateaus

Josefina Flores Coni, Juan Dellepiane, Gisela Cassiodoro, Rafael Goñi, and Agustín Agnolin

Abstract This work states that hunting guanaco (*Lama guanicoe*) in plateaus from Southern Patagonia increased progressively during the Late Holocene (ca. 2500 years BP) and entailed effective technologies combined with new demographic configurations and mobility strategies among hunter-gatherer groups (extensification processes and population convergences). These strategies include different technological aspects; technology is conceived as part of a total system and not only as a list of artifacts or instruments. Therefore, the construction of stone structures known as parapetos would have been a key aspect in the progressive use of plateaus for the procurement of faunal resources. The region under study comprises the Strobel Plateau and the area of Pampa del Asador-Guitarra Lake Plateau and Asador Plateau (Santa Cruz province´s steppe, Patagonia, Argentina). A high frequency of hunting blinds characterizes these areas which could have been part of different procurement modalities. Their functionality was not necessarily only one; it could have been variable according to different objectives and necessities in time and space. Sets of hunting blinds augmented along time, increased progressively and created an archaeological landscape supplied with the adequate technology to mark, establish and claim complete fields for hunting in wide and open areas. Thus, information was provided for the present and future generations regarding the places for acquiring prey and social contact. Therefore, communication was delivered as to which were the places with a high energetic return that guaranteed success of seasonal mobility from different places in the region.

Keywords Late Holocene · Plateaus · Hunting blinds · Strategies

---

J. Flores Coni (✉) · J. Dellepiane · A. Agnolin
Instituto Nacional de Antropología y Pensamiento Latinoamericano (INAPL), Consejo Nacional de Investigaciones Científicas y Técnicas (CONICET), Buenos Aires, Argentina

G. Cassiodoro
INAPL, CONICET, Universidad de Buenos Aires (UBA), Buenos Aires, Argentina

R. Goñi
INAPL, Universidad de Buenos Aires (UBA), Buenos Aires, Argentina

© Springer Nature Switzerland AG 2021
J. B. Belardi et al. (eds.), *Ancient Hunting Strategies in Southern South America*,
The Latin American Studies Book Series,
https://doi.org/10.1007/978-3-030-61187-3_11

11.1 Introduction

The central-western portion of Santa Cruz province (Patagonia, Argentina) comprises highlands and plateaus, which were used by hunter-gatherer groups in the past for seasonal hunting of guanaco (*Lama guanicoe*), the main prey in Southern Patagonia. Our study areas are the Strobel Plateau, Guitarra Plateau, Asador Plateau, and Pampa del Asador (Fig. 11.1). The successful colonization of these environments occurs during the Late Holocene, referring to the last 2500 years, and was connected to the use of lower environments in the meso region (Goñi 2010).

According to the peopling models established for the region (see Goñi 2010), hunter-gatherer occupations were highly conditioned by climatic and environmental variations, in a scenario characterized by progressive aridity with epic droughts during the global scale episode known as the Mediaeval Climatic Anomaly (MCA) (Stine 1994). New demographic conditions and new general mobility strategies, as extensification[1] and population convergence processes (in terms of Goñi 2010 and Belardi and Goñi 2006), were adopted in this environmental context.

Thus, this study assesses the characteristics of the different long-term technological strategies Patagonian hunter-gatherers implemented and aims to highlight the progressive efficiency in this environment´s exploitation and the better procurement of prey. It is important to take into account that the continuous construction of hunting blinds over more than 1000 years was the key to the sustained use of plateaus, for hunting guanacos as well as for social interaction.

11.2 Palaeoclimatic Conditions

As previously mentioned, human peopling models for the region state that paleoclimatic and paleoenvironmental aspects conditioned this process. In this section, we summarize the main variations recorded during the Holocene. For the central-western portion of Santa Cruz province, sedimentological research in lacustrine basins allowed to establish a paleoenvironmental panorama in this spatial scale. Analysis carried out by Stine and Stine (1990) in Cardiel Lake (south of Strobel Plateau)

---

[1]Extensification is understood as a process "… that prioritizes a more intense use of extensive spatial ranges connected to permanent settlements. This had to incorporate very wide areas, previously little frequented or only frequented in terms of transit, such as plateaus, basaltic plateaux and/or high pampas. Likewise, some sectors which were previously permanent settlements or recurrently used, were given a transit role or were less visited" (authors' translation) (Goñi 2000). Binford (2001, 2008) used the concept of extensification in an ethnographical sense. It was deeply related with the new organization of American hunter-gatherers when horses were introduced in the continent by European conquerors. The main examples to introduce this concept were the Great Plains societies in North America and the Tehuelche society in Patagonia. However, in this paper the use of the concept of extensification is based on an archaeological perspective, using Binford´s frames of references (2001), like environmental information and Effective Temperatures (ET), as useful tools to identify cases of the processes under study (Goñi 2010, 2016, 2018).

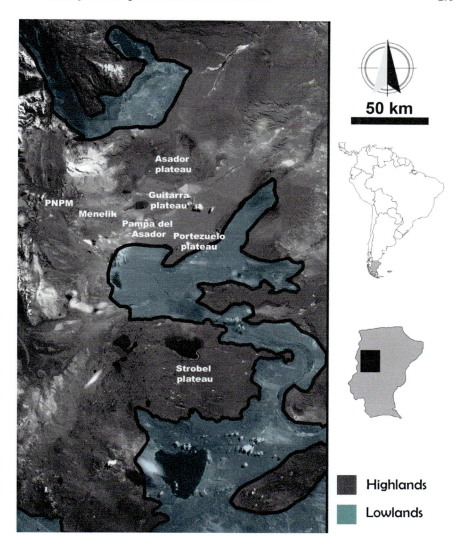

Fig. 11.1 Map with the location of the study areas: plateaus and highlands from central-western Santa Cruz province, Patagonia, Argentina

recognized variations in moisture levels during the Holocene. Thus, between 10,100 and 7000 years BP a very humid moment was recorded; a drier one took place between 7000 and 5500 years BP; a humid period occurred between 5500 and 4500 years BP; another drier period extended between 4500 and 3000 years BP and an even drier one happened from 2200 years BP onwards, with a very dry moment at around 900 years BP, related to the Medieval Climatic Anomaly (Stine and Stine 1990; Stine 1994).

Moreover, high-resolution sub-bottom seismic profiles as well as sedimentological analysis (Gilli et al. 2001; Gilli 2003; Markgraf et al. 2003) also confirmed these variations. These studies also pose the existence of a period of great humidity between 11,200 and 6700 years BP and a high variability in the sequence of humid and dry moments after 1870 years BP. Furthermore, changes in the direction and intensity of winds took place, specifically the western southern ones, known as the Southern Westerlies. In the Middle Holocene (between 6800 and 5300 calibrated years BP), a readjustment of winds occurs, with an intensification at 49° south latitude; this tendency increased during the Late Holocene (1800-1200 calibrated years BP) (Gilli et al. 2005).

11.3 Research Background

For more than 20 years ongoing archaeological investigations were led by our research team in plateaus and highlands form central-western Santa Cruz province (Espinosa and Goñi 1999; Goñi et al. 2011–2012; Re et al. 2017, among others). Different types of sites and archaeological materials were registered in this region. Hunting blinds stand out (Figs. 11.2 and 11.5), which were built by the accumulation of rocks forming a short wall, without using mortar. They are semi-circular constructions, even though some circular or straight structures have been found (Cassiodoro 2011; Cassiodoro and Flores Coni 2010; Flores Coni 2014, 2018, 2019a; Goñi et al. 2011–2012; Gradin 1959–1960, among others).

This work focuses on the available information for stone structures located in Strobel Plateau and the area of Pampa del Asador-Guitarra Lake Plateau. We present a synthesis of the chronology, frequency, distribution, and dimensions of hunting blinds, as well as the associated archaeological record that has been registered in

Fig. 11.2 Examples of hunting blinds in plateaus and highlands from central-western Santa Cruz province, Patagonia

more than 20 years of research and that has been published in several papers and thesis (Aragone 2009; Aragone and Cassiodoro 2005–2006; Aragone et al. 2010; Cassiodoro 2011, 2016; Cassiodoro and Flores Coni 2010, 2019; Cassiodoro and Dellepiane 2019; Cassiodoro and Tessone 2014; Cassiodoro et al. 2016; Dellepiane 2014, 2018, 2019; Dellepiane and Cassiodoro 2019; Dellepiane and Flores Coni 2016; Espinosa and Goñi 1999; Flores Coni 2014, 2018, 2019a; Goñi 2000–2002; Goñi et al. 2010, 2011–2012, 2016; Pasqualini et al. 2016; Re et al. 2017). We also include the first available information on frequencies and dimensions of hunting blinds from the Asador Plateau. Given the great amount of information, some examples are specific for some sectors of the areas under study.

It is worth to mention that a great number of hunting blinds do not present sedimentary deposition due to the local climatic conditions, with strong winds and severe erosive processes (Flores Coni 2018). Nevertheless, many hunting blinds sites were excavated; so far, 31 m^2 were excavated. Samples for chronologic dates were obtained from positive excavations; bone remains have enabled faunal analysis which provided exceptional information for this kind of environment (Aragone 2009; Dellepiane 2014, 2019).

11.4 Environment and Prey

We take into account ecological and environmental variables in order to provide an objective frame of reference for human behavior. Thus, we initially highlight that guanaco (*Lama guanicoe*) has been the main and most frequent prey in steppes from the interior of southernmost continental Patagonia since the Early Holocene (Miotti 2012). Based on this premise, human behavior´s logic throughout time is tied to this animal´s ethology: gregarious, territorial and with a predictable behavior which has a seasonal mobility (Kaufmann 2009).

A second aspect to consider refers to the ecological and geographical environment that held the scenario for human peopling in the region. In this case, highlands are the focal point, given their seasonal availability. These are broad basaltic plateaus from the Miocene (Ramos 2002) between 800 and 1400 m a.s.l., which comprise a great amount of shallow lakes or wetlands (Lancelotti 2009); for instance, there are more than 1000 in the Strobel Plateau. These plateaus are steppe environments characterized by a semi-desert climate with template-cold temperature and rainfalls between 200 and 400 mm. Seasonality in these environments is highly marked given their latitudinal location (between 45° and 50° south) as well as their altitude. Winters are cold with plenty of snowfall and the availability of new pastures starts toward the end of spring and beginning of summer (November/December). Therefore, primary productivity of these areas becomes available for guanaco herds in those moments where they start their migration from lowlands (below 300 m a.s.l.) toward the highlands in search of an environment with good sustenance for massive birth and the following immediate mating stage. This would be the most adequate moment of the year for hunter-gatherer populations to climb to plateaus from different directions, in small groups as well as in pluri-familiar groups, to take advantage of the concentration of prey including offspring and sub-adults, highly prized for their hide.

11.5 Demographic Conditions

Another important aspect posed in this work is related to low demography. According to Binford (2001), hunter-gatherers who base their diet and sustainability in terrestrial animals present a low demography, calculated in 3.4 human beings every 100 km^2; thus, a population of 1100 to 1500 people were estimated for the entire region under study (350 km long in the north–south axis, and 150 km long in the east–west axis). Moreover, in environments where prey offer low failure probability or low risk at their encounter, as it is our case, a low demography may be kept (Binford 2007). Therefore, under low diversification (it must be borne in mind that the main prey is guanaco); we could assume a low demography (see Belardi and Goñi 2006). In this context, highlands with a seasonal and logistical use would have had a significant role in social interchange for populations with such a low demography (see Belardi and Goñi 2006).

11.6 Hunting Blinds and Provisioning of Places

Provisioning of places implies the distribution of resources in terms of anticipating future needs (Binford 1979). According to this author, site furniture is related to the items that go with the place, such as fireplace rocks, fireplaces, anvils, etc. Within this frame, discarding artifacts in specific places of the landscape, sectors of redundant use, either annually or seasonally, represent a significant benefit for hunter-gatherer groups (Kuhn 1992).

The technological provisioning of places may imply many different alternatives and aims. In general terms, a place can be equipped with structures and artifacts, either with logistical or residential aims. As regards structures, beyond the construction of residential structures, other examples are hunting blinds, burial structures, storage structures, etc. Also, a variety of artifacts exist that can be deposited in specific places with the objective of reuse a posteriori. Some of them might be projectile points, grinding artifacts, raw material, etc. (Binford 1979; Kuhn 1992; Martínez 1999, among others). Thus, the presence of artifacts with particular characteristics in specific points of the landscape can occur in relation to planning the reuse of specific spaces (Binford 1979).

This study affirms that the cumulative character of an archaeological landscape contains diagnostic information about the organizational properties of the original system and it is not isomorphic with the dynamic functions of the social system of the past. Artifacts´ associations in sites do not appear organized; what seems organized is behavior related to the environment *per se* (Binford 1987: 22). Through this perspective the evidence about the archaeological landscape is constructed as well as the technological strategies implemented through time, in which hunting blinds are an essential feature of it. Therefore, we assume that their study offers an important medium for the analysis of past organizational systems.

11.7 Hunting Blinds Chronology

More than 20 years of systematic surveys in plateaus from the region allowed archaeological excavations in different hunting blinds. Zooarchaeological samples were recovered and have been dated through AMS. Thus, 24 dates have been obtained for stone structures from the Pampa del Asador, Guitarra Plateau, and Strobel Plateau (specific data has been pertinently published elsewhere—Cassiodoro and Tessone 2014; Cassiodoro et al. 2019; Dellepiane 2019; Dellepiane and Cassiodoro 2019; Goñi 2000–2002; Goñi et al. 2010; Re et al. 2017; Rindel 2009).

These chronologies start around 2000 years BP (Goñi 2000–2002) (Fig. 11.3), which coincide with specific environmental processes of a regional humidity drop (Stine and Stine 1990).

As from 1000 years BP a persistent use of stone structures is registered. A clear example is provided by some of the 50 hunting blinds in site K116, located in the Strobel Plateau (Goñi et al. 2016; Re et al. 2017) which provided evidence on dates ranging between 900 and 1100 years BP (Fig. 11.4). Results from t test (Student) on average differences (t: 7.31 gl: 4) establish that the null hypothesis of equality between samples cannot be rejected, with a significance level of 0.05. Therefore, contemporaneous occupations are evident and thus, open up the possibility of communal hunting based on the evidence that structures from this site could have functioned simultaneously (Goñi et al. 2016) (Fig. 11.4).

This cumulative process of structures construction implies that after 500 years BP, Pampa del Asador, Guitarra Plateau, and Strobel Plateau held a landscape supplied with hunting blinds. Moreover, two additional aspects should be taken into account. Firstly, the reuse of structures in time; secondly, the simultaneity in the use of different structures. As regards the former, some cases are relevant such as sites in Pampa del Asador: CP2C where structure 3 evidences an occupation gap of at least 836 years; CP6 structure 9 with a lapse of 1200 years, and CP2A structure 4 with approximately 1840 years. Concerning the second aspect, site K116 in the Strobel Plateau has already been highlighted but it is worth to mention that chronologies from this site have equal averages with site CP2A structure 2 and CP6 structure 12 in Pampa del Asador. Moreover, four of the samples from both structures from CP6 do not present significant statistical differences (t: 3.31 < 0.05) (Dellepiane and Cassiodoro 2019).

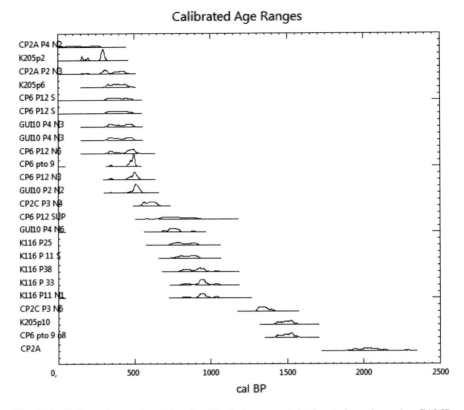

Fig. 11.3 Calibrated ages for all hunting blinds (*parapetos*) in the study region using CALIB. REV 7.0.1 program (CALIB RADIOCARBON CALIBRATION PROGRAM, Copyright 1986–2013; Stuiver and Reimer 1993), Southern Hemisphere calibration curve (Hogg et al. 2013) and two sigma ranges. Left axe: site names; CP: Cerro Pampa; GUI: Guitarra; K: Strobel

11.8 Characteristics of Sample and Hunting Blinds

In our study region, 535 structures have been recorded so far, using GPS. The Strobel Plateau registers the highest frequency followed by the Guitarra Plateau (Table 11.1 and Fig. 11.5). Other highlands inside the study region also register hunting blinds, though in lower frequencies: in Parque Nacional Perito Moreno (PNPM) (n: 12) and nearby Estancia Menelik (n: 4) (Cassiodoro et al. 2016; Molinari and Ferraro 2004) (Fig. 11.1). Also, in Portezuelo Plateau, eastwards from Pampa del Asador, recent surveys found one structure (Fig. 11.1).

Other structures have been registered through remote sensing (Fig. 11.6). So far, more than 72 structures have been recorded using satellite images (Dellepiane 2018).

11 Technological Strategies and Guaranteed Return …

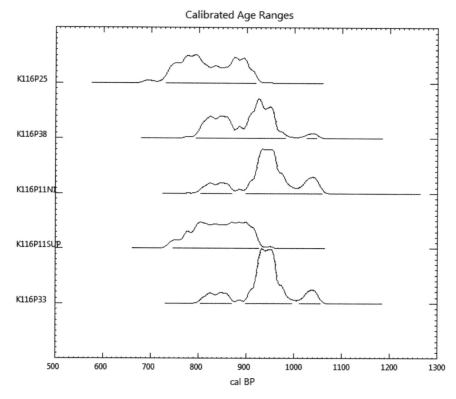

Fig. 11.4 Probability distributions for dates in hunting blinds from site K116, located in the Strobel Plateau, Santa Cruz, Patagonia, using CALIB. REV 7.0.1 program (CALIB RADIOCARBON CALIBRATION PROGRAM, Copyright 1986–2013; Stuiver and Reimer 1993), Southern Hemisphere calibration curve (Hogg et al. 2013) and two sigma ranges

Table 11.1 Number of hunting blinds recorded in our study areas

Area	N hunting blinds
Asador Plateau	32
Pampa del Asador	34
Guitarra Plateau	84
Strobel Plateau	368
Total	**535**

11.8.1 Characteristics of Stone Structures

Different aspects measured on stone structures reflect variability in their characteristics. Firstly, many different sizes have been registered (Table 11.2) as well as

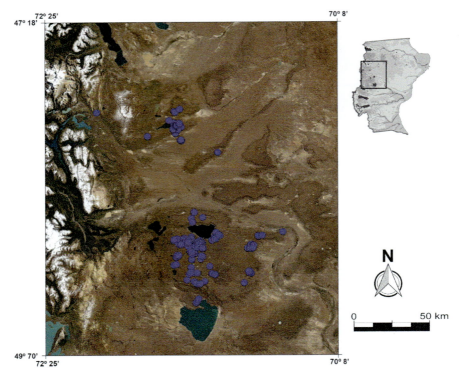

Fig. 11.5 Distribution of hunting blinds in central-western Santa Cruz, Patagonia, Argentina

varied morphologies. As regards the latter, the most frequent morphology corresponds to arch forms, even though circular and linear structures have also been found (Cassiodoro 2011; Cassiodoro et al. 2016; Flores Coni 2018, 2019a; Goñi et al. 2011–2012). Their walls are usually oriented against the prevailing westerly winds and immediately available rocks were used in their construction.

Secondly, regarding their emplacement, the construction of hunting blinds has been variable and there is no clear pattern. They can be found near water: shallow lakes or rivers, and also in open plains (Cassiodoro et al. 2016; Flores Coni 2019a).

Lastly, an important characteristic refers to the fact that hunting blinds can be found isolated or in groups. These can be formed by two or more structures, with groups that can reach up to 50 hunting blinds (that is the case of the aforementioned site K116 located in the Strobel Plateau—Fig. 11.7) (Cassiodoro et al. 2016; Dellepiane and Flores Coni 2016; Flores Coni 2014, 2019a; Goñi et al. 2016).

Fig. 11.6 Structures from Patagonia identified through satellite images. 1, 2, and 3: images with examples from the Guitarra Plateau. 4: Hunting blind from the Guitarra Plateau

Table 11.2 Average size of hunting blinds for each of the areas considered in central-western Santa Cruz province, Patagonia

Average size	Length (m)	Depth (m)	Height (m)
Asador Plateau (n:25)	2.99	2.36	0.79
Pampa del Asador (n:29)	4.04	1.72	0.59
Guitarra Plateau (n:55)	3.51	2.66	0.74
Strobel Plateau (n:180)	4.64	1.67	0.58

11.8.2 Archaeological Record in Hunting Blinds

Lithic material has been recorded in hunting blinds as well as faunal and ceramic material. Nevertheless, some hunting blinds do not present evidence of any kind. Lithic material found in some hunting blinds consists of a great number of flakes were found and a low diversity of tools mainly represented by projectile points, end scrapers and retouched flakes (Cassiodoro 2011; Cassiodoro and Flores Coni 2019; Flores Coni 2018, 2019a). In the Strobel Plateau, many of the hunting blinds present

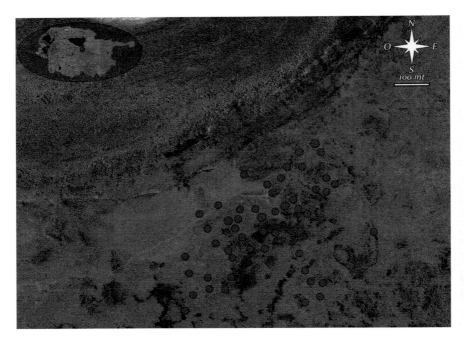

Fig. 11.7 Site K116 located in the Strobel Plateau, Patagonia. More than 50 hunting blinds were recorded

only one or two classes of artifacts, mainly projectile points and flakes (Flores Coni 2018).

Projectile points designs correspond to those related to the Late Holocene; two different stems widths were recorded, which are related to different weapon systems (Fig. 11.8). Frequencies are similar between stem widths over and less than 10 mm. The latter corresponds to the use of bow and arrow, dated in 900 years BP in the region (Goñi et al. 2019). Both types of projectile point can be found in association with hunting blinds; thus, diverse hunting strategies were developed through time and structures were reused. The presence of stone bolas adds variability to the array of weapons associated with hunting blinds (Agnolin et al. 2019).

Many aspects of the materials found in hunting blinds allow assessing provisioning strategies of the structures themselves. That could be the case of the Strobel Plateau where no sources of raw materials have been found and all lithic resources had to be transported from elsewhere (Flores Coni 2019b). In this case, the presence of discarded artifacts in the structures provides an example of provisioning in a context of unavailable local raw materials. Table 11.3 shows non fractured tools, cores, and medium to big flakes (4 to 12 cm long) found in 125 hunting blinds from the Strobel Plateau. Numbers are interesting given the fact that they reflect what was left in the structures after using them. We will resume this topic in the discussion section in terms of raw material storage.

Fig. 11.8 Different morphologies and sizes of projectile points in hunting blinds from Pampa del Asador, Patagonia

Table 11.3 Tools, cores, and flakes raw materials from hunting blinds in the Strobel Plateau, Patagonia, Argentina

	Obsidian	Siliceous rocks	Basalt	Others	Total
Tools	71	36	10	28	145
Cores	9	11	–	5	25
Flakes	30	52	18	77	177
Total	110	99	28	110	347

In addition, the presence of grinding artifacts and ceramic herds in structures from Pampa del Asador also reflect this idea (Cassiodoro 2011; Cassiodoro and Flores Coni 2019; Dellepiane and Cassiodoro 2019). So far, more than 81 ceramic remains have been recorded in three hunting blinds and 19 grindstones in five of the excavated hunting blinds. Also, hammer stones were found in all structures which are directly related to the availability of raw materials in this area (Espinosa and Goñi 1999).

More than 7200 bones were recovered from structures in all the study areas (Dellepiane 2019). Taxonomic structure is mainly represented by guanaco (*Lama guanicoe*) (n: 3100 NISP); the presence of other species is almost nonexistent. In relation to guanaco, the high frequency of immature individuals reflects the potential exploitation of their skins and the seasonal use of these basaltic plateaus (Dellepiane 2019).

Moreover, a wide range of variability has been recorded in bone assemblages as regards the representation of skeletal parts and processing evidence. Skeletal parts profiles indicate the presence of very incomplete bone assemblages with a low proportion of axial elements and a diverse use of the appendicular segment. Within this context, upper, middle, and inferior extremities predominate differentially according to the stone structure under study. Additionally, some cases have been recorded where anatomic assemblages exhibit a higher global completeness and a more balanced profile between both skeletal sectors.

Processing evidence has been identified in all cases though in variable frequencies: some bone assemblages stand out with very low values, while others exhibit NISP frequencies over 30%. This evidence shows that a variable number of tasks were carried out (Dellepiane 2019; Dellepiane and Cassiodoro 2019; Goñi et al. 2011–2012). Thus, some stone structures may have been related to procuring activities and with the initial processing of prey, while others could have been part of residential camps such as temporary settlements within a logistical and/or seasonal context (Dellepiane 2019; Dellepiane and Cassiodoro 2019; Dellepiane and Flores Coni 2016; Goñi et al. 2011–2012).

11.9 Discussion

Our study´s main interest is to evaluate in which way certain technological strategies, such as provisioning places with hunting blinds in broad areas grant a high hierarchy to certain environments which were not part of hunting groups' mobility during the great part of the Holocene. Moreover, this work discusses this process in terms of guanaco procurement but also in terms of the opportunity these broad areas offer for social interaction of populations with low demography. Therefore, social strategies for interaction, communication, aggregation, convergence, mobility, and logistics generate long-term technological strategies that will guarantee energetic return allowing the continuity of the former social strategies in a regional scale.

Reasonably, continuous provisioning of places makes sense from an ecological perspective. As mentioned before, during the Late Holocene when climatic conditions were defined by growing aridity, these environments offered broad spaces of good primary productivity and strong seasonality. Thus, the main prey in the past (guanaco) migrated in mass toward these highlands tying human groups to its mobility; this is the only case of isomorphic mobility between hunters and prey, similar to a pastoralist mobility (Goñi 2018). The energetic return that these environments potentially produced and guaranteed was certainly a first ranked seasonal resource for Patagonian hunters during the Late Holocene. Meat, fat, and marrow, or raw materials such as leather, bones, sinews, etc., were the most abundant resources that supported this logistical and seasonal mobility of hunters. It should be considered that under these conditions, a strategy that implied resources diversification was not an option, given the fact that there is no such diversity in a local scale and it would have entailed a mobility tied to oceanic coasts (Atlantic or Pacific), which presents no archaeological or isotopic correlate (García Guraieb et al. 2015; Goñi 2010).

An important aspect to discuss refers to the cumulative and additive character of structures in time. Its importance stands in that this is a positive argument in relation to the colonization of these environments and their functionality on a regional scale. The presented chronology places most of the hunting blinds in the Late Holocene, as from 2000 years BP, and appears more concentrated between 1300 and 300 years BP when the introduction of horses in Southern Patagonia radically modified mobility patterns. In other words, in a 1000 years lapse a great social provisioning developed where the construction of new structures did not necessarily imply that previous ones were not reused; on the contrary, many are the cases in which structures were used for long periods (that is the case of Pampa del Asador) (Cassiodoro 2011). In fact, ethnoarchaeological studies have shown that the existence of previous infrastructure will condition the selection of different types of camps in populations with residential mobility (Haas et al. 2019). Moreover, distances between sets of hunting blinds became shorter throughout time and created an archaeological landscape which gets denser in a contemporary context.

Additionally, the nature of this archaeological landscape—isolated cases, groups, etc., different forms, sizes, and quantities—poses the existence of a great degree of variability in hunting and settlement strategies implemented in these highlands during the Late Holocene (Cassiodoro et al. 2016).

As stone structures remain, this technological strategy would have allowed a better optimization of resources, with a less investment in the provisioning of places. According to the experimental work of Morgan et al. (2018), the construction of semi-circular hunting blinds with similar dimensions to the ones registered in our study areas would imply a construction time of approximately three hours for two people. Thus, in three hours a structure with a potential use of 1800 years (such as the previously cited case of Pampa del Asador—CP2A) can be built. In other words, hypothetically, in one summer all hunting blinds from our study areas could have been constructed. Time spent in the construction of hunting blinds decreased along time given that space and environment augmented their provisioning and therefore, return was higher and it was guaranteed according to the technological investment model (Bettinger 2009). The conclusion is that the provisioning of plateaus was not costly in terms of energy and social collaboration and provided high benefits in the long term. This supports the idea of a more effective and general technological strategy on a regional scale. Thus, during the Late Holocene plateaus became environments that guaranteed high return with low cost in the long run.

Another aspect is the low variety of weaponry along time, something common to groups who depended upon hunting, as Oswalt (1976) proposed for ethnographic hunter-gatherers. Low demography conditions, the local environmental productivity, and the almost unique prey are initial conditions for posing a low technological replacement rate along time.

In addition, discarding artifacts manufactured in different raw materials in a context where there is no availability of sources is congruent with technological strategies of permanent provisioning and can be interpreted as potential raw material reservoirs. These sorts of caches (sensu Binford 1980) can be part of a process of landscape lithification as proposed by Martínez and Mackie (2003–2004). From this perspective, permanently adding technology to the landscape supports the idea of a planning strategy with forecast and anticipation of the reoccupation of high productivity environments during the Late Holocene.

Thus, the accumulative construction of hunting blinds along time and in broad open spaces generated a landscape equipped with the adequate technology to establish and claim complete hunting grounds. Therefore, these strategies are potentially informative, in the present and toward the future, about which are the places to obtain prey and social contact. Hence, these communicate about which may be the places with highest energetic return. Thus, they will guarantee the success of seasonal mobility from nearby lowlands. At the same time, an opportunity appears for populations of low demography to aggregate or converge in a common space in the wide geography of Southern Patagonia (Goñi 2010; Belardi and Goñi 2006). Therefore, this strategy entails not only an energetic return but also a social return: the possibility of interaction, communication, sharing information, couples and goods in broad scales such as the plateaus from Southern Patagonia.

This work has proposed the existence of a variety of social, economic, and consequently, technological strategies for the procurement of the main animal resource and its derivatives. Hence, technological strategies can be seen as the factor that favors this energetic procurement but that also favors the endurance of major social strategies.

Acknowledgements Funding for this research came from Universidad de Buenos Aires (UBACYT N° 20020170100150BA) and Ministerio de Cultura de la Nación of Argentina (INAPL). We thank the organizers of this workshop for the possibility of publishing this work. Our acknowledgments also go for Asociación Identidad (Perito Moreno), Municipalidad de Perito Moreno and Municipalidad de Gobernador Gregores (Santa Cruz), and for Goldcorp. We specially thank support from local estancias (= ranches) in the study areas, mainly Laguna Verde, Lago Strobel, La Paloma, Sierra Colorada, Las Tunas, Cerro Pampa, Sierra Andía, El Delfín, La Criolla, Dos Hermanos, Pecho Blanco, La Verde, and La Nativa.

References

Agnolin A, Flores Coni J, Goñi R (2019) Las bolas y el viento: análisis de la distribución de bolas en las cuencas de los lagos Cardiel y Strobel. In: Otero JG, Sbovoda A, Banegas A (eds) Arqueología de Patagonia: El pasado de las Arenas. Altuna Impresores, Buenos Aires, pp 81–92

Aragone A (2009) Los conjuntos arqueofaunísticos de los sitios Médanos Lago Posadas (cuenca baja) y Parapetos Cerro Pampa (meseta alta), Provincia de Santa Cruz. In: Salemme M, Santiago F, Alvarez M, Piana E, Vázquez M, Mansur E (eds) Arqueología de Patagonia: una mirada desde el último confín. Editorial Utopías, Ushuaia, pp 679–692

Aragone A, Cassiodoro G (2005–2006) Los parapetos de Cerro Pampa: registro arqueofaunístico y tecnológico (noroeste de la provincia de Santa Cruz). Arqueología 13:131–154

Aragone A, Dellepiane J, Rindel D (2010) Análisis de parapetos en ambientes mesetarios del noroeste de Santa Cruz, Patagonia meridional: propiedades del registro arqueológico y su integración con líneas de evidencia arqueofaunísticas. In: Bárcena R, Chiavazza H (eds) Arqueología Argentina en el Bicentenario de la Revolución de Mayo, XVII Congreso Nacional de Arqueología Argentina V, Zeta Editores, Mendoza, pp 1841–1846

11 Technological Strategies and Guaranteed Return … 309

Belardi JB, Goñi R (2006) Representaciones rupestres y convergencia poblacional durante momentos tardíos en Santa Cruz (Patagonia argentina). El caso de la meseta del Strobel. In: Fiore D, Podestá M (eds) Tramas en la Piedra. Producción y usos del arte rupestre. World Archaeological Congress, Sociedad Argentina de Antropología and Asociación Amigos del Instituto Nacional de Antropología, Buenos Aires, pp 85–94

Bettinger R (2009) Hunter-gatherer foraging: five simple models. Eliot Werner Publications, New York

Binford L (1979) Organization and formation processes: looking at curated technology. J Anthropol Res 35(3):255–273

Binford L (1980) Willow smoke and dogs' tails: hunter-gatherer settlement systems and archaeological site formation. Am Antiq 45(1):4–20

Binford L (1987) Data, relativism and archaeological science. Man 22:391–404

Binford L (2001) Constructing frames of reference: an analytical method for archaeological theory building using ethnographic and environmental data sets. University of California Press, Berkeley, Los Angeles, London

Binford L (2007) The diet of early hominids: some things we need to know before "reading" the menu from the archaeological record. In: Roebroeks W (ed) Guts and brains: an integrative approach to the hominin record. Leiden University Press, Leiden, pp 185–222

Binford L (2008) ¿Por qué se usa la frase "a igualdad de condiciones" cuando se postulan generalizaciones, se desarrollan argumentos de causalidad o cuando se construye teoría? Relaciones de la Sociedad Argentina de Antropología XXXIII:29–59

Cassiodoro G (2011) Movilidad y uso del espacio de cazadores-recolectores del Holoceno tardío: estudio de la variabilidad del registro tecnológico en distintos ambientes del noroeste de la provincia de Santa Cruz. South American Archaeology Series 13, British Archaeological Reports (International Series). Archaeopress, Oxford

Cassiodoro G (2016) Variabilidad tecnológica en sectores altos del centro-oeste de Santa Cruz durante el Holoceno medio y tardío. Arqueología 22(2):335–359

Cassiodoro G, Dellepiane J (2019) Registro arqueológico del oeste de la meseta del lago Guitarra (Santa Cruz): un aporte desde la teledetección. Relaciones de la Sociedad Argentina de Antropología XLIV 1:187–194

Cassiodoro G, Flores Coni J (2010) Los parapetos del sitio Guitarra 10 (meseta del lago Guitarra, Santa Cruz): una aproximación tecnológica. In: Bárcena R, Chiavazza H (eds) Arqueología Argentina en el Bicentenario de la Revolución de Mayo, XVII Congreso Nacional de Arqueología Argentina. UNCuyo-CONICET, Mendoza, pp 1871–1876

Cassiodoro G, Flores Coni J (2019) Análisis comparativo del registro lítico del conjunto de parapetos Guitarra 10 (Meseta del lago Guitarra, Santa Cruz, Argentina). Comechingonia. Revista de Arqueología 23(1):303–324

Cassiodoro G, Tessone A (2014) Análisis radiocarbónico y de isótopos estables en residuos cerámicos del centro-oeste de Santa Cruz (Patagonia). Relaciones de la Sociedad Argentina de Antropología XXXIX 1:293–299

Cassiodoro G, Goñi R, Pasqualini S (2016) Variabilidad del registro arqueológico en sectores altos de Santa Cruz: tendencias generales en el uso del espacio. In: Mena F (ed) Arqueología de la Patagonia de mar a mar. CIEP-Ñire Negro ediciones, Coyhaique, pp 224–234

Cassiodoro G, Guichón F, Re A (2019) Diseños sobre soportes móviles y comunicación en el centro-oeste de Santa Cruz durante el Holoceno tardío. In: Otero JG, Sbovoda A, Banegas A (eds) Arqueología de Patagonia. El pasado en las arenas. Instituto de Diversidad y Evolución Austral, Puerto Madryn, pp 29–40

Dellepiane J (2014) Zooarqueología de espacios mesetarios. Patrones de subsistencia y obtención de recursos en el centro-oeste de Santa Cruz durante el Holoceno tardío. Facultad de Ciencias Sociales, Universidad Nacional del Centro de la provincia de Buenos Aires, Olavarría. Unpublished Graduate Thesis

Dellepiane J (2018) Uso de imágenes satelitales para el reconocimiento de parapetos en el centro-oeste de Patagonia meridional. Arqueología 24:259–269

Dellepiane J (2019) Poblamiento y uso del espacio de sectores mesetarios del centro-oeste de Santa Cruz durante el Holoceno tardío. Una aproximación zooarqueológica. Facultad de Filosofía y Letras, Universidad de Buenos Aires, Unpublished doctoral Thesis

Dellepiane J, Flores Coni J (2016) Aspectos tecnológicos y faunísticos en sitios a cielo abierto: variabilidad del registro en los parapetos de la meseta del Strobel, Provincia de Santa Cruz. In: Mena F (ed) Arqueología de la Patagonia: de mar a mar. CIEP-Ñire Negro ediciones, Coyhaique, pp 245–255

Dellepiane J, Cassiodoro G (2019) Estructuras de caza o campamentos temporales? Registro arqueológico de parapetos del sitio Cerro Pampa 6 (Santa Cruz). In: Otero JG, Svoboda A, Banegas A (eds) Arqueología de Patagonia: el pasado en las arenas. Altuna Impresores, Buenos Aires, pp 361–372

Espinosa S, Goñi R (1999) Viven! Una fuente de obsidiana en la Pcia. de Santa Cruz. In Soplando en el Viento. Actas de las III Jornadas de Arqueología de la Patagonia. Edición INAPL-Universidad Nacional del Comahue, Buenos Aires, pp 177–188

Flores Coni J (2014) Análisis de la variabilidad de parapetos en la meseta del Strobel (Santa Cruz). Relaciones de la Sociedad Argentina de Antropología XXXIX(2):551–557

Flores Coni J (2018) Poblamiento humano y uso del espacio en la meseta del Strobel (provincia de Santa Cruz). Un análisis sobre la variabilidad tecnológica durante el Holoceno. Facultad de Filosofía y Letras, Universidad de Buenos Aires, Unpublished doctoral Thesis

Flores Coni J (2019a) Tecnología de parapetos en Patagonia meridional: el caso de la meseta del Strobel. Relaciones de la Sociedad Argentina de Antropología XLIV(1):131–153

Flores Coni J (2019b) Population convergence in the Strobel Plateau: a discussion based on the study of lithic raw materials variability. J Archaeol Sci: Rep 24:473–485

García Guraieb S, Goñi R, Tessone A (2015) Paleodemography of Late Holocene hunter-gatherers from Patagonia (Santa Cruz, Argentina): an approach using multiple archaeological and bioarchaeological indicators. Quatern Int 356:147–158

Gilli A (2003) Tracking late Quaternary environmental change in southernmost south America using lake sediments of lago Cardiel (49°S), Patagonia, Argentina. Swiss Federal Institute of Technology, Unpublished PhD Dissertation

Gilli A, Anselmetti F, Ariztegui D, Beres M, McKenzie J, Markgraf V (2005) Seismic stratigraphy, buried beach ridges and contourite drifts: the Late Quaternary history of the closed Lago Cardiel basin, Argentina (49°S). Sedimentology 52:1–23

Gilli A, Anselmetti F, Ariztegui D, Bradbury J Platt, Kelts K, Markgraf V, McKenzie J (2001) Tracking abrupt climate change in the Southern Hemisphere: a seismic stratigraphic study of Lago Cardiel, Argentina (49°S). Terra Nova 13(6):443–448

Goñi R (2000–2002) Fechados radiocarbónicos y registro arqueológico en la cuenca de los lagos Salitroso/Posadas (Santa Cruz). Cuadernos del Instituto Nacional de Antropología y Pensamiento Latinoamericano 19:666–668

Goñi R (2010) Cambio climático y poblamiento humano durante el Holoceno tardío en Patagonia Meridional. Una perspectiva arqueológica. Facultad de Filosofía y Letras, Universidad de Buenos Aires, Unpublished doctoral thesis

Goñi R (2016) Extensification in archeology. Poster 81st Annual Meeting SAA, Orlando, FL, USA

Goñi R (2018) Extensification in archaeology. In: Book of abstracts XVIII° Congress UISPP. FCR, Paris, p 345

Goñi R, Cassiodoro G, Rindel D (2011–2012) Poblamiento de mesetas: Arqueología de Pampa del Asador y Cerro Pampa (Patagonia Meridional). Cuadernos del Instituto de Antropología y Pensamiento Latinoamericano 23(1):21–36

Goñi R, Cassiodoro G, Re A, Guichón F, Flores Coni J, Dellepiane J (2010) Arqueología de la Meseta del lago Guitarra (Santa Cruz).XVI CNAA. Arqueología de la meseta del lago Guitarra (Santa Cruz). In: Bárcena R, Chiavazza H (eds) Arqueología Argentina en el Bicentenario de la Revolución de Mayo, XVII Congreso Nacional de Arqueología Argentina, V. UNCuyo-CONICET, Mendoza, pp 1923–1928

Goñi R, Cassiodoro G, Flores Coni J, Dellepiane J, Agnolin A, Guichón Fernández R (2016) Estrategias de caza y movilidad. Parapetos del sitio K116 (Meseta del Strobel, Santa Cruz). In: Mena F (ed) Arqueología de Patagonia: de Mar a Mar. Ediciones CIEP/Ñire Negro, Santiago, pp 441–449

Goñi R, Re A, García Guraieb S, Cassiodoro G, Tessone A, Rindel D, Dellepiane J, Flores Coni J, Guichón F, Agnolin A (2019) Climate changes, human peopling and regional differentiation during the late Holocene in Patagonia. Quatern Int 505:4–20

Gradin C (1959–1960) Tres informaciones referentes a la meseta del lago Strobel (prov. de Santa Cruz, Argentina). Acta Praehistorica III/IV:144–149

Haas R, Surovell T, O'Brien M (2019) Dukha mobility in a constructed environment: past camp use predicts future use in the Mongolian Taiga. Am Antiq 84(2):215–233

Hogg A, Hua Q, Blackwell P, Niu M, Buck C, Guilderson T, Heaton T, Palmer J, Reimer P, Reimer R, Turney C, Zimmerman S (2013) Shcal13 Southern Hemisphere calibration, 0–50,000 years Cal Bp. Radiocarbon 55(4):1889–1903

Kaufmann C (2009) Estructura de edad y sexo en guanaco. Estudios actualísticos y arqueológicos en Pampa y Patagonia. Sociedad Argentina de Antropología, Buenos Aires

Kuhn S (1992) On planning and curated technologies in the middle Paleolithic. J Anthropol Res 48(3):185–214

Lancelotti J (2009) Caracterización limnológica de lagunas de la Provincia de Santa Cruz y efectos de la introducción de Trucha Arco iris (Oncorhynchus mykiss) sobre las comunidades receptoras. Universidad Nacional del Comahue, Bariloche, Unpublished doctoral thesis

Markgraf V, Platt B, Schwalb A, Burns S, Stern C, Ariztegui D, Gilli A, Anselmetti F, Stine S, Maidana N (2003) Holocene paleoclimates of southern Patagonia: limnological and environmental history of Lago Cardiel, Argentina. The Holocene 14(4):581–591

Martínez G (1999) Tecnología, subsistencia y asentamiento en el curso medio del río Quequén Grande: un enfoque arqueológico. FCNyM, Universidad Nacional de La Plata. Unpublished doctoral thesis

Martínez G, Mackie Q (2003–2004) Late Holocene human occupation of the Quequén Grande River valley botton: settlement systems and an example of a built environment in the Argentine Pampas. Before Farming 1:1–27

Miotti L (2012) El uso de los recursos faunísticos entre los cazadores-recolectores de Patagonia: tendencias espacio/temporales de las estrategias durante el Holoceno. Archaeofauna 21:137–162

Molinari R, Ferraro L (2004) Estancia Menelik: Implicancias para el manejo de recursos culturales en la zona de amortiguación del Parque Nacional Perito Moreno. In: Civalero T, Fernández P, Guráieb G (eds) Contra Viento y Marea. Arqueología de Patagonia. INAPL-SAA, Buenos Aires, pp 625–634

Morgan C, Webb D, Sprengeler K, Black M, George N (2018) Experimental construction of hunter-gatherer residential features, mobility, and the costs of occupying "persistent places". J Archaeol Sci 91:65–76

Oswalt W (1976) An anthropological analysis of food-getting technology. John Wiley, New York

Pasqualini S, Cassiodoro G, Dellepiane J (2016) Logistic mobility on plateaus in center-west Santa Cruz, Argentina: an anthracological, technology and archaeofaunal approach. Quatern Int 422:135–151

Ramos V (2002) El magmatismo neógeno de la Cordillera Patagónica. In: Haller MJ (ed), Geología y recursos naturales de Santa Cruz. XV Congreso Geológico Argentino (El Calafate) Relatorio 1. Buenos Aires, pp 187–200

Re A, Goñi R, Flores Coni J, Guichón F, Dellepiane J, Umaño M (2017) Arqueología de la meseta del Strobel Argentina (Patagonia meridional): 15 años después. Relaciones de la Sociedad de Antropología 42:133–158

Rindel D (2009) Arqueología de momentos tardíos en el noroeste de la Provincia de Santa Cruz (Argentina): una perspectiva faunística. Facultad de Filosofía y Letras, Universidad de Buenos Aires, Unpublished doctoral thesis

Stine S (1994) Extreme and persistent drought in California and Patagonia during Mediaeval Time. Nature 369:546–549

Stine S, Stine M (1990) A record from Lake Cardiel of climate change in southern South America. Nature 345:705–708

Stuiver M, Reimer P (1993) Extended 14C database and revised CALIB radiocarbon calibration program. Radiocarbon 35:215–230

Chapter 12
Hunting Blinds in the Southern End of the Deseado Massif: Collective Hunting Strategies During the Late Holocene

Nora V. Franco, Lucas Vetrisano, Brenda L. Gilio, Natalia A. Cirigliano, and Pablo E. Bianchi

Abstract The Southern End of the Deseado Massif (SDM, Patagonia, Argentina) is part of a morphostructural region with seasonal shallow lakes and streams highly dependent on rainfall. The area is rich in rock shelters and both primary and secondary sources of high-quality siliceous rocks. To the South there are basaltic plateaus and open plains where no such sources have been identified. Although a relatively big space was explored, rock structures forming groups were located in only a small part of it. In this paper we seek to analyze the reasons for their location and the way in which they were used. In order to do this, we present information related to their frequency, characteristics, and the archaeological context recovered. In addition, in order to understand the way in which they were used, the visibility of nearby environments was analyzed with Geographical Information Systems, using a DEM (Digital Elevation Model) developed by the Argentine *Instituto Geográfico Nacional* (IGN). Results obtained indicate that the rock structures were built in places higher than the surroundings, using immediately available rocks. According to the visibility analysis, they worked in an articulated way as part of collective hunting strategies. The characteristics and composition of the artifact assemblages recovered indicate that different activities took place at these sites during the Late Holocene. The identification of the hunting blinds in a specific area within the SDM and their absence in the remaining study area to the North and South suggest that this area was selected for planned collective hunting.

Keywords Deseado Massif · Patagonia · Hunter-gatherers · Hunting blinds · Collective hunting strategies

---

N. V. Franco (✉) · L. Vetrisano · N. A. Cirigliano · P. E. Bianchi
IMHICIHU-CONICET, Buenos Aires, Argentina

B. L. Gilio
CIT Santa Cruz-CONICET, Río Gallegos, Argentina

N. V. Franco
Universidad de Buenos Aires, FFyL, Dpto. Cs. Antropológicas, Buenos Aires, Argentina

© Springer Nature Switzerland AG 2021
J. B. Belardi et al. (eds.), *Ancient Hunting Strategies in Southern South America*,
The Latin American Studies Book Series,
https://doi.org/10.1007/978-3-030-61187-3_12

12.1 Introduction

The Deseado Massif is a morphostructural region of 60,000 km^2 located near the center of the Santa Cruz Province, North of the Chico River, in Southern Patagonia. The region was shaped by volcanic activity during the Jurassic (De Giusto et al. 1980). It has plenty of caves and rockshelters as well as excellent raw materials for high-quality flintknapping, which are more abundant to the North of our study area (e.g. Panza et al. 1998; Cattáneo 2000; Panza and Haller 2002; Miotti and Salemme 2003; Cattáneo 2004; Echeveste 2005; Paunero et al. 2007; Hermo 2008; Paunero 2009; Skarbun 2009; Franco et al. 2015a).

The Southern End of the Deseado Massif (SDM) is characterized by its heterogeneity, with different resources—such as high-quality raw materials, caves, rockshelters, and water—varying over distances of 2 km or more. Water is a critical resource in the region today, and the differences in availability and reliability between areas may have influenced hunter-gatherer strategies in the past, as previous studies have shown, both here and to the North of the Massif (Brook et al. 2013; Mosquera 2018). In the study area there are several closed depressions in volcanic and sedimentary rocks that contain seasonal shallow lakes and, occasionally, permanent bodies of water. To the South of the Deseado Massif, there are several low plateaus formed by interbedded lava flows and till deposits (Coronato et al. 2008). Caves are less common but there are springs and small streams. Raw material availability is also markedly different between the Deseado Massif and the area to its South, where sampling has shown that high-quality siliceous rocks are far less abundant, and primary sources of siliceous rocks have not been found yet (Franco et al. 2015b). These differences imply a landscape change between the Southern Deseado Massif and other spaces farther to the South.

The oldest dates of human occupation in the Southern Deseado Massif were obtained at La Gruta 1, where there are dates of ca. 10,840 years BP. The site overlooks a nearby shallow lake and the earliest human occupations correspond to a period more humid than present times (Franco et al. 2010, 2013; Mancini et al. 2012; Brook et al. 2015). Evidence for human occupation is more abundant around 9000–8000 years BP, also during a wetter period, according to palynological and faunistical information (Aguerre 2003; Aguerre and Pagano 2003; Durán et al. 2003; Mancini et al. 2012; Franco et al. 2013; Brook et al. 2015). The area shows human presence until the Late Holocene, although there is no continuous record of utilization at any locality (Aguerre 2003; Rubinos Pérez 2003; Brook et al. 2013; Franco et al. 2013). These discontinuities, which are also apparent at other sites in the Southern Deseado Massif (e.g. Paunero et al. 2007; Paunero 2009; Skarbun 2009; Brook et al. 2013; Mosquera 2018) are consistent with low population densities and the existence of arid periods, as suggested for Patagonia by different researchers (e.g. Borrero 1994–1995; Miotti and Salemme 2004; Brook et al. 2013; Mosquera 2018). During the Late Holocene, three different periods of human occupation were identified in La Gruta 1, one centered around ca. 3400 years BP, one between ca. 1800 and 1400 years BP and the other at ca. 400 years BP (Franco et al. 2013; Brook et al. 2015).

An area of 2000 km² within the Southern Deseado Massif (SDM) was explored using both systematic transects and unsystematic samplings, mainly on foot. Until the moment, open rock structures were identified only in the southern part of the area. They correspond to three archaeological localities which, from East to West, are La Gruta, Melisa, and La Barda, an area of 31.6 km², less than 1.58% of the total explored area. Most of the identified rock structures formed groups. In the three cases (La Gruta, Melisa, and La Barda) several rock structures are located on top of small hills, close to and, in some cases, overlooking small depressions occupied by temporary shallow lakes, suggesting their use as hunting blinds (HBs). In this paper we seek to analyze reasons for the location chosen and the way in which rock structures were used. In order to do this, we give information related to their frequency, characteristics, and archaeological context. In addition, in order to understand the way in which they were used, the visibility of nearby environments was analyzed with Geographical Information Systems, using a DEM (Digital Elevation Model) developed by the Argentine *Instituto Geográfico Nacional* (IGN).

12.2 General Background

The first studies on hunting blinds in Patagonia were done by Gradin in the late 1950s and early 1960s. Based on his findings in the Lake Strobel and Cardiel plateaus (Fig. 12.1), he classified them according to their shape, dividing them between semi-circular, arc, right angled, and incomplete circles (Gradin 1959–1960a, b). The author recognized more than a hundred of these structures that were widespread across the

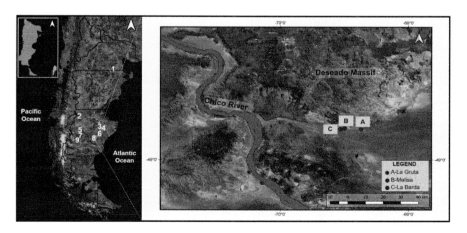

Fig. 12.1 Hunting blinds mentioned in the text: 1. Somuncurá plateau, 2. Lake Buenos Aires; 3. Piedra Museo and Parque Nacional Bosques Petrificados; 4. Bajo Grande, La Primavera and Aguada del Cuero localities; 5. Cerro Pampa; 6. Cerro Vanguardia; 7. Strobel plateau; 8. La Barda, Melisa and La Gruta localities; 9. Lake Cardiel

space. Although they were of different size and shape, they were always facing the predominant winds, which blow from the West, as a way to prevent animals from smelling the occupants (Gradin 1959–1960b). In later articles, Gradin (1971, 1976) reports hunting blinds in the Somuncurá plateau—in North Patagonia—and in the Lake Buenos Aires (Fig. 12.1), closer to our study area. On the basis of his findings, he suggests that these structures would have served two different functions: to give shelter to the hunter-gatherers and to serve as blinds spots during hunting parties. The location of these structures—in higher or lower topographies—and the association with water sources (shallow lakes and wet meadows) would have determined their function. According to this author, historical sources mentioned the utilization of similar structures as small habitational units that could be inhabited by four to six people, using guanaco (*Lama guanicoe*) leather to build the roof. They were frequently occupied in relation to hunting parties and showed association to faunal remains resulting from butchering activities.

In the last decades, different researchers have focused on hunting blinds in Patagonia in relation to various topics such as their distribution and characteristics, zooarchaeology, lithic technology, visibility, rock art and, in few cases, the relationship between morphology, visibility, accessibility, and location of the structures (e.g. García and Pérez de Micou 1979; Gradin 1996; Martinic 2002; Miotti et al. 2004; Magnin 2010; Re 2010; Aragone et al. 2010; Borrero et al. 2011; Goñi et al. 2011–2012; Belardi et al. 2013; Cassiodoro et al. 2014; Dellepiane and Flores Coni 2016; Miotti et al. 2016; Belardi et al. 2017; Dellepiane 2018). We will focus here on the research done closer to our study area and we will make a special mention to the paper by Miotti et al. (2016), who applied viewshed analysis to evaluate the relation between different stone structures and their location in space

During an archaeological rescue project in Cerro Vanguardia (central Deseado Massif, Fig. 12.1), almost 95 km to the North of our study area, Hermo and Vázquez (1999) recognized the presence of a series of semicircular structures of anthropic origin. They were characterized as hunting blinds, in part because of its similarities with those identified by Gradin in the Strobel, Buenos Aires, and Somuncurá plateaus (Gradin 1976, 1996). Lithic artifacts (projectile points, bolas, and flakes) were recovered during the field works, both inside and outside of the structures. These hunting blinds are located on high places and characterized as part of stalking and hunting strategies, because of their direct relation to critical resources: water (shallow lakes), fuel, shelter (caves), and lithic raw material. The author's hypothesis is that the existence of similarities between these strategies and those used at the plateaus, can be attributed to the development of activities by human groups on a large area that includes both spaces.

As part of her doctoral thesis, Magnin (2010) presented the analysis of a varied set of stone structures identified in the Deseado Massif in the localities of Bajo Grande, Piedra Museo, Monumento Nacional Bosques Petrificados, Aguada del Cuero, and La Primavera (Fig. 12.1), around 150 km to the North of our study area. Most of them were hunting blinds, which the author divides in two categories. Category N° 1 includes structures of semicircular shape and small size with a N-S orientation, while the structures that encompass category N° 2 are bigger in size and diverse in shape,

12 Hunting Blinds in the Southern End of the Deseado Massif … 317

ranging from semicircular to circular. The height of the structures ranges between 45 and 64 cm, their width varies between 96 and 298 cm and their length between 128 and 438 cm. In a latter paper, Magnin et al. (2015) use line of sight, viewshed, and least cost paths analysis to generate hypotheses related to hunter-gatherers' strategies in the case of La Primavera archaeological locality (Fig. 12.1). These analyses were integrated with other lines of evidence, mainly from lithic artifacts associated with hunting activities. The results obtained allow them to propose at least the development of three different strategies: 1) the use of a rock structure to monitor sectors with a high natural accessibility; 2) the use of more than one structure to monitor sectors of high natural accessibility, as part of possible group hunting strategies; and 3) the hunting in open spaces or the use of special topographies.

Belardi and Goñi (2006) have postulated that the Strobel Plateau, nearly 124 km to the West of our study area (Fig. 12.1), was intensely utilized as a hunting space during summer, when the guanaco groups were moving along the lakes. According to them, at a supraregional scale, the plateau was a point of convergence—although not necessarily during the same time lapse—that attracted hunter-gatherers from nearby areas due to its availability of resources. Their assumption is based on the examination of two sets of information: the archaeological findings obtained in different sites located on the Lake Cardiel basin (Fig. 12.1) and ecological data, specifically related to faunal distribution and water availability. These hunting blinds were subjected to a more detailed analysis by Flores Coni (2014), in order to categorize this type of structures and account for their variability. They were considered as grouped when there was an association—in terms of visibility and internal structuring—between them, as well as a separation of 50 m or less. A high proportion of hunting blinds is located near shallow lakes, due to the attractiveness of these areas for the local fauna. They present great differences in shape and size, as much as in the rocks used in their construction. The author concludes that the hunting blinds would have had different functions in relation to their location, as part of an anticipated strategy for the use of space, involving redundancy and reutilization (Flores Coni 2014).

Rindel and colleagues (2007) identified hunting blinds in Cerro Pampa locality (Fig. 12.1), 170 km to the Northwest of our study area. The locality is characterized by the presence of abundant water sources, with variable availability. Guanaco was the most exploited taxon, although there were also cut marks on *choique* (*Pterocnemia pennata*). Non-indigenous species such as horse (*Equus caballus*) and sheep (*Ovis aries*) were also present. In the case of guanaco, the prevalence of body parts with low economic value suggests that primary butchering took place at these sites. Lithic tools (end scrapers and projectile points) and debitage were also recovered. The authors conclude that Cerro Pampa was utilized by hunter-gatherer groups as part of a logistical strategy developed during the late Holocene, with seasonal and redundant uses of the space, involving the frequent utilization of the hunting blinds.

Belardi et al. (2017) synthesize previous research about this topic in the already mentioned western basaltic plateaus and in the central Deseado Massif. Their main objective is oriented toward the study of hunting tactics developed by hunter-gatherers during late Holocene times. They focus on the analysis of hunting blinds location, distribution, and spatial arrangements across the space and conclude that communal hunting seems to have been more important in the western basaltic plateaus. They recognized an individual tactic as well as different communal tactics, which relate to the location of a group of hunting blinds in the plains (tactic 2), near the entrance or exit of guanacos to the ponds (tactics 3 and 4), on the downward slope of the plateau (tactic 5) or on the plains between ponds (tactic 6). In the case of linear arrangements of hunting blinds, they understand that the hunter-gatherers used natural narrows in order to direct guanacos to them (tactic 7).

A final mention must be done, regarding the viewshed analysis performed by Miotti et al. (2016) at the Somuncurá plateau, in order to evaluate the relationship between morphology, visibility, accessibility, and location of rock structures positioned in different landscape units. The results obtained allowed them to recognize the organization of the landscape structure with spaces related to domestic and control activities. The radiocarbon dates indicate that these rock structures correspond to the Late Holocene (Miotti et al. 2016).

12.3 Methodology

The rock structures analyzed here were located as part of the surveys carried out in our study area. In order to define which rock structures could be considered as hunting blinds (HBs), we took into account the previous definitions developed by other researchers in Patagonia. In our case we defined the hunting blinds as open structures made of the accumulation of rocks in a variety of ways. Each of the hunting blinds was described considering several characteristics:

a. Morphology: in arc, semicircular, circular, in angle and linear, following Gradin (1959–1960b)
b. Quantity of rows of cobbles or blocks used in the construction of the wall, as well as the incorporation of natural outcrops into their construction
c. Raw material provenance (immediately available or not)
d. Height of the wall from the ground, including any natural feature used in the wall
e. Measurements in regard to the overall size of the hunting blinds, taking into consideration the particularities of each form, e.g., the cord length and the height of the segment, in the case of semicircular structures. They are indicated as measurements 1 and 2 (Fig. 12.2)
f. GPS (Global Positioning System) position
g. Altitude
h. Main cardinal orientation of the wall of the structure

In addition, through the use of Geographic Information Systems (GIS), viewshed analyses were performed with the aim of evaluating the spatial relationship between each one of the hunting blinds as well as between them and the topography. This kind of spatial analysis can be defined as the identification of a set of locations or points in a landscape that are visible from a specific viewpoint, based solely on topography and with a given maximum viewing distance (Wheatley and Gillings 2000; Llobera

Fig. 12.2 Diagram of the structures showing the measurements taken into account: A: ARC MORPHOLOGY: Measurement 1—Major axis; Measurement 2—Semi-minor axis. B: SEMICIRCULAR MORPHOLOGY: Measurement 1—Cord length; Measurement 2—Height of the segment. C: CIRCULAR MORPHOLOGY: Measurement 1—Diameter

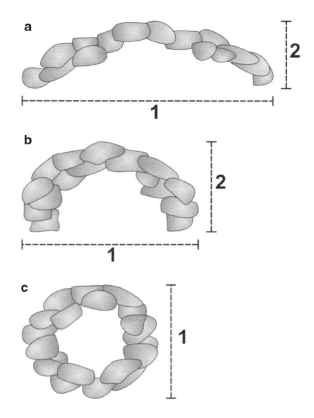

2003; García et al. 2006; Magnin et al. 2015; Miotti et al. 2016). Viewsheds were calculated using the Global Mapper 17 software and a raster Digital Elevation Model (DEM) developed by the Argentine *Instituto Geográfico Nacional* (2018), with an approximate spatial resolution of 30 m (1 arc per second). Once the viewpoint was established, which in this case coincided with the geographical location of each hunting blind, the algorithm calculates a new binary raster, where the cells with a value of 1 are visible and those with a value of 0 are invisible (García et al. 2006). A maximum viewing perimeter of 5 km was defined. After comparing the views registered in the field with different results obtained with the viewshed analysis, the observer height was established at 1 m, taking into account that humans could have used the hunting blinds as a way of hiding from potential prey (Gradin 1959–1960b, 1976). The azimuth, i.e., the horizontal angle that limits the visual exploration, was established in 360°. We use ArcMap 10 software to calculate the visibility area from each HB (Tables 12.2, 12.5, and 12.7).

In all the cases we registered the archaeological evidence related to the structures, i.e., found within the hunting blinds or up to distances of 5 m from them. Several surface collections were done, both through transects and grids located in selected places. In order to explore the possibility of stratigraphic findings, we dug several test pits both inside the area limited by the structures and outside them, within a hypothetical toss area. Test pits had dimensions between 25 and 50 cm and reached the base rock or between 20 and 32 cm depths, if there were no findings. The artifact composition recovered in each one of the archaeological localities was analyzed following the criteria proposed by Aschero (1975, 1983). Cores were categorized as a category on its own, due to the kind of information they can provide. In addition, the main characteristics of projectile points and end scrapers were compared to those of the regional record as a way to estimate the hunting blinds chronology.

12.4 Results

As it has been mentioned, results are presented divided by archaeological localities from East to West. In the three cases, the hunting blinds are located nearby shallow lakes that depend on rainfall. As previously mentioned, water is a critical resource in the area and the lakes and ponds tend to serve as a place of attraction to guanaco groups, which have been the main prey during the whole period of human occupation of the area and Patagonia in general.

12.4.1 Hunting Blinds Characteristics and Visibility of Nearby Spaces

12.4.1.1 La Gruta

At La Gruta locality six hunting blinds (HBs) were located during our surveys (Figs. 12.1, 12.3, and 12.4). They are close to a shallow lake that lies within a big depression, which was bigger during more humid periods in the past (Brook et al. 2013, 2015). The total dispersion of the structures is an area of 0.1 km^2. All

Fig. 12.3 View of each of the shallow lakes mentioned in the article. 1: La Gruta; 2: Melisa; 3: La Barda

Fig. 12.4 Some of the hunting blinds discussed in the article. 1: La Gruta HB B; 2: La Gruta HB F; 3: Melisa HB B; 4: Melisa HB D; 5: La Barda HB C; 6: La Barda HB F

the hunting blinds are semicircular in shape (Figs. 12.3 and 12.4) and are built using immediately available rocks. Some of the structures take advantage of naturally outcropping boulders to use as the base of the walls. The ones closer to the shallow lake—HBs A, B, and C—have the same orientation, pointing to the Southwest, in the general direction of the shallow lake. The others (HBs D, E, and F) face West, facing also the lagoon (Table 12.1). It is also worth considering that in the region the winds blow predominantly from the West, so this kind of orientation could prevent the dissemination of the hunters' scent.

Hunting blinds dimensions are highly variable (Table 12.1), varying between 271 and 680 cm in the case of the cord length and between 136 and 442 cm in the case of the segment height. With only one exception, wall height ranges between 50 and 61 cm, in this last case including the natural outcrop (Table 12.1).

The viewshed analyses allowed us to further differentiate between HBs. Table 12.2 indicates the visibility to other HBs, as well as those to the shallow lake, the general

Table 12.1 Summary of HBs characteristics at La Gruta locality

Name	Morphology	Rows of rocks	Wall height (cm)	M. 1 (cm)	M. 2 (cm)	Altitude (masl)	Cardinal orientation
HB A	Semicircular	1 (plus outcrop)	94	680	442	309	SW
HB B	Semicircular	2	50	272	170	288	SW
HB C	Semicircular	1 (plus outcrop)	61	476	204	283	SW
HB D	Semicircular	2	55	816	272	298	W
HB E	Semicircular	2	55	340	136	297	W
HB F	Semicircular	2	60	476	204	297	W

Legend: HB: hunting blind; M.: measurement

Table 12.2 Visual coverage and visibility from the different HBs at La Gruta locality

HB	Visual coverage				Visibility (km^2)
	Other HBs	Lagoon	Depression	S plateau	
A	B – C – D – E – F	T	T	T	23
B	D	T	P	P	8
C	D – E	P	P	P	7
D	A - C - E - F	T	P	T	12
E	A - C - D - F	P	P	T	11
F	A - B - E	P	P	T	9

Legend: HB: hunting blind; T: total; P: partial

depression, and the plateau located to the South. The total visibility from each hunting blind (HB) is also indicated.

The structure named HB A stands out as the one with the most extensive viewshed, largely due to its higher altitude (309 masl, Tables 12.2 and 12.3). It is located 250 m away from the shallow lake and 30 m above it in altitude.

HB B (Fig. 12.5) is the closest to the shallow lake, 170 m away from it and 9 m above it. It lies 670 m to the Southeast of HB A. HB C is 200 m away from HB B and 350 m away from the shallow lake, while it is 9 m above it. The rest of the hunting blinds, HBs D, E, and F are situated 930 m to the Southeast of HB C, 1000 m to the East of the shallow lake, and 30 m above it. They are aligned from West to East and are separated less than 20 m from each other.

HB A is the only hunting blind that visually covers all the other structures, as well as most of the shallow lake and its surroundings (Table 12.2). Based on this, we interpret that this hunting blind could have served for spotting the movements of prey and, at the same time, for sending indications, through visual signals, to the other hunting blinds. The position of HB A, located in a hill much higher than the shallow lake and with a steep slope, suggests that the hunters stationed in it did not get

Table 12.3 Summary of hunting blinds characteristics at Melisa archaeological locality

Name	Morphology	Rows of rocks	Wall height (cm)	M. 1 (cm)	M. 2 (cm)	Altitude (masl)	Cardinal orientation
HB A	Semicircular	4	65	272	136	332	W
HB B	Semicircular	3	40	272	136	297	W
HB C	Semicircular	2	55	204	136	324	W
HB D	Circular	1	66	250	–	330	–
HB E	Semicircular	2	55	204	68	327	W
HB F	Semicircular	2	45	204	102	324	W
HB G	Semicircular	1	65	272	68	326	W

Legend: HB.: hunting blind; M.: measurement

12 Hunting Blinds in the Southern End of the Deseado Massif ... 323

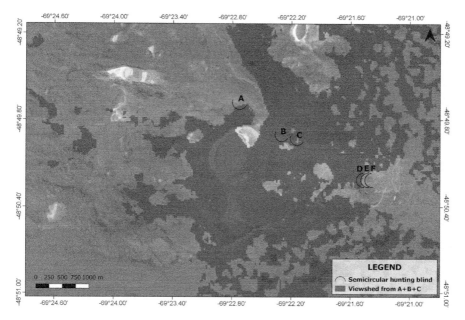

Fig. 12.5 Map of La Gruta locality showing the combined viewsheds from HBs A, B, and C

involved directly with the prey. In this sense, all the other HBs lie to the East, further away from HB A. This eastward position could also be related to the fact that the slopes that led to the shallow lake's depression are more pronounced toward the West and the Southwest, where some parts of the edge of the plateau even have sandstone cliffs. A gentler slope to the East could imply a better route for the guanacos leaving the depression.

HBs B and C are the closest to the shallow lake and almost at its level. Together they visually cover all of the shallow lake and its basin (Table 12.2); this could mean that the hunters using them would be more involved in the interception of prey. However, they cannot see each other, so they would have depended on HB A for coordination (Fig. 12.5).

The easternmost hunting blinds, HBs D, E, and F, are very close between them, allowing coordination. Although they lie 1800 m to the Southeast of HB A, they could have used visual signals to communicate, as they are intervisible (Fig. 12.5). Due to the distance involved this kind of visual signals would be the only available way to communicate.

As we mentioned before, the location of HB A suggests that it was not able to work on its own and so it seems to have been used together with HBs B and C, which have better locations in order to intercept prey. Also, due to its higher altitude in relation to the shallow lake, it probably would not have worked alone. The cluster comprising HBs D, E, and F contrast with this situation. Their combined viewshed allows the spotting of prey in the shallow lake and its depression, as it covers all of

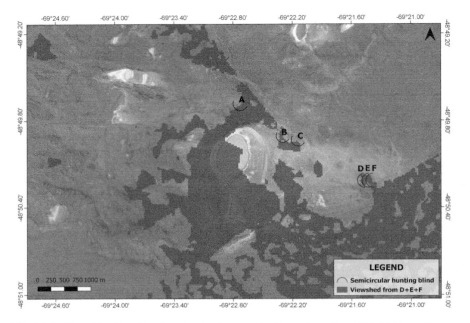

Fig. 12.6 Map of La Gruta locality showing the combined viewsheds from HBs D, E, and F

its southern half (Fig. 12.6). In this sense, these hunting blinds could be independent of the rest, working as a separate group. In addition, it is worth noting that between these three hunting blinds and the two closest to the shallow lake lie two paths that, running between small hills, lead outside the depression toward the Northeast. This path is better covered by the westernmost structures: HBs A, B, and C. HB D and HB E only cover it partially, while HB F has almost no visuals of the area.

12.4.1.2 Melisa

This locality comprises seven hunting blinds located in a small hill to the North side of a shallow lake (Figs. 12.3 and 12.4). They are closer between them than in the previous case, scattered in an area of less than 0.04 km^2, with a difference in altitude of less than 15 m between them. The shallow lake is 20 m below the lowest hunting blind. All the structures face to the West and are semicircular in shape (Fig. 12.4, Table 12.3) with the exception of one that is fully enclosed, taking a circular shape. Although it is a closed structure, we included it within the description because it is closely related to the other ones. A different function can probably be attributed to it.

All the hunting blinds were built using rocks immediately available, but the walls vary in the amount of rows and their overall size. In this case, there is less variability in the cord length, which ranges between 204 and 272 cm, while the variation of the segment height is bigger.

The viewshed analysis allows us to divide the space visually covered from the hunting blinds in four sectors: the shallow lake itself, the small hills and streams to the West, the slope of the hills South of the shallow lake, and a bigger stream to the East. The shallow lake is the least visible sector, fully covered only by HB B and F, and partially covered by HB A and E (Table 12.4).

Overall, most of the structures visually cover the surroundings of the shallow lake to the South, the West, and the East (Figs. 12.7 and 12.8). In this sense, it seems that their objective was not only to spot the guanacos within the shallow lake, but also to spot their movements entering or leaving it. This means that even in the case that the hunting blinds were not contemporaneous they would have worked mainly spotting the surroundings of the shallow lake.

The low hills to the South of the shallow lake are better covered by HBs A, B, E, and F (Fig. 12.7). All these HBs also cover the hills and streams to the West, which have a general slope toward the shallow lake. The functioning of these structures as a group would have been possible as there is good intervisibility among them. HBs C and D are two more hunting blinds that cover the area further South, but do not have good coverage of the West side (Table 12.4). In regard to the stream that runs in a NW-SE direction, to the East of the shallow lake and the hunting blinds, it is also well covered by most of the structures (Table 12.5, Figs. 12.7 and 12.8). This means that the spotting of all the surroundings of the shallow lake, to the West, to the East, and to the South could have been coordinated, as some hunting blinds cover more than one sector at the same time or they can communicate with other structures that cover these other sectors. If we consider the streams at both sides, West and East, as possible passageways to the shallow lake, both have the same amount of coverage, with four hunting blinds providing full coverage and two more providing partial coverage. The only difference between the coverage of each sector is that the viewshed of the West sector is associated with the view of the land to the South, while there is no such association regarding the East sector. This implies the

Table 12.4 Visual coverage and visibility from the different HBs at Melisa locality

HB	Visual coverage					Visibility (km^2)
	Other HBs	Lagoon	W hills	S hills	E stream	
A	B - D - E	P	T	T	P	13.39
B	A	T	T	T	–	7.66
C	E - F	–	–	P	T	13.34
D	E - F	–	P	T	T	12
E	D - F	P	T	T	T	10
F	E	T	T	T	P	13.39
G	–	–	–	–	T	6.13

Legend: HB: hunting blind; T: total; P: partial

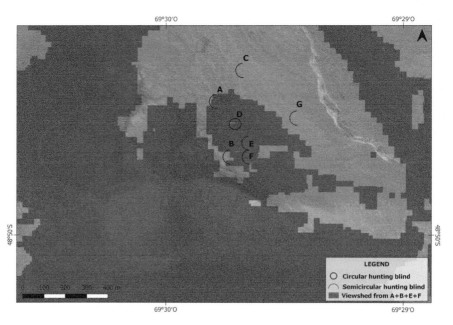

Fig. 12.7 Map of the Melisa locality showing the combined viewsheds from HBs A, B, E, and F

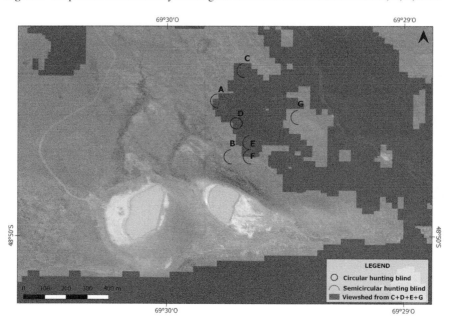

Fig. 12.8 Map of the Melisa locality showing the combined viewsheds from HBs C, D, E, and G

12 Hunting Blinds in the Southern End of the Deseado Massif …

Table 12.5 Summary of HBs characteristics at La Barda locality

Name	Morphology	Rows of rocks	Wall height (cm)	M. 1 (cm)	M. 2 (cm)	Altitude (masl)	Cardinal orientation
HB A	Arc	2	45	408	68	339	W
HB B	Semicircular	1	20	204	68	337	S
HB C	Semicircular	2	60	272	68	340	NW
HB D	Semicircular	1	50	204	102	335	NW
HB E	Arc	1	60	680	68	335	SW
HB F	Semicircular	4	85	306	136	343	W
HB G	Arc	1	41	306	17	324	W
HB H	Semicircular	1	30	136	68	379	W
HB I	Semicircular	1	46	204	102	324	NW
HB J	Arc	1	40	340	136	487	S
HB K	Semicircular	1	33	102	68	596	W
HB L	Semicircular	1	28	500	68	347	SW

Reference: HB. Hunting blind; M.: measurement

intention of establishing the visual coverage of a larger area, further in distance and with a general Southwest-Northeast direction. The larger visual coverage would be useful to spot the guanacos with enough anticipation. In this case, it would mean that the hunters waited for the guanacos to enter the shallow lake from the West. Once they faced the hunting blinds, guanacos could be forced toward the eastward stream as a way out of the shallow lake, hence the need for the hunters to cover both sectors at the same time. A fact that supports this interpretation is that the hunting blinds which lie closer to the eastern stream—HBs D, E, F, and G—are also the ones visually covering it.

A final mention involves HB G. Although its viewshed includes the eastern stream, it seems that it was not meant to coordinate actions with other hunting blinds. It does not offer a view to other structures and it cannot be seen from any other structures, forbidding the use of visual signals. It is also 100 m away from the nearest structure, making it impossible to hear or to speak with the hunters stationed at any other structure. The only sector that this hunting blind covers is the eastern stream which is well covered by several structures that lie near it. In this sense, HB G could serve as an additional post for hunters that waited for the guanacos to be routed toward the stream.

12.4.1.3 La Barda

La Barda locality is merely 1.8 km eastwards from Melisa. In this case 12 HBs were identified during fieldwork. They are located in a hill South of the shallow lake

(Figs. 12.1, 12.3, and 12.4), divided in two groups separated by 345 m. The western group lies in the highest part of the hill and includes HBs A, B, C, D, E, and F (see some examples in Fig. 12.4). They are separated from each other by distances ranging between 140 and 25 m, in an area of 15,000 m^2. The eastern group is located in an almost plain sector of the hill slope to the Southeast. It is composed by HBs G, H, I, J, and K, which are separated from each other by distances ranging between 125 and 2 m and dispersed over an area of 4000 m^2. The only exception to this grouping is HB L, which is located to the Northeast on top of a small plateau that has a small cliff facing the shallow lake to the Southwest. Although this set of hunting blinds is larger than the previous cases, it also shows certain homogeneity, repeating some of the characteristics previously observed. This is the case of the rocks used, which are immediately available in all the cases (Table 12.6). Most of the hunting blinds are semicircular in shape, having the remaining four cases an arc morphology (Table 12.5). The height of the walls varies, but in almost all the cases it is made of a single row of rocks. The only exceptions are two structures with two rows and one which has four rows. This last case has the highest wall, reaching 85 cm, which is 25 cm more than the next in height. The overall dimension of the structures is rather heterogeneous.

The main difference with respect to the previous cases lies in the orientation of the hunting blinds, which is very heterogeneous. Most of the structures again have a general westward orientation, more specifically 5 face the West, 3 the Northwest, and 2 the Southwest, but 2 more face the South. As mentioned above, because almost all of the structures lie in two groups, close to each other and in the same terrain feature, the topography and their location in relation to the shallow lake does not

Table 12.6 Visual coverage and visibility from the different HBs at La Barda locality

Location	HB	Visual coverage					Visibility (km^2)
		Other HBs	Other group	Hill	South	W	
W group	A	–	–	–	–	T	7
	B	D - E - G - H - I - J	T	T	T	P	13
	C	G - H - I	T	T	P	T	14
	D	E - G - H - I - J	T	T	P	–	11
	E	D - G - H - I - J	T	T	P	–	11
	F	L - J	P	P	P	T	17
E group	G	B - D - E - H – I -K	T	T	T	–	10
	H	B - D - E - G - I -K	T	T	T	–	9
	I	B - D - E - G - H- K	T	T	T	–	9
	J	B – D – E – G - L	T	T	T	–	15
	K	B – D - E	P	P	T	–	9
N	L	F	–	–	–	P	17

Legend: HB: hunting blind; W group: Western group; E group: Eastern group; N group: Northern group; S: South; W: west of the shallow lake; T: total; P: partial seem to explain their different orientations. HB L, the hunting blind exceptionally located in the northern plateau, seems to be oriented toward the shallow lake.

The viewshed analysis shows that besides certain intervisibility between hunting blinds and the visual coverage of the hill where the structures are located, the areas mostly covered are the West and South of the shallow lake. The hunting blinds that provide some kind of additional coverage are HBs A, F, J, and L, although some of them are rather isolated in terms of intervisibility and distance to other structures (Table 12.6).

HB A cannot be seen from any other structure and it does not provide coverage of any structure either. It is also spatially isolated as it lays 80 m away from the nearest structure. It provides some kind of additional coverage as its viewshed to the West of the shallow lake is considerably wider than that of the other structures (Table 12.6). In this sense it could be interpreted as an individual hunting blind or as serving another purpose. HB F only has intervisibility with HB L and it cannot be seen from any other HB, while the nearest structure lies 140 m away (Table 12.6). As mentioned before, HB L is too far away to the NE and it also cannot be seen from any other structure, making it even more isolated. In order to coordinate actions with other hunting blinds, these three structures would depend on the shared viewshed of the hill itself and the South of the shallow lake (Fig. 12.9).

The HBs providing coverage that are better suited for coordinated actions are HBs J and I, as they have coverage of HB G and intervisibility with most of the western group of hunting blinds (Table 12.6, Fig. 12.9). The fact that some of these structures

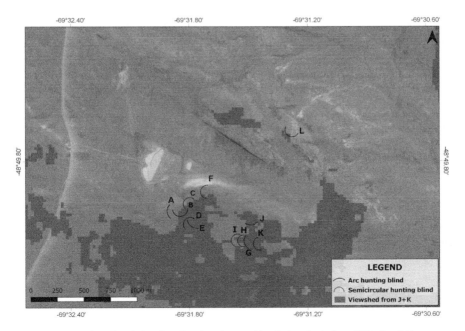

Fig. 12.9 Map of La Barda locality showing the combined viewsheds from HBs J and K

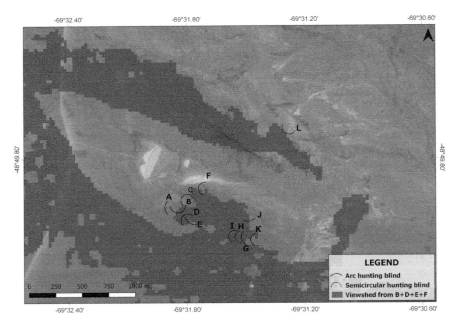

Fig. 12.10 Map of La Barda locality showing the combined viewsheds from HBs B, D, E, and F

are more isolated compared to the rest opens up the possibility that they could have worked as a separate group and, eventually, correspond to other time spans, or with some other purpose besides spotting prey.

As we mentioned before, the rest of the hunting blinds lie clustered in two groups. The structures that form each group have enough intervisibility to have worked coordinated as a whole (Figs. 12.10, 12.11, and 12.12). Also, as there is almost total intervisibility between both groups, they could have worked together as well. The land they can spot to the South has a general slope to the SE that leads to several streams and shallows. The good visual coverage of the hunting blinds is due to their higher position, between 10 and 20 m above the terrain to their South. If this area was a passage for the guanacos to reach the shallows, while moving following the slope, the two groups of hunting blinds would have a chance of interception from West to East.

12.4.2 The Archaeological Record Related to the Hunting Blinds

Artifacts related to the rock structures were recovered on the surface in all the archaeological localities. Flakes and blades without retouch (included within the debitage category in Table 12.7) are the most frequent kind of artifacts recovered: 94.23% of

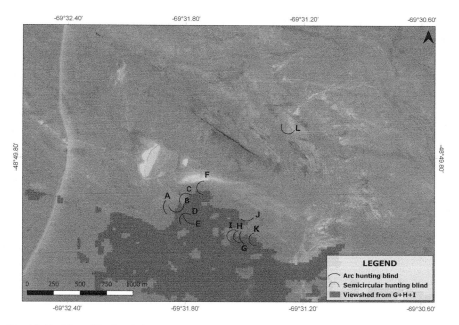

Fig. 12.11 Map of La Barda locality showing the combined viewsheds from HBs G, H, and I

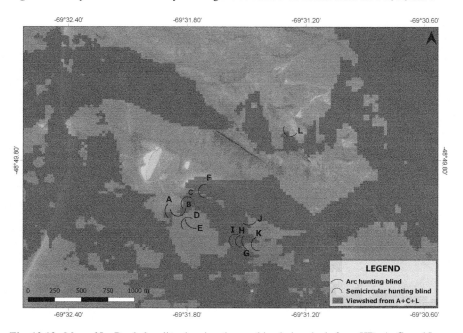

Fig. 12.12 Map of La Barda locality showing the combined viewsheds from HBs A, C, and L

Table 12.7 Artifacts recovered on the surface at the three archaeological localities, within or close to the rock structures

Artifacts recovered	La Gruta	Melisa	La Barda
Debitage	1486	1359	88
Cores	45	20	3
Projectile points	8	3	11
Bolas	2	0	0
End scrapers	21	24	2
Sidescrapers	9	5	7
Knives	0	1	1
Drills	1	0	0
Bifacial artifacts	6	20	1
Notches	1	0	0
Hammer stone	1	0	0
Total number	1580	1432	113

the sample in the case of La Gruta, 94.56% in the case of Melisa, and 81.48% in La Barda archaeological localities.

12.4.2.1   La Gruta

In this case, most of the tools recovered on the surface are unifacial (Table 12.8). End scrapers are the most frequent type of tool recovered (more than 42% of the tool sample). Unifacial tools also include sidescrapers, drills, and notches. Bifacial artifacts were also recovered, including projectile points. Most of them are proximal ends of medium and/or small stemmed ones. A bifacial unstemmed resharpened projectile point was also discarded at the site. The sample includes a bifacial

Table 12.8 Comparison of dimensions of the hunting blinds located at the different archaeological localities

Locality	*n*	Variable	Max	Min	Mean	SD
La Gruta	6	Height of the wall	94	50	62.5	15.93
		Cord length	816	272	510	205.13
		Height of the segment	442	136	238	109.65
Melisa	7	Height of the wall	65	40	55.86	10.33
		Cord length	272	204	239.71	34.3
		Height of the segment	200	68	120.86	46.36
La Barda	12	Height of the wall	85	20	44.83	17.58
		Cord length	680	102	305.17	162.91
		Height of the segment	136	17	80.75	33.32

Legend: Max: maximum; Min: minimum

preform of a projectile point, broken during the manufacturing process, indicating the flintknapping of this kind of tools next to the hunting blinds. *Bolas* are also part of the sample. The presence of cores and the existence of rejuvenation flakes also points out to manufacture activities being done at the site. In this sense, the presence of primary and secondary flakes would also point in this direction. Blades with sizes consistent to those recovered in Central and South Patagonia during the Late Holocene (Aschero 1987; Gradin et al. 1979) were recovered, suggesting that they were discarded during this time period. They were used as blanks for different types of tools. End scrapers vary in width between 15 and 35 mm, and in thickness between 4 and 18 mm, allowing us to attribute them to Late Holocene times.

Test pits were carried out in the interior of HB D (2), in the exterior of HB E (1), and the interior and exterior or HB F (3). In all the cases, test pits were dug close to the hunting blind walls, where sedimentation allowed it. Very few lithic debris as well as small bones without cultural marks were recovered.

12.4.2.2 Melisa

In this case, most of the tools recovered on the surface are unifacial, most of them being endscrapers (more than 45% of the tool sample; Table 12.7). There is a high percentage of bifacial artifacts (more than 43% of the tools), composed of projectile points and a preform. Cores were also recovered at the site. The presence of the cores and a rejuvenation core flake indicates that initial stages of artifact manufacture were taking place at the site. The existence of a resharpening flake suggests last stage manufacturing activities also took place at the site. Blades were recovered and also used as blanks for endscrapers, with widths of less than 29 mm and thickness less than 9 mm. Their sizes are consistent with the ones recovered in other places of Central and South Patagonia during the Late Holocene (i.e. Aschero 1987; Gradin et al. 1979), and most of the assemblage can tentatively be attributed to this time frame.

In the case of Melisa, two test pits were carried out in the interior of HB C, which show almost no sediment accumulation. In the case of HB G, two test pits were made in its interior; only one bone without cultural marks was recovered in one of them, very close to the hunting blind wall. Although there was sediment in the case of HBs F and D, the test pits made in the interior of each one provided no findings (Fig. 12.4).

12.4.2.3 La Barda

The small quantity of artifacts in the case of La Barda is surprising, especially taking into account that the number of hunting blinds in this area is higher than the ones at La Gruta and Melisa. This can probably be related to a different use of this space and/or to the location of this place very close to an old road and a ranch. Its owner, according to local inhabitants, had an important collection of projectile points and other artifacts, which was destroyed in a fire. La Barda is also nowadays located besides the access of a mining company. In this case, sidescrapers are the most frequent tools and only two endscrapers were recovered, both of them fragmented. Surprisingly, projectile points are an important part of the sample (50% of the tool sample). Most of them are bifacially stemmed projectile points, which according to the bibliography can be attributed to Late Holocene times (i.e. Aschero 1987; Gradin et al. 1979; Guráieb 2000, 2004).

A test pit made in the interior of HB G, underneath the wall, provided only small debris, without any datable material, while a test pit made in the interior of HB C did not provide archaeological material.

12.4.3 Comparison Between Cases and Estimated Chronologies

Data obtained show that the number or hunting blinds is roughly the same at La Gruta and Melisa localities, while in the case of La Barda it almost doubles it (Tables 12.1, 12.3, 12.5, and 12.8). The minimum variability in Measure 1, which is the cord length in most of the cases, and in the height of the wall corresponds to Melisa, while Measure 2, which is the height of the segment in most the cases, has the smallest variation in the case of La Barda. The shorter records of Measure 1 have also been identified in Melisa, while the ones of La Gruta are the longest ones.

Altitudes oscillate between 288 masl (in the case of La Gruta) and 596 masl (La Barda). Altitudes increase from East to West (La Gruta: 288–309 masl; Melisa: 297–332 masl; La Barda: 324–596 masl). In the case of La Gruta and Melisa, hunting blinds are located between 9 and 30 m above the shallow lakes. Most of the hunting blinds in the case of La Barda seems to have been related to spaces located to its South, and are located between 10 and 20 m above this terrain.

If we compare the results obtained at the three archaeological localities, most of the hunting blinds are semicircular (n=20, 80% of the sample). A circular structure was identified at Melisa, and four in arc shape in the case of La Barda.

As we mentioned before, the prevailing winds come from the West and due to their strong nature in the region, this could be an additional factor worth considering to explain the general westward orientation of the hunting blinds. The three localities comprise 25 HBs, 11 of them (including all the structures in Melisa with the exception of the circular one) face the West, 8 face the Southwest, 3 the Northwest, and 2 the South. This could imply that the hunting blinds could have been utilized to help hiding from the prey but in a way that could also help to prevent the dissemination of the hunters' scent.

The HBs' orientation, along with some of the tools recovered (projectile points and *bolas*) point to the utilization of these spaces for hunting activities. This is specially the case at La Barda locality, where there is a high frequency of projectile points. It must be mentioned, however, that in this case the sample is small. Cores were introduced to most of the hunting blinds. The presence of core rejuvenation flakes suggests that initial stages of artifact manufacture took place at the HBs. In addition, preforms of bifacial projectile points and tool resharpening flakes indicate that manufacturing activities took place at least in the cases of La Gruta and Melisa. The presence of end and sidescrapers in all the archaeological localities, in addition to drills and notches in the case of La Gruta, suggest that other activities took place at these localities. They were probably related to hide processing.

Although test pits were carried out in each one of the localities, in some cases both in the interior and exterior of the hunting blinds, datable material could not be recovered. However, the characteristics of some of the tools can give us clues about their chronologies. Bifacially stemmed projectile points, which both in Central and South Patagonia have chronologies attributed to the Late Holocene, were recovered at the three localities, suggesting that hunting blinds can probably correspond to this period. For example, in the case of the South of Lake Argentino, the so-called Fell IV stemmed projectile points were dated at ca. 2000 years BP, although the date should be used with caution due to the small size of the sample (Franco 2002). In Lake Posadas, the same type of projectile points was dated at ca. 1420 years BP (Guráieb 2000, 2004). In the case of the small bifacially stemmed projectile points, they have chronologies of ca. 650 years BP at the steppes North of Lake Argentino (Franco 2002), and of ca. 490 years BP at Salitroso Lake (García Guraieb et al. 2007). In central Patagonia, medium and small stemmed projectile points have dates between 1600 and 160 years BP (Aschero 1987; Gradin et al. 1979; Sacchi 2013). Although we recovered a few samples of unstemmed projectile points in relation to HBs, which could be related to earlier times, their very low frequency could mean that they were discarded before the construction of the rock structures. Until the moment, most of the evidence related to the HBs seems to correspond to the Late Holocene, as indicated also by the small size of the end-scrapers recovered and the utilization of small blades as blanks (Aschero 1987; Gradin et al. 1979).

12.5 Discussion and Perspectives

Rock structures were identified in the extreme South of the Deseado Massif, in an area of 36.2 km^2. Until the moment, similar structures were not identified in the remaining 2000 km^2 explored through systematic and unsystematic samples, both to the North and South. Most of the structures are open ones, similar to some identified in the central Deseado Massif, some 150 km to the North of the area (Hermo and Vázquez 1999; Magnin 2010) and in the high plateaus of the Northwestern Santa Cruz province, located around 140 km to the west of our study area (Gradin 1959–1960a, 1976; Goñi 2000–2002; Belardi and Goñi 2006; Espinosa et al. 2009; Aragone et al. 2010; Cassiodoro and Flores Coni 2010; Goñi 2010; Magnin 2010; Cassiodoro et al. 2013; Belardi et al. 2017; Re et al. 2017). In these cases, they were mostly attributed to hunting activities.

The composition of the lithic record recovered (e.g., projectile points, *bolas*, endscrapers, sidescrapers, and drills) suggests that, in addition to hunting, other activities took place near the HBs, as for example, hide processing. Flintknapping activities also took place at these sites, as the presence of cores, core rejuvenation flakes and broken bifacial preforms suggest. Flintknapping activities while watching game is an expected activity, as suggested by ethnographic information from other spaces (Binford 1978).

Although the test pits made at the HBs did not provide datable material, the morphology of the projectile points and the dimensions of the end scrapers made on blades, suggest that they can be attributed to the Late Holocene. The quantity of tools recovered in stratigraphy at La Gruta is small. However, the characteristics of the artifacts recovered at the HBs are similar to those recovered at the Late Holocene both at La Gruta locality (Cirigliano 2016) and in spaces to the North (Aschero 1987; Gradin et al. 1979). This is consistent with information obtained to the Northwest, where hunting blinds have dates between ca. 2010 and 170 years BP (Goñi 2000–2002; Goñi et al. 2000–2002, 2010).

In all the cases identified at the Southern Deseado Massif, hunting blinds are located in places higher than the surroundings, with and without direct visibility of the nearby shallow lakes. Both immediately available rocks and outcrops were used for their construction. Visibility analysis performed indicates that most of them worked together, in a coordinated manner. These results indicate that, in the Southern Deseado Massif, hunting would have been a collective planned strategy. Following Belardi et al. (2017), the case of La Gruta seems to correspond to tactic 4, with hunters waiting for guanacos to leave the shallow lakes. Melisa could correspond to tactic 3 or 4, where guanacos are intercepted entering or leaving the shallow lake. Finally, in the case of La Barda, most of the hunting blinds can be interpreted as tactic 5, with the guanaco moving downward the slope. In all the cases, some of the structures could have worked isolated (tactic 1) or have had a different function.

The fact that, until the moment, hunting blinds were recovered only in the extreme South of the Massif and not in the remaining explored area poses some questions for further research. As we mentioned before, to the South of the Massif there is a change in the landscape in the form of open plains and basaltic plateaus with different water and lithic raw material availability.

We can think that the presence of hunting blinds is related to the existence of shallow lakes and shallows. However, there are other lagoons and shallows more to the North and to the South of the area where hunting blinds were not located and which were archaeological surveyed. We believe it is possible that the presence of hunting blinds is related to the change in the landscape between the Massif and spaces to the South, a hypothesis that requires additional research. During earlier times, some differences were identified between the Southern End of the Deseado Massif and spaces more to the North and South, such as the presence of caches during periods more humid than the present (Franco et al. 2018, 2019), suggesting that humans were using these spaces in a planned way. During the Late Holocene, the information obtained points to the existence of collective planned hunting strategies in the Southern End of the Deseado Massif.

Acknowledgements Funding was provided by PICT 2015-2038 (ANPCyT). We want to acknowledge the assistance of the managements of the Triton Mining Company S.A. and Piedra Grande S.A. mines, especially Claudio Iglesias, Ricardo Silva, and Carolina Negre. We also appreciate the support and help of the Gobernador Gregores authorities (Sr. Pablo Ramírez and Marcelo Cebeira), Mrs. María and Betty from 17 de Marzo ranch, all the workers of Minera Piedra Grande S.A. and all the people who took part of the fieldwork, specially P. Ambrústolo, C. Compagno Zoan, M. V. Fiel, A. Acevedo, and B. Pollard. We also wish to thank two anonymous reviewers, whose comments improved the quality of the manuscript, and the organizers of the Workshop and editors of this volume for their invitation.

References

Aguerre AM (2003) La Martita: ocupaciones de 8000 años en la Cueva 4. In: Aguerre A (ed) Arqueología y Paleoambiente en la Patagonia Santacruceña Argentina. Nuevo Offset, Buenos Aires, pp 29–61

Aguerre AM, Pagano MI (2003) Fauna de las ocupaciones de 8000 años de la Cueva 4 de La Martita: Guanaco. In: Aguerre A (ed) Arqueología y Paleoambiente en la Patagonia Santacruceña Argentina. Author edition, Buenos Aires, pp 71–85

Aragone AC, Dellepiane JM, Rindel D (2010) Análisis de parapetos en ambientes mesetarios del noroeste de Santa Cruz, Patagonia Meridional: propiedades del registro arqueológico y su integración con líneas de evidencia arqueofaunística. In: Bárcena JR, Chiavazza H (eds) XVII Congreso Nacional de Arqueología Argentina. Arqueología Argentina en el Bicentenario de la Revolución de Mayo (V). Universidad Nacional de Cuyo, Facultad de Filosofía y Letras, INCIHUSA-CONICET, Mendoza, pp 1841–1846

Aschero CA (1975) Ensayo para una clasificación morfológica de artefactos líticos aplicada a estudios tipológicos comparativos. CONICET unpublished internal report

Aschero CA (1983) Ensayo para una clasificación morfológica de artefactos líticos aplicada a estudios tipológicos comparativos. CONICET unpublished internal report. Revisión 1983

Aschero CA (1987) Tradiciones culturales en la Patagonia Central: Una perspectiva ergológica. In: Comunicaciones de las Primeras Jornadas de Arqueología de la Patagonia, ed. Dirección de Cultura de la Provincia del Chubut, 17–26. Rawson

Belardi JB, Goñi R (2006) Representaciones rupestres y convergencia poblacional durante momentos tardíos en Santa Cruz (Patagonia argentina). El caso de la meseta del Strobel. In: Fiore D, Podestá M (eds) Tramas en la piedra. Producción y usos del arte rupestre. World Archaeological Congress, Sociedad Argentina de Antropología and Asociación de Amigos del Instituto de Antropología, Buenos Aires, pp 85–94

Belardi JB, Espinosa S, Barrientos G, Carballo Marina F, Re A, Campan P, Súnico A, Guichón F (2013) Las mesetas de San Adolfo y Cardiel Chico: estrategias de movilidad y tácticas de caza de guanacos en el SO de Santa Cruz. In: Zangrando FJ, Barberena R, Gil AF, Neme GA, Giardina MA, Luna L, Otaola C, Paulides SL, Salgán LM, Tívoli AM (eds) Tendencias teórico metodológicas y casos de estudio en la arqueología de la Patagonia. Museo de Historia Natural de San Rafael, Altuna Impresores, Buenos Aires, pp 261–270

Belardi JB, Carballo Marina F, Madrid P, Barrientos G, Campan P (2017) Late Holocene guanaco hunting grounds in southern Patagonia: blinds, tactics and differential landscape use. Antiquity 91(357):718–731

Binford L (1978) Dimensional analysis of behavior and site structure: learning from an Eskimo hunting stand. Am Antiq 43:330–361

Borrero LA (1994–1995) Arqueología de la Patagonia. Palimpsesto. Revista de Arqueología 4:9–69

Borrero LA, Borrazzo KB, Garibotti I, Pallo MC (2011) Concentraciones de pilas de rocas en la Cuenca Superior del río Santa Cruz (Argentina). Magallania 39(2):193–206

Brook GA, Mancini MV, Franco NV, Bamonte F, Ambrústolo P (2013) An examination of possible relationships between paleoenvironmental conditions during the Pleistocene-Holocene transition and human occupation of southern Patagonia (Argentina) east of the Andes, between 46° and 52° S. Quatern Int 305:104–118

Brook GA, Franco NV, Ambrústolo P, Mancini MV, Wang L, Fernández PM (2015) Evidence of the earliest humans in the Southern Deseado Massif (Patagonia, Argentina), Mylodontidae, and changes in water availability. Quatern Int 363:107–125

Cassiodoro G, Flores Coni J (2010) Los parapetos del sitio Guitarra 10 (Meseta del Lago Guitarra, Santa Cruz): una aproximación tecnológica. In: Bárcena JR, Chiavazza H (eds) XVII Congreso Nacional de Arqueología Argentina. Arqueología Argentina en el Bicentenario de la Revolución de Mayo (V). Universidad Nacional de Cuyo, Facultad de Filosofía y Letras, INCIHUSA-CONICET, Mendoza, pp 1871–1876

Cassiodoro G, Flores Coni J, Dellepiane L (2013) Cronología y asentamiento en la meseta del Guitarra (Santa Cruz): El sitio Cañadón Guitarra 3. In: Zangrando FJ, Barberena R, Gil AF, Neme GA, Giardina MA, Luna L, Otaola C, Paulides SL, Salgán LM, Tívoli AM (eds) Tendencias teórico metodológicas y casos de estudio en la arqueología de la Patagonia. Museo de Historia Natural de San Rafael, Altuna Impresores, Buenos Aires, pp 297–306

Cassiodoro G, Ré A, Rindel D (2014) Estrategias de caza en espacios altos de Patagonia meridional durante el Holoceno tardío: evidencia arqueofaunística, tecnológica y rupestre. In: Cassiodoro G, Ré A, Rindel D (eds) Integración de diferentes líneas de evidencia en la Arqueología Argentina. Aspha Ediciones, Buenos Aires, pp 113–137

Cattáneo GR (2000) El paisaje y la distribución de recursos líticos en el Nesocratón del Deseado. In: Miotti L, Paunero R, Salemme M, Cattaneo R (eds) Guía de Campo de la visita a las localidades arqueológicas, Taller Internacional del INQUA International Workshop "La Colonización del Sur de América durante la transición Pleistoceno-Holoceno". INQUA International Workshop, La Plata, pp 26–35

Cattáneo GR (2004) Desarrollo metodológico para el estudio de fuentes de aprovisionamiento lítico en la Meseta Central Santacruceña, Patagonia Argentina. Estudios Atacameños 28:105–119

Cirigliano NA (2016) Movilidad de grupos indígenas y aprovechamiento de materias primas entre el extremo sur del Macizo del Deseado y la cuenca del río Santa Cruz durante los últimos 2.000 años (Provincia de Santa Cruz, Argentina). Unpublished doctoral thesis, Facultad de Filosofía y Letras, Universidad de Buenos Aires, Buenos Aires

Coronato A, Coronato F, Mazzoni E, Vázquez M (2008) Physical geography of Patagonia and Tierra del Fuego. In: Rabassa J (ed) Late Cenozoic of Patagonia and Tierra del Fuego. Developments in Quaternary Science vol. 11. Elsevier, Amsterdam, pp 13–56

De Giusto JM, Di Persia CA, Pezzi E (1980) Nesocratón del Deseado. Geología Regional Argentina 2:1389–1430

Dellepiane J (2018) Uso de imágenes satelitales para el reconocimiento de parapetos en el centro-oeste de Patagonia meridional. Arqueología 24(2):259–269

Dellepiane J, Flores Coni J (2016) Aspectos tecnológicos y faunísticos en sitios a cielo abierto: variabilidad del registro en los parapetos del sitio K116 (meseta del Strobel, provincia de Santa Cruz). In: Mena F (ed) Arqueología de la Patagonia: de mar a mar. Andros Impresores, Santiago, pp 245–255

Durán V, Gil A, Neme G, Gasco A (2003) El Verano: ocupaciones de 8900 años en la Cueva 1 (Santa Cruz, Argentina). In: Aguerre A (ed) Arqueología y Paleoambiente en la Patagonia Santacruceña Argentina. Nuevo Offset, Buenos Aires, pp 93–120

Echeveste H (2005) Travertinos y jasperoides de Manantial Espejo, un ambiente Hot Spring Jurásico: Macizo del Deseado, Provincia de Santa Cruz, Argentina. Latin American Journal of Sedimentology and Basin Analysis 12(1):33–48

Espinosa S, Goñi R, Flores Coni J (2009) Aproximación tecnológica al uso de pampas y bajos en la meseta del lago Strobel. In: Salemme M, Santiago F, Álvarez M, Piana E, Vázquez M, Mansur M (eds) Arqueología de Patagonia: una mirada desde el último confín (2). Editorial Utopías, Ushuaia, pp 977–984

Flores Coni J (2014) Análisis de la variabilidad de los parapetos de la Meseta del Strobel (Santa Cruz). Relaciones de la Sociedad Argentina de Antropología 39(2):551–557

Franco NV (2002) Estrategias de utilización de recursos líticos en la cuenca superior del río Santa Cruz. Unpublished doctoral thesis. Buenos Aires: Facultad de Filosofía y Letras, Universidad de Buenos Aires

Franco NV, Ambrústolo P, Martucci M, Brook GA, Mancini MV, Cirigliano NA (2010) Early human occupation in the Southern part of the Deseado Massif (Patagonia, Argentina). Current Research in the Pleistocene 27:13–16

Franco NV, Ambrústolo P, Acevedo A, Cirigliano NA, Vommaro M (2013) Prospecciones en el sur del Macizo del Deseado (Provincia de Santa Cruz). Los casos de La Gruta y Viuda Quenzana. In: Zangrando FJ, Barberena R, Gil AF, Neme GA, Giardina MA, Luna L, Otaola C, Paulides SL, Salgán LM, Tívoli AM (eds) Tendencias teórico metodológicas y casos de estudio en la arqueología de la Patagonia. Museo de Historia Natural de San Rafael, Altuna Impresores, Buenos Aires, pp 371–378

Franco NV, Ambrústolo P, Vetrisano L (2015a) Materias primas líticas y su utilización en las cuencas de los ríos Chico y Santa Cruz (provincia de Santa Cruz, Patagonia argentina). Intersecciones en Antropología 16(1):113–123

Franco NV, Borrero LA, Lucero G (2019) Human dispersal in the Atlantic slope of Patagonia and the role of lithic availability. Paleoamerica 5(1):88–104

Franco NV, Cirigliano NA, Vetrisano L, Ambrústolo P (2015b) Raw material circulation at broad scales in Southern Patagonia (Argentina): the cases of the Chico and Santa Cruz River Basins. Quatern Int 375:72–83

Franco NV, Cortegoso V, Lucero G, Durán V (2018) Human ranking of spaces and the role of caches: case studies from Patagonia (Argentina). Quatern Int 473:278–289

García Guraieb S, Goñi R, Bosio L (2007) Lesiones traumáticas en un entierro del Lago Salitroso (Santa Cruz, Argentina). In: Morello F, Martinic M, Prieto A, Bahamonde G (eds) Arqueología de Fuego-Patagonia. Levantando piedras, desenterrando huesos... y develando arcanos. Ediciones CEQUA, Punta Arenas, pp 375–380

García L, Metcalfe-Wood S, Rivera T, Wheatley DW (2006) Análisis de pautas de visibilidad en la distribución de monumentos megalíticos de Sierra Morena Occidental. In: Grau Mira I (ed), La aplicación de los SIG en la arqueología del paisaje. Universidad de Alicante, Alicante, pp 181–200

García L, Pérez de Micou C (1979) Aproximación a un análisis funcional de parapetos pertenecientes al complejo Patagoniense en la meseta de Somuncurá, provincia de Río Negro. Sapiens 4:139–144

Goñi R (2000–2002) Fechados radiocarbónicos y registro arqueológico en la cuenca de los lagos Salitroso/Posadas (Santa Cruz). Cuadernos del Instituto Nacional de Antropología y Pensamiento Latinoamericano 19: 666–668

Goñi R (2010) Cambio climático y poblamiento humano durante el Holoceno tardío en Patagonia Meridional. Una perspectiva arqueológica. Unpublished doctoral thesis, Buenos aires: Facultad de Filosofía y Letras, Universidad de Buenos Aires

Goñi R, Barrientos G, Cassiodoro G (2000–2002) Condiciones previas a la extinción de las poblaciones humanas del sur de Patagonia: una discusión a partir del análisis del registro arqueológico de la cuenca del lago Salitroso. Cuadernos del Instituto Nacional de Antropología y Pensamiento Latinoamericano 19:249–266

Goñi R, Cassiodoro G, Rindel D (2011–2012) Poblamiento de mesetas: Arqueología de Pampa del Asador y Cerro Pampa (Patagonia Meridional). Cuadernos del Instituto Nacional de Antropología y Pensamiento Latinoamericano 23(1):21–36

Gradin C (1959–1960a) Petroglifos de la meseta del lago Strobel (prov. de Santa Cruz, Argentina). Acta Praehistorica 3–4:123–143

Gradin C (1959–1960b) Tres informaciones referentes a la meseta del Lago Strobel (Prov. De Santa Cruz, Argentina). Acta Praehistorica 3–4:144–149

Gradin C (1971) Parapetos habitacionales en la Meseta de Somuncurá, provincia de Río Negro. Relaciones de la Sociedad Argentina de Antropología 5(2):171–185

Gradin C (1976) Parapetos de piedra y grabados rupestres de la meseta del lago Buenos Aires. Actas y Memorias del IV Congreso Nacional de Arqueología Argentina (Primera parte). Revista del Museo de Historia Natural de San Rafael II(1/4):315–337

Gradin C (1996) Grabados y parapetos de la zona sur de la meseta del Lago Buenos Aires (prov. de Santa Cruz). In: Gómez Otero J (ed) Arqueología: Solo Patagonia. CENPAT-CONICET, Puerto Madryn, pp 173–184

Gradin CJ, Aschero CA, Aguerre A (1979) Arqueología del Área Río Pinturas (Provincia de Santa Cruz). Relaciones de la Sociedad Argentina de Antropología XIII(N.S.):183–227

Guráieb AG (2000) Características tecnológicas y de composición de los conjuntos artefactuales líticos del Área 2 de Excavación de CI1. Arqueología 10:215–225

Guráieb AG (2004) Before and after the hiatus. Lithic technology in Cerro de los Indios 1. Before Farming: Anthropology and Archaeology of Hunter-Gatherers 2:1–19

Hermo D (2008) Los cambios en la circulación de las materias primas líticas en ambientes mesetarios de Patagonia. Una aproximación para la construcción de los paisajes arqueológicos de las sociedades cazadoras-recolectoras. Unpublished doctoral thesis. La Plata: Facultad de Ciencias Naturales y Museo, Universidad Nacional de La Plata

Hermo D, Vázquez M (1999) Cuánto que caminamos: Primeros resultados de las prospecciones en Cerro Vanguardia y Monumento Natural Bosques Petrificados. In: Diez-Marín C (ed) Actas del XII Congreso Nacional de Arqueología Argentina III. Facultad de Ciencias Naturales y Museo, Universidad Nacional de La Plata, La Plata, pp 475–483

Instituto Geográfico Nacional (2018) Geodesia. Modelos Digitales de Elevación. Recovered from https://www.ign.gob.ar/NuestrasActividades/Geodesia/ModeloDigitalElevaciones/Búsqueda. Accessed May, 2018

Llobera M (2003) Extending GIS-based visual analysis: the concept of 'Visualscapes'. International Journal of Geographical Information Sciences 17:25–48

Magnin LA (2010) Distribuciones arqueológicas en la Meseta Central de Santa Cruz. Implicancias para los estudios de uso del espacio y movilidad de sociedades cazadoras recolectoras. Unpublished doctoral thesis. La Plata: Facultad de Ciencias Naturales y Museo, Universidad Nacional de La Plata

Magnin L, Hermo D, Weitzel C (2015) Estrategias de caza en la localidad arqueológica de La Primavera, Santa Cruz (Argentina): Análisis de visibilidad y accesibilidad mediante SIG. In: Sepúlveda Retamal M, Alday Mamani C, Castillo Fuentes C, Oyaneder Rodríguez A (eds) Actas del XIX Congreso Nacional de Arqueología Chilena. Universidad de Tarapacá and Andros Impresores, Santiago de Chile, pp 63–67

Mancini MV, Franco NV, Brook G (2012) Early human occupation and environment South of the Deseado Massif and South of Lake Argentino. In: Miotti L, Salemme M, Flegenheimer N, Goebel T (eds) Southbound: late Pleistocene peopling of Latin America, current research in the Pleistocene special edition. Center for the Study of the First Americans, College Station, pp 197–200

Martinic M (2002) Estructuras de piedra en la Patagonia austral oriental. Anales del Instituto de la Patagonia 30:103–115. Serie Ciencias Humanas

Miotti L, Salemme M (2003) When Patagonia was colonized: people mobility at high latitudes during Pleistocene-Holocene transition. Quatern Int 109–110:95–111

Miotti L, Salemme M (2004) Poblamiento, movilidad y territorios entre las sociedades cazadorasrecolectoras de Patagonia. Complutum 15:177–206

Miotti L, Salemme M, Hermo D, Magnin L, Rabassa J (2004) Yamnago 137 años después: otro lenguaje para la misma región. In: Civalero MT, Fernández P, Guráieb AG (eds) Contra viento y marea. Arqueología de Patagonia. Instituto Nacional de Antropología y Pensamiento Latinoamericano and Sociedad Argentina de Antropología, Buenos Aires, pp 775–795

Miotti L, Terranova E, Blanco R, Marchionne L, Hermo D, Magnin L (2016) Entre basaltos y lagunas: las estructuras de piedra de la meseta de Somuncurá. Apuntes para la reflexión de los patrones de movilidad de los cazadores-recolectores. In: Mena F (ed) Arqueología de la Patagonia: de Mar a Mar. CIEP/Ñire Negro Ediciones, Santiago de Chile, pp 256–266

Mosquera B (2018) Análisis de la información radiocarbónica de sitios arqueológicos del Macizo del Deseado, provincia de Santa Cruz, Argentina. Intersecciones en Antropología 19:25–36

Panza JL, Haller MJ (2002) El vulcanismo Jurásico. In: Haller M (ed) Geología y Recursos Naturales de Santa Cruz. Relatorio del XV Congreso Geológico Argentino (I). Asociación Geológica Argentina, Buenos Aires, pp 89–101

Panza JL, Marin G, Zubia M (1998) Hoja Geológica 4969-I "Gobernador Gregores", Provincia de Santa Cruz. Boletín 239. Buenos Aires: SEGEMAR

Paunero R (2009) Arqueología en la Meseta Central: La María y Cerro Tres Tetas. In: Mirelman S, Tauber A, Espinosa S, Palacios ME, Campán P, Álvarez P, Luque E (eds) Estado Actual de las Investigaciones realizadas sobre Patrimonio Cultural en Santa Cruz. Dirección de Patrimonio Cultural, Subsecretaría de Cultura de Santa Cruz, Río Gallegos, pp 185–194

Paunero RS, Frank AD, Skarbun F, Rosales G, Cueto M, Zapata G, Paunero M, Lunazzi N, Del Giorgio M (2007) Investigaciones arqueológicas en sitio Casa del Minero 1, Estancia La María, Meseta Central de Santa Cruz. In: Morello F, Martinic M, Prieto A, Bahamonde G (eds) Arqueología de Fuego-Patagonia. Levantando piedras, desenterrando huesos y develando arcanos. Ediciones CEQUA, Punta Arenas, pp 577–588

Re A (2010) Representaciones rupestres en mesetas altas de la provincia de Santa Cruz. Circulación de información en espacios de uso estacional. Unpublished doctoral thesis. Buenos Aires: Facultad de Filosofía y Letras, Universidad de Buenos Aires

Re A, Goñi R, Flores Coni J, Guichón F, Dellepiane J, Umaño M (2017) Arqueología de la meseta del Strobel (Patagonia meridional): 15 años después. Relaciones de la Sociedad Argentina de Antropología XLII(1):133–158

Rindel D, Cassiodoro GE, Aragone AC (2007) La utilización de mesetas altas durante el Holoceno tardío: el sitio Cerro Pampa 2 Ojo de Agua (Santa Cruz). In: Morello F, Martinic M, Prieto A, Bahamonde G (eds) Arqueología de Fuego-Patagonia: Levantando piedras, desenterrando huesos...y develando arcanos. Ediciones CEQUA, Punta Arenas, pp 649–662

Rubinos Pérez A (2003) Recopilación y análisis de las fechas carbono 14 del norte de la provincia de Santa Cruz (Argentina). In: Aguerre A (ed) Arqueología y Paleoambiente en la Patagonia Santacruceña Argentina. Author's edition, Buenos Aires, pp 1–25

Sacchi M (2013) A un paso de la laguna: Análisis lítico del sitio Bajo de la Laguna 2, provincia de Santa Cruz. Comechingonia virtual VII 2:216–233

Skarbun F (2009) La organización tecnológica en grupos cazadores recolectores desde las ocupaciones del Pleistoceno final al Holoceno tardío en la Meseta Central de Santa Cruz. Unpublished doctoral thesis. La Plata: Facultad de Ciencias Naturales y Museo, Universidad Nacional de La Plata

Wheatley D, Gillings M (2000) Vision, perception and GIS: developing enriched approaches to the study of archaoelogical visibility, in 321 edition, NATO Science Series A: Life Sciences. In: Lock GR (ed) Beyond the map: archaeology and spatial technologies. IOS Press, Amsterdam, pp 1–27

Chapter 13
Hunting Landscapes in the North Margin of Lake Viedma (Southern Patagonia, Argentina): Preys, Strategies and Technology

Juan Bautista Belardi, Flavia Carballo Marina, and Gustavo Barrientos

Abstract The aim of this paper is to describe and discuss the strategies and technology implemented by Late Holocene hunter-gatherers to hunt their most prominent animal resources, guanaco (*Lama guanicoe*) and choique (*Rhea pennata pennata*), in different settings in the north margin of Lake Viedma (Santa Cruz province, Argentina). In order to do that, we use archaeological distributional data from different altitudinal levels, namely lakeshore dunes (255–275 m.a.s.l), mid-altitude plains or *pampas* (276–900 m.a.s.l.), and Del Tobiano basaltic plateau ($\geq$900 m a.s.l.). The *pampas*, particularly the grounds below 400 m.a.s.l., may have been used by both species as their wintering grounds (although their permanence in this environment could have occurred throughout the year), while the mid-altitude plains and the plateau seem to have been primarily used by the guanaco as grazing and calving grounds from late spring to early fall, the months in which most of its surface is free of snow. Likely, differences in seasonality, topography and use of these environments by the guanaco and choique social groups may have forced people to adopt different hunting strategies, tactics and weaponry. Frequency variations in the presence of projectile points and bolas at different altitudinal levels have been observed. In the *pampas*, evidence suggests that guanaco hunting was aided by the use of bow and arrows and/or throwing weapons, such as spears and bolas, the latter likely also used in the hunting of choique. In the plateau, on the other hand, guanaco hunting tactics involved the use of blinds either by individuals or small groups of hunters who were mainly equipped with throwing weapons and/or bow and arrows. The archeological record of the plateau shows a logistic hunting-oriented strategy as well as a residential use during summer months. Artifact density and variety at lakeshore dunes

---

J. B. Belardi (✉)
CIT Santa Cruz, Consejo Nacional de Investigaciones Científicas y Técnicas (CONICET),
Universidad Nacional de La Patagonia Austral, Unidad Académica Río Gallegos (UNPA-UARG),
ICASUR, Rio Gallegos, Santa Cruz, Argentina

F. C. Marina
ICASUR, UNPA-UARG, Rio Gallegos, Santa Cruz, Argentina

G. Barrientos
CONICET, UNLP-FCNyM, La Plata, Argentina

© Springer Nature Switzerland AG 2021
J. B. Belardi et al. (eds.), *Ancient Hunting Strategies in Southern South America*,
The Latin American Studies Book Series,
https://doi.org/10.1007/978-3-030-61187-3_13

suggest a greater intensity of occupation of these grounds, probably linked to a more residential use—either seasonal (fall/winter) or year-round—made possible by the availability, although in variable density throughout the year, of guanaco and choique. Consequently, the regional archeological landscape exhibits evidence of integration and complementarity of the different altitudinal levels in the northern margin of the Lake Viedma, at least during the Late Holocene.

Keywords Lake Viedma · Late Holocene · Guanaco · Choique · Hunting

13.1 Introduction

Hunting has played a key role in the organization of past foraging societies (Binford 2001; Kelly 1995; Lemke 2018), due to the fact that the distribution and availability of prey determine human strategies in landscape use, especially at high latitudes where the supply of nutrients is mostly reliant upon this kind of subsistence activity (e.g. Binford 1981; Frison 2004). There lies the importance of studying the relation between human populations and their prey, since hunting strategies and tactics exert a clear influence on other components of social organization (e.g. Binford 1978; Aschero and Martínez 2001; Frison 2004; Moreno 2012; Bar-Oz and Nadel 2013; Borrero 2013).

From the onset of human settlement in southern Patagonia by the end of the Pleistocene (around 12,000 cal. yr BP; Martin and Borrero 2017; Pérez et al. 2016) to historical times, the guanaco (*Lama guanicoe*) has been the main prey of continental hunter-gatherers (e.g. Borrero 2001; Miotti 1998; Mengoni Goñalons 1999). The choique (*Rhea pennata pennata)*, which is a medium-size flightless bird, was also a prey but a secondary or complementary one (Belardi 1999; Fernández 2010; Giardina 2010; among others).

The Lake Viedma Basin, located in the southwestern portion of Santa Cruz province in southern Patagonia (Argentina), is an optimal setting to evaluate the interaction between landscape features, hunter-gatherers and their prey. This study is focused on the northeastern area of Lake Viedma, mainly between the shoreline and Del Tobiano Plateau, which corresponds to a steppe ecosystem (Fig. 13.1). An altitudinal gradient can be observed in a reduced spatial scale of about 10.5 km from the lakeshore to the edge of Del Tobiano Plateau. The width of this strip of land approximately corresponds to the maximum distance foragers are willing to walk round-trip in a single day, i.e., 20–30 km, or 10–15 km one way (Kelly 1995: 133). From south to north there is a succession of three main altitudinal levels (a) lakeshore dunes (255–275 m.a.s.l.), (b) mid-altitude plains or *pampas* (276–900 m.a.s.l.), which are wide open plains made up of glacial deposits, and (c) Del Tobiano basaltic plateau (901–1100 m.a.s.l.) (Figure 13.1). Altitudes of the lakeshore dunes and the mid-altitude plains should only be taken as a reference, since they tend to slightly increase westward. Seasonal variations in rainfall (mainly snowfall) and temperature determine

13 Hunting Landscapes in the North Margin of Lake Viedma ...

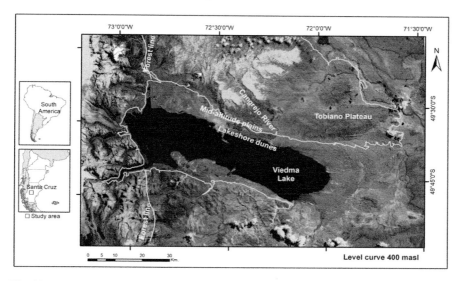

Fig. 13.1 Map of Lake Viedma with altitudinal levels

that the altitude of 400 m.a.s.l. is the boundary between wintering grounds (all-year-round living grounds) and summer grounds or *veranadas*, suitable for habitation from late spring to early fall. This altitudinal segmentation, which determines the differential availability of grassland, is nowadays utilized by livestock breeders to manage sheep (Sturzenbaum and Borrelli 2001) and governs the mobility of guanaco and choique (Belardi et al. 2019b).

The organization of this contribution is as follows. Firstly, we will introduce the characteristics of the different altitudinal levels on the northern shore of Lake Viedma, their use by guanaco and choique populations and the results of distributional archaeological studies. On these grounds, variability in landscape use by hunter-gatherer populations will be assessed together with the identification of the implemented weapon systems, the latter understood as the type of weapon plus its mode of propulsion and use (sensu Aschero and Martínez 2001; Ratto 1991). Then, we will describe the likely tactics deployed for prey hunting, which were inferred on the basis of the differential frequency, characteristics and location of hunting blinds[1] (Belardi et al. 2017) and remnants of weaponry (i.e. lithic projectile points and bolas). Finally, we will discuss the way in which Late Holocene human societies articulated the different altitudinal levels of the steppe around guanaco and choique hunting.

---

[1] Blinds are unique structures mostly found in the western plateaus of Santa Cruz. Hunting blinds in high hills have been identified toward the east and outside plateau areas, but in a much lower proportion (see Belardi et al. 2017).

13.2 Lake Viedma Basin: Paleoenvironmental Evolution and Current Seasonality

Lake Viedma (250 m.a.s.l.), which flows into the Atlantic Ocean through La Leona and Santa Cruz rivers, has an elongated shape and is oriented from West to East as a result of Quaternary glacial dynamics. It is 78 km long, covering a total area of 1088 km^2, which makes it a natural temperature regulator. Its headwaters are connected to the Southern Patagonian Ice Field, a natural barrier hampering or impeding human circulation toward the Pacific slope of the Andes (Fig. 13.1). As a consequence, it can be considered a marginal area regarding its potential use in comparison with other areas located eastward (Borrero 2004).

The northeast bank of the lake is framed by basaltic plateaus of Miocene age, among which Del Tobiano Plateau (900–1100 m.a.s.l.) outstands. West of the Cangrejo River, the plateau gives rise to a mountain relief that hinder human circulation to the north (Fig. 13.1). Therefore, lakeshore dunes constitute a steppe corridor whose vegetation is characterized by a patchy distribution of shrubs (such as molle, *Schinus sp.*), sub-shrubs and gramineous species, which are associated with natural drainage systems (Oliva et al. 2001).

In the Holocene, Wenzens (1999) indicated a series of glacial advances in the area of the Viedma and Argentino lakes, which took place between 8500 and 7500 cal years BP and, again, between 5800–5500 cal years BP. These were followed by Neoglacial advances, originally proposed by Mercer (1976): Neoglacial I, with ages between 4500–4200 years BP, Neoglacial II, between 2700-2200 years BP, and Neoglacial III, corresponding to the Little Ice Age. Such fluctuations resulted in greater seasonality at the western end of Lake Viedma (Kaplan et al. 2016; Strelin et al. 2014), which probably caused its intermittent use or abandonment and a higher concentration of human occupations around the shoreline.

The study of the sediments at the bottom of Lago del Desierto, an elongated lake northward from Lake Viedma Basin indicate that, around 850 years cal AD, the Medieval Climatic Anomaly (MCA) started, a warm period that lasted about 600 years (Kastner et al. 2010). After the MCA the environment became colder and wetter during the Little Ice Age, which ended around 1750 years cal AD (Masiokas et al. 2009). It is believed that an expansion in the *Nothofagus* forest took place during this period (Bamonte 2012), but this expansion never reached the study area.

In winter, snow accumulates on the plateau more than in other altitudinal levels, being the lakeshore dunes practically free of this coverage. For this reason, wintering fields that concentrate local groups of guanaco extend between the coastline and the 400 m level, well within the *pampas*. In addition, in this area there are rocks suitable for knapping—from the glacial moraines that surround the lake and the dragging material of the rivers that flow into it—and firewood, coming from both small molle groves and driftwood from the *Nothofagus* forest located westward (Fig. 13.1). Additionally, molle groves and lakeshore dunes provide shelter for human occupation. In biogeographical terms, finally, these fields are corridors of variable width connecting the steppe with the forest.

13.3 Prey Availability at Different Altitudinal Levels

Guanaco is a medium-size gregarious camelid (90–120 kg) that is considered a generalist herbivore that feeds on a wide variety of plants (Puig et al. 1997; Muñoz and Simonetti 2013; Barri et al. 2014; Arias et al. 2015). The diet of guanaco varies seasonally depending on the productivity of its habitat, exhibiting a preference for woody species when the availability of grasses decreases (Puig et al. 1997). Its behavior is seasonally territorial with a social structure based on a polygynous mating system. The basic social units are family groups, male groups and solitary individuals (González et al. 2006), even though these units are usually transient (Franklin 1982; Ortega 1985; Merino 1988). Current guanaco population density in Southern Patagonia is high (1.1–7.4 individuals/km^2) and very variable across the landscape (Travaini et al. 2015 and references therein). Basaltic plateaus, where the availability of guanaco is seasonal (from late spring to early fall; Puig 1986; Ortega and Franklin 1995; Puig and Videla 1995), are the preferred calving areas. The high population density in these zones is due to the presence of different social groups. Although estimating their distribution and density in the past is really difficult, it seems to have been similar or even higher than today. Under this assumption, a high seasonal availability of prey is expected, particularly in Late Holocene times (Belardi et al. 2019b).

Choique is a large flightless bird, with an adult weight between 17 and 24 kg. It is a social animal that lives in groups whose size vary seasonally. The largest groups can be seen during the reproductive and breeding season (Daciuk 1978), which starts in August (mid-winter). In southern Patagonia, specifically, egg hatching takes place from the end of October till December (Manero 2019, pers. communication to J.B.B.). Habitat selection according to the relief type, suggests the use of two kinds of Patagonian steppe described in order of preference: (a) steppe with hills and plains, (b) steppe with hills, mountains and plateaus (SAG 2002). In relation to this, Pedrana et al. (2011) have found a positive association between choique presence and primary productivity that is typically associated with open and flat areas, which favor the "watch and run" anti-predator strategy (González-Urrutia et al. 2018). Our own observations, mainly restricted to the summer months, indicate that although choiques are found in the plateaus in that season, their presence in such environments is less than that recorded at the bottom of the basins.

Summarizing, throughout the year the lakeshore dunes concentrates various social groups of guanaco and choique. The highest population density in this zone can be observed in winter, when these prey animals adopt a rather linear distribution around the lake. Evidence of this is observed in the record of guanacos killed by winter stress. The *pampas* hold a lower density of prey, principally of guanaco, with a more heterogeneous distribution. Basaltic plateaus, finally, present a high summer concentration of different social groups and age classes of guanaco; due to habitat preferences, population density of choique in this season is lesser than in lower altitudinal levels.

The above generates a series of questions about the influence of the mostly seasonally-driven distribution of both prey species on the hunting strategies implemented by Late Holocene hunter-gatherers in the Lake Viedma Basin. Such questions refer mainly to the degree of that influence, to the existence or not of a resulting differential exploitation of guanaco and choique at each altitudinal level, and to the way in which all these aspects are expressed archeologically. We will try to address them in the remaining sections of this chapter.

13.4 Archaeological Information

13.4.1 Chronological Frame

Available radiocarbon dates indicate the presence of hunter-gatherer populations in the Lake Viedma Basin between 3670 and 970 radiocarbon years BP (i.e. 4230–740 years cal BP). This chronology was obtained at the site Punta del Lago 1 (PL1), located in a sandstone canyon (500 m.a.s.l), between the lakeshore and Del Tobiano Plateau (Belardi et al. 2019a). In addition, there are isolated radiocarbon dates from surface and open-air contexts from the lower *pampas* which, together with evidence of the use of the Tehuelche-Aonikenk reserve called Lake Viedma, indicate that the occupations reached the twentieth century (Belardi et al. 2016; Nuevo Delaunay et al. 2017).

Despite the relatively small chronological range of human occupation recorded in the Lake Viedma Basin, there is no reason to think that the area could not have been occupied since the Early Holocene, as occurs in other nearby lake basins such as San Martín-Tar and Argentino, located north and south respectively (Belardi et al. 2013; Franco and Borrero 2003). It is significant, in this sense, that in PL1 more than 30 panels with rock art—mostly engravings—were recorded in which techniques (painting, engraving and superficial and shallow scratching) and motifs overlap. The paintings, which are found in very low frequency, are in red color; there are one guanaco figure similar to those described as Style B of the Pinturas River (Gradin 2001) and an anthropomorphic figure with a headdress, in both cases assignable to the Early Holocene (Belardi et al. 2019a). Engraved guanacos have been recorded on Del Tobiano Plateau, whose design would be assignable to the Middle Holocene (Re 2017).

13.4.2 Distributional Data and Landscape Use

At the northern margin of Lake Viedma, archaeological information was obtained through a distributional perspective, which considers the archaeological record as relatively continuous in space, with recognizable variations in its density (Borrero

13 Hunting Landscapes in the North Margin of Lake Viedma ...

Table 13.1 Distributional information in relation to altitudinal levels. References: SU: sample units

Altitudinal levels		Area (m^2)	N SU	N SU with artifacts/ (%)	N artifacts	Density (10^{-5}. m^2)
Wintering grounds	lakeshore dunes 255–275 masl	162,000	107	29/ (27.10)	263	1600
	low *pampas* 276–400 masl	383,250	411	42/ (10.21)	134	340
Veranada grounds	high *pampas* 401–900 masl	120,000	120	37/ (30.83)	255	2100
	Del Tobiano basaltic plateau 901–1100 masl	155,000	90	8/ (8.88)	14	9

et al. 1992; Dunnell and Dancey 1983; Foley 1981). Under this perspective, the unit of analysis is not the site but the artifact (Thomas 1975).

Linear transects were implemented in each of the altitudinal levels: lakeshore dunes, *pampas* (differentiated in low and high) and Del Tobiano Plateau. In all of them erosion predominates over deposition, which is why archaeological visibility is good ($\geq$50%). The frequency of sampling units with artifacts is used as an approximate measure of spatial continuity in landscape use, and artifact density as a relative measure of intensity of use (Table 13.1).

There are differences in both continuity and intensity of landscape use at different altitudinal levels (Table 13.1). The high *pampas* are the one with greater intensity of use, in a relatively continuous way. This is a large space furrowed by canyons that dissect sandstone outcrops; it combines the offer of shelter and suitable panels for rock art in a local context of relative scarcity of rockshelters. *Mallines* (small wetlands) originate on the canyon floor, increasing the availability of water in the spaces located between the plateau and the lakeshore. In the *pampas*, the highest concentrations of artifacts come from discrete knapping events on locally available rocks (flintknapping "on the go"). As it has been already said, on this altitudinal level is the site PL1 that shows the consumption of guanaco and a high frequency of panels with rock art, reflecting the intensity of use of the high *pampas* by human populations (Belardi et al. 2019a).

Lakeshore is the second altitudinal level with greater density of archaeological materials. It is characterized by the presence of deflated dunes, small molle groves, driftwood and rocks suitable for the elaboration of artifacts either by knapping or by pitting, abrasion and polishing. Like the high *pampas*, it shows discontinuity in the artifact distribution (27.10%) but with marked peaks of artifact density. Sectors with guanaco bones and high artifact frequency and richness are few and mostly associated with blowouts (e.g. San Agustín, Santa Margarita 1 and 2 and Médano de Kaikén Aike 1 site). Several metates and a mano with red pigments were recorded at the site San Agustin, the last suggesting the existence of site furnishing. The high frequency of blades and blade cores manufactured with immediately available basalts also stands out. Blades—as pieces with long and parallel edges—would have been used in guanaco processing. The residential use of the lakeshore dunes during winter or throughout the year is proposed.

The low artifact density and the remarkable discontinuity in the distribution of artifacts in the lower *pampas* could be due to the fact that it is the transit corridor to and from the coast. The only thing that makes this pattern vary is the presence of a sandstone shelter with evidence of occupation located east of the lake, at the site Punto Singular 6, Farallón de Arenisca 4 (PS6 FA4) (Belardi et al. 2016).

Distributional artifact evidence shows that Del Tobiano Plateau is the place with the highest discontinuity and least artifact density. However, high artifact frequencies occur at the foot of the basalt cliffs that enclose small lakes and in the inner space and immediate surroundings of hunting blinds. In the latter, a high frequency of fragmented stemmed projectile points is found—likely resulting from the replacement of broken points—and microflakes, byproducts of the thinning of bifaces and edge resharpening. Spatial variations in the frequencies of blinds, their topographic location and the dimensions and diversity of sizes of the recovered projectile points were the basis for the modeling of different guanaco hunting tactics by stalking—both individual and group—that would have focused on guanaco calves or *chulengos*. The hunting tactics were mainly deployed around lakes—where the entrance and exit of the groups of guanaco that come to drink water could be controlled—and at narrow basaltic passages between depressions where guanaco circulation could be monitored, so the diversity of tactics responds to the use of favorable topographic conditions (Belardi et al. 2017). It must be mentioned that no archaeofaunal remains were recovered at these sites. On the other hand, basalt cliffs surrounding the small lakes where hunting blinds occur were used as panels for rock engravings. The engraved motifs are similar to those found in other plateaus of the west and interior of Santa Cruz. This is evidence of the information flow through social interaction nets and population convergence in the plateaus, which should be understood as the use—not necessarily synchronic—of this altitudinal level by groups of hunters from neighboring areas (Belardi and Goñi 2006).

13.4.3 Weapon Systems

Three weapon systems have been identified so far: bow and arrow, lithic tipped spears and bolas.

While lithic bolas can be the remnants of different weapon systems (Vecchi 2010; Aschero 2019) they will be treated here as a single group. These weapon systems are considered to be proportionally biased on the lakeshore and in the *pampas*, since lithic projectile points of different size and bolas are equally identified and gathered by contemporary amateur collectors. This impact over the archaeological record must be lower in the plateau because of the low intensity in current use. Based on regional archaeological data, it is likely that the three weapon systems have been simultaneously used, at least during the last 1000 years.

Projectile points were assigned to different weapon systems based on the width of the stems (Churchill 1993; Ratto 1991): >10 mm corresponds to spears (hand-throwing spears) and <10 mm to arrows. Only 24 points have kept the stems. Those which have lost it were considered undetermined. The highest frequency of projectile points ($N = 34$) were found in Del Tobiano Plateau (71%), mainly in relation to hunting blinds; spear points predominate (Table 13.2, Fig. 13.2). All of them are triangular stemmed points, a characteristic design since at least 3000 BP (Vetrisano and Franco 2019). No blanks (bifaces) were found. Points were mainly made of black obsidian (79.4%) from the Pampa del Asador, located 200 km northwards (Espinosa and Goñi 1999), followed by 8.8% of chert and basalt and just 3% of dacite.

Table 13.2 Frequency of lithic projectile points according to weapon system and altitudinal level

Lithic heads	Wintering grounds		*Veranada* grounds		Total
	Lakeshore dunes	Low *Pampas*	High *Pampas*	Del Tobiano basaltic plateau	
Arrow	–	1	2	1	4
Hand-throwing spear	3	1	1	15	20
Undetermined	1	1	–	8	10
Total and (%)	4 (12)	3 (8.5)	3 (8.5)	24 (71)	34

Fig. 13.2 Lithic projectile points. From left to right: the first four points (with the exception of the second one that has no stem) were assigned to hand-throwing spears and the last two points were assigned to arrows

Stone bolas were also classified according to the altitudinal levels and analyzed considering their state of preservation, i.e., whole bolas or half bolas. At the same time, polyhedra (initial reduction stage), preforms and flakes were recognized, categories that allow to identify manufacturing processes. The fragments of finished bolas and preforms correspond to pieces that have less than 50% of its original mass preserved (Vecchi 2010). Thirty eight artifacts were identified (Table 13.3, Fig. 13.3) manufactured in plutonic (68.4%) and volcanic (29%) rocks, which are

Table 13.3 Frequency of stone bolas and derived products according to altitudinal level

Bolas and related artifacts	Wintering grounds		*Veranada* grounds		Total
	Lakeshore	Low *Pampas*	High *Pampas*	Del Tobiano basaltic plateau	
Polyhedron	3	–	–	–	3
Stone bola	4	2	–	–	6
Half bola	2	1	–	–	3
Bola fragment	5	–	–	–	5
Blank	8	3	1	–	12
Blank fragment	2	–	–	–	2
Flake	6	1	–	–	7
Total and (%)	30 (79)	7 (18)	1 (3)	–	38

Fig. 13.3 Blanks at different manufacturing stages, flakes and stone bolas from Médano de Kaikén Aike 1 site

locally available. Only one of the stone bolas has been polished and has an equatorial groove.

The lakeshore is the zone that shows the highest frequency of stone bolas and artifacts linked to their manufacturing sequence ($N = 30$) in contexts corresponding to the last 2000 years BP. Only one preform was found in the high *pampas*, while no bolas or preforms were found in the plateau.

13.5 Discussion and Conclusions

The results of the distributional studies carried out in the north margin of Lake Viedma indicate a low intensity of use by human populations throughout the Holocene. However, based on variations in densities and spatial continuity of artifact distributions it is possible to recognize differences in landscape use. Thus, the upper *pampas* and the lakeshore are identified as those altitude levels of greater preeminence in terms of intensity of use, followed by Del Tobiano Plateau. In addition, on each level it is possible to recognize differences in the frequency of projectile points (Table 13.2) and bolas (Table 13.3). The same happens with the presence or absence of hunting blinds, reflecting the use of different weapons systems and hunting tactics in each zone. This is the likely consequence of the seasonal use of the different altitudinal levels by local groups of guanaco and choique.

Del Tobiano Plateau is a circumscribed space with a high seasonal concentration of guanaco (and likely less of choique). It would have acted as a guanaco hunting ground. Projectile points of at least two weapons systems were used in conjunction with hunting blinds, located in such a way as to take advantage of topographic accidents (Hitchcock et al. 2019, for an ethnographic case that relates weapons and blinds systems). The different stalking tactics would have involved both individual and communal hunting events and are a reflection of an equipped landscape, built especially for hunting. This situation would have occurred from the Middle Holocene onwards, once the plateaus of western Santa Cruz were incorporated into the cultural geography of the hunting populations (Goñi 2010). The availability and predictability of prey in line with the supply of rocks and the facility for the construction of hunting blinds (Morgan et al. 2018) would have led to the redundant use of basaltic cliffs that surround the small lakes as shelters and panels for rock art (engravings). From the above, it is possible to propose the use not only logistic but also residential of the plateau by family groups from late spring to late summer. In this way, a "seasonal window" of resources would have been used in a sustained manner. These are conditions under which the plateaus would act as places for population convergence (Belardi and Goñi 2006), a fact that would have been consolidated throughout the Late Holocene.

The use of the plateau, at least from the south, would have been articulated from the lakeshore and from the rock shelters located in the low and high *pampas*. This does not necessarily imply that the low *pampas* and the lakeshore were unoccupied during spring-summer, but that the groups of foragers would have been less numerous there. Thus, hunting pressure on wintering fields would be decompressed, even when the highest frequency of guanaco is found on the plateau.

Now, why is there no record of bola discards in Del Tobiano Plateau? If such weapons had been used, they would have been expected to be found in open-air settings and near the hunting blinds where broken bolas could be replaced. There would also be a high rate of fractures because of the basaltic substrate and, consequently, a high rate of discards. However, there is no single evidence of bolas or of their manufacturing. Even though this could be an expected result on account of sample size, in other high plateaus such as the Strobel (central west section of the Santa Cruz province) there are records of bolas, although in a much smaller proportion than that of projectile points (Agnolin et al. 2019). This fact is worth mentioning due to the wide dimensions of the Strobel Plateau and the intensity of archaeological research carried out there in the last two decades (Re et al. 2017). A disparity between the archaeological representation of projectile points and bolas is also evident in San Adolfo and Cardiel Chico plateaus (observations made by this research team), located between Del Tobiano and Strobel plateaus. To sum up, the bola can be considered a weapon system which would not fit the hunting tactics used in Del Tobiano Plateau—and in plateaus in general—, at least until historical moments in which hunter-gatherer populations introduced the horse (Nuevo Delaunay 2013). Then, why is there a predominance of projectile points in the plateau? Since both weapon systems coexisted at low altitudinal levels, the difference must have laid on the type of prey, the guanaco, and in the building of hunting blinds, which are unique structures of plateaus. Thus, the answer must be found in the interrelationship between guanacos, blinds and points. On the other hand, the absence of bolas may be associated with the difficulties of replacing the raw material used for their manufacture, which is mainly found around the lakeshore. Although nothing could impede the access of hunters with bola provisions to the plateau, weapon systems with projectile points offered an easier possibility for replacement: with the same weight, the frequency of blanks/complete points is much higher than that of bolas. In this sense, the difference also lies on the transportation cost of blanks/complete artifacts of weapon systems.

Another striking feature of the regional archaeology is the absence of hunting blinds in the *pampas* and lakeshore. Could it be related to the low availability of rocks suitable for their construction (i.e. large and angular blocks)? It is a remarkable fact that where there were appropriate rocks (e.g. sandstone) and there were topographic situations similar to those of the plateaus, for some reason blinds do not seem to have been a viable option. However, it cannot be ruled out that in these lower altitudinal levels, such facilities may have been made with perishable materials, such as branches (e.g. O'Connell et al. 1988). Evidence against the latter is the absence, in the *pampas*, of relative discrete concentrations of fractured projectile points and microflakes such as those found inside the hunting blinds in Del Tobiano Plateau. This absence seems not to be related to formational processes given that flintknapping events were recognized across the *pampas*. In sum, in the shore and intermediate *pampas* implemented hunting tactics seem not to have required the use of blinds but of the three weapon systems described above. Such tactics could have been carried out both individually and in groups and would have been both by stalking and interception, taking advantage of landscape features.

The relative high frequency of bolas in the lower *pampas* and, especially on the lakeshore (Table 13.3), would be linked to two aspects. Firstly, with the hunting of the choique, that can be performed using hunting tactics such as persecution, stalking (both individually and communally) and encircling (communal) (Vecchi 2010). During the reproductive season (August–October; i.e. mid–winter to early spring), individuals of this species are aggregated in these altitudinal levels in large groups (8–15 individuals), a situation that could have favored their capture. However, archeological sites on the coast of the lake lack archaeological evidence supporting this, likely due to taphonomic biases (see, among others, Belardi 1999; Cruz 2007). Secondly, with the availability of raw materials, since it is on the coast of the lake where the rocks used for the manufacture of bolas are available. Here, the presence of bola workshops is part of a characteristic supra-regional pattern, at least during the last 2500 years AP. In this sense, bola workshops were also recognized on the coast of Lake Cardiel (Belardi et al. 2003; Agnolin et al. 2019), Lake Tar (Belardi et al. 2010) and Lake Argentino (Borrero et al. 1998–1999; Franco et al. 1999).

The only space that can be used throughout the year, the lakeshore, would have articulated the use of the other levels. In general terms, complementarity occurs on a very simple environmental basis: as the *pampas* start to get clear from snow, the highest levels begin to be used and, on the contrary, as they start to be covered with snow, prey and people tend to occupy the lower altitudinal levels. As mentioned, during winter the distribution of guanaco and choique would have been linear, following the coastal contour and, as the summer progressed, its distribution could have been more continuous, occupying all the available space although, in the case of guanaco, with a preference for the plateau. These vertical, short-distance displacements of prey could have been followed by people, allowing their exploitation within the same home range.

West from the Cangrejo River, where the plateau topography ends and the Andean Mountains start, there is an abrupt change in altitudinal levels (Fig. 13.1). This rendered the complementarity between wintering and *veranada* grounds really difficult. As a consequence, there was a higher intensity of use by hunter-gatherer groups to the East of Cangrejo River, where seasonality is lower.

In view of the foregoing, the complementarity of the altitudinal levels can be inferred, regarding the possibilities of seasonal use, prey availability and the weapons systems used for hunting. This complementary pattern has already been noticed in the neighboring basins of the Cardiel (Rindel et al. 2017), Tar-San Martín (Belardi et al. 2010) and Argentino (Franco and Borrero 1996) lakes. Thus, this pattern is a remarkable characteristic of the Southern Patagonian lacustrine basins, where significant altitudinal differences can be reached within short distances.

Acknowledgements The studies were financially supported by Universidad Nacional de la Patagonia Austral, Unidad Académica Río Gallegos, Project 29/A360-1 and the CONICET, PIP-11220120100622CO (Res. 4316). We like to thank Ana Rojo, from Estancia Punta del Lago; to Sergio Raggi, from Estancia La Margarita; to Carlos Marcú, from San Agustín, to Christian Rivera, from Estancia Santa Margarita, to José Rojo from Estancia San José and to Patricia Halborsen, from Estancia La Quinta for their hospitality and help during field work. We are indebted to Patricia Campan, Pablo Binaghi and Nicolás Sepúlveda for their collaboration with this research and to Daniel Grima for designing the map. Luis Borrero and Gustavo Martínez read the manuscript and offered their suggestions. Two anonymous reviewers made other comments that helped improve the manuscript.

References

Agnolin A, Flores Coni J, Goñi R (2019) Las bolas y el viento: análisis de la distribución de bolas en las cuencas de los lagos Cardiel y Strobel, Santa Cruz In: Gómez Otero J, Svoboda A, Banegas, A (eds) Arqueología de la Patagonia: el pasado en las arenas. CONICET-IDEAUS, Buenos Aires, pp 81–92

Arias N, Feijóo S, Quinteros P, Bava J (2015) Composición botánica de la dieta del guanaco (*Lama guanicoe*) en la Reserva Corazón de la Isla, Tierra del Fuego (Argentina): utilización estacional de *Nothofagus* spp. Bosque (Valdivia) 36(1):71–79

Aschero C, Martínez J (2001) Técnicas de caza en Antofagasta de la Sierra, Puna Meridional argentina. Relaciones de la Sociedad Argentina de Antropología NS 26:2015–2041

Aschero C (2019) Cazadores-recolectores, sistemas de armas y arte rupestre: más allá del río Pinturas. In: Laguens A, Bonnin M, Marconetto B, Costa da Silva T (eds) Libro de Resúmenes XX Congreso Nacional de Arqueología Argentina: 50 años de arqueologías. Facultad de Filosofía y Humanidades, Universidad Nacional de Córdoba, Córdoba, pp 1444–1446

Bamonte F (2012) Cambios paleoecológicos y su posible relación con las ocupaciones humanas durante el Holoceno en el SO de Santa Cruz, Argentina. Unpublished doctoral thesis, Universidad Nacional de Mar del Plata

Bar-Oz G, Nadel D (2013) Worldwide large-scale trapping and hunting of ungulates in past societies. Quat Int 297:1–7

Barri FR, Falczuk V, Cingolani AM, Díaz S (2014) Dieta de la población de guanacos (*Lama guanicoe*) reintroducida en el Parque Nacional Quebrada del Condorito, Argentina. Ecología Austral 24:203–211

Belardi JB (1999) Hay choiques en la terraza. Información tafonómica y primeras implicaciones arqueofaunísticas para Patagonia. Arqueología 9:163–185

Belardi JB, Goñi RA, Bourlot TJ, Aragone AC (2003) Uso del espacio y paisajes arqueológicos en la cuenca del lago Cardiel (Provincia de Santa Cruz, Argentina). Magallania 32:95–106

Belardi JB, Goñi RA (2006) Representaciones rupestres y convergencia poblacional durante momentos tardíos en Santa Cruz (Patagonia argentina). El caso de la meseta del Strobel. In: Fiore D, Podestá MM (eds) Tramas en la piedra. Producción y usos del arte rupestre. World Archaeological Congress, Sociedad Argentina de Antropología y Asociación Amigos del Instituto Nacional de Antropología, Buenos Aires, pp 85–94

Belardi JB, Espinosa S, Carballo Marina F, Barrientos G, Goñi R, Súnico A, Bourlot T, Pallo C, Tessone A, García Guraieb S, Re A, Campan P (2010) Las cuencas de los lagos Tar y San Martín (Santa Cruz, Argentina) y la dinámica del poblamiento humano del sur de Patagonia: integración de los primeros resultados. Magallania 38(2):137–159

Belardi JB, Barrientos G, Bamonte F, Espinosa S, Goñi R (2013) Paleoambientes y cronología de las ocupaciones cazadoras recolectoras de las cuencas de los lagos Tar y San Martín (provincia de Santa Cruz). Intersecciones en Antropología 14:459–475

Belardi JB, Espinosa S, Carballo Marina F, Barrientos G, Campan P, Súnico A (2016) Desde la meseta del Cardiel Chico a la margen norte del lago Viedma (provincia de Santa Cruz, Argentina): nuevos datos sobre el paisaje arqueológico. In: Mena F (ed) Arqueología de Patagonia: de Mar a Mar. Ñire Negro Ediciones, CIEP, Coyhaique, Chile, pp 411–420

Belardi JB, Carballo Marina F, Madrid P, Barrientos G, Campan P (2017) Late Holocene guanaco (*Lama guanicoe*) hunting grounds in Southern Patagonia: blinds, tactics and differential landscape use. Antiquity 91(357):718–731

Belardi JB, Carballo Marina F, Barrientos G, Campan P (2019a) Punta del Lago 1: implicaciones para la arqueología de la margen Norte del lago Viedma (Santa Cruz). In: Gómez Otero J, Svoboda A, Banegas A (eds) Arqueología de la Patagonia: el pasado en las arenas. CONICET-IDEAUS, Buenos Aires, pp 351–359

Belardi JB, Carballo Marina F, Borrero LA, Grima D (2019b) Disponibilidad de campos de invernada e intensidad de uso del espacio en cuencas lacustres del Sur de Patagonia (Santa Cruz). In: Gómez Otero J, Svoboda A, Banegas A (eds) Arqueología de la Patagonia: el pasado en las arenas. CONICET-IDEAUS, Buenos Aires, pp 251–258

Binford LR (1978) Dimensional analysis of behaviour and site structure: learning from an Eskimo hunting stand. Am Antiq 43:330–361

Binford LR (1981) Bones: ancient men and modern myths. Academia Press, New York

Binford LR (2001) Constructing frames of reference: an analytical method for archaeological theory building using ethnographic and environmental data sets. University of California Press, Berkeley and Los Angeles

Borrero LA, Lanata JL, Ventura BN (1992) Distribuciones de hallazgos aislados en Piedra del Aguila. In: Borrero LA, Lanata JL (eds) Análisis *espacial en la arqueología patagónica*. Ediciones Ayllú, Concepción del Uruguay, Entre Ríos, pp. 9–20

Borrero LA, Franco N, Carballo Marina F, Martín FM (1998–1999) Arqueología de Estancia Alice, Lago Argentino. Cuadernos Instituto Nacional de Antropología y Pensamiento Latinoamericano 18:31–48

Borrero LA (2001) Cambios, continuidades, discontinuidades: Discusiones sobre arqueología Fuego-patagónica. In: Berberián E, Nielsen A (eds) Historia Argentina Prehispánica, Tomo II. Editorial Brujas, Córdoba, pp 815–838

Borrero LA (2004) The archaeozoology of Andean "Dead Ends" in Patagonia: living near the Continental Ice Cap. In: Mondini M, Muñoz S, Wickler S (eds) Colonisation, migration, and marginal areas: a zooarchaeological approach. Oxbow Books, Oxford, pp 55–61

Borrero LA (2013) Estrategias de caza en Fuego-Patagonia. Comechingonia. Revista de Arqueología 17:11–26

Churchill S (1993) Weapon technology, prey size selection, and hunting methods in modern hunter-gatherers: implications for hunting in the Paleolithic and Mesolithic. In: Peterkin GL, Bricker H, Mellars PA (eds) Hunting and animal exploitation in the later Paleolithic and Mesolithic of Eurasia. American Anthropological Association, Washington, DC, pp 11–24

Cruz I (2007) The recent bones of the Río Gallegos Basin (Santa Cruz, Argentina) and their preservation potential. In: Gutiérrez MA, Miotti L, Barrientos G, Mengoni Goñalons G, Salemme M (eds) Taphonomy and zooarchaeology in Argentina. Bar International Series 1601, England, pp 161–170

Daciuk J (1978) Notas faunísticas y bioecológicas de Península Valdés y Patagonia. XXIII. Estudio bioecológico y etológico general del ñandú petiso patagónico y de los tinámidos de Península Valdés, Chubut, Argentina. Physis, Sección C, 38(95):69–85

Dunnell R, Dancey WS (1983) The siteless survey: a regional scale data collection strategy. In: Schiffer M (ed) Advances in archeological method and theory, vol 6. Academic Press, New York, pp 267–287

Espinosa S, Goñi R (1999) Viven!! Una fuente de obsidiana en la provincia de Santa Cruz. In: Instituto Nacional de Antropología y Pensamiento Latinoamericano y la Universidad Nacional del Comahue (eds) Soplando en el viento. Actas de las III Jornadas de Arqueología de la Patagonia. San Carlos de Bariloche, pp 177–188

Fernández PM (2010) Cazadores y presas. 3.500 años de interacción entre seres humanos y animales en el noroeste de Chubut. Fundación de Historia Natural Félix de Azara, Buenos Aires

Franco NV, Borrero LA (1996) El *stress* temporal y los artefactos líticos. La cuenca superior del río Santa Cruz In: Gómez Otero J (ed) Arqueología. Solo Patagonia. Ponencias de las II Jornadas de

Arqueología de la Patagonia. Publicación del Centro Nacional Patagónico (CONICET), Trelew, pp 341–348

Franco NV, Borrero LA, Belardi JB, Carballo Marina F, Martin F, Campan P, Favier Dubois C, Hernández Llosas MI, Stadler N, Muñoz S, Borella F, Cepeda H, Cruz I (1999) Arqueología del cordón Baguales y sistema lacustre al sur del lago Argentino. Praehistoria 3:65–86

Franco NV, Borrero LA (2003) Chorrillo Malo 2: initial peopling of the upper Santa Cruz basin, Argentina. In: Bonnichsen R, Miotti L, Salemne M, Flegenheimer N (eds) Ancient evidence for paleo South Americans: from where the South winds blow. Center for the Studies of the First American & Texas A&M University Press, Texas, USA, pp 149–152

Franklin WL (1982) Biology, ecology, and relationship to man of the South American camelids. In: Mares M, Genoways H (eds) Mammalian biology in South America. University of Pittsburgh, Pittsburgh, pp 57–489

Frison G (2004) Survival by hunting: prehistoric human predators and animal prey. University of California Press, Berkeley

Foley R (1981) Off-site archaeology: an alternative approach for the short-site. In: Hoder I, Isaac G, Hammond N (eds) Pattern of the past: studies in honour of David Clarke. Cambridge University Press, Cambridge, pp 157–183

Giardina MA (2010) El aprovechamiento de la avifauna entre las sociedades cazadoras recolectoras del sur de Mendoza: un enfoque arqueológico. Unpublished doctoral thesis, Universidad Nacional de La Plata

González BA, Palma RE, Zapata B, Marín JC (2006) Taxonomic and biogeographical status of guanaco *Lama guanicoe* (Artiodactyla, Camelidae). Mammal Rev 36:157–178

González-Urrutia M, Muñoz-Pedreros A, Norambuena HI (2018) Historia natural del ñandú del sur *Rhea pennata pennata*. Gestión Ambiental 36:23–45

Goñi RA (2010) Cambio climático y poblamiento humano durante el Holoceno tardío en Patagonia Meridional. Una perspectiva arqueológica. Unpublished doctoral thesis, Universidad de Buenos Aires

Gradin C (2001) El arte rupestre de los cazadores de guanaco de la Patagonia. In: Berberian E, Nielsen A (eds) Historia Argentina Prehispánica, Tomo II. Editorial Brujas, Córdoba, pp 839–874

Hitchcok RK, Crowell A, Brooks A, Yellen JE, Ebert J, Eber I, Osborn AJ (2019) The ethnoarchaeology of ambush hunting: a case study of ≠ Gi Pan, Western Ngamiland, Botswana. Afr Archeol Rev 36(1):119–144

Kaplan MR, Schaefer JM, Strelin JA, Denton GH, Anderson RF, Vandergoes MJ, Finke RC, Schwartz R, Travis SG, García JL, Martini MA, Nielsen SHH (2016) Patagonian and Southern South Atlantic view of Holocene climate. Quat Sci Rev 141:112–125

Kastner S, Enters D, Ohlendorf C, Haberzettl T, Kuhn G, Lücke A, Mayr C, Jean-Louis Reyss R, Wastegard S, Zolitschka B (2010) Reconstructing 2000 years of hydrological variation derived from laminated proglacial sediments of Lago del Desierto at the eastern margin of the South Patagonian Ice Field, Argentina. Glob Planet Chang 72:201–214

Kelly R (1995) The foraging spectrum: diversity in hunter-gatherer lifeways. Smithsonian Institution Press, Washington

Lemke A (ed) (2018) Foraging in the past: archaeological studies of hunter-gatherer diversity. University Press of Colorado, Louisville

Masiokas MH, Luckman BH, Villalba R, Delgado S, Skvarka P, Ripalta A (2009) Little Ice Age fluctuations of small glaciers in the Monte Fitz Roy and Lago del Desierto areas, South Patagonian Andes, Argentina. Palaeogeogr, Palaeoclim, Palaeoecol 281:351–362

Martin FM, Borrero LA (2017) Climate change, availability of territory, and Late Pleistocene human exploration of Ultima Esperanza, South Chile. Quat Int 428:86–95

Mengoni Goñalons GL (1999) Cazadores de guanaco de la Estepa Patagónica. Sociedad Argentina de Antropología. Serie Tesis Doctorales, Buenos Aires

Mercer JH (1976) Glacial history of Southernmost South America. Quaternary Research 6:125–166

Merino ML (1988) Estructura social de la población de guanacos en la costa norte de Península Mitre, Tierra del Fuego, Argentina. Cuartas Jornadas Argentinas de Mastozoología, Tucumán, Argentina

Miotti L (1998) Zooarqueología de la Meseta Central y costa de Santa Cruz. Un enfoque de las estrategias adaptativas aborígenes y los paleoambientes. Museo Municipal de Historia Natural, Secretaría de Gobierno, Departamento de San Rafael, provincia de Mendoza, San Rafael

Moreno E (2012) The construction of hunting sceneries: interactions between humans, animals and landscape in Antofalla Valley, Catamarca, Argentina. J Anthropol Archaeol 31:104–117

Morgan C, Webb D, Sprengeler K, Black M, George N (2018) Experimental construction of hunter-gatherer residential features, mobility, and the cost of occupying "persistent places". J Archeol Sci 91:65–76

Muñoz AE, Simonetti JA (2013) Diet of guanaco in sheep-free rangeland in Tierra del Fuego, Chile. Ciencia de Investigación Agraria 40(1):185–191

Nuevo Delaunay A (2013) Tecnología lítica y asentamientos modernos: análisis de un conjunto de bolas líticas del siglo XX. In: Zangrando F, Barberena R, Gil A, Neme G, Giardina M, Luna L, Otaola C, Paulides L, Salgan L, Tívoli A (eds) Tendencias teórico-metodológicas y casos de estudio en la arqueología de Patagonia. Museo de Historia Natural de San Rafael, Sociedad Argentina de Antropología, Instituto Nacional de Antropología y Pensamiento Latinoamericano y Secretaría de Cultura, Altuna Impresores, pp 469–474

Nuevo Delaunay A. Belardi JB, Carballo Marina F, Saletta MJ, De Angelis H (2017) The incorporation of glass and stoneware among Southern continental Patagonia and Fueguian hunter-gatherers from XVIII th to XX th century. Antiquity 91(359):1330–1343

O' Connell J, Hawkes K, Jones B (1988) Hadza hunting, butchering, and bone transport and their archeological implications. J Anthropol Archaeol 44(2):113–161

Oliva G, González L, Rial P, Livraghi E (2001) El ambiente en la Patagonia Austral. In: Borrelli P, Oliva G (eds) Ganadería ovina sustentable en la Patagonia Austral. Tecnología de Manejo Extensivo. Ediciones Instituto Nacional de Tecnología Agropecuaria, Buenos Aires, pp 19–82

Ortega I (1985) Social organization and ecology of a migratory guanaco population in Southern Patagonia. Unpublished PhD Dissertation, Iowa State University

Ortega IM, Franklin W (1995) Social organization, distribution and movements of a migratory guanaco population in the Chilean Patagonia. Revista Chilena de Historia Natural 68:498–500

Pedrana J, Bustamante J, Travaini A, Rodríguez A, Zapata S, Zanón Martínez JI, Procopio D (2011) Environmental factors influencing the distribution of the Lesser Rhea (Rhea pennata pennata) in southern Patagonia. Emu - Austral Ornithology 111 (4):350–359

Pérez SI, Postillone MB, Rindel D, Gobbo D, González PN, Bernal V (2016) Peopling time, spatial occupation and demography of Late Pleistocene-Holocene human population from Patagonia. Quat Int 425:214–223

Puig S (1986) Ecología poblacional del guanaco (Lama guanicoe, Camelidae, Artiodactyla) en la Reserva Provincial de La Payunia (Mendoza). Unpublished doctoral thesis, Universidad de Buenos Aires

Puig S, Videla F (1995) Comportamiento y organización social del guanaco. In: Puig S (ed) Técnicas para el manejo del Guanaco. UICN-Gland, Switzerland, pp 97–118

Puig S, Videla F, Cona M (1997) Diet and abundance of the guanaco (*Lama guanicoe*) in four habitats of northern Patagonia, Argentina. J Arid Environ 36:343–357

Ratto N (1991) Análisis funcional de las puntas de proyectil líticas de sitios del sudeste de la Isla Grande de Tierra del Fuego. Arqueología 1:151–179

Re A (2017) Grabados de guanacos en la Patagonia austral. Intersecciones en Antropología 18:135–147

Re A, Goñi R, Flores Coni J, Guichón F, Dellepiane F, Umaño M (2017) Arqueología de la meseta del Strobel (Patagonia meridional): 15 años después. Relaciones de la Sociedad Argentina de Antropología, XLII 1:133–158

Rindel D, Goñi R, Belardi JB, Bourlot T (2017) Climatic changes and hunter-gatherer populations: archaeozoological trends in Southern Patagonia. In: Monks GG (ed) Climate change and human responses: a zooarchaeological perspective. Springer, The Netherlands, pp 153–172

SAG (2002) Propuesta de enmienda para transferir *Pterocnemia pennata pennata* desde el Apéndice I al Apéndice II de CITES. XII Conferencia de las Partes de CITES, Santiago, Chile

Strelin JA, Kaplan MR, Vandergoes MJ, Denton GH, Schaefer JM (2014) Holocene glacier history of the Lago Argentino basin, Southern Patagonian Icefield. Quat Sci Rev 101:124–1455

Sturzenbaum P, Borelli P (2001) Manejo de riesgos climáticos. In: Borrelli P, Oliva G (eds) Ganadería Ovina Sustentable en la Patagonia Austral. Tecnologías de Manejo Extensivo. INTA and ErreGé, Santa Cruz y Buenos Aires, pp 255–270

Thomas DH (1975) Nonsite sampling in archaeology: up the creek without a site? In: Muller L (ed) Sampling in archaeology. University of Arizona Press, Tucson, pp 61–81

Travaini A, Zapata SC, Bustamante J, Pedrana J, Zanón J, Rodríguez A (2015) Guanaco abundance and monitoring in Southern Patagonia: distance sampling reveals substantially greater numbers than previously reported. Zool Stud 54:23

Vecchi RJ (2010) Bolas de boleadora en los grupos cazadores recolectores de la Pampa Bonaerense. Unpublished doctoral thesis, Universidad de Buenos Aires

Vetrisano L, Franco N (2019) El registro arqueológico al aire libre y bajo roca en el extremo meridional del Macizo del Deseado: La integración de información de superficie y estratigráfica. In: Gómez Otero J, Svoboda A, Banegas A (eds) Arqueología de la Patagonia: el pasado en las arenas. CONICET-IDEAUS, Buenos Aires, pp 339–350

Wenzens G (1999) Fluctuations of outlet and valley glaciers in the Southern Andes (Argentina) during the past 13,000 years. Quat Res 51:238–247

Index

A

Active traps, 86, 103–106
Actualistic Study, 60, 65, 73
Andean forest, 211
Antofagasta de la Sierra, 3, 5–8, 14, 20, 21, 24–26, 28
Archaeofaunal, 65
Archaeology, 4, 70, 84, 140, 262, 354
Argentina, 1, 5, 7, 34, 36, 63, 77, 84, 87, 102, 114, 117, 126, 139, 224, 262, 294, 295, 302, 305, 344
Argentine Andes, 141
Artiodactyls, 87, 88, 91
Atlantic coast, 87, 89, 105, 126, 129, 215

B

Bow and arrow, 20, 21, 24, 51, 68, 76, 84, 101, 105–107, 138–141, 149, 151, 152, 245–248, 262, 272, 278, 283–285, 304, 350

C

Choique, 190, 213, 214, 216, 217, 219, 243, 245, 246, 248, 344, 345, 347, 348, 353, 355
Collective hunting strategies, 260–262, 285
Current hunters, 77

D

Deseado Massif, 263, 264, 268, 270, 283, 284, 314–317, 335, 336
Diet breadth models, 176, 179, 199

F

Fishing, 76, 77, 114–116, 123, 126, 128–130, 145

G

Guanaco, 51, 75, 76, 84, 86–89, 91–98, 102, 103, 105, 106, 114, 143, 170, 177, 185, 186, 190–192, 197–201, 210, 213–219, 224, 240, 244–246, 260–262, 268, 270, 272, 274, 275, 279, 280, 282, 283, 285, 294, 297, 298, 305, 306, 316–318, 323, 325, 327, 330, 336, 344–350, 353–355

H

Holocene, Northwestern Argentina, 1–3, 7, 9, 14, 20, 21, 23, 24, 26–28
Hunter gatherers, 114, 116, 127, 130, 177, 178, 210, 211, 247, 316–318
Hunting, 1–5, 9, 11, 12, 160–166, 168, 170–172, 344, 345, 348, 350, 351, 353–355
Hunting blinds, 11–17, 19, 24, 103, 262–264, 269, 272, 277, 279, 283–285, 294, 296–308, 315–325, 327–330, 332–336
Hunting practices, 2, 28, 152, 210, 215, 217, 244, 247, 248, 260, 262, 272

L

Lake Viedma, 344–346, 348, 353
Landscape, 7, 8, 12, 15–17, 19–21, 23–25, 27, 54, 85, 87, 103, 106, 107, 211,

© Springer Nature Switzerland AG 2021
J. B. Belardi et al. (eds.), *Ancient Hunting Strategies in Southern South America*,
The Latin American Studies Book Series,
https://doi.org/10.1007/978-3-030-61187-3

261, 262, 268, 277, 280, 283–285, 349, 353
Late Holocene, 60, 68, 70, 76, 87, 88, 91, 102, 105, 107, 130, 139, 177, 185, 247, 264, 272, 275, 282, 284, 285, 294, 296, 304, 306–308, 345, 347, 348, 353
Late Prehispanic Period, 34, 36, 50, 52–54
Lithic weapons, 67, 69
Lithic weights, 124, 129, 130

M

Micropogonias furnieri, 115, 119, 122, 123, 126, 127, 129, 130
Middle Holocene, 9, 26, 28, 70, 103, 113, 114, 116, 117, 125–127, 130, 186, 270, 282
Myocastor coypus, 60, 63, 64

N

Niche breadth, 54
Northwest Patagonia, 176, 177, 179, 190, 191, 198, 199
Nutritional Ecology, 176, 179, 199

P

Pampa and Patagonia, 160, 171
Pampa grasslands, 84
Patagonia, 103, 152, 201, 244, 246, 268, 314–316, 318, 320, 333, 335

Patagonian plateaus, 260, 261, 283, 284
Plateaus, 294–299, 305, 307, 308
Pleistocene/Holocene, 262–264, 268–270, 275, 276, 279, 282, 285
Pogonias cromis, 115–117, 119, 122, 123, 126–130
Projectile points, 33–35, 37, 38, 41, 44, 46–51, 53, 139, 141–147, 150, 151, 153

R

Rheas, 159–163, 165, 168, 170–172
Rock art, 261, 263, 269, 272, 274, 279, 280, 284, 285

S

Sierras of Córdoba, 34, 36, 52
Spears, 216, 218, 219, 233, 237, 245–247
Steppe, 210–214, 217–220, 223–225, 233, 237–240, 244–248
Strategies, 294, 299, 304, 306–308

W

Weapons, 2, 15, 20, 23, 24, 261–263, 272, 278–280, 283–285
Weapon system(s), 33, 34, 84, 89–91, 98, 101, 102, 105–107, 139–141, 149, 151–153